TimeOut
Berlin

Penguin Books

PENGUIN BOOKS

Published by the Penguin Group
Penguin Books Ltd, 27 Wrights Lane, London W8 5TZ, England
Penguin Books USA Inc., 375 Hudson Street, New York, New York 10014, USA
Penguin Books Australia Ltd, Ringwood, Victoria, Australia
Penguin Books Canada Ltd, 10 Alcorn Avenue, Toronto, Ontario, Canada M4V 3B2
Penguin Books (NZ) Ltd, 182-190 Wairau Road, Auckland 10, New Zealand

Penguin Books Ltd, Registered Offices: Harmondsworth, Middlesex, England

First published 1993
Second edition 1995
Third edition 1998
10 9 8 7 6 5 4 3 2 1

Copyright © Time Out Group Ltd, 1993, 1995, 1998
All rights reserved

Colour reprographics by Precise Litho, 34-35 Great Sutton Street, London EC1
Printed and bound by William Clowes Ltd, Beccles, Suffolk NR34 9QE

Edited and designed by

Time Out Guides Limited
Universal House
251 Tottenham Court Road
London W1P OAB
Tel + 44 (0)171 813 3000
Fax+ 44 (0)171 813 6001
Email guides@timeout.co.uk
http://www.timeout.co.uk

Editorial

Managing Editor Peter Fiennes
Editor Dave Rimmer
Deputy editor Kevin Ebbutt
Researcher John Fitzsimons
Indexer Dorothy Frame

Design

Art Director John Oakey
Art Editor Mandy Martin
Designers Benjamin de Lotz, Scott Moore
Scanner Operator Chris Quinn
Picture Editor Kerri Miles
Picture Researcher Michaela Freeman

Advertising

Group Advertisement Director Lesley Gill
Sales Director/Sponsorship Mark Phillips
Advertisement Sales (Berlin) Runze & Casper Verlagsservice

Administration

Publisher Tony Elliott
Managing Director Mike Hardwick
Financial Director Kevin Ellis
Marketing Director Gillian Auld
General Manager Nichola Coulthard
Production Manager Mark Lamond
Accountant Catherine Bowen

Features in this guide were written and researched by:

Introduction Dave Rimmer. **History** Frederick Studemann. **Berlin Today** Frederick Studemann. **Berlin By Season** Lisa Ellis. **Architecture** Francesca Rogier. **Sightseeing** Frederick Studemann, Dave Rimmer, Ed Ward. **Museums** Holly Austin, Julie Emery, Dave Rimmer. **Art Galleries** Dominic Eichler. **Accommodation** Kevin Cote, Sophie Lovell. **Restaurants** Dr JJ Gordon, Dave Rimmer, Ed Ward, Julie Wedow. **Cafés & Bars** Kevin Cote, Timothy Mohr, Dave Rimmer, Ed Ward. **Shopping & Services** Dave Rimmer, Dominica Spencer, Trevor Wilson. **After Hours** John Fitzsimons, Dave Rimmer. **Cabaret** Priscilla Be. **Children** Kevin Cote. **Clubs** Timothy Mohr, Mark Reeder, Dave Rimmer. **Dance** Julie Wedow. **Film** Andrew Horn. **Gay & Lesbian** Lisa Ellis, Christopher Nicholas. **Media** Frederick Studemann. **Music: Classical & Opera** Dr JJ Gordon. **Music: Rock, Folk & Jazz** Biba Kopf, Timothy Mohr. **Sport & Fitness** Timothy Mohr, Trevor Wilson. **Theatre** Dr JJ Gordon. **Trips out of Town** Dave Rimmer, Ed Ward. **Essential Information** Kevin Cote, John Fitzsimons, Dave Rimmer, Frederick Studemann. **Getting Around** John Fitzsimons, Dave Rimmer, Ed Ward. **Business** Holly Austin. **Women** Lisa Ellis. **Further Reading** Dave Rimmer.

The editor will remain ever-undyingly grateful to: Chris & Nadine Auty, Matthew Collin, Kevin Cote, Stephanie Dosunmu, Daniel Duesentrieb, Omar Elshami, John Fitzsimons, Volker Hauptvogel, Doris Jaud, Annie Lloyd, Yasmin Röcker, Fernando Rodriguez, Janet Street-Porter, Fred Studemann, Trevor Wilson. Further gratitude is due to Mark Reeder, Torsten Jurk, Marcus Nifch and everyone at MFS. Plus love and kisses to Gosto Babka von Gostomski, Chaos, Claus Erbstzorn, Stefan Fiebig and everyone at the Pinguin Club.

Photography by Hadley Kincade except: pages 5, 8, 9, 11, 12, 15, 16, 17, 18, 19, 21, 22 **AKG London**; page 6 **Mary Evans Picture Library**; page 92 **Uwe Walter/Galerie Eigen & Art**; page 107 **Propeller Island**; page 184 **British Film Institute**; page 206 **Bungalow Records**; page 210 **DHR**; page 228 **AKG London**; pages 231, 232, 233, 234, 235, 236 **Image Bank**.

Contents

About the Guide

This is the third edition of the *Time Out Berlin Guide*, one of our ever-expanding series on the world's most vital cities. This latest version has been shaken out, dusted down, held up to the light, paraded before a team of specialists and taken down the *Imbiß* for a good hot meal. We've reassessed Berlin's attractions, searched out the new and the up-and-coming, and tried to discern the future shape of this still unifying city.

Although any trip to Berlin will be enhanced with a copy of this *Guide*, it is not only a book for casual visitors and tourists. While listing the main sights and major monuments, we've also roved the city in search of its most crucial cafés, darkest dives, grooviest galleries, sharpest shopping opportunities and most happening clubs. We aim to highlight not only the traditional must-sees, but also aspects of Berlin as the Berliners know it – places that tourists seldom see.

date advice, so we always want to hear if you've been ripped off, badly treated, or otherwise given the runaround.

Details, details, details

All information was checked and correct at the time of going to press, but please bear in mind that Berlin is still changing as the two halves of the city are finally sewn back together. Little stays the same for long in this town. Clubs, bars, restaurants, galleries and other cultural venues wink in and out of existence. Even street names still change from time to time.

Addresses & telephone numbers

In listing addresses we've included both the district name and the five-digit postcode. You don't need the district name when addressing a letter, but very few people are going to be able to direct you to 'Berlin 10783'. Telephone numbers in Berlin can be anything from four to eight digits long.

Prices

Prices, where listed, should be treated as guideline rather than gospel. Fluctuating exchange rates, inflation and the particular circumstances of the volatile Berlin economy can cause prices, especially in shops and restaurants, to change rapidly. So do expect some fluctuation. But if prices vary wildly from those we have indicated here, ask if there's a good reason. If not, take your custom elsewhere and then, please, let us know. We try to give the best and most up-to-

Credit cards

Compared the UK or USA, credit cards are still not widely used in Berlin. The larger shops will take them, and many of the more expensive restaurants, but you can basically forget about using them in clubs, galleries, bars, theatres, concert halls and cinemas. In Berlin, cash is king. We've used the following abbreviations for the major credit cards: Amex – American Express; EC – EuroCard; DC – Diner's Club; JCB – Japanese credit card; MC – Mastercard; V – Visa.

To boldly go

In chapters without listings, such as History or Architecture, names of places **highlighted in bold** are fully listed elsewhere in the book and can be found in the index.

Right to reply

It should be stressed that the information we offer in this *Guide* is impartial. No institution or enterprise has been included because they advertise in our publications. Rigorous impartiality and cosmopolitan criticism are the reasons why are guides are so successful and well-respected. But if you disagree with us, please, let us know. Your comments on places you have visited are always welcome – you'll find a reader's reply card in the back of this book.

There's an on-line version of this *Guide*, as well as all the weekly events listings information for Berlin and other international cities at:
http://www.timeout.co.uk

Introduction

I always experience a certain feeling of relief when the plane taxis to a halt and I find myself once more back in Berlin. It's not just that Tegel and Tempelhof are two of Europe's most hassle-free airports, although that certainly helps. It's more that, in this city of night but not of sleep, where social and cultural experiment has been the norm for decades, where the gruff tolerance of Berliners balances a rugged and generous cosmopolitanism, it is somehow possible to be truly myself.

So long a city of the past, carved in two by geopolitical circumstance and left adrift by the tides of the twentieth century, Berlin is now in the final stages of becoming a city of the future – capital of Europe's most powerful country, with a fancy new city centre and a souped-up twenty-first-century infrastructure. Most noticeable where the forests of cranes looms over Potsdamer Platz and the Spreebogen, construction continues everywhere. Whatever it might represent elsewhere, in this city the millennium is first and foremost a deadline. Berlin's twentieth century ended a decade early with the breach of the Wall on 9 November 1989.

But despite the frantic pace of change since then, in Berlin there is still somehow that most precious commodity, time. It's not like the sleepiness of

Vienna, or some Mediterranean *mañana* vibe. But the city retains an unhurried quality, valuing the space to reflect and take stock of things. Here the examined life really is the only one worth living.

And in Berlin it truly is possible to live a different kind of life, to reinvent yourself – even if only for an evening or a weekend. It is, for example, one of the world's great gay cities. Or take nightlife, another of Berlin's most resounding strengths. Unlike in many cities, where people are shoehorned into some leisure conglomerate's notion of what constitutes an acceptable social space, in Berlin the bars and clubs, free to open as long as they like, spring up in response to certain scenes, to certain moods and desires, certain notions about how life should be lived – and fuelled by a firm commitment to pursue the high as far as it will go.

For it's an extreme sort of city – the darkness and intensity of its culture (its 'decadence', if you like) balanced by relaxed summers when café life spills emphatically out on the streets, and where it's possible, at the end of a short S-Bahn ride, to go swimming in a forest lake. As often as not, Berlin turns weakness into strengths, making the most of its fringe position. When no one was interested in German music, Berlin tactically retreated into resolutely uncommercial territory and then came exploding back with techno, a music about as extreme as it's possible for music to get. The margins battered their way back into the mainstream so effectively that by 1997 the annual techno carnival, the Love Parade, was drawing over one million attendees. Likewise the art scene. Faced with a lack of the monied patrons necessary to fuel a commodity-based art market, the mushrooming Mitte gallery scene, like the club culture with which it often interacts, made the most of available spaces left behind by the twists and turns of history and spat back in the eye of commercialism with a frutiful determination to experiment.

Berlin, then, is no ordinary city – a capital that's not yet a seat of government, a unified city that is still divided, a place where the unexpected has space to happen and sooner or later usually does. After the year 2000, with the first stages of construction complete and the federal government installed, the city will change forever. But for now, in the spaces between past and future, between east and west, Berlin still offers an experience of life unique to this battered, restless, determinedly individualistic metropolis.
Dave Rimmer

Capital for Trade Fairs and Conventions!

For full programme details and relevant information please contact:

Messe Berlin GmbH · Messedamm 22 · D-14055 Berlin
Tel. ++49/30/30 38-0 · Fax ++49/30/30 38-23 25
http://www.messe-berlin.de
E-Mail marketing@messe-berlin.de

||||| Messe Berlin

Berlin in Context

Key Events

1237 Cölln first mentioned in a church document.
1307 The towns of Berlin and Cölln officially united under the rule of the Ascanian family.
1319 Last of the Ascanians dies.
1359 Berlin joins the Hanseatic League.
1411 Friedrich of Hohernzollern is sent by the Holy Roman Emperor to bring peace to the region.
1447-48 The 'Berlin Indignation'. The population rebels and locks Friedrich II and his courtiers out of the city.

1535 Accession of Joachim I Nestor, the first Elector to embrace Protestantism. The Reformation arrives in Berlin.
1538 Work begins on the Stadtschloß.
1618-48 Berlin and Brandenburg are ravaged by the Thirty Years War – the population is halved.
1640-88 Reign of Friedrich Wilhelm, the Grand Elector.
1662-68 Construction of the Oder-Spree canal.
1672 Jewish and Huguenot refugees begin to arrive in Berlin.
1695 Work begins on Schloß Charlottenburg.
1701 Elector Friedrich III, son of the Grand Elector, has himself crowned Friedrich I, King of Prussia. Work begins on the German and French cathedrals at the Gendarmenmarkt.
1713-40 Reign of King Friedrich Wilhelm, who expands the army and gives Berlin the character of a garrison city.
1740-86 Reign of Friedrich II – Frederick the Great – a time of construction, military expansion and administrative reform.
1788-91 Construction of the Brandenburg Gate by Karl Gottfried Langhans for King Friedrich Wilhelm II. Johann Schadow adds the Quadriga.

1806 Napoleon marches into Berlin on October 27. Two years of French occupation. The Quadriga is shipped to Paris.
1810 Wilhelm von Humboldt founds the university.
1813 Napoleon is defeated at Grossbeeren and Leipzig.
1814 General Blücher brings the Quadriga back to Berlin and restores it on the Brandenburg Gate.

1837 Foundation of the Borsig Werke marks the beginning of Berlin's expansion into Continental Europe's largest industrial city.
1838 First railway line, from Berlin to Potsdam.
1840 Friedrich Wilhelm IV accedes to the throne. With a population of around 400,000, Berlin is the fourth largest city in Europe.
1848 The 'March Revolution' breaks out. Berlin briefly in the hands of the revolutionaries.
1861 Accession of King Wilhelm I.
1862 Appointment of Otto von Bismarck as Prime Minister of Prussia.
1871 Following victory in the Franco-Prussian war, King Wilhelm I is proclaimed German Emperor and Berlin becomes the Imperial capital.
1879 Electric lighting comes to Berlin, which also boasts the world's first electric railway. Three years later telephone services are introduced. The city emerges as Europe's most modern metropolis.
1888 Kaiser Wilhelm II comes to the throne.
1890 Kaiser Wilhelm II sacks Bismarck.

1894 Completion of the Reichstag.
1902 First underground line is opened.
1914-18 World War I.
1918 On November 9, Kaiser Wilhelm abdicates, Philip Scheidemann proclaims Germany a republic and Karl Liebknecht declares Germany a socialist republic. Chaos ensues.
1919 Spartacist uprising is suppressed by the Freikorps.

1920 Attempted right-wing coup lead by Wolfgang Kapp.
1923 Hyperinflation – one dollar is worth 4.2 billion marks.
1926 Joseph Goebbels comes to Berlin to take charge of the local Nazi party organisation.
1927 Berlin boasts more than 70 cabarets and nightclubs.
1933 Hitler takes power.

1936 The 11th Olympic Games are held in Berlin.
1938 Kristallnacht, November 9. Jewish homes, businesses and synagogues in Berlin are stoned, looted and set ablaze.
1939 Outbreak of World War II, during which Berlin suffers appalling devastation.
1944 A group around Colonel Count von Stauffenberg attempts to assassinate Hitler. Most are subsequently executed at Plötzensee prison.
1945 Germany signs unconditional surrender on May 8.

1948-49 The Berlin Blockade. The Soviets cut off all transport links to west Berlin. For 11 months the city is supplied by the Allied Airlift.
1949 Foundation of Federal Republic in May and of the German Democratic Republic on October 7.
1953 The June 17 uprising in East Berlin is suppressed.
1958 Krushchev issues the 'Berlin Ultimatum'.
1961 The Wall goes up on August 13.
1965 Students stage a sit-down protest on the Ku'damm.
1968 Student leader Rudi Dutschke is shot.
1971 Erich Honecker succeeds Walter Ulbricht as East German head of state. Signing of the Quadrapartite Agreement formalises Berlin's divided status.
1980-81 The 'Hot Winter' of violent protest by squatters.
1987 East and West celebrate Berlin's 750th birthday.

1989 On November 9, the Wall comes down.
1990 October 3, formal German Reunification.
1994 The last of the Allied military leave Berlin.

History

From twin trading town to divided metropolis – enduring wars, revolution and totalitarianism of all types – Berlin has taken every punch that history could find to throw at it.

Ascanian origins

Berlin's origins are neither remarkable nor auspicious. It emerged sometime in the twelfth century from swamp-lands that pioneering German knights had wrested from the Slavs. The name Berlin is believed to be derived from the Slav word *birl*, meaning swamp.

Facing off across the Spree river, Berlin and its twin settlement Cölln (on what is now Museum Island) were founded as trading posts half-way between the older fortress towns of Spandau and Köpenick. Today the borough of Mitte embraces Cölln and old Berlin, and Spandau and Köpenick are outlying suburbs. The town's existence was first recorded in 1237, when Cölln was mentioned in a church document.

The Ascanian family, who held the title of Margraves of Brandenburg, ruled over the twin towns and the surrounding region. Eager to encourage trade, they granted special rights to merchants with the result that Berlin and Cölln emerged as prosperous trading centres linking east and west Europe. In 1307 the two towns were officially united.

In the thirteenth century, construction began on the Marienkirche and Nikolaikirche churches, both of which still stand. The latter gave its name to the **Nikolaiviertel**.

The early years of prosperity came to an end in 1319 with the death of the last Ascanian ruler. This opened the way for robber barons from the outlying regions, eager to take control of Berlin. However, despite political upheaval and the threat of invasion, Berlin's merchants did manage to continue business. In 1359 the city joined the Hanseatic League of free-trading European cities (more prominent members were Hamburg and London).

The Hohernzollerns arrive

But the threat of invasion remained. Towards the end of the fourteenth century two powerful families, the Dukes of Pommerania and the notoriously brutal von Quitzow brothers, began to vie for control of the city.

Salvation came with Friedrich of Hohernzollern, a nobleman from southern Germany sent by the Holy Roman Emperor in 1411 to bring peace to the region. Initially, Friedrich was well received. The bells of the Marienkirche were melted down to be made into weapons for the fight against the aggressors. (In a strange echo of history, the Marienkirche bells were again transformed into tools of war in 1917, in the reign of Kaiser Wilhelm II, the last of the Hohernzollerns to rule.)

Having defeated the von Quitzow brothers, Friedrich officially became Margrave. In 1416 he took the further title of Elector of Brandenburg, denoting his right to vote in the election of the Holy Roman Emperor – titular head of the German-speaking states.

But with peace and stability came the gradual loss of Berlin's independent traditions as Friedrich consolidated his power. In 1442 foundations were laid for the Berlin castle and a royal court was founded. Disputes began to erupt between the patrician classes (representing trade) and the guilds (representing crafts).

The Nikolaikirche – still standing today.

Increasing social friction culminated in the 'Berlin Indignation' of 1447-48 when the population rose up in rebellion. Friedrich's son (Friedrich II) and his courtiers were locked out of the city and the foundations of the castle were flooded. But within months, the uprising collapsed and the Hohernzollerns returned triumphant. While merchants were forced to shoulder new restrictions, courtiers were exempted from communal jurisdiction. The city began to lose economic impetus and Berlin was transformed from an outlying trading post to a small-sized capital (in 1450 the population was 6,000).

Reformation & debauchery

The Reformation arrived in Berlin and Brandenburg under the reign of Joachim I Nestor (1535-71), the first Elector to embrace Protestantism. Joachim strove to improve the cultural standing of Berlin by inviting artists, architects and theologians to work in the city. In 1538 Caspar Theyss and Konrad Krebbs, two masterbuilders from Saxony, began work on a Renaissance-style palace. The building took a hundred years to complete and evolved into the bombastic Stadtschloß which stood on the Spree island, until the East German government demolished it in 1950.

Joachim's studious nature was not reflected in the behaviour of his subjects. In a foretaste of Berlin's later reputation for debauchery and decadence, self-indulgence characterised life in the late sixteenth-century city. Repeated attempts to clamp down on excessive drinking, gambling and loose morals had little effect. Visiting the city, Abbot Trittenheim remarked that 'the people are good, but rough and unpolished, they prefer stuffing themselves to good science'.

After stuffing itself with another 6,000 people, Berlin left the sixteenth century with a population of 12,000 – double that of a hundred years earlier.

WAR & RECONSTRUCTION

The outbreak of the Thirty Years War in 1618 dragged Berlin on to the wider political stage. Although initially unaffected by the conflict between Catholic forces loyal to the Holy Roman Empire and the Swedish-backed Protestant armies, Berlin was eventually caught up in the war which was to leave the German-speaking states ravaged, divided and weakened for over two centuries.

In 1626 Imperial troops occupied Berlin and plundered the city. In the following years Berlin was repeatedly sacked and forced to pay special taxes to the occupying forces. Trade collapsed and its hinterland was laid waste. To top it all, there were four serious epidemics between 1626 and 1631 which claimed thousands of lives. By the time the war ended in 1648, Berlin had lost a third of its housing stock, the population had fallen to less than 6,000 and municipal coffers were greatly depleted.

The Great Elector

Painstaking reconstruction was carried out under the reign of Friedrich Wilhelm (later known as the Great Elector). He succeeded his father in 1640, but chose to see out the war in exile. Influenced by

The 'Residenzstadt' of Berlin, Cölln and Friedrichswerder – today the core of Mitte.

Dutch ideas on town-planning and architecture (he was married to a Princess of Orange), Friedrich Wilhelm embarked on a policy that linked urban regeneration, economic expansion and solid defence.

New fortifications were built around the city and a garrison of 2,000 soldiers established as Friedrich expanded his 'Residenzstadt'. In the centre of town, the Lustgarten was laid out opposite the palace. Running west from the palace the first Lindenallee (avenue of lime trees: Unter den Linden) was created.

To revive the economy, housing and property taxes were abolished in favour of a modern-style sales tax. With the money that was raised, three new towns – Friedrichswerder, Dorotheenstadt and Friedrichstadt – were built. (Together with Berlin and Cölln, today these make up the Mitte borough.) In the late 1660s a canal linked the Spree and Oder rivers, confirming Berlin's position as an east-west trading centre.

But Friedrich Wilhelm's most inspired policy was to encourage refugees to settle in the city. First to arrive were over 50 Jewish families from Vienna. In 1672 the first Protestant Huguenot settlers arrived from France. The influence of the new arrivals was pronounced, bringing new skills and industries.

The growing cosmopolitan mix laid the foundations for a flowering of intellectual and artistic life. By the time the Grand Elector's son, Friedrich III, took the throne in 1688 one-fifth of Berlin's population spoke French. This legacy can be seen in the many French words that still pepper Berlin dialect today, such as *Boulette* (hamburger) and *Etage* (floor).

In 1695 work commenced on **Schloß Charlottenburg** to the west of Berlin. A year later the Academy of Arts was founded. And in 1700, intellectual life was further stimulated by the founding of the Academy of Sciences under Gottfried Leibniz. The construction of the German and French cathedrals at the **Gendarmenmarkt** in 1701 gave Berlin one of its most beautiful squares. Five years later the Zeughaus (Armoury), now the **Deutsches Historisches Museum**, on Unter den Linden was completed, .

In 1701 Elector Friedrich III took a step up the hierarchy of European nobility when he had himself crowned Prussian King Friedrich I (not to be confused with the earlier Elector). In little more than half a century, Berlin had progressed from a devastated town to a thriving commercial centre with a population of nearly 30,000.

The Prussians are coming

The common association of Prussia with militarism can broadly be traced back to the eighteenth century and the efforts of two men: King Friedrich Wilhelm I and his son Friedrich II – also known as Friedrich the Great. Although they hated each other and had very different sensibilities (Friedrich Wilhelm was boorish and mean, his son sensitive and philosophical), together they launched Prussia as a major military power and in the process gave Berlin the character of a garrison city.

King Friedrich Wilhelm (1713-40) made parsimony and militarism state policy – and almost succeeded in driving Berlin's economy into the ground. The only thing that grew was the army, which by 1740 numbered 80,000 troops. Many of these were deployed in Berlin and billeted in the houses of ordinary citizens.

With a king more interested in keeping the books than reading them, intellectual life suffered. Friedrich had no use for art so he closed down the Academy of Arts; instead he collected soldiers, and swapped a rare collection of Oriental vases with the King of Saxony for a regiment. The Tsar got a small gold ship in exchange for 150 Russian giants.

But the obsession with all things military did have some positive effects. The king needed competent soldiers, so he made school compulsory; the army needed doctors, so he set up medical institutes. Eventually Berlin's economy also picked up on the back of demand from the military. City administration was reformed. Skilled immigrants (this time mostly from Saxony) met the increased demands. The result was a population boom (from 60,000 in 1713 to 90,000 in 1740) and a growth in trade and manufacturing.

Friedrich the Great

While his father collected soldiers, Friedrich the Great deployed them in a series of wars with Austria and Russia (from 1740-42, 1744-45 and 1756-63 – the Seven Years War) in a bid to win territory in Silesia in the east. Initially, the wars proved disastrous. The Austrians occupied the city in 1757, the Russians in 1760. However, with a mixture of luck and military genius, Friedrich finally emerged victorious from the Seven Years War.

When not fighting, the king devoted his time to forging a modern state apparatus (he called himself 'first servant of the state'; Berliners called him 'Old Fritz') and transforming Berlin and Potsdam. This was partly through conviction – the king was friends with Voltaire and brought him to live at Potsdam, and Old Fritz saw himself very much as an aesthetically-minded Enlightenment figure – but was also a political necessity. He needed to convince enemies and subjects that even in times of national crisis he was able to afford grand projects.

So Unter den Linden was made into a grand boulevard. At the palace end, the Forum

Friedrich the Great debates with Voltaire.

Fredericianium, constructed by the architect von Knobelsdorff, comprised the opera house, the St Hedwigskathedrale, the Prince Heinrich Palace (now the **Humboldt University**) and the state library. Although never fully completed, the Forum remains one of Berlin's main attractions.

To the west of Berlin, the **Tiergarten** was landscaped and a new palace, the Schloß Bellevue (now the Berlin residence of the German president), was built. Friedrich also decided to replace a set of barracks at the Gendarmenmarkt by a theatre, now called the **Konzerthaus**.

To encourage manufacturing and industry (particularly textiles), advantageous excise laws were introduced. Businesses such as the KPM (Königliche Porzellan-Manufacture) porcelain works were nationalised and turned into prestigious and lucrative enterprises.

Legal and administrative reforms also characterised Friedrich's reign. Religious freedom was enshrined in law; torture was abolished; and Berlin became a centre of the Enlightenment. Cultural and intellectual life blossomed around figures such as Moses Mendelssohn, the philosopher, and Gottfried Lessing, the poet.

By the time Friedrich died in 1786, Berlin had a population of 150,000 and was the capital of one of Europe's grand powers.

ENLIGHTENMENT'S END

The death of Friedrich the Great also marked the end of the Enlightenment in Prussia. His successor, Friedrich Wilhelm II, was more interested in spending money on architecture than wasting his time with political thought. Censorship was stepped up and the king's extravagance plunged the state into an economic and financial crisis. By 1788 over 14,000 people in the city were dependent on state and church aid. The state apparatus began to crumble under the weight of incompetent and greedy administrators. When he died in 1797, Friedrich Wilhelm II left his son with huge debts.

However, the old king's expensive love of classicism left Berlin with its most famous monument: the **Brandenburg Gate**. It was built by Karl Gottfried Langhans in 1789, the year of the French Revolution, and modelled on the Propylaea in Athens. Two years later, Johann Schadow added the Quadriga, a sculpture of a bare-chested Victoria riding a chariot drawn by four horses. Originally one of 14 gates marking Berlin's boundaries, the Brandenburg Gate is now the geographical and symbolic centre of the city.

If the king did not care for intellect, then the emerging bourgeoisie did. Towards the turn of the century, Berlin became a centre of German Romanticism. Literary salons flourished, and remained a feature of Berlin's cultural life into the middle of the nineteenth century.

Despite censorship, Berlin still had a platform for liberal expression. The city's newspapers welcomed the French Revolution so enthusiastically that in the southern German states Jacobins were referred to as 'Berliners'.

The Napoleonic wars

In 1806 Berlin came face to face with the effects of revolution in France: following the defeat of the Prussian forces in the battles of Jena and Auerstadt on 14 October, Napoleon's army headed for Berlin. The king and queen fled to Königsberg and the garrison was removed from the city. On 27 October Napoleon and his army marched through the Brandenburg Gate. Once again Berlin was an occupied city.

Almost immediately, Napoleon set about changing the political and administrative structure. He called together 2,000 prominent citizens and told

A triumphant Napoleon enters the city.

them to elect a new administration called the Comité Administratif. This body oversaw the city's day-to-day administration until the French troops left in 1808.

Napoleon decreed that property belonging to the state, the Hohernzollerns and many aristocratic families be expropriated. Priceless works of art were removed from palaces in Berlin and Potsdam and sent to France: even the Quadriga was taken from the Brandenburg Gate and shipped to Paris. The city also suffered financially. With nearly 30,000 French troops stationed in the city, Berliners had no choice but to supply them with accommodation and food. On top of this came crippling war reparations.

When the French left, a group of energetic, reform-minded aristocrats, grouped around Baron vom Stein, seized the opportunity to introduce a series of wide-ranging reforms in a bid to modernise the moribund Prussian state. One key aspect was the clear separation of state and civic responsibility, which gave Berlin independence to manage its own affairs. A new council was elected, based loosely on the Comité Administratif (though only property owners and the wealthy were entitled to vote). In 1810 the philosopher Wilhelm von Humboldt founded the university. All remaining restrictions on the city's Jewish population were removed.

Other reforms included the introduction of a new and simplified sales tax. A newly created 'trade police' was established to monitor trading standards. Generals Scharnhorst and Gneisenau completely overhauled the army.

Although the French occupied Berlin again in 1812 on their way home from the disastrous Russian campaign, this time they were met with stiff resistance. A year later the Prussian king finally joined the anti-Napoleon coalition and thousands of Berliners signed up to fight. When Napoleon tried to capture the city once more, he was defeated at nearby Grossbeeren. This, together with a subsequent defeat for the French in the Battle of Leipzig, marked the end of Napoleonic rule in Germany.

In August 1814, General Blücher brought the Quadriga back to Berlin, and restored it to its place on the Brandenburg Gate. One symbolic addition was made to the statue: an Iron Cross and Prussian eagle were added to the staff in Victoria's hand.

Biedermeier & Borsig

The burst of reform initiated in 1810 was short-lived. Following the Congress of Vienna (1814-15), which established a new order for post-Napoleonic Europe, King Friedrich Wilhelm III reneged on promises of constitutional reform. Instead of a greater unity among the German states, a loose

alliance came into being: dominated by Austria, the German Confederation was distinctly anti-liberal.

In Prussia itself, state power increased. Alongside the normal police, a secret service and vice squad were set up. The police president had the power to issue directives to the city council. Book and newspaper censorship increased. The authorities sacked Humboldt from the university he had set up.

With their hopes for lasting change frustrated, the bourgeoisie withdrew to their salons. It is one of the ironies of this time that although political opposition was quashed, a vibrant cultural movement flourished. Academics like Hegel and Ranke lectured at the university and enhanced Berlin's reputation as an intellectual centre. The period became known as Biedermeier after a fictional character embodying bourgeois taste, created by Swabian comic writer Ludwig Eichrodt.

Another legacy of this period is the range of neo-classical buildings designed by Karl Friedrich Schinkel, such as the Neue Wache (now the **Mahnmal** – a memorial to the victims of war) on Unter den Linden.

For the majority of Berliners, however, the post-Napoleonic era was a period of frustrated hopes and bitter poverty. Industrialisation swelled the ranks of the working class. Between 1810 and 1840, the city's population doubled to around 400,000, making Berlin the fourth-largest city in Europe. But most of the new arrivals lived in slums, in conditions which would later lead to riots and revolution.

INDUSTRIAL REVOLUTION

Prussia was ideally equipped for the industrial age. By the nineteenth century it had grown dramatically and boasted one of the greatest abundances of raw materials in Europe.

It was the founding of the Borsig Werke in the Chausseestraße in 1837 that established Berlin as the workshop of continental Europe. August Borsig was Berlin's first big industrialist. His factories turned out locomotives for the new railway network which had started with the opening of the Berlin to Potsdam line in 1838. Borsig also left his

Early industry – the Borsig Werke in 1862.

mark through the establishment of a suburb (Borsigwalde) that still carries his name.

The other great pioneering industrialist, Werner Siemens, set up his electrical engineering business in a small house near Anhalter Bahnhof. The first to manufacture telegraph equipment in Europe, Siemens personified the German industrial ideal with his combination of technical genius and business savvy.

The Siemens company also left a permanent imprint on Berlin through the building of a new suburb (Siemensstadt) to house its workers. With the growth of companies like these, Berlin became continental Europe's largest industrial city.

1848 and all that

Friedrich Wilhelm IV's accession to the throne in 1840 raised hopes of an end to repression; and initially, the new king did appear to want genuine change. He declared an amnesty for political prisoners, relaxed censorship, sacked the hated justice minister and granted asylum to political refugees.

Political debate thrived in coffee houses and wine bars. The university was another focal point. In the late 1830s, Karl Marx spent a term there, just missing fellow alumnus Otto von Bismarck. In the early 1840s Friedrich Engels came to Berlin in order to do his military service.

The thaw didn't last long. Friedrich Wilhelm IV shared his father's opposition to constitutional reform. Living and working conditions for the majority of Berliners worsened. Rapid industrialisation had also brought sweat-shops, 17-hour days and child labour.

This was compounded in 1844 by harvest failure which drove up prices for potatoes and wheat. Food riots broke out on the Gendarmenmarkt when a crowd stormed the market stalls. It took the army three days to restore order.

Things came to a head in 1848, the year of revolution across Europe. Berliners seized the moment. Political meetings were held in beer-gardens and in the Tiergarten, and demands made for internal reform and a unification of the German-speaking states. At the end of one demonstration in the Tiergarten, there was a running battle between police and demonstrators on Unter den Linden.

On 18 March, the king finally conceded to allowing a new parliament, and made vague promises about other reforms. Later that day, a crowd of 10,000 which had gathered to celebrate the victory were set upon by soldiers. Shots were fired and the revolution began. Barricades went up throughout central Berlin and demonstrators fought with police for 14 hours. Finally the king backed down (again). In exchange for the dismantling of barricades, the king ordered his troops out of Berlin.

Days later, he took part in the funeral service for the 'March dead' – the 183 revolutionaries who had been killed – and also promised more freedoms.

Berlin was now ostensibly in the hands of the revolutionaries. The city was patrolled by a Civil Guard, the king rode through the streets wearing the revolutionary colours (black, red, gold) and seemed to embrace the causes of liberalism and nationalism. Prussia, he said, should 'merge into Germany'.

But the revolution was short-lived. When pressed on unification, the king merely suggested that the other German states send representatives to the Prussian National Assembly. Needless to say, this offer was rebuffed.

Leading liberals instead convened a German National Assembly in Frankfurt in May 1848. At the same time, a new Prussian Assembly met in what is now the Konzerthaus on the Gendarmenmarkt to debate a new constitution. Throughout the summer and autumn of 1848, reforming fervour took over Berlin.

THE BACKLASH

The onset of winter, however, brought a change of mood to the city. Using continuing street violence as pretext, the king ordered the National Assembly to be moved to Brandenburg. In early November he brought troops back into the city and declared a state of siege. Press freedom was once again restricted. The Civil Guard was dissolved, followed shortly by the National Assembly. On 5 December the king delivered his final blow to the liberals by unveiling a new constitution fashioned to his own tastes.

Throughout the winter of 1848/49 thousands of liberals were arrested or expelled. A new city constitution, drawn up in 1850, reduced the number of eligible voters to five per cent of the population, or around 21,000 people. Increased police powers meant that the position of police president was more important than that of mayor.

By 1857 the increasingly senile Friedrich Wilhelm had gone quite literally mad. His brother Wilhelm acted as regent until becoming king on Friedrich's death in 1861.

Once again, the peoples' hopes were raised: the new monarch began his reign by appointing liberals to the cabinet. The building of the **Rotes Rathaus** (Red Town Hall) gave the city council a headquarters to match the size of the royal palace. Built between 1861 and 1869, the Rathaus was named for the colour of its bricks, and not (yet) political persuasion of its members.

But by 1861, the king found himself in dispute with parliament around proposed army reforms. The king wanted to strengthen his direct control of the forces. Parliament wouldn't accept this, so the king went over its members' heads and appointed a new prime minister: Otto von Bismarck.

The Iron Chancellor

An arrogant genius who began his career as a diplomat, Bismarck was well able to deal with unruly parliamentarians. Using a constitutional loophole to rule against the majority, he quickly pushed through the army reforms. Extra-parliamentary opposition was dealt with in the usual manner – oppression and censorship. Dissension thus suppressed, Bismarck turned his mind to German unification.

Unlike the bourgeois revolutionaries of 1848 who desired a Germany united by popular will and endowed with political reforms, Bismarck strove to bring the German states together under the authoritarian dominance of Prussia. His methods involved both astute foreign policy and outright aggression.

Wars against Denmark (1864) and Austria (1866) brought the post-Napoleonic order to an abrupt end. Prussia was no longer the smallest of the Great Powers but an aspiring initiator of geopolitical change. The defeat of Austria confirmed the primacy of Prussia among the German-speaking states.

Victory on the battlefield boosted Bismarck's popularity across Prussia, but not in Berlin. He was defeated in his Berlin constituency in the 1867 election to the newly created North German League (a Prussian-dominated body linking the northern states and a stepping stone towards overall unification).

Bismarck's third war – against France in 1870 – revealed his scope for intrigue and opportunism. He exploited a dispute over the succession to the Spanish throne to provoke France into declaring

Bismarck – intriguer and opportunist.

war on Prussia. Citing the North German League and treaties signed with the southern German states, Bismarck brought together a united German army under Prussian leadership.

Following the defeat of the French army on 2 September, Bismarck moved quickly to turn a unified military campaign into the basis for a unified nation. The Prussian king would be German emperor: beneath him would be four kings, 18 grand-dukes and assorted princes from the German states which would retain some regional powers. (This arrangement formed the basis for the modern federal system of regional Länder.)

On 18 January 1871, King Wilhelm was proclaimed German Kaiser (emperor) in the Hall of Mirrors in Versailles.

In just nine years, Bismarck had united Germany, forging an empire that dominated central Europe. The political, economic and social centre of this new creation was Berlin.

Imperial Berlin

The coming of empire threw Berlin into one of its greatest periods of expansion and change. The economic boom (helped by five billion gold francs extracted from France as war reparations) led to a wave of speculation. Farmers in Wilmersdorf and Schöneberg became millionaires overnight as they sold off their fields to developers.

During the decades following German unification, Berlin emerged as Europe's most modern metropolis. This period was later dubbed the Gründerzeit (foundation years).

The Gründerzeit was marked by a move away from traditional Prussian values of thrift and modesty, towards the gaudy and bombastic. In Berlin, the change of mood manifested itself in numerous monuments and buildings. Of these the **Reichstag**, **Siegessäule** (Victory Column), the **Berliner Dom** and the **Kaiser-Wilhelm-Gedächtniskirche** are the most prominent.

Superficially, the Reichstag (designed by Paul Wallot and completed in 1894) represented a weighty commitment to parliamentary democracy, but in reality Germany was still in the grip of conservative, backward-looking forces. The authoritarian power of the Kaiser remained intact, as was demonstrated by the decision of Kaiser Wilhelm II to sack Bismarck in 1890 following disagreements over policy.

BERLIN BOOMS

When Bismarck began his premiership in 1861, his offices in the Wilhemstraße overlooked potato fields. By the time he lost his job in 1890, they were in the centre of Europe's newest and most congested city. Economic boom and growing political and social importance attracted hundreds of thousands of new inhabitants to the city. At the time

Kaiser Wilhelm II – ill-advised facial hair.

of unification in 1871, 820,000 people lived in Berlin; by 1890 the population had nearly doubled.

The growing numbers of the working class were shoved into hastily built *Mietskasernen* tenements (literally, rental barracks) which mushroomed across the city – particularly in Kreuzberg, Wedding and Prenzlauer Berg. Poorly ventilated and hopelessly overcrowded, the *Mietskasernen* (many of which still stand) are characterised by a series of inter-linked courtyards. They became both a symbol of Berlin and a breeding ground for social unrest.

The Social Democratic Party (SPD), founded in 1869, quickly became the voice for the city's have-nots. In the 1877 general election it won over 40 per cent of the vote in Berlin. Here was born the left-wing reputation ('Rotes Berlin' – 'Red Berlin') which has followed the city into the late twentieth century.

In 1878 two assassination attempts on the Kaiser gave Bismarck an excuse to classify Socialists as enemies of the state. He introduced a series of restrictive laws to curb the 'red menace', and outlawed the SPD and two other progressive parties.

The ban existed until 1890 – the year of Bismarck's sacking – but did little to stem support for the SPD. In the general election held that year, the SPD dominated the vote in Berlin. And in 1912 it won over 70 per cent of the Berlin vote to become the largest party in the Reichstag.

Kaiser Bill

Famed for his ridiculous moustache, Kaiser Wilhelm II came to the throne in 1880 and quickly became (in many people's eyes) the personification of the new Germany: bombastic, awkward and unpredictable.

Like his grandmother Queen Victoria he gave his name to an era. Wilhelm's epoch is associated with showy militarism and foreign policy bungles leading to a world war that cost the Kaiser his throne and Germany its stability.

The Wilhemine years were also characterised by further explosive growth in Berlin (the population rose to two million by 1910 and by 1914 had doubled again) and a blossoming of the city's cultural and intellectual life. The Bode Museum was built in 1904 and in 1912 work began next door on the **Pergamon Museum**. In 1912 a new opera house was unveiled in Charlottenburg (later destroyed by wartime bombing; the **Deutsche Oper** now stands on the same site). Expressionism took off in 1910 and the Kurfürstendamm became the location for many new art galleries. Although Paris still remained ahead of Berlin in the arts, the German city was fast catching up.

By the time of his abdication in 1918, Wilhelm's reign had also seen the emergence of Berlin as a centre of scientific and intellectual development. Six Berlin scientists (including Albert Einstein and Max Planck) were awarded Nobel Prizes.

In the years immediately preceding World War I, Berlin appeared to be loosening its stiff collar of pomposity. Tangoing became all the rage in new

Pre-World War I, tango was all the rage.

clubs around the Friedrichstraße – though the Kaiser promptly banned officers in uniform from joining in the fun. Yet despite the progressive changes, growing militarism and international tension overshadowed the period.

Germany was not alone in its preparedness for war. By 1914 Europe was well and truly armed and almost waiting to tear itself apart. In June 1914 the assassination of Archduke Franz Ferdinand provided the excuse. On 1 August war was declared on Russia and the Kaiser appeared on a balcony of the royal palace to tell a jubilant crowd that from that moment onwards, he would not recognise any parties, only Germans. At the Reichstag the deputies, who had virtually unanimously voted in support of the war, agreed.

World War I & revolution

No one was prepared for the disaster of World War I. After Bismarck, the Germans had come to expect quick, sweeping victories. The armies on the Western Front settled into their trenches for a war of attrition that would cost over a million German lives. Meanwhile, the civilian population began to adapt to austerity and shortages. After the 1917 harvest failed, there were outbreaks of famine. Dog and cat-meat started to appear on the menus in the capital's restaurants.

The SPD's initial enthusiasm for war evaporated and in 1916 the party refused to pass the Berlin budget. A year later, members of the party's radical wing broke away to form the Spartacus League. Anti-war feeling was voiced in mass strikes in April 1917 and January 1918. These were brutally suppressed, but when the Imperial Marines in Kiel mutinied on 2 November 1918 the authorities were no longer able to stop the force of the anti-war movement.

The mutiny spread to Berlin where members of the Guards Regiment came out against the war. On 9 November the Kaiser was forced into abdication and subsequent exile. This date is weirdly layered with significance in German history; it's the anniversary of the establishment of the Weimar Republic (1918); Kristallnacht (1938); and the fall of the Wall (1989).

It was on this day that Philip Scheidemann, a leading SPD member of parliament and key proponent of republicanism, broke off his lunch in the second-floor restaurant of the Reichstag. He walked over to a window overlooking Konigsplatz (now Platz der Republik) where a crowd had massed and declared to them: 'The old and the rotten have broken down. Long live the new! Long live the German Republic!'

At the other end of Unter den Linden, Karl Liebknecht, who together with Rosa Luxemburg headed the Spartacus League, declared Germany a Socialist republic from a balcony of the occupied royal palace. (The balcony was the same one the Kaiser used when he spoke to Berliners on the eve of the war, and has been preserved as part of the Staatsratsgebaude, State Council building, of the East German government.)

Liebknecht and the Spartacists wanted a Communist Germany similar to Soviet Russia; Scheidemann and the SPD wanted a parliamentary democracy. Between them stood those still loyal to the vanished monarchy. All were prepared to fight their respective corners. Barricades were erected in the city centre and street battles ensued.

It was in this climate of turmoil and violence that Germany's first attempt at republican democracy – later known as the Weimar Republic – was born.

Terror & instability

The revolution in Berlin may have brought peace to the Western Front, where hostilities were ended on 11 November, but in Germany it unleashed a wave of political terror and instability. The new masters in Berlin, the SPD under the leadership of Friedrich Ebert, ordered renegade battalions of soldiers returning from the front (known as the Freikorps) to quash the Spartacists who launched a concerted bid for power in January 1919.

Within days, the uprising had been bloodily suppressed and Liebknecht and Luxemburg went into hiding. On 15 January Freikorps officers traced them to a house in Wilmersdorf and put them under arrest. They were then taken to a hotel near **Zoo Station** for interrogation. Between the hotel and Moabit prison, the officers murdered both of them and dumped Luxemburg's body over the Liechtenstein Bridge into the Landwehr Canal. Today a plaque marks the spot.

Four days later, the national elections returned the SPD as the largest party: the Social Democrats' victory over the extreme left was complete. Berlin was deemed too dangerous for parliamentary business, so the government swiftly decamped to the quaint provincial town of Weimar from which the first German republic took its name.

Germany's new constitution ended up being full of good liberal intentions but riddled with technical flaws. And this left the country wide open to weak coalition government and quasi-dictatorial presidential rule.

Another crippling blow to the new Republic was the Versailles Treaty, which set the terms of peace. Reparation payments (set to run until 1988) blew a hole in a fragile economy already weakened by war. Support for the right-wing nationalist lobby was fuelled by the loss of territories in both east and west. And restrictions placed on the German military led some right-wingers to claim that Germany's soldiers had been 'stabbed in the back' by Jews and left-wingers at home.

In March 1920, a right-wing coup was staged in Berlin under the leadership of Wolfgang Kapp, a civil servant from east Prussia. The recently returned government once again fled the city. For four days Berlin was besieged by roaming Freikorps. Some of them had taken to adorning their helmets with a new symbol: the Hakenkreuz or swastika.

Ultimately a general strike and the refusal of the army (the Reichwehr) to join Kapp brought an end to the putsch. But the political and economic chaos in the city remained. Political assassinations were commonplace. Food shortages lead to bouts of famine. Inflation started to escalate.

There were two main reasons for the precipitate devaluation of the Reichsmark. To pay for the war, the increasingly desperate imperial government had resorted simply to printing more money – a policy continued by the new republican rulers. The burden of reparations also lead to an outflow of foreign currency. In 1914 one dollar bought just over four Reichmarks; by 1922 it was worth over seven thousand. And one hyperinflationary year later, one dollar was worth 4.2 billion marks. Workers needed suitcases to carry the near-worthless bundles of notes that made up their salaries. Wheelbarrows replaced wallets as almost overnight the savings of millions were wiped out.

In the same year, 1923, the French government sent troops into the Ruhr industrial region to take by force reparation goods which the German government said it could no longer afford to pay. The Communists planned an uprising in Berlin for October but lost their nerve.

In November a young ex-corporal called Adolf Hitler, who led the tiny National Socialist Party (NSDAP or Nazi), launched an attempted coup from a beer-hall in Munich. His programme called for armed resistance against the French, an end to the 'dictatorship of Versailles' and punishment for all those – especially the Jews – who had 'betrayed' Germany at the end of the war.

Hitler's first attempt at power came to nothing. Instead of marching on Berlin, he went to prison. Inflation was finally brought down with the introduction of a new currency (one new mark was worth one trillion old ones).

But the overall decline of moral and social values that had taken place in the five years since 1918 was not so easy to restore.

The Golden Twenties

Joseph Goebbels came to Berlin in 1926 to take charge of the local Nazi party organisation.

On arriving, Goebbels observed: 'This city is a melting-pot of everything that is evil – prostitution, drinking houses, cinemas, Marxism, Jews, strippers, negroes dancing and all the off-shoots of modern art'.

The term 'evil' is better applied to Goebbels himself, but his description of 1920s Berlin was not far wrong. During that decade the city overtook Paris as continental Europe's arts and entertainment capital and in the process added its own decadent twist. 'We used to have a first-class army', mused Klaus Mann, the author of *Mephisto*, 'now we have first-class perversions.'

By 1927 Berlin boasted over 70 cabarets and night-clubs. At the Theater des Westens, near Zoo station, cabaret artist Josephine Baker danced to a packed house. Baker also danced naked at parties thrown by playwright Karl Volmoeller in his flat on Pariser Platz. 'Berlin was mad! A triumph!' she later recalled.

While Brecht's *Threepenny Opera* played at the Theater am Schiffbauerdamm, Berlin's Dadaists were gathered at the Romanisches Café on Tauentzienstraße (later destroyed by bombing – the **Europa-Center** now stands on the site) There was a proliferation of avant-garde magazines reflecting new ideas in art and literature.

But the flipside of all the frenetic enjoyment was an underbelly of raw poverty and glaring social tension reflected in the works of painters like George Grosz and Otto Dix. In the music halls, Brecht and Weill used a popular medium to ram home points about social injustices.

In architecture and design, the revolutionary ideas emanating from the Bauhaus school in Dessau (it briefly moved to Berlin in 1932 but was closed down by the Nazis a year later) were taking concrete form in building projects such as the **Shell House** building on the Landwehr canal, the Siemenstadt new town, and the model housing project Hufeisensiedlung (Horse Shoe Estate) in Britz. Furniture, ceramics, sculptures and sketches created in the Bauhaus workshop from 1919 until 1933 are kept in the **Bauhaus Archiv-Museum für Gestaltung**.

Street-fighting years

The stock market crash on Wall Street and the onset of global depression in 1929 ushered in the brutal end of the Weimar Republic.

The fractious coalition governments that had just managed to hold on to power in the brief years of prosperity in the late 1920s were no match for rocketing unemployment and a surge in support for extremist parties.

Already by the end of 1929 nearly one in four Berliners were out of work. The city's streets became a battleground for clashes between Nazis, Communists and social democrats. Increasingly the police relied on water cannons, armoured vehicles and guns to quell street-fighting across the city. One May Day demonstration left 30 dead and several hundred wounded. At Bülowplatz (now Rosa-Luxemburg-Platz) where the Communist

1932 – street violence reaches crisis point.

party, the KPD, had its headquarters, there were regular battles between Communists, the police and Nazi stormtroopers (the SA). In August 1931 two police officers were murdered on Bülowplatz. One of the men accused of the murders (and later found guilty, albeit by a Nazi court) was Erich Mielke, a young Communist, later to become the head of East Germany's secret police, the Stasi.

In 1932 the violence in Berlin reached crisis level. In just six weeks over the summer, 300 street battles left 70 people dead. In the general election in July, the Nazis took 40 per cent of the vote and became the largest party in the Reichstag. Hermann Göring, one of Hitler's earliest followers and a wounded veteran of the beer-hall putsch, was appointed Reichstag president.

The prize of government, however, still eluded the Nazis. At the elections held in November, the Nazis lost two million votes across Germany and 37,000 in Berlin where the Communists emerged as the strongest party. (In 'Red' Wedding, over 60 per cent voted for the KPD.)

The election had been held against the backdrop of a strike by the 20,000 public transport employees who were protesting against planned wage cuts. The strike had been called by the Communists and the Nazis who vied with each other to capture the mass vote and bring the Weimar Republic to an end. Under orders from

Moscow, the KPD shunned all co-operation with the SPD in a possible broad left-wing front.

As Berlin headed into another winter of depression, almost every third person was out of work. A city survey recorded that almost half of Berlin's inhabitants were living four to a room and that a large proportion of the city's housing stock was unfit for human habitation. Berlin topped the European table of suicides.

The new government of General Kurt von Schleicher ruled by presidential decree. Schleicher had promised President von Hindenburg he could tame the Nazis into a coalition. When he failed, his rival Franz von Papen successfully overcame Hindenburg's innate dislike for Hitler and manoeuvred the Nazi leader into power. On 30 January 1933, Adolf Hitler was named Chancellor and moved from his headquarters in the Hotel Kaiserhof in Glinkastraße (it was central and his favourite band played there) to the Chancellery two streets away in the Wilhelmstraße.

That evening, the SA staged a torchlight parade through the Brandenburg Gate and along to the Chancellery. Looking out from the window of his house next to the Gate, the artist Max Liebermann remarked to his dinner guests: 'I cannot eat as much as I'd like to puke.'

The Nazis take control

The government Hitler now led was a coalition of Nazis and German Nationalists led by the media magnate Alfred Hugenberg. Together their votes fell just short of a parliamentary majority so another election was called for March. In the meantime, Hitler continued to rule by decree.

The last relatively free election of the Republic was also the most violent. Open persecution of Communists began. The Nazis banned meetings of the KPD, shut down Communist newspapers and broke up SPD election rallies.

On 27 February a fire broke out in the Reichstag. It was almost certainly started by the Nazis, who used it as an excuse to step up the persecution of opponents. Over 12,000 Communists were arrested. Spelling it out in a speech at the Sportspalast two days before the election, Goebbels said: 'It's not my job to practise justice, instead I have to destroy and exterminate – nothing else.'

The Nazis still didn't achieve an absolute majority (in Berlin they polled 34 per cent), but that no longer mattered. With the support of his allies in the coalition, Hitler pushed through an Enabling Law giving him dictatorial powers. By summer, Germany had been declared a one-party state.

Already ad hoc concentration camps – known as brown houses after the colour of the SA uniforms – had sprung up around the city. The SS established itself in the Prinz Albrecht Palais where it was later joined by the secret police, the Gestapo.

Adolf entertains at the Sportpalast.

After the death of President Hindenburg in August 1934, Hitler had himself named Führer (leader) and made the armed forces swear a personal oath of allegiance to him. Within less than two years, the Nazis had subjugated Germany to their will.

Planning & persecution

A brief respite came with the Olympic Games in August 1936. In a bid to persuade foreign participants and spectators that all was well in the Reich, Goebbels ordered the removal of anti-Semitic slogans from shops. 'Undesirables' were also moved out of the city and the pavement-side display cases that held copies of the rabidly racist Nazi newspaper *Der Stürmer* ('The Stormtrooper') were dismantled.

The Games themselves, which were mainly held at the newly-built **Olympia Stadion** in Charlottenburg, were not such a success for the Nazis. Instead of blond, Aryan giants sweeping the field, Hitler had to watch the African-American Jesse Owens clock up medals and records. Whenever Owens won, Hitler fled the stadium so as not to have to shake hands with the real star of the Games.

The Games did work, however, as public relations. Foreign observers left Berlin glowing with reports about a strident and healthy nation. But had any of the foreign visitors stayed, they would have seen the reality of Hitler's policy of co-ordinating all facets of life in Berlin within the Nazi doctrine.

As part of a nationwide campaign to remove what the Nazis considered to be *Entartete Kunst* (degenerate art) from German cultural life, works of modern art were collected and brought together in a touring exhibition designed to show the depth of depravity in contemporary ('Jewish dominated') culture. But Nazi hopes that these 'degenerate' works would repulse the German people fell flat. When the exhibition arrived at the Zeughaus in Berlin in early 1938, thousands queued for admission. The people loved the paintings.

After the exhibition, the paintings were sent to auction in Switzerland. Those that remained unsold were burnt in the fire station in Köpenicker Straße. More than 1,000 oilpaintings and 4,000 watercolours were destroyed.

TOTALITARIAN TOWN-PLANNING
Shortly after taking power, Hitler ordered that the lime trees on Unter den Linden be chopped down to give Berlin's boulevard a cleaner, more sanitised form. This was just the first step taken in Nazi urban planning.

Hitler's plans for the redesign of Berlin reflected the hatred the Nazis felt for the city. Hitler entrusted young architect Albert Speer with the

Just to the north of Berlin near Oranienburg, a concentration camp, **Sachsenhausen**, was set up.

Along the Kurfürstendamm squads of SA stormtroopers would go 'Jew baiting' and on 1 April 1933, the first boycott of Jewish shops began. A month later Goebbels, who became Minister for Propaganda, organised a book-burning, which took place in the courtyard of the university on Unter den Linden. Books by Jews or writers deemed degenerate or traitors were thrown on to a huge bonfire.

Berlin's unemployment problem was tackled through a series of public works programmes, growing militarisation, which drew new recruits to the army, and the 'encouragement' of women to leave the workplace.

Following the policy of *Gleichschaltung* (co-ordination), the Nazis began to bring all aspects of public life under their control. With a few exceptions, party membership became obligatory for doctors, lawyers, professors and journalists.

During the Night of the Long Knives in July 1934, in an orgy of killing, Hitler settled some old scores with opponents within the SA and Nazi party. At Lichterfelde barracks, officers of the SS shot and killed over 150 SA members. Hitler's predecessor as Chancellor, General von Schleicher, was shot together with his wife at their home in Wannsee.

The onset of war meant that Speer only built a fraction of what was intended. Hitler's new Chancellery was constructed in under a year and finished in early 1939. It was demolished after the war. On the proposed east-west axis, a small section around the Siegessäule was widened for Hitler's fiftieth birthday in April 1939.

PERSECUTION

Of the half million Jews living in Germany in 1933 over a third lived in Berlin. The Jewish community had played an important role in Berlin's development and their influence was especially prevalent in the financial, artistic and intellectual circles of the city.

The Nazis wiped out these centuries-old traditions in 12 years of persecution and murder. Arrests soon followed the initial boycotts and acts of intimidation. From 1933 to 1934, many of Berlin's Jews fled to exile abroad. Those who stayed were to be subjected to legislation (the Nuremberg Laws of 1935) that banned Jews from public office, forbade them to marry Aryan Germans and stripped them of citizenship. Jewish cemeteries were desecrated and the names of Jews chipped off war memorials.

Berlin business institutions that had been owned by Jews – such as the Ullstein newspaper group and the Tietz and Wertheim department stores on Alexander and Potsdamerplatz – were 'Aryanised'. The Nazis either expropriated the owners or forced them to sell at ridiculously low prices.

On 9 November 1938, a wave of 'spontaneous' acts of vandalism and violence against Jews and their property began in response to the assassination of a German diplomat in Paris by a young Jewish emigré. Jewish businesses and houses across Berlin were stoned, looted and set ablaze. A total of 24 synagogues were set on fire. The Nazis rounded up 12,000 Jews and took them to Sachsenhausen concentration camp.

Nazis organise the boycott of Jewish shops.

job of recreating Berlin as a metropolis to 'outtrump Paris and Vienna'. The heart of old Berlin was to be demolished and its small streets replaced by two highways stretching 37 kilometres (23 miles) from north to south and 50 kilometres (30 miles) from east to west. Each axis would be 90 metres (100 yards) wide. Crowning the northern axis would be a huge Volkshalle (People's Hall) nearly 300 metres (328 yards) high with space for over 150,000 people. Speer and Hitler also had plans for a triumphal arch three times the size of the Arc de Triomphe and a new Führer's palace 150 times bigger than the one occupied by Bismarck. The new city was to be called Germania.

World War II

Since 1935, Berliners had been taking part in practice air-raid drills, but it was not until the Sudeten crisis of 1938 that the possibility of war became real. At that juncture Hitler was able to get his way and persuade France and Britain to let him take over the German-speaking areas of northern Czechoslovakia.

But a year later, his plans to repeat the exercise in Poland were met with resistance in London and Paris. Following Germany's invasion of Poland on 1 September 1939, Britain and France declared war on the Reich.

Despite a huge Nazi propaganda exercise and spectacular early victories, most Berliners were horrified by the war. The first air-raids came in

Roll-call at Sachsenhausen.

early 1940 when the RAF bombed Pankow and Lichtenberg.

In 1941 following the German invasion of the Soviet Union, the 75,000 Jews remaining in Berlin were required to wear a yellow Star of David and the first large-scale and systematic deportations to concentration camps began. By the end of the war in May 1945, only 5,000 Jews remained in Berlin.

Notorious assembly points for the deportations were Putlitzstraße in Wedding, Große Hamburger-straße and Rosenstraße in Mitte. On 20 January 1942, a meeting of the leaders of the various Nazi security organisations in the suburb of Wannsee agreed on a 'final solution' to the Jewish question. They joked and drank brandy as they sat around discussing mass murder.

The turning-point in the war came with the surrender of the German army at Stalingrad on 31 January 1943. In a bid to grab some advantage from this crushing defeat, Goebbels held a rally in the Sportpalast where he announced that Germany had now moved into a state of 'total war'. By summer, women and children were being evacuated from Berlin and schools were shut down. By the end of 1943, over 700,000 people had fled Berlin.

The 'Battle of Berlin', which the RAF launched in November 1943, began to reduce much of the city centre to rubble. Between then and February 1944, over 10,000 tonnes of bombs were dropped on the city. Nearly 5,000 people were killed and around a quarter of a million made homeless.

THE JULY PLOT

On 20 July 1944, a group of officers, civil servants and former trade unionists launched a last ditch attempt to remove Hitler through assassination and bring an end to the war. But Hitler survived the explosion of a bomb placed at his eastern command post in East Prussia by Colonel Count von Stauffenberg.

That evening Stauffenberg was killed by firing squad in the court-yard of army headquarters in Bendlerstraße, now Stauffenbergstraße. The other members of the plot were rounded up and put on trial at the People's Court near Kleistpark and subsequently executed at **Plötzensee** Prison.

In early January 1945, the Red Army launched a major offensive that carried it on to German soil. On 12 February, the heaviest bombing raid killed over 23,000 people in little more than an hour.

As the Red Army moved into Berlin's suburbs, Hitler celebrated his last birthday on 20 April in his bunker behind Wilhelmstraße. Three days later, Neukölln and Tempelhof fell. By 28 April, Alexanderplatz and Hallesches Tor were in the hands of the Red Army.

The next day Hitler called his last war conference. He then married his long-time companion Eva Braun and committed suicide with her the day after. As their bodies were being burnt by loyal SS

officers, a few streets away a red flag was raised over the Reichstag. The city officially surrendered on 2 May. Germany's unconditional surrender was signed on 8 May at the Red Army command centre in Karlshorst.

Devastation & division

When Bertolt Brecht returned to Berlin in 1948 he encountered 'a pile of rubble next to Potsdam'. Nearly a quarter of all buildings in the city had been destroyed. The human cost of the war was equally startling – around 80,000 Berliners had been killed, not including the thousands of Jews who would not return from the concentration camps.

There was no gas or electricity and only the suburbs had running water. Public transport had all but completely broken down. In the first weeks following capitulation, Red Army soldiers went on a rampage of random killings and rapes. Thousands of men were rounded up and transported to labour camps in the Soviet Union. Food supplies were used up and later the harvest in the war-scarred land around the city failed. Come winter, the few remaining trees in the Tiergarten and other city parks were chopped down for firewood.

Clearing the rubble was to take years of dull, painstaking work. The Trummerfrauen or 'rubble women' cleared the streets and created mountains

'Rubble women' cleared the post-war debris.

of brick and junk – such as the Teufelsberg, one of seven such hills which still exist today.

The Soviets stripped factories across the city as part of a programme to dismantle German industry and carry it back to the Soviet Union. As reparation, whole factories were moved to Russia.

Under the terms of the Yalta agreement which divided Germany into four zones of Allied control, Berlin was also split into four sectors, with the Soviets in the east and the Americans, British and French in the west. A Kommandatura, made up of each army's commander and based in the building of the People's Court in Elßholzstraße, administered the city.

Initially the administration worked well in getting basics, like the transport network, back to some form of running order. But tensions between the Soviets and the western Allies began to rise as civilian government of city affairs returned. In the eastern sector, a merger of the Communist and Social Democratic parties (which had both been refounded in summer 1945) was pushed through to form the Socialist Unity Party (SED). In the western sector, however, the SPD continued as a separate party.

Events came to a head after elections for a new city government in 1946. The SED failed to get more than 20 per cent of the vote, while the SPD won nearly 50 per cent of all votes cast across the city. The Soviets vetoed the appointment to office of the SPD's mayoral candidate, Ernst Reuter, who was a committed anti-Communist.

THE BERLIN AIRLIFT

The situation worsened in spring 1948. In response to the decision by the Western Allies to merge their respective zones in western Germany into one administrative and financial entity and introduce a new currency, the Soviets walked out of the Kommandatura. In late June, all transport links to west Berlin were cut off and the blockade of the city by Soviet forces began. Three 'air-corridors' linking west Berlin with western Germany became life-lines as Allied aircraft transported thousands of tonnes of food, coal and industrial components to the beleaguered city.

Within Berlin, the future division of the city began to take permanent shape as city councillors from the west were drummed out of the town hall. They moved to Schöneberg Town Hall in the west. Fresh elections in the western sector returned Reuter as mayor. The **Freie Universität** was set up in response to Communist dominance of the Humboldt University in the East.

Having failed to starve west Berlin into submission, the Soviets called off the blockade after 11 months. The blockade also convinced the Western Allies that they should maintain a presence in Berlin and that their sectors of the city should be linked with the Federal Republic which had been founded in May 1949. The response from

Allied aircraft broke the Soviet blockade.

the East was the founding of the German Democratic Republic on 7 October. With the birth of the 'first workers' and peasants' state on German soil', the formal division of Germany into two states was complete.

The Cold War

During the Cold War, Berlin was the focal point for stand-offs between America and the Soviets. Far from having any control over its own affairs, the city was wholly at the mercy of geopolitical developments. Throughout the 1950s the 'Berlin Question' remained high on the international agenda.

Technically the city was still under Four Power control, but since the Soviet departure from the Kommandatura and the setting up of the German Democratic Republic with its capital in East Berlin (a breach of the wartime agreement on the future of the city), this counted for little in practice.

In principle the Western Allies adhered to these agreements by retaining ultimate authority in West Berlin while allowing the city to be integrated as far as possible into the West German system. (There were notable exceptions such as the exemption of West Berliners from conscription and the barring of city MPs from voting in the West German parliament.)

Throughout the 1950s the two halves of Berlin began to develop separately as the political systems in East and West evolved. In the East, Communist leader Walter Ulbricht set about creating Moscow's most hard-line ally in eastern Europe. Work began on a Moscow-style boulevard – called Stalinallee – running east from Alexanderplatz. Industry was nationalised and subjected to rigid central planning. Opposition was kept in check by the newly formed Ministry for State Security: the Stasi.

West Berlin landed the role of 'Last Outpost of the Free World' and as such was developed into a showcase for capitalism. As well as the Marshall Plan, which paid for much of the reconstruction of western Germany, the Americans poured millions of dollars into West Berlin to maintain it as a counterpoint to Communism. The West German government, which at the time refused to recognise East Germany as a legitimate state, demonstrated its commitment to seeing Berlin reinstated as German capital by holding occasional parliamentary sessions in the city. The prominence accorded West Berlin was later reflected in the high profile of its politicians (Willy Brandt for example) who were received abroad by prime ministers and presidents – unusual for mere mayors.

Yet despite the emerging divisions, the two halves of the city continued to co-exist in some abnormal fashion. City planners on both sides of the sectoral boundaries initially drew up plans with the whole city in mind. The transport system crossed between East and West, with the underground network being controlled by the West and the S-Bahn by the East.

Movement between the sectors (despite 'border' checks) was relatively normal as Westerners went East to watch a Brecht play or buy cheap books. Easterners went West to work, shop or see the latest Hollywood films.

The secret services of both sides kept a high presence in the city, and there were frequent acts of sabotage on either side. Berlin became espionage capital of the world.

Reconstruction & refugees

As the effects of American money and the West German 'economic miracle' took hold, West Berlin began to recover. A municipal housing programme meant that by 1963 200,000 new flats had been built. Unemployment dropped from over 30 per cent in 1950 to virtually zero by 1961. The labour force also included about 50,000 East Berliners who commuted over the inter-sector borders.

In the East reconstruction was slower. Until the mid-1950s East Germany paid reparations to the Soviet Union. And to begin with there seemed to be more acts of wilful destruction than positive construction. The old palace, which had been only slightly damaged by bombing, was blown up in 1950 to make way for a parade ground which later evolved into a car park.

In 1952 the East Germans sealed off the border with West Germany. The only way out of the 'zone' was through West Berlin and the number of refugees from the East rose dramatically from 50,000 in 1950 to over 300,000 in 1953. Over the decade, one million refugees from the East came through West Berlin.

THE 1953 UPRISING

In June 1953, partly in response to the rapid loss of skilled manpower, the East German government announced a ten per cent increase in working 'norms' – the number of hours and volume of output that workers were required to fulfil each day. In protest, building workers on the Stalinallee

(now Karl-Marx-Allee) downed tools on 16 June and marched towards the government offices in the old Air Ministry on Leipzigerstraße. The government refused to relent and by the next day strikes had broken out across the city. Communist party offices were stormed and red flags torn from public buildings. By midday the government had lost control of the city and it was left to the Red Army to restore order. Soviet tanks rolled into the centre of East Berlin where they were met by stones thrown by demonstrators.

By nightfall the uprising was crushed. According to official figures 23 people died, though other estimates put the figure at over 200. There followed a wave of arrests across East Berlin with more than four thousand people being detained. The majority went on to receive stiff prison sentences.

The 17 June uprising only furthered the wave of emigration. By the end of the 1950s it was almost possible to calculate the moment when East Germany would cease to function as an industrial state through the loss of skilled labour. Estimates put the loss to the East German economy through emigration at around DM100 billion. Ulbricht stepped up his demands on Moscow to take dramatic action.

In 1958, the Soviet leader Nikita Khrushchev tried to bully the Allies into relinquishing West Berlin with an ultimatum calling for an end to the military occupation of the city and a 'normalisation of the situation in the capital of the GDR', by which he meant Berlin as a whole. The ultimatum was rejected and the Allies made clear their commitment to West Berlin. Unwilling to provoke a world war but needing to prop up his ally, Khrushchev backed down and sanctioned Ulbricht's alternative plan for a solution to the Berlin question.

The Wall

Throughout the early summer of 1961 rumours began to spread in the city that Ulbricht intended to seal off West Berlin with some form of barrier or reinforced border. Emigration had reached a highpoint as 1,500 East Germans fled West each day and it became clear that events had reached a crisis point.

However, when in the early hours of the morning of 13 August units of the People's Police (assisted by 'Working Class Combat Groups') began to drag bales of barbed wire across Potsdamer Platz, Berlin and the world were caught by surprise.

In a finely planned and executed operation (overseen by Erich Honecker, then Politburo member in charge of security affairs), West Berlin was sealed off within 24 hours. As well as a fence of barbed wire, trenches were dug, the windows in houses lining or straddling the new border were bricked up, and tram and railway lines were inter-

1962 – another brick in the Wall.

rupted: all this under the watchful eyes of armed guards. Anyone trying to flee West risked being shot, and in the 29 years the Wall stood, nearly 80 people died trying to escape. Justifying their actions, the East Germans later claimed they had erected an 'Anti-Fascist Protection Barrier' to prevent a world war.

Days later the construction of a brick wall began. When it was completed, the concrete part of the 100-mile (160km) fortification ran to 70 miles (112km); 23 miles (37km) of the Wall ran through the city centre. Previously innocuous streets like Bernauer Straße (where houses on one side were in the East, those on the other in the West) suddenly became the location for the world's most sophisticated and deadly border fortifications.

The initial stunned disbelief of Berliners turned into despair as it became clear that (as with the 17 June uprising) the Western Allies could do little more than make a show of strength. President Kennedy dispatched American reinforcements to Berlin and for a few tense weeks, American and Soviet tanks squared off at **Checkpoint Charlie**. Moral support from the Americans came with the visit of Vice-President Lyndon Johnson a week after the Wall was built. And two years later Kennedy himself arrived and spoke to a crowd of half-a-million people in front of the Schöneberg Town Hall. His speech linked the fate of West Berlin with that of the free world and ended with

John F Kennedy: 'I am a doughnut!'

the now famous statement 'Ich bin ein Berliner!' (Literally, alas, 'I am a doughnut'.)

In the early years the Wall became the scene of many daring escape attempts (all documented in the **Museum Haus Am Checkpoint Charlie**) as people abseiled off buildings, swam across the Spree river, waded through ancient sewers or simply tried to climb over the Wall.

But as the fortifications along the Wall were improved with mines, searchlights and guard dogs, and as the guards were given orders to shoot, escape became nearly impossible. By the time the Wall fell in November 1989 it had been 'updated' four times to incorporate every conceivable deterrent.

In 1971, the Four Powers met and signed the Quadrapartite Agreement which formally recognised the city's divided status. Border posts (such as the infamous Checkpoint Charlie) were introduced and designated to particular categories of visitors – one for foreigners, another for West Germans and so on.

Tale of two cities

During the 1960s, with the Wall as infamous and ugly backdrop, the cityscape of modern Berlin (both East and West) began to take shape. On Tauenzienstraße in the West the Europa-Center was built and the bomb-damaged Gedächtniskirche was given a partner – a new church made up of a glass-clad tower and squat bunker.

In the Tiergarten, Hans Scharoun laid out the Kulturforum as West Berlin's answer to the Museuminsel complex in the East. The first building to go up was Scharoun's **Philharmonie,** which was completed in 1963. Mies van der Rohe's **Neue Nationalgalerie** (which he had originally designed as a Bacardi factory in Havana) was finished in 1968.

In the suburbs work began on concrete mini-towns, Gropiusstadt and Märkisches Viertel. Conceived as modern-day solutions to housing shortages, they would later develop into alienating ghettos.

In the East, the **Alexanderplatz** was rebuilt along totalitarian lines and the **Fernsehturm** (television tower) was finished. The historic core of Berlin was mostly cleared to make way for parks (such as the Marx-Engels Forum) or new office and housing developments. On the eastern outskirts of the city in Marzahn and Hohenschönhausen work began on mass-scale housing projects.

In 1965, the first sit-down was staged on the Kurfürstendamm by students protesting against low grants and expensive accommodation. This was followed by political demonstrations as students took to the streets to protest against the state in general and the Vietnam war in particular. The first communes were set up in Kreuzberg, thereby sowing the seeds of a counter-culture which was to make that district famous.

In 1967 and 1968, the student protest movement came into increasingly violent confrontation with the police. One student, Benno Ohnesorg, was shot dead by police at a demonstration against the Shah of Iran, who visited the city in June 1967. A year later the students' leader, Rudi Dutschke, was shot by a right-winger. Demonstrations were held outside the offices of the newspaper group Springer whose papers were blamed for inciting the shooting. It was out of this movement that the Red Army Faction (also known as the Baader-Meinhof gang) was to emerge. It was often to make headlines in the 1970s, not least through a series of kidnappings of high-profile city officials.

NORMALISING ABNORMALITY

The signing of the Quadrapartite Agreement confirmed West Berlin's abnormal status and ushered in an era of decline as the frisson of Cold War excitement and 1960s rebellion petered out. More than ever, West Berlin depended on huge subsidies from West Germany to keep it going.

Development schemes and tax-release programmes were introduced to encourage business to move to the city (to keep the population in the city, Berliners also paid less income tax), but still the economy and the population declined.

At the same time there was growth in the number of *Gastarbeiter* (guest workers) who arrived from southern Europe and particularly Turkey, to take on jobs (mostly menial and low-paid) which most Germans shunned. Today there are over 120,000 Turks in the city, largely concentrated in Kreuzberg.

By the late 1970s, Berlin seemed to have reached the depths of decline. The city government was discredited by an increasing number of scandals, mostly connected with the property world. In East Berlin Erich Honecker's regime (he succeeded Ulbricht in 1971), which had begun in a mood of reform and change, became increasingly repressive. Some of East Germany's best writers and artists, who had previously been willing to support socialism, left the country. The Communists were glad to be rid of them. From its headquarters in Normannenstrasse (a building which now incorporates the **Ministerium für Staatssicherheit** museum), the Stasi directed its policy of mass observation and increasingly succeeded in permeating every part of East German society. Between East and West there were squalid exchanges of political prisoners for hard currency.

The late 1970s and early 1980s saw the rise of the squatter movement (centred in Kreuzberg), which brought violent political protest back on to the streets. The problem was only diffused after the Senate caved in and gave squatters rent contracts.

In 1987 Berlin celebrated its 750th birthday twice, as East and West vied to outdo each other with exhibitions and festivities. In the East the Nikolaiviertel was restored in time for the celebra-tions and Honecker began a programme to do the same for the few remaining historical sites which had survived both wartime bombing and post-war planning. The statue of Frederick the Great riding his horse was returned to Unter den Linden.

The fall of the Wall

But restored monuments were not enough to stem the growing dissatisfaction of East Berliners. The development of perestroika in the Soviet Union had been ignored by Honecker who stuck hard to his Stalinist instincts. Protest was increasingly vocal and only initially beaten back by the police.

By the spring of 1989, the East German state was no longer able to withstand the pressure of a population fed up with Communism. Throughout the summer, thousands fled the city and the country via Hungary, which had opened its borders to the West. Those who stayed began demonstrating for reforms.

By the time Honecker was hosting the celebrations in the Volkskammer (People's Chamber) to mark the fortieth anniversary of the GDR on 7 October 1989, crowds were demonstrating outside and chanting 'Gorby! Gorby!' to register their opposition. Honecker was ousted days later. His successor, Egon Krenz, could do little to stem the tide of opposition. In a desperate bid to defend through attack, he decided to grant the concession

November 1989 – the Wall is chipped away.

East Germans wanted most – freedom to travel. On 9 November 1989 the Berlin Wall was opened, just over 29 years after it had been built. As thousands of East Berliners raced through to the sound of popping corks, the end of East Germany and the unification of Berlin and Germany had begun.

Reunifying Berlin

With the Wall down, Berlin was once again the centre-stage of history. Just as the concrete division of the city defined the split of Europe, so the freedom to move again between east and west marked the dawn of the post-Cold War era.

Unsurprisingly such an auspicious moment went to Berlin's head and for more than a year the city was in a state of euphoria. Between November 1989 and October 1990 the city witnessed the collapse of communism and the first free elections (March 1990) in the east for more than 50 years; economic unification with the swapping of the tinny Ostmark for the Deutschmark (July 1990); and the political merger of east into west with formal political unification on 3 October, 1990. (It was also the year Germany picked up its third World Cup trophy. The team may have come from the west, but in a year characterised by outbursts of popular celebration, easterners cheered too.)

But unification also brought many problems for Berlin. To start with two distinct halves had to be made into one whole. Traffic jams on the roads between east and west were catastrophic. The telephone system in the west was modern; in the east it was antediluvian. Western infrastructure was in decent working order; in the east it was falling apart.

COLLAPSE & CONSTRUCTION

Challenges also came from the collapse of a command economy where jobs were provided regardless of cost or productivity. The Deutschmark put hard currency into the wallets of easterners, but it also exposed the true state of their economy. Within months thousands of companies across the east cut jobs or closed down altogether.

Overseeing this process of transformation was the Treuhandanstalt, a state agency responsible for the restructuring of eastern industry. Based first at Alexanderplatz and later in the former Reich air ministry on Wilhelmstraße, this behemoth gave highpaid employment to thousands of western yuppies and put hundreds of thousands of easterners on the dole. Understandably, the Treuhand soon became hated in the east and a target for popular anger.

In spring 1991 the head of the Treuhand, Detlev Karsten Rohwedder, was assassinated at his home in western Germany. The killing appears to have been the work of remnants of the Red Army Fraktion (RAF) who in a stroke of opportunism sought to hitch their clapped out ideological wagon to the frustrations of easterners.

In Berlin the killing of another state employee, Hanno Klein, drew attention to another dramatic change brought about by unification: a property boom. The biggest boost to the market ironically came from Bonn where in summer 1991 parliament voted to shift the seat of national government back to Berlin. Klein was responsible for drawing up a controversial master plan for the development of the new/old city centre where the Wall stood. Who killed him remains unknown.

But optimism about Berlin's rebirth as a metropolis proved premature. Having voted to move, Bonn delayed the actual transfer. Federal truculence in turn contributed to a dampening of spirits in Berlin where nerves were already frayed. The scrapping of federal subsidies to west Berlin cut private incomes and municipal services. The construction boom turned Berlin into one big building site.

The drift to normality

In summer 1994 the remaining Russian, US, British and French troops left Berlin. Their departure marked the formal end to the city's unique Cold War status. But it also deprived Berlin of the added internationalism which accompanied occupation. Without its status as capitalist bulwark or communist showcase, Berlin was on the way to becoming like any other big European city.

The drift to normality also brought the end to much of west Berlin's old coziness. Deprived of government incentives companies either slimmed down or quit the city altogether for western Germany or the rediscovered hinterland of Brandenburg. The Senate found itself facing near bankruptcy and began a painful round of cuts in culture, education and municipal services.

Perhaps in a bid to save Berlin from itself, the city embarked on a plan to merge with Brandenburg. On paper this made sense. Berlin's status as city-state was another Cold War anomaly. Redressing that would also relieve Berlin of an added tier of administration; as the capital of the merged state would have been Potsdam. But while the politicians pushed for merger, the people – particularly in Brandenburg, where resentment of the big city ran high – were unimpressed. In a referendum in both states in spring 1996 the merger plan was rejected.

The 1990s has been Berlin's decade. It began with events which not only changed the city, but also shook the world. But, perhaps perversely, the 1990s has also a decade when, unusually in its history, Berlin had no formal role to play on the national or European stage. No longer a symbol of dictatorship or ideological division; not yet the centre of a democratic Germany. But in the frustrating vacuum of anticipation, Berlin spent the 1990s doing what it had done so often in the past: regenerating itself out of the wreckage left by history's great turns.

Berlin Today

**Relentless change is the only constant in building-site Berlin, but a
new European metropolis is rising from the ashes of history.**

Berlin – 'forever in the process of becoming'.

Karl Scheffler, an Austrian art critic, took one
look at all the construction activity he could see
in Berlin and concluded that the city 'is forever
in the process of becoming and never in the state
of being'.

As a passing comment his words neatly capture
the city's fundamental restlessness – so essential
to Berlin and one of its particular charms. Few
other cities in Europe, and certainly none other in
Germany, appear to offer so much promise as
Berlin. With everything changing, opportunities
abound. With no firm establishment in place, newcomers and outsiders have a better chance of
putting ideas into action.

But curiously enough, Scheffler was not refer-
ring to contemporary Berlin. The late Herr
Scheffler was writing about Berlin at the turn of
the century when the after-burn of Bismarck's
original unification of Germany was rapidly trans-

forming the small-scale capital of Prussia into the
grandiose centre of an arriviste imperial power.

That Scheffler's words still read true now at the
end of the century, when Berlin is in the state of
becoming (once again) Germany's capital city, is
revealing. Yes, Berlin in the late 1990s is unique
among European cities. Where else, after all, can
you walk through a massive open-heart surgery
operation as the two halves of a city – each beat-
en for decades to a different ideological drum – are
painstakingly stitched together? But seen in the
context of the city's own history, the process of
transformation and regeneration engulfing Berlin
in the late 1990s is not an entirely novel experience.

Whether after the Thirty Years War, the
Napoleonic invasion or 1945 devastation after the
crushing of Nazism, Berlin has repeatedly had to
pick itself up and rebuild in the wake of one of history's great wipe-outs.

Yet while the present transformation may be
in keeping with Berlin's history, it hardly offers
its inhabitants the comfort that tends to come
with tradition. When historians come to write up
the 1990s, they will look back on a period in
which the city and its people seemed to lose their
way in the midst of so much relentless change.
The situation before the Wall came down may
have been one of normalising the abnormal, but
Berlin's citizens had grown used to such cer-
tainties as that situation offered. Now easterners can no longer count on the persistent
presence of an omnipresent state which may
have limited personal freedoms but also provided cradle-to-grave security. Westerners,
meanwhile, are having to learn to live in a new
world where public subsidies are no longer so
generous, taxes no longer lower than elsewhere
in the country, and the pace of life no longer so
amenable to artistic experimentation and the
exploration of personal space.

Money now plays a profound role in the life of
the city. This is new. In the old days the tab was
picked up either by the federal government in
Bonn or smoothed away in the fantasy financing
of the communist system – neither of whom ever
seemed to question the bill. Speculative investment matched with public money is physically
transforming Berlin with brash real-estate developments and infrastructure upgrades. But the
lack of cash in municipal coffers has lead to

East meets west – brand-name burgers and communist landmarks.

painful cuts in services, especially in education and culture, while restraints on personal spending have affected daily life all over the city.

The effects are not hard to spot. Central west Berlin has become shabbier and quieter as less money is spent in and on such glossy former showcases as the Ku'Damm. The city's large student population – some 130,000 – which once enjoyed something of a charmed existence, is now rumbling with discontent as budget cuts limit places and threaten to introduce fees (*see page 245* **The student's lot**). Meanwhile, the artistic community is frankly appalled that the 'Weltstadt' Berlin no longer has the funds to subsidise their latest creative urges. They claim the city is losing its edge and becoming more provincial.

And in many ways this is true. The departure of the Allied forces in 1994 also removed an international edge from the city. Against that Berlin has seen a fresh influx of foreigners – from nouveau riche Russians attracted by the city's location as convenient first port-of-call in 'the West' to itinerant Europeans and North Americans drawn to the Berlin's enduring reputation as an 'edgy' place. Though these new arrivals have bolsterd the city's claim to cosmopolitanism, they are unlikely to have the kind of profound impact on city life caused by previous generations of immigrants such as the French Huguenots or White Russians.

Another feature of present-day Berlin is the disorientation caused by the almost literal moving of the ground under one's feet as the city's centre of gravity moves (or returns) to the east. While construction mushrooms around Potsdamer Platz and the Spreebogen, and northern Mitte asserts itself as the new centre of fashion, art and nightlife, bits of old west Berlin are suffering. The streets north and south of the Kurfürstendamm, which once used to be considered central, now seem deserted by comparison. Schöneberg and Kreuzberg, formerly the beating heart of bohemian Berlin, are now relatively quiet inner-city areas, ripe for gentrification. Against that the classically narrow roads of Mitte and more boastful streets of Prenzlauer Berg change almost on a weekly basis as buildings are renovated and new shops, bars and restaurants move in.

The east is not only the most popular destination for leisure pursuits. The government, when it arrives, will be in the east – as will most of the paraphernalia that goes with it, such as embassies and offices for lobbyists and the media. For students arriving in Berlin today, it is no longer the Freie Universität housed out in Dahlem whch offers the most promise, but rather the Humboldt on Unter den Linden.

As well as watching the centre stage lurch eastwards, Berliners have also been confronted with the competing attractions of the hinterland of

Brandenburg. Lower-priced greenfield sites decorated with juicy financial and material incentives have lured many companies out of town. The prospect of a truly suburban home has persuaded many young families to move to Brandenburg. According to the DIW economic research insitute, from the year 2000 such migration will annually cost Berlin some DM400m in lost taxes and spending. The problem is compounded by the fact that those who move out still want to use the city's educational, cultural and health services.

Unsurprisingly, the challenges presented by all of the above have been difficult to meet. The Senate, the city's government, appears in a state of shock – unable, or unwilling, to make the necessary policy changes demanded by events around it. Empty coffers demand cuts be made. But when it comes to making the incision everyone insists on being an exception. The result is a painfully slow decision-making process which benefits no one.

Part of the problem is whereas west Berlin once enjoyed strong local governments equipped with the sense of purpose necessary to see the city through some trying times, united Berlin has been ill-served by an unwieldy grand coalition between Christian Democrats (CDU) and Social Democrats (SPD). The reason for this unfortunate alliance of giants – who spend as much time arguing with each other as they do actually running the city – is the Party of Democratic Socialism (PDS), the successor to East Germany's ruling Socialist Unity Party, as the communists called themselves here.

Despite all the mainstream western parties' efforts to bury it, the PDS has proved a resilient force, regularly picking up over 20 per cent of the vote in east Berlin. At city level this means that neither of the big parties – the CDU or SPD – could govern alone or in a coalition of their preference with, say, the Greens. At a national level support for the PDS in Berlin has secured it three direct seats and thus entry into the Bundestag.

While the policies of the PDS are half-baked, the party has been an effective motivator of eastern disappointment with unification. The PDS also contributed towards the failure in 1996 of a plan to merge the city-state of Berlin with Brandenburg. While the other parties generally backed the plan, the PDS came out against it and successfully played to eastern fears in Brandenburg of being dominated by Berlin. (To be fair, some west Berliners were also nervous about 'eastification', though in general the city voted for the plan while Brandenburgers rejected it.)

But in the midst of the gloom there are signs of renaissance. The media and film industries have boomed in recent years, partly due to the influx of new talent attracted by the city's restless state. Mitte's art scene is attracting galleries not only from west Berlin, but even from as far away as Cologne. The most visible signs of the new Berlin

On yer bike – getting the message across.

emerging can already be seen in the buildings which are now being completed. Architecturally, most are nothing special. But in the midst of all the standard steel and glass modules, there are a few gems. *See chapter* **Architecture**.

Some improvements have come directly out of present hardships. For instance, the acute lack of cash has forced the city to take a radical approach towards the sprawling public sector. Assets, such as the electricity and gas companies, have been sold off, partly to foreigners eager to break into heavily protected and over-priced German markets. As such Berlin is positioning itself as a pioneer among German cities, many of whom eventually have to make similar decisions. The wholesale reconstruction of eastern infrastructure means that Berlin is becoming one of Europe's most modern cities – 60,000 kilometres of new fibre optic cable, for example, makes Berlin the continent's most wired metropolis.

It is that position as pioneer which Berlin is now seeking to achieve. The arrival of the federal government will certainly help. Politicians and civil servants may not make the place more exciting. But once the national (and possibly international) headlines are being made in Berlin as newly rebuilt capital of the continent's biggest and most powerful nation, the standing of the city will once again rise to that of a major European metropolis.

Berlin by Season

The city's cultural calendar is crowded all year round.

Summer in Berlin is marvellous. The streets bustle with activity; cafés, bars and restaurants spill out on to the pavements; and people become more helpful and friendly as they emerge from what seems like a prolonged period of hibernation. This is largely due to the severity and length of the Berlin winter which can see temperatures plummet as low as minus 20°C, and which turns the sky into a static, grey blanket for months on end.

However, the extremes in the weather seem to have little affect on the city's cultural calender which is packed all year round. Taking in a broad spectrum of events and festivals, from classical music, theatre, jazz and sport to gay pride, techno mardi gras and world music concerts, there is something for every visitor, whenever they come.

Information

Berlin Tourismus Marketing

Europa-Center, Budapester Straße, Charlottenburg, 10787 (250 025/fax 2500 2424). U2, U9/S3. S5, S6, S7, S9 Zoologischer Garten. **Open** 8am-10pm Mon-Sat; 9am-9pm Sun. Reduced opening hours on public holidays. **Map D4**
Among everything you might expect from a tourist office, you can also pick up a copy of *Berlin – The Magazine* (DM3), a publication in English and German offering information on three months of cultural and sporting events in the city.
e-mail: information@btm.de
http: www.berlin.de
The main tourist information office, with branches at Tegel Airport and the Brandenburg Gate.
Branches: im Brandenburger Tor, Unter den Linden, Mitte. (250 025); Airport Service Flughafen Tegel (250 025).

Messe Berlin Trade Fair and Exhibition Grounds

Messedamm 22, Charlottenburg, 14055 (30 380). U2 Kaiserdamm. **Open** 8am-6pm Mon-Fri.
Helpful, multi-lingual staff provide details on trade fairs.
e-mail: marketing@messe-berlin.de

Spring

Musik Biennale Berlin

Philharmonie, Matthäikirchstraße 1, Schöneberg, 10785 (254 880). U1 Kurfürstenstraße/bus 148 And other venues. Contact: *Berliner Festspiele, Budapester Straße 50, Tiergarten (254 890).* **Dates** 1998 and every other year in March. **Admission** varies.
After unification, this former East German festival highlighting trends in contemporary serious music was spared extinction and put on the west Berlin life support system. Held every other year, the ten-day event invites international avant-garde and modern composers and musicians to present music that is anything but harmonious. *See also chapter* **Music: Classical & Opera**.

International Tourism Trade Fair Berlin

Messe Berlin Trade Fair and Exhibition Grounds, Messedamm 22, Charlottenburg, 14055 (30 380). U2 Kaiserdamm. **Open** 10am-6pm. **Dates** early March. **Admission** DM21.
Berliners dub this enormous tourism and travel trade fair 'the world's biggest travel agency'. Although you can't make bookings during the six-day fair, you can pick up enough brochures to open a recycling plant, and get information on the world's most popular or obscure destinations directly from people who live there. It's around the world in a day – if you can get through the crowds in the exhibition halls.

Urbane Aboriginale

Haus der Kulturen der Welt, John-Foster-Dulles-Allee 10 (397 870). S3, S5, S6, S9 Lehterstadt. Podewil, Klosterstraße 68, Mitte, 10179 (247 496). U2 Klosterstraße.
Contact: *Freunde Guter Musik eV, Erkelenzdamm 11-13, Kreuzberg, 10999 (615 2702).* **Dates** spring.
Admission DM18-25 per performance.
This festival of iconoclastic music and performance has been introducing experimental, avant-garde artists from different nations to Berlin since 1985. Between ten and 40 musicians, theatre, dance and performance groups and soloists spend about a week demonstrating that the world's underground art world is a strange beast indeed.

Berliner Halbmarathon

Contact: *Berlin Marathon, Alt-Moabit 92, Moabit, 10559 (302 5370).* **Date** first Sun in April. **Admission** *participants* DM30, *spectators* free.
As its name suggests, this 21-kilometre (13 mile) run is half the stretch of the summer marathon. Starting point is on the Karl-Marx-Allee. Participants usually number around 4,000.

May Day Riots

Around Kollwitzplatz, Prenzlauer Berg. **Date** afternoon of May 1.
The May Day Riot has become an annual fixture since 1987 when 'Autonomen' engaged in violent clashes with police before going on to smash, loot and eventually burn down their local supermarket. These days the action, along with the few remaining squatters, has shifted from Kreuzberg to Prenzlauer Berg. There are usually a number of tense confrontations between police and protesters during the course of the afternoon, but these days it seems it is only the truly inebriated, or tourists from Stuttgart, who stay to the bitter end.

Theatertreffen Berlin

Contact: *Berliner Festspiele, Budapester Straße 50, Tiergarten, 10787 (254 890).* **Dates** end of April and beginning of May. **Admission** varies.
The best that German-speaking theatre has to offer. A jury of experts picks about a dozen of the most intriguing new productions from theatres in Germany, Austria and Switzerland. The winning companies get a trip to Berlin where they perform their piece two or three times during the fortnightly meeting. There is also a smaller Youth Theatre Meeting at the end of May that runs along the same principles. Venues vary from year to year, so check the local press for details.

German Open

LTTC Rot Weiss eV, Gottfried-von-Cramm-Weg 47-55,
Grunewald, 14193 (895 7550). S3 Grunewald or bus
119, 186 Hagenplatz. **Dates** 20th week of the year, in
May. **Admission** DM40-DM80 for seats, DM20 for day
ticket with access to all courts except centre court.
The Internationale Tennismeisterschaften von Deutschland
für Damen, as the German Open is subtitled, is the fifth
largest international women's tennis championship in the
world. Not just a chance for Steffi to bag another $900,000,
it's also a week-long get-together of Germany's rich and
famous. Come match point, the focus switches to the annual gala ball and other glitzy social affairs. Mortals have a
hard time getting tickets – centre court games are sold out
a year in advance. Day tickets with access to all eight courts
except centre court, however, are affordable, available and
worthwhile during the first few days of the tournament.

Deutsche Pokalendspiele

German Football Cup
Olympiastadion, Charlottenburg, 14053 (30 06 33). U2
Olympia-Stadion. **Tickets & Information** *Berliner*
Fußball Verband, Humboldtstraße 8A, Grunewald, 13407
(896 9940). **Date** May/June. **Admission** DM20-DM120.
Berlin's football frenzy, when 65,000 fans drink and dance
in the aisles of a sold-out Olympic stadium.

Import Messe Berlin

Messe Berlin fair grounds, Messedamm 22,
Charlottenburg, 14055 (303 80). U2 Kaiserdamm. **Open**
10am-8pm. **Dates** late March. **Admission** DM14.
Four-day trade fair for the world's importers, exporters and
producers of textiles, leather wear, jewellery, glass, ceramics, carpets and furniture. Stock up on ethnic goods and
cheap western clothing at the consumer market for almost
the same prices you would pay in Bali, Brazil or Botswana.

Summer

Berlin Philharmonie at the Waldbühne

Waldbühne, Glockenturmstraße/cr Passenheimer Straße.
14053, U2 Olympia-Stadion, shuttle buses run for major
events. **Date** June. **Admission** DM27-DM58.
Often judged to be the world's greatest orchestra, the Berlin
Philharmonic ends its season with an open-air concert at the
Waldbühne. The event marks the arrival of summer for
22,500 Berliners, who, once darkness sets in, light up the
venue with thousands of candles, lighters, matches, and pro-
hibited but smuggled-in sparklers. Memorable music for the
masses. The atmospheric Waldbühne is one of Berlin's best
summer venues for big-name rock bands. It hosts an Oldie
Night (DM48-DM58) each Aug or Sept, giving bygone stars
a chance to feel loved again. Films shown on the arena's huge
screen are a major party a few nights a week throughout
summer. See local press for details.

Deutsch-Französisches Volksfest

German-French Festival
Kurt-Schumacher-Damm, Tegel, 13405 (213 3290). U6
Kurt-Schumacher-Platz. **Dates** mid-June until mid-July.
Admission DM2,50.
Berlin's largest Volksfest features Europe's biggest travel-
ling rollercoaster, lots of wine, frogs' legs, snails and other
French specialities, and the model of a different French town
highlighted every year.

Christopher Street Day Parade

Begins at Adenauerplatz, marches through the
Brandenburg Gate and finishes at the Rotes Rathaus.
Date end of June. **Admission** free. Evening parties at
different venues DM10-DM35.
Commemorating the 1969 riots at the Stonewall Bar in
Christopher Steet, New York, which marked the beginning

Café culture comes into its own in summer.

of modern gay liberation. The Saturday parade and week-
long festival are a popular celebration of Berlin's lesbian and
gay community and have developed into one of the most
flamboyant summer tourist attractions. *See also chapter* **Gay**
& Lesbian Berlin.

Love Parade

Date second Sat in July. **Admission** free for parade,
varies for the official raves in the evening.
A kind of techno/house Mardi Gras, this spectacular event
has come along way since its inception in 1989 when a couple of vans began blasting out techno to a few bemused shoppers on the Kurfürstendamm. In 1997, the Love Parade
attracted over one million ravers who partied aboard, alongside and behind floats sponsored by clubs, record labels,
magazines and posses from all over Europe. The ensuing
raves and parties, known collectively as 'The Weekend of
Love' carried on for days. However, in addition to the euphoria, the parade also stokes up a fair amount of controversy.
In 1997 it was almost cancelled after a legal battle with environmentalists over its route through the Tiergarten public
park, and at the time of writing it was still not clear whether
or where it would take place in 1998. There has even been
talk of the event moving to Paris. However, despite the uncertainty, few believe that the city would let go of an event
which generates so much publicity and, perhaps more impor-
tantly, so much money – particularly if it's the French who
want it.

Bach-Tage Berlin

Philharmonie, Matthäikirchstraße 1, Schöneberg, 10785,
(254 880). U1 Kurfürstenstraße and bus 148.
Schloß Charlottenburg, Spandauerdamm,
Charlottenburg, 14059 (329 911). U1 Sophie-Charlotte-
Platz.

Schauspielhaus, Gendarmenmarkt, Mitte, 10117 (2090 2157). U6 Französische Straße.
Plus various churches throughout Berlin.
Contact: *VDMK, Kaiserdamm 31, Charlottenburg, 14057 (301 5518).* **Dates** first two weeks of July in years with odd numbers. **Admission** DM10-DM50.
Despite a series of hot summers since 1970, this nine-day festival paying tribute to the work of Bach and other baroque composers has lured some 16,000 to 20,000 classical music buffs indoors every other year. They come to hear top international baroque orchestras and soloists perform in a series of about 30 concerts. Since the fall of the Wall the festival has expanded to classical music venues in east Berlin, and historical sites in the capital's surroundings, such as Schloß Sanssoucci in Potsdam. (*See chapter* **Trips out of Town**.)

Jazz in July
Quasimodo, Kantstraße 12A, Charlottenburg, 10623 (312 8086). U2, U9/S3. S5, S6, S7, S9 Zoologischer Garten. **Dates** two to three weeks beginning early July. **Admission** DM30-DM45.
More summertime music: This time in the smokey cellar of the Quasimodo. Organisers pick up top jazz acts already on their way to large European festivals. Recent headliners have included Branford Wynsalis, Maynard Ferguson, Bill Evans, Lenny White, Defunkt and Artie Shepp. This excellent venue (*see chapter* **Music: Rock, Folk & Jazz**) is in tune with seasonal trends, and concerts are usually packed out.

Deutsch-Amerikanischer Volksfest
German-American Festival
Hüttenweg, Zehlendorf, 14195 (401 3889). U2 Oskar-Helene-Heim. **Dates** late July to mid-Aug. **Admission** DM2,50.
The Allies may be gone now, but the joint German/American festival they established in 1961 continues. There are lots of rides, gambling, and stalls selling alcohol, German specialities and authentic American junk food. Tacky, but Berliners lap it up.

Heimatklänge
See chapter **Music: Rock, Folk & Jazz** for details.
Berlin's biggest world music event. Through July and August, for four nights a week plus Sunday afternoons, the Tempodrom hosts acts from all corners of the globe. Expect anything from a chanting Mongolian shaman to an orchestra of Patagonian nose flautists. The concerts have only one thing in common: they're free.

Hofkonzerte
Schultheiss Brauerei, Schmiedehof, Methfesselstraße 28-48, Kreuzberg, 10965 (780 030). U6 Platz der Luftbrücke.
Podewil, Klosterstraße 68, Mitte, 10179 (24 74 96). U2 Klosterstraße.
Dates every weekend in July, Aug. **Admission** varies.
Inside the red-brick Schultheiss brewery next to the Kreuzberg, there's jazz on Friday and classical concerts on Saturday evenings. While the Schultheiss concerts present local musicians, Podewil schedules artists from across Europe. If it rains, concerts move indoors. At both there's veggies and wurst, wine and, of course, beer.

Tango Sommer
Podewil, Klosterstraße 68, Mitte, 10179 (247 496). U2 Klosterstraße. **Dates** late June to mid Aug, Thur from 9pm. **Admission** DM20-DM30
Held in the courtyard of the Podewil arts centre, 'Tango Summer' has proved tremendously popular since its launch in 1996. Attracting a mixed crowd, it is a perfect opportunity to show off your foot and body-work, or simply to soak up the summer sun and the music, played live by orchestras from Europe and Argentina.

Classic Open Air
Gendarmenmarkt, Mitte, 10117 (2090 2488). U6 Französische Straße. Contact: *Media On-Line office open May-July.* **Date** four days (Thur-Sun) in July. **Admission** DM25-DM115.
Established in 1990, this four-day festival is already a fixture in the calendars of classical music-lovers. Organisers schedule big names such as José Carreras or Montserrat Caballe for the opening concert and fill the rest of the programme with lighter-weight but still quality talent. Set in one of the city's most beautiful squares, the festival provides a perfect place to sit beneath the setting sun and rising stars and enjoy the music. Many Berlin orchestras take part, and soloists are engaged from all over Europe. Regular features are the Strauß concert and the 'Eternal Songs' closing concert, with classical and rock hits.

Internationale Funkaustellung
International Electronics Exhibition
Messe Berlin Trade Fair Grounds, Messedamm 22, Charlottenburg, 14055 (30 380). U2 Kaiserdamm. **Open** 10am-7pm. **Dates** late Aug 1999 and every other year. **Admission** DM22; DM16 concs.
All that is new, up, and coming in the world of consumer electronics comes to town during this nine-day trade fair. World market leaders present the latest in eclectic electrics: from audio, TV, video, camcorder and digital photography, to antennae, satellite reception stations and mobile communication. The exhibition is visited by upwards of 370,000 people each year.

Berliner Festwochen
Berlin Festival Weeks
Philharmonie, Matthäikirchstraße 1, Schöneberg, 10785, (254 88-0). U2 Kurfürstenstraße and bus 148.
Schauspielhaus, Gendarmenmarkt, Mitte, 10117 (2090 2157). U6 Französische Straße.
Plus various other venues.
Contact: *Berliner Festspiele, Budapester Straße 50, Tiergarten, 10787 (254 890).* **Dates** through Sept. **Admission** varies.
The cultural summer closes with a month of events, concerts and performances highlighting a different nation or artistic theme. The emphasis is on classical music and international theatre, accompanied by various exhibitions, author readings and seminars.

Berliner Marathon
For details see chapter **Sport & Fitness**.
Berlin's biggest sporting event is also the world's third largest marathon. Sprinters are led past most of Berlin's landmarks on their 42 km (26-mile) trek through ten districts. About 20,000 runners take part, and if the weather is fine, they're cheered on by a million spectators. Two-thirds of participants come from Germany; the other third from all over the world, so finding a hotel room over this weekend is next to impossible. Don't plan on leaving the city – traffic is re-routed into an incomprehensible labyrinth.

Autumn

Art Forum
Messedamm 22, Charlottenburg, 14055 (30 380). U2 Kaiserdamm. **Open** 10am-6pm. **Dates** late September early October. **Admission** DM20; DM10 concs.
Set up in 1996 as a networking opportunity for gallery owners and artists, this five-day fair of contemporary art attracts many of Europe's leading galleries as well as thousands of lay enthusiasts from all over the continent. Non-trade visitors are advised to take a guide, preferably some one familiar with the art scene who can chart a meaningful course though the dozens of hangar-type halls, each of which houses scores of exhibitions.

Oktoberfest

At different venues each year. Check local press for details or call promoters on 213 3290. **Dates** end Sept-Oct. **Admission** DM2 adults, children free.
Nothing like being at Bavaria's beer bash, but Berlin's version provides a good excuse to guzzle beer until it doesn't matter where you are. Partake of charcoal-grilled sausages and other German specialities after you've made the rounds – much of the fest is comprised of stomach-wrenching rides.

JazzFest Berlin

For details see chapter **Music: Rock, Folk & Jazz**.
Jazz dominates the cultural scene for four days each autumn. The whole jazz spectrum is on offer, performed by a mixed bag of internationally renowned artists and the originators of local and German jazz projects. Going strong since 1964, the festival often is accompanied by sub-festivals highlighting specific categories of contemporary music, photo exhibitions and concerts at other venues.

Jüdische Kulturtage

Jewish Culture Days
Various venues. Contact: *Jüdisches Gemeindehaus, Fasanenstraße 79/80, Charlottenburg, 10623 (880 280).* **Dates** two to three weeks in Nov. **Admission** varies.
Annual arts and cultural festival of the city's principal Jewish organisation, the Jüdisches Gemeindehaus. Venues around town provide space for an extensive programme of theatre, music, film, readings, panel discussions, dance and workshops. Past themes have included 'Jewish Life in Eastern Europe' and, 'Jewishness from California', and have brought the likes of Allen Ginsberg, Kathy Acker and Jeffery Burns to Berlin. It's usually an impressive presentation of dynamic Jewish art and thinking in a city where Judaism is too often perceived of as a calcified, withdrawn community.

Leaf it out – another autumn in Berlin.

Winter

German Tattoo Convention

Huxley's Neue Welt, Hasenheide 108-114, Kreuzberg, 10967 (627 9320). U7, U8 Hermannplatz. **Dates** three days in Dec. **Admission** DM30 for day ticket.
Hundreds of long-haired, leather-wearing Lemmy lookalikes perform their art on any part of flesh you may choose to tattoo. There are food vendors and an increasing number of stands displaying jewellery to stick through holes in your nose, nipples, lip and clit.

Christmas Markets

Marx-Engels-Platz. S3, S5, S6, S9 Hackescher Markt; Kaiser-Wilhelm-Gedächtniskirche, Breitscheidplatz. U2, U9/S3. S5, S6, S7, S9 Zoologischer Garten.
Dates starting last week of Nov to Dec 27. **Admission** free.
Yuletide markets speckle the capital throughout the holiday season. Handicrafts, decorations and traditional gingerbread, roasted candied almonds, cinnamon stars, piping-hot spiced Glühwein and plenty of good cheer on offer. Two of the best are those listed above, and the one in Marx-Engels-Platz includes rides and games.

New Year's Eve

At 'Silvester' thousands of Berliners of all ages climb Berlin's heights to watch the firework spectacle that explodes over the city as church bells ring in the New Year. Popping champagne corks make about as much noise as the scene in the sky on the Teufelsberg at the northern tip of the Grunewald, and the Kreuzberg, the hill after which that area is named. The Brandenburg Gate has also become a popular place to congregate since the Wall came down; although those suffering from claustrophobia are advised to remain on the edge of the crowd as it can become quite overwhelming. Note that there is no 'firework code' in Germany and Berliners have

few qualms launching rockets in all directions and flinging bangers at other people. Meanwhile, most clubs and bars are open and stay that way the whole night long.

Internationale Grüne Woche

Green Week
Messe Berlin Trade Fair Grounds, Messedamm 22, Charlottenburg, 10455 (30 380). U2 Kaiserdamm. **Open** 9am-6pm. **Dates** Jan. **Admission** DM20; DM10 concs.
Berlin's annual farm show is actually a ten-day orgy of food and drink from the far corners of Germany and the world. Hordes of Berliners and visitors flock to the exhibition halls to sample German gastronomic specialities and exotic foods, but nothing's free, so if you want to eat, bring your wallet.

Berlin International Film Festival

For details see chapter **Film**.
One of the world's major film festivals, the 'Berlinale' features at least 300 movies each year by directors from around the globe. Injecting a shot of glamour in to the life of the city, it is attended by the glitterati of the international film industry as well as hordes of members of the public. The section which atttracts the most attention is the Competition which culminates in the award of the prestigious golden and silver bears. But this is only one small part of a festival renowned for its incredible diversity.

VideoFest

Podewil Klosterstraße 68, Mitte, 10179 (2472 1907). U6 Klosterstraße. **Dates** mid-Feb, **Admission** varies.
Running parallel to the Berlinale, the Videofest is one of the largest events of its kind in the world. Bringing together artists from over 40 different countries, it presents recent productions in video art, television, computer animation, the internet. Each year there are symposia on specific topics, a retrospective and a popular 'Gays & Lesbians' evening. The programme starts daily at noon and fasts forward into the early hours.

Architecture

As a new city centre rises in former no-man's land, Berlin remains a patchwork of imperial splendour, industrial might, avant-garde edge and totalitarian tendencies.

Once tourists came to see the Wall. Now the stilted, red Info-Box, with its assorted exhibits about the current reconstruction of downtown Berlin, is the number one tourist attraction. Mesmerised by the sight of hundreds of cranes, visitors leave the city with the mental image of a single, raw building site.

Sadly, most of the new architecture – despite a glittering credit list of international names – is pretty disappointing. But then Berlin, shaped by the rise of the modern era, yet very much a product of its long history as a military outpost, was never a beautiful city in the first place.

This is in part because it is relatively young. From small beginnings as two thirteenth-century riverside villages, Berlin did not become a fully-fledged city until after the creation of the empire in 1871. In this period of growth known as the Gründerzeit, an 1862 development plan gave the city its characteristic courtyard apartment blocks, or Mietskaserne.

Many valuable buildings were destroyed in World War II, but traces of Berlin's industrial might and imperial splendour, which peaked around 1910, can still be found.

Division rendered space a finite and thus precious commodity in the western sector, injecting politics into even the most mundane projects. Reunification and the return of Berlin's role as capital meant the return of corporate architecture and a new ring of development beyond the periphery. At the same time, works of various periods are pitted against one another in the city's never-ending 'search for identity', reinterpreting history to accommodate economic and political will.

Stadtmitte – a cored city

Perhaps the greatest irony is the planned commemoration in special stone markers of the city's most famous structure, the Wall. Dismantled with breathtaking speed after 1990, it carved the

Gendarmenmarkt – *unusually for William I, it has nothing to do with the military. Page 32.*

*Classic Karl Friedrich Schinkel: the Neue Wache (now the **Mahnmal**) on Unter den Linden.*

historic core away from the western districts. Thus most of the oldest monuments are in the former east. The earliest are the churches belonging to the Wendish/Slavic trading and fishing towns of Berlin and Cölln (colonised by Germans around 1237): the **Marienkirche** and the Nikolaikirche. The latter is enclosed in the **Nikolaiviertel** along with other reconstructed landmarks (like the 1571 pub Zum Nussbaum and also the baroque Ephraimpalais) and prefab townhouses simulating Dutch gables. All were built by the East Germans a few decades after they levelled nearly all of the original medieval fabric.

Also demolished was the Stadtschloß (City Palace), whose recently excavated foundations in front of the **Palast der Republik** on the Spree island date to the reign of Elector Joachim II (begun 1538). The Schloßbrücke crossing to Unter den Linden, with sculptures by Daniel Rauch, and the Neptunbrunnen ('Neptune fountain', modelled on Bernini's great fountains in Rome, now relocated south of the Marienkirche) are two of the remaining palace-related artifacts.

In 1647, the Great Elector, Friedrich Wilhelm II (1640-1688) hired Dutch engineers to transform the route to the Tiergarten, the royal hunting forest, into the tree-lined boulevard of Unter den Linden. It led westward toward Schloß Charlottenburg, built in 1695 as a summer retreat for Queen Sophie-Charlotte. Over the next century, the Elector's 'Residenzstadt' expanded to include Berlin-Cölln and the extension of Friedrichswerder to the south-

west. Traces of the wall that enclosed them can still be seen on Waisenstraße in Mitte. Two further districts, Friedrichstadt (begun 1688) and Dorotheenstadt (begun 1673, named after the Great Elector's Dutch queen), expanded the street grid north and south of Unter den Linden. All were united under one civic administration in 1709.

Andreas Schlüter, an architect in the court of Elector Friedrich Wilhelm III (1688-1713, crowned King Frederick I of Prussia in 1701), also built the alte Marstall (Royal Stables, 1687) in Breite Straße and the baroque Zeughaus (Royal Arsenal; Nering and de Bodt, 1695-1706; now the **Deutsches Historisches Museum**). The bellicose ornamentation of the Zeughaus embodies Prussian militarism, yet concealed within the square courtyard are Schlüter's 22 gruesome masks of dying warriors – a reminder of war's horrors.

William I, the Soldier King (1713-1740), imposed conscription and subjugated the town magistrate to the court and military elite. The economy catered to the army, now comprising 20 per cent of the population, a fairly constant percentage until 1918. To spur growth in Friedrichstadt, the frugal king forced people to build new houses in a stripped down classical style – naturally with room for quartering his soldiers.

Space was also set aside for a public square, the Gendarmenmarkt, where twin churches were built in 1701, one for French Huguenots recently welcomed to Berlin by the Great Elector, who valued their expert skills.

After the population reached 60,000 in 1710, a new customs wall enclosed four new districts – the Spandauer Viertel, Königstadt, Stralauer Vorstadt and Köpenicker Vorstadt; all now parts of Mitte. Built in 1737, the 14km border remained the city limits until 1860. Geometric squares later marked three of the fourteen city gates in Friedrichstadt. At the square-shaped Pariser Platz, the axial gateway to the Tiergarten, Langhans built the **Brandenburg Gate** in 1789, a triumphal arch later topped by Schadow's quadriga. The stately buildings around the square were levelled after the war, but are being reconstructed today, including the **Adlon Hotel**, the **Academie der Künste**, and the French, British and American embassies. The Oktagon, or Leipziger Platz, together with neighbouring Potsdamer Platz, evolved into a major commercial centre on the road to Potsdam. The busy traffic node at the circular Rondell, later Belle-Alliance-Platz (now Mehringplatz), was finally closed in by a depressing 1960s housing project; still at its centre is the Friedensäule ('Peace Column', a lesser cousin to the Seigessäule) topped by Daniel Rauch's statue of Victoria (1843).

Schinkel and his disciples

Even with the army, the Berlin population did not reach 100,000 until well into the reign of Frederick the Great (1740-1786), which was marked by Enlightenment ideas and absolutist politics. The military successes of the French-speaking 'philosopher king' provided the means to embellish Berlin and Potsdam.

Many of the monuments along Unter den Linden stem from his vision of a 'Forum Fredericianum'. Though never completed, the unique ensemble of neoclassical, baroque and rococo monuments that did evolve includes the **Humboldt University** (Knobelsdorff and Boumann, 1748-53, palace of Frederick's brother Prince Heinrich until 1810); the **Staatsoper** (Knobelsdorff and Langhans, 1741-3); the Prinzessinnenpalais (1733; now the **Operncafé**) and the Kronprinzenpalais (1663, expanded 1732; Unter den Linden 3). Set back from the Linden on Bebelplatz are the alte Bibliothek, reminiscent of the curvy Vienna Hofburg (Unger, 1775-81; part of the university) and the pantheon-like St Hedwigs-Kathedrale, a gift to Berlin's Catholics (Legeay and Knobelsdorff, 1747-73).

Not long after the Napoleonic occupation, the prolific Karl Friedrich Schinkel became Berlin's most revered architect under Prince Friedrich-Wilhelm IV. Drawing from early classical and Italian precedents, his early stagesets experimented with perspective, while his inspired urban visions served the cultural aspirations of an ascendant German state. His work includes the colonnaded **Altes Museum** (1828) overlooking the Lustgarten, and the Neue

Wache (1818; now the **Mahnmal**), the royal guardhouse next to the Zeughaus, whose classical form lent itself well to Tessenow's 1931 conversion into a World War I memorial.

Other Schinkel masterpieces include the Schauspielhaus at Gendarmenmarkt (1817-21, now the **Konzerthaus**), the neo-gothic brick Friedrichwerdersche Kirche (1830, now the **Schinkel-Museum**) and the cubic Schinkel-Pavillon (1825) at **Schloß Charlottenburg**. One of his many collaborations with garden architect Peter Joseph Lenné is **Schloß Glienecke** with its picturesque ensemble of classical follies in a park overlooking the Havel near the Glieneckebrücke that connects Berlin to Potsdam.

Generations of Schinkel disciples built up nineteenth century Berlin after his death in 1841. One follower, Stüler, satisfied the king's desire to supplement the Altes Museum by designing the Neues Museum (1841-59; Bodestraße). Originally home of the Egyptian collection, it mixed new wrought iron technology with classical architecture, terracotta ceiling coffers and elaborate murals. (A partial restoration of this bomb-damaged treasure is planned, with an addition by English architect David Chipperfield.) By the turn of the century, the Museum Island comprised the neo-classical Alte Nationalgalerie (1864, also Stüler, with an open stairway framing an equestrian statue of the king;

Modern life in a Bruno Taut Siedlung.

Bodestraße); the triangular Bodemuseum (1904, von Ihne; Am Kupfergraben); and the sombre grey **Pergamon Museum** (1906-9, Messel and Hoffmann) – a stark contrast to the tasteful polychromy of the earlier neo-renaissance Martin-Gropius-Bau (1881, Gropius and Schmieden; Stresemannstraße 110, Kreuzberg).

Historicism and eclecticism

As the population boomed after 1865, doubling to 1.5 million by 1890, the city began swallowing up neighbouring towns and villages. Factory complexes and worker housing gradually moved to the outskirts. Many of the new market halls and railway stations used a vernacular brick style with iron trusses, such as the Arminiusmarkt in Moabit (Blankenstein, 1892; Bremer Straße 9) and Franz Schwechten's Romanesque Anhalter Bahnhof (1876-80, now a ruin; Askanischer Platz, Kreuzberg). Brick was also used for civic buildings, like the neo-Gothic **Rotes Rathaus** (1861-69), while the orientalism of the beautiful gold-roofed **Neue Synagoge** on Oranienburger Straße (Knoblauch and Stüler, 1859-66) made use of colourful masonry and mosaics.

Historicism gave way to wild eclecticism as the nineteenth century continued. This was true of public buildings as well as the many new apartment blocks, or Mietskaserne, whose decorative plaster façades typically belied plain interiors, dark courtyards and overcrowded flats. Eclecticism was also rampant among the increas-ingly lavish Gründerzeit villas of the fashionable suburbs that formed a green ring around the city, especially in the south-west, like Dahlem and Grunewald. There the modest yellow-brick vernacular of Brandenburg was rejected in favour of elaborately modelled plaster and stone.

The Kurfürstendamm, a tree-lined shopping boulevard developed in the 1880s, soon helped the 'new West' to rival the finery of Leipziger Straße. In outer suburbs such as Nikolasee and Wannsee private homes hit new heights of scale and splendour – especially those by Muthesius which were inspired by the English country house, such as Haus Freudenberg in Zehlendorf (1908; Potsdamer Chausee 48).

The new metropolis

In spite of the overscaled bombast of works such as the new **Berliner Dom** (1905, Raschdorff) or the monumental **Reichstag** (1894, Wallot), an attempt at greater restraint and stylistic clarity was made around the turn of the century. The Wilhelmine era's paradoxical mix of reformism and conservatism elicited an architecture of Sachlichkeit ('objectivity'), often as disdainful of art nouveau (or Jugendstil) as it was of eclecticism.

Heavy, vertical massing, compressed forms, low-hanging mansard-style roofs and 'reduced' ornamentation typified Prussian bureaucracy in the many public buildings of Ludwig Hoffmann, city architect from 1896-1924. These include the Stadthaus in Mitte (1919; Jüdenstraße) and the

Rampant orientalism – the **Neue Synagogue** *on Oranienburger Straße.*

baroque-flavoured Rudolf-Virchow-Krankenhaus in Wedding (1906; Augustenburger Platz 1), whose pavilion system was innovative for its time.

Perhaps most severe is the stripped-down classicism of Alfred Messel's Pergamon Museum, while Kaufmann's **Hebbel-Theater** (1908) and the **Hackesche Höfe** lean more towards a restrained Jugendstil. Messel's bold Warenhaus Wertheim at Leipziger Platz is long gone (except for the underground safe-deposit box room, now part of the **Tresor** nightclub), as are most of the Wilhelmine department stores, but a Bruno Schmitz building once housing a turn-of-the-century food automat at Friedrichstraße 167 (1905) has something of the period.

The population climbed to three million shortly after 1900 (another million or so already lived in the outskirts). To help meet the housing shortage, cooperatives began building affordable apartment blocks. Some had a country-house flair, like those built by Messel (Sickingenstraße 7-8, Moabit, 1895, or Stargarder Straße 30, Prenzlauer Berg, 1900). Parallel to this, larger ensembles were developed – forerunners of the Weimar-era housing estates. In the suburb of Staaken, built for World War I munitions workers (1917), Schmitthenner explored a vernacular style with gabled brick terraces arranged like a medieval village. Taut and Tessenow substituted coloured stucco for ornament in the terraced housing of Gartenstadt Falkenberg in Altglienicke (1915), part of an unbuilt larger town plan.

Prior to the incorporation of metropolitan Berlin in 1920, many suburbs had become fully fledged cities with their own town halls, such the massive Rathaus Charlottenburg (1905; Otto-Suhr-Allee 100) and Rathaus Neukölln (1909; Karl-Marx-Straße 83-85). Neukölln's Reinhold Kiehl also built the Karl-Marx-Straße Passage (1910), now home of the **Neuköllner Oper**, and the Stadtbad Neukölln (1914; Ganghofer Straße 3-5), whose niches and mosaics evoke a real Roman atmosphere. Special care was also given to many suburban stations of the period, such as the sachlich/jugendstil S-Bahnhof Mexikoplatz in Zehlendorf (1905, Hart and Lesser), set on a lovely garden square with shops and restaurants, or U-Bahnhof Dahlem-Dorf, whose half-timbered style goes even further to capture a countrified look.

Radical Weimar reform

The work of many pioneers, particularly in commercial and industrial structures, helped make Berlin the birthplace of modern architecture. One of the earliest was Behrens, who reinterpreted the factory with a new monumental language in the façade of the Turbinenhalle at Huttenstraße in Moabit (1909) and several other works for the AEG, for whom he also designed lamps and fit-

Going up! The soon-to-be Sony building.

tings. But after 1918, the radical times of Weimar Germany gave birth to an equally radical architecture. This was not only able to make a final aesthetic break with the Wilhelmine compromise, but also gave formal expression to long-awaited social and political reforms.

The influence of men such as Tessenow and Behrens, mixed with Dutch modernism, cubism, Russian constructivism, engineering works and even some Japanese design, inspired the 'neues Bauen' movement to exploit the new technology of glass, steel and concrete. Thanks to the 1920 incorporation, a socialist administration, post-war housing demand and the new city architect Martin Wagner, architects could explore the new functionalism to their hearts' content, using clean lines and a machine aesthetic bare of ornament.

In spite of rampant inflation, Wagner oversaw the construction of several hundred thousand units. To do so economically, the city became the builder of a new form of social housing. Wagner and his colleagues developed the *Siedlung* (housing estate) within the framework of a 'building exhibition' of experimental prototypes – typically a collaboration among such architects as the brothers Taut and Luckhardt, Gropius, Häring and Salvisberg. Standardised dwelling sizes kept costs down and amenities like tenant gardens, schools, public transport and shopping areas were offered when possible. The best-known 1920s Siedlungen include Taut's Hufeisen-Siedlung (1927; Bruno-Taut-Ring, Britz), arranged around a communal garden, and Onkel-Tom's-Hütte (Haring and Taut, 1928-29; Argentinische Allee, Zehlendorf) centred around Salvisberg's U-Bahn station with shops. Most Siedlungen were housing only, such as the Ringsiedlung (Goebelstraße, Charlottenburg) or Siemensstadt (both Scharoun and others, 1929-32).

Traditional-looking 'counter-proposals' with pitched roofs were made by more conservative designers led by Tessenow in Am Fischtal, Zehlendorf (Mebes, Emmerich, Schmitthenner, et al, 1929).

Many larger infrastructure projects and public works were also built by avant-garde architects under Wagner's direction. Outstanding examples are the rounded U-Bahn station at Krumme Lanke (Grenander, 1929), the totally rational Stadtbad Mitte (1930; Gartenstraße 5-6), the Messegelände (Poelzig and Wagner, 1928), the ceramic-tiled Haus des Rundfunks (Poelzig, 1930; Masurenallee 10, Charlottenburg), and the twin office blocks on the southern corner of Alexanderplatz (Behrens, 1932). Beginning with his expressionist Einsteinturm in Babelsberg, Erich Mendelsohn distilled his own brand of modernism, characterised by the rounded forms of the Universum Cinema (1928; now the **Schaubühne**) and the elegant corner solution of the IG Metall building (1930; Alte Jacobstraße 148, Kreuzberg). Before emigrating – as did so many

other architects, Jewish and non-Jewish – Mendelsohn was able to build a few private homes, including his own at Am Rupenhorn 6 in Charlottenburg (1929).

Grand designs and demolition

In the effort to remake liberal, free-thinking Berlin in their image, the Nazis undertook a form of spatial reeducation. This included banning modernist trademarks such as flat roofs and slender columns in favour of traditional architecture, and shutting down the Bauhaus school, brought to Berlin from Dessau by Mies van der Rohe. Hitler dreamt of reforming Berlin into a mega-capital named 'Germania'. Designed by Albert Speer, its crowning glory was to be a grand axis lined with the embassies of newly subjugated countries and dominated by a massive copper dome at its northern end. At some 16 times the size of St Peter's in Rome, its inhuman scale was meant to instill fear in the observer. Design work was halted by the war, but not before demolition was begun in the Tiergarten and Schöneberg.

Hitler's notion was that Germania would someday leave picturesque ruins à la ancient Rome. But ruins came sooner than expected. Up to 90 per cent of some districts were destroyed by Allied bombing. Literally mountains of rubble were moved to the city's edge, creating new terrain, such as the Teufelsberg in Charlottenburg. Apartment blocks – reconstructed by women survivors – were

Bauhaus modernism meets Stalinist monumentalism on Karl-Marx-Allee.

stripped of their ornate exteriors, and many façades still bear signs of the three weeks of street combat prior to capitulation.

One of the most insidious legacies of fascism was its landscape of bunkers and secret tunnels – often reused by the East Germans as listening stations. And much of the above-ground fascist architecture, recognisable by its stripped-down, severely abstracted classicism, typically in travertine, has been used almost without interruption. In the west, Sagebiel's **Tempelhof airport** (1941) and the **Olympic Stadium** (March, 1936) are among those still in use. In the east, the former Reichsluftfahrtministerium (Sagebiel, 1936; Leipziger Straße 5-7, Mitte), served the GDR administration, albeit refurbished with socialist murals, while the frightening Reichsbank (Wolff, 1938; Am Werderschen Markt, Mitte), to a design personally chosen by Hitler over competition entrants Mies and Gropius, became home to the central committee of the Communist Party.

The two Berlins

The Wall, erected in a single night in 1961, introduced a new and more cruel reality which soon acquired a sense of permanence. Following the military zones, the balance of the urban network shifted as the Wall cut off the historic centre from the west, suspending and Brandenburg Gate and Potsdamer Platz in no-man's land, while the outer edge followed the 1920 city limits.

Post-war architecture is a mixed bag, ranging from the crisp linear brass of 1950s storefronts to concrete 1970s mega-complexes. Even though architects east and west had learned from the same modernist sources, city planning quickly became the tool of opposing ideologies. Early joint planning efforts led by Scharoun were scrapped.

Radical interventions brought many architectural casualties both east and west. Losses included Schinkel's Bauakademie, the Stadtschloß and much of the Fischerinsel, clearing a sequence of wide spaces from Alexanderplatz to Marx-Engels-Platz.

In West Berlin, Anhalter Bahnhof was left in ruins and Schloß Charlottenburg narrowly escaped the same fate. But the commonalities were masked by the design rhetoric of opposing showcase projects. The Hansa-Viertel in the West, part of the 1957 Interbau Exhibition for the 'city of tomorrow', brought the International Style back to Berlin with no less than 53 architects, 19 of them foreign – including Oskar Niemeyer, Avar Aalto and Le Corbusier.

Around the same time, the Stalinallee (1951-54, now Karl-Marx-Allee, Mitte and Friedrichshain) pushed the socialist cause. The Frankfurter Tor segment was designed by Herman Henselmann, a Bauhaus modernist who momentarily agreed to abandon free-form layouts in favour of a monu-

Jewish Museum – on the cutting edge.

mental axis. Funnily enough, both the Hansa-Viertel and Karl-Marx-Allee are now some of Berlin's most desirable housing – although the latter is far noisier. East and west stylistic differences diminished in the 1960s and 1970s, when Siedlungen reached even greater dimensions: the West's Gropiusstadt in Britz and Märkisches Viertel in Reinickendorf (1963-74) were mirrored in the East by equally massive, if shoddier, prefab housing in Marzahn and Hellersdorf.

To replace the cultural institutions lost to the west, Dahlem became the site of the Egyptian museums and the new **Freie Universität**, with a daring rusted-steel exterior (Candilis Woods Schiedhelm, 1967-79). Scharoun conceived a 'Kulturforum' on the site cleared for Germania, designing two masterful prizes: the **Philharmonie** (1963) and the **Staatsbibliothek** (1976). Other additions were Mies' slick **Neue Nationalgalerie** (1968), and the Kunstbibliothek (1994), but the plan, never finished, left the door open to endless debate. The US presented Berlin with Hugh Stubbin's Kongresshalle in the Tiergarten (1967, now **Haus der Kulturen der**

Welt), an entertaining futuristic work which needed seven years of rebuilding after its embarassing 1980 collapse. East German architects brewed their own version of futuristic modernism in the enlarged, vacuous Alexanderplatz with its **Fernsehturm** (1969), the muraled Haus des Lehrers nearby (Henselmann, 1961-64), and the quite enjoyable cinemas, the **International** (Kaiser, 1964) and the Kosmos (Kaiser, 1960-62; Karl-Marx-Allee 131, Friedrichshain).

Modernist urban renewal gradually gave way to historic preservation after 1970. This happened first in the West, when, largely in response to squatters, the public-private Internationale Bauausstellung (IBA) was dedicated to both 'careful renewal' of the Mietskaserne and 'critical reconstruction' with infill projects for 'missing teeth' in areas near the Wall. Projects included schools and recreation centres, such as Langhof's cascaded pool at Spreewaldplatz in Kreuzberg (1988), and the huge catalogue includes names both local and foreign, from Ungers, Sawade, and Behnisch to Krier, Siza, Moore and Hertzberger. The irreverent organicism of the prolific Ballers (1982-84; Fraenkelufer, Kreuzberg) contrasts sharply with the neo-rationalist work of Eisenman (1988; Kochstraße 62-63, Kreuzberg) or the postmodernism of Aldo Rossi (1988; Wilhelmstraße 36-38, Kreuzberg) – all architects who had rarely built until then.

In the East, the renewal of inner-city areas became economically attractive by the late 1970s as funds for new housing ran dry. East-bloc preservation focused mainly on Prenzlauer Berg and infill projects on northern Friedrichstraße, imitating western postmodernism. Progress was slow, and after 1990, unfinished work was demolished, but places like the Nikolaiviertel were infused with good old capitalist culture.

Critical reconstruction

While the task of joining east and west was a unique challenge, the first impulse of the city fathers – former West Berliners – was to erase the memory of 40 years of division. This overshadowed conflicts with the Nazi heritage. The former Luftsfahrtministerium became the HQ of the Treuhand privatisation agency; the Reichsbank took control of the ministries of trade and construction.

Critics have decried the notion of 'Berlinische Architectur' – imposing homogenised historicism and a five-storey cornice height limit in Friedrichstadt – as a denial of Berlin architecture's rich variety.

The new version of 'critical reconstruction' includes the American Business Center filling Checkpoint Charlie (Philip Johnson, SOM, Lauber and Wöhr, 1996-98) the Friedrichstadt Passagen shopping malls (Ungers, Cobb/Fried/Pei, Nouvel,

1993-5), supposedly home of designer shoes and French clothing, though many of the retail units remain empty. By constrast, Hans Kollhoff's internet-age concoction for Alexanderplatz proposes to help eradicate the memory of the GDR by evoking the Rockefeller Center, only with a dozen highrises. The disputed project awaits approval – and the revival of the glutted office market.

The recolonisation of the centre is focused on a dismaying campaign to rebuild the Stadtschloß and the £3 billion reconstruction of Potsdamer Platz. The latter is founded on a notorious land deal between the Social Democrats and Daimler-Benz, who soon shared their windfall with Sony. Larger than many downtowns, a denser and higher rendition of the old plan is being built by an array of local and big-name architects (Piano, Grassi, Rossi, Rogers, Jahn, Isozaki, et al). In a twist on the notion of preservation, Sony transplanted one of the last real pieces of Wilhelmine Berlin – the Kaisersaal café in the old Esplanade Hotel – moving it about 50 metres to make room for its new building. The entire project was no less a feat of engineering, with scuba divers pouring foundations below the water table, and a special logistics centre keeping track of the removal of millions of tons of soil – enough truckloads to circle the globe several times.

The marketability of so much new commercial space remains questionable, especially since late capitalist corporate architecture has arrived well in advance of the government. Bonn's slowness in making good on its 1991 decision to move the government to Berlin actually caused a real estate collapse, but after lengthy delays work is finally underway on the Spreebogen government centre. The **Reichstag**, retrofitted and domed by Sir Norman Foster, will be joined by a new federal Chancellery by Axel Schultes, all built above a massive tunnel for rail and road traffic, with a new bridge by Santiago Calatrava.

A few jewels now underway are Daniel Libeskind's deconstructivist Jewish Museum zigzagging on Lindenstraße in Kreuzberg, the skeletal Stock Exchange on Fasanenstraße in Charlottenburg by Nicholas Grimshaw, and the sleek new **Velodrom** in Prenzlauer Berg.

Despite widespread disappointment with some of the completed large developments (few seem to love Piano's Debis building on Reichpietschufer), the best work may be yet to come in more modest projects.

Key questions still remain after the first wave of the post-Wall boom. To retain the city's three airports and/or build a new one? Will the massive development around Lehrter Bahnhof – intended as a new main railway station – still go ahead as planned? But with construction of every kind certain to continue for years to come, Berlin is putting on a whole new face for the millennium.

Sightseeing

Sightseeing

The scars and memorials of a turbulent history speckle the diverse districts of this sprawling city.

A relatively young city and never a particularly beautiful one, Berlin is not a conventional sightseeing destination in the same way as, say, Rome or Paris. Few would come here just to look at churches. But this isn't to say that there's nothing to see. Berlin's fascinating history has left scars and reminders all over this huge town, while a new future on the global stage is only just beginning to take shape out of the many construction sites that currently dominate the centre – and have become a tourist attraction in themselves.

Most of the stuff that could properly be described as unmissable – either because you really ought to see it or simply because you couldn't avoid it if you tried – is in and around the Mitte district. Such historical sights include the Brandenburg Gate, the grand structures of Unter den Linden, Alexanderplatz and the remnants of the old Jewish Quarter.

But this is only a small segment of this enormous, sprawling city – carved up by rivers and canals, punctuated by pockets of green and fringed with lakes and forest. During its rapid growth in the latter part of the nineteenth century, it gobbled up a number of small communities and then, in the mid-twentieth century, became two cities with a wall between them. Today the Wall is down and the small towns exist only as names on the map, but there are still big differences between one part of town and another.

From beginnings as a small fortified enclave on an island in the Spree (now the Museuminsel), Berlin soon expanded into what is now the borough of Mitte. For many years, that's pretty much how it stayed: the court preferred the pleasures of Potsdam or Königsberg and Berlin remained little more than a trading town. But towards the end of the seventeenth century, Kaiser Friedrich Wilhelm took a town that had been devastated by war and disease and started shaping it into a modern metropolis – establishing a harbour, building Schloß Charlottenburg, and encouraging immigration, particularly of Jews and Huguenots.

Within a century, Berlin had been transformed into one of Europe's great cities: a military, commercial and cultural centre. This expansion was dwarfed by the enormous boom that started in 1871, when Berlin was named the capital of the newly unified German Reich. By the 1920s Berlin had become a world city, ranked with New York,

London and its perennial rival, Paris. Greater Berlin was officially divided into 20 *Bezirken*, or boroughs. Today there are 23, the extra ones having been added to East Berlin after 1949.

Hitler hated Berlin (and, it must be added, Berlin largely returned the compliment) and directed Albert Speer to turn it into something more to his liking – the megalopolis of Germania, capital of the Thousand-Year Reich. World War II slowed down his plans, and only a few buildings (such as Tempelhof airport or the Olympiastadion) and some grandiose street plans (the East-West Axis including the grand Großer Stern roundabout at the Siegessäule in the Tiergarten) were completed.

The Allies then bombed the city into submission, leaving a good half of it completely uninhabitable. Massive rebuilding was necessary on both sides of the Cold War divide. As an island now stranded in the middle of East Germany, West Berlin had to come up with novel solutions, since there was nowhere for it to expand. This explains the number of modern Dachbau, or roof-top, extensions of old buildings. East Berlin was under heavy pressure to serve as a showcase for the glories of communism, so what little money there was mostly went into architectural showpieces that were both cheap and overblown (such as Alexanderplatz). The rest either remained soot-encrusted and bullet-pocked, or else was flattened and flat-blocked.

This chapter concentrates first on the central boroughs. Beginning with the area around Potsdamer Platz, it then moves clockwise through Mitte, Prenzlauer Berg, Kreuzberg, Schöneberg, Charlottenburg and Tiergarten. There follows a brief section on other interesting neighbourhoods, divided into east and west, and then a look at places to go among the woods and waterways on the outskirts of town.

Bars, cafés, restaurants and other venues mentioned and highlighted **in bold** can be found listed in the relevant chapters.

Around Potsdamer Platz

At Potsdamer Platz, the once and future centre of town, you'll find scores of tower cranes rising from the building project intended to make this the city's new commercial centre. Since this once-bustling intersection was bombed flat and then

*Sign of former times – all that remains of **Checkpoint Charlie** is a barrier and watchtower.*

wound up just on the east side of the Wall, it was a literal no-man's land for many years, and today's construction will transform it once again into an area of corporate skyscrapers and seats of power. At the time of going to press, the Debis building had already risen from the dust and the Sony building was beginning to take shape. To the north, the Reichstag is acquiring its new Sir Norman Foster dome and beyond that construction proceeds on the Spreebogen government quarter and Lehrter Stadtbahnhof, intended to be the city's new main train station.

Every day there appears more evidence of what is to come. But for now, the forest of tower cranes can in itself be quite beautiful, especially at night, and the **Info-Box** – the stilted red thing on Leipziger Straße – provides an interactive glimpse at the likely look of the finished project.

While Lehrter Stadtbahnhof goes up, off Anhalter Bahnhof, once the city's main rail terminus, only a tiny piece remains. You'll find it along Stresemannstraße from Potsdamer Platz, preserved in its bombed state near the S-Bahn station that still bears its name. Another ruin near the station is a section of the eighteenth-century city wall that was excavated and reconstructed for the city's 750th birthday celebration in 1987.

Elsewhere on Stresemannstraße there's the popular **Hebbel-Theater** and the cosy **Plantation Club**. The Bauhaus-designed Europahaus was heavily bombed during the War, but the lower stories remain, and the Café Stresemann on the corner is a popular local hangout. Nearby, the Martin-Gropius-Bau, one of the city's best museums, is undergoing renovation until the year 2000. Next to it is a deserted patch of ground that once held the Prinz Albrecht Palais, which the Gestapo took over as its headquarters. In the basement, thousands of political prisoners were held and tortured to death, and the land was flattened after the War. In 1985, during an acrimonious debate over the design of a memorial to be placed on the land, a group of citizens cut the wire surrounding it and staged a symbolic 'excavation' of the site. To their surprise, they hit the Gestapo's basement, and immediately plans were made to reclaim the site. Today, the **Topographie des Terrors** exhibition there, with a ground-level photographic display of the site's history, and railings over which one can look down into the cells, is undergoing renovation, which will result in a more formal visitors' centre and permanent display.

From here, it's a quick walk to the beginning of Friedrichstraße, where the notorious Checkpoint Charlie once stood, now memorialised with a museum as the valuable real-estate has been claimed by yet more new buildings.

Checkpoint Charlie

Friedrichstraße, Mitte, 10117. U6 Kochstraße/U2, U6 Stadtmitte. **Map F4**
The world's most famous border crossing now features Phillip Johnson's American Business Center. There is nothing left of the border post here except an old barrier and watchtower preserved for posterity. The actual checkpoint itself is on display at the **Allied Museum**. Just down Friedrichstraße from where the border used to be is the **Haus am Checkpoint Charlie**, an interesting museum documenting the history of the Wall.

Info Box

*Leipziger Platz 21, Mitte, 10117 (226 6240). U2, S1, S2
Potsdamer Platz.* **Open** 9am-7pm daily; 9am-9pm Thur.
Entry free; observation platform DM2. **Map E4**
Where some see mud and construction cranes, others see a
city transforming itself, and the huge construction site on
Potsdamer Platz has become a major tourist attraction. To
explain the huge changes being wrought in the area, a number of the players, including Daimler-Benz, Sony, Deutsche
Bahn and the Federal Government have installed exhibitions
in this striking red structure that floats over the mess. Many
exhibitions are bilingual, many are interactive, using computers, and some of them may even be working when you
visit. The view from the top helps you visualise what you've
learned inside, and don't miss the replica of the world's first
traffic-light, which was installed at Potsdamer Platz, standing outside.

Mitte

When the Wall was up, the idea of this part of town
calling itself Mitte – 'middle' – seemed just a bit
ludicrous. True, it was the place where the city was
born on the sand islands in the Spree, and before
World War II it had been the hub of the city. But
it wasn't central to East Berlin, and, despite inter-
national-quality hotels, the International Business
Centre at Friedrichstraße station and the
Fernsehturm looming above Alexanderplatz, it
didn't seem too important. In the reunited city,
though, Mitte has regained its title as centre of the
city in every way possible: culturally, scenically,

The restored Sophienstraße in Mitte.

administratively. With the historic old buildings
scrubbed until they shine, an influx of capital promoting new construction, and a new energy from
youthful settlers, Mitte is back in the middle again.

Friedrichstraße

What post-War West Berlin pretended the
Kurfürstendamm was, Friedrichstraße had been
and will be again: Berlin's answer to the Champs
Élysées or Fifth Avenue – that is, if customers
finally start coming to the sleek new shops that
have sprung up there. The street starts at
Hallesches Tor in Kreuzberg and ends at
Oranienburger Tor in Mitte, but the best way to
explore it is to take the U-Bahn to Kochstraße and
Checkpoint Charlie, and start walking north.
What's most evident is money; a huge amount has
been poured into this part of the street, with office
buildings and upmarket shopping malls largely
awaiting tenants. One exception is the
Friedrichstadt Passagen, into which **Galeries
Lafayette** bravely moved early on. Also worth
noting is the **Dussmann Das Kulturkaufhaus**,
a cultural department store which is seeking to
take the place that both FNAC and Virgin's
Megastore failed to capture in the west.

Looming over the nearby plaza, a white building with a black stripe down the side, is the
Internationales Handelzentrum, (International
Trade Centre) – the building from which East
Germany conducted its trade in cheap consumer
durables and coal, getting technology, raw materials and hard currency in return. The state held
the monopoly in this trade, of course, and shortly
after the government fell, most of the officials in
this building were indicted for extortion.
Friedrichstraße station is currently undergoing
renovation as part of the city's master plan to modernise its rail services; this formerly grim building
is being totally gutted in the process. The station
interior was once notable mostly for its ability to
confuse, since this was the main East-West gateway for all categories of people (both East and
West German and foreigners) and necessitated a
warren of passageways and interior spaces to
maintain security. For the time being, the maze-
like quality of the place remains – access to the various lines changes almost daily due to
construction. Make sure you're not in too much of
a hurry if you have to use this facility.

Following the train tracks to the east along
Georgenstraße, one comes upon a succession of
antique stores, bookshops, and cafés in the *Bogen*,
or arches, ending at Museuminsel. The building
just to the north of the train-station is known as

Opposite: *Get your fake Wall chunks here –
hawker of communist kitsch in front of the*
Brandenburger Tor. *See page 49.*

THE HARD ROCK CAFE. GREAT FOOD.
GREAT MEMORABILIA. THE BEST ROCK 'N ROLL
Meinekestr. 21, 10719 Berlin • Nähe Ku'Damm
Telefon 88 46 20 • Fax 884 62 88/89

Fernsehturm – 'the Pope's revenge'. Page 55.

the Tränenpalast ('Palace of Tears'), since it was where departing visitors left their eastern friends and relations who could not follow them back home. Today, it's a concert and cabaret venue, and a piece of the Wall can be seen in its beer garden.

North on Friedrichstraße, the **Metropol Theater** is a survivor of the bombing, now putting on translated Broadway hits and cabaret in the attached Distel Cabaret, but threatened with cost-cutting closure. Crossing the river on the wrought iron Weidendammerbrücke, one turns left on Schiffbauerdamm towards the **Berliner Ensemble** theatre, with its bronze statue of Brecht, who directed the company from 1948-1956, surrounded by quotations from his works. The **Berliner Ensemble Casino**, a former canteen for theatre workers, has become a popular bar. Behind it, at Schumannplatz, stands the Deutsches Theater, another of the city's important companies. The rest of Schiffbauerdamm features assorted riverside restaurants and bars, including **StäV**, **Ganymed** and **Broker's Bier Börse**,.

Back on Friedrichstraße is the **Friedrichstadt-palast**, a large variety theatre that was one of the entertainment hot-spots during the GDR, since they took hard currency, and still pulls the crowds today, albeit mostly grannies from out of town. Billboards featuring the leggy chorines are inescapable in the area.

Communism's very last gasp

Though east Berlin may these days seem to have been totally taken over by designer shops, brand-name burger joints and conceptual art galleries, communism is in fact alive and well and living at the corner of Mohrenstraße and Glinkastraße, just north of Checkpoint Charlie.

In a display case outside the North Korean embassy – located, appropriately enough, next to a fresh-faced women's fitness centre – you can find photos of beaming collective farm workers bringing in the harvest.

The Great Leader Kim Jong Il is a frequent picture of good health and generally credited with responsibility for everything from the dawn of the sun to the provision of running water. (The general secretary's unfortunate inability to provide food for his starving population goes unmentioned.)

Power stations and generously designed Palaces of The People are a recurring theme. Spontaneous acts of mass exuberance and sweet smiling children, whose very existence has been made possible by socialism, add a rather jolly

note to the display case, which is well-tended and regularly updated.

In another blast from the past, the embassy is rumoured to be the centre of European operations for North Korea's intelligence service. The weekly Pyongyang to Schönefeld flight – operated by Air Koryo – is suspected of being a conduit for all manner of naughty and subversive goods.

But if anyone reckons North Korea is about to follow its erstwhile ally East Germany down the rocky road to unification and oblivion, think again. A particular gem of a snap shows the dapper and well-armed troops of the Korean People's Army who, as the caption succinctly puts it, 'listen with great joy to the special communique of the Central Committee and the Central Military Committee of the Korean Workers' Party announcing that the Commander-in-Chief, Comrade Kim Jong Il has been elevated to the post of General Secretary of the Korea Workers' Party'.

All is well in the state of North Korea. But hurry while stocks last.

Gendarmenmarkt – one of the high-points of Frederick the Great's vision for Berlin.

Museuminsel and Unter den Linden

From the Hohenzollern Dynasty to the Weimar Republic to the Nazis to the GDR, the entire history of Berlin can be found around here. It's also the place where the city came into being, so the plethora of museums and historical sites is no accident. That said, it can also be easily covered in an afternoon if you're not going into the museums, since this concentration of history is easily walked, starting at the **Brandenburg Gate**.

Berlin's famous gate was the scene of much partying after the Wall came down, having been sandwiched between the East and West walls for nearly 30 years. Once, only the monarch could drive through the central arch of the Gate; today it's available to taxis and the 100 bus, and, on some days, to all. Immediately to the east of the Gate is Pariser Platz, site of the 1994 visit by US President Clinton, but more usually host to *Bratwurst* stands and hawkers of communist souvenirs.

This is now a major construction site, with the newly reconstructed **Adlon Hotel** back at its old address, and the Gate no longer stands in isolation. Among the new buildings will be the US Embassy, standing on the ground it inhabited before World War II, and a memorial to victims of the Holocaust.

Leading east from the Gate is Unter den Linden. Originally laid out to connect the town centre with the Tiergarten, Unter den Linden, which begins at the Brandenburger Tor, got its name from the *Linden* (lime trees) that shaded its sidewalks. Hitler, concerned that they obscured the view of his parades, had them felled, but they've been replanted. Between the Gate and the Spree, the side-streets were laid out in a grid by the Great Elector for his Friedrichstadt, which he hoped would provide the model for Berlin's continued growth.

The western end of Unter den Linden is all recent, having been badly bombed, and among the glories of Soviet-influenced architecture is the Russian and Ukranian Embassy (formerly the Soviet Embassy) with a large bust of Lenin (who, as a student, worked in the nearby Staatsbibliothek) hiding under a box in the front.

Humboldt University is now integrated into Berlin's university system, and its grand old façade has been restored, as have the two statues of the Humboldts, between which booksellers set up their tables in good weather. Across the street, Bebelplatz, the site of the huge Nazi book-burning (noted by a plaque on the west wall and Micha Ullmann's wonderful monument set into the Platz itself) is framed by the Kommodie and the **Deutsche Staatsoper**, whose cafés and restaurants are appropriately glitzy.

A statue of Frederick the Great (taken down by the GDR, it suddenly and mysteriously reap-

*Lit up like a wall of neon, the **Europa-Center** looks best at night. See page 63.*

peared one night when the party line on him changed) usually points toward the river at this point, although restoration has it out of sight until 1999.

A few blocks south of Unter den Linden lies the Gendarmenmarkt, one of the high-points of Frederick the Great's grandiose vision for the city. Here, the two cathedrals, the Französischer Dom (now the **Hugenotten Museum**, dedicated to the Protestant Huguenots, who fled here from persecution in France in the seventeenth century) and the Deutscher Dom (current home of the 'Questions of German History' exhibit which was formerly in the Reichstag) frame the **Konzerthaus**. This was once a theatre (the Schauspielhaus) and is now home to the Deutsches Symphonie-Orchester Berlin.

The island where Berlin started life as a small thirteenth-century trading town is divided in half by Werder Straße. The northern part has a collection of museums, and is, therefore, known as Museuminsel, while the southern half (although much enlarged by landfill) was once a neighbourhood for the city's fishermen, and is now a pleasant residential area with a couple of quiet hotels and some restaurants. Across a bridge is the **Märkisches Museum** (which houses an exhibition of circus history), and Köllnischer Park, in which you can visit Maxi and Tilo, the official Berlin bears.

For the most part, the museums on Museuminsel are more impressive seen from the outside than the inside. Just as well, really, given that currently many of them are closed. The Alte Nationalgalerie, the Bode Museum and the Neues Museum are all undergoing renovation and reorganisation and won't reopen until sometime after the year 2000. The Altes Museum, from 1830, currently hosts the major works of the Alte Nationalgalerie's collection.

The **Pergamon-Museum** is still open. This is a showcase for three important bits of ancient architecture: the Great Altar of Pergamon (a Greek temple-complex in what is now Turkey), the Blue Gate of Babylon, and the Market of Augustus from Caesarium. On Museuminsel's eastern edge is the **Berliner Dom**, now once again holding Sunday services after decades of living under communist opprobrium.

Continuing east on Karl-Liebknecht-Straße, one comes to the shell of the Palast der Republik. Don't even think of going into this asbestos-contaminated relic of the GDR: it has been closed to the public since 1990. Built in the mid-1970s (a sadly obvious fact) as the main parliamentary chamber of the GDR, it also contained discos, bars and a bowling alley.

The Palast der Republik replaced what was left of the war-ravaged Prussian castle, residence of the Kaisers, which was heavily bombed and lay in

Schinkel

More than any other architect, Karl Friedrich Schinkel, born in 1781, was responsible for trying to give Berlin a complete and distinctive look. Schooled in the ideals of Greek architecture, he developed his own neoclassical style after principles of monumental simplicity and geometrical clarity. His journeys to Italy inspired many of his designs: he would paint during his stays there and return to Berlin brimming with ideas. But the occupation of Berlin in 1806 by French troops stopped nearly all building activity and Schinkel had to work as a restauranteur.

After the French left, Friedrich Wilhelm III made Schinkel curator of monuments. In this capacity he was commissioned to build the Neue Wache on Unter den Linden (now the **Mahnmal**), the **Altes Museum** (1824-30) and the Schauspielhaus (now the **Konzerthaus**). The latter was built on the foundations and six Ionic columns of Langhan's earlier state theatre (1800-1802), which had burned down. Designed and built from 1818 to 1821, the Schauspielhaus is characterised by a classical simplicity in an early German neoclassical style.

For the **Friedrichswerderesche Kirche**, Schinkel proposed a classical design, but the Crown Prince argued successfully for a gothic style. Other places to see Schinkel's work include his pavilion at **Schloß Charlottenburg** (1824), the monument at Viktoria Park in Kreuzberg, **Schloß Glienicke**, and the Nikolaikirche (1830-37) in Potsdam. *See also chapter* **Architecture**.

ruins until 1952, when the GDR levelled it, leaving only the bit of the façade from which Karl Liebknecht proclaimed the German Republic in 1917. Arguments continue about whether to rebuild this Stadtschloß, as it was called (the original plans are still on file), totally renovate the existing structure, or grace the site with some new postmodernist structure. One way or another, though, the communist Palast will soon see some sort of change.

Just beyond the Palast is the Marx-Engels Forum, one of the few remaining monuments to the old boys; the huge statue of Karl and Fred begs one to take a seat on Karl's big lap. Surrounding the statue are bronze reliefs of members of the proletariat freeing themselves from their oppressors, and aluminum stelae etched with photographic images of more of the same.

The Elephant Gate at the **Zoologischer Garten**. *See page 64.*

Brandenburger Tor

Brandenburg Gate
Pariser Platz, Mitte, 10117. S1, S2 Unter den Linden.
Map E4
Constructed in 1791 and designed by Langhans after the Propylaeus gateway into ancient Athens, the Gate was built as a triumphal arch celebrating the Prussian capital city. It was first called the Friedenstor (Gate of Peace) and is the only remaining city gate left from Berlin's original 18. (Today U-Bahn stations are named after some of the other city gates, such as Hallesches Tor and Schlesisches Tor.)

The Quadriga statue, a four-horse chariot with Victory driving, designed by Schadow, sits on top of the gate. This has had a particularly turbulent history. When Napoleon conquered the city in 1806 he decided to take the statue home with him and held it hostage until his defeat in 1814. The Tor was later a favourite place for Nazi rallies. It suffered severe damage during World War II, but was repaired in 1956-7, and again after everyone had partied around it in 1990. During the lifespan of the Wall, the iron cross was taken out of the hand of the Quadriga. The current Quadriga is a 1958 copy of Schadow's eighteenth-century original.

Mahnmal (Neue Wache)

Unter den Linden 5, Mitte, 10115. S3, S5, S7, S9, Hackescher Markt. **Map F3**
The Mahnmal was once known as the Neue Wache when it served as a guardhouse for the royal residences in the area, and is today a memorial to the German dead in the last war, with a simple reproduction of a Käthe Kollwitz statue in its centre. The police presence is there in case someone takes exception (as some did at its rededication in 1993) to the inclusion of the Jews in that number.

Berliner Dom

Berlin Cathedral
Lustgarten, Mitte,10178 (202 690). S3, S5, S6, S9 Hackescher Markt. **Open** 9am-7pm Mon-Sat; 11.30am-7pm Sun. **Admission** DM5; DM3 concs. Photo permission DM3. **Map F3**

The dramatic Berliner Dom is at long last healed of its war wounds. Built at the turn of the century in lavish Italian Renaissance style, it was almost completely destroyed during World War II and remained a ruin until 1973, when restoration work began. It's always looked fine from the outside, but now that the internal work is complete, it's fully restored, crammed with Victorian detail, including dozens of statues of eminent German Protestants, and holding weekly services after many years of existing in the displeasure of the GDR. Its lush nineteenth-century interior is hardly the perfect acoustic space for the frequent concerts held there, but it's definitely worth a visit to see the crypt containing about 90 sarcophagi of the Hohenzollern dynasty.

Friedrichswerdersche Kirche

Werderscher Markt, Mitte,10117 (208 1323). U2 Hausvogteiplatz. **Open** Tue-Sun 10am-6pm. **Admission** DM4; DM2 concs; free to all Sun. **Map F3**
Built according to a design by Karl Friedrich Schinkel during the 1820s, the Friedrichwerdersche church currently houses the Schinkel-Museum, a collection of the artist/architect's sculptures. The neo-Gothic structure was, like almost everything else in the area, destroyed during World War II, but was successfully restored and re-opened in 1987.

Museum of German History (Zeughaus)

Unter den Linden 2, Mitte, 10115 (203 040). S3, S5, S6, S9, Hackescher Markt. **Open** 10am-6pm Mon, Tue, Thur-Sun. **Admission** free for most exhibits. **Map F3**
The Zeughaus is a former armoury with a deceptively peaceful pink façade that currently houses the Museum for German History. Its exhibitions no longer have the peculiar slant that made the place a favourite place for western tourists to visit in GDR times, but it has frequent exhibitions on GDR-related themes, and is well worth visiting, especially at Christmas, when its gift shop has one of the finest selections of traditional German handcrafts in the city. *See chapter* **Museums**.

FiLm
Guide

'Without doubt, the "bible" for film buffs.'
British Film and TV Academy News

Updated annually to include over 11,500 films from around the world and fully cross-referenced with extensive indexes covering films by genre, subject, director and star, this A-to-Z directory is the ultimate guide for movie lovers.

The *Time Out* Film Guide is available at a bookshop near you.

The Scheunenviertel & Oranienburgerstraße

If the area below Friedrichstraße station is the new upmarket face of Mitte, the Scheunenviertel and Oranienburgerstraße is the face of its new bohemia. Once so far out of town that the highly-flammable hay barns (*Scheunen*) were built here, this was also historically the centre of Berlin's Jewish community.

Immediately following the fall of the Wall, the Scheunenviertel became a magnet for squatters who had access to the list of buildings supposedly wrecked by lazy urban developers who checked them off as gone in order to meet quotas but did nothing at all to them. With many of the other buildings in disrepair, rents were cheap, and the new residents soon learned how to take advantage of city subsidies for opening galleries and other cultural spaces. Result: the Scheunenviertel became Berlin's hot new cultural centre.

The first of these art-squats was Tacheles, on Oranienburger Straße near the corner with Friedrichstraße. Originally built as a shopping arcade, Tacheles was already falling apart when Berlin was bombed. Squatted by artists immediately following the Wall's fall, it became a rather arrogant arbiter of hip in the neighbourhood, offering studio space to artists, performance spaces for music, and several bars and discos. In 1997, the city presented the squatters with an opportunity to buy at a very low rate and was spurned, so eviction looms as we go to press. The sculpture garden out back is nice when the weather's good, but the future is cloudy for this latter-day institution. This is still a lively corner, though, with **Freßco**, **Obst & Gemüse** and the **Mitte Bar** across the road from Tacheles, **Oscar Wilde** round the corner in Friedrichstraße and **Shift** gallery just opposite the end of Oranienburger.

A bit further down Oranienburger Straße is the **Neue Synagogue**. This important piece of Jewish history drew a lot of young people to Berlin in the early 1990s, many of them American Jews, and a renaissance occurred in the neighbourhood: cafés, Jewish restaurants and galleries opened, and the end is still not in sight. (Many tourists initially think the building on the corner of Oranienburger Straße and Tucholskystraße is the Synagogue, but it's a former postal building, albeit a very ornate one, currently undergoing renovation to house the Berliner Galerie's collection while the Martin-Gropius-Bau is closed.) Among the thriving venues on and around this stretch are **Café Oren**, **Café Orange**, **Café Beth** and **Silberstein**.

Turning into Große Hamburger Straße is to walk right into the middle of Berlin's Jewish history. On the right, on the site of a former old age home, there is a memorial to the thousands of Berlin Jews who were forced to congregate at this site before being shipped off to die in the concentration camps. Following Jewish tradition, many visitors put a stone on the memorial in remembrance of those who died. Behind the memorial is a park which was once Berlin's oldest Jewish cemetery; the only remaining gravestone is of the father of the German Jewish renaissance, Moses Mendelssohn, who founded the city's first Jewish school, next door at number 27. A few others can be seen in a pile in the park's southeast corner.

Across the street at number 15-16 is *The Missing House*, an artwork by Christian Boltanski, in which the walls left blank by a bombed-out house have the former residents' names and occupations inscribed at the location of each one's former apartment. The Sophienkirche, from which nearby Sophienstraße gets its name, sits behind wrought-iron fences a little further on, and is much better looking from the outside than inside, although it is one of the few remaining Baroque churches in the city.

At the end of Oranienburger Straße, at the corner of Rosenthaler Straße, is the Hackesche Höfe, built in 1906-7 by some young Jewish idealists as just what it is today, a mixed-use complex with nine courtyards. The Hackesche Höfe never took off, despite its lovely art deco design, but, having miraculously survived two wars, it was restored from the old plans in the mid-1990s, and today is

Schloß Charlottenburg. *See page 65.*

The Kurfürstendamm – dedicated to separating you from your Deutschmarks.

an upmarket collection of shops, galleries, theatres, cabarets, cafés, restaurants, and a cinema – way too many places to list them all here. It's worth a wander not only to see the buildings, but also because there's always something going on there, particularly on weekends. Across the street, towards the S-Bahn station, a 'new' Hackesche Höfe is going up, and meanwhile, the area around the station is another welter of bars, restaurants, and galleries.

Neue Synagogue

Oranienburger Straße 28-30, Mitte, 10117 (2840 1316). S1, S2 Oranienburger Straße. **Open** 10am-6pm Sun-Thur (last entry 5.30pm); 10am-2pm Fri (last entry 1.30pm). **Closed** Sat and Jewish holidays. **Admission** DM8; DM4,50 concs. **Tours** 2pm and 4pm Sun; 4pm Wed; DM3, DM1,50 concs.
Built in 1857-66 as the Berlin Jewish community's showpiece, this was the synagogue attacked during Kristallnacht in 1939 (50 years to the day before unification), and Allied bombs damaged the rest of the interior in 1945. The façade remained intact, however, and the Moorish dome has been reconstructed and given a spanking new gilding. Inside is an excellent exhibit of Jewish life in Berlin (only in German, unfortunately for the large number of English-speaking tourists who visit it) and a glassed-in area protecting the ruins of the sanctuary, a reminder for the ages of what has been lost.

Sophienstraße & Auguststraße

Sophienstraße is a jewel in Mitte: an eighteenth-century street restored in 1987 for the city's 750th anniversary, and lined with handcrafts ateliers which have replicas of old merchants' metal signs hanging outside of them. The brick façade of the Handwerker Verein at number 18 is particularly impressive, and the interior has several galleries, as well as a theatre space in what was once an old Jewish ballroom.

At 20-21 is the Sophie-Gips Höfe, which came into being when Erika and Rolf Hoffmann were denied permission to build a gallery for their huge collection of contemporary art in Dresden. Instead, they bought this complex, restored it, and installed the art here, along with their private residence, which includes an Olympic-sized swimming-pool. Tours of the **Sammlung Hoffmann** are available, but there are also text, earth and light works integrated into the structure, which can be seen at all times, as well as galleries, cafes, and offices. Beyond, it's worth noting **Johanna Petzold**'s wonderful shop of wood and straw handcrafts, the window of the book/stamp/postcard dealer, or, at night, the venerable **Sophienclub**, next to the Sophienstraße entrance to the Hackesche Höfe.

Running from Oranienburger Straße to Rosenthaler Straße (emerging two blocks north of Sophienstraße) Auguststraße is the core of Berlin's new art district, its many galleries including such important venues as **Eigen + Art** and **Kunstwerk Berlin**, although important galleries are also found on surrounding streets.

A popular open-house day every six Sundays (the *Galerierundgang*) has proven too popular, and many galleries have pulled out, but it may continue in attenuated form (look for a booklet in any participating gallery) and the street makes a good afternoon's stroll on any day of the week, possibly

Science-fictional scene for concerts and meetings: the International Conference Centre.

with a stop for refreshment at **Hackbarths** or **Ici**, or to watch a football game at the pitch by Kleine Hamburger Straße.

Alexanderplatz and surrounds

Visitors who have read Alfred Döblin's classic *Berlin Alexanderplatz* or seen the multi-part television film by Fassbinder may arrive here and wonder what happened. What happened was that, in the early 1970s, Erich Honecker decided that this historic square should reflect the glories of socialism, and tore it all down to erect a masterpiece of commie kitsch: gapingly wide boulevards, monotonous white buildings filled with cafés and shops, and, of course, the impressive golf-ball-on-a-knitting-needle, the **Fernsehturm** (Television Tower), from whose observation deck and revolving restaurant one can gain a fantastic view of the city on a clear day.

At ground level, capitalism's neon icons sit incongruously on Honecker's erections, a giant Panasonic television blares news, weather, and commercials at busy shoppers, the goofy clock with the 1950s-style atom design on the top tells the time in (mostly) socialist lands all over the world, and at the Markthalle, one can sip a beer at the brew-pub or buy a brand-name burger. Plans are afoot to raze Alexanderplatz once again, which will doubtless result in an equally ugly collection of non-communist architecture. Even the Fernsehturm may fall in this latest vision for the square, plans for which look a bit

like the Rockefeller Center, only with twice as many skyscrapers.

Fernsehturm

Television Tower
Alexanderplatz, Mitte, 10178 (242 3333). S3, S5, S6, S9/U2, U5, U8 Alexanderplatz. **Open** *April-Oct* 9am-1am daily; *Nov-Feb* 10am-midnight daily. **Admission** DM8; DM4 children 3-16; children under-3 free; last admission half an hour before closing. *Telecafé* open *Mar-Oct* 10am-1am daily; *Nov-Feb* 10am-midnight daily; last admission one hour before closing, entry only via elevator. No handicapped admitted due to evacuation restrictions.
Map G3
Built in the late 1960s at a time when relations between East and West Berlin were at their lowest ever ebb, the 365-metre tower – its ball-on-spike shape visible from all over the city – was intended as an assertion of communist dynamism and modernity. Shame that such television towers were a West German invention. Shame, too, that they had to get Swedish engineers to build the thing. Atheist communist authorities were also displeased to note a particular phenomenon: when the sun shines on the tower, reflections on the ball form the shape of a cross. Berliners dubbed this stigmata 'the Pope's revenge'. Nevertheless, they were proud enough of the thing to make it one of the central symbols of East Germany's capital; its silhouette even used to form the 'i' in 'Berlin' on all eastern tourist information. No longer is it flaunted, but Berliners have grudgingly come to like this modernist monstrosity. It may be ugly, but it's a great way to orient yourself early on a visit to Berlin, as much of the city is visible from the top. Wend your way through the cheap tourist attractions in the lobby, take the elevator to the observation platform and you'll find a view of Berlin unbeatable by day or night – particularly looking westwards, where it takes in the whole of the Tiergarten and surrounds. If heights make you hungry, take a twirl in the revolving Telecafé restaurant, which offers an even better view plus a full menu of snacks and meals – including, for those who want something light, 'leg of lamp'.

Nikolaiviertel
Mitte, 10178, S3, S5, S6, S7, S9/U2, U5, U8
Alexanderplatz. **Map G3**
The oldest area in Berlin, centred around the Nikolaikirche, built around 1230, with its awful DDR reconstruction job and odd collection of artifacts that purports to tell the ancient history of Berlin. The eighteenth century neighbourhood was completely destroyed during the war, and the reconstruction job here isn't too bad, though obviously prefabricated, with a good selection of restaurants, cafés, and overpriced shops, and a definite old-time European feeling that's rare in Berlin.

Rotes Rathaus
Red Town Hall
Rathausstraße 10, Mitte, 10178 (240 10). S3, S5, S6, S7, S9/U2, U5, U8 Alexanderplatz. **Open** 8am-6pm Mon-Fri. **Admission** free. **Map G3**
Berlin's town hall sits just off Alexanderplatz. This magnificent building was built during the 1860s of terracotta brick. The history of Berlin up to that point is illustrated in a series of 36 reliefs on the façade. During communist times, it served as East Berlin's town hall – which made its old nickname, 'Red Town Hall' (because of the colour of the façade), especially fitting. West Berlin's city government workers moved here from their town hall, Rathaus Schöneberg, in 1991. Guided tours are run by arrangement, phone for details.

St Marienkirche
Alexanderplatz, Mitte, 10178 (242 4467). S3, S5, S6, S9 Hackescher Markt. **Open** 10am-noon, 1-4pm Mon-Thur; noon-4pm Sat, Sun. **Admission** free. **Map G3**
The St Marienkirche is one of Berlin's few remaining medieval buildings. Just inside the door, a wonderful Berlinish Dance of Death fresco dating from the fifteenth century is being painstakingly restored, and fans of organ music shouldn't miss a concert on the eighteenth century Walther organ here, considered this famous builder's masterpiece. The St Marienkirche hit the headlines in 1989 when the new civil-rights movement chose it for one of the first sit-ins in the city, since churches were one of the few places large numbers of people could congregate without state permission.

Stadtmauer (City Wall)
Littenstraße/Waisenstraße, Mitte, 10179. U2 Klosterstraße. **Map G3**
Long before the infamous Wall, Berlin had another wall; the medieval city wall of the original thirteenth- to fourteenth-century settlement. There's almost as much left of this wall as there is of the more recent one. Built along the wall is the old (and extremely popular) restaurant Zur Letzten Instanz, which takes its name from the neighbouring law court from which there was no further appeal. There's been a restaurant on this site since 1525. The building is one of four old houses that have been reconstructed.

Prenzlauer Berg

If the fall of the Wall has precipitated a renaissance in any neighbourhood in Berlin, it is surely Prenzlauer Berg. Long described as grey and depressing, an area of workers' houses unrelieved by any sites of historical or touristic interest, these days the east Berlin district is having its façades renovated, its streets cleaned, and its buildings newly inhabited by everyone from artists to yuppies. Galleries and cafés have sprung up, and hundred-year-old buildings are having central heating, bathrooms and telephones installed for the very first time.

Funkturm *and Messegelände. Page 65.*

Built around the turn of the century during the construction boom, Prenzlauer Berg seems to have had more visionary social planners than some of the other neighbourhoods that date from the same period. It has wider streets and pavements, giving the area a distinctive, open look that is unique in Berlin. Although many of the buildings still await restoration, looking down a street in which some have been scrubbed and painted, one gets the feeling of a nineteenth-century boulevard.

The hot centre of Prenz'lberg, as its inhabitants call it, is LSD, the section bounded by Lychner Straße on the east, Danziger Straße on the south, and Schönhauser Allee on the west. Starting at Senefelder Platz U-Bahn, walk up Schönhauser Allee, noting the Jewish graveyard, Berlin's oldest, and fairly gloomy even by local standards due to its closely-packed stones and canopy of trees. At Sredzkistraße stands an old brewery that houses a huge furniture store, and the **Kulturbrauerei**, a theatre venue and club.

The streets to the east of here are alive with other clubs, restaurants, and shops. One block of Husemannstraße was lovingly restored by the GDR for the city's 750th birthday and is today lined with boutiques, cafés like **November**, restaurants like **Ostwind** and **Restauration 1900**, and an agency that hires horse-and-buggy rigs for special events.

The Landwehrkanal – placidly separating Kreuzberg from Kreuzberg.

Husemannstraße feeds into Kollwitz Platz, one of the prettiest spots in the area, a small park dedicated to the painter and social reformer Käthe Kollwitz, whose statue stands in the park. It was in the Café Westphal (now a Greek restaurant) that the first meetings of East Berlin dissidents were held in the early 1980s, until they got too big and had to be moved to the nearby Gethsemanekirche. Taking Knaackstraße off Kollwitzplatz (turn east by the **Gugelhof** restaurant) brings one past a nicely-restored synagogue to another square containing a small park with a water-tower. Today there are apartments in the water-tower, but the Nazis had a small prison in its basement, a fact acknowledged by a plaque. Again, this park is bounded by bars and cafés such as **Pasternak**, **Kommandatura** and **Anita Wronsky**, and is one of the centres of social life in Prenzlauer Berg.

Heading north on Prenzlauer Allee, one comes to Ernst Thälmann Park, named for the leader of the pre-1933 Communist Party in Germany. In its north-west corner stands the Zeiss Planetarium, a great GDR interior space that once hymned Soviet cosmonauts and still runs programmes on what's up there in space. Considering the wide expanse of sky visible from almost any street in Prenz'lberg, it seems a fitting symbol for the whole neighbourhood.

*The **Siegessäule**, war memorial and film set, rises above Straße des 17 Juni. See page 68.*

Another hot centre at the moment is the area around Kastanienallee, which has become a main commercial street with a decided Prenz'lberg flavour. The Volksbühne's **Prater** branch has a wonderful beer-garden, and the Schmalzwald club at the Prater is a major venue for weirdness. On and around Schönhauser Allee are also dozens of gay venues – the is the centre of the eastern scene.

Prenzlauer Berg is undergoing such rapid change at the moment that new places to go and things to do appear almost daily. Like the more bohemian parts of Mitte, it hums with energy and creativity, much of it generated by the same artists, writers and musicians who lived here before the Wall came down. It's also taken over as the venue of the traditional Mayday riots, which formerly occurred in Kreuzberg, as well as a new one, on the Day of German Unity (October 3), so be warned. The rest of the year, whether you're gallery-hopping, seeing a band at the **Knaack Club**, eating in one of its restaurants or drinking in one of its many bars, you're sure to feel the energy.

Kreuzberg

Back in November 1994, one of the last Kreuzberg demonstrations attempted, rather pathetically, to prevent the opening of the Oberbaumbrücke. During the Cold War, this bridge across the Spree and into Friedrichshain was a border post and spy-exchange venue. Only pedestrians, most of them eastern old-age pensioners, could cross. Its open-

Viktoriapark's cheery, fake waterfall cascades to the foot of the Kreuzberg.

ing to the traffic that now surges across it was effectively the fall of one of the last pieces of Wall. But it was also the fall of the Kreuzberg of old.

In the 1970s and 1980s, the half of Kreuzberg that lies north of the Landwehrkanal was off at the western edge of West Berlin. Enclosed on two sides by the Wall and mostly ignored by the rest of the city, its decaying tenements came to house Berlin's biggest, and most militant, squatting community. The area was full of punky left-wing youth on a draft-dodging mission and Turks who came here because the rents were cheap and people mostly left them alone. The air was filled with the smell of hashish, the sound of Turkish pop music and the clamour of political activity.

No area of west Berlin has changed quite so much since the Wall came down. This once isolated pocket found itself recast as desirable real estate in the centre of the unifying city. Gentrification began to rear its well-coiffed head while Mitte and Prenzlauer Berg asserted themselves as the new centres of radical energy and underground nightlife. The entire alternative art scene uprooted and moved east into the Scheunenviertel and these days even the Mayday riots – long an essential Kreuzberg tradition – take place in Prenzlauer Berg (*see chapter* **Berlin By Season**).

But though young bohemia has largely moved on, enough of the anarchistic old guard stayed behind to ensure that the area still has a distinct atmosphere. The northern half of Kreuzberg continues to be an earthy kind of place, full of cafés, bars and clubs, dotted with small movie theatres,

and an important centre for the city's gay community. It's just much, much quieter and a lot less radical than it used to be.

One thing hasn't changed. It's still the capital of Turkish Berlin, the world's fifth-largest Turkish city. The area around Kottbusser Tor, with its kebab shops, Galatasaray supporters' club bars and Anatolian travel agents, is the hub of Turkish Berlin. The open-air **Turkish Market** stretches along the Maybachufer every Tuesday and Friday. Görlitzer Park, once an important train station, turns into the world's largest outdoor Turkish barbecue on fine weekends. The area is full of doner takeaways and Turkish grocery stores, while at night Turkish street gangs defend their territory – mostly from other Turkish street gangs.

Oranienstraße is northern Kreuzberg's main drag, still full of bars and capable of bustling with weekend nightlife. Former punk venue **SO36** now hosts some of Berlin's most important gay one-nighters and **Roses**, the dyke/queer cruise bar, is along the road. Funky dance music booms from the **Schnabelbar** while the Kreuzberg old guard eat and drink at **Rote Harfe**. There are still more bars on this street than anyone could handle in one single night out, and the area to the north and west of here is home to even more – including excellent places such as **Café Anal**, **Markthalle** and **Abendmahl**. More gentrification can be seen beyond on Köpenicker Straße, and fans of art deco in the service of commerce are urged to check out the gigantic warehouse on Pfuelstraße, which runs for a block towards the Spree.

South across Skalitzer Straße, Oranienstraße changes into Wiener Straße, running alongside the old Görlitzer Bahnhof, where bars and cafés such as **Madonna** and **Morena** welcome what's left of the old Kreuzberg crowd. A couple of blocks further south lies the Paul-Linke-Ufer, the border with Neukölln, lined with canal-bank cafés that provide a favourite spot for weekend brunch.

The U1 line runs overhead through the neighbourhood along the middle of Skalitzer Straße. The onion-domed Schlesisches Tor U-Bahn station was once the end of the line. These days it continues one more stop across the Spree to Warschauer Brücke. Otherwise, you can walk across the Oberbaumbrücke into Friedrichshain and find the East Side Gallery, one of the longest remaining stretches of Wall, which runs along Mühlenstraße on the north bank of the river and has been painted by various artists in work that commemorates the end of the Cold War.

Around Bergmannstraße

The southern part of Kreuzberg, the one that actually has the 'cross hill' in Viktoriapark for which the borough is named, has both a lot of life and contains some of the most picturesque corners of west Berlin.

Viktoriapark is the natural way to enter the area. It has a cheery, fake waterfall cascading down the hill, the large outdoor summer beer garden at Golgotha, and lots of paths that wind their way up to the summit of the Kreuzberg. At the top stands Schinkel's 1821 monument commemorating victories in the Napoleonic Wars (most of the streets hereabouts are also named after battles and generals of the period) and from here there is a commanding view over this relatively flat city. With the Schultheiss brewery at your back, the landmarks of both east and west spread out before you: Friedrichstraße dead ahead, the Europa-Center off to the left, construction around Potsdamer Platz in between the two, and the Fernsehturm over to the right. The view is better in winter, when the park's trees are bare. But then the waterfall only gets turned on in summer, so there's something to be said for every season.

Back on ground-level, walking along Kreuzbergstraße (passing **Osteria No. 1**) until it crosses Mehringdamm takes one on to Bergmannstraße, the hub of neighbourhood activity. Bucking the general tendency of anything in Berlin to move eastwards, this street of cafés and junk-shops, groceries and record stores these days seems livelier than ever. It leads down to Marheinekeplatz, where stands one of Berlin's several market halls and, among the cafés behind it, the **Tres Kilos** restaurant. Zossener Straße also bustles, and includes the **Freßco** café, **Space Hall** record shop (pick of the bunch, although

Brussels sprouts at Winterfeldtplatzmarkt.

there are several others in the area) and **Grober Unfug** comic store among its many businesses.

Bergmannstraße continues east to Sudstern, past several large cemeteries, and eventually comes to the Hasenheide, the other of the neighbourhood's large parks, with its famous outdoor cinema in summertime, and another good view from atop the Rixdorfer Höhe.

If you've ever seen 'old Berlin' in a movie, chances are it was filmed in the streets just to the south of Bergmannstraße. Many buildings in this neighbourhood survived the wartime bombing and the area around Chamissoplatz has been immaculately restored. The cobbled streets are lined with houses still sporting their Prussian façades and illuminated by gaslight at night. This is one of the most beautiful parts of this largely unbeautiful city, and also contains **Ristorante am Chamissoplatz**, an excellent neighbourhood Italian joint, and two theatres: **Theater Zerbrochene Fenster**, which occasionally features English-language performances, and **Friends of Italian Opera**, which always does. The old water tower on Fidicinstraße has been restored and also holds occasional performance events.

The edge of this area is dominated by the hulking presence of the Columbushaus, a red-brick monster that once had a Nazi prison in its basement and is currently used by the Police for automobile registration. Beyond that, just across the border into the borough of the same name, stands the huge Tempelhof Airport. Once the central airport for the city, it was begun in the 1920s and later greatly expanded by the Nazis. The largest building in Berlin – and one of the largest in the world – its curving bulk looms with a distinctly authoritarian ominousness.

Tempelhof was where Lufthansa Airlines started, but its place in the city's affections was cemented during the Berlin Airlift of 1948-49, when it served as the base for the 'raisin-bombers', which flew in and out at a rate of one a minute, bringing much needed supplies to the blockaded city and tossing sweets and raisins to kids waiting nearby as the planes taxied in. The monument forking towards the sky in the nearby Platz der Luftbrücke commemorates the pilots who flew these missions, as does a photo-realist painting stuck over in a corner of the terminal building. After commercial flights to Tempelhof were discontinued in the early 1970s, it became the centre of the US air operation in Berlin. Today it's once more a civil airport catering to small airlines running small planes on short-hop European routes.

This uses only a tiny fraction of the enormous structure, other parts of which have been converted into entertainment venues, such as Hangar II, which occasionally houses club called, of course, **Hangar II**.

Schöneberg

Both geographically and in terms of atmosphere, Schöneberg lies midway between Kreuzberg and Charlottenburg. It's a diverse part of town, mostly built in the late nineteenth century boom but these days veering from the 'alternative' to the upmarket and accommodating all points in between. Though largely devoid of conventional sights, it's rich in intriguing reminders of Berlin's recent history. The nightlife isn't bad either.

Schöneberg means 'beautiful hill' – oddly, because the borough's mostly as flat as a pancake. It does have an island, though: the triangular Schöneberger Insel, carved away from the rest of the city by the broad railway cuttings that these days carry S-Bahn lines 1 and 2, with an elevated

Flak tower and flatblock on Pallasstraße.

stretch of line S45/46 providing the southern boundary. In the 1930s it was known as the Rote Insel ('Red Island'), because approached mostly over bridges and thus easy to defend, the area was one of the last to resist the Nazification of Berlin. Walking between the island and Kreuzberg's Viktoriapark, there's a fine view of central east Berlin from the Monumentenbrücke. Around here can be found the pocket-sized **Scheinbar** cabaret and the agreeable **Café Aroma** Italian restaurant. On the north-west edge of the island is the St Matthäus-Kirchhof, a large graveyard and last resting-place of the Brothers Grimm.

The Langenscheidtbrücke – named for the dictionary publishers which ■■ its offices on the western side – leads one towards the Kleistpark intersection, where you'll find both the excellent **Zoulou Bar** and yet another worthy Italian joint, **Petite Europe**.

Here Schöneberg's main street is called Haupstraße to the south and Potsdamer Straße to the north. Hauptstraße leads south-west in the direction of Potsdam. David Bowie and Iggy Pop once resided at number 152 – Bowie in a big, first-floor apartment at the front, Pop in a more modest Hinterhof flat. The **Odeon** cinema, favourite haunt of Anglophone movie-goers, lies in this direction, but it's a good, long walk. The Dominikuskirche nearby is one of Berlin's few baroque churches.

North along Potsdamer Straße from Kleistpark U-Bahn is the entrance to the Kleistpark itself – an eighteenth-century double colonnade which was moved here from near Alexanderplatz in 1910. The park was once Berlin's first botanical gardens. The mansion in it was formerly a law court (here is where the 1944 July Bomb Plotters were sentenced to death), and after the War, it was the headquarters for the Allied Control Council. After the signing of the Ost-Verträge in 1972, which recognised the separate status of East and West Germany, the building stood virtually unused save for occasional meetings, at which the Americans, British, and French would observe a ritual pause, as if expecting the Soviet representative, who had last attended in 1948, to show up. In 1990, a Soviet finally did wander in and the Allies held a last meeting here to formalise their withdrawal from the city in 1994. This may be the place where the Cold War ended.

On the northwest corner of Potsdamer Straße's intersection with Pallasstraße stood the Sportpalast, site of many Nazi speeches including Goebbels' 'Total War' speech of 1944. West along Pallasstraße from here is a block of flats straddling the road and resting on the south side atop a Nazi flak tower the planners were unable to destroy. It, along with some of the used-furniture shops on nearby Goebenstraße, featured in Wim Wenders' *Wings of Desire*.

Isherwood lived at Nollendorfstraße 17.

Nollendorfplatz to the north and west is the centre of nighttime Schöneberg. Outside Nollendorfplatz U-Bahn, the memorial to the homosexuals killed in concentration camps is a reminder of the immediate area's history: Christopher Isherwood chronicled Berlin from his rooming house at Nollendorfstraße 17, and today Motzstraße is one of the hot centres of Berlin's gay life. At number 5 can be found the **Mann-O-Meter** information centre and further along are bars and clubs such as **Tom's Bar**, **Hafen** and **Scheune**.

South of Nollendorfplatz along Maaßenstraße, one comes to Winterfeldplatz, site of a lively twice-weekly market where the locals come to pose and occasionally buy things. Winterfeldtstraße has many antiquarian bookshops and at night the area is full of bars and restaurants.

From here and down Goltzstraße you can watch Schöneberg's café society watch you from the trendy places that mingle with pricey, but interesting shops. This is the scene as Goltzstraße crosses Grünewaldstraße and turns into Akazienstraße. This street ends up back at Hauptstraße, but a left turn before this on Belziger Straße brings one eventually to Rathaus Schöneberg, from whose steps John F. Kennedy announced that he was a Berliner in 1963, and Berlin mayor Walter Momper welcomed the East Berliners in 1989.

Perhaps the best way to get to know Schöneberg, though, is through its many lively restaurants, bars, and cafés – sipping a cappuccino at the **Café Berio**, tucking into a hearty plateful of Alsatian food at the **Storch**, downing a beer at the **Pinguin** or **Zoulou**. Talk to the locals. They won't mind. This is one of the most cosmopolitan areas of Berlin and most of them were once strangers here themselves.

Zoo area

Although it's not as important as it once was, Zoo Station is still the arrival-point for many visitors to Berlin, and nearly everyone winds up there at some point in their visit. It's the gateway to the centre of the former West Berlin, and, obviously, it's got the Zoo, which is worth checking out, especially if you're travelling with kids.

The surrounding area, with its mixture of sleaze and shopping, huge cinemas and bustling crowds (during the daytime, anyway) is the gateway to the Kurfürstendamm, once the main shopping street of West Berlin and still laying claim to that title in some respects. The discos and bars along Joachimsthaler Straße are best avoided – the opening of the **Beate Uhse Erotik-Museum** actually added a touch of class to the area – but the rest of this district is worth a wander.

The **Zoo Palast** cinema is one of the central venues of the Berlinale Film Fest, whose offices on Budapester Straße are nearby, and Amerika Haus and the **British Council**, next-door neighbours on Hardenbergstraße, are English-language oases whose libraries are useful, and whose message boards are worth checking for events and contacts. Breitscheidplatz, with the ruined **Kaiser-Wilhelm-Gedächtniskirche** rising in its midst, is a hangout for punks demanding *Kleingeld* (spare change), and the **Europa-Center**, whose Mercedes star can be seen from much of the rest of the city, is a sort of monument to the West Berlin of the past. It looks neon-lit at night.

The tubular steel sculpture in the divider on Tauentzienstraße was commissioned for the city's 750th anniversary in 1987 and nicely represents the then divided city in that the two halves twine around each other but never meet. The street runs along past KaDeWe, Berlin's most prestigious department store, to Wittenbergplatz. The U-Bahn station here has been wonderfully restored with wooden kiosks and old ads on the walls. Outside stands a memorial to those who died in concentration camps, looking eerily like a departure board in a train station.

A block further is the huge steel sculpture at an der Urania (no, we've never seen anybody skateboard it) with its grim monument to children killed in traffic by Berlin's drivers. This marks the end, or the beginning, of 'downtown'.

Europa-Center
Breitscheidplatz 5, Charlottenburg, 10789. S3, S5, S6, S7, S9/U2, U9 Zoologischer Garten. **Map D4**
The Europa-Center, a skyscraper attached to a shopping area and cultural centre, was built in the mid-1960s and looks it. Tacky and nasty, it houses a tourist information centre, around 100 stores, restaurants, the largest of Berlin's many Irish pubs, cinemas, a hotel (**Hotel Palace**, *see chapter* **Accommodation**) and Die Stachelschweine, a cabaret. It even contains a very luxurious (and expensive) sauna facility, with a pool that allows you to swim outside and back in again, even in the middle of winter. Ignore all that and head up to the observation platform for a dizzying look at the area. The strange sculpture in front of the Center was erected in 1983 and has become a congregating place for tourists, punks and others. It is officially called Weltenbornen (Fountain of the Worlds'), but like everything else in Berlin, it has a nickname: the Wasserklops ('water meatball').

KaDeWe

Tauentzienstraße 21-24, Schöneberg, 10789 (21 210).
U1, U2, U15 Wittenbergplatz. **Open** 9.30am-8pm Mon-
Fri; 9am-4pm Sat. **Credit** AmEx, DC, EC, MC, V.
Map D4
The Kaufhaus des Westens – 'Department Store of the West'
– is Germany's largest luxury department store and one of
the biggest on the Continent. It's most famous for its food
hall on the sixth floor, and rightly so, even if the show of opu-
lence can get a little overpowering. The array and variety of
food is mind-boggling: Wurst-lovers will think they have
died and gone to heaven, but vegetarians should make a
point of steering clear of the meat departments. There are
numerous places to stop, eat and drink when the sight of all
that food makes you hungry.

Kaiser-Wilhelm-Gedächtniskirche

Kaiser-Wilhelm-Memorial-Church
*Breitscheidplatz, Charlottenburg, 10789 (218 5023). S3,
S5, S6, S9/U2, U9 Zoologischer Garten.* **Open** 9am-7pm
Mon-Sat. *Old tower* 9am-4pm Mon-Sat. *Guided tours*
1.15pm Wed-Fri. **Admission** free. **Map D4**
One of Berlin's best-known sights, at its most dramatic by
night. The neo-Romanesque church was built at the end
of the nineteenth century in honour of – you've guessed it
– Kaiser Wilhelm I. Much of the structure was destroyed
during an air raid in 1943. Today it serves as a stark
reminder of the damage done by the war, although some
might argue that the bombing has improved what was
originally a profoundly ugly structure. The ruin of the
tower is flanked on either side by modern extensions,
tubes with stunning blue stained-glass windows that glow
eerily at night which contain the sanctuary in use today
by the congregation.

Zoologischer Garten

*Hardenbergplatz 8, Tiergarten, 10787 (254 010). S3,
S5, S6, S7,S9/U2, U9 Zoologischer Garten.* **Open** *zoo*
9am-6pm daily summer, 9am-5pm winter; *aquarium* 9am-
6pm daily. **Admission** *zoo* DM12; DM6 children; DM10
students; *aquarium* DM12; DM6 children; DM10 students;
combined DM20; DM10 children; DM16 students.
Map C4
The Zoological Garden, Germany's oldest zoo, opened in
1844. With 16,000 animals from 1,700 species, it is by some
way the largest in the world. It is also one of the most
important, with more endangered species in its collection
than any zoo in Europe save Antwerp's. Given its age, it
has some surprisingly modern exhibits: try not to trip over
the mouse deer running through the Vietnamese rain-for-
est, which has no bars, and chance an encounter with a similarly unencumbered rhinoceros, separated from you only
by a trench. The Zoo is huge, so if you're with kids, zero-
ing in on some specific areas is a better idea than trying to
see the whole thing at once. The aquarium is also one of the
world's most varied, including more than 500 species displayed in four sections: Oceanic, Freshwater, a Crocodile
Hall and an Insectarium. For the brave, there's a 'petting
zoo' with carp.

Charlottenburg

Once upon a time before the Wall fell, Charlottenburg *was* Berlin to most tourists. They stayed in
Kurfürstendamm hotels, did their shopping in the
same place, and if they were museum-goers, went
to the complex around **Schloß Charlottenburg**
to catch a bit of culture. There's more of Berlin to
see these days, but Charlottenburg maintains a
central position in the cultural and commercial life
of the city.

Around the Kurfürstendamm

Named for the Prussian Kurfürst (Elector), who
was one of the princes responsible for electing the
Holy Roman Emperor, the Kurfürstendamm, or
Ku'damm, has long been a popular street, the
hangout of the *demi-monde* in the 1920s, lined with
trees and plenty of surviving old buildings. With
cinemas (mostly showing dubbed Hollywood fare),
restaurants (from the venerable **Bovril** to assorted burger joints), chic shops and offices, it's a street
dedicated to separating you from your
Deutschmarks. It's also very long, running westwards for a couple of miles almost to the edge of
the Grunewald and gradually getting quieter as it
approaches Halensee.

Off the downtown stretch, the side-streets to the
south are a bit quieter, albeit even more upmarket
– especially Fasanenstraße – and Bleibtreustraße
to the north has more shops and some of the most
outrageous examples of nineteenth-century
Gründerzeit architecture in Berlin.

Kantstraße more or less parallels the Ku'damm
to the north, and has still more shops to look in.
Savignyplatz, once a training-ground for British
spies, has a tiny red-light district, numerous for-
eign-correspondent offices and more chic places,
particularly the restaurants and cafés on and
around Grolmannstraße (such as **Café Savigny**,
Ashoka, **Toto**, **Samadhi** or **Florian**) and the
shops in Savignypassage such as **Bucherbogen**
or **Canzone**. This is also the main area for finding budget accommodation – Berlin's biggest concentration of pensions and small hotels can be
found on the streets hereabouts.

Concerts & Conferences

The International Conference Centre (ICC) at the
top of Neue Kantstraße looks like something out
of *Raumschiff Enterprise* (Star Trek), and is used
for large gatherings from pop concerts to political
rallies. Next door, the even larger Messe- und
Ausstellungsgelände (Trade Fair and Exhibition
Area) plays host to trade fairs ranging from electronics to food to aerospace, and from the
Funkturm (Radio Tower) on top, one can get a
panoramic view of western Berlin. Nearby, Hitler's
impressive Olympic Stadium is home turf for the
useless Hertha BSC football club and other sports
and concert events. Its swimming pool is popular
in the summertime. The Maifeld, once the parade-
ground for the British Army, is now open to the
public, again for concerts and other large gatherings, and the Waldbühne beyond is Berlin's most
popular outdoor concert and cinema venue in the
summer.

Funkturm

Radio Tower
Messedamm, 14055 (30 380). U2 Theodor-Heuss-Platz.
Open 10am-11pm daily. **Admission** DM5; DM3

Watching the wildlife

London has foxes. New York City was once commonly supposed to have alligators. Miami has turkey vultures. Anchorage occasionally gets invaded by polar bears. And Berlin? Berlin has bunny rabbits.

You'll see them in the most unlikely places: a small patch of wasteground off some busy square; hopping around the courtyard of an apartment block. In the old days they used to hang around in no-man's land, frolicking among the border defences, safe from human predators. The Tiergarten, originally laid out as a royal hunting ground, is full of rabbits. So full that the city government recently tried to curb the bunny population by sending out teams of hunters at dawn – and stopped again after this caused an outcry.

The rabbit population is also subject of much debate around the time of the annual Love Parade. Environmentalists have tried to get Berlin's dance music festival banned because of

the effect that hundreds of thousands of partying ravers have on the Tiergarten wildlife. Presumably rabbits just don't like techno, despite their fondness for thumping their paws on the ground.

Meanwhile Berlin's rats – reckoned to number around three for every one human inhabitant – are currently on the move. Construction has involved the Spree being diverted around Lehrter Stadtbahnhof and the Tiergarten tunnel has affected the flow of an underground river that normally runs east to west under central Berlin. This has altered Berlin's water table and rats, as a result, are scrambling. Strangely, as the rest of the city moves eastwards, the rats are joining the sinking western ship. You can see them scuttling along the Spree and into Charlottenburg.

One other creature deserves mention. When walking in the woods on the outskirts of town, beware of rampaging wild boar.

---

children, students. DM3; DM1 students to restaurant only. **Map A4**
The 150-metre (164-yds) Funkturm was built in 1926 and looks not unlike a smaller version of the Eiffel Tower. The Observation deck is at 126 metres (138yds). Vertigo-sufferers should seek solace in the restaurant, which is only 55 metres (60yds) from the ground. At the foot of the tower is the Deutsches Rundfunkmuseum (German Broadcasting Museum): *see chapter* **Museums**.

Olympiastadion
Olympic Stadium
Charlottenburg, 14053 (300 633). U1 Olympia-Stadion. **Open** 10am-5.30pm daily, except event days. **Closed** November to April. **Admission** DM3; children DM1,50; concs DM2,50.
Built from 1934 to 1936 for Hitler's 1936 Olympic Games (an attempt at Aryan propaganda that was gloriously sunk by Jesse Owens). The 76,000-seat stadium still hosts sporting events like football games and track and field athletics, as well as rock concerts. *See* **Nazi Architecture** *box and also chapter* **By Area**.

Around Schloß Charlottenburg

Impressive though a lot of the buildings on the long street variously named Bismarckstraße or Kaiserdamm are, the building that brought Charlottenburg into being is still the ruler here. Coming into view as you walk up Schloßstraße, Queen Sophie Charlotte's summer palace – **Schloß Charlottenburg** – was intended to be Berlin's answer to Versailles. Today, the Schloß is most interesting as a park: the guided tours are conducted only in the German language, and the museums on the grounds proper are mostly of

interest to specialists, but the grounds easily transport the visitor back to the eighteenth century.

The museums across the street are another matter, though: the **Ägyptisches Museum**, the Museum of Greek and Roman Antiquities, the **Bröhan Museum** (art deco and art nouveau) and the **Museum für Vor und Frühgeschichte** are all worth visiting.

For those who like to wander, the streets just south of Bismarckstraße, particularly those named for philosophers (Leibnitz, Goethe, Schiller and others) have a lot of interesting small shops selling antiques, books, and the fashions that the well-to-do residents of Charlottenburg sport in the cafés and restaurants in this area

Gedenkstätte Plötzensee
Plötzensee Memorial
Huttigpfad, Charlottenburg, 13627 (344 3226). Bus 123. **Open** 8am-6pm daily *March to September*; 8.30am-5.30pm *October, February*; 9.30am-4.30 pm *November, January*; 9.30am-4pm *December*. **Admission** free.
Map C2
The Nazis executed 2,500 political prisoners here. In a single night in 1943, 186 people were hanged in groups of eight. Hitler ordered the hangings to be done with piano wire, so the victims would slowly strangle rather than die from broken necks. In 1952 it was declared a memorial to the victims of Fascism. There is little to see today, apart from the execution area with its meat hooks upon which victims were hung, and a small room with an exhibition of death warrants and pictures of some of the leading members of the resistance. Booklets in English are available from the information office. The stone urn near the entrance is filled with earth from National Socialist concentration camps. Today the rest of the prison is a juvenile corrective centre.

Grave matters

Where to leave that single red rose for Marlene Dietrich? In the Friedenauer Friedhof, a tiny cemetery in a quiet neighbourhood (U9 Friedrich-Wilhelm Platz). Marlene's grave in the far right corner is so understated that it nearly fades into the background. A copper angel turned blue with age fittingly marks the row where Marlene lies.

The gravestone reads simply 'Here I stand on the marker of my days'; with the name 'Marlene' and the years 1901-1992. Berlin still seems ambivalent, at best, about the return of the star. Marlene hasn't yet been added to the list of the cemetery's famous interred – officially that is. One fan wrote on the list of the cemetery's famous dead at the entrance, 'Marlene Dietrich, the most beautiful woman in the world'. But someone else has added, 'not including her face and figure'.

Heinrich Mann, author of *Professor Unrath*, the novel on which *The Blue Angel* film was based, lies in east Berlin, in one of Berlin's oldest cemeteries, the Friedhof der Dorotheenstädtischen und Friedrich-Werderschen Gemeinden (U6 Zinnowitzer Straße). A bronze bust of Mann tops his headstone. A characteristic cigar stub can sometimes be seen balanced on the simple stone marking the grave of Bertolt Brecht and his wife, Helene Weigel. Philosopher GWF Hegel and Carl Friedrich Schinkel, the architect of the Schauspielhaus (now the Konzerthaus) and the Altes Museum are also buried here.

Europe's largest Jewish cemetery is deep in east Berlin. Wander around the Neuer Jüdischer Friedhof in Weißensee on a melancholy afternoon (Tram 28 or 58 to Smetanastraße). Magnificent mausoleums, some inlaid with mosaics, line the inside wall. While strolling among the shroud-like trees and ivy-entangled black gravestones, packed tightly together, watch for the grave of the Mendel family. The asymmetric white-stone memorial was designed in 1923 by Bauhaus founder Walter Gropius.

In Große Hamburger Straße are the remains of another Jewish cemetery, the Alter Jüdischer Friedhof, which was destroyed by the Nazis in 1938. A marker to the philosopher Moses Mendelssohn is one of the few that can still be seen.

Tiergarten

Originally a hunting-preserve for the local princes, the park for which this borough is named is surely one of the nicest in Europe. It was opened to the public when the Brandenburg Gate was dedicated, and they're still coming: on a sunny day in summertime it hosts thousands of nature-lovers, joggers, kids, football players and Turkish barbecues. It's so lovely there you may be tempted to pitch a tent, but don't: it's illegal. On the park's outskirts, there are lots of hints of the past: a stretch of Tiergartenstraße contains the mostly still-shuttered remains of the pre-war Embassy Row. Just beyond is the Kulturforum, where one can find the **Neue Nationalgalerie**, the **Staatsbibliothek**, and the **Philharmonie**, home to the world-renowned Berlin Philharmonic Orchestra and famous for offering near-perfect acoustics and vision from all of its 2,200 seats. The **Musikinstrumenten Museum** is tucked away in a corner of the Philharmonie complex. Also in this area is the **Bauhaus Archiv**, documenting the famous design school which moved to Berlin from Weimar after that city elected a Nazi city council.

Even the street which cuts through the park as its main thoroughfare, the Straße des 17 Juni, has a Cold War reference, memorialising in its name the East Berlin worker's strike in 1953, although the street itself, with its Nazi lampposts and huge roundabout at the Großer Stern, is largely a piece of Hitler's plan for Germania. The **Siegessäule** ('Victory Column') in the Großer Stern was moved there from in front of the Reichstag, where Hitler complained that it spoiled his view. The area of park to the south-west of the column is one of the city's main gay cruises. To the east, 17 Juni runs past the **Sowjetisches Ehrenmal** and into the Brandenburg Gate (on the other side it becomes Unter den Linden), with a couple of small monuments in the divider strip proclaiming freedom for those behind the Wall.

The **Haus der Kulturen der Welt** (formerly the Kongreßhalle), is an impressive bit of modern architecture whose reflecting pool contains a Henry Moore sculpture. The Haus was designed by Hugh Stubbins, its nearby carillon by Bangert Jansen Scholz Schultes. A gift from the Americans known to the locals as the 'pregnant oyster', it collapsed shortly after being opened – an event that provided the name for one of Berlin's best-known bands, Einstürzende Neubauten. Today, it houses superb exhibits of world culture and hosts musical ensembles and cinema screenings from far-off lands. Alongside the building runs In den Zelten, a street with a history as long as it is short, hav-

Straße des 17 Juni – every Sunday the site of Berlin's best and busiest flea market.

ing been a campground for Huguenot refugees, the site of Berlin's first coffee-house, and for a short time in the 1930s, Dr Magnus Hirschfeld's ground-breaking Institute for Sexual Research.

Schloß Bellevue, a minor palace from 1705 and once a guest house for the Third Reich, just off the Großer Stern, now houses the German President when he's in town: a flag flying from its roof is the signal he's in. When he is, there are a few more soldiers in the nearby Englischer Garten than make for a comfortable stroll. Like its more famous cousin in Munich, this garden came about because King Ludwig I of Bavaria decided that the reason why there weren't constant revolutions in England was because of the plentiful, green open spaces in the cities. The idea caught on, and these gardens became such an integral part of German life that Lenin once commented that revolution in Germany was impossible because it would require people to step on the grass.

Just beyond the Schloß at the Großer Stern, there is a monumental statue of Bismarck set back from the road, flanked by statues of Prussian generals Moltke and Roon, reminders of the past which, judging from the constantly reappearing graffiti, seem to have a few people worried.

Behind Schloß Bellevue, bounded by Bachstraße, Altonaerstraße, and the Tiergarten, is the Hansaviertel, a post-war housing project whose buildings were designed by a who's who of architects in a competition. Although perhaps of most interest to specialists, it still manages to draw busloads of architecture students from all around the world, who see something other than a group of fairly sterile, modern buildings. *See chapter* **Architecture**.

Siegessäule
Victory Column
Straße des 17 Juni, Tiergarten, 10785 (391 2961). S3, S5, S6, S9 Bellevue. **Open** 1pm-5.30pm Mon; 9am-6pm Tue-Sat. (Last admission 5.30pm). **Admission** DM2; DM1 concs. **Map D3**
The Tiergarten's biggest monument is the Siegessäule, built from 1871 to 1873 to commemorate the Prussian campaigns against Denmark (1864), Austria (1866) and France (1870-71). On top of the column is an eight-metre (26-foot) high gilded Goddess of Victory by sculptor Friedrich Drake, and captured French cannons and cannon-balls, sawn in half and gilded, provide the decoration of the column proper. Fans of Wim Wenders' *Wings of Desire* can climb the 285-step spiral staircase to the viewing platform to the top for a fine view.

Sowjetisches Ehrenmal im Tiergarten
Soviet War Memorial
Straße des 17 Juni, Tiergarten, 10557. S1, S2 Unter den Linden.
The impressive Soviet War Memorial, once the only piece of Soviet property in West Berlin, stands on the north side of the street just across Entlastungsstraße and was built during 1945-6 from marble that came from Hitler's Reich chancellery. Once, this monument posed quite a problem: built in the British Zone, it was surrounded by a British military enclosure, which was guarded by the Berlin Police, all to protect the monument and the two Soviet soldiers who stood 24-hour guard. Today, one can walk right up to the memorial and read its Russian inscriptions when it's not undergoing renovation. The two tanks flanking it are alleged to have been the first two Soviet tanks into Berlin, but this is probably legend. The memorial hit the news in January 1990 when it was defaced, allegedly by neo-Nazis, despite being guarded round the clock. Some East Germans accused the still-communist government of a put-up job.

The **Tiergarten** – a picturesque place to stick your oar in, among many other delights.

Reichstag

Platz der Republik Tiergarten, 10557 (39 770). S1, S2
Unter den Linden.

The Reichstag, hugely imposing with its grand lawn stretching towards the Tiergarten now in tatters, is currently a huge building-site. Designed by Frankfurt architect Paul Wallot, in Italian High Renaissance style, the Reichstag was completed in 1894 to house the government of Bismarck's united Germany. It was burned on 17 February 1933. The Nazis may or may not have done this themselves but they blamed it on an educationally subnormal, partially-sighted Dutchman Marius van der Lubbe and certainly used it as an excuse to clamp down on communists and suspend basic freedoms. Today, after a memorable wrapping by Christo which turned the front lawn into Berlin's major party venue, it is undergoing extensive renovation, including a dome to designs by Sir Norman Foster, and will become the home of the German Parliament when the government moves from Bonn.

Tiergarten

Tiergarten, 10785. S3, S5, S6, S7, S9 Tiergarten.

Hunting grounds of the Prussian electors since the sixteenth century, the Tiergarten was turned into a park in the eighteenth century. During the war, bombs damaged much of it, and in the desperate winter of 1945-46 almost all the trees that were left were cut down for firewood. The park was left as a depressing collection of wrecked monuments and sorry-looking shrubbery interspersed with vegetable plots. Rehabilitation began in 1949 with the symbolic planting of a young lime tree by then-mayor Ernst Reuter. Some of the trees were donated by Queen Elizabeth II. A stone on the Großer Weg, the large path in the park, is inscribed with names of the German towns that contributed trees. Today the bucolic Tiergarten is one of the largest city parks in Europe. Take a stroll on the lovely Löwenbrücke (Lion Bridge), a major gay cruising area at night, which is marked by four huge iron lions, or just get lost roaming through the 167-hectare (412-acre) park.

Gedenkstätte Deutscher Widerstand

Memorial of the German Resistance
Stauffenbergstraße 13-14, Tiergarten, 10785 (26 540).
U2 Kurfürstenstraße. **Open** 9am-6pm Mon-Fri; 9am-1pm
Sat, Sun. **Admission** free.

An exhibition chronicling the German resistance to National Socialism is housed here. The building is part of a complex known as the Bendlerblock, which was owned by the German military from its construction in 1911 until 1945. At the back is a memorial to the conspirators killed during their attempt to assassinate Hitler at this site on 20 July 1944.

Shell House

corner of Reichpietschufer and Stauffenbergstraße,
Tiergarten, 10785. U1 Kurfürstenstraße.

Designed by Emil Fahrenkamp in 1932, the Shell House, these days offices for the electricity company BEWAG, is a curvaceous architectural masterpiece. But though it survived the war, it's now standing up to the march of time too well. The undulating façade, for which it is named, is being restored. It was a leading piece of modern architecture and is a must-see for fans of twentieth-century architecture.

Going underground

Berlin's U- and S-Bahn stations offer a whole underground landscape. The Märkisches Museum station on the U2 line in Mitte shows the history of Berlin in a series of relief maps, from the thirteenth century medieval settlement until, well... not quite the present.

The last map, commissioned before the Wall came down, is of Berlin in the 1980s – that is to say, East Berlin. The government only allowed their side of the city to be depicted.

Both the S- and U-Bahn stations at Alexanderplatz are worth a look. The S-Bahn station has a huge curving glass canopy which reaches from floor to ceiling, through which you can glimpse the trunk of the **Fernsehturm** and pieces of Alexanderplatz. The underground station, the biggest on the whole network, has shops and stalls and art on the walls instead of the usual ads.

Much of the south-western stretch of the U1 line is worth exploring. The building at Dahlem-Dorf, stop for all the Dahlem museums on the U2 line, is a pun: Dorf means small village and the station resembles a thatched country house. Strange benches on the platform are modelled as male and female forms. The Wittenbergplatz stop, near KaDeWe, was renovated to look like it did in the 1920s, right down to the glazed-tile and art deco adverts. Many of the stations in between these two are distinctly gothic.

The stop near Schloß Charlottenburg and the nearby art museums is a work of art itself: a row of mosaics line the walls at Richard-Wagner-Platz, on the U7. These were salvaged from a turn-of-the-century hotel on Potsdamer Straße, the Bayernhof, shortly before it was torn down in 1975. One depicts the Tannhäuser, from Wagner's opera of the same name.

At the Spandau end of the U7 line things get quite postmodern. The Zitadelle stop is a space-age interpretation of the nearby medieval citadel. At Rathaus Spandau ornate lamps hang from a very high ceiling above incredibly wide platforms.

Twenty-seven stops eastwards, on a stretch which dates from the 1930s, Hermannplatz is magnificent looking with its blocky pillars and lofty ceilings.

Anhalter Bahnhof used to be Berlin's largest train station. Now there is nothing left of the old station above ground save a small chunk of pitted façade – first it was wrecked by bombs, then blown up by city planners – and now only the S1 and S2 trains stop underground.

Don't mention the Wall!

In East German officialese it was known as the 'Anti-Fascist Protection Barrier'; in West Berlin it was simply Die Mauer; to the rest of the world it was the Berlin Wall. For 28 years it stood there, an historical reality made implacably concrete, snaking for 97 miles (155km) around the perimeter of West Berlin.

One of the most secure stretches of frontier in the world, 80 people were shot trying to get over it. Star of stage, screen and radio, and handy backdrop for visiting politicians, it achieved the status of global symbol long before it was breached on November 9 1989.

And now there is bugger all left of it.

The most central surviving stretch of Wall runs along Niederkirchner Straße, just off Wilhelmstraße (U2, S1, S2 Potsdamer Platz), between the Luftfahrtsministerium and the **Topograpy of Terror** (*see chapter* **Museums**). It is a pock-marked piece, a block or two long, much of it chipped away by tourists with hammers. The remainder is now protected by a wire fence.

A longer stretch, now known as the East Side Gallery and commemorating the Wall's tradi-tional function as graffiti canvas, can be found along Mühlenstraße by the river Spree (S3, S5, S6, S9 Berlin Hauptbahnhof). This is decked by mostly political work from various international artists and is billed as the world's largest outdoor picture gallery.

From the S-Bahn lines running across the Spree west of Friedrichstraße, you can see a length of Wall, graphically divided into 28 segments, each of them representing a year from 1961-1989.

For each year there is a body count of people killed trying to get over – over the years at least 80 people died trying. If you want to view this at ground level, it's at the corner of Reinhardstraße and Schiffsbauerdamm (S1, S2 Unter Den Linden).

There are also small hunks of Wall all over town. A few displaced slabs are still lying around on Potsdamer Platz. There is a piece at one of the Tauentzienstraße entrances to the Europa-Center and another in Pariser Platz outside the Akademie der Kunst building. Various hotel lobbies also boast their very own chunks of Wall. Lo, how the mighty has fallen.

Other hoods

Because Berlin's underlying soil is sandy, until recently large buildings haven't been built here, which means that the city sprawls. On the other hand, the U-Bahn and S-Bahn system will whisk you to some of its lesser-known neighbourhoods in minutes. Here are some suggestions for further exploration.

West Berlin

To the north, the city eventually gives itself up to block after block of industrial works and housing for the people who work there, and while the Moabit section of Tiergarten has some charm, particularly along the river, it's harder to defend areas like Wedding and Reinickendorf. One sight in Wedding, although most easily approached from Mitte, is worth the trip: the Gedenksstätte Berliner Mauer, a section of the Wall without graffiti (it was on the east side, since the Wall was actually two walls with a no-mans'-land in the middle) that has been preserved by the Berliner Museum. It lies between Bernauer Straße and Invalidenstraße near the Nordbahnhof S-Bahn station.

Southern West Berlin was the American Sector, and sections like Steglitz, Dahlem, and Zehlendorf contain some of the city's wealthiest residences. Besides the museum complex (*see chapter* **Museums**), Dahlem is the home of the **Freie Universität**, some of whose departments occupy former villas seized by the Nazis from their Jewish owners. In Zehlendorf, Mexikoplatz is a beautifully-preserved plaza with one of the city's best-known left-wing book-stores in its S-Bahn station. Elsewhere in Zehlendorf, the Onkel-Toms-Hütte development is a historically-important collection of workers' houses designed in the 1920s and 1930s by architects like Bruno Taut, Hugo Häring, and Otto Rudolf Solvisberg, painted in unique colours only available from one company in Germany, and today lived in by workers in professions that are a long way away from those the original inhabitants toiled at. Take the U-Bahn to Onkel-Toms-Hütte and walk down Onkel-Tom-Straße towards the woods. (*See also chapter* **Architecture**.)

Otherwise, Zehlendorf's main claim to fame these days is the many empty buildings left by the departing American troops, used as housing for students and asylum-seekers as of this writing.

Perhaps the best way to ogle the mansions in Steglitz and Dahlem is by car or bicycle, wandering down the streets wondering at the mélange of architectural styles and trying to guess which Steglitz mansion is the one Helmut Kohl has bought in anticipation of the government moving to Berlin in 1999.

Another southern district, Neukölln, was a pocket south-east of Kreuzberg until the Wall came down, and now is the most direct neighbour of Schönefeld Airport. Karl-Marx-Straße here is a major shopping district, but the Rixdorf section around Richard-Schadoma-Platz is charming because of the many old buildings that remain there. Further south, at Britz-Sud, the Bruno-Taut-Ring, a horseshoe-shaped housing estate, is a fine example of Bauhaus architecture.

One other tourist attraction in a seldom-visited neighbourhood should be mentioned: in a tiny graveyard just off the Südwest Korso in Friedenau, southwest of Schöneberg is Marlene Dietrich's grave. Like most graveyards here, this one has a card with the location of some of the more prominent residents by its gateway, giving their names and occupations. Dietrich has not been formally added to this list, but a fan has scrawled her name and 'Most Beautiful Woman in the World' so she's easy to find. *See* **Grave matters** *page 66.*

South of Charlottenburg and west of Schöneberg lies Wilmersdorf. This is a mostly boring district of smart apartments that nonetheless has many bars and cafés and a lot of street life at night in the area around Ludwig-Kirch-Platz.

Botanischer Garten

Botanical Garden
Königin-Luise-Straße 6-8, Zehlendorf, 14195 (830 060). S1 Botanischer Garten/U9 Rathaus Steglitz. **Open** 9am until sunset daily. **Admission** DM6; DM3 concs.
The Botanical Garden was landscaped at the beginning of this century on a 42-hectare (104-acre) plot of land. Today it is home to approximately 18,000 species of plants, and includes 16 greenhouses and a museum with displays on herbs and dioramas of flowers. *See also chapter* **Museums**.

East Berlin

This side of town is generally thought of as a wasteland of decaying communist apartment blocks, but there's still a lot of the flavour of old Berlin in the east, particularly in the up-and-coming districts of Treptow and Friedrichshain. The latter has the Volkspark Friedrichshain, a huge park with assorted bits of socialist-realist art, an open-air stage and an early twentieth-century fountain of fairy tale characters among lush greenery. The graves of the fighters who fell in March 1848 in the battle for German Unity are here.

Not all of the neighbourhoods here are universally attractive: especially if you're not white, it's best to avoid Marzahn's grim housing projects after dark, although its Biesdorf district is quite nice and has a small park with a castle in it.

Another place worth a visit is Treptower Park, with its immense **Soviet War Memorial** and pleasant picnic area. From here, several excursion boats leave in the summer for trips along the Spree,

and there are other boats with restaurants on them. The park continues to the south, where it becomes the Plänterwald, site of a big amusement park.

Fans of urban living can see plenty of examples of East-bloc apartment buildings in the east, built on a plan that is echoed unchanged in the outlying areas of any major Warsaw Pact city. Of particular note is the long string of Soviet-style 'Zuckerbäcker' apartment buildings lining Frankfurter Allee, constructed along a utopian scheme that made each a miniature model of an ideal communist society, with all classes of workers included in each building. Artists were given the top floors. These buildings, although somewhat ratty today, are listed as having architectural and historical value, and are presently being restored. As for Frankfurter Allee, it continues in a straight line nearly to the Polish border.

Soviet War Memorial

Treptow, 12435, S6, S8, S9, S10 Treptower Park.
Treptower Park is home to a huge, sobering monument to the Soviet soldiers who died in the war against Hitler, as well as a mass grave for 5,000 of them. As you walk down the tree-lined avenue you arrive at a statue of Mother Russia, weeping for her dead children. Fascinating, if heavy-handed, white stone reliefs, set up almost as stations of the cross and bearing quotations from Stalin, depict the story of how the Soviets triumphed over Fascism. On top of the tomb at the far end of the park is a huge statue of a valiant, square-jawed Soviet soldier, clasping a child in one arm, and with the other smashing a swastika. Don't miss it.

Outskirts

The obscure New York songwriter David Ackles once wrote a song called *Subway to the Country* about wishing he could jump on the underground and get out where the land was green. Well, David, come to Berlin: at end-stations like Königs Wusterhausen and Strausberg Nord you can do just that, particularly if you take a bicycle and are willing to pedal for 30 minutes or so. Even some of the closer-in stations, particularly in the east, can offer pleasant surroundings of two-family houses with backyards filled with fruit-trees.

Grunewald

The largest of Berlin's forests is also its most visited; on a fine Sunday afternoon, its lanes and paths are as packed as the Kurfürstendamm, but with walkers, runners, cyclists, horse-riders and dog-walkers. This is because it's easily accessible by S-Bahn.

There are several restaurants next to Grunewald station, and on the other side of the motorway at Schmetterlingsplatz, open during the season (April to October). Follow Schildhornweg (past the Sandgraben, from which high-quality Berlin sand was dug for building and to supply its glass industry), to Teufelssee, a tiny lake which is packed with bathers in summer.

The near-by Teufelsberg is a product of wartime devastation: a railway was laid from Wittenbergplatz, along Kurfürstendamm, to carry rubble from the city centre for depositing in a great pile at the terminus here. There are great views from the summit, on which sits a now-disused American electronic listening post.

To the south, there are kiosks for sausages, drinks and ice creams at the Großer Stern on Hüttenweg (also an exit from the motorway) in the summertime. It's a busy pitstop for hundreds of cyclists pelting up the paths, Kronprinzessinweg and Königsweg, parallel to the road.

At Grunewaldsee, the Jagdschl

oß (hunting lodge) is a good example of hundreds of such buildings which once maintained the country life of the Prussian Junkers (landed gentry). There is bathing by the lake in the summer, including a nudist section; for some reason, it is also a favourite promenade for chic dogs and their owners, who refresh themselves in the deer-horn-bedecked Forsthaus Paulsborn.

A kilometre east through the woods, Chalet Suisse is an over-the-top Swiss-themed restaurant popular with families because of its extensive playground and petting zoo. A ten-minute walk takes you to the **Allied Museum**. Also nearby, the **Brücke Museum** houses surviving works by the influential Brücke group (including Kirchner, Heckel and Schmidt-Rottluff), known for their impressionistic views of Berlin.

Krumme Lanke and Schlachtensee are nice urban lakes (along the south-eastern edge of Grunewald – take the U1 to Krumme Lanke or the S1 to Schlachtensee), perfect for a picnic, swimming and rowing.

Half way up the Havelchaussee, the Grunewaldturm (Grunewald Tower), built in 1897 in memory of Wilhelm I (aka 'Kaiser-Wilhelm-Turm'), has an observation platform 105 metres (115 yards) above the lake with views as far as Spandau and Potsdam. There is a restaurant at the

Tyrannical town-planning

Hitler and his pet architect Albert Speer had grandiose plans for Berlin — or Germania, as it was to be renamed.

Once the rest of the world had been subjugated, the capital of the Thousand Year Reich would be equipped with dinky features like a monstrous hall with a dome 16 times the size of St Peter's in Rome, a triumphal arch three times as tall as the one in Paris, a chancellery that would require visiting diplomats to take a chastening quarter-mile hike once inside the building, and a Führer's palace no less than 150 times the size of Bismarck's.

Well, war put a stop to all that and Allied bombs demolished much of what the Nazis actually did build. Some fine examples of fancy fascist architecture did, however, survive.

Fans of tyrannical town-planning might start with Flughafen Tempelhof (Tempelhofer Damm, U6 Platz der Luftbrücke). Originally opened in 1923, this was greatly expanded by the Nazis and had its place in Speer's plan for Germania. Not only the largest building in Berlin but one of the largest in the world, its 400 metre quarter-circle form is probably best appreciated from the air. At ground level it's impossible to take in all at once.

Somehow the Luftfahrtsministerium – the Nazi air ministry (corner of Leipziger Straße and Wilhelm Straße, U2, S1, S2 Potsdamer Platz) – survived wartime bombardment and went on to house various East German ministries until the Wall came down and the Treuhand moved in. Overbearing and bureaucratic, this is totalitarian architecture at its bleakest. The finance ministry is now scheduled to set up house here when it arrives from Bonn.

The Olympiastadion in Neu-Westend (*see listing below*), set for Leni Riefenstahl's least boring film *Olympiad*, orchestrates height, space and enclosure in a way that is both chilling and thrilling. Built as a Nazi showpiece for the world on the occasion of the 1936 Olympics, this actually does what fascist architecture was intended to do: impress.

Other remnants of the Third Reich include offices around Fehrbelliner Platz (U1, U7 Fehrbelliner Platz) which are now used by the city Senate; the Finanzamt at Bismarkstraße 48 (U2 Bismarckstraße), where the Nazi eagle now clutches the street number instead of a swastika; the Reichsbank building at Werderscher Markt in Mitte (U2 Hausvogteiplatz); and the ruins of the Gestapo HQ at the Topography of Terror (*see listing*).

There are also assorted blank, grey concrete Nazi flak towers around town, including one on Pallasstraße near the junction with Potsdamer Straße, one up at Humboldthain which has had a park landscaped around it, and one on Albrechtstraße in Mitte which until recently housed a club called Bunker.

The Wannsee – a big sweep of water in constant use by all manner of craft.

base, the Ausflugsrestaurant am Grunewaldturm, and another on the other side of the road, Waldhaus Wildspezialitäten, both with garden terraces. A short walk along Havelufer brings you to the ferry to Lindwerder Island, which also has a restaurant, Lindwerder Insel Restaurant.

Jagdschloß Grunewald

On the shore of the Grunewaldsee, Zehlendorf, 14193 (813 35 97). S3, S5 Grunewald. **Open** 10am-6pm Tue-Sun. **Admission** DM4; DM2 concs.
Built by Kurfürst Joachim II von Brandenburg in 1542, who described it as zum grünen Wald ('in the green wood') thus coining the name of the forest in which it stands. Considerably altered by Graf Rochus zu Lynar and Frederick the Great (1770), much of the Renaissance façade was pulled down and thrown into a nearby pit. Later excavations unearthed this pit and recently the building has been restored to its original sixteenth-century appearance.

Wannsee

Strandbad Wannsee is the largest inland beach in Europe. Between May and September it becomes the most popular resort in Berlin, with service buildings housing showers, toilets, cafés, shops and kiosks. There are boats and pedaloes and hooded, two-person wicker sunchairs for hire (enquire about these at the entrance), a children's playground and separate sections for nudists and the severely disabled.

The waters of the Havel are extensive and in summer are warm enough to make swimming comfortable; there is a strong current, so do not stray beyond the floating markers. The rest of the open water is in constant use by ferries, speed- and sailing boats and waterskiers.

Beyond the Strandbad lie the Wannseeterrassen, a couple of rustic lanes on the slopes of the hill, at the bottom of which private boats and yachts are moored. There is a good view from the restaurant Wannseeterrasse, but less remarkable food. A small bridge takes you across to Schwanenwerder, once the exclusive private island retreat of Goebbels and now home to the international think-tank, the Aspen Institute.

The town of Wannsee to the south is clustered around the bay of the Großer Wannsee and dominated by the long promenade, Am Großen Wannsee, which is scattered with hotels and fish restaurants. Also here is the **Gedenkstätte Haus der Wannsee-Konferenz** (Memorial House of the Wannsee Conference). Here, in January 1942, a meeting of prominent Nazis chaired by Reinhard Heydrich laid out plans for the extermination of the Jewish people – the 'Final Solution'. The house, an elegant Grunderzeit mansion, is now a museum documenting the Holocaust.

A short distance from S-Bahnhof Wannsee along Bismarckstraße is a little garden in which the German dramatist, Heinrich von Kleist, shot himself in 1811; the beautiful view of the Kleiner Wannsee was the last thing he wanted to see. On

Schloß Pfaueninsel – *built in 1793 for Friedrich Wilhelm II's mistress, Wilhelmine Encke.*

the other side of the railway tracks is Düppler Forst, a little-explored forest including a nature reserve at Großes Fenn at the south-western end. Travelling on the S-Bahn to Mexikoplatz and then the 629 Bus to Krummes Fenn brings you to **Museumsdorf Düppel**.

Strandbad Wannsee
Wannseebadweg, Nikolassee, 14219 (803 5450). S1, S3, Nikolassee. **Open** 7am-8pm daily. **Admission** DM5; DM3 concs.

Gedenkstätte Haus der Wannsee-Konferenz
Am Grossen Wannsee 56-58, Zehlendorf, 14109 (805 0010) S1, S3, S7 Wannsee, then bus 114. **Open** 10am-6pm Mon-Fri; 2pm-6pm Sat, Sun. **Admission** free.
A lovely house with a grim history, and at present writing, the only Holocaust museum in Berlin.

Museumsdorf Düppel
Clauertstraße 11, Zehlendorf, 14163 (802 6671). Bus 115, 211. **Open** April to Sept 3pm-7pm Thur; 10am-5pm Sundays and holidays. **Admission** DM10; DM3 concs.
A working reconstruction of a medieval Brandenburg village, and a great place to take the kids. *See chapter* **Children**.

Pfaueninsel

'Peacock Island', a 98-hectare (242-acre) non-smoking island in the Havel River is part of the Potsdam complex (though within Berlin's borders) and is reached by the shortest private ferry ride in the city, hourly from 8am-6pm daily.

The island was inhabited in prehistoric times, but wasn't mentioned in archives until 1683. Two years later the Grand Elector presented it to Johann Kunckel von Löwenstein, a chemist who experimented with alchemy and produced instead 'ruby glass', examples of which are on view in the castle. But it was only at the start of the Romantic Era that the island's windswept charms began to attract more serious interest. In 1793, Friedrich Wilhelm II purchased it and built a Schloß for his mistress, Wilhelmine Encke. But he died in 1797 before they had a chance to move in. Its first residents were the happily married couple, Friedrich Wilhelm III and Queen Luise. The island was later added to and adorned. A huge royal menagerie was developed, with enclosed and free-roaming animals (most of which were moved to the new Tiergarten Zoo in 1842). Only peacocks, pheasants, parrots, goats and sheep remain.

Surviving buildings include the Jakobsbrunnen (Jacob's Fountain), a copy of a Roman temple; the Kavalierhaus (Cavalier's House), built in 1803 from an original design by Schinkel; and the Swiss cottage, also based on a Schinkel plan. All are linked to each other by winding, informal paths laid out in the English manner by Peter Joseph Lenné. A walk around the island, with its extreme quiet, its monumental trees and rough meadows, and its breathtaking views of the waters of the Havel and the 'mainland' beyond, provides one of the most

Pfaueninsel – 'Peacock Island' – formerly a royal menagerie, now a public pleasure garden.

complete sensations of escape from urban living to be had within the borders of Berlin.

Back on the mainland, a short walk south along the bank of the Havel, is the Blockhaus Nikolskoe, a recreation of a huge wooden chalet, built in 1819 by Friedrich Wilhelm II for his daughter Charlotte, and named after her husband, the future Tsar Nicholas of Russia. There is a magnificent view of the Havel from the terrace, where you can also enjoy an excellent choice of mid-price Berlin cuisine, or just coffee and cakes in the afternoon. The nearby Kirche St Peter und St Paul (Church of St Peter and St Paul) dates from 1834-37 and has an attractive interior.

Schloß Pfaueninsel

(805 3042). Open *Apr-Sept* 10am-5pm daily; *Oct* 10am-4pm daily. Guided tours every hour.

Glienicke

The centre of this park (now a conference centre) and its outbuildings, which are being restored, is Schloß Glienicke. Although closed to the public, its surrounding park invites a walk along the Havel, which is a nice way to get to Moorlake, at which there's a cafe in the old hunting lodge. Close by the park, the suspension bridge over the Havel (1909), was named Brücke der Einheit (Bridge of Unity) because it joined Potsdam with Berlin; the name continued to be used even when, after the building of the Wall, it was painted different shades of olive green on the east and west sides and used only by Allied soldiers and for top-level exchanges of spies and dissidents (Anatoly Scharansky was one of the last in 1986).

Schlösser & Park Glienicke

on the Königstraße, Zehlendorf, 14109 (805 3041). Bus 116. The palace is closed to public.
A hunting lodge designed by Schinkel for Prinz Carl von Preußen, who quickly became notorious for his ban on all women visitors. On at least one occasion, Prinz Carl's wife was turned away at the gate by armed guards. The Prinz adorned the walls of the gardens with ancient relics collected on his various holidays around the Mediterranean, and decided to simulate a walk from the Alps to Rome in the densely wooded park, laid out by Pückler in 1824-50. The summerhouses, fountains and follies are based on Italian models, and the woods and fields surrounding them make an ideal place for a Sunday picnic, since this park is little-visited.

Spandau

Berlin's western neighbour and eternal rival; the home of Rudolf Hess, the city's last Nazi chieftain, until 1987; a little baroque town which seems to contradict everything about the city of which it is now, reluctantly, a part: Spandauers still talk about 'going into Berlin' when they head off to the rest of the city, although the rest of us can easily get there on the U7, getting off at Zitadelle or Altstadt Spandau. The original charter of the town lies in the Stadtgeschichtlichesmuseum in the Zitadelle and dates from 1232, a fact which Spandauers have relied on ever since to assert their legitimacy before Cölln and Berlin to be the historical heart of the capital.

The old town centre of Spandau is mostly pedestrianised, with two- and three-storey eighteenth-century townhouses interspersed between burger joints and department stores. One of the prettiest examples is the former Gasthof zum Stern in Carl-Schurz-Straße; older still are the houses in Kinkelstraße (until 1933, Judenstraße) and Ritterstraße; but perhaps the best preserved district is across Am Juliusturm in the area bounded by Hoher Steinweg, Kolk and Behnitz. Steinweg contains a fragment of the old town wall from the first half of the fourteenth century; Kolk has the Catholic garrison church (Alte Marienkirche dating from 1848); and in Behnitz, at number five, stands the Heinemannsche Haus, perhaps the finest late-baroque townhouse in Berlin.

At Reformationsplatz, the brick nave of the Nikolaikirche dates from 1410-1450, the west tower having been added in 1468, and with further additions by Schinkel. All these landmarks, of course, had to be thoroughly restored after the last war.

One of the most pleasant times to visit the town is in the weeks before Christmas, when the market square has a Nativity scene with real sheep. The Konditorei (bakery/café) on Reformationsplatz is excellent.

Probably the most notorious of Spandau's recent residents was Rudolf Hess, Hitler's deputy, imprisoned in the Allied Gaol after the Nuremberg Trials, where he remained (alone after 1966) until his suicide on 17 August 1987. Once he'd gone, the nineteenth-century brick building at Wilhelmstraße 21-24 was demolished to make way for a supermarket for the British Forces – who have now left the city. Hess's story has attracted controversy for decades, but, until the official documents are released by the British government, there's still little evidence to contradict the official version: that Hess parachuted into Scotland in 1940 in a private attempt to negotiate an end to the war with Britain.

Zitadelle (Juliusturm, Palas)

Am Juliusturm, Spandau, 13599 (33 911). U7 Zitadelle. Open 9am-5pm Tue-Sun Admission Juliusturm, Palas, & Stadtgeschichtlichesmuseum DM5; DM3 concs. Tours noon and 3pm daily, DM5; DM3 concs.
The oldest building here (and the oldest secular building in Berlin) is the Juliusturm, probably dating back to an Ascanian *(see chapter* History) water fortress from about 1160; the present tower, with 154 steps and walls measuring up to 3.6 metres (4 yards) thick, was home until 1919 to the 120 million Goldmark reparations, stored in 1,200 boxes, which the French paid to Germany in 1874 after the Franco-Prussian War. In German financial circles, state reserves are still referred to as 'Juliusturm'.

Köpenick and its Schloßinsel – one of the most sought-after areas of east Berlin.

Stadtgeschichtlichesmuseum Spandau

Spandau Museum of Local History
*Am Juliusturm, Spandau, 13599 (3391 264). U1
Zitadelle.* **Open** 9am-5pm Tue-Fri; 10am-5pm Sat, Sun.
Admission DM1,50; DM1 concs. Combined with
Juliusturm/Palas ticket.
Located in the Palas, which has stones in its cellar dating
back to 1200; the base of the south front contains Jewish
tombstones from 1244-1347, when Spandau was the only
place guaranteeing safety for Jewish graves, but these can
only be seen on the twice-daily guided tour. The bulk of the
Zitadelle, however, was designed in 1560-94, in the style of
an Italian fort; its purpose was to dominate the confluence
of the Spree and Havel rivers. Since then it has been used as
everything from garrison to prison to laboratory. Today,
most of the huge 300m (328yd) by 300m site (except for the
museums and a few galleries) is under restoration and archeological excavation and not accessible to the public.

Köpenick

The name Köpenick is derived from the Slavonic
copanic, meaning place on a river. The Altstadt
(old town) stands at the confluence of the Spree and
Dahme, and having escaped bombing, decay and,
worse, development by the GDR, still maintains
much of its eighteenth-century character.

Köpenick's imposing Rathaus (Town Hall) is a
good example of Wilhelmenisch civic architecture.
It was here, in 1906, two years after the building's
completion, that Wilhelm Voigt, an unemployed
cobbler, disguised himself as an army captain and
ordered a detachment of soldiers to accompany him
into the Treasury, where they confiscated the town
coffers. He entered popular folklore as the
Hauptmann von Köpenick (Captain of Köpenick),

and was pardoned by the Kaiser because he'd
shown how obedient Prussian soldiers were.

His theft is re-enacted every year during the
Köpenicker Sommer festival (late June), when a
parade of locals in period costume marches to the
town hall steps.

Köpenick, of all the areas of east Berlin, was and
still is the most sought after, with handsome and
increasingly affluent shops, cafés and restaurants
clustered around the old centre, the Kiez. With its
old buildings and extensive riverfront, it's a fine
place for a Sunday afternoon Bummel, or wander
– a great Berlin tradition.

On the Schloßinsel island stands Köpenick's
Schloß. Occasional open-air concerts are held here
in summer, and the late-medieval Kunstgewerbe-
museum (Museum of Applied Art) houses a collection of porcelain, glass, gold and Berlin iron. It
was here in the Weapons Room in 1730 that
Friedrich Wilhelm I ordered the trial for desertion
of his son (the future Frederick the Great) who had
attempted to flee to England with his friend (also,
probably, his lover), Lieutenant von Katte. The
couple were betrayed and the courtmartial sentenced them both to two years' imprisonment, but
the King then altered the verdict, forcing his son
to watch von Katte's decapitation from his cell.

A few minutes' walk from the castle is the Kiez.
The little streets, lined with narrow, cramped houses, are being restored and taken over by the new
east Berlin *Schickeria*, or trendies. There's now a
good choice of art galleries and antique dealers.

Museums

While the museum scene keeps ringing the changes, there's still plenty to stimulate both body and mind.

If you came to Berlin just to visit its many museums, you've arrived at the wrong time. Renovation and reorganisation as the city spruces itself up for the millennium mean that no less than 14 major museums are closed until sometime after the year 2000. This doesn't mean there's nothing to see – far from it: it does, for example, make a trip to the Dahlem complex in south-west Berlin more daunting given that instead of the usual five museums, you'll currently find only two.

Despite the temporary closures, many museums are still clustered around the Museuminsel in Mitte (**Altes Museum**, **Pergamon**), around Schloß Charlottenburg (**Ägyptisches Museum**, **Bröhan-Museum**, **Museum für Vor und Frühgeschichte**, and **Schloß Charlottenburg** itself) and in Dahlem (**Museum für Europäische Volkskunde**, **Museum für Völkerkunde** and the nearby **Brücke-Museum**).

English guided tours of most state museums can be arranged by appointment. For Dahlem, Charlottenburg, Tiergarten and so forth contact the *Besucherdienst* at Dahlem (*830 1466*); open 8am-noon Mon-Fri. The Pergamon (*2090 5555*) is open 8am-4pm. In both cases give at least 14 days' notice. Guided tours in English for up to 25 people, costing around DM80 plus admission, last about an hour. As a general rule, the larger museums are more likely to have either booklets or information sheets in English. However, a lot of museums have little or no information in English available: where this may be a problem, we have indicated it in the review.

Archaeology & ancient history

Ägyptisches Museum

Egyptian Museum
Schloßstraße 70, Charlottenburg, 14059 (320 911). U2 Sophie-Charlotte-Platz/U7 Richard-Wagner-Platz. **Open** 9am-5pm Tue-Fri; 10am-5pm Sat, Sun. **Admission** DM8 combined ticket for Egyptian, antique, prehistoric, and romantic galleries; DM4 concs; DM4 single museum; DM2 concs; free Sun. **Map B3**
Just across the street from Schloß Charlottenburg and one of the most popular museums in Berlin, mainly because of the bust of Egyptian Queen Nefertiti. This piece of art, crafted in 1350 BC, was buried for more than 3,000 years until German archaeologists dug it up earlier this century. Nefertiti has a room to herself on the second floor. Also notable are a mummy and sarcophagi, a papyrus collection and the Kalabasha Gate. Despite the museum's popularity,

no English booklets are available. But you could invest DM30 in a rather expensive hardback book which has full-colour pictures of the museum's main exhibits.

Pergamon Museum

Am Kupfergraben, Mitte, 10178 (2090 5555). S3, S5, S6, S9 Hackescher Markt. **Open** 9am-5pm Tue-Sun. **Admission** DM4; DM2 concs; free first Sun of month. **Map F3**
The Pergamon Museum is dedicated to ancient spaces. Equipped with the gates, altars and gathering places of antiquity, it's the next best thing to being there. The vast Hellenistic Pergamon Altar (from which the museum takes its name) dates from 180-160 BC. It is made of white marble and carved with figures of the gods. The Market Gate of Miletus, a two-storey Roman gate erected in AD 120, once provided access to a public market and was large enough to contain a few shops of its own. In an adjoining room, the Babylonian Processional Street leads to The Gate of Ishtar, a striking cerulean and ochre tiled structure. It is the reconstruction of a street built during the reign of King Nebuchadnezzar (605-562 BC). Built between 1909 and 1930, the Pergamon is a relative newcomer to the Museuminsel, on which it stands, but is one of the most significant archaeological museums in the world.

Museum für Vor und Frühgeschichte

Primeval and Early History Museum
Spandauer Damm 20, Charlottenburg, 14059 (320 911). U2 Sophie-Charlotte-Platz/U7 Richard-Wagner-Platz. **Open** 9am-5pm Tue-Fri; 10am-5pm Sat, Sun. **Admission** DM4; DM2 concs; free Sun. **Map B3**
The evolution of Homo Sapiens from 1,000,000 BC to the Bronze Age is the subject of this museum next to the west wing of the palace. Keep an eye out for the sixth-century BC grave of a girl buried with a gold coin in her mouth. Beats Christmas pudding. Information is available in English.

Art & architecture

Altes Museum

Lustgarten, Mitte, 10178 (2090 5555). S3, S5, S6, S9 Hackescher Markt. **Open** 9am-5pm Tue-Sun. **Admission** DM4; DM2 concs; free first Sun of the month. **Map F3**
Opened as the Royal Museum in 1830, this originally housed all the art treasures on Museum Island. It was designed by the ubiquitous Karl Friedrich Schinkel and is considered one of his finest buildings. The entrance rotunda is particularly magnificent. The museum is currently hosting the major works of the Alte Nationalgalerie which, like so many Berlin museums, is undergoing renovation.

Bauhaus Archiv-Museum für Gestaltung

Klingelhöferstraße 13-14, Tiergarten, 10785 (254 0020). Bus 109, 116, 124, 129. **Open** 10am-5pm Mon, Wed-Sun. **Admission** DM5; DM2,50 concs. **Map D4**
Walter Gropius, founder of the Bauhaus school, designed this modern white building, just across the canal from the **Grand Hotel Esplanade** (*see chapter* **Accommodation**). The museum presents furniture, ceramics, metal objects,

The neo-classical **Altes Museum** – *Karl Friedrich Schinkel in fine mid-season form.*

prints, sculptures, photographs and sketches created in the Bauhaus workshop from 1919 until 1933. Designs and models by Gropius, Ludwig Mies van der Rohe and paintings and drawings by Paul Klee, Georg Muche, Wassily Kandinsky and Oskar Schlemmer are also on show. For architecture experts and novices, a computer exhibition in German and English provides a useful context to the museum. There's a cafeteria, plus a library with Bauhaus documents (open 9am-1pm Mon-Fri).

Bröhan-Museum

Schloßstraße 1A, Charlottenburg, 14059 (321 4029). U2 Sophie-Charlotte-Platz/U7 Richard-Wagner-Platz. **Open** 10am-6pm Tue-Sun. **Admission** DM6; DM3 concs. **Map B3**

The Bröhan Museum, across from the Egyptian Museum, offers a welcome break for those weary of tourist traps. This quiet, private museum contains three levels of art nouveau and art deco pieces that businessman Karl Bröhan began collecting in the 1960s. The wide array of paintings, furniture, porcelain, silver, vases and sculptures dates from 1890 up to 1939. Hans Baluschek's paintings of social life in the 1920s and 1930s, and Willy Jaeckel's series of portraits of women are the pick of the bunch.

Brücke-Museum

Bussardsteig 9, Zehlendorf, 14195 (831 2029). U1 Oskar-Helene-Heim, then bus 115. **Open** 11am-5pm Mon, Wed-Sun. **Admission** DM7; DM3 concs.

Some distance from the other Dahlem museums, an exhibit dedicated to the work of *Die Brücke* (The Bridge), a movement of artists established in Dresden in 1905 and credited with introducing Expressionism to Germany. On display are oils, water colours, drawings and sculptures by the main members of the movement: Schmidt-Rottluff, Heckel, Kirchner, Mueller and Pechstein. The 'Mahler Der Brucke' (Artists of The Bridge) exhibition runs until September 1998 to be followed by 'Der Blaue Reiter und seine Kunstler' until January 1999. Although a little out of the way, the Brücke is definitely worth seeing: a connoisseur's museum, small but

satisfying and coherently arranged, full of fascinatingly colourful work. Wander through the fancy neighbourhood of Dahlem to the museum's location on the edge of the Grunewald.

Ephraim-Palais

Poststraße 16, Mitte, 10178 (240 020). U2, U5, U8/S3, S5, S7, S9 Alexanderplatz. **Open** 10am-6pm Tue-Sun. **Admission** DM6; DM4 concs; free Wed. **Map G3**

In the Nikolaiviertel, this is part of the Foundation of City Museums. It was built in the fifteenth century, remodelled into a bourgeois home in the late baroque style of the late seventeenth century, and is now home to temporary art exhibitions. Its soft, chandelier-lighting, parquet floors and spiral staircase add a refined touch to exhibited works without overwhelming them. Recent exhibitions include the acclaimed 'Stadtbilder' – nineteenth- and twentieth-century painters from Berlin – and a well-presented show devoted to the Berliner Secessionists.

Gemäldegalerie

Picture Gallery

Stauffenbergstraße 40, Tiergarten, 10785 (266 2100). U2 Potsdamer Platz. **Open** 9am-5pm Tue-Fri; 10am-5pm Sat, Sun. **Admission** DM5; DM3 concs. **Map E4**

The Gemäldegalerie has an astonishing number of works by most of art history's big boys, including Rubens, Dürer, Breughel, Holbein, Raphael, Gainsborough, El Greco, Canaletto and Caravaggio. Room after room of paintings await exploration. There are works by German, Dutch and Italian artists from the thirteenth- to the sixteenth century; French and English paintings from the eighteenth century; Dutch, French and Flemish works from the seventeenth century; Italian baroque and rococo; and many Spanish paintings. Devotees of Rembrandt won't be disappointed by the 20 or so of his canvases displayed here, which constitute one the world's largest collections of his works. Also on display is a version of Botticelli's famous *Venus Rising* (the complete painting is in Florence) and Correggio's brilliant *Leda With The Swan*. Look also for Lucas Cranach's

Fountain of Youth (1546), depicting old, haggard women entering a pool and emerging from the other side young and beautiful again.

Georg-Kolbe-Museum

Sensburger Allee 25, Charlottenburg, 14055 (304 2144). Bus 149, 105; or a 15-minute walk from U2 Theodor-Heuss-Platz. **Open** 10am-5pm Tue-Sun. **Admission** DM5; DM3 concs.

Georg Kolbe's former studio in a quiet neighbourhood of Charlottenburg has been transformed into a showcase for his work. The Berlin sculptor, regarded as Germany's best in the 1920s, mainly focused on naturalistic human figures. The museum features examples of his earlier, graceful pieces, as well as his later sombre and larger-than-life works created in accordance with the ideals of the Nazi regime. One of his most famous pieces, *Figure for Fountain*, is outside in the sculpture garden.

Hamburger Bahnhof, Museum für Gegenwart Berlin

Invalidenstraße 50-51, Mitte, 10557 (2090 5555). S3, S5, S7, S9 Lehrter Stadtbahnhof. **Open** 9am-5pm Tue-Fri; 10am-5pm Sat, Sun. **Admission** DM12; DM6 concs. **Map E3**

Opened with much fanfare in 1997 and housed in a huge and expensive refurbishment of a former train station near both Lehrter Bahnhof, scheduled to become the city's new central station, and what will soon be the new government quarter. The exterior features a stunning fluorescent light installation by Dan Flavin, which is worth whizzing by at night to observe. The permanent exhibition within comes principally from the bequested Marx Collection. It includes wings for works by Andy Warhol and Joseph Beuys along with works by Bruce Nauman, Amseln Kiefer and many others – lots of macho metal and grey art from the 1980s. Some relief is on the first floor – the sculptures of Rosemarie Trockel and charming pre-pop Warhol drawings from the 1950s. The Museum has one of the best art bookshops in Berlin and is the venue for large retrospectives of artists such as Sigmar Polke. It also has an 'Aktionraum' hosting various events such as performances and symposia, plus a video archive of all Joseph Beuys' performances that were taped.
Bookshop

Käthe-Kollwitz-Museum

Fasanenstraße 24, Wilmersdorf, 10719 (882 5210). U3 Uhlandstraße. **Open** 11am-6pm Wed-Sun. **Admission** DM6; DM3 concs. **Map C4**

Käthe Kollwitz's powerful work embraces the full spectrum of life, from the joy of motherhood to the pain of death. Charcoal sketches and sculptures by this Berlin artist (1867-1945) are housed in a beautiful four-storey villa on one of Berlin's most elegant streets. Guided tours on request.

Kunstgewerbe

Museum of Applied Art
Matthaikirchplatz, Tiergarten, 10875 (266 2902). U1 Kurfürstenstraße. **Open** 9am-5pm Tue-Fri; 10am-5pm Sat, Sun. **Admission** DM8; DM4 concs. **Map E4**

Opposite the Philharmonie, the Kunstgewerbe holds a collection of European arts and crafts from the Middle Ages to the present day. The top attractions are the ecclesiastical goldsmith works from the eleventh- to the fifteenth century.

Neue Nationalgalerie

Potsdamer Straße 50, Tiergarten, 10785 (266 2651). U1 Kurfürstenstraße. **Open** 9am-5pm Tue-Fri; 10am-5pm Sat, Sun. **Admission** DM4; DM2 concs. **Map E4**

Bauhaus Archiv-Museum – *modernism on display. See page 78.*

The modern building, designed in the 1960s by former Bauhaus president Ludwig Mies van der Rohe, houses German and international paintings from the twentieth century. It's strong on German expressionists and surrealists, like Max Beckmann, Otto Mueller, Ernst Ludwig Kirchner, Paul Klee and Max Ernst. The Neue Sachlichkeit is also well represented by George Grosz and Otto Dix. Many major non-German twentieth-century artists are also featured: Picasso, de Chirico, Léger, Munch, Wols, Dubuffet and Dali among them. However, the pleasure of the gallery really is in discovering lesser known artists like Ludwig Meidner, whose post-World War I apocalyptic landscapes exert the great, garish power of the most action-packed Marvel comic centrefold.

Note: Its nineteenth-century exhibits are now part of the Alte Nationalgalerie's collection; this has in turn been moved for the time being to the **Altes Museum** (*see above* **Art & architecture**).

Schinkel-Museum

Werderscher Markt (in the Friedrichwerdersche Kirche), Mitte, 10117 (208 1323). U6 Französische Straße. **Open** 9am-5pm Tue-Sun. **Admission** DM4; DM2 concs. **Map F3**

The brick church was designed by Karl Friedrich Schinkel and completed in 1830. Its war wounds were repaired in the 1980s and it reopened in 1987 as an homage to the architect that gave it life. Statues by Schinkel, Schadow and others stand inside, rubbing shoulders with the visitors in the soft light from the stained glass windows. Photographs and histories of those of his architectural masterworks that didn't survive the war (such as the Prinz-Albert-Schloß) are also on display.

Schloß Charlottenburg

Luisenplatz and Spandauer Damm, Charlottenburg, 14059 (320 911). U2 Sophie-Charlotte-Platz/U7 Richard-Wagner-Platz. **Open** *Apr-Oct* 9am-5pm Tue-Fri, 10am-5pm Sat, Sun; *Nov-Mar* closed. **Admission** *combination ticket for all palace buildings* DM15, DM8 concs. *single admissions* Historic rooms DM4; Knobelsdorff Flügel DM3, DM1,50 concs; Neringbau, Schinkel or Belvedere DM2,50, DM1,50 concs; Mausoleum DM1; pfg50 concs. Galerie der Romantik DM4, DM2 concs. Free Sun, holidays. **Map B3**

Queen Sophie-Charlotte was the impetus behind this sprawling palace and garden. Sophie's husband built it in 1695 as a modest summer home for the 'philosophical Queen'. Later kings also summered here, tinkering with and adding to the buildings. Unless you have a whole day to spend, it's best to tackle only a part of the Schloß. The central and oldest section houses the bedrooms of its original residents, Sophie-Charlotte and her husband. The apartments can only be seen during guided tours in German; English group tours have to be arranged several weeks in advance.

Highlights of the newer west wing are the living quarters of Frederick the Great, including his collection of eighteenth century paintings. The Romantic Gallery downstairs includes the beautifully bleak work of Caspar David Friedrich, alongside the paintings of Schinkel and a number of lesser German romantics. The Schinkel Pavilion, named for the architect who designed it, used to be a small summer house. Built in 1825, it contains sculpture, drawings, furniture, porcelain and more paintings by the indefatigable Karl Friedrich Schinkel.

The Belvedere, a former tea house, contains three storeys of choice porcelain from the eighteenth and nineteenth centuries, including some fine pieces by KPM Berlin, once porcelain-makers to the Kaiser. Carl Gotthard Langhans, architect of the Brandenburg Gate, designed the Belvedere in 1788. The Mausoleum contains the tombs of Queen Louise, King Friedrich Wilhelm III, Kaiser Wilhelm I and Kaiserin Augusta.

*The **Brücke-Museum** – small, satisfying and full of colourful work. See page 79.*

Botany

Botanisches Museum

Botanical Museum
*Königin-Luise-Straße 6-8, Zehlendorf, 14191 (830 060).
U1 Dahlem-Dorf/S1 Botanischer Garten.* **Open** Oct-Feb
9am-5pm Tue-Sun; *March, Sept* 9am-6pm Tue-Sun; *April,
Aug* 9am-7pm Tue-Sun; *May, July* 9am-8pm Tue-Sat; *June*
9am-9pm Tue-Sat. **Admission** (to gardens and museum)
DM6; DM3 concs.
Within the Free University's Botanical Gardens (*see chapter*
Sightseeing), this museum is meant to show behind the
scenes of the plant kingdom. There are fossils and dioramas
showing plantlife through the ages, examples of mushrooms,
sponges, leaves, seeds and woods in vitrines, as well as the
different types and uses of things like rice, tobacco, hemp,
and cotton. There is no information in English, and the museum looks like it was finished around the time the Wall went
up and never redecorated since, but it's free with a ticket for
the gardens, and the cross-section of the California Redwood,
as well as the herbs stolen from ancient Egyptian and Roman
graves, are both worth seeing.

Cabaret & circuses

Märkisches Museum

*Am Köllnischen Park 5, Mitte, 10179 (308 660). U2
Märkisches Museum.* **Open** 10am-6pm Tue-Sun.
Admission DM3; DM1 concs. **Map G4**
Circus and variety show paraphernalia are displayed at the
Märkisches Museum: old clown costumes, posters and brief
histories of circuses and performers. In the back, and perhaps the most interesting exhibit, is a selection of programmes and newspaper articles from the scandalous
variety shows and cabaret acts that made Berlin notorious
in the 1920s. The highlight of the museum is the stuffed body
of a famous circus lion that gave up the ghost in 1987. The
rest of the museum is a bit stuffy and static, but diehard cir-
cus-lovers shouldn't be disappointed.

Commodities

Hanf Museum

Hemp Museum
*Mühlendamm 5, Mitte, 10178 (242 4827). U2
Klosterstraße/Alexanderplatz.* **Open** 10am-8pm Tue-Fri;
noon-8pm Sat, Sun. **Admission** DM5. **Map G3**
The world's largest hemp museum, with the aim of teaching the visitor about the uses of hemp throughout history,
as well as touching on the controversy surrounding the
herb today. There are a few booklets to leaf through in
English, as well as books in their shop including *Growing
Marijuana in Cool Climates* and *Industrial Hemp* about
hemp-based products. The exhibit starts with the history
of hemp-growing and interesting displays of the plant's
many traditional uses in textiles and industry – from ropes
and sails to wigs and beauty cream. There is then a section
on its medicinal properties, including a 1900 advert tout-
ing hashish as 'the ideal cure for callouses and warts'.
Another section is devoted to hemp's cultural meaning,
including a display of hookahs and pipes and explanations
of the plant's uses around the world. (In Vietnam it's used
as a spice, while the Turks have used it as a drug since
ancient times.) Finally, there is a section on the current controversy surrounding the legalisation of hemp. The café
(which doubles as a video-viewing and reading-room) has
cakes made both with and without hemp. Everything,
though, is guaranteed THC-free.

Zucker Museum

Sugar Museum
*Amrumer Straße 32, Wedding, 13353 (3142 7574). U9
Amrumer Straße.* **Open** 9am-5pm Mon-Wed; 11am-6pm
Sun. **Admission** DM4,50; DM2 concs. **Map D1**
Any museum devoted to the chemistry, history and political
importance of sugar would have problems thrilling the pun-
ters. But the Zucker does have a very unusual collection of
sugar paraphernalia. Most interesting is a slide show on the
slave trade, on which the sugar industry was so dependent.
Something to ponder on over a coffee.

Ethnology

Museum für Völkerkunde

Ethnological Museum
*Lansstraße 8, Zehlendorf, 14195 (830 1438). U1
Dahlem-Dorf.* **Open** 9am-5pm Tue-Fri; 10am-5pm Sat,
Sun. **Admission** DM4; DM2 concs.

The Ethnological Museum is much too big to be covered in
one visit. Eight regional departments cover two floors:
Oceanian, American, African, East Asian, South Asian, West
Asian and European, as well as Music Ethnology. There is
also an educational department which includes a junior
museum and museum for the blind. No need to bother with
all the collection, though, as some sections are pretty tedious
(the early American exhibits, for instance, can easily be
bypassed). But the South Sea (Südsee) collection should not
be missed, nor should the beaded artefacts from Cameroon:
the beaded throne is quite amazing (although it looks less
than comfy). The displays themselves are a joy – no doubt
the curators had a lot of fun putting them together. The most
interesting collection contains New Guinean masks and effi-
gies suspended from the ceiling in well-lit cabinets; a large
assortment of boats and canoes; a number of curious façades;
even a fully intact men's clubhouse. The figure of a woman,
suspended over the doorway with her legs wide open, just
goes to show that boys have always been boys.

Museum für Europäische Volkskunde

Museum of European Ethnology
*Im Winkel 6-8, Zehlendorf, 14195 (839 0101). U1
Dahlem-Dorf.* **Open** 9am-5pm Tue-Fri; 10am-5pm Sat,
Sun. **Admission** DM4; DM2 concs.

Traditional clothes, jewellery, furniture, cooking utensils and
toys of the people of Europe, from the Rhine to Silesia, are
collected at the Volkskunde. Exhibits are artfully arranged
and informative. Particularly worth seeing is the traditional clothing, much of which was still worn regularly up to the
first half of this century. The displays of weaving and spinning machines are also admirable. The museum is near but
not a part of the immense Dahlem complex (of which the
Museum für Völkerkunde is currently the only open component), but down the street and around the corner – just follow the sign at the U-Bahn station.

History

See also **Schloß Charlottenburg** *under* **Arts &
Architecture**.

Allied Museum

*Outpost, Clayallee 135, Zehlendorf, 14195 (818 1990).
U1 Oskar-Helene-Heim.* **Open** 10am-6pm Tue-Sun; 10am-
8pm Wed. **Admission** free

The Allied forces arrived as conquerors, kept West Berlin
alive during the 1948 Luftbrücke ('Airlift'), and left many
Berliners with tears in their eyes when they finally went
home again in 1994. Housed in what used to be a cinema for
US Forces personnel (shows used to begin with a cinematic
montage of American military might, while the audience
stood for the Stars and Stripes), the exhibition is mostly
about the period of the Blockade and Luftbrücke, documented with photos and such, but also tanks, weapons,
weapons, uniforms, cookbooks and music of the period.
Outside you can find the building that was once the stop-
and-search centrepiece of Checkpoint Charlie.

Anti-Kriegsmuseum

Anti-War Museum
*Brüsseler Straße 21, Wedding, 13353 (4549 0110). U9
Amrumer Straße.* **Open** 4pm-8pm daily. **Admission**
free. **Map D1**

All human life is there – the **Käthe-Kollwitz-Museum**. *See page 81.*

The original was founded in 1925 by Ernst Friedrich, author of the book *War Against War*. It was destroyed in 1933 by Nazi storm troopers, and Friedrich fled to Brussels. There he had another museum from 1936-1940, at which point German troops once again showed up and trashed the place. In 1982 a group of teachers including Tommy Spree, grandson of Friedrich, reestablished the museum in West Berlin. It now hosts changing exhibitions (for example on the work of Gandhi, or prosecution of Kurds in Turkey), as well as a permanent display including some grim World War I photos and artifacts from the original museum, children's war toys, information on German colonialism in Africa, pieces of anti-Semitic material from the Nazi-era, and World War II memorabilia including a medal of honour awarded to German mothers who bore lots of children, and a 1940s air-raid shelter in the cellar. In addition, there is a 15-minute video in German on Friedrich and his work. Information on the museum and copies of *War Against War* are available in English, but the exhibitions themselves are only in German. Call ahead to arrange a tour in English with director Tommy Spree, who is British.

Museum Berliner Arbeiterleben

Museum of Berlin Working-Class Life
Husemannstraße 14, Prenzlauer Berg, 10435 (442 2514). U2 Eberswalder Straße. **Open** 10am-3pm Mon-Thur. **Admission** free, donations welcomed.
Map G2
A reconstruction of a Berlin worker's flat, as it would have been at the turn of the century. It's an interesting way to tell the story of everyday life in Berlin, with all kinds of articles on display, ranging from a stove-heated curling iron to a weirdly shaped baby carriage. The front room is set aside for changing exhibitions.

Deutsches Historisches Museum

Unter den Linden 2, Mitte, 10117 (203 040). S3, S5, S6, S9/U6 Friedrichstraße. **Open** 10am-6pm Mon, Tue, Thur-Sun. **Admission** free. **Map F3**
The Zeughaus, where this is housed, was built as an arsenal in 1706 and is one of Berlin's most beautiful baroque buildings. During the latter half of the nineteenth century, it served as an army museum, and until the end of World War II possessed the largest historical collection of weapons in Europe. During the GDR era, the museum made German history serve the needs of its incumbent rulers. Once the Wall came down, a sign went up on the door promising 'everything must be revised and seen in a new light', and a new curator was brought in from west Germany on the promise of staging themed historical exhibitions, such as The Art Of Memory about holocaust memorials, 'to make people think'. The GDR has not been forgotten, though. There's also a fine collection of the bizarre official souvenirs representatives of socialist organisations used to present to each other – stuff like commemorative Sputnik plates and workers-of-the-world-unite paperweights.

Deutsch-Russisches Museum Berlin-Karlshorst

German-Russian Museum
Zwieseler Straße 4, corner of Rheinsteinstraße, Karlshorst, 10318 (509 8609/508 8329). S3 Karlshorst. **Open** 10am-6pm Tue-Sun. **Admission** free.
Built between 1936-38, this place was used until 1945 as a German Officers' Club. After the Soviets took Berlin, it was commandeered as a headquarters for the military administration and it was here, during the night of 8-9 May 1945, that German commanders signed the final and unconditional surrender of the Nazi army, thus ending the war in Europe. It was also here, five years later, that Soviet General Chuikov authorised the first Communist government in the GDR. The building now houses a museum which looks at the German-Soviet relationship over the

past 80 years. Divided into 16 small rooms including the Allied flag-adorned conference room in which the Nazis surrendered, it takes us through two world wars, one cold one; assorted pacts, victories and capitulations; and varying degrees of hatred and camaraderie. The permanent exhibit includes lots of photos, memorabilia, documents, campaign maps, video footage and propaganda posters. Buy a guide in English for DM4, the exhibits are explained in German and Russian. Interesting enough to warrant a couple of hours.

Museum Haus am Checkpoint Charlie

Friedrichstraße 44, Kreuzberg, 10969 (253 7250). U6 Kochstraße. **Open** 9am-10pm daily. **Admission** DM8; DM5 concs; DM4,5 for groups of ten or more.
Map F3
An essential trip for anyone interested in the Wall and the Cold War. The museum opened not long after the GDR government constructed the Berlin Wall in 1961 with the purpose of documenting those grisly events that were taking place. The exhibition charts the history of the Wall, and gives details of the ingenious and hair-raising ways people escaped from the GDR – as well as exhibiting some of the contraptions that were used, such as suitcases and a weird car with a propeller. There's also a display about non-violent revolutions – including information about Mahatma Gandhi, Lech Walesa and, of course, the peaceful 1989 upheaval in East Germany.

Gedenkstätte Haus der Wannsee-Konferenz

Am Grossen Wannsee 56-58, Zehlendorf, 14109 (805 0010). S1, S3, S7 Wannsee, then bus 114. **Open** 10am-6pm Mon-Fri; 2pm-6pm Sat, Sun. **Admission** free.
On January 20 1942, a grim collection of prominent Nazis – Heydrich and Eichmann among them – gathered here on the Wannsee to draw up plans for the Final Solution, making jokes and sipping brandy as they sorted out the practicalities of genocide. Today, this infamous villa has been converted into a place of remembrance, with a standing photo exhibition about the conference and its consequences. Call in advance if you want to join an English-language tour, otherwise all information is in German.

Hugenotten Museum

Gendarmenmarkt, Mitte, 10117 (229 1760). U6 Französische Straße. **Open** noon-5pm Tue-Sat; 11am-5pm Sun. **Admission** DM3; DM2 concs. **Map F3**
An exhibition on the history of the French Protestants in France and Berlin-Brandenburg is displayed in the Französischen Dom, the congregation's main church. The museum chronicles the religious persecution Calvinists suffered (note the bust of Calvin on the outside of the church) and their subsequent immigration to Berlin after 1685, at the invitation of the Hohenzollerns. The development of the Huguenot community is also detailed with paintings, documents and artefacts. One part of the museum is devoted to the history of the church, in particular the effects of World War II. The church was bombed during a Sunday service in 1944 and remained a ruin until the mid-1980s. Other exports from France can be found in the wine restaurant upstairs.

Luftwaffe Museum

Air Force Museum
Entrance on Ritterfelddamm, Gatow, 14089 (3687 2601). U7 Rathaus Spandau, then bus 135 to Gutsstraße. **Open** 10am-5pm (last admittance 4pm) Tue-Sun. **Admission** free.
On the western fringes of the city at one of the airbases integral in the Berlin Airlift (and a 25-minute walk from the nearest bus stop!), this is a 'museum in progress'. An old hangar houses much of the exhibit, which includes information on the history of the Luftwaffe as well as pieces of an entire

Museum für Europäische Volkskunde.

fighter and surveillance planes from the beginning of the century through to 1970s NATO equipment. There's a World War I tri-plane, a restored Handley Page Hastings (as used in the Airlift) and an Antonov An-2 from the East German air force. Outside are more recent aircraft, including modern fighter planes and helicopters. Plans for providing English brochures by summer 1998.

Ministerium für Staatssicherheit Forschungs- und Gedenkstätte Normannenstraße

Stasi Museum
Ruschestraße 59, Lichtenberg, 10365 (553 6854/fax 553 68 53). U5 Magdalenenstraße. **Open** 11am-6pm Tue-Fri; 2pm-6pm Sat, Sun. **Admission** DM5; DM3 concs.
These days one almost needs evidence that communism ever happened. This museum, housed in part of what used to be the gruesome headquarters of the Ministerium für Staatssicherheit (the *Stasi* – East German equivalent of the KGB), offers some proof. You can look round the old offices of secret police chief Erich Mielke and view displays of bugging devices and spy cameras concealed in books, plant pots and Trabant car doors. There's also a lot of communist kitsch: tasteless furniture, tacky medals, banners and busts of Marx and Lenin.

Nikolaikirche

Nikolaikirchplatz, Mitte, 10178 (240 020). U2 Klosterstraße. **Open** 10am-5.30pm Tue-Sun. **Admission** DM3; DM1 concs. **Map G3**
Inside Berlin's oldest congregational church, from which the Nikolai Quarter takes its name, is an interesting historical collection chronicling Berlin's development from its founding (c1230) until 1648. Old tiles, tapestries, stone and wood carvings – even old weapons and punishment devices – are on display. Part of the collection includes photographs of the

extensive wartime damage, plus examples of how the stones melted together in the fiery heat of bombardment. Reconstruction of the church was completed in 1987, in time to celebrate Berlin's 750th anniversary.

Postmuseum Berlin

An der Urania 15, Schöneberg,10787 (7501 6891). U1, U2 Wittenbergplatz/U4 Nollendorfplatz. **Open** 9am-5pm Mon-Thur; 10am-4.30pm Sat, Sun. **Admission** free. **Map D4**
A potentially boring subject is presented in a captivating manner at the Postmuseum. Using several short videos, exhibits and displays for kids to push, pull and turn, the museum traces the Prussian/German postal system from the late nineteenth century to the present day. The videos of Berlin's city life over the past century make for fascinating viewing and provide an insightful glimpse into the city's pre-war history.

Topographie des Terrors

Stresemannstraße 110, Kreuzberg, 10963 (2548 6703). S1, S2 Anhalter Bahnhof. **Open** 10am-6pm Tue-Sun. **Admission** free. **Map F4**
The Topography of Terror is a piece of waste ground where once stood the Prinz Albrecht Palais, headquarters of the Gestapo. It was from here that the Holocaust was directed, and where the Germanisation of the east was dreamt up. You can walk around – small markers explain what was where – before examining the fascinating exhibit documenting the history of Nazi state terror. This is housed in some former basement cells of the Gestapo complex. The catalogue (DM10 and available in English) is excellent. A surviving segment of the Berlin Wall runs along the northern boundary of the site and, at the time of going to press, a library and document centre was being added.

Gay

Gründerzeit Museum

Hultschiner Damm 133, Hellersdorf, 12623 (567 8329). S5 Mahlsdorf, turn right and walk 500m through village and across main road, museum is in an old farmhouse on right. **Open** 10am-6pm Wed, Sun (guided tours only). **Admission** DM4.
A famous private museum, founded and still managed by Charlotte von Mahlsdorf, half-Jewish survivor of the Third Reich and the late GDR's most notorious transvestite. The Gründerzeit is housed in an old farmhouse and each room is decorated in the 1870-1910 style. In the basement is a recreation of a gay bar.

Schwules Museum

Gay Museum
Mehringdamm 61, Kreuzberg, 10961 (693 1172). U6, U7 Mehringdamm. **Open** 2pm-6pm Wed-Sun; tours 5pm Sat. **Admission** DM7; DM4 concs. **Map F5**
This museum, opened in 1985, is the first and still the only one in the world dedicated to the research and public exhibition of homosexual life in all of its forms. The museum, its library and archives are staffed by volunteers and function thanks to private donations, including bequests (such as the archive of GDR sex scientist Rudolf Klimmer). On the ground floor is the actual museum, which (in rather limited space) houses temporary exhibitions that include photography, video, installations, sketches, sculpture, and so forth. More impressive are the library and archives on the third floor. Here can be found 5,000 books, 3,000 international periodicals, as well as collections of photos, posters, TV, film and audio footage, all available to be borrowed. Information about the whole place is available in English and a host of other languages; catalogues of previous exhibitions are also available. *See also chapter* **Gay & Lesbian Berlin**.

A masquerade of perversions

In 1919, pioneering sex researcher Dr Magnus Hirschfeld established an Institut für Sexualwissenschaft near where the **Haus der Kulturen der Welt** (*see chapters* **Sightseeing** *and* **Music: Rock, Folk & Jazz**) now stands. Christopher Isherwood lived next door, and in *Christopher and his Kind* later recalled the contents of Hirschfeld's museum:

'Here were whips and chains and torture instruments designed for the practitioners of pleasure-pain; high-heeled, intricately decorated boots for the fetishists; lacy female undies which had been worn by ferociously masculine Prussian officers beneath their uniforms. Here were the lower halves of trouser-legs with elastic bands to hold them in position between knee and ankle. In these and nothing else but an overcoat and a pair of shoes, you could walk the streets and seem fully clothed, giving a camera-quick exposure whenever a suitable viewer appeared.'

An exhibit about Hirschfeld is one of the delights promised by the **Beate Uhse Erotik-Museum**, whose red neon sign gleams out over the corner of Kantstraße and Joachimsthaler Straße, advertising a collection that crowns the flagship retail outlet of Germany's biggest sexshop chain.

'One metropolis sets before us a world of openness!' gushes the museum's blurb. 'At a time when all borders have been overcome, your imagination need not be limited by bounderies! [sic] You are invited to a journey through a fascinating world.'

Decorated in rich colours, with new age music playing and mutedly phallic pillars dotted about, the three floors of this 'fascinating world' contain rather too many oriental prints, a selection of rather stupid showroom dummy tableaux, and glass cases containing early Japanese dildos, Andean penis flutes, Javanese erotic dagger hilts, seventeenth-century chastity belts, a giant coconut that looks like an arse and a vase used in the film *Caligula*.

The Hirschfeld exhibit is but a few boards of dry documentary material, worthily considering the history of his Institute, which was eventually closed by the Nazis. Not a pair of Prussian officer's lacy undies nor a flasher's trouser-bottom kit in sight. And of all the people who mill around the Erotik-Museum (a much dodgier crowd than one might find in, say, the Pergamon) few seem to bother checking out this small corner.

This is also the only section that has very much to do with Berlin, apart from an inadequate item about satirist Heinrich Zille and a corner documenting Frau Uhse herself – which went from Luftwaffe piloting and postwar potato-picking to annual sex-aid sales of over DM100 million, taking in the time when east German hands reached out eagerly for the 600,000 catalogues the company distributed there after the fall of the Wall.

This seems strange for a city with such a 'decadent' reputation. But then the museum is only one component of a Beate Uhse complex that also includes a sex shop, video booths and

Natural History

Museum für Naturkunde
Museum of Natural History
Invalidenstraße 43, Mitte, 10115 (209 38591). U6 Zinnowitzer Straße. **Open** 9.30am-5pm Tue-Sun. **Admission** DM5; DM2,50 concs. **Map E3**
Berlin's Museum of Natural History is one of the world's largest and best organised. It's also one of the oldest: the kernel of the collection dates from 1716. A 12-metre tall skeleton of a brachiosaurus greets you in the first room, which is full of dinosaurs, each thought to be around 150 million years old. Take a look at the archaeopteryx, perhaps the most perfectly preserved that has yet been unearthed. Even the feathers can be seen clearly. Another room has an enormous collection of fossils, from trilobites to lobsters. Other highlights include the skeleton of a giant armadillo and the vast insect collection (not for the squeamish). The animal collection, assembled in the 1920s, almost makes you feel like you're at the zoo – except that these critters are stuffed. And the immense mineral collection is a wonder: row upon row of rocks, set up exactly as

they were when the building first opened in 1889. Don't miss the meteor chunks in the back of the room. The museum, part of the Humboldt University, has over 60 million exhibits in its collection.

Music

Musikinstrumenten Museum
Tiergartenstraße 1, Tiergarten, 10785 (254 810). Bus 129, 148, 248, 341. **Open** 9am-5pm Tue-Fri; 10am-5pm Sat, Sun. **Admission** DM4; DM2 concs; free under-12s; free Sun. **Map E4**
Over 2,200 string, keyboard, wind and percussion instruments dating back to the 1500s are crammed into this small museum next to the Philharmonie. Among them is an assortment of rococo musical clocks, for which eighteenth century princes commissioned jingles from Mozart, Hadyn and Beethoven. The place comes alive during tours, when guides play such obsolete instruments as the Kammerflugel (Bach played one in the court of Friedrich The Great). Concerts are held on the first Saturday of the month.

all the rest. Just marketing, then? Well, here's Isherwood again, looking back at the myth of 1920s Berlin:

'Wasn't Berlin's famous "decadence" largely a commercial "line" which the Berliners had instinctively developed in their competition with Paris? Paris had long since cornered the straight girl-market, so what was left for Berlin to offer its visitors but a masquerade of perversions?'

In other words, it was always just marketing. But given this history, the weirdest thing about Uhse's modern 'masquerade of perversions' is its utterly heterosexual, high-street respectability.

Beate Uhse Erotik-Museum
Joachimsthaler Straße 4, Charlottenburg, 10623 (886 0666). S3, S5, S6, S7, S9/U9 Zoologischer Garten. **Open** 9am-midnight daily. **Admission** DM10; DM8 concs. **Map C4**

Theatre

Brecht-Haus
Chausseestraße 125, Mitte, 10115 (282 9916). U6 Zinnowitzer Straße/Oranienburger Tor. **Open** 5pm-7pm Tue-Fri, every half hour; 5pm-6.30pm Thur, every half hour; 9.30am-noon Sat, every half hour. **Admission** DM4; DM2 concs. **Map F2**
Brecht's home, from 1948 until his death in 1953, has been preserved exactly as he left it. Tours of the house last about half an hour and give interesting insights into the life and reading habits of the playwright. The window at which he worked overlooked the grave of Hegel in the Dorotheenstädtische und Friedrichswerdersche Friedhof, which is where Brecht, too, is buried (*see chapter* **Sightseeing**). His wife, the actress Helene Weigel, continued living here until she died in 1971. The Brecht archives are kept upstairs. Phone in advance for tours in English. The Kellerrestaurant near the exit serves 'select wines and fine beers and Viennese cooking in the style of Helene Weigel', in case you want to extend your Brecht-Weigel experience. *See chapter* **Restaurants**.

Transport

Museum für Verkehr und Technik
Museum of Transport and Technology
Trebbiner Straße 9, Kreuzberg, 10963 (254 840). U1, U7 Möckernbrücke. **Open** 9am-5.30pm Tue-Fri; 10am-6pm Sat, Sun. **Admission** DM5; DM2 concs; DM1 groups of ten or more. **Map E5**
Opened in 1983 in the former goods depot of the once thriving Anhalter Bahnhof, the Museum für Verkehr und Technik is a quirky collection of industrial objects. The rail exhibits have pride of place, with these station sheds providing an ideal setting for locomotives and rolling stock from 1835 up to the present day. On view are also exhibitions on the industrial revolution; street, rail, water and air traffic; computer technology and printing technology. Oddities, such as vacuum cleaners from the 1920s and a large collection of sextants, make this a fun spot for implement enthusiasts. Behind the main complex is an open-air section with two functioning windmills and a smithy. The Spectrum annex, in an old railway administrative building, houses 200 interactive devices and experiments. *See also chapter* **Children**.

Art Galleries

The limelight has shifted east to shine on a fresh and fertile art scene which provides thought-provoking extremes.

Among the war ruins, massive building sites and pastel concrete renovations, contemporary art in Berlin is currently enjoying renewed energy and international attention. Politicians, property developers, young commercial gallerists and a diverse assortment of artists are all contributing to a scene characterised by a variety of different and often conflicting visions. This fervent activity is uniquely set against Berlin's historical landscape of bombastic collections and monuments, and the work of dissident and counter-cultures.

Without having to cover much ground you can experience thought-provoking extremes. Erika and Rolf Hoffmann's private collection of international display-case art is, for example, just around the corner from conceptual galleries such as **Projektraum** and temporary spaces such as Asian Art Now. The costly re-development of **Hamburger Bahnhof** (*see chapter* **Museums**) is, meanwhile, not far from a number of ambient makeshift bars that are also in some sense art projects. Clubs and bars have been reinvigorated in Berlin in the 1990s as the hippest site for underground or alternative art actions. There artists might be broadcasting on the net, exhibiting sardonic urban video or collaborating with DJs.

Generally speaking (there are some important exceptions) work by historical figures of German art is still found in the older galleries in and around Charlottenburg, but gallery-goers who've been to Berlin before – even as recently as a couple of years ago – won't recognise the rest of the scene. Mitte is now where international contemporary and cutting-edge work is found, and galleries spring up in the east like weeds once did. Mitte and neighbouring Prenzlauer Berg are also home to most alternative and temporary exhibitions. In the last year or so many galleries have moved from Kreuzberg, Charlottenburg and even from Cologne to Mitte. The limelight has shifted east.

An easy way to orient yourself in the Mitte scene is to attend a Rundgang ('walk around'). On a Rundgang evening the Mitte galleries all open at the same time, allowing visitors to stroll from one to another. There are mutterings that these won't continue because the mood on the Auguststraße 'art mile' is turning less social and more aggressively commercial – some new gallerists don't want their showrooms damaged by the non-

purchasing public that the Rundgang attracts – but it seems that for now they will, but quarterly rather than monthly. You will need to check listings (*see below*) for dates.

In the lead-up to 2000 a few of Berlin's venues are undergoing major renovations and will be closed – most notably the Martin-Gropius-Bau which normally hosts major international travelling exhibitions and which until 1997 was also the home of the Berlinische Galerie's collection of Berlin art since 1870. There is talk of that collection moving into the Postfuhramt on the corner of Oranienburger Straße and Tucholskystraße in Mitte, but for the time being some of it can be viewed at Willy-Brandt-Haus (Stresemannstraße 28, Kreuzberg, 10963). Tacheles, meanwhile, the alternative art centre in a squatted former shopping arcade and long the principal landmark of the Mitte scene, has lost its battle against property developers and the city government.

There are two new major events on the Berlin art calendar: Art Forum Berlin, an international art fair, and the Berlin Biennale. The former, established in 1996, takes place late October at the Messehallen unter dem Funkturm (for details contact European Galleries, Projektgesellschaft GmbH, 8855 1643). It is impressive, as art fairs go, and attracts galleries and attention worldwide. The first Be rlin Biennale, intended to be a large-scale international exhibition, is scheduled for October 1998 (for details, contact the Berlin Biennale office on 2859 9148).

Listings & information

Most galleries provide free copies of the *Mitte Gallery Guide* and/or *Berliner Galerien* (which covers all Berlin). Both have maps; neither list all galleries. Check out also current written material at the galleries, as invitations to forthcoming exhibitions and events are often there for the taking.

The *Berliner Kunstkalender* (DM3), published monthly and available at galleries and museums, is almost too comprehensive, listing everything from postcard shops up. Unless you know who or what to look for it can waste your time. The *Kunstkalender* in the fortnightly listing magazine, *Zitty*, has a more selective version of the same information – useful because temporary galleries, exhibitions and performances are often listed

Arndt & Partner – *conceptualism thrives in the Hackesche Höfe. See page 93.*

nowhere else. Most people in the galleries are receptive to visitors and do speak English if you have questions.

Public galleries & collections

See also chapter Museums *for* Bauhaus Archiv-Museum für Gestaltung, Bröhan Museum, Brücke Museum, Gemäldegalerie, Georg-Kolbe-Museum, Hamburger Bahnhof, Käthe-Kollwitz-Museum, Kunstgewerbe, *and* Neue Nationalgalerie.

Akademie der Künste
Hanseatenweg 10, Tiergarten, 10557 (390 760). U9 Hansaplatz/S3, S5, S6, S7, S9 Bellevue. **Open** 10am-7pm daily. **Admission** DM6 adults; DM4 concessions. **Map D3**
Founded by the Prussian Prince Friedrich III in 1696, the Akademie der Künste is one of the oldest cultural institutions in Berlin. By 1938, however, the Nazis had forced virtually all of its prominent members into exile. Re-established in 1954 to serve as 'a community of exceptional artists' from the world over, its multi-faceted programme now offers a great variety of events ranging from free jazz concerts and poetry readings to performances and film screenings. The Akademie also has a reputation for landmark exhibitions such as the Hundert Jahre Schwule Bewegung ('One hundred years of the gay movement') in 1997.
Café. Group discounts. Wheelchair access.

DAAD Galerie
Kurfürstenstraße 58, Tiergarten, 10785 (261 3640). U2, U4, U15 Nollendorfplatz/U1, U2, U3 Wittenbergplatz. **Open** 12.30pm-7pm daily. **Admission** free. **Map D4**
Above the original Café Einstein, the gallery for the German Academic Exchange Service (DAAD) that initiated an 'Artists-in-Residence' programme in West Berlin in 1965. The list of DAAD-sponsored artists reads like a 'Who's Who' of the international art world. John Armleder, Daniel Buren, Edward Kienholz, Mario Merz and Nam June Paik have all partaken. More recent recipients of this prestigious grant include Andrea Zittel, Steven Pippin and Johan Grimonprez. At the time of going to press, DAAD were looking for an exhibition space in Mitte.

Haus am Lützowplatz
Lützowplatz 9, Tiergarten, 10785 (261 3805). U2, U4, U15 Nollendorfplatz. **Open** 11am-6pm Tue-Sun. **Admission** free. **Map D4**
One of the first non-commercial, private galleries to re-open in West Berlin after World War II, the Haus am Lützowplatz shows mostly figurative work of Berlin neo-realists and paintings, sculpture and photography from Hungary, Bulgaria, Russia and Poland.
Wheelchair access from parking lot in the back of the house.

Haus am Waldsee
Argentinische Allee 30, Zehlendorf, 14163 (8091 2234). U1 Krumme Lanke. **Open** 10am-6pm Tue-Sun. **Admission** DM6 adults; DM4 concessions.
The Haus am Waldsee was founded in 1946 by the local arts council, in a villa in the wealthy suburb of Zehlendorf. During the first two decades after World War II the Haus mounted a series of pioneering exhibitions which presented the work of artists who had been banned by the Nazis and, as a result, were almost unknown in Germany at the time: Käthe Kollwitz (in 1946), Hermann Blumenthal (in 1947), Karl Schmidt-Rottluff (in 1948) and Max Ernst (in 1951). But even as late as 1980, with its show Heftige Malerei (violent painting), the gallery broke new ground for those neo-Expressionist Junge Wilde painters who – just three years later – were to be the main attraction of the international Zeitgeist show at the Martin-Gropius-Bau. But that's history. These days you should check what's on before making the trip to the 'burbs.
Group discounts.

Haus der Kulturen der Welt

Kongreßhalle, John-Foster-Dulles-Allee 10, Tiergarten, 10557 (397 870). 100, 248 bus. **Open** usually 11am-7pm Tue-Sun. **Admission** DM4-DM8 adults; DM2-DM4 concs. **Map E3**

A unique institution and an important part of Berlin's cultural life. Funded by the Federal Government and the Berlin Senate, the 'House of World Cultures' was set up in January 1989 to promote artists from so-called Third World countries, mounting spectacular large-scale exhibitions such as contemporary Indian art, Bedouin culture in North Africa and the avant-garde in China. The programme also features film festivals, readings, lectures, panel discussions, concerts and dance performances. Hugh A Stubbins' big oyster-like Kongreßhalle was erected in 1957/58 as America's contribution to Berlin's first international building exhibition. When the original structure collapsed in 1980, the building was rebuilt almost from the ground.

Restaurant. Bookshop. Wheelchair access. Toilets for the disabled.

Hochschule der Künste

Hardenbergstraße 33, Charlottenburg, 10623 (31850). U2, U9 Ernst-Reuter-Platz/S3, S5, S6, S7, S9 Zoo. **Open** 10am-7pm Mon-Sat. **Admission** free. **Map C4**

Enter the main lobby from Hardenbergstraße and you'll find a colourful diversity of student displays ranging from traditional painting to video installations and computer graphics. Most of the Junge Wilde painters are in some way connected with the HdK – either as teachers (Karl-Horst Hödicke, Georg Baselitz) or as former students (Salomé, Helmut Middendorf, Rainer Fetting). The school has once yearly open days and also hosts symposia and other events. *Wheelchair access.*

Künstlerhaus Bethanien

Mariannenplatz 2, Kreuzberg, 10997 (616 9030). U1, U15 Kottbusser Tor or Görlitzer Bahnhof. **Open** 2-7pm Tue-Sun. **Admission** free. **Map G4**

A Berlin institution and a good place to start an art tour of Berlin if you're staying in Kreuzberg. You can also pick up guides and flyers to art and other cultural events from the table just in the front door. Located in a huge nineteenth-century complex of former hospital buildings (the first ward system hospital in Berlin) it was originally squatted in the 1970s and back then hosted alternative art and theatre. These days it offers studio residencies to foreign artists; USA, France, Russia and Japan are often represented (Bruce McLean was one of numerous artists-in-residence to work here) and both Sweden and Australia have permanent studio programmes. There are three main galleries almost permanently running exhibitions by the resident artists (who often sit their own shows too), along with talks, screenings and symposia. Funding cut-backs increasingly threaten the place but Bethanien plans also to open a gallery in Mitte sometime in 1998. In the same building on the ground floor is the Kunstamt Kreuzberg – Kreuzberg's local government art office – which often mounts large thematic exhibitions of contemporary art.

Wheelchair access (ask the door guard for key to elevator).

NGBK

Neue Gesellschaft für bildende Kunst
Oranienstraße 25, Kreuzberg, 10999 (615 3031). U1, U8, U15 Kottbusser Tor. **Open** noon-6.30pm daily. **Admission** free. **Map G4**

An offshoot of the late 1960s student movement, the NGBK has for more than 20 years produced a highly diversified and ambitious programme featuring photography, ethnic art, Berlin art and documentary shows. Exhibitions are consistent and to a high standard. Enter via the ground floor bookshop or via the courtyard to the left of the bookshop.

Bookshop. Wheelchair access.

Deutsche Guggenheim Berlin

Unter den Linden 13-15, Mitte, 10017 (3407 4134). U6 Französische Straße. **Open** 11am-8pm. **Admission** DM8; DM5 students; free on Mondays). **Map F3**

In partnership with Deutsche Bank (and housed in one of their buildings) this is perhaps the least impressive European branch of the Guggenheim museums. The programme features scaled-down versions of Guggenheim travelling exhibitions – it opened in mid-1997 with an exhibition of works by Robert Delaunay.

Kunst-Werke

Auguststraße 69, Mitte, 10117 (281 7325). U6 Oranienburger Tor. **Open** 2pm-6pm Tue-Sun. **Admission** free. **Map F2**

A good starting point for a gallery walk in Mitte. Originally a pioneering but modest undertaking, Kunst-Werke is now the funding-fattened HQ of Klaus Biesenbach (also director of the first Berlin Biennale, scheduled for October 1998, and member of the 1997 Venice Biennale jury, among other things). Opening in the early 1990s, it quickly became the most high-profile venue in Berlin for young and emerging contemporary art. Recently renovated and with a new 'café pavilion' designed by Dan Graham, Kunst-Werke has multiple exhibition rooms and offers studio residencies to young international artists.

NBK

Neuer Berliner Kunstverein
Chausseestraße 128/129, Mitte, 10115 (280 7020/2). U6 Oranienburger Tor. **Open** noon-6pm Tue-Fri; noon-4pm Sat. **Admission** free. **Map F2**

In a new building that could just as easily have housed an insurance office, this is a well-funded *Verein* (society) that hosts mainly curated groups exhibitions by contemporary artists chosen from proposals submitted to a jury of the NBK's members. Choices and results are somewhat variable.

Sammlung Hoffman

Sophienstraße 21, Mitte, 10178 (2849 9121). U8 Weimeister Straße. **Open** 10am-6pm Tue-Fri; 11am-6pm Sat, Sun. Guided tours Sat only by appointment. **Admission** DM10. **No credit cards. Map F3**

This is Erika and Rolf Hoffmann's private collection of international contemporary art, including a charming floor installation work by Swiss video artist Pipilotti Rist and work by Douglas Gordon, Felix Gonzalez-Torres and AR Penck. They offer guided tours through their chic apartment every Saturday by appointment only – felt slippers supplied. For some, this kind of ritzy development signals the beginning of the end for of what was good about Mitte; for others it means the exact opposite. Both camps are exaggerating.

Sammlung Berggruen

Westlicher Stülerbau, Schloßstraße 1, Charlottenburg, 14059 (3269 5814). U2 Sophie-Charlotte-Platz. **Open** 10am-6pm Tue-Fri; 11am-6pm Sat, Sun. **Admission** DM8; DM4 concs. **Map B3**

A satisfying collection compiled by Berggruen, an early dealer of Picasso's in Paris, offering a superb overview of Picasso's oeuvre. Also on display are works of his contemporaries such as Braque, Klee and Giacometti. The collection is on loan to Berlin for at least ten years and is housed in relatively intimate rooms in a building opposite the Schloß Charlottenburg and the Egyptian Museum (*see chapter* **Museums**).

Commercial Galleries

Charlottenburg & the west

The Charlottenburg galleries are generally within walking distance of one another and are nestled

Still room for experiment

While commercial galleries colonise Mitte with expensively renovated spaces and imported artists, it is the area's low-budget and experimental spaces that continue to give Berlin its edge. These are what led the way for the development of the Scheunenviertel as the city's new visual arts quarter, and while the gentrification of the area inevitably means rocketing rents and an increasingly sanitised atmosphere, there is still some room for experiment.

Berlin has been a breeding ground for inter-disciplinary experiments where the 'white cube' gallery model gets put to one side in favour of projects – often in clubs and ambient rooms. Cheap mini-galleries in makeshift spaces, cafés, bookshops and bars – free from the conforming forces on commercial galleries – provide a context for the kind of mixed-discipline and post-conceptual work that has been so prevalent in the 1990s. Die Box, for example, is a private micro-gallery initiative of Katharina Neubert – started three years ago in an apartment near Nollendorfplatz. She exhibits young conceptually orientated locals and similar artists from London (phone 216 5741 for details).

On a larger scale OSMOS, in a ground floor garage-like space in Prenzlauer Berg, is the gallery of Christian Rattemeyer. He organised a programme based around inviting artists that hadn't previously been to Berlin to come and respond with a site-specific work. Particularly successful was a 1997 installation by Rita McBride, inspired by the coloured balconies of GDR housing blocks. The programme continues: phone 444 0215 for details of current activities.

Both galleries **Neu** and **Wohnmaschine** began with low overheads and evolved with their growing profiles into more commercial galleries. In some ways this is seen as a coming of age, others view this cynically and try themselves to remain aggressively alternative. Sniper, for example (in the courtyard of Rosenthaler Straße 39, Mitte), is a combination bar and video installation.

Organisers Heinrich Dubel and Safy Etiel also mount temporary bars, such as the one created for the 1997 Berlin Art Forum where patrons were given a 35mm film (plus voucher for free developing). The Dead Chickens group also runs a bar, which is next door to Sniper. Both have snooty door policies, though, and they probably won't let you in.

Asian Art Now!, Acud and Institut are other group arts projects in Mitte that have experimental programmes. Convex TV, a group experimenting with pirate radio broadcasts and the Net, often also mount temporary events – you'll need to contact them for further details (http://www.art-bag.net/convextv). If they're no longer around by the time you read this, you can be sure that other groups will have swiftly taken their places.

The commercialisation of Mitte continues apace, but as Werner Müller from Zwinger Galerie put it, 'Mitte is not SoHo yet.' For the time being there remains an interesting tension, as these alternative and anarchic projects rub shoulders with the glossy new upmarket concerns – each benefiting from the others' unflattering comparisons

---

between designer stores and restaurants. These days they rarely receive much attention from the press and at the Berlin Art Forum most are conspicuous by their absence. They do, however, remain reliable in their fields of interest, particularly for canvasses by German artists of the pre-1990s generation – something you'd rarely find in Mitte.

As elsewhere in Berlin, none of the following take credit cards.

Fine Art Rafael Vostell

Knesebeckstraße 30, Charlottenburg, 10623 (885 2280).
S5, S7, S9, S75 Savignyplatz. **Open** 11am-7pm Mon-Fri; 11am-6pm Sat, Sun. **Map C4**
An upmarket gallery representing established artists like Francis Bacon, Nam June Paik and Yoko Ono, along with younger Berlin types such as Axel Lischke, Dead Chickens and MK Kähne.

Galerie Barbara Weiss

Potsdamer Straße 93, Tiergarten, 10785 (262 4284).
U15 Kurfürstenstraße. **Open** noon-6pm Tue-Fri; 11am-2pm Sat. **Map E4**
A beautiful conceptual art-orientated gallery in a gracious old apartment down the road from the Neue Nationalgalerie. Gallerist Barbara Weiss represents, among others, Maria Eichorn, Roaul de Keyser, John Miller and Janet Cardiff.

Galerie Volker Diehl

Niebuhrstraße 2, Charlottenburg, 10629 (881 8280).
U15 Uhlandstraße/S3, S5, S6, S7, S9 Savignyplatz.
Open 2pm-6.30pm Tue-Fri; 11am-2pm Sat.
Map C4
Mainly contemporary German, Italian and American painters of the post-war generation are shown, but you may also find minimal sculpture by Donald Judd and work by younger locals. Volker Diehl, a prominent figure in the Berlin art world, helped to organise both the seminal Zeitgeist show in 1982 and the Berlin Art Forum in 1997.
Wheelchair access.

Galerie Anselm Dreher

*Pfalzburger Straße 80, Wilmersdorf, 10719 (883 5249).
U1 Hohenzollernplatz.* **Open** 2-6.30pm Tue-Fri; 11am-
2pm Sat. **Map C5**
Anselm Dreher's unique gallery has been around for more
than 30 years now, uncompromisingly promoting the concrete, minimal and conceptual tendencies in contemporary
art. He was the first in Berlin – and for quite some time the
only one – to show the work of Carl André, Joseph Kosuth,
Jochen Gerz and Ange Leccia.
Wheelchair access.

Galerie Franck + Schulte

*Mommsenstraße 56, Charlottenburg, 10629 (324 0044).
U7 Adenauerplatz/S3, S5, S6, S7, S9 Savignyplatz.*
Open 11am-6pm Mon-Fri; 11am-3pm Sat. **Map C4**
Eric Franck came from Geneva and Thomas Schulte all the
way from New York to challenge the Berlin market with
fresh ideas in April 1991. Now it's one of the main blue-chip,
upmarket galleries. The work of famous Americans dominates. Recent exhibitions have included work by artists such
as Chuck Close and Gordon Matta-Clark, but funky Swiss
video artist Pippilotti Rist has also exhibited here. The
gallery also represents Rebecca Horn, Sol Le Witt, Katharina
Sieverding, Tony Oursler and Robert Mapplethorpe.

Galerie Georg Nothelfer

*Uhlandstraße 184, Charlottenburg, 10623 (881 4405).
U15 Uhlandstraße.* **Open** 2pm-6.30pm Tue-Fri; 10am-
2pm Sat. **Map C4**
Nothelfer, a longtime doyen of the Berlin art world, concentrates on German Informel, Tachism and Lyrical Abstraction
as well as gestural, scriptural and narrative painting by
established European artists such as Pierre Alechinsky,
Arnulf Rainer, Antoni Tàpies and Cy Twombly.

Galerie Eva Poll

*Lützowplatz 7, Tiergarten, 10785 (261 7091). U2, U4,
U15 Nollendorfplatz.* **Open** 10am-1pm Mon; 11am-
6.30pm Tue-Fri; 11am-3pm Sat. **Map D4**
When Eva Poll established her gallery in 1968, it was with
the intention of supporting a local group of young 'critical'
realists who had emerged in the mid-1960s. She currently
represents Harald Duwe, G.L.Gabriel, Maxim Kantor, Ralf
Kerbach, Volker Stelzmann, Hans Schieb and Sabine
Grzimek. The Poll foundation has recently opened rooms at
Gipsstraße 3, Mitte (264 7080).
Wheelchair access.

Raab Galerie

*Potsdamer Straße 58, Tiergarten, 10785 (261 9217/18).
U15 Kurfürstenstraße/129, 148, 248, 348 bus.* **Open**
10am-6.30pm Mon-Fri; 10am-2pm Sat; 10am-4pm First
Sat of the Month. **Map E4**
Ingrid Raab's established gallery is known for representing
the expressive and figurative painting that Berlin used main-
ly to be identified with. Among the exhibited artists are
Markus Lupertz, Elvira Bach, Luciano Castelli, Adolph
Gottlieb, Rainer Fetting and Daniel Spoerri.
Wheelchair access.

Galerie Springer

*Fasanenstraße 13, Charlottenburg, 10623 (312 7063).
U2, U9/S3, S5, S6, S7, S9 Zoologischer Garten.* **Open**
10am-7pm Mon-Fri; 11am-2pm Sat. **Map C4**
Until the end of 1997 this was the gallery of Rudolf Springer,
one of the grand old men of Berlin's art world, who opened
his first gallery as early as 1948. Now his son runs the
gallery. Among the greats Springer has presented are

*Neo Rauch's 'Mitgift'. One of **EIGEN + Art**'s
painters, Rauch's work comes over like
communist pop art. See page 94.*

Alexander Calder, Joan Miró, André Masson, Max Ernst and
Henri Laurens. But he's also had a continuous passion for
German post-war artists (Wols, Ernst Wilhelm Nay, AR
Penck, Jörg Immendorf and Markus Lüpertz).

Mitte

The Scheunenviertel district of Mitte is the
undoubted heart of Berlin's contemporary art
scene, with the Auguststraße 'art mile' as its main
street. We've listed the principal galleries as of
early 1998, but spaces come and go and there are
many others in this neighbourhood – mostly within walking distance of one another along these old
and, for Berlin, uncharacteristically narrow streets.
Many of the galleries are less than a year old; many
of the gallerists are under 30. Temporary galleries
and alternative spaces are a feature of the scene.
See page 91 **Still room for experiment**.

Arndt & Partner

*Auguststraße 35, Mitte, 10119 (280 8123). U8
Rosenthalerstraße.* **Open** noon-6pm Tue-Sat. **Map F2**
Established in 1994 by Matthias Arndt to show international
contemporary art. Exhibited artists include Via
Lewandowsky, Peter Friedl (a conceptual artist responsible
for the 'KINO' sign at Documenta X) and young locals
Johannes Kahrs and Susan Turcot.

Galerie Berlin

*Friedrichstraße 231, Mitte, 10969 (251 4420). U6
Kochstrasse.* **Open** 11am-6pm Tue-Fri; 11am-2pm Sat.
Map F4
Formerly the international branch of the GDR's official art
trade and since November 1990 a thriving private venture.
The owners concentrate on expressive painting from east-
ern Germany including work by artists such as Bernhard
Heisig and Werner Liebmann. They also have works from
early twentieth-century German Expressionism and
Impressionism (Max Beckmann, Käthe Kollwitz, Max
Liebermann).
Wheelchair access.

Galerie Bodo Niemann

*Hackesche Höfe , Hof VI, Rosenthaler straße 40-41,
10178 (2839 1928). U8 Rosenthaler straße.* **Open** 1-7pm
Tue-Fri; noon-6pm Sat. **Map F2**
Known for its exhibitions of photography and figurative and
abstract art from the 1920s, mostly by German artists such
as Hannah Höch, Emil Orlik, Kurt Scheele or photographer
August Sander. At the end of 1997 the gallery moved here
from Charlottenburg and celebrated with a more contemporary exhibition of Sally Mann's controversial photographic
studies of her children.
Wheelchair access with assistance.

Contemporary Fine Arts

*Sophienstraße 21, Mitte, 10178 (283 6580). U8
Weimeister Straße.* **Open** 10am-6pm Mon-Sat. **Map F3**
One of the more upmarket galleries in Berlin, established by
Bruno Brunnet and Nicole Hackert. It's in the Sophien-Gips
Höfe – the same building as the Hoffman Sammlung (*see
above*). This is the place to see expensive British imports such
as Damien Hirst, Sara Lucas and Angus Fairhurst, and big
canvas boys such as Daniel Richter and Olav Christopher
Jenssen. Sigalit Landau, the Israeli artist who caused a stir
at both the Venice Biennale and Documenta X in 1997 with
her container installations, has also exhibited here.

Galerie EIGEN + ART

*Auguststraße 26, Mitte, 10117 (280 6605). S1, S2
Oranienburger Straße/U6 Oranienburger Tor.* **Open** 2-
7pm Tue-Fri; 11am-2pm Sat. **Map F2**
The success of the Auguststraße phenomenon can in a
large part be contributed to charismatic gallerist Gerd
Harry 'Judy' Lybke. Originally from Leipzig he ran an independent gallery there for many years and still does. Shortly
after the collapse of the Wall, he started his second venture in Auguststraße. Since then he's tirelessly promoted
artists from the former East Germany and emerging international artists. Tribute to his effectiveness was the inclusion of five of them in Documenta X. Among those
exhibited here are Dresden painter Neo Rauch, 1997
Turner prize nominee Christine Borland and Carsten and
Olaf Nicolai.
Wheelchair access with assistance.

Galerie Gebauer

*Torstraße 220, Mitte, 10115 (280 8110). U6
Oranienburger Tor.* **Open** noon-6pm Tue-Sat.
Map F3
This first floor gallery exhibits mainly high-profile interna-
tional artists such as Thomas Schütte, Luc Tymans and
(e)Twin Gabriel – a brother and sister duo from the former
GDR known for their sculpture and installation work.

Galerie Hilgemann

*Linienstraße 213, Mitte, 10119 (283 1376). U6
Oranienburger Tor.* **Open** 3-7pm Wed-Sat. **Map F2**
The gallery has a mixed programme with an emphasis on
young Russian neo-avantgarde, particularly from St
Petersburg. In one recent exhibition Julia Straussowa
showed plaster-cast busts of Berlin club DJs.

Galerie Leo Coppi

*Hackesche Höfe, Hof III, Rosenthalerstraße 40/41, 10178
(283 5331). U8 Weinmeister Straße.* **Open** 1-6.30pm
Tue-Fri; noon-6pm Sat. **Map F2**
Doris Leo and Helle Coppi opened this gallery in 1991 to promote a number of painters and graphic artists, most of whom
live and work in east Berlin and Dresden, but it all seems terribly old-fashioned.

Galerie Max Hetzler

*Zimmerstraße 89, Mitte, 10117 (229 2437). U6
Kochstraße.* **Open** 11am-6pm Tue-Sat. **Map F4**
Another new upmarket gallery (recently relocated from
Cologne and closer to Checkpoint Charlie than Auguststraße)
with a proclivity towards architectural discourse.
Established figures such as Günther Förg, Robert Gober, On
Kawara, Jeff Koons, Terry Winters and Christopher Wool
are represented here.
Branch: Schillerstraße 94, 10625 (315 2261).

Galerie neugerriemschneider

*Linienstraße 155, Mitte, 10115 (3087 2810). U8
Weinmeister Straße.* **Open** 11am-6pm Tue-Sat.
Map F2
Another arriviste from Charlottenburg, exhibiting the lat-
est and hippest from the USA, Europe and latterly even
some local talent. Among the artists represented are artists
Franz Ackermann, Sharon Lockhart, Tobias Rehberger and
Rirkrit Tiravanija.

Galerie Paula Böttcher

*Kleine Hamburgerstraße 15, Mitte, 10117 (281 1236).
U8 Weinmeister Straße.* **Open** 2-7pm Mon-Fri; noon-5pm
Sat. **Map F2**
Opened by 25-year-old Paula Böttcher in June 1997, the
gallery is working with young local and international artists.
One of her first shows was entitled 'How to make a good
group show if you've only got one room'. Thirteen artists
answered using models of the gallery.

Klosterfelde

*Linienstraße 160, Mitte, 10115 (283 5305). U6
Oranienburger Straße.* **Open** 11am-6pm Tue-Sat. **Map
F2**
Martin Klosterfelde's narrow ground-floor gallery was formerly a vaulted passageway to a courtyard typical of old
Berlin. The gallery opened in 1996 on the heels of the closure
of a number of larger squats in the same street, in microcosm
reflecting the general state of affairs in Mitte. His programme
to date has been a mix of contemporary Germans such as
painter Nader with his large-scale philosophical oil tableaux
and established artists such as Vito Acconci and Dan
Peterman.

Mehdi Chouakri Berlin

*Gipsstraße 11, Mitte, 10119 (2839 1153). U8
Weinmeister Straße.* **Open** 2-7pm Tue-Fri. **Map F2**
Opened in October 1996 by Mehdi Chouakri (formerly of
Paris) with a slick you-can-eat-off-the-floor type of space, this
gallery has a pan-European/North American programme.
Exhibitions are heavy on conceptual photography and hip-
looking furniture-as-art by the likes of Sylvie Fleury with
her fashionable vacuumable fluffy stuff. Also represented
are John M Armleder, Claude Closky and local Monica
Bonvicini.

Neu

*Charitéstraße 3, Mitte, 10117 (285 7550). U6, S1, S2,
S3, S5, S9, S25, S75 Friedrichstraße.* **Open** 2-7pm Tue-
Fri; noon-4pm Sat. **Map E3**
Formerly in Auguststraße where it was the main hangout
for serious young locals – the resultant scene often com-
pensating for a lack of art on the walls. Alexander Schröder
and Tilo Wermke decided in their second year to move off
the main gallery drag (a short interesting walk from
Oranienburger U-bahn Station towards Charité Hospital)
and actually show some art. This gallery is the main stop
for seeing local talent with emerging reputations in modest
surroundings. Among those represented at Neu are painter
Lukas Duwenhögger, Daniel Pflumm and conceptual Brit
Josephine Pryde.

Shift

*Friedrichstraße 122/123, Hof II, Mitte, 10117 (2859
8631). U6, S1, S2, S3, S5, S9, S25, S75 Friedrichstraße.*
Open 3-7pm Thur-Sun. **Map F3**
A non-commercial collective labour of love in a novel multi-
roomed ground-floor space. They also have a salon on the
first floor of the front building for photography and performance. The main gallery is tucked away on the left-hand side
of the second courtyard around a dark corner that you
wouldn't normally approach. There are often solid shows by
up-and-coming European and American artists. You can
view their programme to date on a specially produced CD-
Rom available at the gallery.
http://www.bin.de/shift.

Galerie Schipper und Krome

*Auguststraße 91, Mitte, 10117 (2839 0139). U6
Oranienburger Straße.* **Open** noon-6pm Tue-Fri; 1-5pm
Sat. **Map F2**
The gallery moved from Cologne to Berlin in 1997, illustrat-
ing Mitte's upmarket trend. This is the place to see work by
the kind of artists currently featured in the important art
magazines. Among others, Vanessa Beecroft, Matti Braun,
Angela Bulloch, Liam Gillick and Raymond Pettibon are
represented.

Galerie Barbara Thumm

*Auguststraße 22, Mitte, 10117 (283 4223). U6
Oranienburger Straße.* **Open** 2-7pm Tue-Fri; 1-5pm Sat.
Map F2
Opened in 1997 with a programme emphasising British
artists (gallerist Barbara Thumm studied in London) and

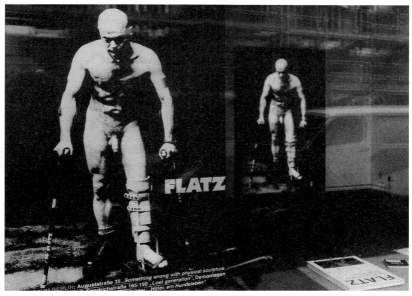

Another installation at **Projektraum Berlin** – *a small space but big on ideas.*

generally known artists that have not previously exhibited in Berlin. Artists represented include Julian Opie, Kerry Stewart, Fiona Banner and Swedish duo Bigert+Bergström.

Galerie Wohnmaschine
(282 0795).
This important experimental gallery originally opened in 1988 in the apartment of owner Friedrich Loock (hence the name, German for 'machine for living'). It survived until recently in the same spot, on the corner of Auguststraße and Tucholskystraße, while Mitte's art quarter grew up around it. At the time of going to press, it was moving into a new but as yet unspecified address. The phone number will stay the same, though, so call for details.

Projektraum Berlin
Auguststraße 35, Mitte, 10119 (2839 1862). U6 Oranienburger Straße. **Open** 2-7pm Thur-Fri; 1-6pm Sat. **Map F2**
Andreas Binder and Mathias Kampl are the directors of this small gallery dedicated to the display of primarily conceptual installation art. Recent exhibitions have included Fred Sandback, Matt Mullican and Sabine Groß.

Zff – Zentrum für Fotografie
Charitestraße 3, Mitte, 10117 (283 5211). U6, S1, S2, S3, S5, S9, S25, S75 Friedrichstraße. **Open** 5-9pm Thur-Sat; noon-4pm Sun. **Map E3**
A recently established group enterprise gallery for the work of classic modernist photography not previously shown in Germany. They also intend to mount exhibitions of young German photographers.

Zwinger Galerie
Gipsstraße 3, Hinterhof, 10119 (2859 8907). U8 Weinmeister Straße. **Open** 2-7pm Tue-Fri; 11.30am-5pm Sun. **Map F2**

A long-established and reputable commercial gallery that in 1997 moved with the crowd from Kreuzberg to an atmospheric courtyard space. Gallerist Werner Müller didn't want to miss out on the international visitors that the Mitte galleries now attract. Artists represented include Bettina Allamoda and Tobias Hauser.

Auctions

Kunstkabinett Gerda Bassenge
Bleibtreustraße 19, Charlottenburg, 10623 (881 8104). U15 Uhlandstraße/S3, S5, S6, S7, S9 Savignyplatz. **Open** 2-6pm Mon-Fri; 11am-2pm Sat. **No credit cards. Map C4**
Gerda Bassenge, the grande dame among Berlin's gallery owners, deals in eighteenth- and nineteenth century engravings, prints and graphic works ranging from Art Nouveau and the Berlin Secessionists (Liebermann, Corinth) to German Expressionism (Kollwitz, Pechstein), and rare books. Auctions are held several times a year. Ring for details.

Galerie Pels-Leusden
Fasanenstraße 25 (at Villa Grisebach), Charlottenburg, 10719 (885 9150). U15 Uhlandstraße. **Open** 10am-6.30pm Mon-Fri; 10am-2pm Sat. **No credit cards. Map C4**
There are two big auctions each year – one in June, the other in late November. The rest of the year you get to see a diversity of exhibitions with a focus on classic modern art.

Auktionshaus Sotheby's
Palais am Festungsgraben, Unter den Linden, behind Neue Wache, Mitte, 10117 (201 0521). S1, S2, S3, S5, S6, S7, S9/U6 Friedrichstraße. **Open** 10am-1pm, 2-5pm, Mon-Fri. **No credit cards. Map F3**
The emphasis is on German Expressionism and contemporary painting. Auctions are held in May and November.

Consumer

Accommodation

From a room full of mirrors to a dorm full of backpackers: a shortage of beds but no shortage of variety.

Berlin is changing fast. New places sprout like mushrooms, others fall victim to redevelopment. Despite a lot of new hotels, Berlin still only has around 50,000 hotel beds (London, by contrast, has 170,000). And although finding accommodation is not quite the nightmare it used to be, it remains particularly difficult to find a room during major holidays, conventions and festivals – especially if you're on a budget. We therefore advise you, whenever possible, to book a good month in advance. Apart from contacting hotels directly, you can also phone **Berlin Tourismus Marketing** (*below*).

Many hotels now have websites which are worth checking for information about facilities and special deals. Some, for example, offer cheaper rates at weekends. If backpacking, you could try contacting Circus Hostel – the staff speak English and should be able to pass you on to another hostel if theirs is full.

Hotels are mainly concentrated in Mitte and around the Zoo and Savignyplatz in the west. The east side of the city is still notably lacking in cheaper options, but new places are opening up all the time, especially around Oranienburger Straße and in Prenzlauer Berg and Friedrichshain. Do check the up-to-date lists available from Berlin Tourismus Marketing, especially if looking for a backpacker hostel. While location is important, it's worth remembering that the Berlin public transport system is excellent. Unless you really are out in the suburbs, you're rarely more than half an hour away from anywhere you might want to be.

For a longer stay, your best bet (besides word of mouth) is either a Mitwohnzentrale or the classified ads in *Zweite Hand*, *Tip*, *Zitty* and the *Berliner Morgenpost*. You can also look on the noticeboards in the foyer of the Hochschule der Kunst at Hardenbergstraße 33 in Charlottenburg, or pin up your own notice. Prices vary wildly, but if you look for something 'auf Zeit' (for a limited period) you can often get something quite reasonable. Expect to pay DM600-DM800 for a two-room flat in the more central districts of Kreuzberg, Prenzlauer Berg and Schöneberg. (In winter, check what kind of heating is available – lugging coal up to the fourth floor every day may not be the kind of authentic Berlin experience you had in mind.)

The listings below aim to give a rounded idea of what to expect from each establishment. Remember to add breakfast to your room price if it is not included. Most hotels offer breakfast as a buffet which can be as simple as coffee and rolls (called *Schrippen* in Berlin) with cheese and salami, or the full works complete with smoked meats, smoked salmon, muesli with fresh fruit and yoghurt, and a glass of sparkling wine.

Our price categories work as follows: a De Luxe hotel is one in which a double room costs DM350 or more; an Expensive hotel is DM220 or more; Moderate is DM125 or more; and the rest are Budget. All prices given are room prices.

Tourist Information

Berlin Tourismus Marketing

Europa-Center, Budapester Straße, Charlottenburg, 10787 (250 025/fax 2500 2424). S3, S5, S6, S7, S9/U2, U9 Zoologischer Garten. **Open** 8am-10pm Mon-Sat; 9am-9pm Sun. Reduced opening hours on public holidays. **Map D4**

This privatised tourist information office, with branches at Tegel Airport and the Brandenburg Gate, can provide an up-to-date hotel guide booklet for free (although the hotels listed have paid to be in it). They also have a photocopied list of youth hostels and camping sites that costs DM1, and another list of private apartments and holiday homes for DM2. *e-mail: information@btm.de*

http: www.berlin.de

Branches: im Brandenburger Tor, Unter den Linden, Mitte. (250 025); Airport Service Flughafen Tegel (250 025).

De Luxe

Berlin Hilton

Mohrenstraße 30, Mitte, 10117 (20230/fax 2023 4269). U2, U6 Stadtmitte. **Rates** *single* DM310; *double* DM350; *suites* DM395-DM1,500; *breakfast* DM33. **Credit** AmEx, DC, EC, JCB, MC, V. **Map F4**

Well-placed on the Gendarmenmarkt across from the German and French Cathedrals and a U-Bahn stop, and offers top-quality rooms and services in a pleasant atmosphere. The lobby is huge and airy, dripping with plants and with a restaurant bang in the middle of it. The standard rooms are blue, grey and rattan, including 14 non-smoking rooms; the 14 suites include the art deco, two-storey Maisonette Suite with a working gramophone (a snip at DM3,000 a night).

e-mail: berlin-hilton@compuserve.com

Hotel services *Bar. Laundry service. Lift. Parking. Restaurants (3). Disco. Sauna. Squash court. Swimming pool. Whirlpool. Fitness centre. Solarium. Bicycle rental.* **Room services** *Minibar. Radio. Room service. Telephone. TV. Hairdryer. Bathrobe.*

Bristol Hotel Kempinski Berlin

Kurfürstendamm 27, Charlottenburg, 10719 (884 340/fax 883 6075). U15, U9 Kurfürstendamm. **Rates** *single* DM330-DM480; *double* DM390-DM540; *suite* DM630-DM1,800; *breakfast* DM32. **Credit** AmEx, DC, MC, V. **Map C4**

Bristol Hotel Kempinski Berlin – *famous, faded and a Kurfürstendamm landmark.*

Perhaps Berlin's most famous hotel, if not its best, the Kempinski exudes a faded charm. But even though the rooms are plush, you never really feel you're living in the lap of luxury, as you certainly should for this price. The Bristol Bar on the ground floor, with its fat leather sofas and lots of old, dark wood, has a long cocktail list and snooty waiters. The Kempinski Eck restaurant is nothing special; but then, neither is the Kempinski Grill.
Hotel services *Bar. Conference services. Cosmetic salon. Laundry service. Lift. Sauna. Solarium. Swimming pool. Restaurants (3).* **Room services** *Minibar. Room service. Telephone. TV.*

Grand Hotel Esplanade
Lützowufer 15, Tiergarten, 10785 (254 780/fax 265 1171). U2, U4, U15 Nollendorfplatz. **Rates** *single DM380-DM480; double DM430-DM530; suite DM980-DM2,600; breakfast DM33.* **Credit** AmEx, DC, MC, V. **Map D4**
One of Berlin's better luxury hotels, by the Landwehr canal and close to the Tiergarten. The entrance is grand, with a huge, gushing wall of water across from the door and hundreds of lights glittering above your head. The lobby is spacious and beautifully decorated, and there are art exhibitions adorning some of the walls on the ground floor. The well-tended rooms are sparkling white and 30 have been set aside for non-smokers. If you decide to stay here, you get the added benefit of being within stumbling-back-to-bed distance of the excellent Harry's New York Bar on the ground floor. Plush, but not intimidating, Harry's features a long, long cocktail list, nightly jazz and welcoming red sofas.
e-mail: info@esplanade.de
http: www.esplanade.de
Hotel services *Bar. Conference facilities. Laundry service. Lift. Parking. Restaurant. Sauna. Swimming pool. Wheelchair access.* **Room services** *Radio. Room service. Telephone. TV.*

Adlon Hotel Kempinski Berlin
Unter den Linden 77, Mitte, 10117 (22 610/fax 2261 2222). S1, S2, S25 Unter den Linden. **Rates** *single DM420-DM590; double DM490-DM660; suite from DM800; breakfast buffet DM39.* **Credit** AmEx, DC, EC, MC, V. **Map F3**
The original Hotel Adlon, world renowned for its luxurious interiors and discreet atmosphere, opened in 1907 but burned down shortly after World War II. The new Adlon, rebuilt by the Kempinski group on the original site, opened in 1997 and aims to pick up where its predecessor left off, ostentatiously listing previous guests such as Albert Einstein, Theodore Roosevelt and Marlene Dietrich as though they only checked out last week. Right by the Brandenburg Gate and handy for Berlin's diplomatic quarter, it has immediately become a first-stop choice for heads of state and the like, but, if you are not a Kennedy or McCartney, expect to be peering up nostrils here. The frostiness of the staff simply has to be experienced to be believed. There are tales of one Condé Nast journalist having trouble getting back to his room because the staff didn't believe he was a guest. Some details: there are 337 rooms including 51 suites, six rooms for allergy sufferers, two for travellers with disabilities and two bulletproof presidential suites. There are also marble and black granite bathrooms, hairdressers, 12 boutiques, and wardrobes in each room with hanging rails that light up. *See* **Rooms at the top** pg 109.
e-mail: Adlon@Kempinski.com
http: www.hotel-adlon.de
Hotel services *Restaurants and bars (7). Business and press centre. Conference and banqueting salons. Fitness spa. Swimming pool. Boutiques. Garage.* **Room services** *ISDN. Fax. PC outlet. Air conditioning. CD. TV. Telephones(2). Shower. WC.*

Hotel Intercontinental
Budapester Straße 2, Tiergarten, 10787 (26020/fax 2602 80760). S3, S5, S6, S7, S9/U2, U9 Zoologischer Garten. **Rates** *single DM345-DM495; double DM395-DM545; suite DM495-DM2,600; breakfast DM32.* **Credit** AmEx, DC, EC, MC, V. **Map D4**
If you're on a generous expense account, this is the place to stay. Extraordinarily plush and spacious, the Intercontinental exudes a sense of luxury. The rooms are large, tastefully decorated and blessed with elegant bathrooms. The lobby is huge and airy; its soft leather chairs are the ideal place to read the paper or wait for your next appointment.
e-mail: berlin@interconti.com
http: www.interconti.com
Hotel services *Bar. Conference facilities. Laundry service. Lift. Parking. Sauna. Swimming pool.* **Room services** *Room service. Radio. Telephone. TV.*

Hotel Palace
Europa-Center, Charlottenburg, 10789 (250 20/fax 262 6577). S3, S5, S6, S7, S9/U2, U9 Zoologischer Garten. **Rates** *single DM295-DM480; double DM390-DM540; suite DM395-DM2,800; breakfast buffet DM31.* **Credit** AmEx, DC, EC, V, MC. **Map D4**
A Best Western hotel in the middle of the Europa-Center. The rooms are luxurious, reasonably spacious and complete with all the amenities. One nice extra is free access to the lavish sauna facilities of the Thermen am Europa Center.
e-mail: hotel@palace.de
http: www.palace.de
Hotel services *Bar. Conference facilities. Laundry service. Lift. Parking. Restaurant (special diets catered to).* **Room services** *Minibar. Radio. Room service. Telephone. TV.*

Maritim pro Arte Hotel Berlin
Friedrichstraße 151, Mitte, 10117 (203 35/fax 2033 4209) S1, S2, S25, S3, S5, S7, S75, S9/U6 Friedrichstraße. **Rates** *single DM235-DM445; double DM260-DM500; suites and apartments DM530-DM2,700; breakfast buffet DM29.* **Credit** AmEx, EC, JCB, V. **Map F3**
On the former site of the Hotel Metropol, this gleaming new edifice calls itself a 'designer hotel' and is certainly one of the most stylish in Berlin. Dripping with huge paintings and designer furniture, the foyer, three restaurants and bar are chic and luxurious. The 403 rooms, apartments and suites all have fax and PC connections, air-conditioning and marble bathrooms. Staff are polite and helpful, particularly when you're dressed to match the surroundings. The Brandenburg Gate and Reichstag and are within walking distance, as are Unter den Linden, the swanky shops of Friedrichstraße and the bars and galleries of the Scheunenviertel.
Hotel services *Bar. Restaurants (3). Parking. Conference facilities (2 halls, 9 rooms). Boutiques. Pool. Sauna. Solarium. Gym. Lifts.* **Room services** *Fax & modem. TV. Pay TV. Telephone. Room service. Safe. Minibar.*

Radisson SAS Hotel
Karl-Liebknecht-Straße 5, Mitte, 10178 (238 28/fax 2382 7590). S3, S5, S6, S7, S9 Hackescher Markt/Alexanderplatz. **Rates** *single DM325-DM455; double DM355-DM485; suites DM650-DM2,000; breakfast buffet DM27.* **Credit** AmEx, DC, EC, JCB, V. **Map G3**
The Radisson is surrounded by new restaurants and shops. The architecture may look suspiciously east German (because it is), but its 540 rooms are modern and comfortable. The hotel is popular with Japanese and American business people, who like to gather in the gold-, black- and maroon-leathered lobby. If they need more room, they simply move into the Conference Centre. There's live entertainment in the bar every evening, a Thank God It's Friday restaurant attached, and Museum Island, the Staatsoper, the Berliner Dom and the Nikolaiviertel are all close at hand.

*Despite its prefabricated east German construction, the **Westin Grand** manages to live up to its name. Page 102.*

e-mail: rs@berzh.rdsas.com
Hotel services *Bar. Conference facilities. Laundry service. Lift. Parking. Restaurant. Swimming pool. Sauna.* **Room services** *Minibar. Radio. Room service. Safe. Telephone. TV.*

The Westin Grand

Friedrichstraße 158-164, Mitte, 10117 (20 270/fax 2027 3362). U6 Französische Straße. **Rates** *single DM265-DM375; double DM295-DM475; suite DM550-DM3,400; breakfast buffet DM29.* **Credit** *AmEx, DC, EC, JCB, V.* **Map F3**
Just around the corner from Unter den Linden, providing five-star luxury in a top location. Gratifyingly elegant, despite its prefabricated east German construction, the hotel manages to live up to its name rather well. Its 35 suites are individually furnished with period décor according to whoever they are named after (try the Schinkel or Lessing suites), and its 358 rooms exude traditional taste, design and comfort. There's a hotel garden with a sun patio and atrium as well as ten bars and restaurants and a non-smoking floor. Best of all is the bombastic staircase and foyer.
e-mail: info@westin.com
http: www.westin.com
Hotel services *Bar. Conference facilities. Laundry service. Lift. Restaurant. Sauna. Swimming pool.* **Room services** *Minibar. Radio. Room service. Telephone. Modem. TV.*

Expensive

Hotel-Restaurant Albrechtshof

Albrechtstraße 8, Mitte, 10117 (308 860/ fax 308 86100). S1, S2, S25, S3, S5, S7, S75, S9/U6 Friedrichstraße. **Rates** *single DM208-DM308; double DM265-DM365; suite DM365-DM465; breakfast incl.* **Credit** *AmEx, EC, MC, V.* **Map F3**
The only hotel in our *Guide* with its own chapel – a member of the Verband Christlicher Hotels (Christian Hotels Association), although it doesn't make a song and dance about it. There is a very pleasant Hof garden for breakfast in the summer and there are three restaurants specialising in local dishes. The staff are kind and the hotel is situated in a quiet, village-like area remarkably close to Friedrichstraße station and several theatres. The décor is universal Posh Hotel Style.
Hotel services *Chapel. Restaurants. Parking. Conference rooms. Three rooms with handicapped facilities.* **Room services** *Shower/bath. WC. Radio. TV. Telephone. Fax. PC-modem connection. Minibar.*

Alexander Plaza Berlin

Rosenstraße 1, Mitte, 10178 (240 010/fax 2400 1777). S3, S5, S7, S75, S9 Hackescher Markt. **Rates** *single DM175-DM275; double DM215-DM315; suite DM255-DM555; apartment monthly from DM2,800; breakfast buffet DM22.* **Credit** *AmEx, EC, DC, V, MC.* **Map G3**
A four-star hotel that outdoes a few of Berlin's five-star giants. Well situated between Alexanderplatz, Museuminsel and Hackescher Markt, this handsome, renovated building houses a delightful modern establishment. Despite the proximity of a dozen building sites and the frisky Mitte nightlife district, the hotel stands in an oasis of quiet near the river. The staff are charming and décor is tasteful. There are 90 rooms, 30 of which are non-smoking and three with facilities for the handicapped. Each room has modem facilities and there is also a fitness centre. The apartments from DM2,800 per month look very good value.
http: www.hotelweb.fr
Hotel services *Garage. Restaurant. Fitness centre. Function rooms (4). Sauna. Solarium. Airport shuttle.* **Room services** *TV. Pay TV. Direct phone. Wake-up call. Modem. Shower. WC. Hairdryer.*

Art'otel Ermelerhaus Berlin

Wallstraße 70-73, Mitte, 10179 (240 620/fax 2406 2222). U2 Märkisches Museum. **Rates** *single DM195-DM275; double DM275-DM355; suite/apartment DM275-DM335; breakfast buffet incl.* **Credit** *AmEx, EC, DC, MC, V.* **Map G4**
On the banks of the Spree, this is a delightful fusion of old and new. The Ermelerhaus building houses both immaculately restored rococo dining rooms and an ultra-modern residential section designed by architects Nalbach & Nalbach. The entire hotel is dedicated to the work of artist Georg Baselitz and all the rooms and corridors contain originals of his work as well as others by AR Penck and Andy Warhol. Besides the art, every detail of the décor has been meticulously attended to, from Philip Starck bathrooms to the Marcel Breuer chairs in the conference rooms. Service is friendly, the views from the top suites across Mitte are stunning, and the food in both restaurants is imaginatively traditional. In summer an old barge moored by the towpath in front of the hotel becomes a terrace with charmingly picturesque views.
e-mail berlin@artotel.de
http: www.artotel.de
Hotel services *Conference facilities. Bar. Restaurant. Garage. Laundry service. Babysitting. Theatre tickets. Foyer internet terminal. Business office with computer, fax and modem.* **Room services** *TV. Pay TV. Radio. Telephone. Desk. Hairdryer.*

Hotel Alexander

Pariser Straße 37, Wilmersdorf, 10707 (881 6091/fax 881 6094). U7 Adenauerplatz. **Rates** *single DM160-DM210; double DM210-DM260; breakfast DM20.* **Credit** *AmEx, EC, DC, JCB, MC, V.* **Map C5**
On a lively street south of the Ku'damm, this self-styled 'art hotel' has rooms with ultra-modern furnishings. The doubles are spacious, the singles are small but cosy. If you don't like the grey marbled wallpaper and metal trimmings of the opulent-looking 'café-bistro', the surrounding area is packed with bars and restaurants. The staff speak English and are friendly and helpful.
Hotel services *Bar. Restaurant. Fax facilities.* **Room services** *Room service. Radio. Telephone. Cable TV. Minibar. Safe.*

Berlin Plaza Hotel

Knesebeckstraße 62, Charlottenburg, 10719 (884 130/telex 184 181/fax 8841 3754). U15 Uhlandstraße. **Rates** *single DM148-DM198; double DM198-DM260; extra bed DM50; breakfast incl.* **Credit** *AmEx, DC, EC, MC, JCB, V.* **Map C4**
Get ready to be dazzled by the Berlin Plaza's mirror and brass foyer, which mixes well with several pink sofas and pieces of modern art from local galleries. The hotel has seven floors (one of which is non-smoking), and was renovated in 1989. Its 131 rooms are tastefully decorated in pink, maroon and white, but are rather small and plain. All double rooms and some singles have both shower and bath. You can mix your own muesli at the breakfast buffet: the food is freshly made and bread is baked on the premises. German specialities are served in the restaurant and bar. As for the prices – you are paying for its location just off the Kufürstendamm.
Hotel services *Bar. Conference facilities. Laundry service. Lift. Parking (DM20 a day). Restaurant.* **Room services** *Hairdryer. Minibar. Radio. Safe. Telephone. TV.*

Hotel Berliner Hof

Tauenzienstraße 8, Schöneberg, 10789 (254 950/fax 262 3065). U1, U2, U15 Wittenbergplatz. **Rates** *single DM195; double DM240; extra bed DM60; breakfast incl.* **Credit** *AmEx, DC, EC, MC, V.* **Map D4**
If you want the west end, you won't get much more central than this: the Europa-Center is next door and the Ku'damm

round the corner. The Berliner Hof's rooms face the back of the hotel and are quiet, spacious and pleasantly decorated. **Hotel services** *Lift. Parking (DM10).* **Room services** *Minibar. Radio. Telephone. TV.*

Holiday Inn Garden Court

Bleibtreustraße 25, Charlottenburg, 10707 (881 4076/fax 882 4685). S3, S5, S7, S9, S75 Savignyplatz. **Rates** *single* DM245; *double* DM285; *suite* DM340-DM420; *children under-12 free; breakfast incl.* **Credit** AmEx, DC, JCB, MC, V. **Map C4**
Quiet, charming hotel just off the Ku'damm. The 73 rooms and suites were renovated in 1989 and, though cramped, are tastefully decorated. The bathrooms, also a bit tight, are bright and clean. The glass-enclosed breakfast room on the fifth floor offers a stunning view of the area. The tiny lobby bar stays open around the clock. There are a few tables and comfortable chairs in the light, elegant lobby.
Hotel services *Bar. Conference facilities. Laundry service. Lift. Parking.* **Room services** *Minibar. Radio. Room service. Telephone. TV.*

Hotel Consul

Knesebeckstraße 8-9, Charlottenburg, 10623 (311 060/fax 312 2060). U2 Ernst-Reuter-Platz. **Rates** *single* DM169; *double* DM215; *suite* DM360. **Credit** AmEx, DC, EC, JCB, MC, V. **Map C4**
When this was known as the Hotel Windsor, it was a place of some note; now the Consul's owners are trying to reinject some of its former glory. But at the moment the place is still sadly dilapidated and only some of the otherwise spacious and comfortable rooms have been renovated. The hotel offers guests special deals on public transport: you can buy a day pass (valid on all buses, trams, U-Bahn and S-Bahn lines) for only DM5. The guest lounge is very relaxing.
Hotel services *Laundry service. Lift. Parking. TV room. Bicycle rental.* **Room services** *Minibar and TV in most rooms. Room service. Radio. Telephone.*

Concept Hotel

Grolmanstraße 41-43, Charlottenburg, 10623 (884 260/ fax 8842 6500). S3, S5, S7, S9, S75 Savignyplatz. **Rates** *single* DM220-DM280; *double* DM280-DM350; *suite* DM350-DM500; *breakfast incl.* **Credit** AmEx, DC, EC, MC, V. **Map C4**
Formerly the Curator Hotel, this has been significantly refurbished and is generally pretty smart. There are conference facilities and a big roof terrace for sunbathing, restaurant and bar. The hotel is quiet and situated in the best smart shopping area with a good restaurant selection nearby. Also well situated for the ICC congress centre. Boring bar.
Hotel services *Bar. Conference facilities. Parking. Sauna. Solarium.* **Room services** *Minibar. Radio. Safe. Telephone. TV. Two rooms equipped for disabled guests.*

Sorat Art'otel Berlin

Joachimstaler Straße 29, Charlottenburg, 10719 (884 470/ fax 8844 7700). U9, U15 Kurfürstendamm. **Rates** *single* DM350-DM330; *double* DM275-DM395; *breakfast buffet incl.* **Credit** AmEx, MC, DC, V. **Map C4**
Just off the Ku'damm in the heart of the west end, this hotel's theme is the work of artist Wolf Vostell – his collages and prints adorn the walls. The rooms are modern, tasteful and big with great bathrooms. Ask to see a couple of rooms as they range from good to great without any apparent relation to the price. The 'Eck Zimmer' (corner rooms) are the best. The breakfast room is a joy with a sumptuous buffet and it opens out into the garden in summer.
e-mail: art-otel@SORAT-Hotels.com
http: www.SORAT-Hotels.com
Hotel services *Parking. Disabled facilities. Non-smoking rooms. Small bar. Conference facilities. Restaurant.* **Room services** *Telephone. Cable TV. Radio. Minibar. Fax/modem connection.*

Hotel Sorat Gustavo Berlin

Prenzlauer Allee 169, Prenzlauer Berg, 10409 (446 610/fax 4466 1661). Tram 1/S8, S10 Prenzlauer Allee. **Rates** *single* DM140-DM270; *double* DM180-DM310; *breakfast buffet incl.* **Credit** AmEx, DC, MC, V. **Map G1**
Almost like a piece of Barcelona in the heart of east Berlin, with all the modern design and bright Mediterranean paintings by artist Gustavo. The rooms are generously proportioned as are the ensuite bathrooms. The breakfast buffet offers sparkling wine and salmon as well as a warm and cold buffet. Nearby night buses run into town if you want to be out really late, and there is a good value car hire company across the road if you want to make trips out east. Sorat style at more reasonable prices than the Sorat Art'otel in town.
e-mail: gustavo@SORAT-Hotels.com
http: www.SORAT-Hotels.com
Hotel services *Garage. Conference facilities. Small foyer bar. Internet access in foyer.* **Room services** *Telephone. Radio. Cable TV. Air-conditioning. Sound-proofed windows.*

Hecker's Hotel

Grolmanstraße 35, Charlottenburg, 10623 (88900/telex 184 954 hhblnd/fax 889 0260). U15 Uhlandstraße. **Rates** *single* DM260; *double* DM310; *extra bed* DM60; *children under-12 free; breakfast* DM20. **Credit** AmEx, EC, DC, JCB, MC, V. **Map C4**
Unremarkable on the outside, quite pleasant inside. They have recently added 27 rooms. Although there's not much of a lobby, the bar/restaurant off the entrance has just been renovated and is a fine place to sit and wait. Rooms are a good size and comfortable, with lots of nice little touches – pencil sharpeners, for example, and fresh fruit. Bathrooms are small, but clean and well-lit. The walk-in closets are easily the best in Berlin. Quiet and comfortable.
Hotel services *Bar. Parking.* **Room services** *Minibar. No-smoking rooms. Radio. Telephone. TV.*

Berliner Congress Center

Märkisches Ufer 54, Mitte, 10179 (27580/fax 2758 2170). S3, S5, S6, S7, S9 Jannowitzbrücke. **Rates** *single* DM175; *double* DM200-DM220; *extra bed* DM40; *children under-12 free; breakfast incl.* **Credit** AmEx, DC, EC, JCB, MC, V. **Map G4**
As the name suggests, an ideal hotel for business guests who need conference facilities. There are 13 conference rooms, three restaurants and a banquet room, and 112 bedrooms. The rooms are comfortable, if a bit dull; the baths are lovely; the airy Wintergarden is a splendid place for a meal.
Hotel services *Bar. Laundry. Lift. Parking (DM20)* **Room services** *Minibar. Radio. Telephone. TV.*

Berlin Hilton Krone

Mohrenstraße 30, Mitte, 10117 (202 30/fax 2023 4269). U2, U6 Stadtmitte. **Rates** *single* DM170-DM210; *double* DM210-DM245; *breakfast* DM33. **Credit** AmEx, DC, EC, MC, JCB, V. **Map F4**
The Krone is part of the same building as its parent, the Berlin Hilton (*above*). This is the affordable, less grand part of the complex, but though the rooms are cheaper, you can still use all of the Hilton services.
e-mail: hilton@compuserve.com
Hotel services *Laundry service. Lift. Parking (DM22 a day). Squash court. Bowling. Swimming pool. Whirlpool. Fitness centre. Sauna. Solarium. Bicycle rental.* **Room services** *Minibar. Safe. Telephone. TV.*

Hotel Luisenhof

Köpenicker Straße 92, Mitte, 10179 (241 5906/fax 279 2983). U8 Heinrich-Heine-Straße. **Rates** *single* DM187-DM230; *double* DM230-DM320; *suite* DM380. **Credit** AmEx, DC, EC, JCB, V. **Map G4**
The beautiful building housing the Luisenhof dates from the late nineteenth century and was the headquarters and sta-

bles of a Berlin coaching company. When the Communists held sway, it was home to the party training centre of the SED. It was reopened after renovation in early 1993 and has been tastefully restored in original townhouse style. It's in the middle of old Berlin, close to the major cultural sights and what is fast becoming the city's business district.
Hotel services *Conference facilities. Fax. Flowers. Laundry service. Lift. Restaurants (2). Photocopying.* **Room services** *Minibar. Fax connection. Radio. Safe. Telephone. TV.*

Hotel Unter den Linden

Unter den Linden 14, Mitte, 10117 (238 110/fax 2381 1100). S3, S5, S6, S7, S9/U6 Friedrichstraße. **Rates** *single* DM99-DM220; *double* DM139-DM270; *suite* DM200-DM350; *breakfast buffet incl.* **Credit** AmEx, EC, DC, MC, V. **Map F3**
The best thing about the sprawling, dated lobby of this 1960s hotel is the Le Corbusier-style chrome and black leather chairs. Images of 1960s spy films come to mind as one takes in the extraordinary clash of décor. The staff are friendly but slow, and the food is nothing special – but who eats in their hotel with all Berlin to choose from? The corridors are stuffy and the rooms cramped but clean. Same goes for the bathrooms despite the age of the tiling. However, there is a café terrace on Unter den Linden, and if you want to walk out of the door in the morning on to Berlin's most famous boulevard without paying Adlon prices, then this is an option.
Hotel services *Bar. Bistro. Conference facilities. Laundry service. Lift.* **Room services** *Minibar. Radio. Telephone. TV.*

Moderate

Hotel am Scheunenviertel

Oranienburger Straße 38, Mitte, 10117 (282 2125/2830 8310/fax 282 1115). S1, S2, S25 Oranienburger Straße/U6 Oranienburger Tor. **Rates** *single* DM120; *double* DM140; *breakfast incl.* **Credit** AmEx, DC, EC, MC, V. **Map F3**
One of the best-value, best-located little hotels in town. In the historical heart and old Jewish Quarter of Berlin, the Museuminsel, Friedrichstraße and Hackesche Höfe are all nearby. By night the area is alive with cafés, bars, clubs and restaurants.Rooms are clean and comfortable, each with WC and good strong shower. The ample buffet breakfast is included in the room price and the staff are friendly and helpful. All in all a superb base from which to explore Berlin, but be sure to book: there are only 18 rooms.
Hotel services *Breakfast room* **Room services** *Telephone. TV.*

Alpenland Hotel

Carmerstraße 8, Charlottenburg, 10623 (312 3970/fax 313 8444). S3, S5, S7, S9, S75 Savignyplatz. **Rates** *single* DM75-DM130; *double* DM110-DM190; *extra bed* DM50. **Credit** MC, V. **Map C4**
The Alpenland is a no-frills, friendly hotel. Renovations were completed in 1993, so the rooms are fresh and clean, as well as reasonably spacious. The large, pristine bathrooms are especially fine, although not every room has its own. Communal toilets are on every floor. Breakfast is taken in the restaurant downstairs, which also has a pleasant bar.
Hotel services *Bar. Restaurant.* **Room services** *Telephone. TV.*

Hotel Bogota

Schlüterstraße 45, Charlottenburg, 10707 (881 5001/telex 184 946/fax 883 5887). S3, S5, S7, S9, S75 Savignyplatz. **Rates** *single* DM68-DM125; *double* DM110-DM180; *extra bed* DM70. **Credit** AmEx, DC, EC, M, V. **Map C4**
More functional than fancy, a 130-bedroom hotel with good service and very good prices. It's slightly to the south of

Kurfürstendamm and is frequented by backpackers, businessmen and tourists. This is made possible by the range of rooms and prices available. About half of the double rooms have showers and toilets and most of them, though plainly furnished, are comfortable. If there are four of you on a small budget, you can take a double room and pay an extra DM50 per person (including breakfast) for the two extra beds.
Hotel services *Lift. TV room.* **Room services** *Telephone.*

Hotel California

Kurfürstendamm 35, Charlottenburg,10719 (880 120/fax 8801 2111). U15 Uhlandstraße. **Rates** *single* DM155-DM175; *double* DM185-DM225; *extra bed* DM50-DM60; *breakfast buffet* DM18. **Credit** AmEx, DC, EC, MC, V. **Map C4**
Smack in the middle of some of Berlin's best shops and right next to a new McDonald's. The unimposing lobby sports a small fountain and a large piece of the Berlin Wall, as well as some deep sofas to sink into after a hard day's sightseeing. The rooms are basic and comfortable. The lift stops only on every half floor, so there are still 12 stairs to climb to your room. The hotel can hire you a bicycle in the summer.
Hotel services *Bar. Conference facilities. Lift. Solarium (DM5 for ten minutes). TV room.* **Room services** *Minibar. Radio. Safe. Sauna. Telephone. TV. Hairdryer.*

Hotel Pension Castell

Wielandstraße 24, Charlottenburg, 10707 (882 7181/fax 881 5548). U7 Adenauerplatz. **Rates** *single* DM90-DM125; *double* DM110-DM160. **Credit** AmEx, EC, V. **Map C4**
Tucked away just off the Ku'damm and near many designer shops, this 22-room pension has friendly staff and good sized rooms. They have recently renovated and now nearly all rooms have shower, WC and TV.
Hotel services *Lift.* **Room services** *TV(most rooms). Telephone.*

Hotel Charlot am Kurfürstendamm

Giesebrechtstraße 17, Charlottenburg, 10629 (323 4051/fax 324 0819). U7 Adenauerplatz/S3, S5, S6, S7, S9 Charlottenburg. **Rates** *single* DM70-DM145; *double* DM116-DM210. **Credit** AmEx, EC, V. **Map B4**
There aren't many better hotels in this price range. It's in a beautiful residential area full of chic shops and great cafés; the historical Jugendstil building has been well restored; it has friendly management; and the 24 bedrooms are spotlessly clean. Not all have showers and toilets, but the communal ones are quite clean. Despite its name, the hotel is actually about five minutes away from the Kurfürstendamm.
Hotel services *Bar. Lift. Parking. TV room.* **Room services** *Telephone. Television.*

Hotel-Pension Elba

Bleibtreustraße 26, Charlottenburg, 10707 (881 7504/fax 882 3246). S3, S5, S7, S9, S75 Savignyplatz. **Rates** *single* DM95-DM128; *double* DM148-DM150. **Credit** AmEx, MC, V. **Map C4**
The Elba is closer to a hotel in atmosphere and size, which is reflected in the prices. But it's known for the friendliness of its staff and is housed in a splendid townhouse in a prime location. Its 18 rooms range from the cramped to the capacious, but all are well equipped with showers and toilets, and have recently been redecorated in plain white and wood.
Hotel services *Lift.* **Room services** *Minibar. Radio. Telephone. TV.*

Hotel-Pension Funk

Fasanenstraße 69, Charlottenburg, 10719 (882 7193/fax 883 3329). U2, U9 Spichernstraße. **Rates** *single* DM65-DM100; *double* DM100-DM160. **Credit** AmEx, MC, V. **Map C5**

In the former apartment of the Danish silent movie star Asta Nielsen. The proprietor does his best to maintain the ambience of a pre-war flat, and the rooms are furnished with pieces from the 1920s and 1930s. The effect is cosy, and the 15 rooms are comfortable and large, even if not all have their own showers. For an extra DM40 per person (including breakfast) you can fit another two people into a double room.
Hotel services *Lift.* **Room services** *Telephone.*

Pension-Gästezimmer Gudrun

Bleibtreustraße 17, Charlottenburg, 10623 (881 6462). S3, S5, S7, S9, S75 Savignyplatz. **Rates** *single* DM95; *double* DM135-DM145. **No credit cards. Map C4**
The former Hotel-Pension Grossmann has now moved down to the first floor. There are only three rooms (and only one with a WC) but they are huge and have a shower and TV. The rooms are not as grand as the palatial exterior suggests but they are clean and comfy and have wonderful old-fashioned furniture. For a small group travelling together or a family they are really good value.
Hotel services *TV room. Room services. Telephone.*

Hotel-Pension Kastanienhof

Kastanien Allee 65, Mitte, 10119 (44 3050/fax 4430 5111). U8 Rosenthaler Platz/ Tram 13, 50, 53. **Rates** *single* DM130; *double* DM160; *2-room apartment* DM180; *breakfast incl.* **Credit** EC, MC, V. **Map G2**
If you can handle the pastel peach and pink décor, the rooms here are generously proportioned and well equipped. The staff are friendly and there is are two breakfast rooms (one non-smoking) and a bar. The hotel is well situated for exploring Prenzlauer Berg and Mitte, lying on the border between the two districts in one of the east's most interesting areas.
Hotel services *Bar. Lift. Parking. Breakfast rooms. Ticket booking.* **Room services** *Shower. WC. Sat-TV. Clock radio. Telephone. Minibar. Safe.*

Pension Kettler

Bleibtreustraße 19, Charlottenburg, 10623 (883 4949/5676/fax 882 4228). S3, S5, S7, S9, S75 Savignyplatz./U15 Uhlandstraße. **Rates** *single* DM110-DM145; *double* DM120-DM180; *breakfast incl.* **No credit cards. Map C4**
The seven quiet and light bedrooms in this grand old building overlook an impressive courtyard. Most of the double rooms and some of the single rooms (rather small for the price) have showers.
Room services *Room service. Telephone.*

Hotel Heidelberg

Knesebeckstraße 15, Charlottenburg, 10623 (313 0103/fax 313 5870). S3, S5, S7, S9, S75 Savignyplatz. **Rates** *single* DM98-DM168; *double* DM138-DM198; *suite* DM218. **Credit** AmEx, EC, MC, V. **Map C4**
Those responsible for decorating obviously got lost somewhere back in the 1960s. The dining room fronts the street and its open door seems to be inviting the public to step in. Except nobody does, and even the guests all seem to dine in the café next door. The rooms, though small and plain, are comfortable enough, with their own showers and toilets. In any event, the Heidelberg's location is central.
Hotel services *Bar. Lift. Parking.* **Room services** *Safe. Telephone. TV.*

Hotel Jurine

Schwedter Straße 15, Mitte, 10119 (443 2990/fax 4432 9999). U2 Senefelderplatz. **Rates** *single* DM150-DM190; *double* DM190-DM240; *breakfast incl.* **Credit** AmEx, DC, EC, V. **Map G2**
This freshly renovated building housing a three-star hotel at the foot of the Prenzlauer Berg is within walking distance of the cafés and restaurants around Kollwitz Platz and has

good transport connections into town. The rooms are bright and airy and the hotel has a friendly, family atmosphere although it has yet to develop much character as it really is brand new throughout. There is a garden and disabled facilities and all rooms have shower or bath and WC.
Hotel services *Conference room. Wintergarden with Terrace. Bar. Garden. Garage.* **Room services** *Shower/bath. WC. ISDN telephone. Pay TV. Satellite TV. Fax.*

Propeller Island City Lodge

Paulsborner Straße 10, Wilmersdorf, 10709 (891 8720/fax 891 8720). U7 Adenauerplatz. **Rates** DM120-DM180; *breakfast self-catering.* **No credit cards. Map F7**
Berlin's most original hotel. If you are looking for something really wild and different, the four rooms in this converted apartment most certainly fit the bill. Artist and musician Lars Stroschen has created each chamber in a different style. The 'Symbol Room', squared off with 300 wacky graphics, looks like a scene from a computer game. In the 'Burgzimmer' you sleep on top of a castle in a Toontown-type fantasy. The 'Spiegelzimmer' has mirrors hanging like sails in a monochrome blue environment. The tiny 'Zwergenzimmer' is full of garden gnomes. And the minimal 'Orangenes Zimmer' is, well, orange. Guests can prepare their own meals in the equally wacky kitchens or order (three days in advance) one of the two set meals on the 'Aphrodisiac Menu' – 'Nautical Ecstasy' (seafood) or 'Harem Meal' (vegetarian). For DM100 extra you can have live sitar accompaniment or belly dancing. Propeller Island is ideal for two couples travelling together as each pair of rooms shares a bathroom/WC and kitchen which is pretty much self-contained. There are no TVs or phones in the rooms and the owner requires cash payment in advance as well as DM100 key deposit. Excellent place.
http: www.propeller-island.net4.com

Pension Silvia

Knesebeckstraße 29, Charlottenburg, 10623 (881 2129/fax 885 0435). S3, S5, S7, S9, S75 Savignyplatz. **Rates** *single* DM55; *double* DM100-DM200; *rooms for three and four can be made up for an extra DM50 per person; breakfast* DM9,50. **No credit cards. Map C4**
This pension has been in business for 100 years and its present owner, Silvia, is an abrasive Saxon with a story or two to tell about the hotel trade. The 15 rooms range in price from the cheap to the moderate, but they are all large, white and airy and have modern bathrooms. The location is convenient and don't be put off by the shabby dining room. You can get a decent breakfast for little more in many of the nearby cafés.
Hotel services *TV room.*

Taunus Hotel

Monbijouplatz 1, Mitte, 10178 (283 5254/fax 283 5255). S3, S5, S7, S9, S75 Hackescher Markt. **Rates** *single* DM120; *double* DM150; *breakfast included.* **Credit** AmEx, DC, MC, V. **Map F3**
A small hotel in a newly renovated building tucked away behind Hackescher Markt S-Bahn station. The interior is plain but clean and the location is excellent – close to the Museum Insel and an ideal base for exploring Mitte nightlife.

Pension Viola Nova

Kantstraße 146, Charlottenburg, 10623 (313 1457/fax 312 3314). S3, S5, S7, S9, S75 Savignyplatz. **Rates** *single* DM90-DM130; *double* DM120-DM160; *breakfast buffet* DM9,50. **Credit** AmEx, DC, EC, MC, V. **Map C4**
This is a popular touristic area – close to Kurfürstendamm and Savignyplatz nightlife, the Viola Nova is one of many similar pensions in the district. Like the others, this is an old, converted Berlin house; the Viola Nova is notable for its friendly owners, its pleasant breakfast room and its value for money.
Room services *Telephone. TV.*

Hotel-Pension Waizennegger

Mommsenstraße 6, Charlottenburg, 10623 (883 1709/ fax 881 4528). S3, S5, S7, S9, S75 Savignyplatz. **Rates** *single* DM100-DM110; *double* DM140-DM180. **No credit cards. Map C4**

In a delightful residential area, slightly off the beaten track, but still close enough to Savignyplatz to be convenient. The owners have made a real effort to make this a home away from home: six cosy rooms, most with shower and toilet, are filled with overstuffed furniture.

Hotel services *Lift.* **Room services** *Television.*

Hotel Westerland

Knesebeckstraße 10, Charlottenburg, 10623 (312 1004/fax 313 6489). S3, S5, S7, S9, S75 Savignyplatz. **Rates** *single* DM115-DM155; *double* DM150-DM210; *triple* from DM185. **Credit** EC, V. **Map C4**

Despite the forbidding exterior (a seedy-looking sign adorns an even seedier burgundy façade), the interior is really very pleasant. The beautiful wooden reception desk is quite stunning, and the breakfast room and bedrooms keep up the standard. Rooms are provided with either a bath or a shower and are very comfortable – if there were ever anything good on German TV, it would almost be worth forgoing the sights of Berlin to luxuriate in some of their armchairs.

Hotel services *Lift. Parking.* **Room services** *Minibar. Radio. Room service. Safe. Telephone. TV.*

Hotel Märkischer Hof

Linienstraße 133, Mitte, 10115 (282 7155/fax 282 4331). U6 Oranienburger Tor. **Rates** *single* DM95-DM145; *double* DM120-DM195; *triple* DM210. **Credit** EC, V. **Map F3**

A family-run hotel that's well placed by the junction of Friedrichstraße and Oranienburger Straße. You'll be within walking distance of some of Berlin's main attractions – the Berliner Ensemble, the Metropoltheater and the Staatsoper – and some of the city's most beautiful districts. The hotel is quiet and intimate, with friendly staff, comfortable though drab rooms and a pension atmosphere. Recommended.

Hotel services *Parking.* **Room services** *Minibar. Radio. Telephone. TV.*

Budget

Artist Hotel-Pension Die Loge

Friedrichstraße 115, Mitte, 10117 (280 7513). U6 Oranienburger Tor. **Rates** *single* DM60-DM90; *double* DM100-DM130; *apartment* DM160-DM190; *breakfast self-service* DM5 *(before 11am)* or DM10 buffet. **Map F3**

It's not quiet here but you are very much in the thick of things as far as nightlife is concerned. This small, friendly, young pension has special reduced rates for artists and musi-

*The century-old **Pension Silvia**. Page 105.*

cians (DM60) and is perfect for small groups travelling together. WC and showers are shared. There is a cosy foyer with comfy sofas and rooms have decorative friezes and borders painted by the owners themselves.
e-mail: die-loge@t-online.de

Hotel-Pension Charlottenburg

Grolmannstraße 32-33, Charlottenburg, 10623 (881 5254). S3, S5, S7, S9, S75 Savignyplatz. **Rates** *single* DM65-DM95; *double* DM100-DM150. *Special rates for school groups.* **No credit cards. Map C4**

The Charlottenburg is on one of the many roads fanning out from the Savignyplatz. It's small and modern, with 19 adequate rooms, but lacks character.

Hotel services *TV room.*

Hotel-Pension Imperator

Meinekestraße 5, Charlottenburg, 10719 (881 4181/fax 882 5185). U9, U15 Kürfurstendamm. **Rates** *single* DM75-DM105; *double* DM130-DM170; *breakfast* DM12-DM20. **No credit cards. Map C4**

One of the best places to stay in Berlin. The building is a huge townhouse and the Imperator occupies the second floor. Its 11 bedrooms are vast and stylishly furnished with a mixture of antique and modern furniture, and all have modern showers. The breakfast and television rooms are gorgeous and the proprietor's taste in paintings is exquisite. Take a look in the kitchen and you'll find one wall plastered with photos of the jazz musicians and artists who have stayed here, Cecil Taylor and John Cage among them.

Hotel services *Conference facilities. Laundry service. Lift. TV room.* **Room services** *Room service.*

Hotel-Pension München

Güntzelstraße 62, Wilmersdorf, 10717 (854 2226/fax 853 2744). U9 Güntzelstraße. **Rates** *single* DM66-DM110; *double* DM90-DM130; *breakfast* DM9. **Credit** EC, V. **Map C5**

Even though the lift looks suspiciously antiquated, it's better to brave this cage than hike up the stairs to the third floor of this residential building. Owned by artists, this pension features lots of natural wood, modern art, and eight bright, cheerful rooms decorated in red, white and bright floral with modern furniture. It makes a welcome change from the average pension; as does its helpful and friendly owner. A five-minute walk will connect you to the U-Bahn. Recommended.

Hotel services *Garage. Lift.* **Room services** *Telephone. TV.*

Hotel-Pension Trautenau

Trautenaustraße 14, Wilmersdorf, 10717 (861 3514). U9 Güntzelstraße. **Rates** *single* DM40; *double* DM70-DM95. **No credit cards. Map C5**

A cheap pension in a residential neighbourhood, with 12 reasonable rooms at more than reasonable prices. The décor is uniquely tasteless: checkerboard floors in the hallways, mismatched floral themes in the rooms, and framed pictures of kittens on the walls. The rooms are small but clean, and some have a shower in the room. The neurotic proprietoress only speaks German and hates it when anglophone tourists start chatting to her in English. Still, it's very cheap and only a five-minute walk to the U-Bahn station.

Hotel services *Lift.*

Hotel Transit

Hagelbergerstraße 53-54, Kreuzberg, 10965 (789 0470/fax 7890 4777). U6, U7 Mehringdamm. **Rates** *single* DM90; *double* DM105. **Credit** AmEx, EC, MC, V. **Map F5**

A converted factory houses this unexpectedly bright, airy hotel. It's excellently located in one of the most beautiful parts of Kreuzberg, handy for Viktoria Park, a host of cafés and restaurants, and an U-Bahn station to head off elsewhere. The rooms are basic but clean and the DM33 dor-

Wacky and colourful, **Propeller Island City Lodge** *is Berlin's most original hotel. Page 105.*

mitory bed is the best value in town. There's also a 24-hour shower/bag deposit service for early arrivals. Three-bed rooms cost DM140, four-bed rooms DM180, five-bed rooms DM220 and six-bed rooms DM260. All rooms have showers and the friendly staff speak English. An excellent place to stay.
Hotel services *Bar. Laundry service. Lift. TV room.*
Room services *Safe.*

Pension-City Galerie
Leibnizstraße 48, Charlottenburg, 10629 (324 2658/fax 324 2658). U7 Adenauerplatz. **Rates** *single* DM70; *double* DM100-DM120. **No credit cards. Map C4**
A pleasant place that offers the amenities of a small bar and a TV room – rare for a pension of its size. The 11 good-sized rooms are located on the first floor of a pretty, tan-coloured building and three of them have showers. It's a cosy place on a busy street in between Kantstraße and the Ku'damm.
Hotel services *Bar. TV room.*

Pension Finck
Güntzelstraße 54, Wilmersdorf, 10717 (861 2940/fax 861 8158). U9 Güntzelstraße. **Rates** *single* DM60-DM70; *double* DM90-DM100. **No credit cards. Map C5**
Pension Finck is on the third floor of a residential building, and directly above another pension, so make sure you get the right one. It's a homely jumble, with lots of knick-knacks hanging on the walls of the lobby and breakfast room. The 14 good-sized rooms are decorated in the same eclectic fash-

ion as the rest of the place, and eight of them have a shower in the room. The toilets are in the hallway. The friendly owner will let you use her telephone at the main desk. The place is right next to a U-Bahn station.
Hotel services *Lift.*

Pension Kreuzberg
Großbeerenstraße 64, Kreuzberg, 10963 (251 1362). U7 Mehringdamm. **Rates** *single* DM70; *double* DM90; *extra bed* DM30-DM40. **No credit cards. Map F5**
A small, friendly pension in a typical, old Berlin building. It's not for the unfit as there are four very steep flights of stairs to the reception. None of the rooms has its own bathroom: there's a communal one on each floor. The reception has a phone, which you may be allowed to use, and there's a very small breakfast room. Cheap and in a good location.

Studentenhotel Hubertusalle
Delbrückstraße 24, Wilmersdorf, 14193 (891 9718/fax 892 8698). S3 , S7 Grunewald. **Open** March-Oct. **Rates** *single* DM45-DM80; *double* DM70-DM110; *triple* DM90-DM126. **No credit cards. Map A6**
The Studentenhotel is right by the Hubertus lake and a good place to stay in the summer. The building is an ugly 1980s construction, the 60 rooms are plain and functional and you'll be sharing a bathroom on the corridor. You can get a meal in the cafeteria until 10pm. The place is packed all the time, so you'll have to book in advance, but it's worth it for prices like these. It's only a ten-minute ride to the centre of town.
Hotel services *TV room.*

BBC WORLD SERVICE
going abroad ?
pack the BBC
keep up with
news
current affairs
sport
music
internet: http://www.bbc.co.uk/worldservice
e-mail: worldservice.letters@bbc.co.uk
fax: +44 (0) 171 557 1258 / 1254
phone: +44 (0) 171 240 3456
address: PO Box 76
Bush House
London WC2B 4PH
quote reference: TO.Berlin.1

Mitwohnzentralen

The agencies listed below will find you anything from a room in a shared house for a week, to a flat to rent for a couple of years. In summer, when Berlin is less crowded, they are useful for finding short-term accommodation. But it may be more difficult at other times of the year. Most agencies accept advance bookings, so book ahead.

If you're staying for a couple of weeks and manage to find something through a Mitwohnzentrale, you will probably pay DM40-DM80 a night. For longer stays, the agencies charge between three and four per cent of the monthly rent. Private rooms can also be booked through the Berlin Tourismus Marketing (*above*).

Erste Mitwohnzentrale
Sybelstraße 53, Charlottenburg, 10629 (324 3031/fax 324 9977). U7 Adenauerplatz. **Open** 9am-8pm Mon-Fri; 10am-6pm Sat. **Map B4**

Mitwohnzentrale
Joachimstalerstraße 17, Charlottenburg, 19445 (919 445/ fax 8826 6940). U15, U9, Kurfürstendamm. **Open** 9am-6pm Mon-Fri; 11am-2pm Sat, Sun. **Map C4**

Mitwohnzentrale Wohnwitz
Holsteinischestraße 55, Wilmersdorf, 10717 (861 8222/fax 861 8272). U7 Blissestraße. **Open** 10am-7pm Mon-Fri; 11am-2pm Sat. **Map C5**

Rooms at the top

'Keep an eye out for fundamentalists!'

Looking for a place to entrap east European plutonium smugglers in a sting operation? Seeking refuge from Islamic fundamentalists armed with grenade launchers? What about a link to upload the database from the health department of a large Polish city before you bid on taking over its hospitals? The extraordinary **Adlon** has been rebuilt to maintain its tradition of catering to the eccentric needs of sophisticated guests.

The largest suites in the 337-room Adlon have bulletproof windows and bomb-proof walls. Not all suites are outfitted with closed-circuit video security, but standard appointments in each room do include a safe, fax machine, two ISDN telephone lines and an interactive laser disc player.

The original Hotel Adlon, built by Lorenz Adlon with the support of Kaiser Wilhelm II in 1907, created a sensation with such technological advances as flushing toilets, running water and electric light switches. It was a natural draw for overbred, obsessive-compulsive royals and aristocrats from the day it opened, and the Adlon name quickly became synonymous with glamour and chic.

The rebuilt version is not a carbon copy of the old Adlon, it's much brighter and lighter in tone inside, but the lobby is laden with imported marble, rich fabrics, and valuable antiques. The interior decoration, by Ezra Attia of London, is so delicately balanced that a dispute ensued with safety inspectors over their mandatory green exit symbols which rudely invade every vista with their caustic glow.

The original Adlon, which was destroyed at the end of World War II, defined the concept of 'luxury hotel' in Europe. It managed everything from intimate soirees through society receptions to large international conferences. Artists, diplomats, journalists, nabobs of all stripes, if they were influential and had favourable impressions of Berlin, a fair portion of that goodwill was probably earned by the hospitality of the Adlon. The biggest challenge for the Adlon today is not so much competing with the other high-class hotels as living up to its own exalted reputation.

The other challenge is shielding guests from the dodgy street traders outside or the unruly crowds who collect for regular celebrations, like New Year's Eve, on Pariser Platz. So far, room service is declining requests for grenade launchers.

more fun...

BERLIN HOTEL
Transit

Hagelberger Strasse 53–54
10965 Berlin-Kreuzberg
Phone (030) 789 04 70 Fax 789 04 777

TWO YOUNG HOTELS IN BERLIN

Typically Kreuzberg: a hotel in a courtyard. Great atmosphere and guests from all over the world. People get together at the bar. 49 large, well-lit rooms, 1 to 6 beds per room, all with showers. Tasty breakfast. And Berlin's "Scene" right out-side the door.

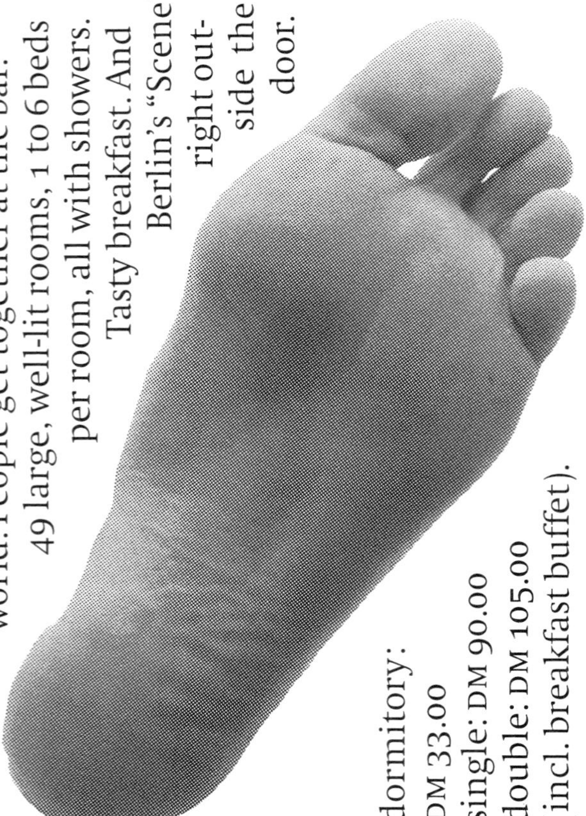

dormitory:
DM 33.00
single: DM 90.00
double: DM 105.00
(incl. breakfast buffet).

*The renovated restaurant at quiet, comfortable **Hecker's**. See page 103.*

Mitwohnzentrale Mehringdamm

Mehringdamm 72, Kreuzberg, 10961 (786 6002/fax 785 0614). U6, U7 Mehringdamm. **Open** 10am-7pm Mon-Fri. **Map F5**

Zeitraum Wohnkonzepte

Horstweg 7, Charlottenburg, 14059 (325 6181/fax 321 9546). U2 Sophie-Charlotte-Platz. **Open** 10am-1pm, 3pm-7pm Mon-Fri. **Map B4**

Youth hostels

Official youth hostels in Berlin (there are three: **Jugendgästehaus-Berlin**; **Jugendgästehaus am Wannsee** and **Jugendheberge Ernst Reuter**) are crammed most of the year so do book ahead. You have to be a member of the YHA for these, which all have single-sex dormitories. At the time of writing there were four new hostels for backpackers under construction: The Backpacker in Köthener Straße by Potsdamer Platz; The Backpacker in Chausseestraße, Mitte; Frederich's in Friedrichshain near Hauptbahnhof; and another 800-bed hostel in Prenzlauer Berg. We had no further details at press time but you should be able to get more information from **Berlin Tourismus Marketing** (*above*) by the time you read this. Otherwise the people at the **Circus Hostel** (*below*) are more than willing to point you towards good value alternatives should they be full.

Mitgliederservice des DJH Berlin-Brandenburg

Tempelhofer Ufer 32, Kreuzberg, 10963 (264 9520/fax 262 0437). U2, U7 Möckernbrucke. **Open** 10am-4pm Mon-Fri.
Otherwise known as the Jugend-Zentrale, this is where you get your YHA membership card. Bring your passport and a passport-sized photo.

Jugendgästehaus-Berlin

Kluckstraße 3, Schöneberg, 10785 (261 1097/8). U2 Kurfürstenstraße. **Rates** DM32 *under-27s*; DM41 *over-27s; breakfast incl.* **Map E4**
Phone for reservations at least two weeks in advance. Sleep in four- to eight-bed dorms.

Jugendgästehaus am Wannsee

Badeweg 1, Zehlendorf, 14129 (803 2034/5). S3 Nikolassee. **Rates** DM32 *under-27s*; DM41 *over-27s; breakfast incl.*
Book as early as possible. Rooms all have four beds.

Jugendheberge Ernst Reuter

Hermsdorfer Damm 48-50, Wedding, 13467 (404 1610). U6 Alt-Tegel, then bus 125. **Rates** DM32 *under-27s*; DM41 *over-27s; breakfast incl.*
Sleep in four- to six-bed dorms.

Jugendgästehaus am Zoo

Hardenbergstraße 9A, Charlottenburg, 10623 (312 9410/fax 401 5283). S3, S5, S6, S7, S9/U2, U9 Zoologischer Garten. **Rates** DM35 a night. No membership required. **Map C4**
Not an official YHA hostel, but not a bad place. Rooms are four- to eight-bed dorms.

Circus Hostel

am Zirkus 2-3, Mitte, 10117 (2839 1433/fax 2839 1484).
U6 Oranienburger Tor/S1, S2, S3, S5, S7, S9, S25, S75,
U6 Friedrichstraße. **Rates** *(per bed per night) DM25 for*
5-bed room; DM25 for 4-bed room; DM28 for 3-bed room;
DM30 for 2-bed room; DM38 for 1-bed room; bedlinen (not
optional) DM3; breakfast not included. **Map F3**
This well-located and newly opened hostel with clean and
bright rooms is heaven for weary travellers on a budget. The
owners are young travellers themselves and have worked
hard to offer good value for money. There is no breakfast,
but if you order in advance they will get deliveries from the
local baker and charge you no more than the cost price. The
hostel is open 24 hours and has single-sex rooms if you want.
The staff strive to help both with your stay and your onward
journey – everything from arranging visas and invites to
Russia to opera tickets and booking your next place of stay.
Their motto is 'If you need help you get it' and disproves all
you have ever heard about grumpy, unhelpful Berliners.
There are only 50 beds so be sure to book. If they are full,
they will suggest alternatives. Highly recommended.
e-mail: circus@mind.de
http: www.mind.de/circus

Camping sites

If you want to explore the camp sites of surrounding Brandenburg, ask for a camping map
from the BTM information offices in Berlin (*above*).
Below we list those within Berlin. They are all
quite far out of town, so check timetables for last
buses if you want to enjoy some nightlife while in
town. Prices don't vary much between sites: for
tents, expect to pay around DM7,50 rent, plus
DM7,50 per person per night: for caravans it's
DM8,50 rent, plus DM7,50 per person per night.

Landesverband des DCC (Deutscher Camping Club)

Geisbergstraße 11, Schöneberg, 10777 (218 6071/72).
Open 10.30am-6pm Mon; 8am-4pm Wed; 8am-1pm Fri.

DCC Kladow

Krampnitzer Weg 111-117, Kladow, 14089 (365 2797).
From Zoo station take Bus 149 to Gatower Straße then
bus 134 south to Krampnitzer Weg then bus 234 (circle
line) to Selbitzer Straße and walk about 6-7 mins
following 'DCC' signs.
Services: *Children's playground. Food shop. Restaurant.*
Shower. Handicapped toilet. Sportsground. Swimming
and bathing in open water.

DCC Dreilinden

Abrechts-Teerofen, Wannsee, 14109 (see 'DDC
Kohlhasenbrück'). From Zoo station take S-Bahn
direction Potsdam, get off at Griebnitzsee, walk back
between station and lake for 20 mins.
Services: *Children's playground. Restaurant. Shower.*

DCC Kohlhasenbrück

Neue Kreisstraße 36, Wannsee, 14109 (805 1737).
From Zoo station take S-Bahn to Griebnitzsee, walk back
between station and lake for ten mins.
Services: *Children's playground. Showers. Laundry*
facilities. Restaurant.

DCC am Krossinsee

Wernsdorfer Straße 45, Köpenick, 12527 (675 8687)
From Zoo station take S-Bahn to Grünau, then Tram 68
to Schmöckwitz, go on by bus 463 to site or walk 20 mins.

Hotel Transit – *a converted factory in one of Kreuzberg's most beautiful corners. Page 107.*

Restaurants

Decent and diverse dining abounds in Berlin – you're sure to spy a Speisekarte to suit.

Berlin is an excellent city for eating. From the lowly sausage stands dispensing Currywurst all over the city to a range of high-quality, top-deutschmark dining-out experiences, the city offers decent eats for every income level. And though traditional German fare maintains its dominance over Berlin's gastronomic life, the city's relatively large immigrant population contribute a vast range of cuisines.

The daily import of fresh ingredients by Berlin's largest ethnic community, for example, guarantees some of the best and most authentic Turkish food outside of Turkey. The city's long-established Italian community, coupled with the German fascination for anything from south of the Dolomites, has resulted in a truly fine spread of Italian restaurants. There are also plenty of Greek, Balkan, Indian, Thai, Russian and Japanese places. Apart from places listed here, however, avoid Berlin Chinese food – it's nearly always awful.

Traditional Berlin cooking is available in pubs, cafés and restaurants all over town and can be heartily splendid value but – based around pork, cabbage, potatoes and still more pork – it's heavy and unhealthy stuff.

Neue deutsche Küche, or new German cuisine, offers some respite with lighter, more imaginative dishes, but remains distinctly inferior to its inspiration, French nouvelle cuisine.

Eating breakfast out is a much-loved tradition in Berlin, and you'll find many places still serving Frühstück – anything from a coffee and croissant to a vast plate of cheeses and cold cuts – until well into the afternoon. Breakfast is more often found in cafés, rather than restaurants, and you'll also find many of them offering reasonably priced light meals. *See also chapter* **Cafés & Bars**.

Lunch is traditionally the day's main meal in Germany, but in Berlin anything goes: whatever you want in the evening – a takeaway snack, a light supper (*Abendbrot*) or a full-blown dinner with all the trimmings – you can find it. This city has a lively dining-out culture. Things are of course a little trickier if you're a vegetarian, but in Berlin, with its large young population and radical political culture, it's never too difficult to find something meatless to eat. *See page 123* **The Hauptstadt for herbivores**.

The eastern side of town still lags behind the west in terms of the diversity of dining options, the quality of food and the overall standard of service, but this gap has been narrowing for years and will continue to do so. Particularly in Mitte and Prenzlauer Berg, east Berlin can now offer a range of eateries that rank among the best in town, even though west Berlin restaurants mostly retain the gastronomic edge if not, these days, the crowds to go with them.

The average prices in our listings – calculated as the cost of one starter and one main course – should be taken as guidelines rather than gospel. We've organised the restaurants in three price bands: Expensive means anything with an average of over DM45; moderate means anything with an average of between DM25-DM44; inexpensive is anything cheaper than that.

Bear in mind that it's possible to eat more cheaply in many of the expensive places, and that adding a bottle or two of wine to your order – rarely cheap in Berlin – is going to hike the cost right up.

We've also included a selection of Imbiße (basically snack bars – some takeaway places, others self-service, sit-down joints) as another route to good gastronomy on a budget.

In restaurants a service charge of 17 per cent is included in the price of a meal, but unless the service has been exceptionally poor, diners usually add an extra tip by rounding up the bill or adding another ten per cent. Tips are handed to the server while paying (or by telling them how much to take) and never left on the table afterwards. Be warned: when you hand over the cash, be careful not to say 'danke' unless you want them to keep the change.

Expensive

Abendmahl

Muskauer Straße 9, Kreuzberg, 10997 (612 5170). U1 Görlitzer Bahnhof. **Open** 6pm-1am daily. **Average** DM45. **No credit cards. Map H4**

The name means 'Last Supper' and the warm decor is enlivened with a little Catholic kitsch. The menu changes regularly and all dishes bear wacky names such as Funf Freunde auf Jesus Trip, Wilkommen in der Wasserlölle and (always on the menu) Flammendes Inferno (Thai fish curry). What you get is inventive and wonderfully presented fish and vegetarian dishes followed by quite spectacular desserts. It's a short menu but the soups are unsurpassable and their seitan dishes alone are worth the trek out to deepest Kreuzberg. Service is charming, efficient and laid-back. An ideal place to linger in good company. Book at weekends.

Maxwell's beautiful façade. See page 116.

Altes Zollhaus
*Carl-Herz-Ufer 30, Kreuzberg, 10961 (692 3300). U1
Prinzenstraße.* **Open** 6pm-11.30pm Tue-Sat. **Average**
Menus at DM80-DM100. **Credit** AmEx, DC, EC, JCB, V.
Map G5
This former customs house on the Landwehrkanal does a
brilliant job of modernising German cuisine, using only the
freshest, locally-grown ingredients, many of them organically-raised. The superb wine-list and attentive service in
pleasant surroundings – plus the healthy-sized portions –
makes this a value-for-money splurge, if that's not something
of a contradiction.

Bamberger Reiter
*Regensburgerstraße 7, Schöneberg, 10777 (218
4282/bistro 213 6733). U4 Viktoria-Luise-Platz.* **Open**
6pm-1am daily. **Kitchen closes** at 10pm. **Average**
DM160, *bistro* DM60. **Credit** AmEx, DC, V; *bistro* no
credit cards. **Map D5**
Franz Raneberger, one of Germany's star chefs, proposes two
set menus of either five or eight courses in this wonderfully
romantic, wood-clad restaurant. Recent delights included
pike-perch, crispy outside and stuffed with tender salmon
and caviar, lamb chops cooked to pink perfection in a
reduced red wine sauce, a cheese board unparalleled in Berlin
and a superb selection of Austrian wines. The adjacent bistro
serves similar food at considerably less painful prices.

Blue Goût
*2nd Hinterhof, Anklamer Straße 38, Mitte, 10115 (448
5840). U8 Rosenthaler Platz.* **Open** noon-1am Mon-Fri,
Sun; 6pm-1am Sat. **Kitchen closes** 11.30pm. **Average**
DM40. *Set menu three courses* DM60. **Credit** AmEx, EC,
MC, V. **Map F2**
A big, airy space with art on the walls and the prices in the
menu, which otherwise includes a good few vegetarian

options among Italian-accented meat and fish dishes. It's a
friendly place, in the second courtyard of the Weiberwirtschaft women's business complex (*see chapter* **Women**)
with a summer garden. A bit out of the way but worth taking the trouble to find. Book at weekends.

Borchardt
*Französische Straße 47, Mitte, 10117 (2039 7117). U6
Französische Straße.* **Open** 11.30am-2am daily. **Kitchen
closes** midnight. **Average** DM60, *lunch* DM45. **Credit**
AmEx, EC, V. **Map F3**
A famous old place now owned by modern-minded Westies
and one of the few central east Berlin restaurants with gen-
uine character: big, airy and bright with mosaics and pillars.
The menu is international with French and Italian influences,
usually including one vegetarian option among the daily specials. It's a popular lunch spot for journalists and diplomats
working in the area. In the evening there are Irish oysters at
DM3,50 apiece and 50g of Persian caviar will set you back
DM135. Courtyard tables in summer.

Bovril
*Kurfürstendamm 184, Charlottenburg, 10707 (881
8461). U7 Adenauer Platz.* **Open** noon-2am Mon-Sat.
Average DM50. **Credit** AmEx, DC, EC, JCB, V. **Map
B5**
A bright bistro on Berlin's magnificent mile, popular among
business, intellectual and artist types – during the film festival it fills out with visiting celebrities – for its selection of light,
German-French meals, exquisitely prepared. The menu
changes daily but the soups are always superb. It's almost
impossible to get a table for their set DM28 lunch, particularly on Saturdays, when it's a favourite after-shopping venue.

Café Einstein
*Kurfürstenstraße 58, Tiergarten, 10785 (261 5096). U1,
U2, U4 Nollendorfplatz.* **Open** 10am-2am daily.
Average DM45. **Credit** AmEx, DC, JCB, V. **Map D4**
Café Einstein models itself on a Viennese coffeehouse, and
the efficient-but-aloof waiters wear tuxedos. Enjoy anything
from one of the wonderful cappuccinos to an expensive if
exquisite full-blown meal, and sit and watch the rest of the
customers. The high-ceilinged main room is always loud and
busy, particularly on Sundays, when Berlin's finest come out
first to sample the famous breakfasts and later to sup
melange and scoff strudel. Summertimes you can eat in the
leafy garden. *See also chapter* **Cafés & Bars**.
Branch: Unter den Linden 42, Mitte, 10117 (204 3632)

Cantamaggio
*Alte Schönhauser Straße 4, Mitte, 10119 (283 1895). U8
Weinmeisterstraße.* **Open** 7pm-midnight daily. **Kitchen
closes** 11.30pm. **Average** DM45. **Credit** DC, V. **Map
G3**
Both the modern Italian menu and the pastel decor punctuated with colourful detail are nicely understated. This is a
bustling place, with a cosmopolitan atmosphere, acquiring
a theatrical atmosphere on weeknights as it draws an after-
show crowd from the nearby Volksbühne. The menu – well-
presented but essentially simple fare – is based around
changing daily specials and familiar regional Italian standards and topped off with an interesting wine list. The only
drawback is the sometimes overstretched service.

Die Quadriga
*Eislebener Straße. 14, Wilmersdorf, 10789 (2140 5650).
U2, S1, S5, S6 Zoologischer Garten.* **Open** 6pm-1am.
Average DM75. **Credit** AmEx, DC, V, MC. **Map D4**
The 'gourmet restaurant' of the Hotel Brandenburger Hof.
Chef Manfred Heissig was named Gault-Millau's 'Discovery
of the Year' in 1996 for his sinfully toothsome, nouvelle-influ-
enced creations such as lobster ravioli with coriander and
shiitake mushrooms. The menu is small, seasonal and
backed-up by a superb wine list. Truly fine dining.

Florian

Grolmanstraße 52, Charlottenburg, 10623 (313 91 84).
S3, S5, S7, S9, S75 Savignyplatz. **Open** 6pm-3am daily.
Kitchen closes at1am. **Average** DM45. **No credit**
cards. Map C4
A light, white restaurant in the attractive area around
Savignyplatz. A sprinkling of celebrities can often be spot-
ted among the members of the film, media and art scene who
cluster around the bar sipping sparkling wine, before sitting
down to order from a small menu of nouvelle European dishes. Nice ambience but overpriced and useless for vegetarians.

Französischer Hof

Jägerstraße 36, Mitte, 10117 (229 3152). U2, U6
Stadtmitte. **Open** 11am-midnight daily. **Average** DM60.
Credit DC, EC, V. **Map F4**
On the splendid Gendarmenmarkt and close to the Hilton
Hotel, the Französischer Hof offers classic German and
French meals. Dress up a bit for this spot; it draws a theatre
and classical music crowd in the evenings.

Hackescher Hof

Rosenthaler Straße 40/41, Mitte, 10178 (283 5293). S3,
S5, S6, S9 Hackescher Markt. **Open** 7am-3am daily.
Kitchen closes 2am. **Average** DM45. **Credit** AmEx,
EC, MC, V. **Map F3**
A huge space at the front of the Hackesche Höfe complex
which was transformed into a hip meeting place for all types
of customers, from the art scene that's taking over the area
to real estate types looking to do the same. Panelled in wood
and furnished with tables with black shiny tops, the room is
tastefully done though it can feel a bit like a canteen when
full of chattering customers. The service is friendly, the food
– new German cuisine – filling if unexceptional. The breakfasts are extremely good and are available early – it's a nice,
quiet time to come. The restaurant's logo and design uses
the old east Berlin traffic-light man. See page 257 **The lit-**
tle traffic light men.

Hakuin

Martin-Luther-Straße 1, Schöneberg, 10777 (218 2027).
U2, U3 Wittenbergplatz. **Open** 4pm-11.30pm Tue-Fri,
except Buddhist holidays; noon-11.30pm Sat, Sun.
Average DM45. **No credit cards. Map D5**
Hakuin provides excellent but expensive Buddhist vegetarian food. In the beautiful no-smoking room people eat quietly amid a jungle of plants and a large fish pool with a gentle
fountain. Fruit curries are often served on bamboo serving
plates, in tune with the décor. Smokers are exiled to a small,
much more boring room next door. A peaceful place.

Hitit

Corner of Danckelmannstraße/Knobelsdorffstraße,
Charlottenburg, 14059 (322 4557). U2 Sophie-Charlotte-
Platz. **Open** noon-1am daily. **Average** DM48. **Credit** V.
Map B4
Completely different from most other Turkish restaurants
in the city, Hitit serves excellent Anatolian/Turkish food in
an elegant setting, complete with Hittite wall-reliefs, stylish
high-backed chairs and pale walls. Choose from over 150
dishes listed, with ample options for vegetarians. Service is
extremely friendly and the atmosphere is calm and sooth-
ing, aided by the small waterfall running down the wall at
the front of the restaurant.

Lubitsch

Bleibtreustraße 47, Charlottenburg, 10623 (882 3756).
U15 Uhlandstraße. **Open** 9.30am-1.30am Mon-Sat; 5pm-
midnight Sun. **Kitchen closes** midnight. **Average**
DM60. **No credit cards. Map C4**
Fashionable feeding trough for the Charlottenburg art crowd
and assorted nouveaux riches – on our last visit the long,
narrow dining area was dominated by an enormous table of
architects. Decor is sleek, service unhurried but profession-

al, food is excellent Neue Deutsche Kuche, perhaps a little
overpriced. Don't sit near the door on a cold evening – opening it wide seems to be their only means of ventilation.

Lutter & Wegner

Schlüterstraße 55, Charlottenburg,10629 (881 3440).
S3, S5, S7, S9, S75 Savignyplatz. **Open** 6.30pm-2am
daily. **Average** DM45. **Credit** AmEx. **Map C4**
Nouvelle cuisine is served elegantly at this Berlin landmark,
established in 1811. It was first a wine cellar in eastern Berlin,
but after World War II re-opened as a restaurant in the West
serving food and selected wines. The enormous wooden bar
and background jazz evoke an old world atmosphere that
attracts a mixed crowd of young and old. Arrogant service
isn't always made up for by the good food and beautiful
ambience: this place definitely has its off nights. But worth
visiting, if only for a drink.

Maxwell

Bergstraße 22, Mitte, 10115 (280 7121). U8 Rosenthaler
Platz. **Open** noon-1am daily. **Kitchen closes** at
midnight. **Average** DM70. *Set menus three courses*
DM60, *five courses* DM92. **Credit** AmEx, DC, EC, MC, V.
Map F2
A western import housed in the beautiful courtyard building of the former Josty brewery, with tables outside in summer. Inside there's both a cosily candle-lit ground floor and
a upper level with a balcony perfect for observing the artistically arranged platefuls of the diners below. This is very
much a see-and-be-seen place at which the light, modern
German menu is good, but disappointing for the price.
(Vegetarians will feel particularly hard-done-by.) Service is
excellent, though. Their interesting art collection includes a
drawing from Damien Hirst's Berlin days.

Modellhut

Alte Schönhauser Straße 28, Mitte, 10119 (283 5511).
U8 Weinmeister Straße. **Open** 6.30pm-2am daily.
Kitchen closes midnight. **Average** DM55. **Credit** V.
Map G3
One of the few new restaurants in Mitte that made the effort
of hiring an architect, and a good one at that. The gold leaf
ceiling and red velvet benches add elegance which for a long
while was not matched by the quality of the food or the service. It was rumoured the kitchen was too high on cocaine to
cope with the orders but a new, sober chef has meanwhile
been appointed and staff make a concerted effort to please a
well-dressed media set. Food is German-French, often merged
with Asian accents. The silver and blue bar downstairs is a
pleasant, quiet place for a digestif (open weekends only).

Paris Bar

Kantstraße 152, Charlottenburg 10623 (313 8052). S3,
S5, S7, S9, S75 Savignyplatz. **Open** noon-1am daily.
Average DM45. **Credit** AmEx. **Map C4**
A classic French bistro that locals either love or hate. The
menu comprises standard, competently cooked French dishes, such as lamb Provençal or soupe de poisson. Art adorns
the walls: some good, some laughable. The waiters are notoriously snooty but can sometimes turn on the charm.
Overrated and ruinously expensive – a dozen Belon Oysters
will set you back a swingeing DM90 – it can nevertheless be
a lot of fun when you get a showbiz crowd in there — for
example, during the Filmfest. Good, quiet lunch spot, too.

Paris Moskau

Alt-Moabit 141, Tiergarten-Moabit, 10557 (394 2081).
S3, S5, S6, S9 Lehrter Stadtbahnhof. **Open** 6pm-
11.30pm daily. **Average** DM60, *set menu* DM70-DM100.
No credit cards. Map E3
Once a railway workers' canteen on the tracks between Paris
and Moscow, this place always has at least one fish dish, and
often poultry and venison with Russian-French influences.
It's fine fare, but all save the most dedicated nouvelle cuisine

*The French bistro **Paris Bar** is a Berlin institution – loved by some and loathed by others.*

fans will blanche at the portion sizes. It used to be a beautiful location, but for the time being it's so near the Lehrter Stadtbahnhof building site that you can hear the construction work while eating.

Sabu
Salzburger Straße 19, Schöneberg, 10825 (787 4483).
U4, U7 Bayerischer Platz. **Open** noon-2pm Mon-Fri;
6pm-midnight daily. **Average** DM45. **Credit** AmEx, EC,
MC, V. **Map D5**
Probably the best Japanese restaurant in Berlin. A smart, white place with a calm atmosphere serving traditional dishes given an individual slant. The tempura is heavenly, the noodle soups are the stuff of legend, and the sushi is so good that this is the restaurant of choice for sushi chefs from other Japanese places. Extravagant set menus hover around DM75. It's on a quiet street and there's a tiny veranda with only a table for two that's wonderful on summer nights, if you can get it.

Sale E Tabacci
Kochstraße 18, Kreuzberg, 10969 (2529 5003). U6
Kochstraße. **Open** 9am-2am daily. **Kitchen closes**
midnight. **Average** DM45. **Credit** AmEx, EC, MC, V.
Map F4
The coolest Italian in town, with a sky-high ceiling and waiters with egos just as lofty. On a bad day customers could be in for a long wait, but in want of a great selection of trendy places to dine they don't seem to care. Standard menu fixtures include fennel and orange salad, inventive pasta combinations and a tiramisu to die for. The fish is always fresh, the vegetables organically grown. A stone's throw from Checkpoint Charlie, it's also a good place for a quick cappuccino.

Schwarzenraben
Neue Schönhauser Straße 13, Mitte, 10178 (2839 1698).
U8 Weinmeister Straße. **Open** *Cafe* from 10am, noon-
3pm lunch, 6.30pm-midnight *dinner; cocktail bar* 9pm-
midnight daily. **Average** DM45. **Credit** AmEx, EC, MC,
V. **Map G3**

An attempt to create a restaurant with world city flair, Schwarzenraben fills out a generous space in a building with a checkered past: it served as a Volkscafe for the poor in the 1890s, a pub peopled by petty thieves and old whores in the 1920s, and a pre-war cinema. Today subdued neutral tones and discreet lighting act as a passepartout for a Gucci-clad, cigar-smoking, model-toting crowd. Bursts of colour are provided by the odd drag queen in pink, or the desserts. As to the food, it's tasty, high-quality Italian cuisine. The selection, however, is limited, as everything is prepared fresh. You can choose from a selection of antipasti and pasta – such as black tagliatelle with jumbo shrimp, cherry tomatoes and basil – but there is only one soup, meat and fish dish offered. After dinner hours, the downstairs Engelspalast bar comes alive. It has a sophisticated, 1950s feel and with English leather arm chairs, good music and 120 cocktails, it is a relaxing place to wind down the evening – or to order a pick-up before heading out to the clubs in the area.

Toto
Bleibtreustraße 55, Charlottenburg, 10627 (312 5449).
S3, S5, S7, S9, S75 Savignyplatz. **Open** noon-midnight
daily. **Average** DM45. **No credit cards**. **Map C4**
A smart Italian place near Savignyplatz, with higher-than-average prices and a short menu. The food is excellent and beautifully prepared. Freshly-made tomato soup and fettuccine with wild mushrooms are both worth spending your Deutschmarks on, and the tiramisu and zabaglione come highly recommended. Service can be chaotic, but it all fits in well with the checked-tablecloth, anything-goes mood of the place.

Udagawa
Feuerbachstraße 24, Steglitz, 12163 (792 2373). S1
Feuerbachstraße. **Open** 6pm-1am daily. **Kitchen closes**
11pm. **Average** DM48. **Credit** AmEx, DC, JCB, MC, V.
The Japanese cooking here well justifies the journey to snoresville Steglitz – sparkling-fresh sushi and sashimi, light and delicate tempura and the whole panoply of classic (and pricey) dishes from the Land of the Rising Yen.

Café Aroma: wake up and smell the coffee.

Vau

Jägerstraße 54-55, Mitte, 10117 (202 9730). U6
Französische Straße. **Open** noon-midnight Mon-Sat.
Average DM85. *Set menus five-courses* DM98, *six-courses* DM179. **Credit** AmEx, DC, EC, MC, V. **Map F4**
Beautifully designed in a modern but conservative style, with dark pillars, dull metal fittings and an arched ceiling, Vau is both innovative and formal. Somehow it's more like London or New York than Berlin – both for the thoughtfulness and quality of its nouvelle international dishes and for the elegantly wealthy crowd who can afford them. The downstairs room is the best feature, with a gorgeous circular bar and lined with what appear to be books but turn out to be bricks of coal. Game is a speciality; vegetarians should go somewhere else. The wine list is huge and authoritative, including a lot of half-bottles and a magnum of Chateau Latour 1961 for DM6,900. Go on, live a little! Service is smooth but perhaps sometimes a little glib.

Moderate

Al Contadino Sotto Le Stelle

Auguststraße 34, Mitte, 10119 (281 9023) U8
Rosenthaler Platz. **Open** 12pm-2am Sun, Tue-Thu; 12pm-3am Fri, Sat. **Average** DM35. **No credit cards. Map F3**
Small, excellent Southern Italian eatery run by a family who make you feel right at home. Huge portions, impeccably prepared and presented, with an authenticity rare in Berlin. It's also open for late dining. They barely speak German, let

alone English, but that hasn't stopped the place from becoming wildly popular: reservations are essential.

Brazil

Gormannstraße 22, Mitte, 10119 (2859 9026). U8
Weinmeisterstraße. **Open** 5pm-2am Mon-Sun. **Average**
DM35. **No credit cards. Map G3**
Usually loud and terribly full, this L-shaped bar and restaurant on a street just off Rosenthaler Straße offers assorted Brazilian dishes – including feijoada, the national dish, a hearty bean stew with chicken.

Café Addis

Tempelhofer Ufer 6, Kreuzberg, 10963 (251 6730). U1,
U6 Hallesches Tor. **Open** 4pm-1am Wed-Mon. **Average**
DM27. **No credit cards. Map F5**
Berlin's small Ethiopian community has turned a funky neighbourhood bar into a first-rate showpiece for its exotic cuisine, spicy stews served on ingera, a towel-like bread. Scoop up bits of the hearty food with your hands from the tray in the centre of your table, and make sure there's a beer (or some homemade Ethiopian honey wine) nearby!

Café Aroma

Hochkirchstraße 8, Schöneberg, 10829 (782 5821).
U7/S1, S2 Yorckstraße. **Open** noon-midnight Mon-Sat;
11am-midnight Sun. **Average** DM35. *Lunch menu*
DM20. **No credit cards. Map E5**
Run by ever so slightly spaced-out young Italians, most of whom enjoy a laugh, this neighbourhood restaurant is always a hubbub of activity and conversation. But though crowded and occasionally a little chaotic, the Sicilian food here is always excellent and the salads are particularly inventive. It's on a quiet, leafy street and there are tables outside in summer. Interesting wine list. Buffet brunch on Sundays, which can be combined with Italian lessons.

Café Oren

Oranienburger Straße 28, Mitte, 10117 (282 8228). S1,
S2 Oranienburger Straße. **Open** 10am-1am daily.
Kitchen closes midnight daily, except 12.30am Sat.
Average DM25. **No credit cards. Map F3**
A Jewish (not kosher) restaurant right next to the New Synagogue and offering inventive fish and vegetarian Middle Eastern specialities. The garlic cream soup is thick and tasty; the salad fresh and crispy; and the soya cutlet breaded with sesame, in a light curry sauce served with fried banana and rice, is heavenly. There's excellent vegetarian borscht and the Orient Express platter, a large selection of meze, is good value at DM17,50. As bustly as Oranienburger Straße outside, it's best to book. Summer tables in the courtyard.

Café Restaurant Jolesch

Muskauerstraße 1, Kreuzberg, 10997 (612 3581). U1
Schlesisches Tor. **Open** 10am-1am daily. **Kitchen
closes** 11.30pm. **Average** DM30. **No credit cards.
Map H4**
Deservedly popular spot serving brilliant interpretations of Austrian cuisine: the goulash is thick with hot paprika and caraway, and the Tafelspitz is tender. There are always at least a couple of inventive vegetarian entrées on the daily menu, and the soups, too, can be ingenious. Dinner reservations suggested.

Casa Portuguesa

Helmholzstraße 15, Moabit, 10587 (393 5506). U9
Turmstraße. **Open** 6pm-1am daily. **Average** DM38. **No
credit cards. Map D3**
Do what the regulars do – despite a commendable bacalhau (salt cod – 24 hours' notice required) ignore the menu and order a fresh salad, an honest vinho verde and whatever fish is chalked up on the board to experience the best grilled fish in Berlin.

*Barkeeper 'Opa' Omar mans the pumps at **Gugelhof**.*

Carpe Diem
Savigny Passage 577, Charlottenburg, 10623 (313 2728). S3, S5, S7, S9, S75 Savignyplatz. **Open** noon-midnight Tue-Sat. **Average** DM40, *set lunch* DM18. **No credit cards. Map D4**
Tapas and other Mediterranean specialities are served under the S-Bahn arches in this imaginatively designed restaurant. The tables are a little too close together for comfort, but it's a lively place with loud music and effusive service. Stick to the tapas and stay away from the menu – it's too expensive and the tapas is better.

Diekmann
Meineckestraße 7, Charlottenburg, 10719 (883 3321). U9, U15 Kurfürstendamm. **Open** noon-1am Mon-Sat; 6pm-1am public holidays. **Average** DM35. *Set menu* DM50. **No credit cards. Map C4**
Just off the Kurfürstendamm, this is a former grocer's shop remodelled into a comely restaurant. It's a big, relaxing space in which they've kept most of the old shop fittings and even have a few odd products adorning the ornate shelves – though these have clearly been chosen for their attractive and colourful packaging, you can also actually buy some of the stuff. The menu, which changes daily, comprises hearty portions of fine German cuisine. The wine list is long, the music classical and the service both friendly and multilingual.

Eiffel
Kurfürstendamm 105, Charlottenburg, 10711 (891 1305). Bus 119, 219, 129 Joachim-Friedrich-Straße. **Open** 9am-2am. **Average** DM35. **Credit** AmEx, EC, V. **Map B5**
Designed with originality, taste and a minimalism that does indeed recall the works of the 'magician of iron' whose name it bears, this restaurant is a pleasant place to have breakfast, lunch or dinner. It offers value-for-money French bistro-style food and does excellent salads. There is a different lunchtime special every day. On the far western stretch of the Kufürstendamm as it rises towards Halensee, it's convenient for meals before, during or after visits to the trade fair grounds. In summer the restaurant stretches out on to the pavement.

Ganymed
Schiffbauerdamm 5, Mitte, 10117 (2859 9046). U6, S1, S2, S3, S5, S6, S7, S9 Friedrichstraße. **Open** 11am-1am Mon-Fri; 9am-1am Sat, Sun. **Average** DM30. **No credit cards. Map F3**
Wine is the star at this renovated holdover from the GDR, the anchor of Mitte's new Restaurant Row. Nothing wrong with the food, either; it's simply not too innovative. Nor need it be, serving as a foil for the small, but exquisitely-chosen list of wines, with an emphasis on German medal-winners.

Gorgonzola Club
Dresdener Straße 121, Kreuzberg, 10999 (615 6473). U1 Kottbusser Tor. **Open** noon-midnight Mon-Thur, Sun; noon-2am Fri-Sat. **Average** DM30. **No credit cards. Map G4**
Relaxed and popular place with a simple Italian menu. In front there's a bar area with tables where you can eat. An appealing main dining area leads through to a rather gloomy back room which is best avoided. Authentic pizzas run between DM9-DM17. Spaghetti, tagliatelli, gnocchi and ravioli are all served with a choice of basic sauces including, of course, gorgonzola. The salad selection is excellent. Handy before or after an English-language movie at the Babylon (*see chapter* **Film**) down the road.

Gugelhof
Knaackstraße 37, Prenzlauer Berg, 10435 (442 9229). U2 Senefelder Platz. **Open** 9am-1am daily. **Average** DM35. *Set menus* DM37, DM53. **Credit** AmEx, DC, EC, MC, V. **Map G2**
On a corner of Kollwitzplatz, a busy establishment that packs them in with South German and Alsatian cuisine. It has a long and complicated meat-heavy menu with a couple of fish and vegetarian options. Specialities include fondue and an excellent Raclette – smoked cheese grilled on a table-top contraption then dished out over baked potatoes and served with pickled onions. Biggest drawback is the lack of elbow room – there really are too many tables for the space – but the bar is generously proportioned and staffed by some of the best in Berlin. (Try a Trester – the German version of grappa.) Frequented by local artists and actors during the week, it fills with tourists and west Berliners at weekends.

Hard Rock Café

Meineckestraße 21, Charlottenburg, 10719 (884 620).
U9, U15 Kurfürstendamm. **Open** noon-2am daily.
Average DM35. **Credit** AmEx, DC, EC, JCB, V. **Map C4**
Very loud, very air-conditioned and pretty pricey, the Hard
Rock can at least boast authentic hamburgers, dozens of
cocktails, good desserts, and the usual load of boring mem-
orabilia from rock stars you would rather forget about.

Heinrich

Sophie-Charlotten Straße 88, Charlottenburg, 14059
(321 6517). U2 Sophie-Charlotte-Platz. **Open** noon-1am
daily. **Average** DM30. **Credit** EC, V. **Map B4**
Named after satirist and illustrator Heinrich Zille, who used to
live at this address, this is the only place in Berlin where you'll
find horse ragout on the same menu as buckwheat pancakes.
A wide spread of vegetarian options rubs shoulders with traditional German standbys and original wooden fittings are
interspersed with Zille's photos of the area at the turn of the
century. Service is courteous and unhurried, wine list is long,
the cheese soup and dandelion salads are particularly good.

India Haus

Feurigstraße 38 (corner Dominicusstraße), Schöneberg,
10827 (781 2546). U4 Rathaus Schöneberg. **Open** 5pm-
midnight Mon-Fri; noon-1am Sat, Sun. **Average** DM25.
Credit DC, EC, V. **Map D6**
Though more and more places are opening, Berlin is not
a great town for Indian food. India Haus is a cut above
most of them. Just off Schöneberg's Hauptstraße, it offers
a long menu, with wide choices for vegetarians. The
almond soup is excellent and the malay kofta delicious,
but avoid the chicken tikka – the bird comes dry and the
sauce is too hot. In the Imbiß part you can stand and eat
cheaply from a smaller menu, before nipping round the
corner to catch a movie in English at the Odeon (*see chapter* **Film**).

Istanbul

Knesebeckstraße 77, Charlottenburg, 10623 (883 2777).
S3, S5, S7, S9, S75 Savignyplatz. **Open** noon-midnight
daily. **Average** DM40. **Credit** AmEx, DC, EC, JCB, MC,
V. **Map C4**

What's on the menu .

The traditional Berlin menu revolves around a
holy trinity of pork, cabbage, and potatoes.
Locals say the signature dish is Eisbein, an
incredibly fatty hunk of pork, but this may be a
ploy to frighten non-Berliners. Although many
restaurants have English translations for their
menus, not all are terribly accurate: we still
remember the Chinese place with the sign in its
window declaring 'We have Crap!' Best, then, to
absorb a little vocabulary before venturing out.

Useful Phrases

I'd like to reserve a table for... people. **Ich möchte
ein Tisch für... Personen reservieren.**
Are these places free? **Sind diese Plätze frei?**
The menu, please. **Die Speisekarte, bitte.**
I am a vegetarian. **Ich bin Vegetarier.**
I am a diabetic. **Ich bin Diabetiker.**
We'd/I'd like to order. **Wir möchten/Ich möchte
bestellen.**
We'd/I'd like to pay. **Bezahlen, bitte.**

Basics

Frühstück breakfast
Mittagessen lunch
Abendessen dinner
Imbiß snack
Vorspeise appetizer
Hauptgericht main course
Nachspeise dessert
Besteck silverware
Brot/Brötschen bread/rolls
Butter butter
Ei/Eier egg/eggs
Spiegeleier fried eggs
Ruhreier scrambled eggs
Gemüse vegetables
Käse cheese
Fleisch meat
Fisch fish
Obst or Fruchte fruit
Nudeln/Teigwaren noodles/pasta

Soße sauce
Salz salt
Pfeffer pepper
Gekocht boiled
Gebraten fried
Paniert sautéed
Nach...Art in the style of...

Soups (Suppen)

Bohnensuppe bean soup
Brühe broth
Erbsensuppe pea soup
Hühnersuppe chicken soup
Klare Brühe mit Leberknödle clear broth with
liver dumplings
Kraftige Brühe mit Flädle hearty broth with
sliced pancakes
Linsensuppe lentil soup

Meat, Poultry, and Game (Fleisch, Geflügel, und Wild)

Ente duck
Ganse goose
Hackfleisch ground meat
Hirsch venison
Huhn/Huhnerfleisch chicken
Hänchen chicken (when served in one piece)
Kaninchen rabbit
Hasen hare
Kohlrouladen cabbage-rolls stuffed with pork
Kotelett chop
Lamm lamb
Leber liver
Nieren kidneys
Puten turkey
Rindfleisch beef
Sauerbraten marinated roast beef
Schinken ham
Schnitzel thinly-pounded piece of meat, usually
breaded and sautéed
Schweinebraten roast pork
Schweinefleisch pork
Speck lean bacon
Truthahn turkey

The oldest Turkish restaurant in Berlin serves well-cooked meals at inflated prices. The menu is extensive, offering a wide selection of starters, meat and fish dishes: vegetarians can opt for a selection of hot and cold meze. From the street you can't see inside: open the door and you could almost be in Constantinople. The interior is dark and lavishly decorated with all manner of Islamic and Turkish paraphernalia. At the weekends belly-dancers perform in the room at the back.

Kamala Siam Kellerspeisebar

Oranienburger Straße 69, Mitte, 10117 (283 2797). U6 Oranienburger Tor. **Open** 1.30pm-midnight daily. **Average** DM27. **Credit** AmEx, DC, EC, V. **Map F3**

Cousin of **Mao Thai** in Prenzlauer Berg (*below*), this labyrinthine white cellar is cramped but they cram you in. There are slim pickings for vegetarians on an otherwise long and varied menu of beef, chicken, pork, duck and fish dishes – try the Pla Thod Grab Lad Prig (DM19), fried pike-perch in a sweet and sour sauce, or go for one of the excellent noo-

dle dishes. Service can be a bit scattier than at their flagship branch, mainly because the warrenous space means you're often out of the waitstaff's sight. Useful location just down the road from the Neue Synagogue and on one of Mitte's main nightlife drags.

Kashmir Palace

Marburger Straße 14, Charlottenburg, 10789 (214 2840). U2 Augsburger Straße. **Open** noon-midnight Sat, 5pm-midnight Sun, Mon, holidays, noon-3pm & 6pm-midnight Tue-Fri. **Average** DM30. **Credit** AmEx, DC, EC, JCB, V. **Map D4**

Possibly the best Indian food in town. In a city where there's no lack of Indian places to eat but a definite deficit of good ones, this up-market curry house is a life saver if you're in bad need of an authentic Mughlai or tandoori dish. The portions are small, the setting is formal and the clientele can include anyone from business-talking Indians to travel story-swapping trekkers of the subcontinent just back from their latest expedition. No one eats with their fingers here.

Wachtel quail
Wurst sausage

Fish (Fisch)

Aal eel
Forelle trout
Garnelen prawns
Hummer lobster
Kabeljau cod
Karpfen carp
Krabben crab or shrimp
Lachs salmon
Makrele mackerel
Matjes raw herring
Miesmuscheln mussels
Schellfisch haddock
Scholle plaice
Seezunge sole
Tintenfisch squid
Thunfisch tuna
Venusmuscheln clams
Zander pike-perch

Herbs and Spices (Kräuter und Gewürze)

Basilikum basil
Kümmel caraway
Kurbiskerne pumpkin-seeds
Mohn poppy-seed
Nelken cloves
Origanum oregano
Petersilie parsley
Sonnenblumekerne sunflower seeds
Thymian thyme
Zimt cinnamon

Vegetables (Gemüse)

Bohnen beans
Bratkartoffeln fried potatoes
Brechbohnen green beans
Champignons mushrooms
Erbsen green peas
Erdnüsse peanuts
Feldsalat lamb's lettuce

Gurke cucumber
Kartoffel potato
Knoblauch garlic
Knödel dumpling
Kohl cabbage
Kurbis pumpkin
Linsen lentils
Möhren carrots
Paprika peppers
Pommes chips
Rosenkohl Brussels sprouts
Rote Bete beetroot
Rotkohl red cabbage
Salat lettuce
Saltzkartoffeln boiled potatoes
Schwarzwurzel comfrey root
Spargel asparagus
Steinpilzen boletus mushrooms
Tomaten tomatoes
Zwiebeln onions

Fruit (Obst)

Ananas pineapple
Apfel apple
Apfelsinen orange (increasingly rare)
Birne pear
Erdbeeren strawberries
Granatapfel pomegranate
Heidelbeeren blueberries
Himbeeren raspberries
Kirsch cherry
Limette lime
Stachelbeeren gooseberries
Zitrone lemon

Drinks (Getränke)

Bier beer
Glühwein mulled wine
Kaffee coffee
Mineralwasser mineral water
Saft juice
Tafelwasser still water
Tee tea
Wein wine

Monday - Sunday 9.00 - 1.00
Sunday Brunch-Buffet
Terrace Seating

Crellestr. 17 10827 Berlin

Tel 781 92 30 FAX 782 06 92

Café Restaurant

The Hauptstadt for herbivores

Germany is notoriously tough for vegetarians, but Berlin is big and cosmopolitan enough to offer meat-free dishes in all price ranges.

First, though, forget traditional German restaurants. If you're lucky you might find an omelette or *Gemüseplatte* – an uninspiring plate of boiled vegetables, occasionally topped off with a slimy boiled egg – but the former will likely be fried in lard and the latter boiled in meat stock. There is also a tendency to sprinkle Speck – pieces of fatty bacon – in anything that doesn't otherwise have meat in it. Presumably this is done according to the notion that a meal without meat isn't a 'proper' eating experience, but this fails to square with a tendency to assure guests that, say, the plain omelette is entirely flesh-free, and then serve the sucker up positively riddled with bacon bits. Ham, for many in Germany, apparently doesn't 'count' as meat.

Neue deutsche Küche places are just as bad. Some of the best and most expensive restaurants in Berlin can offer nothing but asparagus or wild mushroom dishes, and those only when said vegetables are in season (June and September/October respectively).

The best bet is to stick to non-German cuisines: Italian, Indonesian, Greek, Turkish, Indian, Japanese, Lebanese, Mexican and Thai places should all have something more interesting than a salad. So should most of the cooler cafés. Handy phrases to remember are Ich bin (Wir sind) Vegetarier (I am/we are vegetarian); Ich möchte kein Fleisch/keinen Fisch essen (I don't want to eat any meat/fish); Gibt es Fleisch darin? (Is there meat in it?); and Ohne Fleischbrühe (Without meat stock). Bear in mind though, that in a lot of places, especially on the east side, you may be met with blank stares or be taken for a raving lunatic.

Finally, there are one or two top-notch vegetarian places in Berlin – check the listings for **Abendmahl**, **Hakuin** and **Samadhi** – but we've also tried to note which other restaurants of our selection are happy to harbour herbivores.

Kathmandu

Bundesallee 161, Wilmersdorf, 10715 (854 5793). U9, S45 Bundesplatz. **Open** 5pm-midnight Mon-Fri; noon-midnight Sat, Sun. **Average** DM25. **Credit** V. **Map C6**
Germany's first Tibetan-Nepalese restaurant is a find: dome-shaped, ravioli-like momos, a bean soup fit for the Dalai Lama, and a wide range of exotically-seasoned vegetarian and meat dishes. On Tuesday and Thursday there's an all-you-can-eat dinnertime 'Dharma Buffet' for DM15, helpful for students and others on the path of dharma, or else just short on cash, which is the same thing.

Kellerrestaurant im Brecht Haus

Chausseestraße 125, Mitte, 10115 (282 3843). U6 Oranienburger Tor. **Open** 6pm-midnight daily. **Average** DM30. **Credit** AmEx, DC, EC, V. **Map F3**
A small restaurant in the cellar of the house where Brecht lived until his death in 1956. The dark-brown, wooden interior is covered with model stage sets and photographs of Brecht. Some of the dishes (designated on the menu by an asterix) are taken from the cookbook of Helene Weigel, the actress and Brecht's wife. These include roast beef with horseradish sauce, coated in an egg pancake, and fried pork and beef patties, served with green beans and bacon dumplings. Vegetarians may find little, but the creamy cheese soup is recommended. Nice salads too. The wine cellar offers a good selection of French, Italian, German, Portuguese and Californian wines, with prices ranging from DM24 to DM480 for a 1943 Château la Caillon.

Kien-du

Kaiser-Friedrich-Straße 89, Charlottenburg, 10585 (341 1447). U2 Sophie-Charlotte-Platz. **Open** 6pm-midnight Mon-Fri; 4.30pm-midnight Sat, Sun. **Average** DM30. **No credit cards. Map B4**
Despite recent redecoration it still doesn't look much – lots of Buddhas and other south-east Asian paraphernalia littered about – but without question Kien-du serves the best Thai curries in town. There's a huge selection of them too, and though the selection for vegetarians is small, it's very good indeed. Try the beef, potatoes and peanuts in hot yellow sauce or the curried pineapple, bamboo and peppers – then take the edge off with a Singha beer. They're extremely flexible here, and happy to prepare things to your specifications.

Lusiada

Kurfürstendamm 132A, Wilmersdorf, 10711 (891 5869). U7 Adenauerplatz. **Open** 5pm-2am Mon-Wed; 5pm-3am Thur-Sat; 5pm-midnight Sun. **Average** DM25. **No credit cards. Map B5**
A chaotic but nonetheless welcoming restaurant, appealing to prominent Berliners. They come for the laid-back atmosphere and fine Portuguese fish dishes. Great when it's late: you can still eat at 3am.

Marjelichen

Mommsenstraße 9, Charlottenburg, 10629 (883 2676). S3, S5, S7, S9, S75 Savignyplatz. **Open** 5pm-2am Mon-Fri; 5pm-3am Sat; noon-midnight Sun. **Average** DM45. **Credit** DC, EC, JCB, MC, V. **Map C4**
There aren't many places like this anymore. Excellent specialities from East Prussia, Pomerania and Silesia are served here. The atmosphere is one of German Gemütlichkeit (comfort and conviviality): there's a beautiful bar, service is great and the larger-than-life owner likes to recite poetry and sings sometimes, too.

Merhaba

Hasenheide 39, Kreuzberg, 10967 (692 1713). U7 Südstern. **Open** 4pm-midnight Sun-Fri, noon-midnight Sat. **Average** DM40. **Credit** AmEx, V. **Map G5**
A Turkish hot-spot heavy on authentic wines and traditional food. Ignore the main courses and share a selection of spicy appetisers instead. Effusive service but uninspiring decor of mirrors and chrome.

Meat on the street

Berlin's street food can be summed up in two concepts sticks of meat (sausages) and meat on a stick (döner kebab and its relatives). There's not much variety, but subtleties abound.

There are as many kinds of sausages as there are towns in Germany, but here, all you have to remember is red and white. The white *Bratwurst*, the best of which comes from Thuringia, is omnipresent – 'grilled' (which usually means fried) and served with a squirt of mustard and curling out of a bread-roll which is more of a holder than anything. The red includes *Jagdwurst*, also 'grilled', and steamed *Bockwurst* and *Weinerwurst*, which are sold with a smear of mustard and eaten with the hands.

But Berlin's masterpiece is the *Currywurst*, a concoction which sounds so horrible that many are impelled to try it – and wind up liking it. This is either a white or red sausage, deep fried, carved into sections, dusted with curry powder, and smothered with warm ketchup, onions optional. Go ahead – we dare you.

The ubiquitous kebab is purveyed in many forms. Most common is the *Döner*, sold by Turks in either leaf-style (thin slices of beef piled on top of each other) or the more common solid style. Whichever one it is, the ritual remains the same: the vendor takes a quarter of a *peda* – a flat, round Turkish loaf – toasts and presses it, carves thin pieces from the cylinder of meat, and puts them into the bread along with grated lettuce, cabbage, tomatoes, cucumber slices and any of a number of sauces.

The Greeks have *gyros*, which is pork, served with *tzatziki*, a garlicky yogurt sauce, and the Palestinians have *schwarma*, which is lamb seasoned with black pepper and served in a thinner pita bread. Both Turkish and Palestinian places serve falafel, but the Turkish kind is pre-fab and often seems made from compressed wood-chips, while the Palestinians make it fresh on the spot, and often offer a small glass of mint tea for you to drink while it's being made.

Other offers at the Imbiß, or snack-bar, can include the *Boulette*, a hamburger-shaped patty often described, because of its high breadcrumb quotient, as a war between the butcher and the baker which the baker won, and the *Nacksteak*, an incredibly tough piece of whole pork. Chips (*Pommes*) are offered red (with ketchup) or white (with mayonnaise), the latter to the horror of cholesterol-watchers. Turks have a number of other kebaps, including aubergine, zucchini and egg, as well as the *Börek*, a virtually tasteless flaky pastry stuffed with cheese or spinach, and the *Lahmancun*, inaccurately described as 'Turkish pizza'.

Whatever your choice, mild indigestion will be your companion for the next few hours, but you'll be full. After all, that's what street-food is about.

Mesa

Paretzer Straße 5, Wilmersdorf, 10713 (822 5364).U1 Heidelberger Platz. **Open** 4pm-midnight daily. **Average** DM35. **No credit cards**. **Map C6**
Out of the way but worth the effort if Middle Eastern food is what you're after. This classy Lebanese restaurant serves up neat variations on the usual staples. There are lots of lamb and chicken dishes, couscous, and plenty for vegetarians – try the vegetable Rosti that comes with three dipping sauces (DM15) and the spicy lentil soup. It's a classy kind of place, elegant and with a relaxed atmosphere. Egyptian cigarettes are on sale and free Lebanese Chiclets arrive with the bill.

Mao Thai

Wörther Straße 30, Prenzlauer Berg, 10405 (441 9261). U2 Senefelder Platz. **Open** noon-3pm, 6pm-midnight Mon-Sat; noon-midnight Sun. **Average** DM27. **Credit** AmEx, DC, JCB, MC, V. **Map G2**
The flagship of what's becoming an empire (*see above* **Kamala**), Mao Thai may not be the best Thai restaurant in town, but it is one of the prettiest. What the food lacks in fire, it makes up for in presentation and careful preparation, and its signature dish, chicken cooked in a coconut, is both unusual and delicious. Service is tops, and the main problem is getting a table, so reserve.

Offenbach-Stuben

Stubbenkammerstraße 8, Prenzlauer Berg, 10437 (445 85 02). S8, S10 Prenzlauer Allee. **Open** 6pm-2am daily. **Average** DM45. **Credit** AmEx, DC, EC, JCB, MC, V. **Map G1**
Back in communist times this was a rare private restaurant and considered the most desirable place in which to be seen eating in Prenzlauer Berg. The cuisine is fairly international (steaks and roasts and the like); the décor is 1950s in style. Best to book.

Osteria No 1

Kreuzbergstraße 71, Kreuzberg, 10965 (786 9162). U6 Platz der Luftbrücke. **Open** noon-midnight daily. **Average** DM40. **Credit** AmEx, V. **Map F5**
There are a lot of good Italian restaurants in this neighbourhood. This one's just near the foot of the Kreuzberg waterfall. Light, bright and crowded in the evenings with a young, groovy crowd tucking into delicious, if a mite over-priced, Italian food. It does have its off nights, depending on which waiter you get. A popular Sunday lunch spot.

Ostwind

Husemannstraße 13, Prenzlauer Berg, 10435 (441 5951). U2 Senefelder Platz. **Open** 11am-midnight daily. **Average** DM25. **No credit cards**. **Map G2**

Good Chinese food is rare in Berlin, so Ostwind's stabs at authenticity are welcome. True, some of it is pretty bland, but such light dishes as dan-dan noodles sauced with spicy meat and bean-sauce and steamed dumplings with pork and vegetables make a great lunch. Main courses are, by Chinese tradition, keyed to the seasons, and change four times a year. It's not all great, but if you choose carefully, you can be rewarded with superb country cooking of a sort rarely found in Chinese restaurants anywhere.

Pasternak
Knaackstraße 22-24, Prenzlauer Berg, 10405 (441 3399). U2 Senefelder Platz. **Open** noon-2am Mon-Sat, 10am-3am Sun. **Average** DM27. **No credit cards.** **Map G2**
Book at least a day in advance if you want to dine in this small bar and Russian restaurant on Prenzl'berg's chicest corner: it's always crammed to the gunnels, which can be irritating as people constantly brush past you looking for places. Try for a table in the small back room. They also let buskers in to play, so avoid if you don't want ancient Neil Young songs strummed in your left ear. But the atmosphere is friendly and the food fine and filling. Kick off with the Borscht (DM9,50) or the ample fish plate (smoked salmon, trout, mussels and sprats, DM17,50). Then broach the Pelmeni or Wareniki (DM18,50) – sort of Russki ravioli filled with either meat or potatoes – or the hearty Beef Stroganoff (DM26,50).

Ristorante Chamisso
Willibald-Alexis-Straße 25, Kreuzberg, 10965 (691 5642). U6 Platz der Luftbrücke. **Open** 6pm-1am daily. **Average** DM30. **No credit cards.** **Map F5**
This excellent and charming Italian neighbourhood joint on picturesque Chamissoplatz – a wonderfully quiet and leafy spot to sit outside in summer – offers daily menus of fresh pastas, inventive salads and other authentic Italian dishes.

Restauration 1900
Husemannstraße 1, Prenzlauer Berg, 10435 (442 2494) U2 Senefelder Platz. **Open** noon-2am daily **Average** DM30. **Credit** AmEx, EC. **Map G2**
Long gone are the days when you could have a satisfying meal here and pay for it with cheapo Eastmarks, but this landmark private business from the GDR days is still going strong. The food (basically German with Italian touches) is mediocre, but it still fills up – these days mostly with tourists and out-of-towners.

Samadhi
Goethestraße 6, Charlottenburg, 10623 (313 1067). U2 Ernst-Reuter-Platz. **Open** noon-3pm, 6pm-11pm Mon-Fri; 6pm-11pm Sat. **Average** DM33. *Lunch menu* DM14. **No credit cards.** **Map C4**
Small and subdued place serving an international selection of east Asian vegetarian specialities. Dishes are drawn from Thailand, Indonesia, Japan, China, Korea and Vietnam and include the likes of an excellent wun-tun soup, Thai papaya salad and tofu beautifully baked with sesame seeds and served with a peanut and chilli sauce. Dishes marked with a star are served 'sharp as your desire'. There are Asian beers to match and an interesting selection of teas. Saturday is non-smokers' night. Distressingly schmaltzy muzak is the only real drawback.

Santiago
Wörtherstraße 36, Prenzlauer Berg, 10435 (441 2555) U2 Senefelder Platz. **Open** 6pm-2am at least, Mon-Fri; 10am-3am Sat, Sun. **Average** DM35. **Credit** AmEx, EC. **Map G2**
Restauration 1900, next door (*above*), was started by a German woman and her Chilean husband, and this sister restaurant/bar is his baby. Typically, the menu is grilled

steaks and chops, but it's got a better wine list than 1900, and as a lunch stop, it's good value: try the empanada (South American meat pie) with its zingy chilli sauce, or one of the big baguette sandwiches.

Skales
Rosenthaler Straße 12, Mitte, 10119 (283 3006). U8 Weinmeisterstraße. **Open** from 5pm daily. **Average** DM32. **No credit cards.** **Map F3**
The name means stairs in Greek, and there's a massive concrete staircase leading nowhere in the middle of this Greek restaurant. It wouldn't be worth a special trek, but it's a useful stop at the northerly extremity of the Mitte nightlife maelstrom. Service are snooty and uninformed about the menu, but the Greek dishes are tasty and cheap enough. A blandly artsy crowd blends well with the pastel-washed walls and high ceilings.

stäV
Schiffbauerdamm 9, Mitte, 10117 (285 98725). U6, S1, S2, S3, S5, S6, S7, S9 Friedrichstraße. **Open** 11am-1am daily. **Average** DM25. **Credit** MC, V. **Map F3**
A 'ständige Vertretung' ('permanent agency') of the Rheinland in Berlin, stäV hopes to make good money off of homesick Bonners when they get here. Meanwhile, Berliners and Rheinlanders-in-exile can dine on Himmel und Ääde ('heaven and earth': blood sausage with mashed potatoes and apples), raisiny Rheinish Sauerbraten, and drink Cologne's sneakily powerful beer, Kölsch, while puzzling over the political in-jokes on the wall. Good list of Rhein wines, as might be expected.

Storch
Wartburgstraße 54, Schöneberg, 10823 (784 2059). U7 Eisenacher Straße. **Open** 6pm-1am daily. **Kitchen closes** 11.30pm. **Average** DM38. **No credit cards.** **Map D5**
It's hard to recommend Storch too highly. The Alsatian food – one soup starter, a sausage and sauerkraut platter, plus varying meat and fish dishes from the place where German and French cuisines rub shoulders – is both finely prepared and generously proportioned. House speciality is tarte flambée: a crispy pastry base cooked in a special oven and topped with either a combination of cheese, onion and bacon or – as a dessert – with apple, cinnamon and flaming calvados. The cheese board is a wonder and they've a small but especially fine selection of brandy, marc and other digestifs. The cosmopolitan front of house staff are one of the best and nicest crews in Berlin. Long wooden tables are shared by different parties and the atmosphere nearly always buzzes. Not the place for a quiet chat and occasionally you get stuck next to someone you don't like but the only real drawback here is that there's rarely very much for vegetarians – but ask the English-speaking proprietor what he can rustle up (and mention that we told you to do so) and they'll always produce something more than edible. Booking essential and no reservations accepted for after 8pm. Winner of the *Time Out Berlin Guide* Golden Sausage for generosity of spirit and all-round attention to detail.

Tandoory
Prinz-Georg-Straße 10, Schöneberg, 10827 (782 7927). U4 Innsbrucker Platz. **Open** 3pm-midnight daily. **Average** DM30. **Credit** AmEx, EC, V. **Map D6**
Most Berlin Indian places have similar menus, but this one is a little more inventive. Try the Kofta Dilkush, vegetable balls in a mouth-wateringly spicy tomato sauce, or the Paneer Pasanda, filled Indian cheese in a cashew nut sauce. The imported Indian decor is well over the top, the music can tend towards New Delhi honky-tonk, and sometimes it seems like the slowest service in town, so don't come here intending to cram in a quick meal before going a movie at the Odeon round the corner.

Thai Palace

Meierottostraße 1, Wilmersdorf, 10179 (883 2823). U1, U9 Spichernstraße. **Open** 5pm-midnight Sun-Fri, noon-11pm Sat. **Average** DM35. **Credit** AmEx, DC, EC, JCB, MC, V. **Map C5**

A large, beautifully decorated restaurant with immaculately dressed staff. The menu divides into meat and fish dishes, and even though the English translations are bad, at least they help you choose. Anything hot is marked *scharf*. The yellow chicken curry in coconut milk is delicious, the mixed starter recommended, the house wine merely passable.

Thürnagel

Gneisenaustraße 53, Kreuzberg, 10961 (691 4800). U7 Südstern. **Open** 6pm-midnight daily. **Average** DM33. **Credit** MC. **Map F5**

Pricey, fussy fish and vegetarian food is placed before Kreuzberg trendies at Thürnagel. Décor is understated (beige walls and gentle lighting); while the menu gives extraordinarily convoluted descriptions of dishes trying very hard to be inventive.

Trattoria da Enzo

Großbeerenstraße 60, Kreuzberg, 10965 (785 8372) U6, U7 Mehringdamm. **Open** 6pm-midnight daily. **Average** DM30. **No credit cards. Map F5**

A bustling little place that serves up authentic pizzas and good pasta dishes as well as commendable meat and chicken and a decent antipasta selection. Wash it all down with an excellent and philanthropically priced Salentino.

Trattoria Lappeggi

Kollwitzstraße 56, Prenzlauer Berg, 10405 (442 6347). U2 Senefelderplatz. **Open** noon-late daily. **Average** DM38. **No credit cards. Map G2**

This big, lively and fashionable place with windows looking out on to Kollwitzplatz serves up a variety of authentic and well-prepared Italian regional dishes to a mixed clientele of every age and drawn from every scene. The fresh pasta is particularly good. The crew are all Italian and mostly seem to be friends, which adds to the atmosphere although often one suspects they're hamming it up a bit. This being Prenzlauer Berg, there are changing exhibitions of paintings on the walls.

Trattoria Paparazzi

Husemannstraße 35, Prenzlauer Berg, 10435 (440 7333). U2 Senefelderplatz. **Open** 6pm-midnight daily. **Kitchen closes** 11.30pm, closed Mon in Jan. **Average** DM30. **No credit cards. Map G2**

Fairly ordinary-looking menu and chaotic service, but things are not what they seem here. True, many of the menu items are the same as in other Italian restaurants, but the cooking here is of a much higher level than in those places. If you're willing to overlook the rather *laissez-faire* attitude of the waiters, you'll be rewarded with a great meal. Particularly recommended are the Malfatti, pasta rolls seasoned with sage and bound with spinach and cheese, and the Strangelapretti, or 'priest stranglers', spinach, pasta, and cheese balls redolent of oregano and served with thin slivers of ham. Both house wines are superb. Stupid name, though.

Tres Kilos

Marheinekeplatz 3-4, Kreuzberg, 10961 (693 6044). U7 Gneisenaustraße. **Open** 6pm-2am daily. **Average** DM35. **Credit** MC, V. **Map F5**

Popular and young, Tres Kilos serves some of the best Mexican food in town in a big, light, lively space. Service has lately come to seem overstretched, but they try and take care of you here, from the hostess at the door to the crayons for doodling on the tablecloth. The menu is interesting (despite some very weak jokes) with specialities like Pavo y Platano (chicken with banana and peanut sauce) and a rack of lamb in ranchero sauce rubbing shoulders with Tex-Mex stan-

dards and chips with dips. The vegetarian fajitas are surprisingly good as are the margaritas, but avoid the strawberry version. Booking recommended.

Troika

Leipziger Straße 120, Mitte, 10117 (229 1369). U2 Mohrenstraße. **Open** noon-11pm daily. **Average** DM38. **No credit cards. Map F4**

Hearty, rib-sticking Russian specialities (pelmeni, vareniki, borscht, blinis and Keta caviar, home-brewed kvass) which make up in value for what they may lack in culinary refinement. Real winter food – and a favourite with Russian Embassy employees. Mind those vodkas, though – the management slosh out doubles unless you specify otherwise.

Tuk Tuk

Großgörchenstraße 2, Schöneberg, 10827 (781 1588). U7 Kleistpark. **Open** 5.30pm-1am daily. **Kitchen closes** 11.30pm. **Average** DM33. **Credit** EC, MC, V. **Map E5**

Tuk Tuk's cosy interior resembles a bamboo hut, with Indonesian bric-a-brac all over the place. The menu is very long, with a separate section for vegetarians. The gado gado is humdrum, although you get a lot of it, while the rice platter at DM78 for two is excellent value.

Ty Breizh

Kantstraße 75, Charlottenburg, 10627 (323 9932). U7 Wilmersdorfer Straße. **Open** 5pm-1am Mon-Fri; 6pm-2am Sat. **Kitchen closes** 11pm. **Average** DM35. **No credit cards. Map B4**

A mad place. The 'Breton House' specialises in two geographically opposed French cuisines: Breton and Savoyarde. This slight schizophrenia is reflected in le patron's physique; he has half a moustache on his lip, tends to burst into song, opens his oysters with a drill, plays games and performs tricks for the guests, and hand-paints every bill personally. Good, if slightly overpriced – and indisputably unique.

Woolloomooloo

Röntgenstraße 7, Charlottenburg, 10587 (3470 2777). U7 Richard-Wagner-Platz. **Open** noon-1am daily. **Average** DM30. **No credit cards. Map C3**

The name is Aboriginal for 'where the waters cross' – it's close by where two canals intersect the river Spree – and this is an Australian restaurant serving kangaroo or ostrich steak, stir-fried crocodile and other extraordinary delights from Down Under. The cooking inclines towards Pacific Rim, meaning a lot of Thai and Japanese influences on the preparation. An interior of exposed brickwork, good and cheery service. Surprisingly few actual Aussies in evidence, but there's a long and authoritative list of Australian wines.

XII Apostoli

Bleibtreustraße 49 (Savigny Passage), Charlottenburg, 10623 (312 1433). S3, S5, S7, S9, S75 Savignyplatz. **Open** 24 hours daily. **Average** DM40. **No credit cards. Map C4**

It's overcrowded, it's cramped, it's pricey, the service varies from rushed to rude, the music is trad jazz doodling irritatingly at the very edge of perception – but the pizzas are excellent and it's open 24 hours. Good selection of breakfast pastries. Same in all respects for the Mitte branch. **Branch:** Georgenstraße, S-Bahnbogen 177-180, Mitte, 10117 (201 0222).

Zur Nolle

Georgenstraße, S-Bahnbogen 203, Mitte, 10117 (208 1655). U6, S1, S2, S3, S5, S6, S7, S9 Friedrichstraße. **Open** 10am-midnight daily. **Average** DM26. **Credit** AmEx, MC, V. **Map F3**

In a cavernous space under the overhead railway by Friedrichstraße station that was formerly a briefing room for border guards, and before that a 1920s beerhall, Zur Nolle serves German stand-bys and international food to a mix of travellers and local businesspeople. There's a beer garden out back and excellent jazz brunches on Sundays.

Inexpensive

Altberliner Bierstuben
Saarbrückerstraße 16, Prenzlauer Berg, 10405 (442 6130). U2 Senefelderplatz. **Open** noon-2am daily **Average** DM22. **No credit cards. Map G2**
You'll often have to wait a few minutes for a table at this busy restaurant, but fear not, there's also a small bar. Cheap, traditional Berlin food is served in an old Berlin atmosphere. Recommended.

Angkor
Seelingstraße 36, Charlottenburg, 14059 (325 5994). U2 Sophie-Charlotte-Platz. **Open** 6pm-11.30pm Sun-Thur; noon-11.30pm Fri, Sat. **Average** DM25. **No credit cards. Map B3**
Extraordinarily friendly service and exotic décor make this a good spot for dinner. The Cambodian food tends towards the spicy, so think twice before asking for extra hot. Have the cold ricepaper rolls stuffed with shrimp to get the meal off to a flying start; move on to beef with Asian aubergine and coconut sauce; then try the fried bananas for dessert.

Café Asmarino
Grunewaldstraße 82, Schöneberg, 10823 (782 7282). U7 Eisenacher Straße. **Open** 5pm-1am Tue-Sun. **Average** DM18. **No credit cards. Map D5**
Small, quiet and friendly establishment offering Eritrean specialities. These mostly hinge around ingera, a kind of wheat pancake either rolled and stuffed or used to mop up sauces, with beef, chicken and vegetable accompaniments. More interesting than excellent, but a genuine change from more common cuisines.

Café Clara
Clara-Zetkin-Straße 90, Mitte, 10117 (229 2909). U6, S1, S2, S3, S5, S7, S9 Friedrichstraße. **Open** 9.30am-midnight Mon-Fri, 11am-midnight Sat, Sun. **Average** DM15. **No credit cards. Map F3**
Popular lunch spot for businessmen and tourists, the menu changes daily but usually features reasonably priced pasta, and meat and fish dishes. Garden in summer.

Café Hardenberg
Hardenbergstraße 10, Charlottenburg, 10623 (312 2644). U2 Ernst-Reuter-Platz. **Open** 9am-1am daily. **Average** DM15. **No credit cards. Map C4**
Across from the Technical University, this trendy café is usually packed with students discussing philosophy over coffee. Simple, decent plates of spaghetti, omelettes, salads and sandwiches are sold at reasonable prices. It's also a good place for cheap vegetarian food.

Café Nola
Dortmunder Straße 9, Tiergarten, 10555 (399 69 69) U9 Turmstraße. **Open** 6pm-2am daily. **Kitchen closes** 11.30pm **Average** DM22. **No credit cards. Map D3**
Two Swiss chefs bravely attempt California cuisine in this uncharacteristically picturesque corner of Moabit, and, more often than not, succeed. A light hand on the sauces, with fruit and chillies providing some of the flavour, an emphasis on fish and vegetarian entrées, and a well-chosen wine-list with some unusual Chilean and South African bottles, and you've got a refreshingly un-Berlinisch dining experience.

Café Orange
Oranienburger Straße 32, 10117 (282 0028). S1, S2 Oranienburger Straße. **Open** 9am-1am daily. **Average** DM22. **Credit** V. **Map F3**
High ceilings, with beautiful mouldings and light orange walls, make this place easy on the eyes as well as the palate. Basic fare is ubiquitous German-international dishes plus upwardly mobile pizzas. Terribly crowded at night, it's better suited for lunch or a languid breakfast before hoofing it around the Scheunenviertel.

Chandra Kumari
Gneisenaustraße 4, Kreuzberg, 10961 (694 3056). U6, U7 Mehringdamm. **Open** noon-1am daily. **Average** DM20. **No credit cards. Map F5**
This very small restaurant serves superb value Sri Lankan cuisine. Try the astonishing Jackfruit curry. Spicing is on the mild side, but the cooks who work frantically in the open-plan kitchen turn out some of the best, freshest and most reasonably priced Ceylonese delights in town. Always crowded, but worth the wait.

China-Restaurant Sezuan
Danziger Straße 13, Prenzlauer Berg, 10435 (441 4283) U2 Eberswalder Straße. **Open** noon-11.30pm daily . **Average** DM20. **Credit** EC, MC, V. **Map G2**
There's plenty of the standard German-Chinese fare here to keep the punters coming in, but what this place does best is, unsurprisingly enough, authentic Szechuan cuisine. Vegetarians are directed to the strips of tofu skin stir-fried with vegetables and chilli oil, which is not unlike *al dente* pasta, others to the classic tofu with ground-beef sauce. The management speaks English, and will helpfully arrange a selection of the house's best dishes for a large party.

Chop Bar
Pappelallee 27, Prenzlauer Berg, 10437 (444 5502). U2 Eberswalder Straße. **Open** 5pm-1am daily. **Average** DM22. **Credit** EC, MC, V. **Map G1**
West African food, mostly from Ghana and Senegal, is the star here: chicken in a spicy peanut stew, lamb and spinach with ground melon-seeds, and black-eyed-peas stewed with tomatoes. Add one of the Ghanian lagers to your order if you intend to use that tiny dish of pepper-sauce they'll be bringing: it's serious business.

Dodge
Dunkerstraße 80A, Prenzlauer Berg (445 9534). U2 Eberswalder Straße. **Open** 9am-4am Mon-Sat; 8am-4am Sun. **Average** DM14. **No credit cards. Map G2**
Americanophilia runs wild at this popular spot. Scrupulously authentic charcoal-broiled hamburgers – they've even got the pickles right – and Buffalo chicken wings (plus less scrupulously authentic 'Mexican' food) for dinner, or pancakes with maple syrup and a variety of omelettes for breakfast (which is served until 5pm) will make you think you have stumbled into a California luncheonette in 1961.

Großbeerenkeller
Großbeerenstraße 90, Kreuzberg, 10963 (251 3064). U1, U7 Möckernbrücke. **Open** 4pm-2am Mon-Fri; 6pm-2am Sat. **Average** DM22. **No credit cards. Map F5**
Going strong since 1862, this cellar Kneipe is a real Berlin institution among insiders. Berliners from all walks of life come for the substantial 'Hoppel-Poppel' breakfast, home-made meat and potato dishes and, of course, beer.

Henne
Leuschnerdamm 25, Kreuzberg, 10999 (614 7730). U1, U8 Kottbusser Tor. **Open** 10am-7pm Wed-Sun. **Average** DM14. **No credit cards. Map G4**
Only one thing worth bothering with here, because it's vir-

Volker Hauptvogel, owner of **Storch***, celebrates his Golden Sausage award with a relaxing Konigs-Pilsener. See page 125.*

tually all that's on the menu: half a roast chicken. What sets it apart from the tens of thousands of chickens rotating in the window of every Imbiß in the city is that it's organically-raised, milk-roasted, and, in short, the Platonic ideal of roast chicken. Your only other decision is cabbage or potato salad on the side (we vote for cabbage), and what kind of beer (Bavarian Monchshof). Check out the letter from JFK over the bar, regretting missing dinner here, as you wait for your table.

Honigmond

Borsigstraße 28, Mitte, 10115 (285 7505). U6 Zinnowitzer Straße. **Open** 11am-2am daily. **Kitchen closes** 11pm. **Average** DM22. **No credit cards**. **Map F2**

This quiet, neighbourhood place serves up traditional Königsberger Klöpse and beef stew alongside a weekly menu of innovative dishes using strictly fresh local ingredients in surroundings designed to evoke a 1920s nostalgia without overdoing it. Excellent small wine-list, lunch, and remarkable homemade bread.

Jimmy's Diner

Pariser Straße 41, Wilmersdorf, 10707 (882 3141). U2 Hohenzollernplatz. **Open** 4pm-4am Sun-Thur; 4pm-6am Fri, Sat. **Average** DM23. **No credit cards**. **Map C5**

This clean and self-conscious recreation of a 1950s diner, complete with red plastic booths and soda pop posters, serves generous portions of Mexican food and burgers at a good price. The burgers are authentic enough and almost too big to finish, but there's nothing here for vegetarians and the place sometimes gets way too full.

Marché

Kurfürstendamm 14, Charlottenburg, 10719 (882 7578). U9, U15 Kurfürstendamm. **Open** 8am-midnight daily. **Average** DM20. **Credit** V. **Map C4**

Healthy and freshly prepared food is what you'll find here, not ambience. On the busiest stretch of the Kurfürstendamm, this Swiss-owned chain offers vegetables, meats and desserts at various stands, buffet-fashion. Mood livens in summer when tables are set out on the pavement.

Markthalle

Pücklerstraße 34, Kreuzberg, 10977 (617 5502). U1 Görlitzer Bahnhof. **Open** 8am-2am Sun-Thur; 8am-4am Fri, Sat. **Kitchen closes** midnight. **Average** DM22. **No credit cards**. **Map H4**

This unpretentious restaurant and bar, with big chunky tables and wood-panelled walls, has become a Kreuzberg institution. They serve breakfasts until 6pm, a lunch menu from noon, and in the evening a selection of filling and reasonably priced meals, though the kitchen is nothing to write home about. Afterwards pop down into the basement club Privat (*see chapter* **Clubs**) or nip over the road for a drink at Der Goldene Hahn (*see chapter* **Cafés & Bars**). Good selection of grappas.

Petite Europe

Langenscheidtstraße 1, Schöneberg, 10827 (781 2964). U7 Kleistpark. **Open** 5pm-1am daily. **Average** DM25. **No credit cards**. **Map E5**

A rough-and-ready, welcoming neighbourhood Italian joint, serving decent and well-priced nosh. The food's not exceptional but vegetarians get a wide choice for once, and all diners get a free bruschetta while waiting and a free grappa after the meal. Avoid any salad except the rucola variations. The owner works his arse off, and however crowded this bustling place gets (expect a short wait mid-evening) he always has a smile and the prompt service rarely falters. We defy you to finish the Calzone. Relentless Phil Collins in the background earns the only black mark.

Tegernseer Tönnchen

Berliner Straße 118, Wilmersdorf, 10715 (323 3827). U7, U9 Berliner Straße. **Open** 11.30am-midnight daily. **Average** DM23. **No credit cards**. **Map C5**

The old-fashioned décor of this Bavarian-style restaurant lacks polish, but does feel authentically German. Heaped portions of Wiener Schnitzel, Eisbein, Bavarian meatloaf and mounds of potatoes fill most tables. So do big mugs of beer.

Tiergarten Quelle

Stadtbahnbogen 482, Bachstraße, near Haydnstraße, Tiergarten, 10555 (392 7615). S3, S5, S6, S9 Tiergarten. **Open** 11am-midnight Mon-Fri, 11am-1am Sat, Sun. **Kitchen opens** at 5pm **Average** DM15. **No credit cards**. **Map D3**

TU students jam this funky bar for huge servings of the food Grandma made: potatoes with quark and linseed oil, pork medallions with tomatoes and melted cheese with Käsespätzle, mixed grill with sauerkraut, Maultaschen on spinach, stone litre mugs of (unfortunately) Schultheiss beer. The Kaiserschmarren (minced pancakes with rum-soaked raisins and cherries topped with whipped cream) at DM9,50 is a meal in itself. You'll wonder where they buy the giant plates. Tip: go when school's out of session or you'll never get a table.

Imbiß & fast food

All over Berlin you will see the sign Imbiß – a catch-all term embracing just about anywhere you get food but not table service, from stand-up street corner Currywürst or Döner Kebab stalls (see page 124 **Meat on the street**), to self-service snack

Freßco – *a popular snacking spot in Mitte.*

*Waiting for the Wurst – **Konnopke's Imbiß** is quintessentially Berlin.*

bars offering all manner of exotic cuisine. The quality varies wildly, but some excellent, cheap food can be found in these places. Here is a selection of some of the more interesting ones.

Ashoka

Grolmanstraße 51, Charlottenburg, 10623 (313 2066). S3, S5, S7, S9, S75 Savignyplatz. **Open** 11am-1am daily. **Map C4**
A friendly Indian snack bar where good-value, no-frills food is served with plenty of choice for vegetarians – try the banana curry with basmati rice, it's delicious. If Ashoka is full, this street also has two other Indian imbißes and one Indian restaurant.

Freßco

Oranienburger Straße 47, Mitte, 10117 (282 9647). U6 Oranienburger Tor. **Open** *winter* noon-midnight daily; *summer* noon-2am daily. **Map F3**
A popular snacking spot for all those bar-crawling the Oranienburger Straße area. Soups, salads, baguettes, tapas, doughnuts, pasta, Calzone – this Imbiß has it all, in both carnivorous and vegetarian versions, and the menu changes regularly. Be prepared to queue a little, though. The Stresemannstraße branch is usefully over the road from the Hebbel Theater. The branch on Zossener is more of a café than an Imbiß.
Branch: Stresemannstraße 34, Kreuzberg, 10963 (2529 9309); Zossener Straße 24, Kreuzberg, 10961 (6940 1611).

Habibi

Goltzstraße 24, Schöneberg, 10823 (215 3332). U1, U2 Nollendorfplatz. **Open** 11am-3am Mon-Fri, Sun; 11am-5am Sat. **Map D5**
Freshly made Middle Eastern specialities including falafel, kubbe, tabouli and various combination plates. Wash it down with freshly squeezed orange or carrot juice, and finish up with a complimentary tea and one of their excellently sinful pastries. The premises are light, bright and well-run. Everything is excellently presented and served with a flour-

ish. The Winterfeldtplatz branch can get very full; the others stay open only until 2am. Winner of the *Time Out Berlin Guide* Silver Serviette for finest Imbiß chain in town.
Branches: Akazienstraße 9, Schöneberg, 10823 (787 4428); Körtestraße 35, Kreuzberg, 10967 (692 2401).

Konnopke's Imbiß

Beneath the U2 tracks, corner of Dimitroff Straße and Schönhauser Allee, Prenzlauer Berg, 10435 (no phone). U2 Eberswalder Straße. **Open** 5am-7pm Mon-Sat. **Map G1**
The quintessential Berlin Imbiß, going strong under family management since 1930, Konnopke's makes their own Wurst, and serves a large variety of sandwiches, including several vegetarian offerings, which people eat in a sort of Biergarten under the tracks.

Ku'damm 195

Kurfürstendamm 195, Wilmersdorf, 10707 (no phone). S3, S5, S7, S9, S75 Savignyplatz. **Open** noon-2am daily. **Map C4**
Berlin's best-known German Imbiß, and one that's not frequented by tourists. Buy Russian shashlik kebab and Currywurst fresh from the grill.

Kulinarische Delikatessen

Oppelner Straße 4, Kreuzberg, 10997 (618 6758). U1 Schlesisches Tor. **Open** 8am-2am daily. **Map H5**
Why do Berliners eat such bad Turkish food? Probably because they know deep in their hearts that someday they'll come upon a place like this, where the same old selections are done to a Platonic ideal. The Döner's not bad, but it's the vegetarian offerings that make it really special: try an aubergine-falafel combo kebab, a zucchini kebab, or even one of the salads.

Kwang-Ju-Grill

Emser Straße 24, Wilmersdorf, 10707 (883 9794). U7 Hohenzollernplatz. **Open** noon-midnight Sun-Thur; noon-2am Fri, Sat. **Map C5**
There's a hundred different items on the menu of this excellent Korean Imbiß: starters and soups at around DM4, every

Pigging out the KaDeWe way

Instead of sitting in a restaurant or queueing at an Imbiß, the Feinschmecker-Etage (Gourmet Food Hall) on the sixth floor of KaDeWe (*see chapter* **Shopping**) offers a different approach to dining.

You can stop off for anything from a nibble to a full meal at one of the many food stalls that dot the shopping floor. Really it's up to you and your wallet. You can pay DM150 for 50g of Sevruga caviar or snack on a sausage for DM4. Six Belon oysters will cost you around DM30 and there are prawn cocktails no one could finish for DM15. Nouvelle cuisine specialities at the Paul Bocuse stand come in the region of DM35 while sushi is reasonably priced at around DM6

per piece. The choice of cuisine is extraordinary and the quality high.

Perhaps the best approach is to browse around, taking an hors d'oeuvres here and a main course there. Try some of the savoury canapés at DM3 apiece, washed down with a glass of champagne for DM15. Follow it with a brimming bowl of bouillabaisse for DM14. Assorted schnitzels are served up for between DM12-DM18 and vegetarian pasta dishes cost around DM12. If you've got any room left after sampling some of that little lot, KaDeWe also has an extraordinary selection of cakes.

One big plus, or minus, depending on your predilection: there is no smoking allowed.

---

kind of meat and fish dish for between DM10–DM16, and a small selection of vegetarian options. Order at the counter and sit at one of the tables inside or (in summer) out. Wash it down with a hot sake or Chinese beer.

Joseph Lange

Wilmersdorfer Straße 118, Charlottenburg, 10627 (316 780). U7 Wilmersdorfer Straße. **Open** 8.30am-6.30pm Mon-Fri; 8.30am-2pm Sat. **Map B4**
Most savvy sausage shops have an Imbiß in them for customers to check out the goods, and what Lange has going for him is not only some fine Wurst, but a Currywurst that could be Berlin's best. Ask for a Wurst mit Kraut, and specify Scharfketchup, and better get a drink while you're at it: that ketchup is spicy! Wurst and ketchup both available to take home.

Mäcky Messer

Mulackstraße 29, Mitte, 10119 (no phone). U8 Weinmeisterstraße. **Open** 6pm-midnight Tue-Sun. **Map G3**
Mitte's fishiest address, named after the ne'er-do-well gangster in Brecht's Dreigroschenoper, who probably would have lived in the neighbourhood if he hadn't been fictional. The attraction here is not only the sushi, which is very well-made, but also Japanese soups and salads, and a changing array of blackboard specials in the European mode. A find in a city where salt-water fish isn't at the forefront, and the prices, which stretch all the way up to DM18, can't be beat.

Misuyen Asia-Bistro

Torstraße 22, Mitte, 10119 (247 7269). U2 Rosa-Luxemburg-Platz. **Open** 11am-9pm Mon-Sat. **Map F3**
Sometimes, if you look behind the surface of one of Berlin's many 'Asia' imbißes, you'll find something unexpected. In Misuyen's case, it's Laotian food, albeit mixed with the usual greatest hits: some Thai, some Indonesian, some fake Chinese. Lighter and with more fresh vegetables than the usual 'Asia' fare, the Laotian dishes can also be made without MSG if you say the magic words 'ohne Glutamat, bitte'.

Pagoda

Bergmannstraße 88, Kreuzberg, 10961 (691 2640). U7 Gneisenaustraße. **Open** noon-midnight daily. **Map F5**
This essential Imbiß is as good as some of the more costly Thai joints in town, and if the Gesundheitspolizei ('health police') hadn't recently made them remove the tables and chairs (only one toilet so according to German law that

means no one's allowed to sit down), you could make a decent dinner here. Dozens of menu selections, the proper amount of chillis already in the dish, making a dip into the hot-sauce jar only minimally necessary, and fast, friendly service.

Safran

Knaackstraße 14, Prenzlauer Berg, 10405 (no phone). U2 Senefelder Platz. **Open** Sun-Fri 11am-1am, Sat 11am-3am. **Map G2**
'The best falafel in east Berlin,' the counterman says, and he's right, but it doesn't stop there: shredded chicken-breast with herbs, almonds, and pine-nuts (available as a plate or a pita-stuffer), stewed okra with aromatic rice, fish soup, and many other daily specials. Inexpensive, open late, and right in the middle of the hopping Wasserturm area.

Spätzle

Lüneberger Straße S-Bahnbogen 390, Tiergarten, 10557 (no phone). S5, S6, S7, S9 Bellevue. **Open** 9am-8pm Mon-Sat, 11am-8pm Sun. **Map D3**
A lovely little place serving the pastas of Swabia, including, of course, Spätzle (with Bratwurst, lentils, or meatballs), Käsespätzle (with cheese), Maultaschen (like giant ravioli), and Schupfenknudle (a cross between pasta and chips). Wash it down with a brown Berg beer.

Viva Mexico!

Chausseestraße 36, Mitte, 10115 (280 7865). U6 Zinnowitzer Straße. **Open** 11am-11pm daily. **Map F2**
A true find: a Mexican woman and her daughters preparing authentic interior Mexican food in Berlin. Homemade refried beans and four salsas (three of which are good and spicy) to put on your tacos, burritos, and tortas, and a small selection of Mexican groceries. This place would be good in Mexico, let alone Germany, and they do catering, as well. A bit out of the way, but worth the trip.

Vietnam Imbiß

Damaschkestraße 30, Charlottenburg, 10711 (324 9344). U7 Adenauerplatz. **Open** 10am-9pm Mon-Fri. **Map B4**
Berlin is thin on authentic Vietnamese food, but this popular little place serves up a hybrid that's healthy, filling, and inexpensive. The daily special is almost always the star of the show, but most of the regular menu items (the sickly-sweet 'sweet-sour' items excepted) are top-notch. Expect to wait a while if you arrive around noon: the neighbourhood loves this place.

Cafés & Bars

Berlin is Bar City. Now go to it.

Few cities can beat Berlin when it comes to bars. In some parts of town there's a place on every corner and several more in between: wacky bars and tacky bars, yuppie bars and hippie bars, scene bars and obscene bars, cocktail bars and cruisy bars – all of them staying open as long as they feel like and sloshing out the drinks with abandon.

There are cafés too, of course. Berlin has a coffeehouse culture to rival that of any other central European city. But it's often a blurry line that separates the café from the bar. In this town you could have breakfast, lunch, afternoon coffee and cakes, dinner and get horribly drunk all in the same place. But while there is this overlap, and while many establishments function as cafés in the daytime and as bars in the evening, distinctions between the two remain.

In a café you might sit for hours nursing a huge bowl of Milchkaffee with your head stuck into a book or newspaper – there's no minimum charge and rarely any pressure to reorder or move on. Afternoon *Kaffee und Kuchen* – coffee and cakes – is a well-established tradition. Ice cream is another German passion, and many cafés have separate ice-cream menus offering a variety of exotic confections, most of them involving rather too much whipped cream (*Schlagsahne*).

Bars have a different kind of life. While there is still quiet conversation around tables – and table service is the norm in Berlin – people also stand around or perch on stools, eye each other up, harass the bar staff, order rounds of tequila. Aside from the brewery-tied working-class corner pubs (*see page 136* **Inside the Eck-Kneipe**), Berlin bars work hard to establish their own identity in terms of decor, mood, atmosphere, style of service, volume of music and nature of crowd – resulting in both some very cool places and some ridiculously crazy dives. Berlin bars are allowed to be eccentric. The best ones are something between institutions and extended families, each with a scene all of its very own. Despite the explosion of bar and café life in Mitte and Prenzlauer Berg, many of the best individual establishments are still in west Berlin – a lot of eastern ones, particularly around Oranienburger Straße and Rosenthaler Straße, are too young to have acquired much character.

Few Berlin bars take credit cards and many don't have strict opening hours. By law, they only have to close one hour out of 24, and a lot of places ignore even this minor restriction. Others are open-

ended and will keep on serving as long as there are enough customers to make it worth their while, or if the staff themselves are having a good time and can't be bothered to go home yet. Many of the closing times listed here are therefore only approximate and places may stay open later. But if the barstaff have started piling the chairs on the tables and pointedly asking if they can call you a cab, there's bound to be somewhere else open within walking distance. Ask the people behind the bar: that's probably where they're going.

Here we've only been able to list a small selection of places: institutions, landmarks, new arrivals and old favourites. But there are plenty more places to be found on Berlin's buzzing streets.

Mitte

Along Oranienburger Straße and Rosenthaler Straße, in and around the Hackescher Höfe – here is the new axis of Berlin nightlife. Extravagantly designed bars now speckle the whole of northern Mitte, but often it seems like there's less real action than there are crowds desperately seeking some.

Aedes

Hof II, Hackeschen Höfe, Rosenthaler Straße 40-41, Mitte, 10178 (282 2103). S3, S5, S7, S9, S75 Hackescher Markt. **Open** 10am-2am daily. **Credit** EC, V. **Map F3**
Small and stylish Hackescher Hof café fills with insiders who know that the food here is better– and better-priced – than in the larger places in the first Hof. Lots of people from nearby theatres, bars, and offices, and fewer of the young western social climbers who otherwise haunt the Höfe.

Barcomi's

Sophie-Gips-Höfe, Sophienstraße 21, Mitte, 10178 (2859 8363). U2 Weinmeisterstraße/S3, S5, S6, S7, S9 Hackescher Markt. **Open** 9am-10pm daily. **Map F3**
Unlike the Kreuzberg Barcomi's, this new one draws a crowd less interested in macadamia nut-flavoured decaffeinated coffee than an atmosphere unusually serene and unpretentious by Mitte standards. Homemade baked goods and the wide variety of freshly roasted coffees are also a novelty. The inconspicuous entrances to the Höfe open from Sophienstraße and Gipsstraße.
Branch: Bergmannstraße 21, Kreuzberg, 10961 (694 8163).

Berliner Ensemble Casino

Bertold-Brecht-Platz, Mitte, 10117 (28 880). S1, S2, S3, S5, S6, S9/U6 Friedrichstraße. **Open** 9am-midnight Mon-Fri; 4pm-midnight Sat, Sun. **Map F3**
Formerly the canteen for workers at the Berliner Ensemble theatre, 'casino' is a misnomer – it's still basically a canteen. Old GDR fittings remain, as does a self-service system, but somewhere along the way it's acquired a weird cult status.

Café Beth

Tucholskystraße 60, Mitte, 10117 (281 8135). S1, S2 Oranienburger Straße. **Open** 10am-6pm Mon-Thur; 10am-3pm Fri. **Map F3**

Meeting place for the Jewish community in a bistro atmosphere. American and British Jews may puzzle over what gets delivered when they order familiar Kosher favourites, since the knishes and 'Gefüllte Fisch Amerikaner Art' bear scant resemblance to what they get at home, but this café wing of the Congregation Adass Jisroel guarantees kashruth and everything is tasty and well-made. Don't be put off by the gun-toting police in front of Berlin's Jewish-orientated businesses: they're friendly. Jazz accompanies Sunday brunches.

B-Flat

Rosenthalerstraße 13, Mitte, 10119 (280 6249). U8 Weinmeisterstraße. **Open** 9am-3am daily. **Shows** start 10pm. **Map F3**

Typical of the current Mitte trend for overdesign, this cavernous bar has been decked out with great attention to detail and the walls have been carefully insulated to provide good acoustics for the regular jazz shows on the stage at one end. At the other end there's a long bar with drinks detailed in a voluminous brochure stuffed with advertising. Nice fittings, shame about the lack of real atmosphere.

Broker's Bier Börse

Schiffbauerdamm 8, Mitte, 10117 (3087 2293). S1, S2, S3, S5, S6, S9/U6 Friedrichstraße. **Open** 8am-late daily. **Map F3**

Mad little place where 'market forces' dictate the prices of their 15 beers, which rise and fall throughout the evening. One minute there's a run on Radeburger, the next everyone gets bullish about Jever. Tends to get going after the nine-to-fivers come out to play, and can get so full in mid-evening that there are queues outside. Breakfasts, snacks and sausages served.

Café Silberstein – *the skeletal staff?*

Café Silberstein

Oranienburger Straße 27, Mitte, 10117 (281 2095). S1, S2 Oranienburger Straße. **Open** 4pm-4am daily. **Map F3**

Loud and funky bar that deals in a spectacular line of weirdly welded steel furniture and skeletal metal sculptures. You can sit on the things or else buy one to take home (prices run between DM1,000-DM1,500, but they're receptive to barter deals). As elsewhere on Oranienburger Straße, tourists and out-of-towners seem largely to have chased away the locals, but this remains one of the better bars around here.

Gorki Park

Weinbergsweg 25, Mitte, 10119 (448 7286). U8 Rosenthaler Platz/Tram 53, 13 Rosenthaler Platz. **Open** 10am-late daily. **Map F2**

Tiny Russian-run café with surprisingly tasty and authentic snacks – blinis, pierogis and the like. Guests range from students and loafers to the occasional guitar-toting Ukrainian and scenesters having a quiet coffee before heading down to pose at more centrally located bars. Interesting weekend brunch buffet includes a selection of warm dishes.

Hackbarths

Auguststraße 49a, Mitte, 10119 (282 7706). U8 Weinmeisterstraße. **Open** 9am-3am daily. Breakfast from 9am-2pm. **Map F3**

Local trendies and squatters enjoy their coffee here. Good (though microwaved) quiche and vegetable rolls plus a selection of interesting cakes, such as chocolate pear, make it a popular stop for lunchtime snacks. By night it's a disconcertingly busy bar and the art scene's local.

Ici

Auguststraße 61, Mitte, 10117 (281 4064). U6 Oranienburger Tor. **Open** 3pm-3am daily. **Map F3**

Featuring original painting and sculpture from local artists, a copy of Camus will help you feel at home among the self-consciously literary set that inhabits this quiet café. Good selection of wines by the glass.

KDW

Neue Schönhauser Straße 9, Mitte, 10178 (no phone). U2 Weinmeisterstraße/S3, S5, S7, S9, S75 Hackescher Markt. **Open** 10pm-morning daily. **Map G3**

Set up by squatters who live upstairs, this bar and occasional club remains a living museum of post-Unification nightlife. Less hardcore now, it still maintains a strong following among the cool unemployed, poor students, and the very drunk when this is the last place to get a drink. Their gutted basement addition sometimes features interesting club nights, from surf to old-school hip hop.

Mitte Bar

Oranienburger Straße 46, Mitte 10117 (283 3837). U6 Oranienburger Tor. **Open** noon-late. **Map F3**

During the day locals involved with nightlife or students with a few hours' break will congregate for coffee or the first beer of the day. Later it fills with people just finished gawking at the tourist sights of Oranienburger Straße. Still, at night the music is fairly adventurous, the decor dark, and a back room is frequently occupied by a wide spectrum of DJs playing everything from drum 'n' bass to 1960s sleaze.

Odessa

Steinstraße 16, Mitte, 10119 (no phone). U8 Weinmeisterstraße. **Open** 7pm-2am daily. **Map G3**

Beautiful minimalist bar that's unusually quiet for this part of town. Wooden tables in the small back room are complemented by a bar out front, behind which can often be found the well-travelled Lithuanian proprietor. There's no music, nor room for many guests, and only a small, though carefully chosen, selection of drinks, but this is an excellent antidote to too much fake cool on nearby Rosenthaler Straße.

Small beer

Champagne was much in evidence the night the Wall fell, but it was Berlin's beer-lovers who quickly started dancing in the streets. West Berlin made terrible beer, from the so-so big brews of Schultheiss and Berliner Kindl to the virtually undrinkable Engelhardt Charlottenburg Pilsner. On the east side, there was a Schultheiss brewery left over from the days when the brewer was one of Germany's giants, but the beer was much better, and there were other small breweries.

The east's Schultheiss became Berliner Pilsner; Kindl took over management of Berliner Burgerbräu, a family-owned operation on the Müggelsee; and smaller labels – Bärenpils, Rex Pils from Potsdam and Bärenquell from a village in Brandenburg – began showing up in the shops. Berlin's beer scene got something it hadn't had in decades: variety. Burgerbräu makes a pils, a superb export lager, Rotkelschen, and a strong, dark beer, Bernauer Schwarzbier, as well as a winter Dunkler Bock and a super-strong, sweet Maibock. Bärenquell, too, makes an excellent, dry winter bock, as well as its own pils. You almost always have to go east if you want to drink any of these in a bar, although they're available at the retail level everywhere.

But if you want to drink any draught beer in northern Germany, the first thing you have to do is wait. The routine of pouring a beer can take seven to ten minutes: the first squirt of the tap releases foam, which is allowed to fill the glass, left to settle, and then followed by another squirt. Squirt, settle, squirt, settle... you're not too thirsty, are you? Sometimes it pays to order your second beer the minute they've delivered the first.

And no matter how good the beer is, there's another issue which British and American beer-lovers have to confront in Germany: with the exception of those hard-to-find seasonal and specialty beers, ultimately, the compass is small. This is due to the beer-purity law, the *Reinheitsgebot*, passed in 1516, which severely limits the ingredients allowed in brewing, and which, until the Maastricht Treaty, was used to keep imports out of Germany. It never assured that the beer actually tasted good, as veteran Berliners will testify.

Perhaps little surprise, then, that one Berlin beer-drinking custom involves dousing the low-alcohol *Berliner Weisse* with a *Schuß* of sweet syrup – either *rot* (raspberry) or *grün* (woodruff). The resulting fruity beverage is served in a bowl-shaped glass, often sipped through a curved straw, and tastes like wine gums.

But there is hope for the connoisseur in a Kreuzberg storefront. The Bier-Company took advantage of the loosening of restrictions to start selling home-brewing kits, teaching brewing courses, and making their own stout, British and Belgian ale, and a host of other superb brews. Most notable is Turn, which, instead of being hopped with hops, is 'hemped' with low-THC hemp blossoms. Turn's clear, crisp taste belies the fact that it is not classified by the government as a 'beer', and this has allowed the Bier-Company to distribute it to bars tied to major breweries without violating any contracts. The Bier-Company always has three of its creations on tap at the shop (usually including Turn), sells a wide range of international beers, and has everything you need to start brewing yourself.

The Bier-Company
Körtestraße 10, Kreuzberg, 10967 (693 2720). U7 Südstern. **Open** 10am-8pm Mon-Fri; 9am-4pm Sat. **Map G5**

Opern Café
Unter den Linden 5, Mitte, 10117 (200 2269). U6 Französische Straße. **Open** 8.30am-midnight daily. **Map F3**
The café in the elaborately decorated palatial villa next to the Staatsoper is a favoured coffee-stop for Berliners. There are murals of 'Old Berlin', brass light fittings, old ladies Kaffeeklatsching in funny hats, and a huge and handsome selection of cakes. It's a big place but quiet and calm. Meals also served. Tables outside in summer.

Oscar Wilde
Friedrichstraße 112a, Mitte, 10117 (282 8166). U6 Oranienburger Tor. **Open** 11am-2am daily, to 3am Fri, Sat. **Live music** 10.30pm Thur, Fri, Sat. **Map F3**
Irish pub offering the obligatory ingredients of Guinness,

plates of egg and chips, and a big video screen in the back room for watching football on Sky. Live music at weekends.

The Pip's
Auguststraße 84, Mitte, 10117 (282 4512). U6 Oranienburger Tor. **Open** 8pm-1am Mon-Thur, Sun; 8pm-3am Fri, Sat. **Map F3**
Quiet and laid-back cocktail bar decked in blue and orange with absurdly squishy barstools, cool staff, subdued music, and decor that incorporates every cheesy lighting fad ever invented. At the back there's an exceedingly small dancefloor, with soul DJs at weekends. The name is a misspelling inspired by Gladys Knight.

Salon Muff
Krausnickstraße 5, Mitte, 10115 (283 2826). S1, S2 Oranienburger Straße. **Open** from 6pm daily. **Map F3**

off Trabant cars and a bar constructed from old GDR petrol pumps. Nice place for a quiet drink on weeknights, it can get uncomfortably crowded at the weekends.

ZeoBar

in Die Hackeschen Höfe (Hof I), Rosenthaler Straße 40-41, Mitte, 10178 (283 4681). S3, S5, S7, S9, S75 Hackescher Markt. **Open** 6pm-late daily. **Map F3**
Use the entrance and staircase for the Chamäleon Varieté and cinema. The long climb is warranted by the elegant long bar and excellent drinks. The somewhat hidden location allows Zeo to cater to a more discerning, stylish, and relaxed crowd than the ground-floor establishments in Hof I. A frequently changing food menu is also on offer.

Zosch

Tucholskystraße 30, Mitte, 10117 (280 7664). S1, S2 Oranienburger Straße. **Open** 11am-late daily. **Map F3**
A Mitte café of the old school, unscrubbed and unconcerned. The little rooms and small basement concert hall (ska to mod) are always full at night, and the bar area is one of the few in Mitte where people stand around and converse rather than retreating to insular tables. A frequent starting point for students, squatters and grubby scenesters on for an all-night session. During the day things are very laid back, and there are well-priced breakfasts and warm meals.

Prenzlauer Berg

Around Kollwitzplatz and the Wasserturm, expect quiet conversation at the tables of gallery cafés. But every other kind of bar can also be found hidden among Prenzl'berg's leafy streets.

Akba

Sredkistraße 64, Prenzlauer Berg, 10405 (441 1463). Tram 1 Danziger Straße. **Open** 7pm-very late. **Map G2**
The front of the place is a quiet, terribly smoky café that can host an eclectic crowd, especially late at night. Through the back is the Akba Lounge, an excellent mini-club devoted to a wide array of music – everything from cheesy 1960s *Schlager* to contemporary house. The adjacent Tarot bar is a good place for late-night cocktails.

Café Anita Wronski

Knaackstraße 26-28, Prenzlauer Berg, 10405 (442 8483). U2 Senefelderplatz. **Open** 10am-3am daily. **Map G2**

The Pip's *but no Gladys Knight. Page 135.*

On a quiet old street off Oranienburger Straße – if you imagine away the cars, you might still be in the nineteenth century – this is an elegant update of the *Weinlokal* tradition. It's a friendly cellar space, with simple wooden tables, an interesting selection of wines, and a few snacks and antipasti to go with them. Nice contrast to the area's many modernist, over-designed bars.

VEB OZ

Auguststraße 92, Mitte, 10117 (no phone). S1, S2 Oranienburger Straße. **Open** from 9pm daily. **Map F3**
A small bar bizarrely furnished with seats made out of sawn-

Inside the Eck-Kneipe

On many corners, down certain streets, especially in less fashionable quarters, you'll run across the typical Berlin Eck-Kneipe – corner pub. Looking for a little local colour, you may be tempted to wander in. Be prepared.

Inside it's smoky. Strange German pop music oom-pahs from a juke box in the corner. Indigenous fruit machines with rules comprehensible only to the locals click and whirr to themselves as someone absently feeds in coins from time to time. The locals are mostly male, and mostly drunk out of their faces. They all know each other and bellow in thick, barely intelligible

Berlinisch, following arcane native rituals it would take an anthropolgist to unravel and downing huge quantities of *Schnapps* and Schultheiss beer.

Then you walk in. You are a stranger. You have dared to invade their inner sanctum. At worst, you can expect outright hostility. At best, they might try and talk to you. Brits should expect daft conversational openings about the Royal Family (a German obsession), World War II, English food, or that fact that in Britain, as everyone German knows, it is always raining cats and dogs.

If you're looking for a quiet drink, forget it.

Friendly café on two levels with scrubbed floors, beige walls, hard-working staff and as many tables crammed into the space as the laws of physics allow. Excellent brunches.

Café November

Husemannstraße 15, Prenzlauer Berg, 10435 (442 8425)
U2 Eberswalder Straße. **Open** 10am-2am daily. **Map G2**
Especially nice during the day, when light floods into this bright, white café through show windows offering views of the beautifully restored Husemannstraße. It's a quiet and friendly place. Unusually for this district – and frankly something of a relief – there isn't much art on the walls. Breakfast's served until 4pm and there's a menu of light meals.

Cocktail Bar X

Raumerstraße 17, Prenzlauer Berg, 10437 (443 4904).
U2 Eberswalder Straße/Tram 1, 20 Prenzlauer Allee.
Open from 6pm-late daily. **Map G1**
The music trying so hard to be hip, but never actually getting there, can give the impression of a crap bar. But the half-price happy hour from 6pm-8pm will quickly change your mind, as you work through some of the hundreds of cocktails on the menu. This brings in all sorts of young Prenzlauer Bergers eager to start the night with a fruity, creamy buzz. At which point the loud music and crowds can give the place a party atmosphere hours before any clubs get started. The music's still crap, though.

Eckstein

Pappelallee/corner of Gneiststraße, Prenzlauer Berg
10437 (441 9960). U2 Eberswalder Straße/Tram 13
Raumerstraße. **Open** 9am-2am daily. **Map G1**
This beautiful café, with its broad corner front and deco-ish look, draws one of the most mixed crowds outside of the Hackeschen Höfe. But unlike many cafés around the Wasserturm or Rosenthaler Straße, Eckstein maintains a fol-

lowing among the less-well-scrubbed residents of Prenzlauer Berg, adding a pleasingly old school bohemian feel to a place otherwise clean enough to take your parents to.

Kommandatur

Knaackstraße 20, Prenzlauer Berg, 10405 (442 7725).
U2 Senefelderplatz. **Open** 6pm-7am daily. **Map G2**
A small, smoky place heaving with trendy and often unfriendly Prenzlauer Bergers who are reluctant to share their bar with anyone else. There isn't much room for newcomers, anyway. The charged atmosphere here though, does have a certain spark lacking in some of the area's nicer cafés.

Lampion

Knaackstraße 54, Prenzlauer Berg, 10435 (442 6026).
U2 Eberswalder Straße. **Open** 4pm-3am daily. **Map G2**
Small bar with dozens of umbrellas hanging from the ceiling, bar staff with a penchant for strange martial music and occasional puppet shows in the small theatre at the back.

Prater

Kastanien Allee 7-9, Prenzlauer Berg, 10435 (448 5688).
U2 Eberswalder Straße/Tram 13, 50, 53. **Open** 6pm-
2am; beer garden open all day. **Map G2**
The centrepiece of this four-in-one location is a theatre run by the Volksbühne, but adjoining the main building are three additional attractions: an expansive beer garden shaded by mature trees, a classy swing-era café, and a loony art-bar patronized by people with second-hand clothing and lo-fi sensibilities. The beer garden is one of the largest and most charming in Berlin. The wonderfully restored café offers hearty German meals and occasional live swing music to a crowd heavy on theatre types. The Schmalzwald bar doubles as a workspace for Canadian artist Laura Kikauka and a troupe of trashy underground scenesters.

Seife und Kosmetik

Schliemannstraße 21, Prenzlauer Berg, 10437 (no phone). U2 Eberswalder Straße. **Open** 24 hours daily.
Map G1
In the grand Berlin tradition of bars named after the shops which once occupied the premises: Seife und Kosmetik means 'soap and cosmetics'. Ironic, because a lot of the local fauna in this nicely sleazy late-night dive looks pretty unwashed. The walls could do with a scrub too, but at least all the scribbled graffiti makes a change from the usual Prenzl'berg paintings. Arty, it ain't.

Times

Husemannstraße 10, Prenzlauer Berg, 10435 (442 8076). U2 Eberswalder Straße/Tram 20 Husemannstraße. **Open** 5pm-6am Mon-Sat; 10am-6am Sun. **Map G2**
Benches from old S-bahn trains provide seating for a crowd that can include bartenders and DJs in for an after-hours nightcap, or Finnish architects who can't believe they can continue to get affordable booze well into the wee hours. The only place in the borough to get warm food late at night.

Torpedo Käfer

Dunckerstraße 69, Prenzlauer Berg, 10437 (444 5763).
U2 Eberswalder Straße. **Open** 11am-2am daily. **Map G2**
Bright, roomy bar that also serves breakfast until 6pm, basic bar food thereafter (Chili con carne, mozarella and tomato salad and so on). The menu also lists assorted paintings and sculptures as Ausser Haus (takeaway). Usually full of real nutcases, doubtless drawn here by the excellent coffee.

Friedrichshain

As rents rocket and tourists swarm in Mitte and Prenzlauer Berg, this area is catching a little of the overspill. There are lots of cafés and bars on and

ZeoBar – *discerning, stylish and relaxed.*

around Boxhagener Straße, and a number of odd bars in the area full of squatted houses to the north of Frankfurter Allee.

Abgedreht

Karl-Marx-Allee 140, Friedrichshain, 10243 (294 6808). U5 Petersburger Straße. **Open** 11am-late daily.
Equipped with a mini-cinema and decorated with German film memorabilia, bits of old hardware and pieces of cello-loid. A young crowd, waiters in sweat pants and white-boy dreadlocks, old sofas, sewing machine tables, and Beck's for DM3 a bottle combine to make this a legitimate heir to the semi-legal joints that made Mitte cook in the early 1990s.

Tagung

Wühlischstraße 29, Friedrichshain, 10245 (292 8756). U5 Samariterstraße. **Open** 7pm-late daily.
Small bar decked out in GDR memorabilia and still serving things like Club Cola, the eastern brand. The patrons are twenty- and thirty-somethings and not bitter or sad the way one might expect. Instead, the place seems to provide good laughs and drunken nights for all.

Kreuzberg

No longer the beating heart of Berlin bohemia, but there's still life – and any number of good bars and cafés – on and around Oranienstraße and Wiener Straße in the east of the borough, and around Bergmannstraße to the south-west.

Anker-Klause

Kottbusser Brücke, corner of Maybachufer, Neukölln, 10967 (693 5649). U8 Schönleinstraße. **Open** from 10am Tue-Sun; from 4pm Mon. **Map G5**
Just over the border into Neukölln, but essentially a part of

the Kreuzberg scene, this is a small, often packed, canal-bank pub with moderate prices, an unkempt and youngish crowd, and occasionally interesting musical events.

Bierhimmel

Oranienstraße 183, Kreuzberg, 10997 (615 3122). U1, U8 Kottbusser Tor. **Open** 3pm-3am daily; cocktail bar 3pm-3am Wed-Sat. **Map G4**
From the outside, Bierhimmel is just another Kreuzberg bar, but its secret lies through the padded swing doors at the back. Inside is a cosy, 1950s-style cocktail bar bathed in red. Popular with local drag queens.

Café Adler

Friedrichstraße 206, Kreuzberg, 10969 (251 8965) U6 Kochstraße. **Open** 8.30am-1am Mon-Fri; 10am-1am Sat, Sun. **Map F4**
Next to what used be Checkpoint Charlie, you could once watch history in the making from this elegant corner café. Today you're more likely to see tower cranes and hawkers of fake Wall chunks. Good stop for coffee or light meals.

Café Anfall

Gneisenaustraße 64, Kreuzberg, 10961 (693 6898). U7 Südstern. **Open** 5pm-5am Tue-Sun; from 10pm Mon. **Map G5**
A bohemian mixture in terms of both the constantly chang-ing décor and the punky clientele, Anfall is loud, friendly and kind of strange. Niagara, a few doors along, is similar.

Café Bar Morena

Wiener Straße 60, Kreuzberg, 10999 (611 4716). U1 Görlitzer Bahnhof. **Open** from 9am-5am daily. **Map H5**
Famous breakfasts are served to people who wake up at all hours. Avoid the 'English Breakfast', though – it features the foulest baked beans known to culinary science. In the evening Morena bustles and the service can be rather slow. The music isn't overpowering and the half-tiled walls and parquet flooring give it an art deco feel.

Schnapp-happy

Celebrating an occasion, asserting cameraderie or simply aiming to get drunk and fall over as quickly and as sociably as possible, Berliners down rounds of *Schnapps* at the slightest excuse.

Schnapps, of course, contrary to the belief of many English and Americans, is not a particu-lar type of alcohol. Rather it's a generic term for any kind of spirit, short or chaser. When drunk in rounds, these tend to be things to knock right back rather than stuff to sip and savour. So for-get fine cognac or Highland malt. Though these are popular in Berlin, celebratory drinking is much more likely to feature a shot of iced vodka or a gold tequila (Germans call it 'brown') quaffed the Berlin way with a slice of orange rather than salt and lemon.

The dark and sweet German herb liqueur Jägermeister, long regarded as suitable only for alkies or old men, has lately been making a

comeback. Shooters such as Whodinis, Kamikazes and B-52s are also popular.

Sometimes a *Schnapps* is used to seal a new friendship, or affirm there are no hard feelings after an argument or misunderstanding. Don't be surprised if someone you've been talking to at the bar suddenly orders a round of tequilas. Barkeepers, too, will often pass out a few free shots if they like your face or have enjoyed your sense of humour. It also makes sound business sense – if you have a good time and are made to feel welcome, hopefully you'll return to drink another day.

If you want to feel one of the crowd, no one will object if you take the initiative. Just remem-ber one thing: when chinking glasses, always look your fellow drinkers in the eye. This is an essential part of the ritual, of affirmation through alcohol, and anyone who does other-wise may be taken as at best ill-mannered, and at worst, untrustworthy.

*Chill-out time at the **Haifisch**.*

Café Übersee

Paul-Lincke-Ufer 44, Kreuzberg, 10555 (618 8765). U1 Kottbusser Tor. **Open** 10am-2am daily; breakfast until 4pm daily. **Map G5**

Vines cover the outside, where summer tables offer a popular spot for breakfast overlooking the Landwehr canal. Nothing special inside, though. If it's full, there are a couple more similar places on this stretch of canal bank.

Der Goldene Hahn

Pücklerstraße 20, Kreuzberg, 10997 (618 8098). U1 Görlitzer Bahnhof. **Open** 9pm-3am daily. **Map H4**

A small bar with unpretentious brick walls, old wooden pharmacist's fittings and lots of stuffed chickens, Der Goldene Hahn is relaxed and smart. Nice place for a drink after a bite at the **Markthalle** (*see chapter* **Restaurants**) opposite.

Enzian

Yorckstraße 77, Kreuzberg, 10965 (786 5088). U6, U7 Mehringdamm. **Open** 7pm-3am Mon-Thur, Sun; 7pm-4am Fri, Sat. **Map F5**

Friendly joint owned and operated by Norbert aka 'Der Wahre Heino' (for his occasional and brilliant satirical impersonations of a particularly objectionable German singing star). Decked with Bavarian flags, garden gnomes and other Deutsche kitsch. Both music and clientele are punky and getting on a bit. Sausages for DM2, Schmalzbrot (bread and dripping) for DM1.

Freßco

Zossener Straße 24, Kreuzberg, 10961 (6940 1611). U7 Gneisenaustraße. **Open** 8pm-midnight daily. **Map F5**

Relaxing, roomy and bright new addition to the cafés of the Bergmannstraße neighbourhood. Good coffee and fresh, tasty food – snacks, salads, sandwiches and pastries – chosen not from a menu, but from the display case below the bar. Lots for vegetarians. The two branches – one opposite the Hebbel Theater and the other on the Friedrichstraße end of Oranienburger Straße – are imbißes rather than cafés.

Branches: Stresemannstraße 34, Kreuzberg, 10963 (2529 9309); Oranienburger Straße 48, Mitte, 10117 (281 3128)

Golgotha

Viktoria Park, Kreuzberg, 10965 (785 2453). S1, S2/U7 Yorckstraße. **Open** *Apr-Sept* 11pm-6am daily. **Map E5**

In the middle of Viktoriapark with a dancefloor inside and a beer garden outside. All human life – or as much of it as can be found in this part of Kreuzberg – hangs out here on summer nights. Action sometimes spills into the surrounding shrubbery and the adventure playground next door.

Haifisch

Arndtstraße 25, Kreuzberg, 10961 (no phone). U6, U7 Mehringdamm. **Open** from 9pm-3am Tue-Thur, Sun; 9pm-4am Fri, Sat. **Map F5**

Well-run and friendly bar where the staff are more than competent at shaking cocktails, the music's always hip and tasteful, and the back room, which also houses a sushi bar, is a great place to chill out at the end of an evening.

*Old institution, new management – Chaos reaches for a pint at **Die Rote Harfe**. Page 140.*

Madonna

Wienerstraße 22, Kreuzberg, 10999 (611 6943). U1 Görlitzer Bahnhof. **Open** 11am-3am daily. **Map H5**
Nasty, loud and loved by the Kreuzberg rock crowd, Madonna has been an institution for years. Though clearly past its best, it still seems to manage to cram them in.

Milagro

Bergmannstraße 12, Kreuzberg, 10961 (692 2303). U7 Gneisenaustraße. **Open** 9am-1am Mon-Thur; 9am-2am Fri, Sat; 10am-1am Sun. **Map F5**
A light and friendly café, with excellent breakfasts until 4pm, plus cheap but classy meals until midnight. Disorientating stairs lead to the hospital-like toilets. On a winter's afternoon, the front room can be too dim to read your daily paper.

Die Rote Harfe

Oranienstraße 13, Kreuzberg, 10999 (618 4446). U1, U8 Kottbusser Tor. **Open** 10am-3am Tue-Sun. **Map G4**
Venerable institution lately afforded a new lease of life under the management of Chaos, well-known former punk about town. It's a traditional Berlin bar, with a drinking area out front, café upstairs, occasional live music, and tables at the back where cheap and filling meals are served. The menus usually have mad themes based on current events – in 1997, 'Week Of The Dead' featured Egyptian Lentil Soup 'Dodi', Fish and Chips 'Diana', Vegetarian Indian Curry 'Theresa' and Lasagne 'Versace'.

Schnabelbar

Oranienstraße 31, Kreuzberg (no phone). U1 Kottbusser Tor. **Open** from 10pm daily. **Map G4**
An essential stop on any Oranienstraße crawl and open all night long, this place is recognisable by the metal beak ('Schnabel') which pokes out over the door. Inside there's a long bar and a tiny dance floor, over which some decent DJs can be found spinning funk, soul, rare groove and reggae.

Schöneberg

Though the area continues to fall out of fashion, some veteran institutions survive and still thrive. Most of the action is on and around Winterfeldtplatz and along Goltzstraße, but look out also for hidden bars with a history, such as Pinguin, Zoulou and Ex 'n' Pop.

Café Berio

Maaßenstraße 7, Schöneberg, 10777 (216 1946). U1, U2, U4 Nollendorfplatz. **Open** 9am-midnight daily. **Map D5**
The locals' choice for breakfasts, it also has plenty of home-made cakes and excellent ice cream. Café Berio has been an institution since the 1930s and the tables outside are a prime people-watching spot in summer.

Caracas

Kurfürstenstraße 9, Tiergarten, 10785 (261 5618). U1 Kurfürstenstraße. **Open** from 10pm daily. **Map E5**
A wild, wacky Latin American cellar bar decked in pink plastic flowers. A small alcove has tatty sofas to sink into when you've worked your way through the 20 kinds of rum, or jigged around to salsa on the tiny dancefloor.

Ex 'n' Pop

Mansteinstraße 14, Schöneberg, 10783 (216 5121). U7/S1, S2 Yorckstraße. **Open** from 9pm Tue-Sun. **Map E5**
Once the wild heart of alternative West Berlin and still a hangout for survivors from the crazy mid-1980s, Ex 'n' Pop is quieter these days, but remains a place where the unexpected always stands a chance of happening. Big on theme nights and parties – a small stage stands ready for occasional live acts and performances and occasional DJs play anything

from country to disco to drum 'n' bass to easy listening. Spacious, scruffy, loud and full of characters, including some of the meanest table football players in Berlin. At its best deep on a weekend night.

Fischlabor

Frankenstraße 13, Schöneberg, 10781 (216 2635). U7 Eisenacher Straße. **Open** 9pm-5am daily. **Map D5**
It's tricky to find and looks nothing special from the street, but once inside you'll find two rooms of space-agey décor and occasional DJs playing funk, soul and rare groove.

Green Door

Winterfeldtstraße 50, Schöneberg, 10781 (215 2515). U1, U2, U12 Nollendorfplatz. **Open** 6pm-3am daily. **Map D5**
It really does have a green door, and behind it there's a whole lotta cocktail shaking going on – the drinks menu is enormous. Nice long and curvy bar, perhaps a few too many yuppies. Good location just off Winterfeldtplatz.

Mutter

Hohenstaufenstraße 4, Schöneberg, 10781 (216 4990). U1, U2, U4 Nollendorfplatz. **Open** 9am-4am. **Map D5**
Mutter ('mother') tries, and largely succeeds, to do everything at once: two bars, an enormous selection of wines, beers and cocktails, breakfasts from 9am-4pm, a sushi bar from 6pm plus a lot of other snacks on offer. It's roomy, the decor is heavy on gold paint and the spectacular corridor to the toilets has to be walked to be believed. Always bustling.

Pinguin Club

Wartburgstraße 54, Schöneberg, 10823 (781 3005). U7 Eisenacherstraße. **Open** 9pm-4am daily. **Map D5**
Though a little past its heyday, the Pinguin remains one of the finest bars in Berlin. It's decorated with 1950s Americana and rock 'n' roll memorabilia, plus assorted kitsch bits and pieces, complete with sparkling mirror ball. Owners and staff are all involved in music, one way or another, and good sounds, varying from Dean Martin to drum 'n' bass, are a feature. Take your pick from 156 spirits behind the bar and don't be surprised at the end of the night if everyone starts waltzing. Winner of the *Time Out Berlin Guide* Golden Shot Glass award for best local bar.

Screwy Club

Frankenstraße 2, Schöneberg, 10781 (215 4441). U7 Eisenacher Straße. **Open** 9pm-2am Tue-Thur; 9pm-4am Fri, Sat. **Map D5**
Small, friendly bar decorated with artwork by Chuck Jones and Tex Avery. The barstools, for example, are set on giant Bugs Bunny-style carrots. Specialises in frozen cocktails.

Zoulou Bar

Hauptstraße 4, Schöneberg, 10728 (784 6894). U7 Kleistpark. **Open** 8pm-6am Mon-Thur, Sun; 10pm-9am Fri, Sat. **Map E5**

*Beer served with love: Gosto at the **Pinguin**.*

A small, atmospheric bar with a funky vibe and occasional DJs. It can very crowded between 10pm and 2am; after that the crowd thins out and it's maybe the best time for a visit then. Usually full of staff from nearby bars until the dawn light gets too bright.

Charlottenburg

On the upmarket streets off the Ku'damm and around Savignyplatz, daytime café life bustles among the designer boutiques. There's not so much of a scene at night, though there are plenty of congenial spots for a cocktail before dinner or few brandies later to wind up the night.

Café Hardenberg
Hardenbergstraße 10, Charlottenburg, 10623 (312 2644). U2 Ernst-Reuter-Platz. **Open** 9am-1am daily. **Map C4**
Witness students in their natural habitat, day or night, at the spacious and relaxing Hardenberg, next to the Goethe Institut and opposite the Technical University. Most nurse a drink for hours, listening to classical music or chatting. Others come for the cheap eats. Furnishings include museum posters, plants and ceiling fans.

Café Kranzler
Kurfürstendamm 18, Charlottenburg, 10719 (882 6911). U9, U15 Kurfürstendamm. **Open** 8am-midnight daily. **Map C4**
Dominating the Ku'damm Eck, Kranzler is one of the city's oldest coffee houses. Though a landmark, this hard-to-miss, three-storey tourist trap is on the wane. There's even talk of it moving east. The terrace overlooking the Ku'damm is still a good spot for people-watching in summer, but there are plenty of better places than this.

Café Savigny
Grolmanstraße 53-54, Charlottenburg, 10623 (312 8195). S3, S5, S7, S9, S75 Savignyplatz. **Open** 10am-2am daily. **Map C4**
It's hard to find a table at this small but airy café. Painted nearly entirely white with round arched doorways, the Savigny has a Mediterranean feel and is popular with the media and fashion crowd. Good breakfasts, filled baguettes and cakes. Tables outside in summer, nice bar within.

Diener
Grolmanstraße 47, Charlottenburg, 10623 (881 5329). S3, S5, S7, S9, S75 Savignyplatz. **Open** 6pm-2am daily. **Map C4**
An old-style Berlin bar, named after a famous German boxer. There's no music and the walls are adorned with faded hunting murals and photos of famous Germans you won't recognise – you could almost be in 1920s Berlin.

Dralle's
Schlüterstraße 69, Charlottenburg, 10629 (313 5038). S3, S5, S7, S9, S75 Savignyplatz. **Open** 3pm-2am Mon-Thur, Sun; 3pm-3am Fri, Sat. **Map C4**
Slick sort of hangout for an oldish, formerly fashionable crowd. The décor is predominantly red, so avoid it if you have an aversion to the colour. Staff are efficient, drinks are pricey, snacks are served.

Gasthaus Lenz
Stuttgarter Platz 20, Charlottenburg, 10627 (324 1619). S3, S5, S6, S7, S9 Charlottenburg. **Open** 9am-2am daily; breakfast 9am-noon daily. **Map B4**
An older crowd is drawn to this unpretentious, spacious café nestled in the cluster of bars on Stuttgarter Platz. *Guardian*-reading thirtysomethings will feel at home. No music, which is unusual in this town.

Nothing rusty about **Rost**.

Leysieffer
Kurfürstendamm 218, Charlottenburg, 10719 (885 7480). U15 Uhlandstraße. **Open** 9am-7pm Mon-Wed, Fri, Sat; 9am-8.30pm Thur; 10am-8pm Sun. **Map C4**
Indulge yourself in style at this refurbished café housed in what used to be the Chinese Embassy. Exquisite tortes, fruit-cakes and chocolate confections are served in the high-ceilinged café upstairs. Mounds of truffles and bonbons, beautifully presented, are sold downstairs in the shop.

Rost
Knesebeckstraße 29, Charlottenburg, 10623 (881 9501). S3, S5, S7, S9, S75 Savignyplatz. **Open** 10am-2am daily. **Map C4**
The name means 'rust', but the only thing remotely rusty here is the sign. The interior is designed simply with pale apricot walls and odd white lights extending from the ceiling. Cool, collected and catering to an older crowd, this is also a haunt of the theatre world.

Schwarzes Café
Kantstraße 148, Charlottenburg, 10623 (313 8038). S3, S5, S7, S9, S75 Savignyplatz. **Open** 24 hours daily except Tue. **Map C4**
Open around the clock for coffees and drinks, breakfasts and meals. It used to be all black (hence the name, also a reference to an anarchistic past) but these days the décor has been brightened up. Service can get overstretched when it's crowded, such as early on a weekend morning when clubbers stop by for breakfast on the way home.

Wintergarten im Literaturhaus
Fasanenstraße 23, Charlottenburg, 10719 (882 5414). U15 Uhlandstraße. **Open** 9.30am-1am daily. **Map C4**
The café of the Literturhaus, which has lectures, readings, exhibitions and an excellent bookshop in the basement (*see chapter* **Shopping & Services**). The greenhouse-like sunny winter garden or salon rooms of the café are great for ducking into a book or scribbling out postcards. Breakfast, snacks and desserts are available.

Tiergarten

Not a major nightlife neighbourhood, but still home to Berlin's most crucial coffeehouse and two of its finest cocktail bars.

Bar am Lützowplatz
Lützowplatz 7, Tiergarten, 10785 (262 6807). U1, U2, U4 Nollendorfplatz. **Open** 5pm-3am Sun-Thur; 5am-4am Fri, Sat. Happy hour from 5pm-9pm daily. **Credit** AmEx, DC, JCB, MC, V. **Map D4**
Long bar a longer drinks list. Classy customers in Chanel suits and furs sip expensive, well-made cocktails.

Café Einstein

Kurfürstenstraße 58, Tiergarten, 10785 (261 5096). U1, U2, U4 Nollendorfplatz. **Open** 10am-2am daily. breakfast until 2pm daily; meals served until midnight daily.
Credit AmEx, DC, JCB, MC, V. **Map D4**

Excellent if pricey Viennese-style coffeehouse housed in an old mansion, with hectic, tuxedo-clad waiters, international papers and magazines, and a renowned apple strudel. In summer you can sit in the garden at the back and enjoy a leisurely breakfast. Gets very crowded on Sundays. The new branch in Unter den Linden is vastly inferior. *See also chapter* **Restaurants**.
Branch: Unter den Linden 42, Mitte, 10117 (204 3632).

Harry's New York Bar

Lützowufer 15, Tiergarten, 10785 (261 011). U1, U2, U4 Nollendorfplatz. **Open** from 6pm daily. **Credit** AmEx, DC, JCB, MC, V. **Map D4**

Pricey cocktail bar in the Grand Hotel Esplanade, Harry's is sister to the famous American hangout in 1920s Paris. Berlin's more modern version, started in 1988, is sleek and sophisticated, with portraits of all US presidents and a jazz singer at the piano. Cocktails are expertly mixed.

Kumpelnest 3000

Lützowstraße 23, Tiergarten, 10785 (261 6918). U1 Kurfürstenstraße. **Open** 5pm-5am daily, later at weekends. **Map D4**

A bit of a meat-market, it used to be a brothel, the walls are carpeted and one of the barmen is deaf. You'll find it at its best at the end of a long Saturday night: overcrowded, chaotic and with people attempting to dance to disco classics.

Wilmersdorf

The area around Ludwigkirchplatz bristles with cafés, bars and restaurants.

Berlin Bar

Uhlandstraße 145, Wilmersdorf, 10719 (883 7936). U1 Hohenzollernplatz. **Open** 10pm-7am daily. **Map C5**

Small and thin (if there's someone standing at the bar, it's hard to squeeze by between them and the wall) this venerable institution goes on serving when all else around here has closed. You pay for the privilege, though. After about 4am it's full of people who've finished working in other places.

Galerie Bremer

Fasanenstraße 37, Wilmersdorf, 10719 (881 4908). U15 Uhlandstraße. **Open** 8pm-3am Mon-Sat. **Map C5**

In the front there's an art gallery that's open between noon and six; in the back there's a quiet cocktail bar. It's pricey, but still an excellent place for an undisturbed tête-à-tête or romantic rendezvous.

Zur Weißen Maus

Ludwigkirchplatz 12, Wilmersdorf, 10719 (882 2264). U1, U9 Spichernstraße. **Open** 6pm-4am Mon-Thur, Sun; 6pm-5am Fri, Sat. **Map C5**

The entrance bell and pricey drinks list lend a feeling of exclusivity to this civilised 1920s-style bar. It's decorated in black and orange, with a painting by Otto Dix. Quiet and a good spot to bring an intimate date, it's on the south-east corner of buzzy Ludwigkirchplatz.

Of bouquets and bandits

You won't sit long in a Berlin bar before someone starts trying to sell you something: tomorrow's papers, jewellery, books, novelty lighters, filled baguettes... or a bouquet of long-stemmed roses, usually proffered by a grinning Sri Lankan.

He'll respond spritely to your slightest notice by extending the shrub another length, hoping against hope that by sending him away, you might be sending the wrong – or at least unintended – signal to your date. In this fashion, some people may be coerced into a spontaneous show of affection by buying a long-stem for DM4. But mostly the rose sellers are just nodded away and slip haplessly out into the night on their way to more rejections at the next restaurant.

You might think the rose sellers are cleverly exploiting a niche in the romantic repertoire of otherwise amorously inhibited Germans, but actually they're being ruthlessly exploited themselves. They who each night silently pile out of battered vans on gas-lit sidestreets in nightlife districts all over town are the minions of criminal bands. The Sri Lankans are often smuggled into Germany in freight containers over the Polish or Czech borders. If lucky, they can live in squalid flats and work the rose circuit for a few weeks before being detected by immigration authorities and put in compounds while their applications for asylum are processed. Unlucky ones barely make it out of the containers alive; in summer police routinely discover abandoned lorries at highway rest stops full of half-starved, nearly suffocated refugees.

This is an underworld business, so details about the rose trade are hard to confirm. But barkeepers and restaurant workers say gang leaders buy huge lots of leftover flowers at the wholesale market in the late afternoon, when perishable blossoms are at their cheapest. Lately the same gangs have branched out into hawking weird novelty cigarette lighters shaped like deer or mobile phones.

Rose sellers pay an unconscionable mark-up for a bouquet of salvaged flowers, but if they sell even half, there's still some profit left over. How much of the proceeds are due back to the bandits who smuggled them into Berlin in the first place is unclear, but it is certain that the whole black market operation is immensely lucrative; gang bosses resort to violence to protect their turf.

Shopping & Services

Prestigious projects hit the high street as a retail resurrection rolls on – but Berlin's best buys are away from the main drag.

Berlin can't compete with Paris, London or even Munich in the shopping stakes. During the decades of dictatorship and division it was starved of the supplies vital to a strong retail culture, and most of its once-great department stores and shopping boulevards died. But the past five years have seen startling developments, with the most exciting new shopping areas appearing in east Berlin. Mitte is at the centre of this retail resurrection with prestigious projects – most notably the series of malls that make up the Friedrichstadt Passagen on Friedrichstraße – coming to fruition, and an influential designer enclave taking root in the Scheunenviertel.

While the east has seen a mushrooming of famous international names (Gucci, Galeries Lafayette, Escada, Jean-Paul Gaultier and Donna Karan), the shopping heartland of the west around the Kufürstendamm has responded to the shifting emphasis and waning custom by undergoing a much-needed facelift.

Despite the impressive new sites and the explosion of expensive names across town, however, Berlin still lacks the bedrock of wealthy, cosmopolitan consumers that drives major shopping cities. And these discerning customers are not likely to be attracted by the poor merchandising, appaling visual display and nasty sales techniques still practised in some of the stores across town. Yet, as in so many aspects of life in this city, what Berlin lacks in sophistication it makes up for in spirit. Its young, energetic population feeds a plethora of excellent second-hand shops and flea-markets, music stores and fashion shops. Designers and retailers of every kind make the most of favourable rents, basing themselves in inexpensive and vibrant pockets of the city.

Opening hours

In 1996 parliament liberalised Germany's restrictive shop opening hours, a move bitterly opposed by the unions and small retailers. Shops can now sell goods until 8.30pm on weekdays, and 4pm on Saturdays. Most big stores normally open their doors at 8.30am, newsagents a little earlier, and smaller or independent shops tend to open around at 10am or later.

The hope behind the changes was that increased shopping time would enliven the retail industry, leading to more sales and jobs, but in fact the impact has been limited. While most of the bigger chains and department stores take full advantage of the liberalised later opening laws, many smaller stores have stuck to old practices. So while you can be sure that all big stores in the city centre will stay open until at least 8pm, with independently run shops it's best to phone beforehand to check closing times.

Another hangover from pre-liberalisation days is the *Lange Donnerstag* (long Thursday) when shops were permitted to stay open until 8.30pm. Through force of habit many Berliners still concentrate their late-night shopping on this day, leading to queues at downtown checkouts.

Antiques

Collectors and browsers with an interest in the eighteenth and nineteenth centuries will find many of the better dealers clustered on Keith Straße and Goltzstraße in Schöneberg. The streets surrounding Fasanenplatz (Wilmersdorf) are worth exploring, as is Suarezstraße (Charlottenburg).

There is an understandable dearth of antique shops in the east, the notable exception being the handful of expensive galleries on the lower ground level of Quartier 206 (Friedrichstadt Passagen, Mitte). These showcase fine art, porcelain, crystal and furniture from the 1780s to the late eighteenth century. At the other end of the scale, streets such as Kollwitzstraße and Husemann Straße (Prenzlauer Berg) are home to small, unpretentious *Antiquariaten* selling inexpensive books, household equipment and assorted communist memorabilia. Wherever you choose to shop for antiques in Berlin, you might as well leave your credit cards at home – most shops don't accept them and you can negotiate a much better price for cash. *See also below* **Flea Markets**.

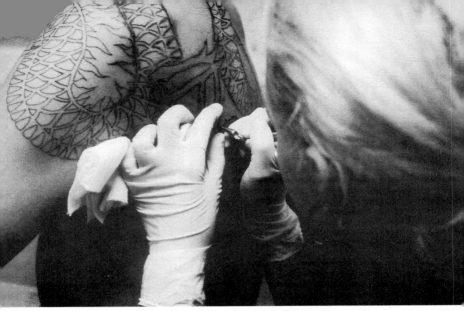

Blut & Eisen – *book early for 'blood and iron', where tattoos don't come cheap.*

Das Alte Bureau

*Goltzstraße 18, Schöneberg, 10781 (216 5950). U7
Eisenacher Straße.* **Open** 3pm-6.30pm Mon-Fri; 10am-
2.30pm Sat. **No credit cards. Map D5**
Antique desks, filing cabinets, chairs and bookshelves for
romantic workaholics.

Jukeland

*Crellestraße 13, Schöneberg, 10827 (782 3335). U7
Kleistpark.* **Open** 2pm-6pm Tue-Fri; 11am-2pm Sat. **No
credit cards. Map E5**
Jukeland has everything you need to turn your home into a
American diner: neon signs, Cadillac couches, diner-style
tables and, of course, juke boxes. There is also a plentiful
supply of adverts and signs from the 1940s and 1950s, and
you may be lucky enough to pick up a lifesize James Dean,
should you so desire.

Lehmanns Colonialwaren

*Grolmanstraße 46, Charlottenburg, 10623 (883 3942).
S3, S5, S7, S75, S9 Savignyplatz.* **Open** 2pm-6.30pm
Mon-Fri; 11am-2pm Sat. **No credit cards. Map C4**
Turn of the century luggage, clothing and furniture deck out
this small shop like a cluttered Victorian parlour. The eccentric stock runs to a colonial theme, so don't be surprised to
come across a stuffed camel, a set of snakeskin luggage or a
guide to hunting big game.

Odeon Art Deco

*Bleibtreustraße 50A, Charlottenburg, 10623 (313 5114).
S3, S5, S7, S75, S9 Savignyplatz.* **Open** 3pm-8pm Mon-
Fri; 11am-4pm Sat. **No credit cards. Map C4**
Superbly restored furnishings and jewellery in the art deco
style, such as mirrored cocktail bars, high-lacquer vanity
tables and outrageous clocks. Prices may be a little steep,
but connoisseurs of the 1920s and 1930s may find the quality justifies the expense.

Schönhauser

*Neue Schönhauser Straße 18, Mitte, 10178 (281 1704).
U8 Weinmeisterstraße.* **Open** noon-8pm Mon-Fri; 11am-
4pm Sat. **No credit cards. Map G3**

All you need to deck out your front room like the flightdeck
of the Starship Enterprise: bright plastic swivel-chairs, GDR
lighting fixtures, bubble TVs, and other design classics of
doubtful taste from the 1960s through to the present day.

Timmerman's Indian Supply

*Berliner Straße 88, Potsdam, 14467 (0331 292076). S1,
S3 Wannsee, then bus 116 to Glienicker Brücke.* **Open**
9am-6pm Mon-Fri; 11am-6pm Sat, Sun. **Credit** EC, MC.
Timmerman's vintage Indian motorcycles are in tip-top condition and make really big toys for really big kids. The beautifully restored 1930s gas station where the machines are
sold is worth the trek to Potsdam in itself.

Ubu

*Bleibtreustraße 55, Charlottenburg, 10623 (313 5115).
S3, S5, S7, S75, S9 Savignyplatz.* **Open** 3pm-6.30pm
Mon-Fri; 11am-2pm Sat. **No credit cards. Map C4**
Impressive collection of vintage travel literature and goods,
including early Baedekers, travelling cases and model ships.

Wolfgaang Haas

*Suarezstraße 3, Charlottenburg, 14057 (321 4570). U2
Sophie-Charlotte-Platz/204 bus.* **Open** 3pm-7pm Tue-Fri;
11am-2pm Sat. **Credit** AmEx, DC, EC, MC, V. **Map B4**
Period, lacquered-timber furniture, glassware, ceramics and
other small antiques dating from 1800 to 1960. There are
classic tables, chairs and cabinets, as well as art nouveau
pieces. The selection of German crystal from the nineteenth
and twentieth centuries is particularly good; the paintings
are all post-1945.

Auctions & Appraisals

Leo Spik

*Kurfürstendamm 66, Wilmersdorf, 10707 (883 6170).
U7 Adenauerplatz.* **Open** 9.30am-1pm, 2pm-6pm Mon-
Fri. **No credit cards. Map B5**
Berlin's only auction house that survived the war was found-
ed in 1919 and specialises in art and antiques from the
Renaissance to classical modern art. Four annual auctions

put paintings, silver, jewellery, furniture and carpets under the hammer each season. The emphasis is on Berlin and German art from local collections or estates, but international valuables are also on offer. No in-house appraisals, but the experts here will point you in the right direction.

Villa Griesebach

Fasanenstraße 25, Charlottenburg, 10719 (882 6811). U15 Uhlandstraße. **Open** 10am-6.30pm Mon-Fri; 10am-2pm Sat. **No credit cards. Map C4**
One of the world's largest auction houses, Villa Griesebach specialises in impressionist and expressionist art, most of it German. Auctions are held in May and November each year and the collections are shown in seven German cities before being auctioned. This elegant villa is also home to one of Berlin's oldest art galleries. Free appraisals on paintings and sculptures that could be considered for a Griesebach auction.

Beauty Salons

Aveda

Kurfürstendamm 29, Charlottenburg, 10719 (8855 2757). U15, U9 Kurfürstendamm. **Open** 10am-8pm Mon-Fri; 10am-4pm Sat. **Credit** AmEx, DC, EC, V. **Map C4**
The hair and beauty salon at the back of the Aveda store offers hair styling and cutting, aromatherapy massage, manicure, pedicure and facials, all using products based on natural flower essences.

Blut & Eisen

Alte Schönhauser Straße 6, Mitte, 10119 (283 1982). U8 Weinmeisterstraße/U2 Rosa-Luxemburg-Platz. **Open** 1pm-7pm Tue, Wed, Fri and Sat; 1pm-9pm Thur. **No credit cards. Map G3**
Book a good three weeks in advance if you fancy a bit of body piercing or tattooing courtesy of 'Blood & Iron', as this is a popular establishment. The three, self-taught staff are native Berliners and walking advertisements for their own artistry. Their work is accomplished and original but doesn't come cheap – they won't touch you for less than DM150, and on average customers leave DM300-DM500 the lighter. No under-14s admitted.

Marie France

Fasanenstraße 42, Charlottenburg, 10719 (881 6555). U15 Uhlandstraße. **Open** 9am-6pm Tue, Wed, Fri; 9am-8pm Thur; 9am-2pm Sat. **No credit cards. Map C4**
The cosmeticians speak English with a French accent and use luxurious French products at this clean, pleasant salon, which has been glamming-up Berliners for more than 30 years. Hot wax depilation is a speciality (DM44 for a half leg), and the salon also offers a full range of relaxing and beautifying treatments.

Silvana Sonsalla Cosmetic

Grand Hotel Esplanade, Lützowufer 15, Schöneberg, 10785 (2547 8252). U1, U2, U4, U15 Nollendorfplatz. **Open** 11am-7pm Mon-Fri, and by appointment. **Credit** AmEx, DC, MC, V. **Map D4**
This most exclusive, yet slightly clinical, beauty salon uses only top-of-the-range products by Bvlgari and Clarita. Not all of the pampering is for women only: men can choose between anti-stress, revitalising and body-care treatments (DM80-DM120). A 90-minute facial costs DM130-DM220.

Condoms

Condomis

Kantstraße 131, Charlottenburg, 10625 (313 50 51). S3, S5, S6, S9/U2, U9 Zoologischer Garten. **Open** 10am-7pm Mon-Fri; 10am-3pm Sat. **Credit** AmEx, EC, MC, V. **Map C4**
While you can buy condoms everywhere in Berlin, you could have more fun here choosing from the mind-boggling selection of coloured or plain, patterned or textured, animal-shaped or fruit-flavoured rubbers.

Letting it all hang out at **Condomis** *– rubbers for every occasion.*

Dublosan

Mühlenfeldstraße 22, Hermsdorf, 13467 (404 6996).
U6 Alt-Tegel. **Open** 9am-1pm Mon-Fri. **No credit cards.**
Wholesale condoms. Minimum order is for 100 condoms,
which will cost at least DM30 – and these can be delivered.

Hair Salons

Berlin hair stylists' technical skills tend to out-
match their judgment and taste. And the state of
the average Berlin barnet might convince you
never to trust your crowning glory to the locals.
That said, the city does boast a few stylists and
colourists that can do a pretty fair job, as well as
some international salons that can cut it with the
best of them. *See also* **Flex/Inch By Inch/Melt-
ing Point** *under Fashion.*

Hanley's Hair Company

Hackesche Höfe, Rosenthaler Straße 40-41, Mitte, 10178
(281 3179). U8 Weinmeisterstraße/S3, S5, S7, S75, S9
Hackescher Markt. **Open** 9am-8pm Mon-Fri; 10am-4pm
Sat. **No credit cards. Map F3**
Friendly, trendy salon run by Thomas Schweizer and
British-born Deborah Hanley. Full range of styling and treat-
ments, with a wash, cut and head massage for DM49 (men)
or DM69 (women).

Kaiserschnitt

Marianenstraße 49, Kreuzberg, 10997 (618 5397). U1
Görlitzer Bahnhof. **Open** 11am-6pm Mon-Fri; 11am-5pm
Sat. **No credit cards. Map H5**
Their name, 'Ceasarian', reveals their fetish for below-the-
belt cuts. The salon's claim to Berlin fame came with its
exclusive pubic hairstyling service in a back room. Heads
of hair also cut; costing around DM50 for both men
and women.

Mod's Hair

Meinekestraße 6, Charlottenburg, 10719 (883 6687).
U15, U9 Kurfürstendamm. **Open** 9am-8pm Mon-Fri;
9am-4pm Sat. **Credit** AmEx, EC, MC, V. **Map C4**
A franchise of the fashionable French chain that can deliver a stylish cut and blow for DM80-DM95 (women) and
DM50-DM60 (men).
Branches: Olivaer Platz 4, Wilmersdorf, 10707 (881
5101); Ludwigkirchstraße 9, Wilmersdorf, 10719 (881
1499).

Udo Walz

Kurfürstendamm 200, Charlottenburg, 10719 (882
7457). U15 Uhlandstraße. **Open** 9am-6pm Mon-Fri; 9am-
2pm Sat. **Credit** AmEx, DC, EC, MC, V. **Map C4**
Udo is the darling of the Berlin hair brigade, and likes to have
his picture taken with Claudia Schiffer. Whether he actually cuts her hair is a different matter. The stylists are well-
trained and friendly (wash, cut and dry, DM110).
Branches: Kempinski-Plaza, Uhlandstraße 181-183,
Charlottenburg, 10623 (885 2221); Hohenzollerndamm 92,
Wilmersdorf, 14199 (826 6108);

Vidal Sassoon

Schlüterstraße 38/39, Charlottenburg, 10629 (884
5000). S3, S5, S7, S75, S9 Savignyplatz. **Open** 9.45am-
6.15pm Tue, Thur; 9am-6.15pm Wed; 9am-7pm Fri;
8.30am-3pm Sat. **Credit** EC. **Map C4**
International safe bet in the hair stakes. A cut from a top
stylist will cost you DM102, and from the 'German Creative
Director' DM138. 'Cut' includes massage, wash, hair treatment, conditioning and styling. Modelling cuts DM15-
DM45. Full colouring and treatments on offer.

Bucherbogen – *all the art that's fit to print.*

Opticians

Brilliant

Schlüterstraße 30, Charlottenburg, 10629 (324 1991).
S3, S5, S7, S75, S9 Savignyplatz. **Open** 10am-7pm Mon-
Wed; 10am-8pm Thur, Fri; 10am-4pm Sat. **Credit** AmEx,
DC, MC, V.
Brilliant has the snappiest frames to be found any where in
this eyewear-conscious town. There are exclusive metal
frames by CK, Yamamoto, Gaultier, Gucci, D & G, Mikli,
Stark Eyes and handmade, platinum-coated frames by
German designer Lunor.

Fielmann

Alexanderplatz/Passage, Mitte, 10178 (242 4507) and
branches. U2, U8, U5, S3, S5, S7, S9 Alexanderplatz.
Open 9am-8pm Mon-Fri; 9am-4pm Sat. **Credit** AmEx,
DC, MC, V. **Map G3**
Germany's biggest chain of opticians. Large selection of
frames and competitive prices. Eye-tests in-house.

Ulrich Schulz

Uhlandstraße 46, Wilmersdorf, 10719 (882 2512). U15
Uhlandstraße. **Open** 9am-6pm Mon-Fri; 9am-1pm Sat
Credit MC, V. **Map C4**
Good selection of designer frames. Contact lenses also available. Known for offering good advice about what spectacles
suit which face. Eye-tests and contact lens fittings sessions
are conducted in-house.

Tanning studios

If you fancy bathing your bod in UV, you're in luck
– there are bronzing parlours all over Berlin. Try
the *Gelbe Seiten* under *Bräunungsstudios*, or keep
your eyes open for the loud neon signs.

City-Sun
First Floor, Tauentzienstraße 16 (entrance in Marburger Straße), Charlottenburg, 10789 (218 8037/8). U1, U15, U2 Wittenbergplatz. **Open** 10am-10pm daily. **Credit** AmEx, EC, MC, V for amounts more than DM20.
Map D4
Sun and beauty oasis, buzzing with towel-clad Venuses and Adonises throughout the year. Eight minutes in a super-intensive frying coffin costs DM6,60. Also an extensive range of massage, nail and make-up services, including permanent lip, eyelid and eyebrow make-up.

Books

Germany is thankfully still blessed with a lively independent book-shop scene, though chain stores are spreading. If the EC succeeds in scrapping the price maintenance system, which keeps many smaller operators in business, then the dominance of the chains will undoubtedly increase.

The British Bookshop
Mauerstraße 83-84, Mitte, 10117 (238 4680). U6 Stadtmitte. **Open** 10am-6pm Mon-Fri; 10am-4pm Sat. **Credit** AmEx, MC, V. **Map F4**
A big shop with a large stock of contemporary and classic fiction, the British Bookshop also boasts comprehensive English-language teaching, travel and children's sections. Good selection of newspapers and magazines. Not the cheapest place in town, though.

Bücherbogen
Kochstraße 19, Kreuzberg. 10969 (251 1345). U6 Kochstraße. **Open** 9.30am-6.30pm Mon-Fri; 10.30am-3pm Sat. **Credit** MC, V, and branches.
Map F4
Great art-book store with particular emphasis on architecture. The branch at Savignyplatz Bogen 593 has more paint-

'Goodness from the east'

The fall of the Wall triggered a cross-town shopping frenzy: easterners rushed to test the west's bananas, Coca-Cola, sex toys and Marlboro cigarettes; while canny westerners picked up cheap Pentacon or Praktica cameras, classical records and even groceries. Most drew the line, however, at purchasing a Trabant.

Most eastern products disappeared from the shops within a year of the fall of the Wall. Gone forever were the 1950s-style logos, shoddily colourful packaging and naively blatant advertising slogans. But easterners' enthusiasm for all things western was quickly tempered by the resentment accompanying the realisation that, for the time being at least, they were destined to remain economic second-class citizens. This had two effects.

The first is that wily old capitalist corporations and newly privatised eastern businesses realised they could exploit surviving loyalty to various old eastern brands. Thus, repackaged, re-formulated and relaunched – really only the names have survived – one can once more find Spee washing powder, Wernesgrüner beer, F6 and Cabinet cigarettes (formerly tasting much like rolled up dogends but now available in fancy light and menthol versions) and various other GDR brands – all of them found in eastern shops, but only rarely on the west side.

The second effect was that disgruntled easterners began demonstrating loyalty to their very own half of Germany by seeking out non-western goods wherever possible. Some supermarket chains now carry foodstuffs with bright-red stickers bearing the legend, 'goodness from the east'.

Even the old socialist product labels for beers and tinned fruit and stewed meats have made a come-back, turning up as the illustrations on a pelmanism-style memory game pack of cards. These sit on the shelves next to a board game about daily life in the good old GDR.

Another marketing success has been the range of t-shirts, postcards, baseball caps and lamps featuring the 'Ampelmännchen' – the stout little green and red fellows on eastern pedestrian crossings who are threatened with extinction at the hands of unimaginative (western) planners. *See page 255* **The little traffic light men.**

Making a commercial play for Ossie-nostalgia, Dussmann (*see* **Bookshops**) has a GDR room devoted to the written works of Marx, Lenin and Engels, statuettes of the same, CD compilations of old *Ost-Schlager*, plus re-issued or updated children's books featuring characters much-loved eastern characters such as Dig and Dag, who travel around getting into trouble, and are these days having adventures in Hollywood.

Fleamarkets such as the Straße des 17 Juni offer GDR literature and records from pop groups such as Die Pudhys and Karat. Look out for some insane light fixtures and household gadgets – particularly the space-age vacuum cleaners from AKA which resemble huge hypodermic needles and clean like demons.

The 'antique' shops, junkshops and antiquarian bookshops around Kollwitzstraße and Husemann Straße in Prenzlauer Berg also offer up the odd gem, if you're prepared to devote a few hours to hunting down the old east.

ing, sculpture and photography books while the nearby S-Bahnbogen branch concentrates more on film.
Branches: Savignyplatz Bogen 593, Charlottenburg 10623 (312 1912); S-Bahnbogen 585, Charlottenburg, 10623 (312 1932)

Dussman Das Kulturkaufhaus
Friedrichstraße 90, Mitte, 10117 (20 250). U6, S1, S2, S3, S5, S7, S9 Friedrichstraße. **Open** 10am-10pm Mon-Fri; 10am-4pm Sat. **Credit** V, EC, MC. **Map F3**
When Peter Dussmann, a millionaire who made his fortune out of office cleaning and maintenance, couldn't find tenants for his new building just north of Unter den Linden he decided to move in himself. The result is a spacious store, spread over three floors, mixing books with CDs, videos with magazines. There's also an internet café with five terminals and an interactive, video-viewing room. Excellent kids section and a little room devoted to artifacts from the old GDR.

Georg Büchner Buchladen
Wörther Straße 16, Prenzlauer Berg, 10405 (442 1301). U2 Senefelderplatz. **Open** 10am-6pm Mon, Tue, Wed, Fri; 10am-7.30 Thur. **Credit** EC. **Map G2**
A friendly independent shop just off Kollwitzplatz in the heart of Prenzlauer Berg. Good range of titles, many devoted to eastern themes.

Hugendubel
Tauenzienstraße 13, Charlottenberg, 10789 (214 060). U1, U2, U15 Wittenbergplatz. **Open** 9.30am-8pm Mon-Fri; 9am-4pm Sat. **No credit cards. Map D4**
After Kiepert, this is the second largest bookshop in Berlin. Its four floors house more than 140,000 books, including a big English-language section and a good selection of comics.

Kiepert
Hardenbergstraße 4-5, Charlottenburg, 10623 (311 880), U2 Ernst-Reuter-Platz. **Open** 9am-8pm Mon-Fri; 9am-4pm Sat. **Credit** AmEx, V, MC, EC. **Map C4**
Berlin's biggest bookshop. Wide selection of fiction and non-fiction, travel guides, maps and a decent selection of foreign language books. Will arrange postal delivery (at DM7 for a standard sized hardback) if necessary. The other branches have much less English-language material.
Branches: Friedrichstraße 63, Mitte, 10117 (201 7130); Georgenstraße 2, Mitte, 10117 (203 9960).

Kohlaas & Co.
Fasanenstraße 23, Wilmersdorf, 10719 (882 5044). U15 Uhlandstraße. **Open** 10am-8pm Mon-Fri; 10am-4pm Sat. **Credit** EC, MC, V. **Map C4**
Elegantly housed beneath the Literaturhaus, this small well-run bookshop aims towards the high-brow. German literature predominates. Service is friendly and helpful.

Marga Schoeller Bücherstube
Knesebeckstraße 33, Charlottenburg, 10623 (881 1112/1122). S3, S5, S7, S75, S9 Savignyplatz. **Open** 9.30am-7pm Mon-Wed; 9.30am-8pm Thur, Fri; 9.30am-4pm Sat. **Credit** MC, V. **Map C4**
This cooperatively owned store is something of an institution. Extensive range of foreign titles, especially new releases from the UK and US. Prices tend to be better than at some other international bookstores. The staff are sweet and helpful and can arrange postal delivery.

Antiquarian and second-hand books
If you're particularly interested in second-hand books, take a walk down Knesebeckstraße in Charlottenburg, Winterfeldtstraße in Schöneberg,

Tiny toys at **Johanna Petzoldt**.

or browse along Kollwitzstraße and Husemann Straße in Prenzlauer Berg. Most places can provide you with a comprehensive list of all the Antiquariaten in Berlin.

Antiquariat
Schönhauser Allee 126, Prenzlauer Berg, 10437 (449 7853). U2 Schönhauser Allee. **Open** 10am-6.30pm Mon-Fri; 9am-1pm Sat. **No credit cards. Map G1**
This bookshop sells quality second-hand books covering all subjects and has a particularly good collection of literature from the GDR.

Antiquariat Senzel
Knesebeckstraße 13-14, Charlottenburg, 10623 (312 5887). U2 Ernst-Reuter-Platz. **Open** noon-6.30pm Mon-Fri; 11am-2pm Sat. **No credit cards.**
You can have a seat in Antiquariat Senzel and enjoy a leisurely read. Most of the books are in German, though odd English and French volumes can be found. Also some beautifully leather-bound tomes and old maps. Well worth a browse.

Düwal
Schlüterstraße 17, Charlottenburg, 10625 (313 3030). S3, S5, S7, S75, S9 Savignyplatz. **Open** noon-6.30pm Mon-Fri; 11am-2pm Sat. **No credit cards. Map C4**
Large store offering everything from recent best-sellers to rare first editions costing thousands of marks. Good selection of foreign titles. They will also buy your old books.

Fair Exchange
Dieffenbackstraße 58, Kreuzberg, 10967 (694 4675). U8 Schönleinstraße. **Open** 11am-6.30pm Mon-Fri; 10am-1pm Sat. **No credit cards. Map G5**
Large selection of second-hand English-language books, with an emphasis on literature.

Grober Unfug
Zossener Straße 32-33, Kreuzberg, 10961 (6940 1491). U7 Gneisenaustraße. **Open** 11am-7pm Mon-Fri; 11am-4pm Sat. **Credit** AmEx, MC, V. **Map F5**
Stockists of comics in all languages, including annuals and comic art from *Viz* to French arty stuff. The new Mitte branch includes a comic gallery.
Branch: Weinmeisterstraße 9b, Mitte, 10178 (281 7331).

Children's clothes & toys
Children's merchandise tends to be very expensive in Germany, so it's probably best for the visiting shopper to steer clear of clothes and shoes. Wooden toys, however, are a German speciality and though pricey, are often original enough to warrant the

KaDeWe – *the Kaufaus des Westens is Berlin's answer to Harrod's. See page 150.*

expense. Puppets from the Dresdener puppet factory and Erzgebirge's delightful candle-mobiles and tiny wooden figures are particularly distinctive.

Stuffed toys are another traditional and important offering of the German toyshop. Steiff and its competitor Sigikid offer beautifully made cuddly animals that are full of character and highly collectible. Steiff claims to have invented the teddy bear a century ago, and you can pick up a Steiff or Sigikid teddy, or one of the hundreds of their other cuddly pets for DM130-DM400. A really huge or exotic beast could set you back thousands. *See also chapter* **Children**.

Berliner Zinnfiguren Kabinet
Knesebeckstraße 88, Charlottenburg, 10623 (313 0802).
S3, S5, S7, S9 Savignyplatz. **Open** 10am-6pm Mon-Thur; 10am-8pm Fri; 10am-3pm Sat. **Credit** AmEx, EC, MC, V. **Map C4**
Armies of tin soldiers line up alongside farm animals and historical characters, all handworked in tin, and painted with incredible attention to detail. Take home an entire battalion of Prussian Grenadiers for DM300. Also a fascinating collection of books on Prussian military history.

Heidi's Spielzeugladen
Kantstraße 61, Charlottenburg, 10627 (323 7556). U7 Wilmersdorferstraße. **Open** 9.30am-6.30pm Mon-Fri; 9.30-4pm Sat. **Credit** EC, V. **Map B4**
Wooden toys, including cookery utensils and child-sized kitchens, are the attraction here. You also find a good selection of books, puppets and wallhangings.

Johanna Petzoldt
Sophienstraße 9, Mitte, 10178 (282 6754). S3, S5, S7, S75, S9 Hackescher Markt. **Open** 10am-6pm Mon-Fri; 10am-3pm Sat. **Credit** AmEx, EC, JCB, MC, V. **Map F3**

Tiny, charming shop filled with traditional handmade wooden figurines, musical boxes and candle-mobiles from the Erzebirge company. Quirky figures depict rural German life, Christmas characters and military types, including British Grenadier guardsmen and drum majors. Appropriate and appealing souvenirs (not just for children), prices range from DM30 for a tiny figure to DM400 for a musical box.

Katrin Georgia
Schlüterstraße 37, Charlottenburg, 10629 (882 5586). S3, S5, S7, S75, S9 Savignyplatz. **Open** 10am-7pm Mon-Fri ; 10am-4pm Sat . **Credit** DC, EC, MC, V. **Map C4**
Exclusive maternity wear, christening gowns and exquisite children's clothing from Italy and France, plus a range of cots, bedding and nursery furnishings designed by Katrin. Take a deep breath before checking out the prices on the exquisite kiddies' clothes.

Michas Bahnhof
Nürnberger Straße 21, Schöneberg, 10789 (218 6611). U1 Augsburger Straße. **Open** 2pm-6.30pm Mon-Fri; 10am-2pm Sat. **Credit** AmEx, DC, EC, V. **Map D4**
Small shop packed with model trains both old and new, and everything that goes with them. Watch out for the antique miniature cars.

Spielen
Hufelandstraße 18, Prenzlauer Berg, 10407 (208 4298). U2 Rosa-Luxemburg-Platz. **Open** 9.30am-7pm Mon-Fri; 10am-3pm Sat. **Credit** AmEx, DC, EC, M, V.
This toy shop was set up in 1992 by an east German with three children and a passion for traditional playthings. She has filled her shop with toys that remind her of her own childhood, mostly handmade from wood by small German manufacturers (tiny working washing mangles and microscopic groceries), handmade puppets, mechanical tin toys and glockenspiels. **Branch**: Neue Schönhauser Straße 8, Mitte, 10178 (281 7183).

Quartier 206 – *new store on the block, but Berliners remain unimpressed.*

Toys 'Я' Us

Am Juliusturm 40-46, Spandau, 13599 (334 2472/334 3059). U7 Zitadelle. **Open** 10am-8pm Mon-Fri; 9am-4pm Sat. **Credit** AmEx, DC, EC, JCB, MC, V.

If you're staying a while it's cheaper than toyshops in the centre of town. No German-made stuff, though.

Tam Tam

Lietzenburger Straße 92, Charlottenburg, 10719 (882 1454). U15 Uhlandstraße. **Open** 10am-6.30pm Mon-Fri; 10am-4pm Sat. **Credit** EC, MC. **Map C4**

A bright, charming shop filled with stuffed animals and wooden toys, including building blocks, trains, trucks, dolls' houses, plus child-sized wooden stoves and household appliances. Taking a child shopping here can turn into a nightmare as all sorts of tempting playthings are well within reach of little hands.

Department stores

Sadly, the halcyon days of the early twentieth century when Berlin's department stores, such as Wertheim and Tietz, were among the finest in Europe (and even celebrated in literature) are gone. Today's high-street offerings, such as Kaufhof, Karstadt and Hertie, are pretty run of the mill concrete blocks offering decently made goods at reasonable prices, but with scant care or attention paid to service and displays. KaDeWe – or the Kaufhaus des Westens – sees itself as a rival to Harrods and has had a post-Wall facelift. But bar its sumptuous food hall, even this – for many years the best Berlin has to offer – doesn't really cut the mustard.

The hugely anticipated opening of Galeries Lafayettes was a big disappointment. The architecture is impressive enough (although the huge glass cone that runs through the building means you scuttle round like you're on a demented roundabout), but it lacks charm and style. Its womenswear and accessories selection is downright awful. Thankfully, there is an even newer kid on the block, the Quartier 206 Department Store, which has a more international flavour with understated service and elegant wares. Unlike other Berlin stores, Quartier 206, which appears to be modelled on Barneys or Bergdorf & Goodman, eschews Italian brands. Although Quartier 206 meets international standards, it remains to be seen whether Berliners will be impressed.

Galeries Lafayette

Französische Straße 23, Mitte, 10117 (209 480). U2/U6 StadtMitte. **Open** 9.30am-8pm Mon-Fri; 9am-4pm Sat. **Credit** AmEx, DC, EC, JCB, MC, V. **Map F3**

KaDeWe

Tauenzienstraße 21-24, Schöneberg, 10789 (212 10). U1, U2, U15 Wittenbergplatz. **Open** 9.30am-8pm Mon-Fri; 9am-4pm Sat. **Credit** AmEx, DC, EC, MC, V. **Map D4**

Karstadt

Wilmersdorfer Straße 118, Charlottenburg, 10627 (311 050). U7 Wilmersdorfer Straße. **Open** 9.30am-8pm Mon-Fri; 9am-4pm Sat. **Credit** AmEx, DC, EC, MC, V. **Map B4**

Kaufhof

Alexanderplatz 9, Mitte, 10178 (2474 3265). S3, S5, S6, S9, U2, U8 Alexanderplatz. **Open** 9am-8pm Mon-Fri; 9am-4pm Sat. **Credit** AmEx, DC, EC, MC, V. **Map G3**

Quartier 206 Department Store

Friedrichstraße 71, Mitte, 10117 (2094 6800). S1, S2, S3, S5, S6, S9, U6 Friedrichstraße. **Open** 10am-8pm Mon-Fri; 10am-4pm Sat. **Credit** AmEx, DC, EC, MC, V. **Map F3**

Wertheim

Kurfürstendamm 231, Charlottenburg, 10719 (880 030). U15, U9 Kurfürstendamm. **Open** 10am-8pm Mon-Fri; 9am-4pm Sat. **Credit** AmEx, DC, EC, MC, V. **Map C4**

Woolworth

Wilmersdorfer Straße 113, Charlottenburg, 10627 (318 6730). U7 Wilmersdorfer Straße. **Open** 9.15am-8pm Mon-Fri; 9am-4pm Sat. **Credit** EC. **Map B4**

Design & household goods

Lots of shops with 'Casa' in the name and window displays conjuring Tuscan homesteads give away Germans' deep love for all things Italian. They also love their bathrooms and kitchens, and there are hundreds of shops catering to a predilection for metallic-finish kitchen units, industrial-sized cooking appliances, acres of chrome and cunningly concealed lighting.

Bale Möbel & Decoration

Savignyplatz 6, Charlottenburg, 10623 (312 9066). S3, S5, S7, S75, S9 Savignyplatz. **Open** 10am-7pm Mon-Wed, 10am-8pm Thur, Fri; 10am-4pm Sat. **Credit** EC. **Map C4**
You'll find no better source in Berlin for rattan furniture, oriental futons, wicker furniture and floor cushions. The glassware and ceramics also run to a far-eastern theme, and there is a lovely selection of hand-sewn Japanese kimonos which start at DM200.

Christiane Teger Wohnkultur

Grolmanstraße 53-54, Charlottenburg, 10623 (313 2977). S3, S5, S7, S75, S9 Savignyplatz. **Open** 11am-7pm Tue-Fri; 10am-3pm Sat. **Credit** AmEx, EC, MC, V. **Map C4**
Beautiful bedlinen from Austria, fine French jacquard tablecloths and Italian nightclothes. As well as these fabulous home textiles, there's a super selection of china, glassware and furniture, all with a natural, slightly rustic edge.

dadriade

Rosenthaler Straße 40-41, Mitte, 10178 (2852 8720). U8 Weinmeisterstraße/S3, S5, S7, S75, S9 Hackescher Markt. **Open** 10am-8pm Mon-Fri; 10am-4pm Sat. **Credit** AmEx, EC, MC, V. **Map F2**
This airy flagship store – the largest worldwide – represents a major investment for these Italian masters of home design. A Mecca for disciples of high style, it is filled with breathtaking tableware, cunningly functional kitchens and steel-and-glass furnishings – much of it designed by style-emperor Philippe Starck. It's here you can track down his Atlantida stacking chairs or Mr Mause coathangers with plastic bristle shoulders – the latter a snip at DM25 each, and by far the cheapest buy in the shop.

J&M Fässler

Europa-Center, Charlottenburg, 10787 (342 7166). S3, S5, S6, S9/U2, U9 Zoologischer Garten. **Open** 10am-

6.30pm Mon-Fri; 10am-6pm Sat. **Credit** AmEx, DC, EC, MC, V. **Map D4**
More than any heart could desire in the way of kitsch German ornaments, from Hummel figurines and cuckoo clocks to Bavarian beer mugs and musical boxes.

Fingers

Nollendorfstraße 35, Schöneberg, 10777 (215 3441). U1, U2, U4 Nollendorfplatz. **Open** 2.30pm-6.30pm Tue-Fri; 11am-2pm Sat. **No credit cards. Map D5**
Splendid finds from the 1940s, 1950s and 1960s, including lipstick-shaped cigarette lighters, vintage toasters, weird lighting fixtures and eccentric china and glassware.

Galerie Weinand

Oranienplatz 5, Kreuzberg, 10999 (614 2545). Bus 129. **Open** only by appointment. **No credit cards. Map G4**
Herbert Jakob Weinand is Berlin's star interior designer and his shop stocks objects for the home made by an international group of interior designers and by Weinand himself.

IKEA

Am Rondell 8, Waltersdorf, 15732 (033 762 660). Take the autobahn 113 to Grunau. **Open** 9.30am-8pm Mon-Fri; 8.30am-4pm Sat. **No credit cards.**
All you could wish for in the way of Scandinavian value-for-money design. Delivery to an address in Berlin costs 10 per cent of the purchase price, up to a limit of DM150.

Glass & Ceramics

Bürgel-Haus

Friedrichstraße 154, Mitte, 10117 (204 4519). U6 Französische Straße. **Open** 9am-8pm Mon-Sat. **Credit** AmEx, EC, M, V. **Map F3**
This distinctive blue-and-cream pottery from the Thüringen region of east Germany makes an inexpensive present for lovers of cosy kitchenware.

Ceramica Atelier

Fraenkelufer 46, Kreuzberg, 10999 (614 4937). U1 Kottbusser Tor. **Open** on appointment. **No credit cards. Map G5**
Fernando Marquina makes sculptural ceramics for the floor and wall. His work is inspired by nature, and costs from DM220 for a small, shell-shaped bowl to DM10,000 for a wall-relief.

Keramikladen

Rykestraße 49, Prenzlauer Berg, 10405 (441 9109). U2 Senefeldplatz. **Open** 11am-6.30pm Tue-Fri; 10am-3pm Sat. **No credit cards. Map G2**
Bright, inexpensive and humourous household ceramics from this collective of five east German potters.

KPM

Wegelystraße 1, Tiergarten, 10623 (3900 9215). S3, S5, S7, S75, S9 Tiergarten. **Open** 9.30am-8pm Mon-Fri; 9am-4pm Sat. **Credit** AmEx, DC, EC, MC, V. **Map D4**
Frederick the Great had a thing about porcelain. So he bought the Königliche Porzellan Manufaktur. You too can eat from a king's plate – and quite inexpensively too if you pick up some seconds at this factory shop. You can fork out for the full-priced version at the Kempinski branch.
Branch: Kempinski Hotel, Kurfürstendamm 27, Charlottenburg, 10719 (884 340).

Paint Your Style

Bleibtreustraße 46, Charlottenburg, 10623 (8855 2223). S3, S5, S7, S75, S9 Savignyplatz. **Open** 11am-10pm daily. **No credit cards. Map C4**
Paint your own crockery. Designs are modern and solid, and prices are reasonable: large vase DM66 and a tile DM6, plus painting an extra DM15 per hour (an hour is usually about

what it takes). Stencils and computer clip-art available for the artistically impaired, and you can even bring your own bottle of booze. A fun place.

Fashion

A quick glance at the average man in the Straße should tell you that Berlin is a long way away from the cutting-edge of style. But this sorry state of affairs seems to be changing; Berliners are waking up to their sartorial responsibilities as citizens of a new 'Weltstadt', and the past five years have seen some interesting developments in retail fashion.

One of the most productive places to hunt for stylish, affordable clothing has sprung up in Mitte's Scheunenviertel. The renovated Hackesche Höfe, and the streets that spider off it, are now home to many of Berlin's designers, their shops and their ateliers. The merchandise on offer may sometimes seem limited, but the advantage of having workshops as part of the store is that styles can be run up quickly in your size and preferred fabric. Many of these shops are on short, cheap rental contracts, so it's best to call and check they're still there before setting out.

Designers of a more hefty calibre are moving into the retail developments on Friedrichstraße, where new shopfronts are slowly filling with high-profile, international labels (*see below*).

But despite all this excitement in the east, for the Berlin shopper there is still no avoiding the pull of the Ku'damm and its affluent offshoots. Here department stores and clothing giants (Gap, Esprit, Laura Ashley, Eddie Bauer) jostle for space with chi-chi boutiques. Most of the designer merchandise is stuff you'd be able to buy back home,

Fashion and folly on Friedrichstraße

Friedrichstraße, east Berlin's new showcase shopping street, is certainly an impressive sight. But with some of the world's best architects and property development companies involved, a superb location at the heart of the new city centre, and a bill of over DM2 billion for new construction, that's precisely what you would expect.

The centrepiece is the Friedrichstadt Passagen, a three-block shopping centre to the east of Friedrichstraße. These architecturally distinct buildings – which include a deco offering from IM Pei, the man who gave the Louvre its glass pyramid – are linked by an underground walkway and are now home to **Galeries Lafayette**, Donna Karan, assorted high-street chain stores and the Berlin branch of Planet Hollywood.

Which is all a bit of change from the bad old days when this was a quiet, gloomy and somewhat paranoid corner of East Berlin. There were a few dowdy shops and the only people about were either westerners ambling up from Checkpoint Charlie, or else secret policemen keeping an eye on them. Friedrichstraße has been transformed.

But behind the glitzy exterior, there are problems. The mix of tenants in the street is awkward, as haute couture rubs shoulders with Bennetton and Hennes & Mauritz. Trade is sluggish, though so far retailers don't seem to be hurting – perhaps because of the cheap rent deals that enticed them to move to Friedrichstraße in the first place. But in both the Friedrichstadt Passagen and elsewhere along the street, many retail units remain untenanted. Tactics for enticement gather pace.

Take the department store **Quartier 206**, occupying the whole top floor of IM Pei's central Friedrichstadt Passagen block. Run by the canny wife of the property fund manager who developed the building, this extraordinary store brings together one of the most impressive mixes of fashion, cosmetics and interiors names in the business – not only the best brands, but those brands' most definitive items. The store actually seems to be a showcase intended to promote the building and draw both upmarket shoppers and other prestigious tenants, rather than operating under any real pressure to shift merchandise.

Likewise, up towards Friedrichstraße station, local office-services mogul Peter Dussmann decided to turn a building he'd developed but was finding difficult to rent into the 'media department store' **Dussman das Kulturkaufhaus**. For Berliners, the comfortable environment and interesting mix of books, CDs and other media is a bonus. But is the venture really viable?

Friedrichstraße is thus clearly some distance from realising the ambition of its planners: to create a serious rival to the Ku'Damm. Like so much else in Berlin, the street remains in a surreal limbo. B ut with acres of designer goods but hardly any shoppers, Friedrichstraße offers some of the weirdest and most wonderful window shopping around.

but cross-town competition for business makes for some lively sales and, when the exchange rate is favourable, you can pick up bargains. The most sophisticated Berlin gets is Fasanenstraße, where you will find the likes of Gucci, Chanel, Tiffany and Bvlgari. Much of the money spent here is Russian; Brits are particularly disdained for looking rather than spending, so don't be surprised if officious assistants ignore you or are openly hostile to enquiries.

The following shops are by no means a comprehensive survey of all that Berlin has to offer, but they aim for a flavour of the more dynamic elements of the city's fledgling fashion culture.

360°

Pariser Straße 23/24, Wilmersdorf, 10707 (883 8596). U7 Adenauerplatz. **Open** 11am-7.30pm Mon-Fri; 10am-4pm Sat. **Credit** AmEx, EC, MC, V. **Map C5**
Designer sportswear and accessories for the outwardly mobile, featuring Quicksilver, Stüssy, Sky & High and Vans shoes. 360° also offers Rollerblades, high-tech snowboards and windsurfing equipment.

Anna von Griesheim

Pariser Straße 44, Wilmersdorf, 10707 (885 4406). U2, U9 Spichernstraße. **Open** 10am-6pm Tue-Fri; noon-4pm Sat. **Credit** AmEx, DC, EC, MC. **Map C5**
Fine city suits, simple daywear and an exquisite range of wedding dresses by this couture-trained designer.

Claudia Skoda *sorts her stock.*

Arrey & Mossina

Pestalozzistraße 106, Charlottenburg, 10623 (3150 4336). U7 Kantstraße. **Open** 11am-8pm Mon-Fri; 11am-4pm Sat. **Credit** EC, MC, V. **Map B4**
Sharp tailoring, muted colours and clever detailing from one of Berlin's most talented designers, flamboyant Russian Katja Mossina. This cleverly designed shop also sells quirky handbags and classic knitwear by Arrey Enow. Just watch the city's media goddesses and social butterflies swarm for the parties presenting the new collections.

Blue Moon

Wilmersdorfer Straße 80, Charlottenburg, 10629 (323 7088). U7 Adenauerplatz. **Open** noon-7pm Mon-Wed; noon-8pm Thur, Fri; 10am-4pm Sat. **Credit** AmEx, EC, MC, V.
For two decades Blue Moon has been a clothing supply house favoured by casual trendies and clubbers. A wide selection of jeans and high-fashion shoes, including Doc Martens and some of the highest platforms in town.

Bramigk

Savigny Passage, Bogen 598, Charlottenburg, 10623 (313 5125). S3, S5, S7, S75, S9 Savignyplatz. **Open** 11am-6.30pm Mon-Fri; 11am-4pm Sat. **Credit** AmEx, EC, MC, V. **Map C4**
Nicola Bramigk specialises in quietly distinctive womenswear in luxurious Italian fabrics (also for sale by the metre). Her sleek, flattering styles can be made up in the fabric and size of your choice.

Brummer

Tauentzienstraße 17, Charlottenburg, 10789 (211 1027). U1, U15, U2 Wittenbergplatz. **Open** 10am-6.30pm Mon-Fri; 10am-4pm Sat. **Credit** AmEx, EC, MC, V. **Map D4**
This 1930s department store was totally revamped to cater to the Anglomania of its owner, and now stocks traditionally 'English' clothing and accessories: impeccable suiting by Hackett, Mulberry leather goods and Penhaligon's fragrances and toiletries for men and women.

Claudia Skoda

Linienstraße 154, Mitte, 10115 (280 7211). U6 Oranienburger Tor. **Open** 11am-7pm Mon-Fri. **Credit** AmEx, DC, EC, MC, V. **Map F3**
Berlin's most established womenswear designer chose to launch her ready-to-wear collection, après skoda, through her new shop (and studio) in Mitte. Using high-tech yarns and innovative knitting techniques, the range bears her signature combination of stretch fabrics and graceful drape effects. Skoda's more costly couture line is available at the Ku'damm branch.
Branch: Skoda Attendance, Kurfürstendamm 50 (885 1009).

Eisdieler

Auguststraße 74, Mitte, 10117 (285 7351). U6 Oranienburger Tor. **Open** noon-7pm Mon-Fri; noon-6pm Sat. **No credit cards. Map F3**
Five young designers pooled their resources to transform this former ice shop in Mitte's bar and gallery quarter. Each partner manages a label under the Eisdieler banner – clubwear, second hand gear, casualwear and sharp street style. Till Fuhrmann jewellery in silver and wood is particularly distinctive, and it's his spikey ironwork adorning the façade.

Escada

Friedrichstraße 176, Mitte, 10117 (238 6404). S1, S2, S3, S5, S6, S9, U6 Friedrichstraße. **Open** 10am-8pm Mon-Fri; 10am-4pm Sat. **Credit** AmEx, DC, EC, MC, V. **Map F3**
German women love the colour and glamour of Escada's pricey offerings and this was one of the first major names to shift east and open a branch in Friedrichstraße. If prices seem

a little steep but you like the styles, try nipping next door into Escada Sport, the slightly cheaper diffusion line.

Evento

Grolmanstraße 53, Charlottenburg (313 3217). S3, S5, S7, S75, S9 Savignyplatz. **Open** 11am-6.30pm Mon, Tue, Wed, Fri; 11am-8.30 Thur; 11am-2pm Sat. **Credit** AmEx, DC, EC, MC, V. **Map C4**

Christine Breuer has been selling her beautifully made womenswear in Berlin since 1982. The boutique's selection is limited but to the point, and the key shapes of the season can be made to order in your choice of colour and fabric for no extra charge.

Flex/Inch By Inch/Melting Point

Neue Schönhauser Straße 2, Mitte, 10178 (283 4836/44). U8 Weinmeisterstraße. **Open** 1pm-8pm Mon; 11am-8pm Tue-Fri; 10am-4pm Sat. **No credit cards**. **Map G3**

Clubware store, hair salon and record shop in one – this is one of the buzziest stores on the street, especially in the evening when Mitte's young, bad and beautiful get their hair cropped and coloured, or pick out an outfit from German rave labels, including Sabotage and Thatcher's. DJs drop by to check out new house, jungle and techno releases.

GB

Auguststraße 77-78, Mitte, 10117 (2839 0103). U6 Oranienburger Tor. **Open** 10am-8pm Mon-Fri; noon-4pm Sat. **No credit cards**. **Map F3**

Chic, understated shop and studio for Guido Bednarz's collection of sharply tailored mens- and womenswear. The range is limited to one or two pieces in each style, with a made-to-measure service if your size isn't available. Prices are reasonable, about DM400 for a tailored jacket.

Groopie Deluxe

Goltzstraße 39, Schöneberg, 10781 (217 2038). U7 Eisenacher Straße. **Open** 11am-8pm Mon-Fri; 11am-4pm Sat. **Credit** AmEx, EC, JCB, MC, V. **Map D5**

Trendy, sexy gear to party in – lots of bright, skimpy numbers, fake fur, accessories and wigs. Labels include local talents Next Guru Now and Beam Me Up.

Hautnah

3rd floor, Uhlandstraße 170, Charlottenburg, 10719 (882 3434). U15 Uhlandstraße. **Open** noon-8pm Mon-Fri; 11am-4pm Sat. **Credit** AmEx, EC, MC, V. **Map C4**

Cult fetish gear for those into latex, leather and stilettos. The shop proudly presents a range of 'English' PVC macs.

Jil Sander

Kurfürstendamm 185, Charlottenburg, 10707 (886 2070). U3, U9 Kurfürstendamm. **Open** 10am-7pm Mon-Fri; 10am-4pm Sat. **Credit** AmEx, DC, EC, JCB, MC, V. **Map C4**

This smart, understated store is a perfect foil for the doyenne of German minimalism. Sander's secret is her sleek silhouette, fine fabrics and Spartan cut, and this combination has won her an international audience who unflinchingly pay her top-dollar prices.

Karstadt Sport

Quartier 205, Friedrichstraße 67, Mitte, 10117 (2094 5000), and branches. **Open** 10am-8pm Mon-Fri; 9.30am-4pm Sat. **Credit** AmEx, DC, EC, M, V. **Map F3**

Huge selection of branded exercisewear and fitness equipment. Large areas are devoted to footwear, swimwear, in-line skating and snow sports. Those tired of shopping can try their luck on the Alpine ski simulator.

Lisa D

Hackesche Höfe, Rosenthaler Straße 40-41, Mitte, 10178 (282 9061). U8 Weinmeisterstraße/S3, S5, S7, S75, S9 Hackescher Markt. **Open** noon-6.30pm Mon-Sat. **Credit** AmEx, DC, EC, JCB, MC, V. **Map F3**

Long, flowing womenswear in subdued shades from this avant-garde designer. Austrian-born Lisa D is a well-known face on the Berlin fashion scene and was one of the first tenants to move into the renovated Hackesche Höfe.

Molotow

Gneisenaustraße 112, Kreuzberg, 10965 (693 0818). U7 Gneisenaustraße. **Open** 2pm-8pm Mon-Fri; 11am-2pm Sat. **Credit** DC, EC, MC, V. **Map F5**

Showcasing local talent, Molotow sells a selection of fashion and millinery from Berlin designers. The clothes are fresh and eye-catching, ranging from futuristic creations to classical sharp tailoring.

Moda Mo

Giesebrechtstraße 17, Charlottenburg, 10629 (324 0025). U7 Adenauerplatz. **Open** 11am-7pm Mon-Fri; 11am-2pm Sat. **Credit** AmEx, DC, EC, MC, V. **Map B4**

Womenswear, millinery and jewellery by predominantly British designers. The hats in particular are worth checking out – a surreal selection from Stephen Jones, Philip Treacy and Berlin-based milliner Fiona Bennett.

New Noise/Scenario

Schönleinstraße 31, Kreuzberg 10967 (691 5064). U8 Schönleinstraße. **Open** 11am-7pm Mon-Fri; 11am-4pm Sat. **Credit** AmEx, DC, EC, MC, V. **Map G5**

A record shop with a good range of drum 'n' bass, house, hip-hop and rarities, plus casualwear from Berlin designers, including Beam Me Up and Next Guru Now.

Nix

Auguststraße 86, Mitte, 10117 (281 8044). U6 Oranienburger Tor. **Open** 2pm-8pm Tue-Fri; noon-4pm Sat. **Credit** EC, V. **Map F3**

Designers Barbara Gebhardt and Angela Herb's atelier and

Tools & Gallery *– fusing fashion and fine art.*

store sells their New Individual X-tras (or NIX) label for men, women and children. This urban collection is unusual in cut, not extravagantly priced and has a dash of humour.

Ozone
Knesebeckstraße 27, Charlottenburg, 10623 (883 1124). S3, S5, S7, S75, S9 Savignyplatz. **Open** 10am-6.30 Mon-Sat. **Credit** EC, MC, V. **Map C4**
Ozone offers everything you need for dance and aerobics activity, from tutus to tap shoes. Children's dancewear (including ballet blocks and leotards) are also on offer, as is a good selection of imported, designer sports wear.

Patrick Hellman
Fasanenstraße 26, Charlottenburg, 10719 (882 4201), and branches. **Open** 10am-7pm Mon-Fri; 10am-8pm Thur; 10am-4pm Sat. **Credit** AmEx, DC, EC, V. **Map C5**
A prolific Berlin retailer with five stores to his name, specialising in international chic for men and women. A bespoke tailoring service offers men the choice of the Hellman design range in a variety of luxurious fabrics, including some by Italian textile maestro Ermenegildo Zegna.

Ralf Setzer
Kurfürstendamm 46, Charlottenburg, 10707 (883 8332). S3, S5, S7, S75, S9 Savignyplatz. **Open** 10am-7pm Mon-Wed; 10am-8pm Thur, Fri; 10am-4pm Sat. **Credit** AmEx, DC, EC, MC, V. **Map C4**
Designer fashion for men and women, from the likes of Helmut Lang, Katharine Hamnett, Paul Smith, Kenzo, Patrick Cox, Massimo Osti and Romeo Gigli. Friendly staff speak English. Ralph's wife runs the branch at Bleibtreustraße, Antonie Setzer Fashion for Women, which offers an intelligent selection of styles from Calvin Klein, Joseph, Ralph Lauren, Miu Miu and others.
Branch: Bleibtreustraße 19, Charlottenburg, 10623 (883 13 50).

RespectMen
Neue Schönhauser Straße 14, Mitte, 10178 (283 5010). U8 Weinmeisterstraße. **Open** noon-8pm Mon-Fri; 11am-4pm Sat. **Credit** AmEx, EC, M, V. **Map G3**
When seen on the rail, Dirk Seidel and Karin Warburg's menswear seems to be traditionally tailored, yet when worn it shows off its contemporary, body-conscious cut. Suits, trousers, jackets and coats can be made to order from the many fabrics on offer. The inventive cut may not appeal to fashion conservatives, but this is some of the most interesting menswear you'll find in Berlin. Also menswear from another local label, Next Guru Now, and British style from Limehaus and John Smedley. Stupid name, though.

Schwarze Mode
Grunewaldstraße 91, Schöneberg, 10823 (784 5922). U7 Kleistpark. **Open** noon-8pm Mon-Fri; 10am-4pm Sat. **Credit** AmEx, DC,EC,V. **Map E5**
Leatherette, rubber and vinyl are among the particular delicacies stocked here for Gummi (rubber) enthusiasts. As well as the fetish fashions, comics and magazines are on offer in Schwarze Mode's sister store next door.

Tools & Gallery
Rosenthaler Straße 34-35, Mitte, 10178 (2859 9343). U8 Weinmeisterstraße/S3, S5, S7, S75, S9 Hackescher Markt. **Open** 10am-8pm Mon-Fri; 10am-8pm Thur-Fri; 10am-4pm Sat. **Credit** EC, MC, V. **Map F3**
Kai Angladegies is not the first retailer to fuse fashion and fine art, but Tools & Gallery is a bold and stylish attempt. The interior is campily decked out in rococo splendour, with candelabras and muslin-draped changing cubicles, and the selection of clothing is equally impressive. Menswear is especially strong and can be altered to fit like a glove. Both that and the women's fashion comes from names such as Kenzo

and Caramelo. The gallery is reached via a beautiful 1860 wrought-iron staircase and features exhibitions of fine art, design and haute couture. Excellent place.

Wicked Garden
Grunewaldstraße 71, Schöneberg, 10629 (782 0455). U7 Eisenacher Straße. **Open** 11.30am-8pm Mon-Fri; 10.30am-4pm Sat. **Credit** AmEx, EC, MC, V. **Map D5**
Katharina Deeken regularly replenishes her supply of young, innovative fashion from designers in London and the US, as well as using homegrown Berlin talent, and her rails feature the work of Helmut Lang, Martin Margiela, Paul Smith and Alexander McQueen.

Second-hand clothes and shoes
Berlin has a huge market in cheaper clothing, with flea markets, junk shops and second-hand stores offering some unique and colourful bargains. The best hunting grounds are around Mehringdamm in Kreuzberg and Prinzenallee in Wedding.

Calypso – High Heels For Ever
Neue Schönhauser Straße 19, Mitte, 10178 (281 6165). U8 Weinmeisterstraße. **Open** noon-8pm Mon-Fri; noon-4pm Sat. **No credit cards. Map G3**
Hundreds of gravity-defying stilettos, wedges and platforms in the vivid shades and exotic shapes of the 1960s and 1970s, almost all in excellent condition. Also a selection of stiletto-toed, thigh-high fetish boots, some in men's sizes. Prices range from about DM40-DM80, but expect to pay up to DM250 for a truly shocking pair of trotters.

Checkpoint
Mehringdamm 57, Kreuzberg, 10961 (694 4344). U7 Mehringdamm. **Open** 10am-6.30pm Mon-Fri; 10am-4pm Sat. **No credit cards. Map F5**
The lurid crayon-coloured walls should grab your attention, but once you've started rummaging though the huge selection of 1970s gear, you'll be lost in the mists of time. Lurex skinny-knit jumpers, printed bellbottoms (DM39), leather coats and jackets (DM125-200), and even wedding dresses (DM200) from the heyday of Charlie's Angels.
Branch: Monroe, Kollwitzstraße 102, Prenzlauer Berg, 10435 (440 8448).

Colours
1st courtyard, Bergmannstraße 102, Kreuzberg, 10961 (694 3348). U7 Gneisenaustraße. **Open** 11am-8pm Mon-Fri; 10am-4pm Sat. **No credit cards. Map F5**
Row upon row of jeans, leather jackets, t-shirts and dresses, including party stunners and some fetching Bavarian dirndls. The odd gem from the 1950s and 1960s is thrown in too, so it's worth ploughing through for a bargain. Patience and a good eye will be well rewarded. Prices vary from DM5-DM200 depending on condition and vintage.

Garage
Ahornstraße 2, Tiergarten, 10787 (211 2760). U1, U2, U4 Nollendorfplatz. **Open** 11.30am-8pm Mon-Fri; 10.30am-4pm Sat. **No credit cards. Map D4**
One of the cheapest second-hand shops in Berlin: tons of clothing priced at DM25 per kilo. It's surprisingly well organised, given the barracks-like nature of the place. Particularly good for cheap, last-minute party outfits.

Humana
Karl-Liebnecht-Straße 30, Mitte, 10178 (242 3000). U2, U5, U8, S3, S5, S7, S9 Alexanderplatz. **Open** 10am-6.30pm Mon-Wed, Fri; 10am-8pm Thur; 10am-4pm Sat. **No credit cards. Map G3**
Huge Humana charity megastores are sprouting all over the city, selling acres of cheap second-hand clothing, house-

hold textiles, fur and leather. This is the biggest and most central, but more are opening all the time. They usually have a 'trend' section of more fashionable, original numbers and this is always worth hunting through for a sensational bargain.

Made in Berlin
Potsdamer Straße 106, Tiergarten, 10785 (262 2431). U1 Kurfürstenstraße. **Open** 10am-8pm Mon-Fri; 10am-4pm Sat. **No credit cards. Map E4**
The sister store of Garage (*above*), where all the 'better stuff' supposedly goes. It's still pretty cheap with dresses and jackets in the DM40-DM60 range.

Sterling Gold
Paul-Lincke-Ufer 44, Kreuzberg, 10999 (611 3217). U8 Schönleinstraße. **Open** noon-8pm; 11am-4pm Sat. **No credit cards. Map G5**
Michael Boenke couldn't believe his luck when he was offered a warehouse full of 'prom' dresses on a trip to the States. He shipped them straight back to Berlin. These wonderful ball- and cocktail gowns, dating from the 1950s to the 1980s, are in terrific condition and attract the attention of fashion aficionados from Hamburg, Cologne and Düsseldorf. Cocktail dresses in every conceivable shade and fabric range in price from DM70-DM150, but expect to pay up to DM500 for a vintage silk ballgown or elegant wedding dress.

Waahnsinn
Neue Promenade 3, Ecke Hackescher Markt, Mitte, 10178 (282 0029). S3, S5, S7, S75, S9 Hackescher Markt. **Open** noon-8pm Mon-Sat. **No credit cards. Map F3**
Unashamedly tacky clothes and jewellery from the 1960s and 1970s, chosen to outrage the eye and complement the plastic egg chairs and lava lamps also on sale. Not the cheapest second-hand clobber in Berlin, but in good condition and running along a strong party-girl theme.

Shoes & Leather Goods

Bleibgrün
Bleibtreustraße 29, Charlottenburg, 10707 (882 1689). S3, S5, S7, S75, S9 Savignyplatz. **Open** 11am-8pm Mon-Fri; 11am-4pm Sat. **Credit** AmEx, DC, EC, MC, V. **Map C4**
Berlin's best designer shoe shop, with a nifty selection from the likes of Lagerfeld, Maud Frizon and Jan Jansen. Bleibgrün has opened a swanky boutique next door at number 30 which has an equally discriminating choice of cutting-edge womenswear.

Bree
Kurfürstendamm 44, Charlottenburg, 10719 (883 7462). U15 Uhlandstraße. **Open** 10am-7pm Mon-Wed; 10am-8pm Thur, Fri; 10am-4pm Sat. **Credit** AmEx, EC, JCB, MC, V. **Map C4**
This German leather goods company must have a patent on practicality; its durable and easy-to-organise handbags, briefcases, rucksacks and suitcases are sported by many a German professional.

Budapester Schuhe
Kurfürstendamm 199, Charlottenburg, 10719 (881 1707). U15 Uhlandstraße. **Open** 10am-7pm Mon-Wed; 10am-8pm Thur-Fri; 10am-4pm Sat. **Credit** AmEx, DC, EC, JCB, MC, V. **Map C4**
Impressive selection of Italian footwear from the likes of Prada, Dolce & Gabanna and Ferragamo plus men's handmade classics from Austrian Ludwig Reiter. Average price is DM400-DM500 per pair, or you can wait for sales when prices are slashed by around 50 per cent.
Branch: Friedrichstraße 81, Mitte, 10117 (2038 8110)

Penthesileia
Linienstraße 106, Mitte, 10115 (282 1152). U6 Oranienburger Tor. **Open** 10am-7pm Mon-Fri; 10am-4pm Sat. **No credit cards. Map F3**

*To **Witt** – Berlin's most extensive suitcase parts assortment, m'lud.*

Named after the Amazon queen, this is showroom, shop and workspace for Sylvia Müller and Anke Runge, who design and make their highly individual range of handbags and rucksacks. Shapes are novel and organic – sunflowers, cones, shells and hearts – and crafted from calfskin and nubuck.

Trippen
Hackesche Höfe, Rosenthaler Straße 40-41, Mitte, (28 39 13 37). U8 Weinmeisterstraße/S3, S5, S7, S75, S9 Hackescher Markt. **Open** noon-7pm Mon-Fri; 10am-4pm Sat. **Credit** EC, V. **Map F3**
Not the most reassuring name for a shoeshop, But Trippen is home to an idiosyncratic selection of foot fashion designed by Angela Spieth and Michael Oehler. Oddly shaped wooden-soled platforms, heels that shoot out at right angles and 'horned' toes are just a few of the surprises here.

Shoe Makers and Repairs

Breitenbach
Bergmannstraße 30, Kreuzberg, 10961 (692 3570). U7 Gneisenaustraße. **Open** 8am-1pm, 2pm-6.30pm Mon-Fri; 10am-2pm Sat. **Credit** AmEx, EC, MC, V. **Map F5**
Gentlemen's shoe- and bootmaker, who also provides first-class repairs for men's and women's footwear. A made-to-measure pair of leather shoes costs upwards of DM350.

Picobello
KaDeWe, Tauentzienstraße 21, Schöneberg, 10789 (212 10). U1, U2, U15 Wittenbergplatz. **Open** 9.30am-8pm Mon-Fri; 9am-4pm Sat. **No credit cards. Map D4**
They'll heel and sole shoes while you wait, and also engrave and cut keys. There are branches all over Berlin, often to be found in department stores.

Luggage Repair

Kofferhaus Meinecke
Meineckestraße 25, Wilmersdorf, 10719 (882 2262). U9 Kurfürstendamm. **Open** 10am-7pm Mon-Fri; 10am-4pm Sat. **Credit** AmEx, DC, MC, V. **Map C4**
Specialists in Samsonite, Delsey, Airline, Traveller, Rimova and Picard, they'll repair all baggage within two to three days. Repairs are not delivered but a new suitcase can be delivered within the city.

Witt
Hauptstraße 9, Schöneberg, 10827 (781 4937). U7 Kleistpark. **Open** 9am-6pm Mon-Wed; 9am-8pm Thur; 9am-2pm Sat. **Credit** AmEx, DC, EC, MC, V. **Map E5**
Probably Berlin's most extensive suitcase spare parts assortment, including patches. Luggage repairs can be completed in a day, and if damage has resulted during a flight and you have written airline confirmation of this, the repairs will be billed to the airline. Evening delivery possible.

Accessories

Kaufhaus Schrill
Bleibtreustraße 46, Charlottenburg, 10623 (882 4048). S3, S5, S7, S75, S9 Savignyplatz. **Open** 11am-7pm Mon-Fri; 11am-4pm Sat. **Credit** AmEx, EC, MC, V. **Map C4**
Feather boas, sequins, tiaras. A sea of pearls, shocking colours, frills and loud, fruity patterns.

Les Dessous
Fasanenstraße 42, Wilmersdorf, 10719 (883 3632). U1 Spichernstraße. **Open** 10am-6.30pm Mon-Fri; 10am-3pm Sat. **Credit** AmEx, DC, EC, V. **Map C5**
A beautiful shop with unusually friendly sales assistants for the area, featuring luxurious lingerie, silk dressing gowns

and fabulous swimwear by Capucine Puearari, Eres, Marvel, Ferre, La Perla, Malizia and Andres Sarda.

Rio
Bleibtreustraße 52, Charlottenburg, 10623 (313 3152). S3, S5, S7, S75, S9 Savignyplatz. **Open** 11am-6.30 Mon-Wed; 11am-8pm Thur; 11am-6.30pm Fri; 10am-4pm Sat. **No credit cards. Map C4**
Eye-catching costume jewellery, including a stunning selection of earrings from Vivienne Westwood, DKNY and Hervé van der Straeten. Plus Rio's own sophisticated range of luminescent frosted-glass necklaces, bracelets and earrings designed by the shop's owner Barbara Kranz.

Tagebau
Rosenthaler Straße 19, Mitte, 10119 (2839 0890). U8 Weinmeisterstraße/S3, S5, S7, S75, S9 Hackescher Markt. **Open** 11am-8pm Mon-Fri; 10am-4pm Sat. **No credit cards. Map F3**
Six young designers share this spacious store-cum-workshop specialising in jewellery, fashion, millinery and furniture. The work of all these designers has in common a sculptural quality which, when combined with the generous space with spot-lighting picking out the displays, gives this shop the impression of a gallery.

Handmade jewellery

Feinschmeide
Windscheidstraße 24, Charlottenburg, 10627 (323 4048). U2 Sophie-Charlotte-Platz. **Open** 11am-6pm Tue-Fri, and by appointment. **No credit cards. Map B4**
Inventive, hand-crafted metalwork brooches, earrings and necklaces. Also on display are steel candleholders, chairs and sculptures.

Fritz & Fillman
Dresdener Straße 20, Kreuzberg, 10999 (615 1700). U1, U8 Kottbusser Tor. **Open** 11am-6pm Tue-Fri; 11am-2pm Sat. **Credit** V. **Map G4**
Highly original designs from these two Berliners plus work from goldsmiths all over Germany. A dazzling range of rings attracts many brides and grooms-to-be, with prices ranging from hundreds to thousands of marks. They also work to commission and offer jewellery-making courses.

Treykorn
Savignyplatz 13 (Passage), Charlottenburg, 10623 (312 4275). S3, S5, S7, S75, S9 Savignyplatz. **Open** 11am-7pm Tue-Fri; 11am-4pm Sat. **Credit** AmEx, DC, EC, MC, V. **Map C4**
This smart gallery specialises in metal- and stone-worked jewellery, with styles ranging from the ultra-modern to contemporary classics. There's always something new to see as stock changes every five weeks. Treykorn also hosts three major exhibitions a year showing the work of jewellery designers from all over the world.

Costume & formal-wear hire

Graichen
Klosterstraße 32, Spandau, 13581 (331 3587). U7 Rathaus Spandau. **Open** 10am-6pm Mon-Fri. **No credit cards.**
Tuxedos, shirts and long eveningwear for women. Bridal gowns, too. Rental fees for black-tie run from DM120-DM200, and womenswear from DM90-DM400.

Theaterkunst
Eisenzahnstraße 43/44, Grunewald, 10709 (864 7270). U1, U7 Fehrbellinerplatz. **Open** 8am-4.30pm; 8am-3.30pm Sat. **No credit cards.**
Three warehouses crammed floor to ceiling with period cos-

tume (including shoes, hats and jewellery, but unfortunately no wigs) to let you live out any historical fantasy. Because of the immense choice on offer allow time to browse and be fitted and to go back later to collect. Founded in 1908, their impressive collection was destroyed during the last war and re-established in 1951. Staff know their stuff and give good advice, and a free alterations service means costumes fit like a glove. Elaborate rococo outfits cost up to DM900 to hire; costumes from more recent times cost around DM250.

Spitze

Weimarer Straße 19, Charlottenburg, 10625 (313 1068). *U7 Kantstraße.* **Open** 2pm-6.30pm Mon-Fri; 11am-2pm Sat. **Credit** EC, V. **Map C4**
A goldmine for glamourous clothes and accessories, Spitze will rent out some of its nuggets for a third of the sale price. Period suits, tuxes and top hats, or cocktail and ballgowns can be hired for an average of DM100 per night. Evening gloves, handbags, shoes and other accessories also available.

Dry-cleaning & alterations

Good laundry and dry-cleaning services are in short supply, and almost non-existent in the east, so to have a much-loved garment cleaned it's worth a trip west. Many fashion designers offer an alterations or made-to-measure service as part of the cost of their garments, or for a small charge. If you need a zip fixing or rip mending, alterations shops all over town (many of them Turkish) will usually provide a next-day service. Consult the *Gelbe Seiten* under *Änderungsschneidereien*.

Kim Jang Woon

Pestalozzistraße 69, Charlottenburg, 10627 (327 5151). *U7 Wilmersdorferstraße.* **Open** 9am-6pm Mon-Fri; 9am-1pm Sat **No credit cards. Map B4**
Quick turnaround for all manner of alterations. Trouser shortening or taking in from DM16.

Kleenothek

Schönhauser Allee 186, Prenzlauer Berg, 10119 (449 5833). U2 Rosa-Luxemburg-Platz. **Open** 7.30am-7.30pm Mon-Fri; 9am-1.30pm Sat. **No credit cards. Map G2**
Reliable dry cleaners which will also take in laundry for service (machine) washing. Dry cleaning of suits from DM16,80.

Michael Klemm

Wörtherstraße 34, Prenzlauer Berg, 10405 (442 4549). *U2 Senefelder Platz.* **Open** 10am-6pm Mon-Fri. **No credit cards. Map G2**

Not-so-supermarkets

Some years back, a high-spirited segment of the Kreuzberg community celebrated Mayday by burning down a supermarket at Kottbusser Tor. There are days when one sympathises. Berlin supermarkets are crap.

In the UK, the needs of the grocery shopper are met through two complementary institutions.

One is the giant, everything-from-all-over-the-damn-world supermarket. The other is the small, shirt-off-your-back-but-open-all-hours corner shop. In America it's the same, only more so.

And what do we find in Berlin? That unhappy medium, the very worst of both worlds: corner supermarkets. They're small and cramped, are staffed with surly assistants, close on the dot of six, never take credit cards, and only rarely stock everything you need in one location. Want a selection of drinkable wines? Forget it. Looking for an interesting mustard? A visit to six supermarkets might turn up a total of as many brands. Require any herb or spice not commonly used in everyday north German cooking? Out of luck, matey, and it's off to the specialist shop half-way

across town on the ever-more-crowded U-Bahn.

And then when you only want one simple, easy to obtain item – a pint of semi-skimmed or a couple of cucumbers – you run up against queues of 20 for each cashier. This is where the corner shop would come in handy, but apart from a few newsagents adventurously branching out into morning Schrippen (bread rolls), that option is denied us. In other countries, the dilemma would be solved by a 'ten items or less' lane, but that happy innovation has yet to occur to the German retail industry – or else they reckon it would discourage you from buying an eleventh item.

Of the various Berlin chains, the lowest end of the market is served by Aldi, Plus and Penny Markt, which price 'em cheap and stack 'em high. But shopping for groceries in these places, especially for meats and fresh produce, can be a distressing experience. Better ranges can be found at branches of Reichelt and Kaisers. For top quality, your only bet is to pay through the nose and visit the foodhalls of KaDeWe or Galeries Lafayette.

Friendly tailor able to do all types of alterations for both men and women. Will also run up garments on request. Skirts taken in for DM14; jeans patched for DM15.

Nantes
Uhlandstraße 20-25, Charlottenburg, 10623 (883 5746). U3 Uhlandstraße. **Open** 8am-6pm Mon-Fri; 9am-noon Sat. **No credit cards. Map C4**
Recommended by designers, Nantes charges only slightly more than most for dry cleaning (DM14,50 for a man's jacket; DM35 for a ballgown), but takes at least four days. It's worth the wait though for valuable items.

Flea markets

There's many a treat in store at Berlin's flea markets, especially for music lovers, collectors of old books, fans of art deco and those with a fetish for old GDR nick-nacks. It's worth checking out *Zitty* and *Tip* for the most up-to-date listings or for smaller markets in your area.

Berliner Antik & Flohmarkt
Bahnhof Friedrichstraße, S-Bahnbögen 190-203, Mitte, 10117 (208 2645). S1, S2, S3, S5, S6, S9, U6 Friedrichstraße. **Open** 11am-6pm Mon, Wed-Sun. **Map F3**
More than 60 dealers have taken up residence in the renovated arches under the S-Bahn tracks, selling furniture, jewellery, paintings and interesting vintage clothing, some of it from the 1920s and 1930s.

Askanierring/Ecke Flankenschanze
Askanierring, Spandau, 13585 (371 4412). U7 Altstadt Spandau. **Open** 8am-5pm Sat, Sun.
The well-organised jumble of furniture, clothing, books and jewellery is reminiscent of London's Portobello Road before it went upmarket.

Fehrbelliner Platz
Fehrbelliner Platz, Wilmersdorf, 10707 (03322 246723). U1, U7 Fehrbelliner Platz. **Open** 8am-4pm Sat.
A bit of a hodge-podge, with a sprinkling of good dealers between mountains of old clothes, second-hand records, furniture and bric-a-brac.

Straße des 17 Juni
Straße des 17 Juni, Charlottenburg, 10787 (2255 0096). U2 Ernst-Reuter-Platz/S3, S5, S6, S9 Tiergarten. **Open** 8am-5pm Sat, Sun. **Map C4**
Early twentieth-century *objets* of a high quality with prices to match, alongside a jumble of vintage and alternative clothing, second-hand records, CDs and books, and tasty French fries sold at the numerous food stands. Arts and crafts further along the street. Best flea market in town, even though the aisles are insanely cramped.

Brandenburg Gate
Pariser Platz, at the Brandenburg Gate, Mitte, 10117. S1, S2 Unter den Linden. **Open** 9am-dusk daily. **Map E3**
A shadow of its former self, but still the place to pick up Commie kitsch such as Party badges, Russian hats, Soviet uniforms and equipment (including binoculars and watches) and chunks of graffitied plaster said to be from the Wall.

Zille-Hof
Fasanenstraße 14, Charlottenburg, 10623 (313 4333). U15 Uhlandstraße. **Open** 8am-5.30pm Mon-Fri; 8am-1pm Sat. **Map C4**
Located almost next door to the Kempinski Hotel, Zille-Hof is a neat and tidy junk market where you can track down everything from an antique hatpin to a chest of drawers. You'll find the better bric-a-brac indoors, while the real bargains lurk in the courtyard outside.

Flowers

Blumenwiese
Dorotheenstraße 151, Mitte, 10117 (2016 5067). S1, S2, S25, S3, S5, S7, S75, S9, U6 Friedrichstraße. **Open** 7am-8pm Mon-Fri; 8am-8pm Sat, Sun. **Credit** AmEx, DC, EC, MC, V. **Map F3**
Tastefully exotic arrangements are something of a rarity in east Berlin, but Blumenwiese pulls off the most extraordinary floral tributes with panache. That's why this florist numbers the Adlon Hotel among its many corporate clients. Smaller arrangements are also to be recommended and Blumenwiese will deliver within Mitte free of charge, and throughout Berlin for a few marks more. A Fleurop shop.

Eberhard Bohnstedt
Ludwigskirchstraße 11, Wilmersdorf, 10719 (881 93 63). U1 Hohenzollerndamm. **Open** 10am-6pm Mon, Tue, Thur, Fri; 10am-noon Wed; 10am-2pm Sat. **No credit cards. Map B5**
The city's star florist. Seasonal and unusual arrangements, such as green tomatoes, wild roses and begonias.

Fleurop
(713 710). **Open** 7.30am-6.30pm Mon-Fri; 8am-2pm Sat.
Call to have flowers delivered anywhere in the western world. Bouquets start at DM25, but hard-up Romeos can opt for a single flower, delivered to their sweetheart's door for only DM20. Within Germany, your flowers can arrive within an hour, sent via any one of 7,000 shops nationwide.

Food

Aqui Espana
Kantstraße 34, Charlottenburg, 10625 (312 3315). U7 Wilmersdorferstraße. **Open** 9am-7.30pm Mon-Fri; 9am-2pm Sat. **No credit cards. Map B4**
Neighbourhood store stocking Spanish wines and groceries, plus ingredients for Mexican and Latin American dishes, including a full array of dried chillies, flour and corn tortillas and Central-American seafood in the freezer.

Brotgarten
Seelingstraße 30, Charlottenburg, 14059 (322 8880). U2 Sophie-Charlotte-Platz. **Open** 7.30am-6.30pm Mon-Fri; 7.30am-1.30pm Sat; 9am-noon Sun. **No credit cards. Map B4**
Health food store notable for its mixes of muesli, dried fruits and nuts, and its delicious wholesome breads, made with a variety of nuts and seeds. Natural-product sweets are also available.

English Food Shop
Seeburger Straße 3, Spandau, 13581 (332 9420). U7 Rathaus Spandau. **Open** 10am-6pm Mon-Fri; 10am-1pm Sat. **No credit cards.**
Widest selection of British foodstuffs available in Berlin, including English mustards, marmalades, jelly, prawn-cocktail crisps, Marmite and PG Tips. Stick your head in the freezer to find lots more tasty goodies from back home. Also a selection of English-language videos.
Branch: Fechnerstraße 21, Wilmersdorf, 10717 (861 0607)

Fuchs Rabe
Ludwigskirchstraße 3, Wilmersdorf, 10719 (882 3984). U1 Hohenzollernplatz. **Open** 9am-6pm Mon-Wed; 9am-6.30pm Thur-Fri. 9am-2pm Sat. **No credit cards. Map C5**

*Beautiful packaged confitures and chocolates from **Leysieffer** on the Kurfürstendamm.*

Superb selection of cheeses, as good as that at KaDeWe (*below*), plus biscuits and their own speciality breads.

Galeries Lafayette

Franzözische Straße 23, Mitte, 10117 (209 480). U2/U6 StadtMitte. **Open** Mon-Fri 9.30am-8pm; Sat 9am-4pm. **Credit** AmEx, DC, EC, JCB, MC, V. **Map F3**
Prices are quite high in the French-orientated basement food hall of this flash department store. The meat counter offers high-quality cuts, and staff are often happy to help out with cooking suggestions. There is also a good selection of French cheese and wines on offer, but these tend to be expensive.

KaDeWe (Kaufhaus des Westens)

Tauentzienstraße 21-24, Schöneberg, 10789 (21 210). U1, U2, U15 Wittenbergplatz. **Open** 9.30am-8pm Mon-Fri; 9am-4pm Sat. **Credit** AmEx, DC, EC, MC, V. **Map D4**
Most famous for its lavish food hall which takes up the whole of the sixth floor and features foodstuffs from around the globe. Seafood and wurst-lovers will think they've died and gone to heaven, but vegetarians should steer clear of the meat department. The delicatessen is famous for its specialities, and if you crave something even more exotic than what's on offer at any of the gourmet bars, you can order it (by phone using credit-card payment if you're feeling lazy, 213 2455). While complicated orders may take a few days to be fulfilled, same-day delivery is possible until 4pm in Berlin and Potsdam, with a DM10 charge for orders less than DM200. Allow two or three days for delivery of large drinks orders.

Kolbo

Auguststraße 77/78, Mitte, 10117 (no phone). U6 Oranienburger Tor. **Open** 11am-1.45pm, 2.15pm-7pm Tue, Wed, Thur and Sun; 9am-2pm Fri. **Credit** AmEx, EC, MC, V. **Map F3**
Small friendly store and bakery in Berlin's old Jewish quarter selling Kosher food stuffs and wines, plus a selection of books (including Kosher cookbooks) and ritual objects.

Leysieffer

Kurfürstendamm 218, Charlottenburg, 10719 (885 7450), and branches. **Open** 9am-7pm Mon-Wed, Fri, Sat; 9am-8.30pm Thur; 10am-8pm Sun. **Credit** AmEx, EC, MC, V. **Map C4**

Beautifully packaged confitures, teas and hand-made chocolates from this German fine food company make perfect high-calorie gifts. Café upstairs and bakery attached.

Vendemmia

Akazienstraße 20, Schöneberg, 10823 (784 2728). U7 Eisenacher Straße. **Open** 10am-6.30pm Mon-Fri; 10am-2pm Sat. **No credit cards. Map D5**
Bulk importers of first-class Italian wines which are then unceremoniously decanted into bottles bearing photocopied labels. Not the most impressive bottle you can take to a party, but it's good stuff and very cheap.

Weichardt-Brot

Mehlitzstraße 7, Wilmersdorf, 10715 (873 8099). U7, U9 Berliner Straße. **Open** 8am-6.30pm Mon-Fri; 8am-1pm Sat. **No credit cards. Map C5**
The very best bakery in town, Weichardt-Brot grew out of a Berlin collective from the 1960s. Stone-ground organic flour and natural leavens make this a Mecca for bread-lovers.

Whisky & Cigars

Sophienstraße 23, Mitte, 10178 (282 0376). S3, S5, S7, S75, S9 Hackescher Markt. **Open** noon-7pm Tue-Sat. **No credit cards. Map F3**
Two friends sharing a love of single malts are behind this shop which stocks 150 whiskies, and cigars from Cuba, Jamaica and Honduras. Top of the range is a bottle of Milroys Imperial at DM188 or a DM60 Havana Montecristo.

Street Markets

Berlin's many *Wochenmärkte* offer an alternative to stores, and usually sell better, cheaper fresh produce. They are everywhere in Berlin, and you'll probably find one at the end of your road.

The Turkish Market

Maybachufer, Neukölln, 12045. U1, U8 Kottbusser Tor. **Open** noon-6.30pm Tue, Fri. **No credit cards. Map G5**
A noisy, crowded street market just across the canal from Kreuzberg, catering for the needs of the neighbourhood's Turkish community. There are good buys and great tastes to be discovered here.

Winterfeldt Markt
Winterfeldtplatz, Schöneberg, 10781. U1, U2, U4
Nollendorfplatz. **Open** 8am-2pm Wed, Sat. **No credit
cards. Map D5**
Come here on Saturday morning to experience a multi-
cultural, Berlin mix. Everybody shows up to buy their
vegetables, cheese, wholegrain breads, wursts, meats,
flowers, clothes, pet supplies and toys; or simply to meet
over a coffee, beer or falafel at one of the many cafés off
the square.

Food delivery & catering

Food delivery has improved amazingly in the past
five years and whichever area of town you're in,
chances are there's a selection of pizza and Chinese
restaurants that will deliver to your door. Look in
the *Gelbe Seiten*, or keep an eye out for flyers offering special offers.

banchetto
Prinz-Eugen-Straße 17A, Wedding, 13347 (461 9794).
Open orders taken daily 9am-10pm. **No credit cards.**
Catering service providing delicious homemade northern
Italian specialities, with free delivery for orders over DM300.
Final preparations are made in your own home. The menu
offers various warm meals with antipasti, main course, salad
and dessert, cold buffets and party canapés. Banchetto Vini
(455 4409) will deliver wines.

Liberty Pizza
Zehlendorf (801 5048). Prenzlauer Berg (445 0412).
Open orders taken noon-10pm. **No credit cards.**
This delivery and take-away service was started by a home-
sick group of Brooklyn Italians to fill the gap in the market
for thick-crusted American-style pizza.

Rogacki
*Wilmersdorfer Straße 145, Charlottenburg, 10585 (341
4091). U7 Wilmersdorfer Straße.* **Open** 9am-6pm Mon-
Fri; 9am-2pm Sat. **Credit** EC. **Map B4**

The vinyl solution

As capital of the music industry's third-largest
market, Berlin is a record collector's paradise.
The city has over 150 shops supplying records
or CDs and a good percentage also stock second-
hand material. Obviously this is the place to
come and get those hard-to-find German recordings from east and west but Berlin has always
had a youthful and cosmopolitan population, so
the selection and range of musical genres found
in record shops is limitless. Prices for American
visitors will seem a little steep, but in European
terms Germany is reasonably cheap.

It's getting ever harder to find new vinyl but
the second-hand shops are full of the stuff –
mainly due to efficient Germans 'changing
over to CD' – that is, repurchasing an entire
record collection while selling the old one for
next to nothing. German 7-inch singles were
always in picture covers and the onslaught of
the CD has released many of these little gems
to collectors via flea markets for as little as 50
pfennigs a go!

Two Berlin shops specialise in vinyl singles,
both offering a unique purchasing experience.
Platten Pedro is run by a determinedly eccentric chap called, unsurprisingly, Pedro. He
speaks good English, is very helpful and refus-
es to buy or sell CDs. Occasionally he can be
heard on Berlin radio playing rarities from his
collection. The shop is basically Pedro's front
room (he lives in the back) and is literally
packed from floor to ceiling with vinyl. There
are ladders to reach the high stuff. You'll see
hardly any singles because they're tucked away
in hundreds of boxes stacked to the roof in

Pedro's hall. He'll haul down the boxes so you
can browse but it is a lot easier just to tell him
what you're looking for and let him get on with
it. Pedro is not cheap, but if you can't find it
there or he hasn't heard of it then it probably
doesn't exist.

It's three stops on the underground to another experience, this time Berlin's filthiest and
most difficult to find record shop. **2X2** is in an
old factory floor and brims with thousands of
collectable records and CDs. The CDs range
from singles for DM1 to rarities for DM40.
Hidden away in the back is the singles room.
Metal shelves filled with boxes line the wall and
the vinyl is alphabetically arranged within different genres or artists. This is definitely not the
place to go if you only have 15 minutes to
browse. If you can't find the singles room, just
ask and they will open it up for you if they are
in the mood. By the time you've finished browsing, your hands will be black.

See also listings above for **Space Hall** and
Mr Dead & Mrs Free. Log on to *www.plat-
ten.net* for a complete listing of over 750 German
record shops and their specialities, with an
emphasis on Berlin.

Platten Pedro
*Tegeler Weg, Charlottenburg, 10589 (344 1875). U7
Richard Wagner Platz.* **Open** noon-4pm Mon-Fri;
noon-2pm Sat. **No credit cards.**
Opening hours vary according to Pedro's whim, but he's
nearly always there in the afternoons.

2X2
*Wilmersdorfer Straße 60-61, Charlottenburg, 10627
(323 4072). U7 Wilmersdorfer Straße.* **Open** 11am-
6pm Mon-Fri; 11am-2pm Sat. **No credit cards.**

Established in 1928, Berlin's fish institution provides smoked eel, salads, sandwiches, wurst and meat dishes. Party service available, too. Delivery charge DM10-DM35.

Photography
Camera Hire

Wüstefeld
Grolmannstraße 36, Charlottenburg, 10623 (883 7593) U15 Uhlandstraße/S3, S5, S7, S75, S9 Savignyplatz. **Open** 9.30am-7pm Mon-Fri; 10am-4pm Sat. **Credit** MC, V. **Map C4**
In exchange for a glance at your passport or ID card and a credit card deposit you can rent Nikon, Canon, Hasselblad and Leica cameras and photo equipment here. They also offer a professional processing service.
Branches: Schloßstraße 96, Steglitz, 12163 (792 8099).

Processing & passport photos

Photolabor Ladewig
Pestalozzistraße 105, Charlottenburg, 10625 (312 1273). S3, S5, S7, S75, S9 Savignyplatz. **Open** 9am-6pm Mon-Fri; 10am-2pm Sat. **Credit** AmEx, DC, JCB, MC, V. **Map C4**
Overnight processing service which offers the option of hand-developing. Passport photos (four for DM15) can be done while you wait. Also sells camera equipment and carries out repairs. Used by professionals.

Foto Klinke
Friedrichstraße 207-208, Kreuzberg, 10969 (2529 5530), U6 Kochstraße. **Open** 8.30am-6.30pm Mon-Wed; 8.30am-7pm Thur; 9am-2pm Sat. **Credit** MC, V. **Map F4**
Large processing department which can turn around films in an hour. Passport photos (four for DM12,95) arrive in ten minutes. Also stocks a large range of cameras and photo equipment. Branches all over town.
Branches: Schönhauser Allee 105, Prenzlauer Berg, 10439 (444 1380); Potsdamer Straße 141, Schöneberg, 10783 (216 3876).

Records, Tapes, CDs

See also **Flex/Inch By Inch/Melting Point** *under* **Fashion** *and* **Dussman Das Kulturkaufhaus** *under* **Books.**

Canzone
Savigny Passage, Bogen 583, 10623 (313 1578). S3, S5, S7, S75, S9 Savignyplatz. **Open** 10.30am-7pm Mon-Thur; 10.30am-8pm Fri; 10.30am-4pm Sat. **Credit** V. **Map C4**
Rivals with new-kids-on-the-block, Piranha, in the world music market, Canzone stocks hard-to-find CDs that will move you to an oriental, Latin, tango, African or Brazilian beat. Some fascinating belly-dancing videos also on offer.

Downbeat
Dresdener Straße 19, Kreuzberg, 10999 (6160 9326). U1 Kottbusser Tor. **Open** 11am-7pm Mon-Fri; noon-4pm Sat. **No credit cards**. **Map G5**
Staffed by some of Berlin's best reggae DJs, this shop stocks lots of vinyl as well as CDs covering dancehall, roots, hiphop, reggae and drum 'n' bass. A flip through the shelves can often turn up some collector's items and rare originals.

DNS
Alte Schönhauser Straße 39/40, Mitte, 10178 (247 9835). U8 Weinmeisterstraße. **Open** 11am-8pm Mon-Fri; 10am-4pm Sat. **No credit cards**. **Map G3**

Hardwax – *Europe's finest techno store.*

Old vinyl, including some rare finds, as well as the latest pressings in the world of techno.

Gelbe Musik
Schaperstraße 11, Wilmersdorf, 10719 (211 3962). U1 Augsburger Straße. **Open** 1pm-6pm Tue-Fri; 11am-2pm Sat. **Credit** EC, MC, V. **Map C5**
Probably Europe's number-one outlet of avant-garde music, with racks filled with minimalist, electronic, world, industrial and extreme noise. Rare vinyl and import CDs, music press and sound objects make absorbing browsing, and the store is a hang-out for the international and the odd.

Hans Riedl Musikalienhandel
Uhlandstraße 38, Wilmersdorf, 10719 (882 7395). U15 Uhlandstraße. **Open** 8am-6.30pm Mon-Fri; 9am-2pm Sat. **Credit** Visa, MC. **Map F4**
Probably the best address for classical music in Berlin, this huge, slightly old-fashioned shop stocks a wide selection of CDs and sheet music, as well as wind, string and brass instruments. Staff are friendly and exceptionally knowledgeable and the store is patronised by music professionals as well as Berlin's classical music-lovers.
Branch: Konzerthaus, Gendarmenmarkt, Mitte, 10117 (204 1136)

Hardwax
1st courtyard, 3rd floor, Paul-Lincke-Ufer 44A, Kreuzberg, 10999 (6113 0111). U8 Schönleinstraße. **Open** noon-8pm Mon-Fri; 10am-4pm Sat. **No credit cards**. **Map G5**
One of the best places in Europe to buy techno records and a good place to pick up flyers for forthcoming events. Records are filed by label rather than artist, and there is also a small selection of CDs, including the excellent minimalist

releases on their own Chain Reaction label. See Berlin's DJs buying their vinyl on Tuesdays and Fridays when new stock comes in. The mail-order service includes an auction of rarities where you bid by phone, mail, fax or e-mail and the record gets shipped COD to the highest bidder the next day.

Mr Dead & Mrs Free

Bülowstraße 5, Schöneberg, 10783 (215 1449). U1, U2 Nollendorfplatz. **Open** 11am-7pm Mon-Wed; 11am-8pm Thur-Fri; 11am-4pm Sat. **No credit cards. Map D5**
The best place in Berlin for indie-rock, with lots of British, American and Australian imports and a huge vinyl section. Tuesday is when imports arrive and you may find it difficult to squeeze in through the door.

Piranha

Carmerstraße 11, Charlottenburg, 10623 (3186 1421). S3, S5, S7, S75, S9 Savignyplatz. **Open** 1pm-7pm Mon-Fri; 11am-4pm Sat. **Credit** EC, V. **Map C4**
Piranha is a name in Berlin's music scene, running a label, organising events and now also opening a record shop. This friendly store offers over 4,000 CDs and records from all corners of the globe, covering everything from salsa to swing, from klezmer to techno.

Space Hall

Zossenerstraße 33, Kreuzberg, 10961 (694 7664). U7 Gneisenaustraße. **Open** 11am-7pm Mon-Wed; 11am-8pm Thur-Fri; 10am-4pm Sat. **No credit cards. Map F5**
Roomy, friendly shop offering a broad range of new and second-hand CDs at reasonable prices. The huge techno/house vinyl room at the back of the shop has recently expanded into a neighbouring department. They also probably offer the best prices in Berlin when buying CDs.

WOM

Augsburger Straße 36-42, Schöneberg, 10789 (885 7240), and branches. **Open** 10am-8pm Mon-Fri; 9am-4pm Sat. **Credit** AmEx, EC, MC, V. **Map D4**
The World Of Music chain offers a no-frills approach to music retailing, and its wide-ranging selection of CDs includes a good selection of jazz recordings. No classical music.
Branch: Hertie, Wilmersdorfer Straße 118, Charlottenburg, 10585 (315 9170).

Zweitausandeins

Kantstraße 41-42, Charlottenburg, 10625 (312 5017). S3, S5, S7, S75, S9 Savignyplatz. **Open** 10am-8pm Mon-

Fri; 10am-4pm Sat. **Credit** EC. **Map C4**
Huge selection of cut-price CDs covering a broad range of mainstream music.

Perhaps it is the national predilection for bureaucracy, but Germans love stationery – particularly anything with a whiff of office efficiency about it. Notebooks and files are taken very seriously and designed to last. Some even look good. As home to some of the world's best makers of stationery and art supplies, the quality on offer is high.

Ferdinand Braune

Grunewaldstraße 87, Schöneberg, 10825 (7870 3773). U7 Kleistpark. **Open** 9am-6pm Mon-Fri; 9am-2pm Sat. **No credit cards. Map E5**
The best shop in town for the serious artist. Berlin's painters flock here for Herr Braune's hand-blended oil paints, acrylics, sketchbooks and the finest canvas stretches. Delivery service available.

McPaper & Co

Wilmersdorfer Straße 36-37, Charlottenburg, 10585 (341 4666). U2, U7 Bismarckstraße. **Open** 9am-8pm Mon-Fri; 9am-4pmSat. **No credit cards. Map B4**
High-street staple offering decent range of personal, office and school stationery at reasonable prices. More than 50 branches across town.

J Muller

Neue Schönhauser Straße 16, Mitte, 10178 (283 2532). U8 Weinmeisterstraße. **Open** 8am-6pm Mon-Fri. **No credit cards. Map G3**
Friendly, family-run business in the trendy heart of Mitte selling fine stationery and rubber stamps. Also prints business cards and small signs.

Papeterie

Uhlandstraße 28, Charlottenburg, 10719 (881 6363). U15 Uhlandstraße. **Open** 9.30am-7pm Mon-Wed; 9.30am-8pm Thur, Fri; 9.30am-4pm Sat. **Credit** DC, MC, V. **Map C4**
Upmarket stockists of beautifully made note-books, agendas, diaries, photo albums and organisers. Also Mont Blanc pens and gilded pencil sets from Count Faber-Castell.

Bringing it all back home

If you couldn't resist that beautiful Biedermeier wardrobe, an authentic four-foot slab of the Berlin Wall, or any other bulky goods you want shipping back to the UK or USA, try one of the following firms. Alternatively, look in the *Gelbe Seiten* under *Umzüge* (removals).

Atege

Quitzowstraße 11-17, Tiergarten, 10559 (397 3970). U9 Birkenstraße. **Open** 8am-5pm Mon-Thur; 8am-4pm Fri. **No credit cards.**
Worldwide shipping of goods, including precious artpieces.

AGS

Eiswerderstraße 18, Spandau, 13585 (337 8435). U7 Altstadt Spandau. Estimations, by telephone appointment. **No credit cards.**

F+N

Fletcher + Neuhaus, Ketziner Straße 32d, Fahrland, 14476 (8040 2965). **Open** 8am-5pm Mon-Fri. **No credit cards.**
Specialists in removals to the UK and Ireland.

Franzkowiak

Uhlandstraße 83/84, Wilmersdorf, 10717 (873 061). U7 Blissestraße. **Open** 8am-5pm Mon-Thur; 8am-4pm Fri. **Credit** AmEx, DC, EC, MC, V.

Arts & Entertainment

After hours

Where to find what in the wee hours.

Post-club breakfast at the **Schwarzes Café**.

It's a paradoxical kind of place, Berlin. Famed for its nightlife, and justifiably so, it has a round-the-clock drinking culture and a volatile club life in which it's perfectly possible to go out on a Friday night and return home on Monday evening without interrupting the party for longer than it takes to catch a cab or one of the city's frequent night-buses from one venue to the next.

But it is only recently that shop opening hours were extended to 8.30pm on weekdays (4pm on Saturdays). And as it is only the bigger chains and department stores that actually take advantage of this harshly radical liberalisation, you are still pretty much snookered if you want to buy a pint of milk after 6pm. The exorbitantly priced grocery stores attached to 24-hour petrol stations are the only possibility, apart from a few Turkish video shops.

For bars and clubs, see their respective chapters. Here, to help you make it through the night, we list a few late night services, details of all-night transport, and a few locations for both small-hour dining and the very earliest of breakfasts.

See also chapter **Getting Around**.

Changing money

The banks listed below have the longest hours of any in Berlin, including those at the airports. If you have an ATM card, there are machines all over town.

Reisebank AG
In Zoo Station, Hardenbergplatz, Charlottenburg, 10623 (881 7117). U2, U2, S3, S5, S6, S7, S9 Zoologischer Garten. **Open** *7.30am-10pm daily.* **Map C4**
In Hauptbahnhof, Friedrichshain, off Stralauer Platz, 10243 (428 7029). S3, S5, S7, S9, Hauptbahnhof.
Open *7am-10pm Mon-Fri; 7am-6pm Sat; 8am-4pm Sun.*
Among the best rates of exchange and longest opening hours in the city.

Shopping

If you must stock up with food after 8pm, most petrol stations sell basic groceries. BP ones are especially good, and have a bakery counter. In Kreuzberg and Schöneberg, a few Turkish video shops stay open after hours.

Chemists

A list of pharmacies offering Sunday and evening services should be displayed on the door of every pharmacy. For more information, phone:

Apotheken Notdienst
Emergency Pharmaceutical Services
(011 41). **Open** *24 hours daily.*

Transport

Berlin has a comprehensive Nachtliniennetz (night-line network) that covers all parts of town via 60 bus and tram routes running every 30 minutes between 1am-4am.

At weekends the U12 (Ruhleben to Warschauer Straße) and U9 (Osloer Straße to Rathaus Steglitz) lines run all night on Fridays and Saturdays, with trains every 15 minutes.

Night-line network maps and timetables are available from the BVG information kiosks at all stations. Ticket prices are the same as during the day. Buses and trams that run at night are distinguished by an 'N' in front of the number. You'll find a timetable at every bus or tram stop.

If you need a taxi, you should be able to hail one or find a few waiting at a rank. At most bars and restaurants, the staff will call a cab for you. Otherwise, call 261 026 for a 24-hour taxi service.

Petrol

Most petrol stations in the city centre are open 24 hours and sell basic groceries, snacks, soft drinks and cigarettes.

Eating

Most restaurants in Berlin will feed you up to midnight and many German and Turkish Imbißes stay open much later. Below we list a few options for a late-night sit-down dinner, but *see also chapter* **Restaurants** for **Hackescher Hof**, **Hard Rock Café**, **Luisiada** and **Markthalle**, and *see chapter* **Cafés & Bars** for **Times**, **Haifisch**, **Mutter** and **Die Rote Harfe**.

El Burriquito

Wielandstraße 6 (corner of Kantstraße), Charlottenburg, 10625 (312 9929). S3, S5, S7, S9, S75 Savignyplatz. **Open** 7pm-5am daily. **No credit cards. Map C4**
Lively Spanish bar/restaurant where you can stuff yourself with tapas at a ridiculous hour in the morning, or perch at the bar and give yourself some serious hangover material.

Gambrinus

Linienstraße 133, Mitte, 10117 (282 6843). U8 Rosenthaler Platz. **Open** noon-4am Mon-Sat. **Average** DM15. **No credit cards. Map G3**
Traditional Berlin local restaurant serving variations on the meat, potato and cabbage theme. The tiled walls are covered with pictures of Berlin throughout the ages.

Jimmy's Diner

Pariser Straße 41, Wilmersdorf, 10707 (882 3141). U1 Hohenzollernplatz. **Open** noon-3am, Sun-Thur; noon-6am Fri, Sat. **No credit cards. Map C5**
A recreation of a 1950s diner serving American beers and the usual Tex-Mex staples. Chilli, burgers, ribs and fries make up the bulk of the menu. Useless for veggies.

Presse Café

Corner of Hardenbergstraße and Joachimstalerstraße, Charlottenburg, 10623. (312 2644). U2, S3, S5, S6, S7, S9 Zoologischer Garten **Open** 24 hours daily. **No credit cards. Map C4**
Just opposite Bahnhof Zoo train and bus stations, the Pressecafé has a pleasantly transient ambience. A good place to wait for the U-bahn to start up again.

Schwarzes Café

Kantstraße 148, Charlottenburg, 10623 (313 8038). S3, S5, S7, S9, S75 Savignyplatz. **Open** 24 hours daily except Tuesdays. **No credit cards. Map C4**
Young and friendly, if occasionally overstretched, service and mixed clientele. Good coffee and cheesecake round the clock. Excellent spot for post-club breakfasts.

XII Apostoli

Georgenstraße, S-Bahnbogen 177-180, Mitte, 10117 (201 0222). U6, S1, S2, S3, S5, S6, S9 Friedrichstraße. **Open** 24 hours daily. **No credit cards. Map F3**
Popular upmarket pizzeria and croissanterie. If you want a DM200 bottle of wine at six in the morning, this is the place. **Branch:** Bleibtreustraße 49 (Savigny Passage), Charlottenburg, 10623 (312 1433).

Zwiebelfisch

Savignyplatz 7-8, Charlottenburg, 10623 (312 7363). S3, S5, S7, S9, S75 Savignyplatz. **Open** noon-6.30am daily. **No credit cards. Map C4**

Greet the morning German-style with a plate of salami and great German Pils. Otherwise, just drink the superb coffee and wander home through Savignyplatz.

Imbiß & fast food

Bagels & Bialys

Rosenthaler Straße 46-48, Mitte, 10178 (283 6546). U8 Weinmeisterstraße/S3, S5, S7, S9 Hackescher Markt. **Open** 9am-3am Mon-Thur, Sun; 9am-4am Fri, Sat. **Map F3**
Sandwiches, kebabs, bagels – a selection of snacks from various cultures, all of it good and fresh.

City Imbiß

Oranienburger Straße, corner of Linienstraße, Mitte, 10117 (no phone). U6 Oranienburger Tor. **Open** 10am-5am daily. **Map F3**
The usual range of German snacks – Currywurst, Bouletten, Kartoffelsalat – available deeper into the night than at most places around here. Favoured haunt of local winos.

Freßco

Oranienburger Straße 47, Mitte, 10117 (282 9647). U6 Oranienburger Tor. **Open** *winter* noon-midnight daily; *summer* noon-2am daily. **Map F3**
Soups, salads, baguettes, tapas, doughnuts, pasta, Calzone – this Imbiß has it all, and in both carnivorous and veghead versions. Be prepared to queue a while: this place is understandably popular.

Habibi

Goltzstraße 24, Winterfeldtplatz, Schöneberg, 10781 (215 3332). U1, U4 Nollendorfplatz. **Open** 11am-3am Mon-Fri, Sun; 11am-5am Sat. **Map D5**
Arab specialities are served in this favourite stop for ravenous night owls in the busy Winterfeldtplatz neighbourhood. The branches don't stay open quite so late.
Branches: Akazienstraße 9, Schöneberg, 10823 (787 4428); Körtestraße 35, Kreuzberg, 10967 (692 2401).

Traube

Dimitroffstraße 24, Prenzlauer Berg, 10405 (441 7447). U2 Eberswalder Straße. **Open** 9am-5am daily. **Map G2**
Excellent Turkish imbiß off the Kollwitzplatz that offers salads and vegetarian snacks as well as kebabs and chicken.

Post Office

The main post office in Zoo station is open to midnight, operating all services. You can also phone long-distance, fax, and collect your post-restante.

Photocopying

Copyhaus

Grunewaldstraße 18, Schöneberg, 10823 (235 5380). U7 Eisenacher Straße. **Open** 8am-12pm Mon-Sat; 1pm-9pm Sun. **Credit** EC, MC. **Map D5**

Trigger

Pohlstraße 69, Tiergarten, 10785 (261 6037). U1 Kurfürstenstraße. **Open** 9am-2am Mon-Fri; 1pm-2am Sat, Sun. **No credit cards. Map E5**
Copy, fax and translation service into the night.

Video

Most video shops have no films in English: the best place to go is **Videodrom** in Kreuzberg.

Cabaret

Forget Sally Bowles. Modern Berlin cabaret offers acrobats and gender-benders, poets and satirists, and dancing girls up the butt.

Life is another kind of cabaret now, old chum. So if you're longing to see a real Berlin cabaret of the 1920s – sorry. The original clubs are long gone, although sometimes the feeling can be recaptured – it all depends on who's playing.

Still, the modern Berlin cabaret scene is truly coming into its own, without nostalgia to hold it back. In places like **Chamäleon, UFA Fabrik,** and **Kalkscheune** you can see anything from Burlesque talkshows to poetic jesters to drag queen theatre. Several venues have invested big money into recreating the look of an old Berlin cabaret but it's mostly just wishful thinking. The shows in these places are strictly tourist fluff. But **Wintergarten** does have gorgeous décor and can be lots of fun, especially if someone else is picking up the tab – table service in these places does not come cheap. This type of show is called 'varieté', meaning you can expect clowns, acrobats, magicians, dancing girls and maybe a snazzy band.

Other places might call the show a 'revue', which may include some of the characters mentioned above but mainly consists of song and dance and/or comedy sketches. This is what most of us would call cabaret. The German form of the word is *Kabarett*. Shows billed as such have little in common with varieté – Kabarett is political satire sprinkled with original songs. This has always had a strong following in Berlin. **Kartoon**, with its rousing and witty performers, is one of the premier exponents of the genre, but if you don't speak perfect German, forget it.

In the **Roter** and **Grüner Salon**, by contrast, there is something for everybody. These two separate clubs inside the **Volksbühne** (*see chapter* **Theatre**) host such a variety of acts that the shows can't be shoehorned into one particular category. It is, in the end, the performers that make the evening. Here we list a few to watch out for:

Worthwhile acts working in German include: Teufelsberg Productions (clever drag cabaret); Stepinskis (tap-dancing female comediennes); Lonely Husbands (slick but cosy male trio with fun musical numbers); Die Spreedosen (endearing drag theatre); New Comedian Harmonists (hysterical male acappella). Interesting Anglophone entertainers include: Rick Maverick (stand-up comedy and poetry); Gayle Tufts (stand-up comedy with pop tunes); Bridge Markland (gender-bending performance); Priscilla Be (sardonic spoken-word).

Traditional

Chez Nous
Marburger Straße 14, Tiergarten, 10789 (213 1810). U2, U9, S3, S5, S6, S7, S9 Zoologischer Garten. **Open** *box office* 7.30pm-1am daily. **Showtimes** 8.30pm and 11pm daily. **No credit cards. Map D4**
A glamourous revue with classic drag queen numbers. Lots of feathers, falsies and celebrity lookalike lip-synching.

Friedrichstadtpalast
Friedrichstraße 107, Mitte, 10117 (2326 2474). U6, S2, S3, S5, S6, S7, S9 Friedrichstraße. **Open** 6pm-1am daily; *box office* noon-7pm Tue-Sun. **Admission** DM14-DM77. **No credit cards. Map F3**
Big venue, big shows – Las Vegas-like musical variety and revues, usually packed with working-class German tourists.

Kleine Nachtrevue
Kurfürstenstraße 116, Schöneberg, 10787 (218 8950). U1, U2, U3 Wittenbergplatz. **Open** 9pm-4am Mon-Sat. Shows lasting for 40 minutes on and off throughout the evening. Sat two longer shows starting at 10.30pm and 12.30am. **Admission** DM30 minimum charge. **Credit** AmEx, DC, V. **Map D4**
A gem. Opened by Sylvia Schmidt, a talented chanteuse who also appears in the show, the club is intimate sexy and as close to old Berlin as one can get.

La Vie en Rose
Europa Center, Tiergarten, 10789 (323 6006). S3, S5, S6, S7, S9, U2, U9 Zoologischer Garten. **Open** 10am-midnight Tue-Sun. **Showtimes** 9pm Sun-Thur; 10pm Fri, Sat. **Admission** DM25-DM60 **Credit** AmEx, DC, EC, V (drink minimum). **Map D4**
Dancing girls up the butt with all the glitter you can stand. The shows in this slightly seedy little venue – often choreographed to chart hits and golden oldies – edge on soft porn.

Wintergarten Varieté
Potsdamer Straße 96, Tiergarten, 10785 (250 0880). U1, U15 Kurfürstenstraße. **Open** *box office* 7.30pm-midnight daily. **Showtimes** 8pm Mon-Sat; 3.30pm, 8.30pm Sun. **Admission** DM39-DM73. **No credit cards. Map E4**
A classy place, run by astute impresario Andre Heller. The shows are slick, professional and very mixed – excellent acrobats, magicians and Denis Lacombe, one of the best clowns around, but often quite terrible dancing girls.

Modern

Kalkscheune
Johanisstraße 2, Mitte, 10117 (2839 0065). U6 Oranienburger Straße/S1 Oranienburger Tor. **Open** 10am-7pm daily for telephone booking; one hour before show. **Showtimes** vary. **No credit cards. Map F3**
Close to the feeling of an old cabaret. A listed building from the 1840s which houses a cabaret, lounge and party room. The Sunday afternoon poetry cabaret is eclectic and popular. In the evening there's Tanja's Nacht Café where this

The **Kleine Nachtrevue** – *about as close to old Berlin as you're going to get. Page 168.*

young diva sings her original tragic chansons and hosts a show with guests ranging from warped to wonderful.

UFA Fabrik
Viktoriastraße 10-18, Tempelhof, 12105 (755 030). U6 Ullsteinstraße. **Open** *box office* 10am-5pm daily. **Admission** and **Showtimes** vary. **No credit cards.**
A large complex including a cinema, classrooms, a gallery, cafe, disco and two theatres. Offers a huge selection of entertainment and is a good source of cabaret information.

Chamäleon Varieté
Hackesche Höfe, Rosenthaler Straße 40-41, Mitte, 10178 (282 7118). S3, S5, S6, S7, S75, S9 Hackesche Markt. **Open** *box office* 10am-6pm Mon-Fri. **Showtimes** 8.30pm-2am. **Admission** DM18-DM39. **No credit cards. Map F3**
A beautiful old theatre with classy and comfortable table seating, a surprisingly modern attitude and a flair for the adventurous. Hang on for the enjoyable late show where new talent shines and acts from other venues around town drop by to strut their stuff.

Bar Jeder Vernunft
Spiegelzelt, Schaperstraße 24, Wilmersdorf, 10719 (883 1582). U9 Spichernstraße. **Open** *box office* 11am-6pm Mon-Sat. **Showtime** 8.30pm **Admission** DM14-DM50. **No credit cards. Map C5**
This renovated circus tent is in a city park-like setting. The inside is lined with mirrors and on stage you can see some of Berlin's most celebrated entertainers. Friday and Saturday late-night shows are generally free and well-attended.

Kartoon
Französische Straße 24, Mitte, 16117 (204 4756). U6 Französische Straße. **Open** 9am-4pm Tue-Sun. **Admission** DM25. **No credit cards. Map F3**
Over 20 years old, this club has paid its dues and stands as one of the most popular places for Kabarett in Berlin. But if you don't speak fluent German or have a good understanding of local politics, the shows here won't make much sense.

Alternative

Scheinbar
Monumentenstraße 9, Schöneberg, 10829 (784 5539). U7 Kleistpark. **Open** from 8pm Wed-Mon. **Admission** DM10-DM20. **No credit cards. Map E5**
A hip and intimate storefront club exploding with fresh talent. One of the most experimental and fun-loving cabarets in town, with an excellent house troupe of their own and a selection of guest performers. Wednesday night's open stage is often pretty wild.

Theater im Keller
Weserstaße 211, Neuköln, 10247 (623 1452). U7 Hermannplatz. **Open** from 8pm Fri, Sat. **Admission** DM36. **No credit cards. Map H5**
Cosy and kitsch is the mood in this small but adventurous club presenting mainly exotic drag revue, but also featuring some very good, real, female chanteuses.

Cafe Theater Schalotte
Behaimstraße 22, Charlottenburg, 10585 (341 1485). U7 Richard-Wagner-Platz. **Open** from 8pm daily. **Admission** DM25. **No credit cards. Map B3**
A friendly and comfortable café with a nice-sized theatre where a well-chosen assortment of acts can be seen. The European Acappella Festival every November is worth catching.

Roter Salon/Grüner Salon
Volksbühne, Rosa-Luxemburg-Platz, Mitte, 10178 (2406 5807/3087 4806). U2 Rosa-Luxemburg-Platz. **Open** *box office* 10am-6pm. **Admission** DM18-DM25. **No credit cards. Map G3**
Sometimes the atmosphere in these two separate performance spaces can really take you back to the secret cabarets of the 1920s – you can get the feeling that you're doing something deliciously illegal. But these small clubs are actually legitimate and very open-minded. Expect anything from drag talkshows to acid house parties.

Children

Germans invented the idea of childhood, then speedily took measures to check its spread.

The first foreign word most of us utter is also one of the most beautiful metaphors produced by any language: kindergarten. A garden of children? A garden for children? However you translate it, the semantics of kindergarten are German; a product of progressive, mid-nineteenth century thought that changed our perception of human development forever. German educators like Friedrich Froebel practically invented childhood. They helped show that kids were more than simply inferior, downsized-versions of adults.

Keep all this in mind when visiting Berlin with your own children. It helps explain everything from why modern Germans seem to have backward notions about museum technology to why many of them can make you feel ill at ease for having the nerve to appear in public with your toddler.

Oddly, the association between kids and gardens does not mean children are allowed to run free on grassy areas in urban parks or formal squares. (Not advisable anyway, because the one thing even law-abiding Berliners refuse to do is curb their dogs.) After Germans got around to identifying the concept of childhood, it seems they wasted no time in establishing strict boundaries within which it should be practised.

As a result, Berlin has a wealth of impressive outdoor playgrounds where children can climb, slide, hop and splash to the point of exhaustion. Many are located in scenic parks, such as the Tiergarten, or quiet shady lots where you can chill out on a bench as the kids burn off excess energy.

ZOOS AND ELEVATED VIEWS

The Berlin Zoologischer Garten (Zoo) and Aquarium are the classic attractions for young tourists. Older kids might go for the thrill of heights: the **Funkturm**, **Fernsehturm** and **Siegessäule** (*see chapter* **Sightseeing**) all have observation platforms that are good for a rush. Other elevations provide quirky views of the city for adults and cost-free fun for the kids. You can stand on 25 million cubic metres of debris– dragged out of the downtown area by widows as soon as the smoke cleared in 1945 – at Teufelsberg in Grunewald. The overgrown site is the place to take kites on windy days, sledges in the snow, and fireworks on New Year's Eve. Closer to downtown, more rubble mountains are at the Volkspark Friedrichshain, which also features a 'fairytale fountain' incorporating sculpture groups

Alexanderplatz – a kids-eye view.

based on the Grimm brothers' stories. (Wilhelm and Jacob, along with a couple of other Grimms, are buried in the graveyard of St Matthew's Church in Schöneberg). Another off-beat, no-fee thrill: in the park next to Märkische Museum there's a bear pit with live animals, a medieval reference to the beast in the city's coat of arms (yup: Bear-lin).

Most places have reduced entrance fees for children, and public transport is free for kids under six. Buses can be entered with buggies from rear doors, and though most U-Bahn stations are not yet equipped with lifts, they aren't very deep. Prams are not allowed on escalators in theory, but few parents pay heed.

Shopping for Children

Necessities are easily found in any shopping district. Traditional wooden toys are widely available, but these often appeal more to parents' fantasies than to those of modern children. Look out also for the pricey but highly collectable German stuffed-toy brands Steif and Sigikind. *See chapter* **Shopping & Services**.

Bärenstark

Georgenstraße 2, Mitte, 10117 (208 2590). U6, S2, S3, S5, S6, S7, S9 Friedrichstraße. **No credit cards. Map F3**
New and antique teddy bears in what's almost a museum of plush kiddie companions. Flea market nearby under the S-Bahn arches.

Hennes & Mauritz (H&M)

Kurfürstendamm 234, Charlottenburg, 10719 (882 3844). U15 Uhlandstraße. **Open** 10am-7pm Mon-Wed; 10am-8pm Thur, Fri; 9am-4pm Sat. **Credit** AmEx, DC, EC, JCB, V. **Map C4**

Specialises in trendy baby, kids and young adults fashions and accessories. This branch is for babies and toddlers but a full range is at other H&M outlets all over town.

Kaufhaus des Westens (KaDeWe)
Wittenbergplatz, Charlottenburg, 10789 (212 10). U1, U2, U12 Wittenbergplatz. **Open** 9.30am-6.30pm Mon-Fri; 9.30am-8.30pm Thur; 9am-2pm Sat. **Credit** AmEx, DC, EC, JCB, V. **Map D4**
An extensive but expensive children's wear department, a wonderful toy section, a food emporium on the sixth floor, a no-smoking cafeteria in the rooftop atrium, and nappy-changing tables in the toilets.

Baby-sitters

You may be able to arrange a baby-sitter through your hotel. If not, two university student employment agencies can help. Book as early as possible and state that you want an experienced baby-minder. Both have English-speakers available, though the person answering the phone may not speak English. Both services charge DM15 to DM20 per hour, with a DM60 minimum.

Heinzelmaennchen (Freie Universität)
(831 6071). **Open** 7.30am-6pm Mon, Tue, Thur; 7.30am-9pm Wed, Fri.

TUSMA (Technische Universität)
(315 9340). **Open** 8.30am-5.30pm Mon-Fri.

Attractions
Museums

In addition to the museums listed below, also keep in mind: The **Pergamon Museum**'s Greek altar and Babylonian Ishtar Gate awe children as well as adults, and a quick scoot around the museum's highlights is free on Sunday. The **Egyptian Museum**'s bust of Cleopatra and sarcophagi appeal to even pre-schoolers. The **Natural History Museum** (Naturkundemuseum) has the world's largest dinosaur skeleton. The cars used to smuggle people through The Wall at the **Checkpoint Charlie Museum** appeal to kids over about age eight. The Citadel Spandau has a nice interpretive museum and a tower to climb to get an aerial view of the sixteenth-century fortress and environs. And at a special 'kindergalerie' in the Bode Museum, kids can touch and feel to their heart's content.

Berlin has no large-scale, hands-on science museum, and few of the kid-friendly computer gimmicks standard by now in lots of museums around the world. Germans are sceptical about the interface of childhood and technology in general, and specifically of the educational value of anything transmitted via a video screen or keyboard. *See also chapter* **Museums**.

Museum für Verkehr und Technik
Museum of Transport and Technology
Trebbiner Strasse 9, Kreuzberg, 10963 (254 840). U1, U7,

U15 Möckernbrücke. **Open** 9am-5.30pm Tue-Fri; 10am-6pm Sat, Sun. **Admission** DM5; DM2 children. **Map E5**
One of Berlin's most kid-friendly exhibits, the Transport Museum is in the old Anhalter Bahnhof roundhouse and trains comprise the best and biggest part of the exhibition. These sit on the original tracks, and include engines and passenger and freight cars from the eighteenth century to the present. There are also demonstrations of early machines plus computers and gadgets to play with. The Spectrum annex (included in admission) houses 200 interactive devices and experiments, most of them primitive and pretty boring. Expansion was underway at the time of going to press.

Museum für Völkerkunde
Ethnological Museum
Lansstraße 8, Zehlendorf, 14195 (830 1438). U1 Dahlem-Dorf. **Open** 9am-5pm Tue-Fri; 10am-5pm Sat, Sun. **Admission** DM4; DM2 students, children.
More educational than entertaining. Among the masks, totems and tools from the South Seas (well-displayed, with lots to see at child's-eye level) stands a large wooden clubhouse which children may enter and run around in. Children may also board a catamaran-type replica of an eighteenth-century wooden boat from the Tonga Islands. In the basement is a small Junior Museum, with exhibits designed for young people.

Puppentheater-Museum Berlin
Karl-Marx-Straße 135, Neukölln, 12043 (687 8132). U7 Karl-Marx-Straße. **Open** 9am-5pm Mon-Fri; 11am-5pm Sat, Sun. **Map H6**
Hand-made and antique puppets and marionettes from around the world. Also occasional performances – a revelation for kids young enough not quite to have sussed who's pulling the strings. A bit out of the way but worthwhile.

Museum villages & farms

Domäne Dahlem
Königin-Luise-Strasse 49, Zehlendorf, 14195 (832 5000). U1 Dahlem-Dorf. **Open** 10am-6pm daily except Tue. **Admission** DM3; DM1,50 children, students.
On this working farm, children can see how life was lived in the seventeenth century. Craftspeople including blacksmiths, carpenters, bakers and potters preserve and teach their skills. It is best to visit during one of several festivals held during the year, at which children can ride ponies, tractors and hay-wagons. Also open during the week just to commune with the animals. Phone for information on weekend events.

Jugendfarm Lübars
Quickborner Strasse, Reinickendorf, 13469 (415 7027). S1 Wittenau, then bus 221. **Open** 9am-7pm daily except Sat and Mon. **Admission** free.
Lübars was once at the edge of West Berlin, just inside the Wall. The working farms in the charming old village and expansive fields provide a haven from the bustle of the city, and although west Berliners are no longer hemmed in, Alt Lübars is still worth a visit. In the nearby children's farm (Jugendfarm Lübars) one can see farm animals, watch craftspeople at work, and have a bite to eat at the restaurant in the hof. Adjacent is a great playground, and a hill of World War II rubble to climb.

Museumdorf Düppel
Clauertstraße 11, Zehlendorf, 14163 (802 6671). U1 Oskar-Helene-Heim, then bus 115. **Open** mid-April to mid-Oct, 3pm-7pm Thur; 10am-5pm Sun and public holidays. **Admission** DM3; DM1,50 children, students.
A fourteenth-century village, reconstructed around archeological excavations and surrounded by the Düppel Forest. Workers demonstrate handicrafts, medieval technology and farming techniques. Ox cart rides for kids. Small snack bar at exit. A very quiet outing.

Zoos

Berlin Zoologischer Garten (Zoo) and Aquarium

Hardenbergplatz 8, Tiergarten 10623 (254 010). U1,
U2, U12, U9, S3, S5, S6, S7, S8 Zoologischer Garten.
Open 9am-5pm daily except Christmas Eve. **Admission**
zoo only DM11; DM5,5 children; *aquarium only* DM11;
DM5,50 children; *combined admission* DM15; DM7,50
children. **Map D4**

At the edge of the Tiergarten and one block from the
Ku'damm, west Berlin's zoo boasts more species (1,500) than
any zoo in the world. The grounds are nice with a good playground, many snack stands and a restaurant. Highlights
include a children's petting zoo (watch out for butting young
goat), nocturnal house and giant pandas. The aquarium is
also extraordinary and worth a separate rainy day visit to
see tropical fish, lizards, alligators and an insect zoo.

Tierpark Friedrichsfelde

Am Tierpark 125, Friedrichsfelde, 10319 (515 310). U5
Tierpark. **Open** 9am-5pm (ticket office closes 6pm) daily.
Admission DM11; DM5,50 children.

The zoo in east Berlin is larger and more spacious but has
fewer animals than its western counterpart. It's good for long
walks and views of grassland animals (giraffes, deer) in
wide-open spaces. Facilities for children include a petting
zoo where goats, monkeys and other animals can be fed, children's playground and snack stands.

Berlin's **Zoo** – always a place to play.

Entertainment

Children's Films

Most films shown in Berlin are in German but
check listings in *tip* or *Zitty* for the notation OF
(Originalfassung – original version) or OmU (subtitled. The city's annual film festival in February
(*see chapter* **Film**) features several movies for children, many in English. There's also usually something educational running at the **Haus der
Kulturen der Welt** (*see chapter* **By Area**).

Theatre & Circus

For current theatre listings, check *tip* and *Zitty*
magazines. Visiting circuses hang their posters
everywhere around town. There's also a permanent circus show at the **UFA-Fabrik** (Victoria
Straße 13, Tempelhof, 752 8085). Because of the
language problem, the circus is not ideal, but Berlin
has several puppet theatres and, especially around
Christmas, ballet productions such as *The
Nutcracker* and *Cinderella* which could appeal to
non-German speakers.

Berliner Figuren Theater

Yorckstraße 59, Kreuzberg, 10965 (786 9815). S1, S2,
S5 Yorckstraße. **Open** phone for details. **Map F5**

West Berlin's oldest and possibly best puppet theatre. Its traditional repertoire of fairy tales and adventure stories is
aimed at a very young audience, and played by a company
of exquisitely hand-crafted dolls.

Hackesches Hof Theater

Rosenthaler Straße 40-41, Mitte, 10178 (283 2587).
S75, S5, S3, S9 Hackesches Markt. **Map F2**

Features a Sunday brunch programme from 10am comprising a buffet followed by clowns and puppets.

Klecks

Schinkestraße 8/9, Neukölln, 12047 (693 7731). U8
Schönleinstrasse. **Open** phone for details. **Map G5**

A puppet theatre with hand-puppets, marionettes and stick
figures, along with oodles of audience participation. A good
choice for non-German speakers.

Zaubertheater Igor Jedlin

Roscherstraße 7, Charlottenberg, 10629 (323 3777). U7
Adenauer Platz. **Performances** 3.30pm Tue-Sun; 8pm
Thur-Sat. **Admission** DM9-DM32. **No credit cards.**
Map B4

In the days of Houdini, Russian State Circus-trained magician Igor Jedlin would have been world-famous. In these
times of David Copperfield, he occupies a small venue in a
Ku'damm side-street, entertaining kids with technically perfect, showy and thoroughly enjoyable tricks.

Parks & Playgrounds

Parks abound in Berlin. The vast Grunewald is
great for long walks, as is the more central
Tiergarten (*see chapter* **By Area**). Paddle and
rowing boats can be hired near the Cafe am Neuer
See (Thomas-Dehler-Straße) in the Tiergarten, and
just south of the S1 Schlachtensee station in the
Grunewald. You can rent bicycles at the
Grunewald S-Bahn station. Treptower Park, on the
Spree River (*see chapter* **By Area**), has flowers
and trees and standard German food. For a playground paradise, head to the Volkspark on the east
side of Bundesallee in Wilmersdorf. There are

myriad slides and playground paraphernalia, as well as a horizontal ski-lift ride and a pond with ducks. Freizeitpark Tegel has trampolines, table-tennis and paddle-boats. Viktoria Park in Kreuzberg has a great hill for climbing (and for tobogganing), Berlin's only waterfall, a small children's zoo and a good playground.

There are also some excellent playgrounds near various tourist attractions: across the Spandauer Damm from the Schloß Charlottenburg at Klausenerplatz; Schustehruspark on Schustehrus Straße two blocks south of the Egyptian Museum; behind Museum Island just across the footbridge in Monbijoupark; and in the Tiergarten off John-Foster-Dulles-Allee on the way to the Reichstag.

Further afield, the FEZ Köpenik (SE corner of Berlin) is a great place for a day out with the kids. Facilities include a swimming pool, park and miniature railway. **Peacock Island** (Pfaueninsel – *see chapter* **By Area**) is a nice place to spend a quiet afternoon. Peacocks roam this island nature preserve near Wannsee, reachable by a short ferry ride. There's also an unusual castle built by Friedrich Wilhelm II with a small museum inside.

In summer there are plenty of places to go swimming or paddling – both outdoor public pools and lakes on the city outskirts. The Strandbad-Wannsee is the most accessible of the latter – a ten-minute walk from S-Bahn Nikolassee. Boat tours depart from nearby Wannsee harbour and from other points around town. Kids may enjoy the gruesome Moby Dick boat, fashioned as a whale with improbable teeth, which sails from Stern und Kreisschiffahrt on Puskinallee in Treptow. *See also chapters* **By Area** *and* **Getting Around**.

BLUB (Berliner Luft und Badeparadies)
Buschkrugallee 64, Neukölln, 12359 (606 6060). U7 Grenzallee. **Open** 10am-11pm daily. **Admission** all day DM 26; DM 23 students; DM21 children. Slightly lower rates during the summer and for briefer visits.
Pools, a water-slide, waterfalls, a sauna and restaurants.

Freizeitpark Tegel
Schlosspark Tegel, Tegel, 13507 (5307 1504). U6 Alt-Tegel.

FEZ (Freizeit und Erholungszentrum) Köpenik
An der Wuhlheide 250, Köpenik, 12459 (635 1833). S3 Wuhlheide. **Open** 10am-9pm Tue-Fri; 1pm-6pm Sat; 10am-6pm Sun. **Admission** free.

Volkspark
Wilmersdorf. U7, U9 Berliner Straße. **Map C6**

Viktoria Park
Kreuzberg. U6 Platz der Luftbrücke. **Map F5**

Restaurants

Most Berlin restaurants make no special provisions for children. Those with very young children might wish to avoid nicer German restaurants

altogether, but if you make a point of asking if children are welcome before sitting down, the waiting staff are more likely to be helpful. Italian, Greek, Turkish or Asian restaurants and those on the Ku'damm are generally quite friendly to children.

For a really memorable evening, teens enjoy the all-evening medieval dinners served at the Citadel Spandau, complete with period entertainment. *See also chapter* **Restaurants**.

Restaurant am Grunewaldturm
Havelchaussee 62, Wilmersdorf, 14193 (304 1203). S1, S3, S7 Nikolasse, then bus 218. **Open** 10am-10pm daily. **Average** DM50. **Credit** AmEx, EC, V.
The food is unexceptional, but the setting – in the middle of the Grunewald – is pleasant. German families fill the place, and in good weather there are tables in the garden. There's space for children to run around outside, but first run them to the top of the tower for a great view over the region. No-frills mini-golf course also nearby. Book at weekends.

Chalet Suisse
Im Jagen, Zehlendorf, 14195 (832 6362). U1 Dahlem-Dorf. Bus 108. **Open** 11.30am-midnight daily. **Average** DM25. **Credit** AmEx, EC, DC, JCB, MC, V.
At the edge of the Grunewald on a forest path. The food is pricey for the quality, but the fairy-tale setting of this 'chalet' and its gingerbread-house appearance makes it a hit with kids.

Charlottchen
Droysenstraße 1, Charlottenburg, 10629 (324 4717). **Open** 3pm-midnight Mon-Fri; 10am-midnight Sat-Sun . **Average** DM25. **No credit cards. Map B5**
Adults eat in peace in the dining room while the kids tear it up in the rumpus room next door. A unique concept in Berlin. Theatre performances for the kids on Sundays at 11.30am.

Hard Rock Cafe
Meinekestrasse 21, Wilmersdorf, 10719 (884 620). U1, U2, U12, U15 Kurfürstendamm. **Open** noon-midnight daily. **Average** DM30. **Credit** AmEx, DC, EC, JCB, V. **Map C4**
Excellent hamburgers, sandwiches and milkshakes, and a fun decor of rock'n'roll memorabilia. Children generally love the place, are well-treated, and are given colouring books.

Mövenpick
1/30 Europa-Center, Charlottenburg, 10789 (262 7077). U1, U2, U9, U12, S3, S5, S6, S7, S8 Zoologischer Garten. **Open** 8am-midnight Mon-Fri; 8am-1am Sat, Sun. **Average** DM30. **Credit** AmEx, DC, EC, JCB, V. **Map D4**
Features a small play area, children's menu and colouring books for young diners. Usually packed and service can be slow, but the ice cream is great and the early hours and central location make it good for brunch before a zoo visit.

Planet Hollywood
Friedrichstraße 68, Mitte, 10119 (2094 5800). U2, U6 Stadtmitte. **Open** 11.30am-midnight Mon-Thur, Sun; 11.30am-1am Fri, Sat.* **Average** DM20. **Credit** AmEx, EC, MC, V. **Map F4**
You wouldn't be seen dead here without your kids.

TGI Friday's
Karl-Liebknecht-Strasse 5, Mitte, 10178 (2382 7966). U2, U5, U8, S3, S5, S7, S75, S9 Alexanderplatz. **Open** noon-1am Mon-Thur; noon-2am Fri, Sat; noon-midnight Sun. **Average** DM30. **Credit** AmEx, EC, DC, V. **Map G3**
Has a great view, an extensive menu of American multi-ethnic international food and great desserts. The friendly staff all speak English and really welcome children.

Clubs

Berlin's legendary club life has splintered into several scenes.

These are transitional times for Berlin's club scene. Gone are the days when techno was capable of drawing anyone and everyone on to one big dance-floor. The closing of the E-Werk in summer 1997 (even though some smaller part of the former power station complex on Wilhelmstraße now looks likely to reopen) was very much the end of an era which had lasted since the first techno clubs opened in the abandoned spaces of no-man's land and began pounding out the sound of the end of history.

Now everything has fragmented into several distinct but often overlapping scenes, with few clubs representing any kind of consistent musical policy. The gay crowd have retreated back into their own corner. The young ravers get off on mid-period trance and imagine it's original techno. Some of the old crowd leap at any chance to relive some aspect of the actual good old days when techno was fresh, radical, extreme and thumpingly apocalyptic. Others have moved on to drum 'n' bass, furiously appreciating its complex cadences as if they were listening to jazz, but never quite working out how to dance to it. The lively trip hop/hip hop/reggae scene continues in its own vein, very much as a doped up alternative to drum 'n' bass, even though breakbeats sometimes set the tone. And then there are assorted micro scenes: easy-listening extravaganzas, digital hardcore DJs, Goa one-nighters, electro events, fetish clubs.

The diversity of this simmering melting-pot can be interesting and there are definitely good nights out to be had at all levels, but there's really little point in us trying to tell you what kind of music or scene can be found where – everything seems to involve a bit of everything these days, and little stays the same for very long.

The club scene is in fact subject to a greater rate of flux than any other aspect of this ever-changing city. Places wink in and out of existence like subatomic particles. In revising the club listings from the last edition of this *Guide*, we found – apart from a few diehard discos that exist pretty much independently of underground trends (*see below* **Discos**) – only one club that had survived long enough to be included a second time around. This was **Tresor**, still partying on beneath the former no-man's land that is currently Europe's largest building site. Everything else had closed down, moved on, fallen out of fashion or tumbled into trouble with the authorities.

So, don't be surprised if some of the places listed here are no longer around by the time you consult this chapter. We've scurried around in the Berlin night and done our best, but three or four of the clubs we originally intended to include had closed down even in the time it took to compile these listings – some of them just weeks after opening. Who knows how many places will still be there in a year? At the time of writing – February 1998 – the clubs included here were the best Berlin had to offer, and the details we have provided as correct as we could make them.

The trick, therefore, is to plug into the network once you get into town. The best single source for current information about clubs and one-off events is the excellent free magazine *Flyer*. A pocket-sized bi-weekly affair available from clubs, shops and bars all over town, it rigorously lists what's on and where to find it. This should be your bible.

You can also pick up actual flyers, which are produced in sufficient quantity to keep a horde of young graphic artists in work, at the same sort of places. If all else fails try music or clubwear fashion shops such as **Hardwax**, **Downbeat**, **Flex/Inch by Inch/Melting Point**, **Space Hall**, **Groopie Deluxe** and **New Noise** (*see chapter* **Shopping & Services**) but information can also be picked up in various bars and restaurants.

Berlin's a good place to catch international DJs – all the big names of underground dance pass through town sooner or later. Tresor still has a Detroit connection and features a lot of techno's legendary old guard as well as being the best place outside of Frankfurt to catch Sven Väth. Berlin DJs to look out for include:

Paul van Dyk (uplifting trance), Westbam (live sets much better than his records – at least

Hangar II – *where techno crawled off to die.*

Icon – *intense dancefloor, imaginative lighting and cool on just about any night. Page 176.*

the ones he plays in Berlin), Mitja Prince (house and trance on a Chicago-Detroit axis), Valis (sometimes ambient, sometime trip hop and drum 'n' bass), Clé (spacey house, bits of drum 'n' bass), Tanith (a Berlin legend, still playing big beats though less apocalyptic than in the past) and Dr Motte (he doesn't play often, but when he does it's worth it). Interference events imaginatively bring together dance beats and live electronica with an avant-garde edge. Parties organised by the MFS label are usually warm, enjoyable events with a predominantly young crowd and a lot of old insiders around the edges.

The Love Parade weekend in mid-July has traditionally been the premier event on Berlin's club calendar. Over a million people showed up in 1997. At the time of writing, though, it looked unlikely that a 1998 Parade would go ahead. *See page 179* **Don't stop the carnival**.

See page 179

Clubs

Bergwerk
Bergstraße 68, Mitte, 10115 (280 8876). U8 Rosenthaler Platz. **Open** 10am-3am (at least) daily. **Map F2**
The basement club is open daily, populated with people eager to avoid trendy clubs and expensive beer prices. Despite the myriad DJs names in listings, there is in fact only one guy who changes his repertoire depending on the night. Just the sort of idiosyncrasy that makes a place worthwhile for a night of slumming and slamming to the Beastie Boys, whose various incarnations seem to be the starting points for all the different club nights here.

Boom Club
Hof 1, Hackesche Höfe, Rosenthaler Straße 40-41, Mitte, 10178 (326 5368). U8 Weinmeisterstraße/S3, S5, S75, S9 Hackescher Markt. **Open** from 10pm Fri, Sat .
Admission DM15. **Map F3**
An airless shoebox, low-lit and spartan, where it's hard to say whether money should first be spent on the cranky soundsystem, the lack of air-conditioning, the perennially flooded downstairs toilets or the lift that sometimes breaks down ferrying people up to the other toilets. Mostly techno and house, with an underground feel, but regarded as neutral territory by Berlin's various feuding dance factions, making it a popular venue for label parties and events. The one big room can just about hold 500 people, most of whom wake up the next day with headaches from oxygen deprivation.

Delicious Doughnuts Research
Rosenthaler Straße 9, Mitte, 10119 (283 3021). U8 Weinmeister Straße/Rosenthaler Platz. **Open** from 8pm daily. **Peaks** 1am-3am. **Admission** *weekdays* DM5; *weekends* DM10. **Map F3**
Well-established venue on the northern perimeter of the Mitte nightlife district, and one of the few clubs in this area and in its field (drum 'n' bass, trip hop, jazzy groove) to offer an adequately sized dancefloor and DJs all through the week. Though the doormen can be a little surly, it's friendly and reasonably priced within, with a cosy bar out front that does indeed sell doughnuts.

Discount
Gartenstraße 103, Mitte, 10115 (no phone). S1, S2 Nordbahnhof. **Open** from 10pm Thur-Sat. **Admission** DM7-DM15. **Map F2**
In a former Tip supermarket (hence the name), this small place has two rooms: one with a bar and one with a dancefloor. With lots of comfy chairs and a programme of mostly underground house and electro, the vibe is paradoxically industrial but cosy. Berlin's DJ Clé and Munich's DJ Hell are among those who regularly take to the turntables.

Garage

Holzmarktstraße 19-24, Mitte, 10179 (no phone). U8, S3, S5, S7, S75, S9 Jannowitzbrücke. **Open** from 10pm Thur.-Sat. **Admission** DM10-DM15. **Map G4**

Part of a former carwash and near the biggest Aral filling station in Germany. There are three sections: a bar near the entrance, a concrete dancefloor beyond, and a chill-out area in the back that looks like an old East German canteen – absurdly low armchairs, tables too wide to talk across, and two fantastically ugly 'chandeliers'. Thursday to Saturday one-nighters embrace a cross-section of dance styles – trip hop, drum 'n' bass, world beat, very occasional techno and house. Good sound, but sometimes too loud for the space.

GoGo Club

Neue Schönhauser Straße 9, Mitte, 10178 (no phone). U8 Weinmeister Straße/S3, S5, S75, S9 Hackescher Markt. **Open** from 10pm Tue, Thur.-Sat. **Map G3**

Mini-club that hints at how the scene in Mitte originally sprang up – a few red lights, lots of tin foil, scrap metal fixtures, and a 'bathroom' ankle deep in fetid water and puke. Punks in Berlin play abrasive techno, and the DJs here are no exception. In recent years the GoGo also has become a rather unfortunate meeting point for British brickies looking for chemicals and fights.

Hangar II

Columbiadamm 2-6, Tempelhof, 10965. (no phone). U6 Platz der Luftbrücke. **Admission** varies. **Map F6**

Techno has crawled off to die in this cavernous venue for weekend parties (look out for No UFOs nights). Though it's mildly interesting being able to access some of the enormous Nazi-built Tempelhof airport complex, this place really does have all the atmosphere of an aircraft hangar – which is precisely what it is. Here you will find a drab young suburban crowd dancing to mostly moribund mainstream beats (although it does depend very much which DJs are playing), and an overwhelming sense that here the post-Wall party has finally taxied to a halt.

Icon

Cantianstraße 15, Prenzlauer Berg, 10437 (no phone). U2 Eberswalder Straße. **Open** from 10pm Thur-Sun . **Admission** varies. **Map G1**

A tricky-to-locate entrance in the courtyard just north of the junction with Milastraße leads to an interesting space cascading down several levels into a long stone cellar. It's a well ventilated little labyrinth, with an intense dancefloor space, imaginative lighting, good sound and a separate bar insulated enough for conversation to remain possible. Sometimes techno events, sometimes drum 'n' bass. At its best when the core crowd of young Prenzl'berg locals is augmented by a wider audience for some special event, but a cool place on just about any night.

Insel

Alt-Treptow 6, Treptow, 12435 (534 8851). S6, S8, S10 Planterwald. **Open** from 10pm Fri, Sat. **Admission** varies.

Out of the way but a brilliant place – like a miniature castle on a tiny Spree island, with several levels including a top-floor balcony overlooking east Berlin. Once a communist youth club (the 'Island of Youth'), these days it doubles as live venue and colourful club – lots of neon and ultra-violet, goa and gabber, crusties and neo-hippies. A magic mushroom kind of vibe. Great in summer.

Kalkscheune

Johannistraße 2, Mitte, 10117 (2839 0065). U6, S1, S2, S25, S3, S5, S7, S75, S9 Friedrichstraße. **Open** from 8pm-late Fri, from 11pm-morning Sat; other nights varies according to event. **Admission** DM12-DM20. **Map F3**

The 'chalk stable' (presumably what it once was) can be great in the summer when the courtyard bar is open, but in winter everyone has to cram into one big, smoky, poorly-lit, low-ceilinged room. If you don't want to dance, or can't find the space, there's a partitioned area around the attractive wooden bar to retreat to. It's mostly techno and house DJs but there's no real defined scene here – just a lot of people desperately seeking one. Cabaret events on Sundays.

Kalkscheune – *no real defined scene, just a lot of people desperately seeking one.*

Kit Kat Club

Glogauer Straße 2, Kreuzberg, 10999 (611 3833). U7
Görlitzer Bahnhof. **Open** 11pm-8am Wed; 7.30pm-8am
Thur; 11pm Fri-6pm Sat; 11pm Sat-7pm Sun. **Map H5**
You want Berlin decadence? Here it is, late 1990s style –
sex and drugs and uplifting, positive dance music. It's not
in the least bit seedy but no place for the narrow-minded,
with half the crowd in fetish kit, the other half in no kit at
all, and every kind of sexual activity taking place in full
view. Interesting decor includes a variety of useful paraphernalia and some truly extraordinary sexual impressionist paintings by an artist called Träumer. In its way Kit
Kat is the most relaxing club in Berlin. No one has anything
to prove and everyone knows why they're there – and will
almost certainly get it. Around 8am on a weekend morning
is the best time to go, but if you're not dressed up (or down)
enough, you probably won't get in. Be warned: they're not
overly fond of the English, whom they regard as inhibited
and prone to sniggering.

Lime Club

Dircksenstraße 105, Mitte, 10178 (2472 1397). U2, U5,
U8, S3, S5, S7, S9 Alexanderplatz. **Open** from 10pm
Wed-Sat. **Admission** DM10. **Map G3**
Small place, with a private feel, a cliquey but friendly
demeanour and an exceedingly dark dancefloor nicely complemented by a bright, separate bar that's excellent for perch-
ing. Music is mostly trance and house.

Matrix

Warschauer Straße 18, Kreuzberg, 10243 (2949 1047).
U1 Warschauer Straße. **Open** from midnight Fri, Sat.
Admission DM15. **Map H4**
A real hole. The space, under the U-Bahn arches on the
east side of Oberbaumbrücke, could be cool but they've
renovated the life out of it and inflicted on staff and customers alike an absurd computerised drink dispensing system that has to be experienced to be believed. The music
is mostly house and techno but there's no real concept and
atmosphere depends very much on the event. At its best
when hosting DJs such as Hazel B or Patrick Lindsey.

Pfefferberg

Schönhauser Allee 176, Mitte, 10119 (449 6534). U2
Senefelder Platz/Bus N52. **Open** times vary. **Admission**
DM15. **Map G2**
A good venue for world beat and assorted other dance
events. From the outside it looks like some kind of Roman
villa with classical columns you can frolic around in the
summer. Inside there's an adequate dancefloor and separate
bar. Filled with a young and impecunious crowd, it's like
some great big youth club.

Plantation Club

Stresemannstraße 69, Kreuzberg, 10963 (252 2734). S1,
S2, S25 Anhalter Bahnhof. **Open** from 11pm Thur-Sat;
6pm in summer. **Admission** DM5-DM7. **Map F4**
Small and cheerful place in a one-storey concrete structure standing alone near Anhalter Bahnhof. Decked inside
with a daft yet interesting assortment of knick-knacks
(cuckoo clocks, crossed oars, old pub signs and other
nasty ornaments) it has the feel of some old clubhouse or
gang hut. There's a low-lit bar area, a tiny dancefloor, and
a miniature stage beyond, used for spoken word performances on Wednesdays, live music on Thursdays. At
weekends the policy seems to be any kind of crowd-pleasing dance music that isn't techno. It's not a showy crowd
here, although one shaven-headed barmaid does bear a
startling resemblance to a showroom dummy that also
lurks behind the counter. At its best in summer, when
there are tables, gazebos and several grills outside in the
gardens that flank the club – people bring their own
sausages and steaks to indulge in an impromptu barbecue. Cheap drinks.

Privat

Pücklerstraße 34, Kreuzberg, 10997 (617 5502). U1,
U12, U15 Görlitzer Bahnhof. **Open** from 10pm Thur-Sat.
Admission DM5. **Map H4**
In the basement of the Markthalle (*see chapter* **Restaurants**)
this had only just been renovated as we went to press. It's a
small low-ceilinged place which has apparently now been
decorated with comfy chairs and standard lamps and other
stuff intended to evoke a living-room – if there were living-
rooms with a dancefloor at one end and a bar at the other.
At the weekends there'll dance music of various stripes; otherwise, Privat will host occasional live acts and experimental performances. It's a nice space and the people who are
running it know what they're doing, so we expect some fun
nights.

Schleusenkrug

Müller-Breslau-Straße/Tiergartenschleuse, Tiergarten,
10623 (313 9909). S3, S5, S6, S9 Tiergarten. **Open**
from 10.30am-late. **Admission** varies. **Map C4**
It has become a familiar story: a location that for decades
has catered to old couples is discovered by some some young
hipsters and becomes a cheesy-but-cool lounge for under-
groundish events. In this case, the location is a bar and beer
garden directly on the canal in Tiergarten park, and the
crowds descend on it in droves for easy listening, mod, and
indie-pop nights. During the day the place retains much of
its original flavour, hinging on nautical themes and large
glasses of pils.

Schnabelbar

Oranienstraße 31, Kreuzberg, 10999 (615 8534). U1,
U8 Kottbusser Tor/Bus N29. **Open** from 11pm daily.
Admission free. **Map G4**
Popular place with a long bar and a small dancefloor and
DJs most nights of the week. Music is mostly at the jazzy,
hip hop, junglist end of things. It's often heaving at the weekends but people still dance, a doorperson keeps local winos
and crazies at bay and there are frozen margaritas to provide some welcome chill.

SO36

Oranienstraße 190, Kreuzberg, 10999 (6140 1306). U1,
U8 Kottbusser Tor/Bus N29. **Open** from 10pm daily.
Admission varies. **Map G4**
Legendary former Mecca of the punk and post-punk scene,
this long and thin space with bad air-conditioning and few
frills hosts an assortment of club nights. Sound, crowd and
music vary enormously. At the time of going to press:
Mondays was hard techno, Wednesdays was a crucial gay
night, every second Saturday was Gay Oriental Night and
there were also monthly Jane Bond parties for lesbians.
Sometimes there are Goa nights or other one-off parties. *See
also chapter* **Gay & Lesbian**.

Tresor/Globus

Leipziger Straße 126a, Mitte, 10117 (609 3702). U2, S1,
S2 Potsdamer Platz/Bus N²52, 84. **Open** from 11pm
Wed-Sun. **Peaks** 1am-3am weekdays; 3am-6am
weekends. **Admission** DM15. **Map F4**
Pioneering no-man's land club partly in the subterranean
safe-deposit box room of the otherwise vanished pre-war
Wertheim department store, partly in the old Globus bank
building on the surface. This was the place to be in techno's
good old days, and the legend just about manages to linger
in the shadow of all the surrounding construction. Still good
for catching Juan Atkins, Derrick May, Blake Baxter and
other Detroit greats when they pass through town, but Sven
Väth and Paul van Dyk are the only DJs who pack the place
these days. Bonito on Wednesdays (DM5) offers young, up-
and-coming DJs and the summer Trancegarden out back,
with tables and fairy lights among the shrubbery, is the
club's finest feature, complementing two internal dancefloors
and a bar. Often there's no longer much happening and

THE ACTIVE ISSUE NO.172

i·D

i-Deas,fashion,clubs,music,people

£2.50 US$6.7

steady...

Subscribe now to i-D to receive 12 issues
full of the latest i-Deas, fashion, clubs, music and people.

Tresor is unlikely to survive much longer in its current form. There's talk of constructing a 'techno tower' on the site, full of shops and studios.

WMF
Johannisstraße 20-21, Mitte, 10117 (282 7901). U6, S1, S2, S25, S3, S5, S7, S75, S9 Friedrichstraße. **Open** from 11pm Thur-Sun. **Admission** DM15-20. **Map F3**
Fourth incarnation of legendary club that, having hitherto occupied an old shop, the former toilets of Potsdamer Platz U-Bahn station, and some premises including the old circular cocktail bar from the Palast der Republic, has now gone for sort of 1950s eastie decor, including lots of wood-style formica and curiously depressing red neon. Over the years, the various WMFs have been the heart of Berlin's trip hoppy/jazzy/funky scene and a haven for anyone who hated techno but still fancied a 'big' night out. This one plays tech-

no on Saturdays, though, with a trip hop/drum 'n' bass night on Fridays, thus attempting to cater for two mutually exclusive crowds. Only just opened as this *Guide* to press, but the leafy circular courtyard looked promising for summer. Definitely lots of potential but they do need to change the red lighting. Sundays is GMF; *see chapter* **Gay & Lesbian**.

Yaam
Cuvrystraße 50-51, Kreuzberg, 10997 (617 5959). U1 Schlesisches Tor. **Admission** varies. **Map H5**
Another place that had just opened as we went to press. Yaam was formerly down the road in a former bus depot that is now a venue called Arena (*see chapter* **Theatre**). This new space isn't quite as cavernous, but still houses a dance-floor capable of accommodating over 1,000 people. Expect club nights on Fridays and Saturdays, but the real point of Yaam was always the outdoor summer events. With stalls

Don't stop the carnival

Back in July 1989, the first Love Parade was around 150 people dancing their way up the Ku'damm behind one solitary float, much to the amusement of Saturday afternoon shoppers. The banner was 'Friede, Freude, Eierkuchen' – 'peace, joy and pancakes' – and DJ Dr Motte led this techno-fuelled cross between a carnival and a demonstration. In July 1997, the Love Parade meant one million people turning up to party in Berlin. One million people from all over the world – jamming into Ernst-Reuter-Platz, struggling shoulder to shoulder along Straße des 17 Juni and around the Seigessäule, overflowing to crash out in the meadows and bonk in the bushes of the Tiergarten. It was a quite simply boggling mass of humanity, spilling out to spend money all over Berlin. It was dozens of floats, taking hours to inch their way through the hordes, blasting out rhythm and representing clubs, record labels, paraphenalia manufacturers, magazines, radio stations, MTV, Camel cigarettes....

Techno, these days, means cash. Sponsorship. Tie-ins. Massive money-spinning events. One million people at the Love Parade demonstrates how effectively it's battered its way into the mainstream. It's a very long way from the underground phenomenon it was back in 1989, or even from the mid-period Love Parade when it was 'only' a few tens of thousands and it was still possible to argue that the event qualified as a political demonstration. For a long time the event thrived in a fascinating tension. The Parade was so big there was an inevitably anarchic effect on public order – crowds would close down whole streets just by dancing in them. But it was also, in a time of falling tourism and a faltering economy, bringing too much money into Berlin for the authorities to want to ban it. One

million ravers partying all weekend spend a considerable amount of cash. So while police muttered about noise and nuisance, politicians would make half-heartedly approving speeches about techno representing German culture and wave the thing back on its way.

It's never been an easy thing to get together. The original organisers, those who own the rights to the name 'Love Parade', have long since stopped loving each other and retreated into various feuding factions. And though scores of businesses profit indirectly from the event – everyone from the clubs who put on the parties over Love Parade weekend through to hoteliers and shopkeepers – the Love Parade itself doesn't make a *Pfennig*. There has, as a result, despite a decade of exponential growth, never been a permanent Love Parade office.

So each year the event just about manages to pull itself together, and each year it gets ever more unmanageable. At the time of writing it looked to be less than a 50-50 chance that a 1998 Love Parade would happen. The 1997 Parade brought protests and court action from environmentalists, worried about the effect it would have on Tiergarten wildlife. (The authorities brought out twin water cannon the next day to hose all the piss off the trees along the route.) It also inspired a rival Hate Parade attended by factions appalled at the increasing commercialism of the event. And nothing could have summed up the present-day Parade's utter lack of radicalism better than Dr Motte's Hallmark card slogan: 'Let the love shine in your heart.'

If the Love Parade does happen again, it will be on the second Saturday in July. At the time of writing there was talk of it moving to Paris, but there seems to be little foundation to rumours of *un Parade d'Amour*.

serving Indian and African food, all-day caipirinhas, facilities for basketball and skateboarding, and lots of reggae and African music, the old Yaam provided a unique daytime ambience. People used to turn up after tipping out of the clubs, or else slept late and rolled along in the afternoon. It was very popular, attracting an extraordinary mix of people. This new venue has a large courtyard that should be hosting similar events in summers to come.

Discos

Abraxas
Kantstraße 134, Charlottenburg, 10625 (312 9493). U7 Wilmersdorfer Straße. **Open** from 10pm Tue-Sun.
Admission DM10. **Map B4**
A dusky, relaxed disco where you don't have to dress up to get in and where academics, social workers, bank clerks and midwives populate the floor. Flirtation rules. Dance to funk, soul, latino and jazz – like techno never happened.

Far Out
Kurfürstendamm 156, Wilmersdorf, 10709 (3200 0723). U7 Adenauerplatz. **Open** from 10pm Thur-Sun.
Admission DM7. **Map B5**
A non-smoking disco run by Bagwanis with a portrait of the deceased Rajineesh watching over the dancefloor while DJs advise revellers to put their glasses down safely might sound like a highly ridiculous proposition – probably because it is.

Im Eimer
Rosenthaler Straße 68, Mitte, 10117 (282 2074). U8 Rosenthaler Platz. **Open** 11pm-morning Fri, Sat.
Admission DM12. **Map F3**
Set up by members of a legendary east Berlin punk band, the club has never strayed from these roots except that punks now mostly play what Alec Empire calls 'digital hardcore' (*see page 210* **The Empire talks back**). The building has been haphazardly gutted to allow a cathedral ceiling in the basement club, while upstairs another set of rooms stay open even later. Though portions of the crowd are distinctly not squatter types, the genuine item still abounds. Stumbling from the bunkerlike club into bright sunlight at noon sometime, you too may feel more suited to a squat.

Junction Bar
Gneisenaustraße 18, Kreuzberg, 10961 (694 6602). U7 Gneisenaustraße. **Open** from 8pm daily. **Admission** DM8-DM10. **Map F5**
A slightly seedy little scene thrives in the basement disco pick-up joint below the jazz venue of the same name (see *chapter* **Music: Rock, Folk & Jazz**). The DJs aren't all bad – it's mostly soul, funk, disco and rare groove – but there's such a weirdo quotient that some locals refer to it as the Dysfunction Bar, while the rest of the clientele have only delusions of cool. Can be a laugh, though.

Knaack
Greifswalder Straße 224, Prenzlauer Berg, 10405 (442 7060). S8, S10 Greifswalder Straße. **Open** 8pm-4am Wed-Sat. **Admission** DM5-DM15. **Map H2**
Multi-level club that hangs on from eastern beginnings by attracting a very young audience with a changing program of hard, aggressive music in the basement, and generic party music upstairs. The concert hall books a steady stream of interesting international acts.

Metropol
Nollendorfplatz 5, Schöneberg, 10777 (216 4122). U1, U2, U4 Nollendorfplatz. **Open** from 9pm-7am Fri, Sat.
Admission varies. **Map D5**
Dominating Nollendorfplatz, it's a beautiful building – particularly when the twin towers are lit up at night. Once upon a time this was a theatre where Hitler used to come and

Metropol – *beautiful building, but forget it.*

watch Zara Leander musicals. In the 1980s it was one of Berlin's most crucial clubs, but these days it's just an enormous disco without any real crowd – and sometimes without any crowd at all. Inside the complex are assorted bars and dancefloors, currently decorated in an Egyptian theme with pyramids and statues of assorted gods. It also contains the **Loft** concert space (*see chapter* **Music: Rock, Folk & Jazz**). But right now it's not worth a visit unless for some special event. A tragic waste of a potentially brilliant venue.

90°
Dennewitzstraße 18, Tiergarten, 10785 (262 8984). U1, U15 Kurfürstenstraße, U2 Bülowstraße. **Open** 11pm-5am Thur-Sat. **Admission** varies. **Map E5**
One large dancefloor room with a big bar, plus a small back bar where conversation is possible, and decor that switches around frequently. Thursday is an excellent gay night, usually with a drag show from Biggi von Blonde. Fridays and Saturdays draw a young and well-heeled crowd who dance to an assortment of slick soul and house DJs. Dress smart. *See also chapter* **Gay & Lesbian**.

Sophienclub
Sophienstraße 6, Mitte, 10178 (282 4552). U8 Weinmeisterstraße. **Open** from 9pm daily. **Admission** varies. **Map F3**
One of a handful of youth-oriented clubs that existed in east Berlin prior to Unification. Sophien went from jazz roots to accessible acid jazz and funk. Its legendary status in the east made it a favourite destination for west Berliners and visiting celebs after the wall fell, but the club resolutely ignored musical trends. Once a location for avant-garde eastern bands to practice and play, the club now functions as a disco and attracts people looking to party and not terribly concerned about the music. Tuesdays, an exception, continue to be the primary meeting place for the indie pop set.

Dance

Berlin is doing its damnedest to become a world capital of dance.

Despite drastic cuts in funding for all the arts in Berlin, dance is alive and kicking. Whether classically romantic or wildly experimental, companies are rising to the challenge and changing with the cash-strapped times. There are growing pains, but a confidence prevails that Berlin will emerge as a world capital of dance in the next century.

In recent years Berlin-based companies from the independent scene have been making a name for themselves. Berlin is increasingly represented in international competitions by names like Anna Huber, Jo Fabian and Tanzcompagnie Rubato, and for the first time in decades fringe groups can support themselves by touring. Standards have improved markedly with an influx of fresh talent from abroad. British and Dutch dancers in particular have been lured by the legend of 1930s Berlin, when the capital was a hotbed of New German Dance and home to the likes of Anita Berber, Rudolph von Laban and Mary Wigman. Berlin is still a town where there's room to experiment and, despite subsidy cuts, still more money available for fringe projects than in, say, London. Another attraction is the availability of unusual, one-off venues. Ensembles are constantly seeking out quirky locations that provide a unique backdrop to their stagings and reflect the transient nature of a city undergoing extensive reconstruction.

Reconstruction is also what is going on in the field of ballet: the Senate has approved the fusion of the three companies attached to the city's opera houses into one 'Berlin Ballet'. To be in place by 1999, the company will consist of two separate classical and contemporary ensembles. The Senate decision, which will cost some 50 dancers their jobs, is an attempt to cut costs while creating a world-class ballet company – a status none of the three existing groups can claim.

The **Deutsche Oper** (tickets DM14-DM70 – for details of this and other venues in this paragraph *see chapter* **Music: Classical & Opera**) has seen a coming and going of ballet directors since unification. US-born Richard Cragun, a former soloist with the Stuttgart Ballet, has a contract until 1999. He's shifted emphasis towards contemporary dance, searching out young choreographers from different cultural backgrounds to infuse the programme with an international flair. The 'dance-theatre' tradition at the **Komische Oper** (tickets DM5-DM45) was founded by Tom Schilling in 1966 and was under his experimental

direction until he retired in 1993. The company's openness to experiment has continued under Dutchmen Marc Jonkers and Jan Linkens. The **Staatsoper Unter den Linden** (tickets DM12-DM200) is not so adventurous. The programme is heavy on crowd-pleasing classics and the ensemble has tried to acquire status by commissioning big-name choreographers such as Roland Petit, Maurice Béjart and Patrice Bart.

The city says it is dedicated to dance, investing more than DM30 million a year in the classical and contemporary genres. Whether or not Berlin ever achieves its dream of dancing alongside Paris and London, there's always plenty on offer. Check *Tip* or *Zitty* for event listings, or consult:

Tanz in Berlin

Monthly calendar of performances and dance-related events for free at theatres, cafés, hotels and posted on the internet (http://www.kulturbox.de/dance).

Dance venues

Hebbel Theater

Stresemannstraße 29, Kreuzberg, 10963 (2590 0427). U1, U6 Hallesches Tor. **Open** *box office* 4pm-7pm Mon-Sun. **Tickets** DM13-DM45. **Credit** AmEx, EC, MC, V. **Map F5**

This 600-seat Kreuzberg theatre is noted for international avant-garde theatre and dance. Director Nele Herling concentrates on featuring top international dance companies like Bill T Jones, Trisha Brown or Tokyo's Saburo Teshigawara. February's Tanz im Winter is a three-week block of performances highlighting current trends and developments in modern dance. Tanz im August is another such festival during which the Hebbel is just one of the main venues. *Wheelchair access.*

Podewil

Klosterstraße 68-70, Mitte, 10179 (247 496). U2 Klosterstraße. **Open** *box office* 2pm-6.30pm Mon-Fri. **Tickets** DM20, DM15 concs. **No credit cards. Map G3**

This east Berlin cultural centre hosts off-beat experimental art, and dance has a firm place in the programme. Anything from the expressive movement of Parisian hip hop culture to contemporary Portuguese choreographies can be on offer here, and workshops usually run parallel to performances. Tanzwerkstatt, an organisation devoted to booking innovative international ensembles, operates from here.

Theater am Halleschen Ufer

Hallesches Ufer 32, Kreuzberg (251 0941). U1, U7 Möckernbrücke. **Open** *box office* from 7pm before performances. **Tickets** DM25; DM18 concs. **Credit** EC, MC, V. **Map F5**

With one of the best stages in Europe for contemporary dance productions, this theatre acts as a showcase for Berlin's independent dance scene. A home to fringe theatre since 1962, in recent years dance has come to comprise 70 per cent of all performances. The Tanzzeit festival in April and October highlights new dance trends in Berlin, including late night shows and a chance to see works in progress. The theatre co-produces with The Place in London.

Sophiensaele

Sophienstraße 18, Mitte, 10178 (283 5266). U8 Weinmeisterstraße. **Open** *box office* one hour before performances; telephone reservations only, tickets at door. **Tickets** DM10-DM30. **No credit cards**. **Map F3**
Originally the headquarters of a turn-of-the-century trade craft association, this building now serves as a venue for experimental theatre and dance. It owes part of its tremendous success to two of Berlin's most noted choreographers: soloist Sascha Waltz and Jo Fabian with his group 'department'. Productions by these and guest ensembles are staged in various spaces throughout the building, from the downstairs foyer to the first-floor 'marriage hall'. The dilapidated interior oozes history.

Volksbühne

Rosa-Luxemburg-Platz, Mitte, 10178 (247 6772). U2 Rosa-Luxemburg-Platz. **Open** *box office* noon-6pm Mon-Sun. **No credit cards**. **Map G2**
Johann Kresnik's starkly expressive political dance theatre has kicked up storm after storm since his arrival at this house in 1994. His biographical interpretations of Red Army Faction terrorist Ulrike Meinhof, for instance, or Gustaf Gründgens and Nietzsche, have sparked heated debate on why some subjects are still not politically correct after German unity.

Classes

Die Etage

Hasenheide 54, Kreuzberg, 10967 (691 2095). U7 Südstern. **Open** 9am-2pm Mon-Fri; 4pm-8pm Sat. **Map G5**
Courses in modern dance, jazz, tap, pantomime, acrobatics, juggling and flamenco cost an average DM20 for one-and-a-half-hour classes; DM70 per month. The school also conducts a three-year state-recognised dance education with a grounding in classic and modern disciplines.

Maison de la Danse

Pestalozzistraße 60, Charlottenburg, 10627 (323 2043). U7 Wilmersdorfer Straße. **Open** 9.30am-6pm Mon-Fri; 9.30am-7.30pm Thur; 9.30am-1pm Sat. **Credit** EC, MC, V. **Map B4**
Leotards, leg warmers and tutus, jazz, tap and point shoes, and most anything else you might need to waltz your way around Berlin, is on sale at this house of dance.

Schokofabrik

Naunynstraße 72, Kreuzberg, 10997 (615 2199). U1 Kottbusser Tor. **Open** 10am-2pm Mon, Thur; noon-6pm Wed. **No credit cards**. **Map G4**
A former factory, now converted into a women's centre, is complete with café and Turkish bath, and contains two floors for dance and sport. Weekend workshops at an average DM90 in Argentinian tango and other couples dances.

Staatliche Balletschule Berlin und Schule für Artistik

Erich-Weinert-Straße 103, Prenzlauer Berg, 10409 (424 4028). S8, S10 Ernst-Thälmann-Park. **Open** 8am-4pm Mon-Fri. **Map G1**
The ex-GDR's State Ballet School was founded in 1951. It's eight-year course is centred around classical Russian ballet. The school admits children from age ten, and about 15 per cent of its 200 students come from abroad. The State School for Artistry has 40 students, who begin training from the age of 15.

Nele Herling's **Hebbel**. *See page 181.*

Tanz Co-op

(440 8975).
Of no fixed abode but offering daily training for professional dancers from a variety of teachers in a variety of locations. DM10 per class, DM140 per month. Call for details.

TanzFabrik Berlin

Möckernstraße 68, Kreuzberg, 10965 (786 5861). U7, S1, S2 Yorckstraße. **Open** 10am-noon, 5pm-8pm Mon-Thur; 10am-noon Fri. **No credit cards**. **Map E5**
Berlin's largest contemporary dance school, with about 50 classes a week and 600 students. Its courses embrace a wide variety of dance techniques, including Limon, jazz, ballet, contact improvisation, new-dance, tai-chi, yoga, African and Afro-Brasileiro, street dance and samba. Bartenieff fundamentals, developed by former Laban student Irmgart Bartenieff, and Feldenkrais technique are also instructed. Guest workshops are a regular feature. TanzFabrik also has a small company which performs on the tiny in-house stage of its 100-seat theatre or at larger venues.

Tanz Tangente

Kuhligkshofstraße 4, Steglitz, 12165 (792 9124). U9 Rathaus Steglitz. **Open** 3pm-8pm Mon-Fri. **No credit cards**.
Former Wigman student Leanore Ickstadt set up this school 20 years after she first arrived in Berlin in 1961 on a Fulbright scholarship. Today Ickstadt teaches children and conducts advanced workshops. Adult classes are held in contemporary dance, awareness through movement, tap, Feldenkrais and ballet. Visitors to Berlin can take part in five lessons of their choice with a DM118 guest ticket. Those staying longer can register for four-month blocks of one 90-minute class a week: it costs DM80 a month (concessions DM70). Students can take advantage of the Semester Ticket, eight classes for DM154. Professional training in classical ballet is offered Mon-Fri.

Film

Berlin and the big screen have a long history together. The city is full of movie treats – open-air cinemas, one of the world's most important festivals and an entertaining diversity of theatres.

Berlin has always been associated with the movies. As home of the UFA studios, it was the capital of the pre-war film industry, and today hosts one of the world's most important international film festivals.

Germany boasts Europe's largest film-going audience and, since the fall of the Wall, Berlin's screen count has rocketed to almost 200.

As in most European cities, the selection is dominated by Hollywood product, though almost all non-German films are dubbed rather than subtitled. Yet Berlin is also a centre for off and off-off cinemas, called Programm-Kinos, which not only show films in their original language, but also offer alternatives to the Hollywood mainstream.

Oddly enough, though the last few years have seen the demise or regrooving of several traditional haunts, the overall number has not declined, and the number of exclusively English-language theatres has actually increased.

The proliferation of multiplexes and a proposed ban on tobacco advertising in cinemas look likely to begin killing off many of Berlin's smaller theatres, but for now they continue to range from the established (**Odeon**), to the eclectic (**Arsenal**), to the classic (**Zeughaus**), to the weird and wonderful (**Eiszeit**), taking in every level in between.

Summer open-air cinemas – *Freiluftkinos* – are a unique Berlin phenomenon. Air-conditioning is not yet a standard feature of Berlin cinemas so that Berliners still consider the summer as a time to be (oh horror!) outdoors. There are, at present, nine different open-air cinemas in the city's many parks, though only the **Freiluftkino Kreuzberg** offers frequent English programming.

Summers also offer Berlin's Fantasy Film Festival which showcases the latest in fantasy, horror and sci-fi from America, Hong Kong, Japan and Europe along with assorted classics and rarities. Dates and venues vary, but it's usually in June and at the Royal Palast in the Europa-Center as well as in Eiszeit and **Central** (*below*).

For film listings, look for the big Kino posters that go up weekly in U-Bahn stations and on various surfaces around town, or scan *Tip*, *Zitty* or the freebie *[030]*. For movies in English look for the notation OF or OV (Originalfassung or original version), OmU (original with subtitles) or OmE (original with English subtitles). Tickets are cheaper in most theatres on Tuesdays and Wednesdays. No Berlin cinemas take credit cards, so forget about phone booking.

Berlin Film Festival

Berlin's peak movie-going experience is the Berlinale, the world's second largest film festival after Cannes. While the Berlin Festival may not have the glamour of Cannes or Venice, it has them both beat when it comes to audience.

What seems like the whole city turns out for 12 days every February to see arguably the widest and most eclectic mix of any film festival in the world. Each year, around 800 films are presented in seven sections, the most important of which are listed below.

The International Competition

The most visible section in terms of glamour and publicity is also the most conservative in selection, concentrating on major international productions with a heavy (and heavily criticised) accent on America. If you are into glitz, the Competition provides the guest stars, both from the films and in the international jury, who appear nightly in the **Zoo Palast**'s 1,200-seat theatre. Films compete for Gold and Silver Bears and there is often a furore accompanying the announcement of the winners. Since the evening shows are the priciest and most likely to sell out, many go for the afternoon shows or the repeats in the Urania and the **International**. All shows at the Zoo Palast have simultaneous translation over headphones.

International Forum of Young Cinema

Originally created in 1971 in opposition to the Competition, the Forum provides a vital selection of the challenging and eclectic. It's here and in the **Panorama** (*below*) where the real discoveries are to be found – from the latest American indie film to African cinema to midnight shows of Hong Kong action films and never-to-be-seen-again films from eastern Europe. Jody Foster can look pretty small waving from the stage of the Zoo Palast but at the Forum, dialogues between audience and filmmaker are *de rigeur*. Films screen in the large (and often packed) Delphi Cinema as well as at the Arsenal, the Zeughaus and the Akademie der Künste (one stop north from the Zoo at U9 Hansaplatz).

Panorama

Originally intended to showcase films that fell outside the Competition guidelines, the Panorama has spread its wings to give the Forum a run for its money in terms of innovative programming, spotlighting world independent cinema with an accent on gay and lesbian films. Panorama films show in the landmark 1950s cinema, the Filmpalast on the Ku'damm, and repeat in one of the downstairs screening rooms in the Zoo Palast. Most films show with English subtitles.

The exile files

While Berlin was at one time a fertile breeding ground for film talent, much of that talent either fled or was kicked out. Though most are now identified with Hollywood, Berlin has a perverse pride in its famous exiles, many of whom started out together on the otherwise undistinguished 1930 film *Menschen am Sonntag*.

Fritz Lang

Probably the most widely touted of all Berlin's film exiles. As director of M and the Dr Mabuse films, he was a superstar in pre-war Germany. So much so that when

Hollywood beckoned in the 1920s, he refused. His sci-fi extravaganza, *Metropolis*, was a favourite of Hitler's and, as a result, Lang was invited to head the German film industry. Lang said he'd think about it and promptly packed his bags and left on the midnight train. He went on to become a major figure in American cinema, specialising in film noir and crime dramas. He returned to Berlin after the war to remake a 1920s

classic, *The Tiger of Eschnapur*, and stayed to resurrect Dr Mabuse. *Metropolis* is a favourite revival in Berlin – usually with live accompaniment, and sometimes a full orchestra.

Marlene Dietrich

A chorus girl and cabaret performer in 1920s Berlin, Marlene was playing small roles in German films when discovered by Josef von Sternberg for the lead in *The Blue Angel*. She left Berlin shortly after the film was finished and, contrary to popular belief, it was not the vehicle that made her a star. Her fame first came with the Hollywood film *Morocco*, which beat *The Blue Angel* to the screens.

She performed for the American troops during World War II and returning to Berlin after the war, was met with protesters chanting 'Marlene, go home!' Even so she has become a cult figure in Berlin and *The Blue Angel* is frequently revived and often touted as a prime example of the German film industry. When she died, the city had her body brought over for burial and paid a very steep sum to acquire her personal effects.

Billy Wilder

Probably Berlin's most popular film director although he never actually directed a German film. Originally a journalist and gigolo, Wilder wrote scripts and scenarios for such UFA films as *Emil and the Detectives* and *Menschen am Sontag*. He fled Berlin in 1933 and arrived in Los Angeles where his first job was jumping into a swimming pool fully clothed at a Hollywood party. A popular screenwriter in the 1930s with films like *Midnight* and *Ball of Fire*, he finally became a director himself in the 1940s, making *Double Indemnity* and *Sunset Boulevard*. After the war, he returned to Berlin to make *A Foreign Affair* (featuring fellow exile Marlene) and later *One, Two, Three*. Both are popular revivals, along with his comedy, *Some Like It Hot*.

Fred Zinnemann

Assistant cameraman on *Menschen am Sontag*, he abandoned Berlin in the 1930s and worked on shorts for MGM until graduating to feature films in the 1940s. He directed the first screen appearances of both Montgomery Clift (*The Search*) and Marlon Brando (*The Men*). He went on to make *High Noon*, *Oklahoma* and won the Oscar for Best Director with *From Here to Eternity* and *Man for All Seasons*.

Edgar G Ulmer

After starting as a set designer for theatre director Max Reinhardt, he became assistant to FW Murnau, following him to Hollywood to work on *Sunrise* (the first film to win the Oscar for Best Picture). He returned to Berlin and co-directed *Menschen am Sontag*, only to flee in 1933. At Universal he directed Karloff and Lugosi in the stylish-looking *The Black Cat*. A scandal involving a producer's wife got him blackballed from the major studios, but he is credited with 120 films and remains best known as an auteur of low-budget film noir and science fiction. His *Detour* is widely considered the epitome of the noir genre.

Robert Siodmak

A film editor at UFA until he co-directed *Menschen Am Sontag*. He fled Berlin in 1933 and, after working a few years in Europe, finally arrived in Hollywood where, thanks to his brother Curt (*below*) he got his start directing *Son of Dracula* for Universal Pictures. He went on to direct a string of successful noir films such as *Phantom Lady* and *The Killers*, gave Burt Lancaster and Ava Gardner their big-screen breaks and is credited with discovering Tony Curtis. He returned to Berlin in the mid-1950s to make *Escape from East Berlin* and remained in Germany to finish his filmmaking career. His *The Spiral Staircase* is a big revival favourite.

Curt Siodmak

A writer and journalist in Berlin, his first film experience was masquerading as a *Metropolis* extra in order to get an interview with Lang. Later, he co-wrote (uncredited) and helped finance *Menschen am Sontag*. Fleeing Berlin with brother Robert (*above*) in 1933, he wound up at Universal during their horror cycle, at first contributing to the Invisible Man series and later creating the Wolf Man. He was responsible for the subsequent series of monster team-ups beginning with *Frankenstein Meets Wolfman*. Later he wrote various 1950s sci-fi classics such as *Riders to the Stars*, *Earth vs the Flying Saucers* and *Donovan's Brain*. He ended up as a director of grade Z horror films such as *Cucuru, Beast of the Amazon*. In spite of this, he was awarded the German Service Cross in 1992.

Retrospective

A sure bet for sheer movie-going pleasure and, while concentrating on the established mainstream, always an opportunity to catch films that you might never otherwise see on the big screen. Past themes have included Colour, the Cold War, Nazi entertainment films and directors such as Erich von Stroheim or William Wyler. There is also an homage to the work of living film personalities such as Jack Lemmon, Alain Delon or Kim Novack, complete with personal appearances and a gala screening in the Zoo Palast. Films show in the Astor on the Ku'damm and the nearby Paris, and repeat at the Zeughaus and International. Hollywood orientated, but foreign-language films rarely have translation.

Tickets

Tickets can be bought up to three days in advance at either the main ticket office in the Europa Center or at Kino International in east Berlin. On the day of performance they must be bought at the theatre box office and last-minute tickets are often available. Queues for advance tickets can be very long indeed – three-hour waits are not uncommon – so it pays to come early, bring something to read and buy as much as you can in one go. Films are described in a Competition and Panorama catalogue which you can buy at the Berlinale Shop. The Forum has its own catalogue, free at every Forum theatre. Films are usually shown three times; cinemas away from the centre, while not as convenient, are less likely to sell out.

Ticket prices range from DM10-DM25 depending on the show. A full festival pass (Dauerkarte) is available at the Berlinale Shop from December until three days before the festival. At DM250 (bring two passport photos), it's good for all sections but not all theatres or times.

Berlinale Shop

Budapester Straße 48, Tiergarten, 10787 (2548 9254). U2, U9/S3, S5, S6, S7, S9 Zoologischer Garten. **Open** noon-6pm. Dauerkarten (Season Tickets) about DM250. **Map D4**

The place to buy Dauerkarten for the festival. For about DM250 (you'll also need two passport-size photos), you'll be allowed entry during the Berlinale to: all films at the Zoo Palast (before 4pm); films that are part of the competition, and evening screenings of the Panorama films and Retrospectives; and films shown at Delphi-Filmpalast, Akadamie der Künste and the International. Dauerkarten can be obtained by writing to the above address the December before the festival, or by turning up there in person anytime up until three days before the festival begins. Every year the administration will tinker with this or finetune that, so it is always best to pick up a programme from the Europa-Center or Berlinale Shop to get the lowdown on the latest developments. Posters, catalogues and paraphernalia can also be found at both places.

Europa Center

Breitscheidplatz 5, Tiergarten, 10787 (348 0088). U2, U9/S3, S5, S7, S75, S9 Zoologischer Garten. **Open** 11.30am-6.30pm, from 3 days before the Berlinale begins. **Map D4**

International

Karl-Marx-Allee 33 (corner of Schillingstraße), Mitte, 10178 (242 5826). U5 Schilling Straße. **Open** noon-7pm, from three days before festival starts. **Map G3**

Cinemas

Arsenal

Welserstraße 25, Schöneberg, 10777 (218 68 48). U1, U15, U2 Wittenbergplatz, U4 Viktoria-Luise-Platz/119, 129, 146, 185, 249 bus. **Tickets** DM10; DM8 members. **Map D5**

Small cinema with brazenly eclectic programming which includes everything from classic Hollywood to contemporary Middle Eastern cinema, from Russian art films to Italian horror, from Third World documentaries to the ever-popular silent films with live accompaniment. They show many English-language films and sometimes foreign films have English subtitles. Occasionally filmmakers are there to present their work.

Babylon Mitte

Rosa-Luxemburg-Straße 30, Mitte, 10178 (242 5076). U2 Rosa-Luxemburg-Platz/140, 147, 157, 240 bus/15. 17, 63, 71 tram. **Tickets** DM9; DM8 concs. **Map G3**

Not to be confused with **Babylon Kreuzberg** (*below*), this is a landmark building designed by Hans Poelzig – who also designed the classic German silent film, *The Golem*. Due to seemingly never-ending renovations, shows take place in the lobby which has been made into a screening room. Heavy on retrospectives and thematic programming, this can be an opportunity for those interested in east bloc films. Occasional Hollywood films in English and foreign films with English subtitles. They also have periodic series of independent films and often do one night a week's gay programming.

Babylon

Dresdener Straße 126, Kreuzberg, 10999 (614 6316). U1, U15, U8 Kottbusser Tor/247 bus. **Tickets** DM11-DM12; DM9 Tue, Wed. Two screens. **Map G4**

*Arriving early at the **Odeon**. See page 187.*

*Boys will be boys at the cosy **Xenon** – largely dedicated to gay and lesbian programming.*

Twin-screen theatre with varied programming featuring off-Hollywood, indie crossover and UK films. Lately they have become almost totally English-language.

Central
Rosenthaler Straße 39, Mitte, 10178 (2859 9973). U8 Weinmeister Straße. **Tickets** DM11, DM8,50 Tue, Wed. Two screens. **Map F3**
A new cinema on the edge of the Hackesche Höfe, this duplex only rarely offers programming in original English outside of their yearly participation in the Fantasy Film Festival. They do, however, have a daily afternoon programme called 'Non Stop Kino' which each month explores a theme such as jazz, film noir, pulp fiction or video projections of drag racing. Sometimes in English and very affordable – DM5 for you and a guest, stay as long as you like.

Checkpoint
Leipziger Straße 55, Mitte, 10117 (208 2995). U2, U6 Stadtmitte/129, 142 bus. **Tickets** DM9-DM11; DM3-DM6 children. **Map F4**
Hole-in-the-wall cinema that does a lot of strange series programming (including John Waters, gay and lesbiana, vampire films, Marilyn Monroe) that sometimes results in English-language shows. You haven't lived till you've seen Cinemascope in a 50-seat theatre.

Eiszeit
Zeughofstraße 20, Kreuzberg, 10997 (611 6016). U1, U15 Görlitzer Bahnhof. **Tickets** DM11; DM8,50. Two screens. **Map H4**
Definitely the most energetic cinema in town and seemingly run by total film nuts who show things because they really want to see them. Recent renovation has brought them plush seats and Dolby Surround but also a more conserva-tive selection of films to pay the bills. But this also means that we can now sit in comfort for their own special blend of German underground, Hong Kong films, Japanimation, slash films, gangsta films, US indies, occasional performance events and other assorted weirdness, often in English. Also a venue for the annual Fantasy Film Festival, with most films in their original versions.

Freiluftkino Kreuzberg
Mariannenplatz 2, In den Hof Bethanien, Kreuzberg 10997 (no phone). U1, U8 Kottbusser Tor. **Tickets** DM10; DM8,50 Tue, Wed. **Map G4**
Programmed by the crew at Eiszeit, this big-screen Dolby Stereo outdoor summer cinema offers, from June through August, a mix of past cinema hits, cult films and independent cinema as well as strange events such as live Turkish hardcore bands and American 1950s stag films. Many shows are in English. Bring a cushion and, considering the last couple of Berlin summers, maybe an umbrella too.

FSK
Segitzdamm 2, Kreuzberg, 10969 (614 2464). U1, U8 Kottbusser Tor. **Tickets** DM10; DM8 Mon. **Map G5**
Named after the state film rating board, this two-screen off-cinema is deep in the heart of Turkish Kreuzberg. They usually get the German versions, but do have the occasional American or British indie film or documentary, and some Taiwan or Hong Kong films with English subtitles.

Klick
Windscheidstraße 19, Charlottenburg, 10627 (323 8437). S5 Charlottenburg. **Tickets** DM9-DM10; DM7,50 Tue, Wed. **Map B4**
Off-Hollywood and theatrical documentaries, with many films in original English.

Kurbel

*Giesebrechtstraße 4, Charlottenburg, 10629 (883 5325).
U7 Adenauer Platz/101, 109, 119, 129, 204, 219 bus.*
Tickets DM12-DM13; DM9 Tue, Wed. Three screens.
Map B4
All the comforts of a multiplex (including plush seats, air-conditioning and one incredibly raked theatre) with at least two of its three screens showing typical Hollywood fare in original English at any given time. Sneak previews of forthcoming releases every Monday at 11pm – only DM7,50, but you don't know what you've got till it's on.

Moviemento

*Kottbusser Damm 22, Kreuzberg, 10967 (692 4785). U8
Leinestraße, U7 Hermannplatz/141, 144, 241 bus.*
Tickets DM10; DM13 double features; DM15 all-nighters; DM5 children 3pm weekends; DM8 Wed. Three screens. **Map G5**
With the loose and youthful atmosphere in this upstairs cinema, one might think they'd show more in original English than they actually do. Nonetheless, with three small screening rooms (232 seats altogether) there is often something available. Indie crossover, occasional off-Hollywood and new young German films, plus periodic retrospectives on actors or directors, frequent midnight double features and occasional all-night film-o-thons.

Odeon

*Hauptstraße 116 , Schöneberg, 10827 (781 5667). U4
Innsbrucker Platz/S45, S46 Innsbrucker Platz.* **Tickets**
DM13; DM9 Tue, Wed. **Map D6**
Long Berlin's best-loved English-language cinema, deep in the heart of Schöneberg. Though the largest, it's often prone to sell-outs, so it pays to get there a bit early. Shows a reasonably intelligent selection of big mainstream hits from Hollywood and the UK. Spacious, comfortable and friendly.

Olympia

*Kantstraße 162, Charlottenburg, 10623 (881 1978). U2,
U9/S3, S5, S6, S7, S9 Zoologischer Garten.* **Tickets**
DM12, DM9 Tue, Wed. **Map C4**
Another recent recruit to the English-language audience, this cinema often picks up films from Odeon after their run and also shows more independent fare.

Xenon

*Kolonnenstraße 5, Schöneberg, 10827 (782 8850). U7
Kleistpark.* **Tickets** DM10; DM 8,50, DM5 children. **Map E5**
Small cosy cinema in large part dedicated to gay and lesbian programming. Since most of this is indie stuff, mostly from America and Britain, a good deal of their programming is in English. Brought to you by the guys from Eiszeit.

Zeughaus

*Unter den Linden 2, Mitte, 10117 (215 020). S1, S2
Unter den Linden.* **Tickets** DM5. **Map F3**
The last place one might expect English-language films is in the **German Historical Museum** (*see also chapter* **Museums**), but there it is. It often hosts travelling retrospective shows such as Robert Wise, Powell & Pressburger, Douglas Sirk and Hollywood Exiles, and also programmes series on thrillers, westerns and British post-war films. They always make a concerted effort to get the original versions and occasionally foreign films have English subtitles.

Zoo Palast

*Hardenbergstraße 29a, Charlottenburg, 10623 (2541
4777). U2, U9/S3, S5, S6, S7, S9 Zoologischer Garten.*
Tickets DM12-DM14; DM9,50-10,50 Tue, Wed. Nine Screens. **Map C4**
Berlin's flagship theatre since the 1950s and an architectural landmark to boot. Two of their nine screens are able to run a CD of the original track along with the German dubbed

Zoo Palast – *architectural landmark and Berlin's flagship theatre since the 1950s.*

version and, with headphones provided in exchange for some form of ID, you can listen along to whatever Hollywood mainstream hit happens to be running. This is the best kept secret in town and they claim that they themselves never know in advance what films will come with the CD. Calling is tricky, the person who answers often doesn't know, so the best thing is to drop by the theatre and ask.

Video rental

British Council Video Club
Hardenbergstraße 20, Tiergarten, 10623 (3110 9910). U2, U9/S3, S5, S7, S75, S9 Zoologischer Garte/100, 109, 145, 146, 149, 219, 245, X9 bus. **Open** 2pm-6pm Mon, Wed-Fri; 2pm-7pm Tue. Annual membership DM50; DM20 for students or teachers. **Map C4**
Has a selection of British films and TV programmes, to be rented on a weekly basis. Depending on the video it will cost you between DM4 and DM8. Proof of residency needed.

Incredibly Strange Video
Eisenacher Straße 115, Schöneberg, 10823 (215 1770). U7 Eisenacher Straße. **Open** 2pm-10pm Mon-Sat. **Map D5**
A selection of over 3,000 titles in a store that lives up to its name – lots of weird cult movies plus a selection of mainstream fare. Video rentals are DM8 per night for the first one and DM6 for each additional one. Bring a personal ID, and either police registration or enough money for a deposit.

Videodrom
Mittenwalder Straße 11, Schöneberg, 10961 (692 8804). U7 Gneisenaustraße/140, 341 bus. **Open** 3pm-midnight Mon-Sat. **Map F5**
Videodrom is the largest English-language video store in Berlin. With thousands of titles ranging from the ultra-conventional to the ultra-weird, everyone should be able to find something to please. Rental is DM7,50 per night for most films; DM10 for new releases. You'll need personal ID and police registration.

Babelsberg: the dream factory

At the end of World War I, Germany might have been defeated as a military power, but as a filmmaking power it was gearing up to challenge Hollywood for world domination.

While it couldn't claim as many international stars, what Germany did have was an innovative visual sense and a technical sophistication that enabled such super-productions as *Metropolis*, *The Niebelungenlied*, *Asphalt* and *The Last Laugh*.

Berlin was the film capital of Europe and the biggest 'dream factory' was the UFA Studios in the suburb of Babelsberg.

If they couldn't actually beat Hollywood, they could at least create a level of production quality that Hollywood had to strive to surpass, and after pioneering set design, the moving camera and special effects in the 1920s, by the 1930s UFA could boast the biggest sound stages in Europe.

Hollywood struck back by buying off the biggest names. The Nazis later forced a mass exodus of the more interesting people who were left (*see box* **The exile files**). By the end of the 1930s, the studios were nationalised and consolidated under the UFA banner but the 'dream factory' was to go into full gear for the next World War.

Nazi propaganda was not the only result. Goebbels, whose favourite films were *It Happened One Night* and *Lives of a Bengal Lancer* kept ideology on a short leash while filling the screens with comedies, romances, musicals and even a couple of westerns.

When the Russians arrived in Berlin, the Babelsberg Studios were one of their first con-

quests. Under its new name, DEFA, they began making anti-fascist and social issue films and became a major production facility for the Warsaw Pact countries.

But the 'dream factory' never died and the East German studio also tried its hand at musicals, comedies, costume dramas and even a popular series of westerns. Their biggest international successes were children's films.

With the fall of the Wall, the facility was privatised and taken over by a French conglomerate. The 1990s have seen extensive renovations and an influx of production facilities and TV activity on the lot, but the studio has been slow to move back into film production – the factory has been re-tooled, but the dreams are still in development. Oddly enough, their biggest success has been the Babelsberg studio tour – one of the region's main tourist attractions.

Studio Babelsberg
August-Babel Straße 26-53, entrance on Großbeerenstraße, Potsdam, 14482 (0331 721 2750 reservations/721 2755 information). S3 Griebnitzsee, then bus 693 direction Bahnhof Rehbrücke or 20 minutes' walk. **Open** 10am-6pm daily (Mar-Oct). Entrance up to 1 1/2 hours before close. **Tickets** DM28; DM25 concs. Special rates for groups.
This tour of the large studio lot features stunt shows, exhibits featuring some of their historical successes and children's films. There is also a backstage look at the studios themselves including a hands-on visit to the costume and make-up departments. They recently added a special effects exhibit paying tribute to F/X master Ray Harryhausen (*Clash of the Titans*, *Jason and the Argonauts*). A tour (in German) leaves every hour. Considering the trip out there and the cost involved, it is something of a disappointment and not really worth a special trip if your time and/or budget is limited.

Gay & Lesbian

Lively for lesbians and groovy for gays, Berlin is one of the world's homosexual Meccas.

The Berlin gay and lesbian scenes are big and bold, with scores of bars, clubs, shops and organisations – mostly concentrated in Schöneberg, Kreuzberg and Prenzlauer Berg. There are still important differences between east and west but contrasts are disappearing as many well-loved eastern institutions are renovated or replaced altogether, leading to increasingly homogeneous venue styles and clientele.

In the 1920s Berlin became the the first city in the world to have what we might recognise as a large-scale community. The club Eldorado (now a Plus supermarket in Schöneberg's Motzstraße, still an important gay street) attracted Marlene Dietrich, Ernst Roehm (leader of the Nazi SA) and Christopher Isherwood, who lived at nearby Nollendorfstraße 17 and whose novels about the era were later turned into the movie *Cabaret*.

Under the Nazis, gays were persecuted and forced to wear the Pink Triangle in concentration camps where 100,000 died. They are commemorated on the plaque outside Nollendorfplatz U-Bahn station.

Since the late 1960s, Berlin has resumed its role as one of the world's homosexual Meccas. Summer is probably the most exciting time, when all contingents of the sometimes fractious gay and lesbian scenes come together. The Motzstraße gay Street fair in early June is followed by the Christopher Street Day Parade (the Saturday nearest June 27,) a flamboyant annual event where gays and lesbians come together to commemorate the Stonewall riots.

Mixed

In west Berlin gays and lesbians have been treading separate, often militant paths for decades. Relations reached a new low in 1997 when the organisers of a major exhibition marking the centenary of the gay movement were accused of re-writing history after failing to mention key lesbian figures. This rift is reflected in scenes which have long been resolutely divided.

*Kick off the weekend, catch a drag show, and feel the temperature rise at **90°**. Page 193.*

The situation was different in East Berlin. Making common cause under the communists, homosexuals of both sexes shared bars, clubs and other spaces. Despite the emergence of male-only cruise bars such as **Pick Ab!**, many places in the east are still quite genuinely mixed, such as **Schall und Rauch** and **Sonntags club**.

That said, the western half of the city is also changing. The late 1990s have seen a proliferation of mixed gay and lesbian venues such as one-nighters at **SO36** and the unique dyke/queer cruise area that is **Roses**. This trend can in part be attributed to the demise of loss-making women-only venues, but it also goes hand in hand with a new spirit of cooperation – and many private friendships – between younger lesbians and gays.

Here we list a selection of genuinely mixed shops and services, including some key venues for gays and lesbians both.

Anderes Ufer

Hauptstraße 157, Schöneberg, 10827 (784 15 78). U7 Kleistpark. **Open** 11am-2am daily. **Map E5**
Established over 20 years ago, this is the city's oldest gay café and doubles as a space for exhibitions of gay art and photography. Lesbians often make up around 30 per cent of the clientele. A good place to pick up the local free mags and plan your exploration of Berlin over coffee and cakes, salads, sandwiches, soups and alcohol.

Die Busche

Mühlenstraße 11-12, Friedrichshain, 10243 (296 0800). U1, U15, S6 Warschauer Straße. **Open** 9.30pm-5am Wed, Sun; 9.30pm-6am Fri; 10pm-6am Sat. **Admission** DM6-DM9. **Map H4**
Loud, tacky, resolutely mixed and always full, this is one of east Berlin's oldest discos for lesbians and gays, and has been in its current location by the river Spree since the early 1990s. A must for all kitsch addicts and Abba fans.

Gründerzeit Museum

Hultschiner Damm 133, Hellersdorf, 12623 (567 8329). S5 Mahlsdorf, turn right and walk 500m through village and across main road, museum is in an old farmhouse on right. **Open** 10am-6pm Wed, Sun (guided tours only). **Admission** DM4.
A famous private museum, founded and still managed by Charlotte von Mahlsdorf, half-Jewish survivor of the Third Reich and the late GDR's most notorious transvestite. It's in an old farmhouse and each room is decorated in the 1870-1910 style. In the basement is a recreation of a gay bar. Every spring the museum hosts a lesbian and gay garden party.

Kit Kat Club

Glogauer Straße 2, Kreuzberg, 10999 (611 38 33) U1, U15 Görlitzer Bahnhof. **Open** 11pm-8am Wed; 7.30pm-8am Fri; 11pm-6am Fri; 11pm-7am Sat. **Admission** DM10-DM20. **Map H5**
Apart from men-only Thursdays, Kit Kat is essentially a mixed/straight sex club. But anything goes – sex is on the menu and there is no shortage of choice. This makes a great chill-out club at weekends: shed a few layers at the entrance, check out the dancefloor, check out the people. There's no pressure to join in, it can be fun to watch, and who knows what might finally tempt you?

Mitfahrzentrale für Schwule und Lesben

Yorckstraße 52, Kreuzberg, 10965 (216 4020). U7/S1, S2 Yorckstraße. **Open** 9am-8pm Mon-Fri; 10am-4pm Sat-Sun. **Map E5**

Berlin's *Mitfahrzentralen* (ride-sharing services) are clearing houses for those offering or seeking rides. This one caters specifically to a gay and lesbian clientele. Those requesting a ride pay a small fee to the agency and a set (very reasonable) fee to the driver depending on the destination. If you need a travelling companion or help with expenses on your car trip, this is safe and reliable. Recommended for travel within Germany, especially between the larger cities.

Movin' Queer

Liegnitzer Straße 5, Kreuzberg, 10999 (618 6955). **Open** 10am-6pm Mon-Fri. **Map H5**
Lesbians who squatted a house in Kreuzberg over 15 years ago have since bought the property and transformed themselves into a group of astute businesswomen. One of their projects is this agency offering a whole raft of services including reservations at 'gay-friendly' hotels, tours of the city and information about bars, restaurants and events.

Roses

Oranienstraße 187, Kreuzberg, 10999 (615 6570). U1, U8 Kottbusser Tor. **Open** 10pm-5am daily. **Map G4**
Whatever state you're in, you'll fit just fine in this boisterous den of glitter and kitsch on Kreuzberg's main drag, near SO36. It draws customers from right across the sexual spectrum. Dykes, queers, drag-queens, drag-kings – just about everybody meets, mingles and cruises here.

Schall und Rauch

Gleimstraße 23, Prenzlauer Berg,10437 (448 0770). U2/S8, S10 Schönhauser Allee. **Open** 10am-3am daily. **Map F1**
One of the east's most established venues. The relaxed and friendly atmosphere, good selection of food and central location make it an ideal place to spend the afternoon or kick off an evening in Prenzlauer Berg. Brilliant cocktails.

Anderes Ufer – *oldest gay café in Berlin.*

Sonntags Club
*Rhinowerstraße 8, Prenzlauer Berg, 10437 (449 7530).
U2, S8, S10 Schönhauser Allee.* **Open** 4pm-11pm Mon,
Wed, Thu; 4pm-midnight Tue; 6pm-midnight Fri-Sun.
Map G1
Eastern advice and information service for both gays and
lesbians, offering events, exhibitions, poetry readings, dis-
cussions, psychological and social counselling. The café is a
popular meeting place for lesbians, gays, bisexuals and
transsexuals and specialises in sausages.

SO36
*Oranienstraße 190, Kreuzberg, 10999 (6140 1306). U8,
U1 Kottbusser Tor.* **Open** from 10pm daily. **Admission**
DM10 Mon; DM7 Wed. **Map G4**
A key venue for both gays and lesbians. Wednesday at SO
is a fixed date for every gay man, and a lot of lesbians too –
it's a fun-packed, very mixed, sociable evening and the
dancefloor heaves. Monday ('Electric Ballroom') is not completely gay, but the hard techno sound draws a largely male
following. Every second Saturday is Gay Oriental Night,
with belly-dancing transvestites and a multi-cultural, mixed
crowd dancing to their favourite Turkish hits. Monthly Jane
Bond parties are a highlight of the lesbian calendar,bring-
ing together every imaginable manifestation of womanhood,
from bull dykes and femmes to drag kings and transsexuals dancing to house and techno, funk and soul. Check local
press for other sporadic one-nighters happening here.

Verzaubert Internationales Schwullesbisches Filmfestival
Annual international gay and lesbian film festival, taking
place in the last week of November. Films not originally in
English are subtitled. Full film programme and tickets can
be obtained from participating cinemas – in 1997 these were
the **Kurbel**, Delphi, Filmtheater am Friedrichshain and
Yorck. For an overview and list of participating cinemas,
pick up a November copy of *Sergej* or *Siegessäule*.

Gay

You don't need to look for the gay scene in Berlin.
It'll find you in about ten minutes. Some districts,
however, are gayer than others – especially the
areas around Motzstraße and Fuggerstraße in
Schöneberg, and Schönhauser Allee in Prenzlauer
Berg. Bars, clubs, shops, saunas and dark rooms
are so many and various you'll find it impossible
to experience everything on one visit, or even to
choose which facet of the scene to check out first.

The age of consent is 16 – same as for everyone
else. Gays making contact in public is rarely a matter of interest to passers-by, but bigots do exist and
anti-gay violence is a reality. In the west it tends
to be from gangs of Turkish teenagers, in the east
from right-wing skinhead Germans. The most dangerous areas are Kreuzberg and Lichtenberg,
though you're unlikely to go near the latter except
for its train station. The attitude of the authorities
is equivocal, but if you see police hanging around
they're likely to be there for your protection.

The scene here is constantly shifting, so much
listed here may have changed by the time you read
this. **Mann-O-Meter** is the best source of up-to-
the-minute information.

Advice & information
See also above **Sonntags Club.**
AIDS Telefon Beratung Berlin
(19 411). **Open** 10am-noon daily.
Telephone helpline and information service.

Mann-O-Meter
*Motzstraße 5, Schöneberg, 10777 (216 8008). U1, U15,
U2, U4 Nollendorfplatz.* **Open** 3pm-11pm Mon-Sat; 3pm-
9pm Sun. **Map D5**
Efficient and helpful drop-in centre and helpline with an
exhaustive computer database. Regularly updated wall displays detail weekly events in the political, cultural and friv-
olous spheres. Cheap stocks of safer sex materials are
available, and stacks of listings magazines and newspapers
adorn the cosy bar in the back. This should be your first stop
when you arrive. English spoken.

Publications
Gay Info, Sergej and *Siegessäule* are monthly freebies which can be picked up at most venues. Even
without any German, the vital information is simple to decipher. If you do read German, then it is
worth having a look at the monthly national
Manner Aktuell (DM13,80) and maybe consider
investing in a copy of the *Berlin Von Hinten* guide
book, which has some illuminating articles.

Accommodation
Most hotels realise how important gays are to the
health of the city's tourist industry and are courteous and efficient. Here are some options catering
specifically for gay men.

Bed & Breakfast
*c/o Mann-O-Meter (see above). (215 1666/fax 2175
2219).* Reservations taken daily between 5.30pm-9pm.
Great accommodation service for gay men. B&B can fix you
up with a bed from as little as DM35.

City Hotel Connection
*Fuggerstraße 33, Schöneberg, 10777 (217 70 28/29/fax
217 7030). U1, U15, U2 Wittenbergplatz.* **Rates** *single*
DM100; *double* DM140. **Credit** AmEx, MC, V. **Map D5**
Comfortable and spacious rooms (most en-suite), sumptuous
breakfast included, prime location, and next to Connection
Disco. What more could you ask of a gay hotel?

Schall und Rauch
*Gleimstraße 23, Prenzlauer Berg, 10437 (448 0770).
U2/S8, S10 Schönhauser Allee.* **Rates** *single* DM75;
double DM130. **No credit cards. Map F1**
Clean, modern rooms next door to the café of the same name
(*above*). All rooms are en-suite, complete with TV and telephone, and the rate includes breakfast.

Tom's House
*Eisenacher Straße 10, Schöneberg, 10777 (218 55 44).
U1, U15, U2, U4 Nollendorfplatz.* **Rates** *single* DM130
(*summer*), DM90 (*winter*); *double* DM170 (*summer*),
DM130 (*winter*). **No credit cards. Map D5**
An eccentric and unpredictable establishment, with seven
double rooms and one single. Great buffet brunches from
10am-1pm. Some of the leather-clad guests are actually
awake at that hour to enjoy them.

Bars

Charlottenburg/Wilmersdorf

Arc
Fasanenstraße 81, Charlottenburg, 10623 (313 2625).
U9, U2, S3, S5, S7, S9 Zoologischer Garten. **Open**
11am-2am Sun-Thur, 11am-2.30am Fri, Sat. **Map C4**
Under the S-Bahn arches. Rustic chic, exposed brickwork, wood interior, and both light snacks and an à la carte menu. From 8pm you can pop into the Banana Bar next door (also run by the Arc team) and sample their professionally shaken cocktails.

Coxx Café
Nürnburger Straße 17, Charlottenburg, 10789 (213
6155) U1, U15, U2 Wittenbergplatz. **Open** 4pm-2am
daily. **Map D4**
A cool and airy long bar, perfect for relaxing in the middle of west Berlin's shopping district. Best in the afternoons.

Kleine Philharmonie
Schaperstraße 4, Wilmersdorf, 10719 (883 1102). U9
Spichernstraße. **Open** 5pm-3am daily (except 8pm-3am
Sat). **Map C5**
This umbrella-ceilinged parlour serves as a cosy living-room for the older local population. Eccentric décor and barstaff.

Kreuzberg

Café Anal
Muskauerstraße 16, Kreuzberg, 10997 (618 7064). U1,
U15 Görlitzerbahnhof. **Open** 8pm-4am daily. **Map H4**
Tuntenbarock ('faggot-baroque') décor – lawdy it's gaudy – and indolent drinkers, laced with a tasteful fringing of political correctness. Punks, skinheads, students, artists and drop-outs feel at home here. Women-only on Mondays.

Café Sundstrom
Mehringdamm 61, Kreuzberg,10961 (692 44 14). U6,
U7 Mehringdamm. **Open** 12pm-4am Mon-Fri; 12pm Sat-
4am Sun. **Map F5**
Daytimes this place serves as a café where rather uptight, pseudo-intellectuals come to read in solitude or discuss poetry over coffee. Weekends it becomes the entrance to Schwutz disco and the place is transformed into a hectic, fun bar.

Prenzlauer Berg

Darkroom
Rodenbergstraße 23, Prenzlauer Berg, 10439 (telephone).
U2/S8, S10 Schönhauser Allee. **Open** 10pm-6am daily.
Map G1
A cruise bar, of course. And yes there is a darkroom. With the help of a few props (camouflage netting and urinals in the actual darkroom) it generally succeeds in pulling a slightly 'harder' clientele, though on less busy nights things can feel a bit desperate. The monthly Naked Sex Party is a great success; after disposing your clothes in a dustbin liner, feel free to roam about like a piece of trash.

Pick Ab!
Greifenhagenerstraße 16, Prenzlauer Berg, 10437 (445
8523). U2/S8, S10 Schönhauser Allee. **Open** 10pm-late
daily. **Map G1**
Late-night cruise bar – this is the **Tom's** of the east – drawing action-seekers from all over at the weekend, and popular with insomniacs during the week. Like most such bars it tends to fill up best during the winter, when cruising heated backrooms is much more comfortable than roaming freezing parks.

Stiller Don
Erich-Weinert-Straße 67, Prenzlauer Berg, 10439 (449
3651). U2, S8, S10 Schönhauser Allee. **Open** 7pm-4am
daily. **Map G1**
Formerly home to the local avant-garde but now attracting a mixed crowd from all over Berlin. The set-up is like a cosy café, but it gets high-spirited on weekends and Mondays.

Zum Burgfrieden
Wichertstraße 69, Prenzlauer Berg, 10439 (449 9801).
U2, S8, S10 Schönhauser Allee. **Open** 7pm-4am daily.
Map G1
The former flagship of the eastern scene has changed little since reunification. Many west Berliners who used to drop by when in the area have been lost to the new breed of cruise bars. In response they've tried to spruce up the joint with camouflage netting in the rear bar. This doesn't seem to have worked – only the old locals remain. Still, a taste of the east as it was.

Schöneberg

Andreas Kneipe
Ansbacher Straße 29, Schöneberg, 10777 (218 3257).
U1, U15, U2 Wittenbergplatz. **Open** 11am-4am daily.
Map D5
One of the oldest bars in Berlin; you can breathe tradition from the moment you set foot across the threshold. If you want real Berlin atmosphere, this is the place to go.

Café PositHIV
Großgörschenstraße 12, Schöneberg, 10829 (216 8654).
U7 Kleistpark, S1 Großgörschenstraße. **Open** 3pm-
midnight Tue-Thur; from 6pm Sat. **Map E5**
A café for people affected by HIV and AIDS; mainly gay men. There is communal cooking and eating every Thursday lunchtime and there are regular art and craft classes.

Connection Café
Martin-Luther-Straße 19, Schöneberg, 10777 (217
6809). U1, U15, U2, U4 Nollendorfplatz. **Open** 2pm-2am
daily. **Map D5**
On entering it is obvious that this place doesn't belong to the Connection conglomerate on Fuggerstraße. The pot plants, mirrors and glitzy bar are all a little on the tacky side, but it's a well established and popular meeting place.

Hafen
Motzstraße 19, Schöneberg, 10777 (211 41 18). U1,
U15, U2, U4 Nollendorfplatz. **Open** 8pm-4am *(summer)*,
9pm-4am *(winter)*. **Map D5**
A red plush and vaguely psychedelic bar. Popular with the fashion- and body-conscious, especially at weekends, when it provides a safe haven from nearby heavy cruising dens.

Lenz
Eisenacher Straße 3, Schöneberg, 10777 (217 7820/217
7729). U1, U15, U2, U4 Nollendorfplatz. **Open** from
8pm daily. **Map D5**
Crowded and chic cocktail bar. Customers do their best to appear cool and care-free but the underlying vibe is downright cruisy.

Tom's Bar
Motzstraße 16, Schöneberg, 10777 (213 4570). U1, U15,
U2, U4 Nollendorfplatz. **Open** 10pm-6am Mon-Thur;
from 10pm Fri-Sun. **Map D5**
Once described by *Der Spiegel* as climax, or crash-landing of the night, Tom's wide appeal is undiminished with the passage of time. The front bar is fairly chatty, but the closer you get to the steps down to Berlin's busiest dark room, the more intense things become. A huge video screen plays an abstract mix of porn, cartoons and MTV. Men only.

Leather & fetish venues

Some of the best leather-wear designers work and sell their wares in Berlin, exerting great influence over the look of the scene. In fact, they might as well get it over with and declare leather the official fabric of Berlin. There are also plenty of fascinating places to show off your animal hide, including the eternally popular Leather Meeting over the Easter holidays. Information from MSC (Motorsports and Contacts – *see below* **Knast**).

Knast

Fuggerstraße 34, Schöneberg, 10777 (218 1026). U1, U15, U2 Wittenbergplatz. **Open** 9pm-5am daily. **Map D5**
The name means 'jail', and there are chains, helmets, bars and riot sticks galore: so much diversion that the porn videos go almost unnoticed. A small backroom exists although little happens there. The weekend is busiest and cruisiest. MSC (Motorsports and Contacts) Berlin meet here regularly.

New Action

Kleiststraße 26, Schöneberg, 10787 (211 82 56). U1, U15, U2, U4 Nollendorfplatz. **Open** from 8pm Mon-Sat; from 1pm Sun. **Map D5**
Atmospheric and custom-designed bar featuring a pool table, porn videos and backroom. Hosts a bizarre selection of parties and events. Friendly staff.

Scheune

Motzstraße 25, Schöneberg, 10777 (213 85 80) U1, U15, U2, U4 Nollendorfplatz. **Open** 9pm-7am daily; Fri evening-Mon morning continuously. **Map D5**
An otherworldly emporium where fantasy runs riot: camouflage, motorcycles, barrels and bolt holes, slings and arrows of love. The action in the cellar is late and heavy. 'Naked Sex Party' every other Sunday and rubber night every last Friday of the month.

Snax Club

Admission DM18
Best perv party in town, as hardcore as you choose to make it. No fixed dates or venue – check the gay press.

Clubs & one-nighters

90°

Dennewitzstraße 18, Tiergarten, 10785 (262 8984). U1, U15 Kurfürstenstraße, U2 Bülowstraße. **Open** 11pm-5am Thur. **Admission** DM10. **Map E5**
This is the place to kick off your weekend. The glamour for which 90° was famous has become more of a norm in Berlin clubs, but any loss in exclusivity has only made the team of this house night work harder to pull in the punters. The DJs are excellent, the shows are fun, and the Go-Gos are hot.

GMF @ WMF

Johannisstraße 19, Mitte, 10117 (2147 4100). U6 Oranienburger Tor. **Open** 8pm-2am Sunday. **Admission** DM10 8pm-10pm; DM15 after 10pm. **Map F3**
No one was disappointed when GMF finally reopened in this new location. The ultimate Tea-Dance, with an unbeatable line up of DJs (Divinity, Westbam, Jay Ray, to name just a few). The dancefloor is intense and the cocktail lounge (complete with original GDR sofas) is sociable and buzzing.

Connection

Welserstraße 24, Schöneberg, 10777 (241 432). U1, U15, U2 Wittenbergplatz. **Open** 10pm-7am Fri, Sat. **Admission** DM12 (includes drink ticket). **Map D5**

With the lack of anything more exciting on Saturday nights, this place continues to pull the crowds. A hot mixture of esoteric and Top 40 sounds ensure that the dancefloor is constantly packed. Bored with dancing? Not a problem – cruise through into **Connection Garage** (*below*).

Ackerkeller

Ackerstraße 12 HH, Mitte, 10115 (280 7216). S1, S2 Nordbahnhof. **Open** 9pm-3am Tue; 10-late Fri & every second Sat. **Admission** DM3,50. **Map F2**
Grungy hole for gay punks and indie queens. Cheap drinks, hard music and rough decor. Sounds different? It is! Sounds exhilarating? Sorry. But worth checking out as one of the few venues where the more 'alternative' side of Berlin reveals itself to the gay visitor.

SchwuZ

Mehringdamm 61, Kreuzberg, 10961 (693 7025). U6, U7 Mehringdamm. **Open** 11pm-late Fri, Sat. **Admission** DM6-DM10. **Map F5**
Saturday is the main disco night at the Schwulen Zentrum (gay centre). The crowd is mixed but it's basically a politically correct, alternative scene. The music is not exactly mind-blowing (charts hits and oldies) and there is more emphasis on mingling between the bar, the dancefloor and **Café Sundstrom** (*above*) at the front. Friday hosts various one-nighters including the excellent House Boys (look out for flyers) with younger, hipper and vastly superior music.

Saunas

Saunas are popular and you may have to queue, especially on cheaper days. In-house bills can be run up on your locker or cabin number and settled on leaving. Penalties for lost keys.

Apollo City Sauna

Kurfürstenstraße 101, Tiergarten, 10787 (213 2424). U1, U15, U2 Wittenbergplatz. **Open** 1pm-7am daily. **Admission** DM22 a day (DM19 Mon). Short-term cabin reservation. **Map D4**
A sprawling labyrinth of sin – with 130 lockers and 160 cabins, this is easily the largest sauna of its kind in the city. Both dry and damp saunas, a porn video den, a TV lounge, weights room, sun beds and a well-stocked bar. If you don't end up in one of the cabins, there is plenty of action in the dark, cruisy steam-bath, and on the free-for-all mattresses in the 'rest' area. Regular slivovitz *Aufguss*, where the alcohol is poured on to the hot coals to create a steamy and heady atmosphere.

Gate Sauna

Wilhelmstraße 81, Mitte, 10117 (229 9430). U2 Mohrenstraße S1, S2 Unter den Linden. **Open** 11am-7am daily, Fri 11am-Mon 7am continuously. **Admission** DM22 (Wed under 25's DM10, Sat/Sun 7am-12pm 2 for price of 1). **Map F4**
Newest addition to the growing sauna scene, Gate appeals to all ages and houses all the usual facilities. The sling in the basement is a prop most welcomed by the 'Heavy Teddies' who meet here every second Sunday afternoon of the month.

Treibhaus Sauna

Schönhauser Allee 132, Prenzlauer Berg, 10437 (448 4503/449 3494). U2 Eberswalder Straße. **Open** 3pm-7am Mon-Thur; 3pm Fri to 6am Mon continuously **Admission** DM23; DM20 concs; DM20 Tue & Thur for everyone. **Map G2**
Tucked back in the first courtyard (buzz for entry), this has become a big favourite, especially with students, though the clientele covers all ages. Facilities include both a dry and a

damp sauna, whirlpool, cycle jet, solarium and massage room. Cabins equipped with TV and VCR on a first-come, first-served basis. There's also a TV room, bar and imbiß.

Shopping

Bruno's
Nürnberger Straße 53, Wilmersdorf, 10789 (2147 3293). U1 Ausburger Straße; U2, U2, U15 Wittenbergplatz. **Open** 10am-10pm Mon-Sat. **Credit** AmEx, EC, MC, V. **Map D4**
Large and rather plush shop. As well as all the Bruno Gmunder products (Spartacus, Bel Ami books and videos) there is an extensive selection of other reading and viewing material, plus cards, calendars and other paraphernalia.

Black Style
Malmoer Straße 25/25a, Prenzlauer Berg, 10439 (445 9888/fax 445 8679). U2, S8, S10 Schönhauser Allee. **Open** 1pm-6.30pm Mon-Fri; 1pm-8pm Thur; 10am-2pm Sat. **Credit** AmEx, EC, MC, V. **Map G1**
From black fashion to butt plugs – if it can be made out of rubber or latex they've got it. High quality, reasonable prices and big variety makes it a must for fetish fans. Mail order.

Galerie Janssen
Pariser Straße 45, Wilmersdorf, 10719 (881 1590). U3 Uhlandstraße. **Open** 11am-8pm Mon-Thur; 11am-10pm Fri-Sat. **Credit** AmEx, EC, MC, V. **Map C5**
Mainly an art gallery, with some books. Regularly art exhibitions, plus reproductions, posters and cards for sale.

Good Vibrations Toys
Motzstraße 8, Schöneberg, 10777 (2175 2838/fax 2175 2837). U1, U15, U2, U4 Nollendorfplatz. **Open** 8pm Mon-Fri, 10am-4pm Sat. **Credit** AmEx, EC, MC, V. **Map D5**
One-stop shop for sex toys – dildos, handcuffs, condoms and a staggering selection of lubes.

Leathers
Schliemannstraße 38, Prenzlauer Berg, 10437 (442 7786) U2 Eberswalder Straße. **Open** noon-7.30pm Tue-Fri; noon-4pm Sat. **Credit** EC, MC, V. **Map G1**
Attached to a workshop, producing leather and SM articles of the highest quality. No smut here – just well-presented products and helpful staff.

Playground
Courbierestraße 9, Schöneberg, 10787 (218 2164). U2, U4, U15, U1 Nollendorfplatz. **Open** noon-midnight Mon-Sat. **Credit** AmEx, EC, MC, V **Map E1**
All-round gay shop selling a fair selection of leather, rubber, toys, videos and magazines. They also run a in-house piercing service and there are cruisy video cabins to top it all off.

Prinz Eisenherz Buchladen
Bleibtreustraße 52, Charlottenburg, 10623 (313 9936). S3, S5, S7, S9, S75 Savigny Platz. **Open** 10am-6pm Mon-Fri; 10am-4pm Sat. **Credit** EC, MC, V. **Map C4**
One of the finest gay bookshops in Europe, including, among its large English-language stock, many titles that aren't always available in Britain. There's a good art and photography section, plus magazines and postcards. Check out the message board for jobs and accommodation.

Sex shops/Video cruising

Bad Boy'z
Schliemannstraße 38, Prenzlauer Berg, 10437 (440 8165). U2 Eberswalder Straße. **Open** 1pm-1am Mon-Sat, 3pm-1am Sun. **Admission** DM11; DM6 Mon. **Map G1**
A series of lockable cabins equipped with beds, in which a

Gay history on display: **Schwules Museum.**

choice of homo-erotica can be viewed alone or with anyone found lurking around the corridors. There is also a darkroom, if you're feeling more sociable, and a little annex with a sling.

Connection Garage
Fuggerstraße 33, Schöneberg, 10777 (218 1432). U1, U15, U2, U4 Nollendorfplatz. **Open** 10am-1am Mon-Sat; 2pm-1am Sun. **Credit** EC, MC, V. **Map D5**
The folks from **Connection Disco** here bring their expertise to retailing rubber novelties, chains 'n' thangs, t-shirts, magazines – you name it, they've got it. The cruising area (DM13), accessible via door at rear of shop, comes alive at weekends when the Garage and Connection Disco amalgamate into one large venue. Also a cinema on the first floor, video cabins on the ground floor, and the 'Andreas Kreuz' in the cellar!

The Jaxx
Motzstraße 19, Schöneberg, 10777 (213 81 03). U1, U2, U4, U12 Nollendorfplatz. **Open** noon-3am Mon-Sat; 1pm-3am Sun. **Admission** DM15; DM11 Tue. **Map D5**
Busier than many of its competitors (particularly on Tuesdays). When neighbouring bars begin to close, these cruisy corridors fill up quickly as frustrated punters give up on small talk.

Cruising

Cruising is a popular and legal pursuit. As old public toilets are replaced with single occupancy 'City Toilets', most action now takes place in the parks. Avoid the public toilet at Hermannplatz – it has a cruisy reputation but is extremely dangerous.

Tiergarten
S3, S5, S7, S9 Tiergarten
It is surprising that the Löwenbrucke (where the Großer Weg crosses the Neuer See) has not collapsed with the sheer volume of men crossing and hanging out on it. This is the cruising focal point – but this whole corner south-west of the Siegessäule becomes a bit of a gay theme-park in summer.

Volkspark Friedichshain
Bus 100, 157, 257.
As the sun goes down and families pack up their picnics, the area around the Marchenbrunnen monument gradually fills with horny lads. Some activity by day, but it involves walking up the neighbouring slopes and searching for it.

Grunewald
S7, S3 Grunewald.
The woods behind the carpark at Pappelplatz. A popular daytime cruising zone, with trees providing plenty of cover.

Museums

See also above **Gründerzeit Museum**.

Schwules Museum

Mehringdamm 61, 2nd Courtyard, Kreuzberg,10961 (693 1172). U6, U7 Mehringdamm 119, 140 bus. **Open** 2pm-6pm Wed-Sun; library and archive open 2pm-6pm Wed.-Sun. **Admission** DM7; DM4 concs. **Map F5**
Regular exhibitions on gay history in Berlin. Exhaustive archive of gay publications from Germany and around the globe. *See also chapter* **Museums**.

Sport & sunshine

Summer brings out all of Berlin's finery. There is no taboo attached to nudity in large parks or large groups. The most popular places are Strandbad Wannsee (S1, S3 to Nikolassee, then walk or take Bus 157); and the corner of the Tiergarten southwest of the Siegessäule.

Apollo Sports Studio

Hauptstraße 150, Schöneberg,10827 (784 82 03). U7 Kleistpark. **Open** 11am-9.30pm Mon-Fri; 1pm-5pm Sat; 11am-3pm Sun. **Map E5**
A well-equipped fitness studio that is well patronised by gays. Facilities include a weights room, a bar and a sauna. **Branch**: Borodinstraße 16, Weissensee, 13088 (927 42 31).

JJ Menfitness

Wilmersdorfer Straße 82, Charlottenburg, 10629 (324 10 25). U7 Adenauer Platz. **Open** 10am-11pm Mon, Wed, Fri; 7am-11pm Tue, Thu; 10am-6pm Sat, Sun. **Map B4**
Perhaps because men-only, this place can get a little intense if all you really want is a good work-out. But the facilities are good and everything is spotlessly clean.

Manuel Sportstudio

1st courtyard, Joachim-Friedrich-Straße 37, Wilmersdorf, 10711 (892 2080). U7 Adenauerplatz. **Open** 9am-10pm Mon-Fri; 9am-6pm Sat-Sun. **Map B5**
Predominantly gay clientele. Aerobics, small sauna, a bar and a good weights room are among the facilities.

Sommerbad Kreuzberg

Gitschiner Straße 18-31, Kreuzberg, 10969 (616 1080). U1, U15 Prinzenstraße. **Open** 8am-8pm daily *(summer)*. **Admission** DM6, DM4 students/unemployed. **Map G5**
Extremely popular with gays, despite all the families and children. The poolside near the entrance is sociable and chatty in the evening, when many come for an after-work dip.

Stadtbad Wilmersdorf I

Mecklenburgische Straße 80, Wilmersdorf, 10713 (821 0274). U1, S45, S46 Heidelberger Platz. **Open** 8am-11pm Mon-Fri; 8am-6pm Sat, Sun. **Admission** DM5. **Map B6**
Cruisy and sociable pool known as the 'Tuntenaquarium' (Faggot aquarium).

Lesbian

Berlin is a heavenly stomping ground for lesbian women. Few cities can compete with its impressive network of bars, clubs and institutions, a fact borne out by the great number of refugees from other parts of Germany and abroad.

The last few years have seen a shift in emphasis as (mostly unprofitable) women-only cafés make way for a new, revitalised scene populated by largely apolitical, fashion-conscious twentysomethings. But Berlin caters for lesbians of all shapes and sizes. There are a few regular haunts such as the **Schoko Café**, **Begine** (*see chapter* **Women's Berlin**) and **Pour Elle** (*below*); but lesbian nightlife is largely made up of one-nighters in venues concentrated in Kreuzberg, Schöneberg and Prenzlauer Berg.

Yet, for all its vibrancy, Berlin's lesbian community can be difficult to penetrate (as it were). Like many Berliners, dykes are not usually in the business of chatting up strangers, and can, initially, seem a little standoffish. In east Berlin lesbians tend to be more open and friendly.

Help & information

Look out for *Berlin Exclusiv für Sie und Sie*, an ad-financed free map offering an overview of Berlin lesbian life. It can be picked up at **Lesbenberatung** (*below*) and many other places listed here and in *chapter* **Women's Berlin**.

Lesbenberatung

Kulmerstraße 20a, Schöneberg, 10783 (215 2000). U7 Yorckstraße or S1 Großgörschenstraße. **Open** 4pm-7pm Tue, Thur; 2pm-5pm Fri. **Map E5**
Offers counselling in all questions of lesbian life as well as workshops, self-help groups, courses and cultural events.

Cafés, bars & restaurants

Most of Berlin's women-only cafés have closed over the last five years. Most of the remaining ones are at women's centres and survive as such through government subsidy. Mondays are women-only at **Café Anal** and note the café at the **Sonntags Club** (*above*). *See chapter* **Women's Berlin** for further options.

Café Amsterdam

Gleim Straße 24, Prenzlauer Berg, 10437 (213 3232). U2, S8, S10 Schönhauser Allee. **Map G1**
A good bar to get wrecked in, with house and techno DJs on Friday nights. Sells snacks and salads.

Café am Senefelder Platz

Schönhauser Allee 173, Prenzlauer Berg, 10119 (449 6605). U2 Senefelderplatz. **Map G2**
Run by lesbians and attracting a mixed crowd.

Café Seidenfaden

Dircksensstraße 47, Mitte, 10178 (283 2783). S2, S5, S7, S9 Hackescher Markt. **Open** 11am-9pm, Tue, Fri; 11am-6pm Sat, Sun. **Map G3**
Run by women from a rehabilitation and therapy group of former addicts. You'll find it packed at lunchtime and quiet in the evenings. There are cultural events, readings, a monthly exhibition and no drugs at all.

O-Bar

Oranienstraße 168, Kreuzberg, 10999 (615 2809). U1, U8 Kottbusser Tor. **Open** from 9pm daily. **Map G4**

The former hedonistic HQ of Kreuzberg's gay and lesbian scene has gone thorough many changes and owners. Currently recovering its form as a lively, late-night meeting place for young, party-loving lesbians and gays.

Whistle Stop Cafe
Knaackstraße 94, Prenzlauer Berg, 10178 (442 7847). U2 Eberswalder Straße. **Open** from 6pm Mon-Sat; Sun from 10am. **Map G2**
Opened as a women-only café in May 1994, and now admitting men in the hope of averting financial ruin. It's furnished like a snack bar and offers cheap and tasty vegetarian food, exhibitions and monthly jazz concerts.

Clubs & one-nighters

For more details consult the monthly listings freebie *Siegessäule*, available at most venues, and *see above* **SO36** for its assortment of one-nighters.

Café Fatal
SO36, Oranienstraße 190, Kreuzberg, 10999 (6140 1306). U1, U8 Kottbusser Tor. **Open** Sundays from 5pm.
This evening of ballroom dancing is hugely popular, albeit a little tongue-in-cheek. The music is mainly old *Schlager* (cheesy German pop songs). Immaculate foxtrots and tangos tend to degenerate into one long Texas line dance as the evening wears on. Attracts a large lesbian clientele.

Goldfinger at Sparbar
Sparbar, Grunewaldstraße 21, Schöneberg, 10823 (0177 2940082). U7 Eisenacherstraße. **Open** every other Friday from 10pm. **Map D5**
Predatory and stylish lesbians turn up *en masse* to this oestrogen-fuelled, women-only one-nighter.

MS TitaniCa
MS Sanssouci, Gröbenufer 8, Kreuzberg, 10997 (611 1255). U1 Schlesisches Tor. **Open** first Friday of the month from March to November. **Map H4**
Energy-charged women-only party organised by MegaDyke Productions aboard the MS Sanssouci, a boat docked permanently near the Oberbaumbrücke in Kreuzberg. The sweltering lower deck churns out serious house beats. Upstairs gyrates to 1970s disco, 1980s classics and Abba.

Mega-Lesben-Party
Tränenpalast, Reichstagsufer 17, Mitte, 10117 (238 6211). U6, S1, S2, S3, S5, S7, S75, S9 Friedrichstraße. **Map F3**
One-nighter cropping up around once every six weeks – usually at the Tränenpalast ('Palace of Tears'). It's a well-attended rallying point for the diverse factions of Berlin's vast lesbian scene. An upbeat housey soundtrack is interspersed with performances by the likes of contortionist Rose Zone and other unusual artists.

Kato
Schlesiches Tor U-Bahn station, Kreuzberg, 10997 (611 2339). U1 Schlesiches Tor. **Map H4**
In the surprisingly large innards of Schlesisches Tor station, the Kato Club hosts a twice monthly house party for 'Drags and Lesbians'. Call venue for details.

Non Tox
Mühlenstraße 12, Friedrichshain, 10243 (no phone). U1 Warschauer Straße. **Map H4**
A dark passageway flanked by hulking old warehouses leads to this club in the cellar of an old east German factory. Playing a mix of house, funk and soul, it attracts a friendly lesbian and gay crowd on selected evenings. Other features include a dark room equipped with a prison-style bed and lots of communist paraphernalia. See *Siegessäule* for dates.

Die 2 am Wasserturm
Spandauer Damm 168, Charlottenburg, 14059 (252 60). Bus 145. **Open** from 7pm Mon-Sun; disco from 9pm Wed, Sat, Sun. **Map B3**
A romantic garden promises wonderful summer nights. Inside they play oldies like *La Vie En Rose* and *Sex Machine*. Easy-going atmosphere.

Doppelfenster mitNichten
Ackerstraße 12, Mitte,10115 (208 7418). U2 Rosenthaler Platz. **Open** 9pm-2am Wed; 9pm-2pm Tue; 10pm-4am Fri. Women only Wed. **Map F2**
The café of Lambda, a counselling service for gays and lesbians, hosts a women-only disco every other Saturday.

Pour Elle
Kalckreuthstraße 10, Schöneberg, 10777 (218 7533). U4 Viktoria-Luise-Platz. **Open** 9pm-5am daily; men admitted Mon, Wed. **Map D5**
Berlin's oldest lesbian bar/club. The kitsch plush gold décor can be a little overpowering. Attracts older lesbians.

Shops & services

See chapter **Women's Berlin** for **Compania**, an escort agency for lesbians and women.

Sexclusivitäten
Laura Merrit, Fürbringerstraße 2, Kreuzberg (693 6666).
This ring of lesbian call-girls will visit you wherever takes your fancy. Alongside a range of sexual services they give lessons in safer sex and SM. Also on offer are porn videos, dildos, vibrators and other sex toys demonstrated at their legendary 'Fuckerware Parties'. By appointment only.

Biank-Rodalquilar
Schlüterstraße 54, Charlottenburg, 10623 (8855 1902). S3, S5, S7, S9, S75 Savigny Platz. **Open** noon-7pm Mon-Wed; noon-8pm Thur-Fri; 11am-3pm Sat. **Map C4**
Gallery and shop selling exclusive designer jewellery and erotic toys. Some items, such as the *Zauberkugelstaben* (Magic Balls Stick) were designed specifically for lesbians.

Playstixx
*Waldemarstraße 24 , Kreuzberg, 10999 (615 2410). U8 Moritzplatz.***Open** 2pm-7pm Thur or by appointment **Map G4**
The dildos on offer at this unique workshop run by sculptress Stefanie Dörr come in the form of bananas, whales, fists or dolphins. Most are made of non-allergenic, highly durable silicon. Customers can usually try them on before buying.

Lesbian studies
Spinnboden Archiv zur Entdecking und Bewahrung von Frauenliebe
Anklamer Straße 38 (448 5848). **Map F2**
Exhaustive lesbian archive in the **Weiberwirtschaft** women's business centre in Mitte (*see chapter* **Women's Berlin**). Spinnboden has been collecting multi-media material and books on lesbian life since 1973.

Conferences
Berlin Lesbenwoche
Beginning in 1985 as a conference for Berlin lesbians, this week-long get-together has been growing into a more international event. Workshops and discussions take place every October. Call **Lesbenberatung** (*above*) for details.

Media

Berlin's many newspapers, television and radio stations are all fighting hard for a slice of a still not yet unified media market.

Berlin is one of Germany's main media centres. While Hamburg – home to many of the big publishing corporations – may still claim the title of Germany's press capital, Berlin has more daily newspapers (nine) than anywhere else and the number of both German and foreign journalists is steadily increasing ahead of the government's move from Bonn to Berlin. The city has several local and national TV stations while the airwaves are so cluttered with radio stations that operators claim advertising money is being spread too thin for anyone to make a profit. On the media production side Berlin and Babelsberg – a suburb of nearby Potsdam – are important locations for the making of programming.

All this activity is taking place in a time of fundamental change within the media industry, which has seen significant growth since the start of the 1990s. Unification shook up two staid markets. In the East, media was controlled by the Communist Party propaganda apparatus; in the walled-in West a mix of a few well-subsidised public and private companies carved up a cosily finite market.

A truly unified media market has yet to emerge. While western broadsheet readers still opt for *Der Tagesspiegel* and the *Berliner Morgenpost*, easterners have stayed loyal to the *Berliner Zeitung*. The story is the same with the tabloid press. Easterners take the *Kurier* while westerners read the *BZ* or the local edition of *BILD-Zeitung*, Germany's biggest-selling daily.

Finding a product which appeals to both sides of the city is proving expensive for the giant publishing conglomerates who are now engaged in a good old-fashioned newspaper war. Gruner + Jahr, a unit of the Bertelsmann media group, sank DM300 million into the *Berliner Zeitung*, formerly owned by the Communist Party. Holtzbrink, another big player, is responding with a revamp of its *Tagesspiegel*. Meanwhile Axel Springer, long the sole giant of the west Berlin market, is considering what to do with its slightly dowdy titles, the *Morgenpost* and *Die Welt*, a turgid, conservative national.

In circulation terms the *Berliner Zeitung* leads the field, though it has lost thousands of subscribers in the last five years. The *Morgenpost* is second but is also dropping readers fast while the *Tagesspiegel* appears to be holding steady. All three titles are hoping to become the preferred read

for all the civil servants, politicians and lobbyists who arrive with the government in 1999. That will confer national status on what are still essentially local papers. And for the publishers such status is worth the current battle.

For information about Berlin on the net, *see chapter* **Essential Information**.

Foreign Press

A wide selection of international publications can be found at Zoo Station, Internationale Presse over the road on Joachimsthaler Straße and in the Europa-Center. The British Bookshop sells the London papers and a small selection of magazines, as does Dussman on Friedrichstraße (*see chapter* **Shopping & Services**). Many ordinary newsstands, particularly near stations and hotels, also sell some international papers, though selection and regularity can be erratic.

There is currently no Berlin English-language magazine or paper, apart from the bi-monthly business-oriented *International Community*, which is too glossy to use as toilet paper, and even less use for anything else.

Newspapers
National

In line with Germany's federal make-up, the country's newspaper landscape is dominated by local and regional titles. Strictly speaking there are only three national dailies – *BILD*, *Die Welt* and *die tageszeitung* – though in reality the *Frankfurter Allgemeine* and Munich's *Süddeutsche Zeitung* have developed enough of a presence outside their home regions to be considered national titles.

BILD

The flagship of the Axel Springer group sells over four million copies a day and claims to be Europe's biggest daily read – though with all the topless snaps and bite-sized captions between blaring headlines, there isn't much reading, as such. Still, among the junk there are some gems. The page two reports on politics are better informed and more lucidly written than what passes for high-toned analysis in the quality papers. A bastion of the conservative establishment.

Die Welt

BILD stablemate *Die Welt* is a dowdy conservative read. The paper moved to Berlin a few years ago and set about trying to relaunch itself and its fortunes. So far, however, it has had little success and the paper is still making hefty losses. But then as the respectable fig-leaf of the Springer empire, which generates much of its money from racier titles such as *BILD*, the future of *Die Welt* seems secure, if unexciting.

die tageszeitung

The lumpen, generic name (literally 'the daily paper') betrays the leftist roots of the '*taz*' – set up in the late 1970s in Kreuzberg and for years the house-journal of the the alternative 'scene'. While it still makes an effort to track issues such as the travails of squatters and foreigner's rights, the *taz*'s street-fighting days are largely over. It lives on to deliver a wry look at the absurdities of modern life, some of Germany's funniest headlines, and excellent local reporting.

Frankfurter Allgemeine Zeitung

Austere, high-brow rag which was inspiration for the British *Independent*. Pictures only rarely make it on to the front page. Instead the *FAZ* serves up long and complex pieces which often read more like a doctoral thesis than an article of journalism. Conservative in outlook, this is the closest Germany has to a paper of record.

Süddeutsche Zeitung

More liberal and better written than the *FAZ*, the *Süddeutsche* delights in proving that it is possible to be witty and informative and write in German. Published in Munich, the paper is bolstering its Berlin presence through a local print run and extra editorial space devoted to the city.

Handelsblatt

Daily business paper which also delivers decent political coverage. Not an exciting read. It's Holtzbrinck-owned, like *Der Tagesspiegel*, which it supplies with business coverage.

Börsenzeitung

Printed on glossy paper, but with no pictures, the small-circulation *Börsenzeitung* has the most authoritative business coverage, analysis and market statistics of any German newspaper. At DM7, Germany's most expensive daily.

Local

Berliner Zeitung

Following an expensive relaunch this is the fashionable paper of the moment. Despite its eastern roots, the paper is now the most overtly wannabe national. Big name writers – many bought in from the *FAZ* and *Süddeutsche* – offer high quality reporting and analysis.

Der Tagesspiegel

A bit worthy, a bit dull and usually a bit behind on the news, the *Tagesspiegel* still manages to be a quality read. Advertisers love its higher-income, liberal-minded readers. Since buying the paper, the southern German Holtzbrink family (who also own British publisher Macmillan) have done little to bolster resources, despite the pleas of journalists gaping in envy at the *Berliner Zeitung*'s lavish budgets.

Berliner Morgenpost

A staid broadsheet which dares to be dull and doesn't get away with it. Essentially conservative (it is owned by Springer) and petty-bourgeois in its views, the *Morgenpost* is a faithful chronicler of events in the city, but offers little exciting or original. In many ways it's another of those west Berlin institutions which has become a victim of unification. No longer a proud symbol of defiance in the face of communism, it seems destined to become a strictly local matter.

BZ

Another Springer title. A good old-fashioned tabloid which likes to see itself as the voice of the little guy. Unlike its more aspirational rivals, *BZ* has succeeded better in bridging the east-west divide and now sells proportionally nearly as many copies in the east as in its original home base in the west. Whether readers are attracted by its saucy content, its politician-bashing leaders or all the adverts for call girls is unclear.

Neues Deutschland

How the mighty have fallen! Under communism this Party rag sold over a million copies daily. Today the paper (still owned by the PDS, successor to the East German Communist Party) is happy to sell a tenth of that. In the past it was the place to find out what the party line was; today it is an interesting place to catch up on developments in the east – even if they are interpreted through rose-tinted glasses.

Zweite Hand

Classified ads paper published on Tuesdays, Thursdays and Saturdays. Where to find everything from accomodation to zoot suits. The Saturday edition is best for flat-hunting.

Weekly

Die Zeit

A heavyweight read for the liberal intelligentsia. With former chancellor Helmut Schmidt as one of its publishing directors, this Hamburg-based weekly has a high-toned image. The problem is that, with its interminable articles and dusty style, the paper has been losing readers and circulation. Owners Holtzbrink, who bought *Die Zeit* in 1996, have put in a younger editor-in-chief to conduct a radical overhaul.

Die Woche

A relative newcomer. Lighter and more picture-led than *Die Zeit*. One of the few newspapers already to have implemented the controversial grammar reform which is supposed to be introduced across Germany in 1998 but may be scuppered by legal challenges brought by supporters of the existing, somewhat complicated rules of language.

Magazines

Der Spiegel

More an institution than a magazine, *Der Spiegel* has chronicled the Federal Republic right from its beginnings back in the 1940s. Along the way the Hamburg-based weekly has uncovered more scandals and initiated more debates than nearly all other newspapers and magazines put together. No Sunday morning TV or radio broadcast seems complete without an item linked to a report in the next day's *Spiegel*.

Focus

To the chattering classes this colourful mix of news, entertainment and gossip is beyond the pale. To its million-plus readers it is a welcome break from the wordy cynicism of *Spiegel* and *Stern*. The shortish articles are a treat in a country where writers will use three words where one will do, but sometimes the drive to provide quick-fire illumination can leave readers sensationally short-changed.

Stern

The heyday of news pictorials may be over, but *Stern* still manages to shift around a million copies a week of big colour spreads detailing the horrors of war, the beauties of nature and the curves of the female body. Despite attempts to be serious as well, its reputation has never really recovered from the 'Hitler Diaries' fiasco of the early 1980s.

Listings magazines

Berlin is awash with listings freebies, notably *[030]* (music, nightlife, film), *Flyer* (a pocket-sized club guide), *Siegessäule* and *Sergei* (both gay). These can be picked up at bars and restaurants.

Irrepressible **Zitty** *editor Kevin Cote.*

Zitty

Now edited by an irrepressible American, this fortnightly is in the process of being remodelled but seems unlikely to lose the rough-and-ready feel which has made it the magazine of choice for many alternative types. Covers all the bases and is often able to offer the best reportage of events in the city.

Tip

Also fortnightly but more glossy than *Zitty*. Tends to have better film reviews and its listings are easier to read, but beyond the statistics the magazine is an uninspiring read.

Television

Germany is Europe's biggest television market. The cable network, preferred mode of reception for most households, typically offers viewers some 30 channels – mostly offering talk-shows and Hollywood re-re-runs.

Heading the spectrum is the public sector network ARD, which takes its inspiration from the BBC. Composed of regional affiliates – in Berlin's case, Sender Freies Berlin (SFB) – the network remains true to its worthy roots. This means audience share has been dropping as viewers switch to the more commercial channels which emerged after mid-1980s market liberalisation. But ARD can still turn on the quality – its evening news shows *Tagesschau* (8pm) and *Tagesthemen* (10.30pm) remain the most authoritative on the airwaves and the weekly *Tatort* crime-thriller is

arguably the best example of German TV drama. ZDF, the second public sector network, also adopts an earnest approach. Its news shows, *heute* (7pm) and *heute-journal* (9.45pm) are more conservative in tone than those on ARD.

For the commercial channels, news is simply an fig-leaf of respectability over a never-ending mix of game-shows, soaps, films and talk shows. Some of the latter deal with relationship and health issues, a useful medium for bombarding viewers with proto-pornographic accounts of how a cheery sado-masochistic couple from Upper Bavaria bonded at a rubber and latex fair in Leipzig.

Leading the commercial fold are RTL, Pro 7 and SAT-1. All operate according to a populist, ratings-driven mix, though SAT-1 is best for sports, while Pro 7 has a more youthful accent. For a more high-brow view check arte, a Franco-German joint-venture which turns out quality programming to a very small audience. Local programming comes from B1, SFB's local channel, whose flagship *Abendschau* is well worth a glance; ORB, the public sector affiliate in Brandenburg offering an interesting eastern look at the world; and TV Berlin, a cheapo commercial channel dedicated to giving you the latest on that Ku'damm traffic snarl-up. For news junkies n-tv offers rolling coverage of disasters and stock prices. The more internationally minded can choose BBC World, available on antennae as well as cable. Other international channels, such as NBC and MTV, are only available on cable where Viva, a German-language equivalent to MTV, can also be found. Premiere, a pay-tv channel offering films and sports, is being upgraded to digital.

Radio

To prove that more can be less just spend a few moments scanning Berlin's jam-packed FM dial. Too many stations are chasing too few advertising Deutschmarks and the result is low, low budget output and a cut-throat market in which no listener-grabbing gimmick is too absurd.

Among the commercial stations 104,6 RTL (104.6) and Hundert,6 (100.6) offer standard chart pop interspersed with rip-and-read news. Energy (103.4) and Fritz (102.6) tend to be little more cutting edge, while Kiss FM (98.8) offers watered-down funk and groove. Jazzradio (101.6) is a welcome break from the usual mainstream pap. Deutschlandfunk (97.7), similar to Radio 4 in Britain, offers the best coverage of German current affairs and culture. In a similar vein, the BBC World Service (90.2) still has a presence in the city. For a snappier German take on events tune to Info-Radio (93.1), part of the SFB family of stations which continues to dominate the airwaves with everything from multi-lingual broadcasting (SFB4 Multi-Kulti, 106.8) to classical music (101.3).

Music: Classical & Opera

From the tried and traditional to the truly avant-garde, classical Berlin offers a crescendo of choice.

Unless you're in town over summer when the opera houses and concert halls are generally dark, the choice of classical music events in Berlin can be staggering. Whether your tastes lean towards the bread-and-butter classical and romantic warhorses or the truly avant-garde, the German capital is unlikely to disappoint.

The Berlin Philharmonic, under the musical directorship of Claudio Abbado, is always a must-see, although their repertoire is often frustratingly old-fashioned.

The Deutsches Sinfonie-Orchester (formerly the Berlin Radio Symphony Orchestra), helmed by Vladimir Ashkenazy and going from strength to strength, these days give them a run for their money. And don't discount the Berliner Sinfonie-Orchester, which is based at the Konzerthaus and can play superbly.

The Deutsche Staatsoper, Komische Oper and Konzerthaus are all within an easy stroll of one another, near or on east Berlin's grand boulevard, Unter den Linden. While the Staatsoper and the Konzerthaus only occasionally attract the megastars of the classical circuit, and the Komische never does, they all offer a generally excellent standard of performance. Furthermore, concerts in the Konzerthaus and operas at the Komische can be considerably less expensive than those at the Berlin Phil or the Deutsche Oper in the city's western half. But concert-going in the east is no longer the bargain it once was; the complete state subsidy of the days before German reunification has drained away, and as Berlin teeters on the edge of bankruptcy, prices have risen as east Berlin's opera companies and ensembles scramble to stay afloat. You won't exactly break the bank in the east

*The forbidding **Deutsche Oper Berlin** – otherwise known as 'Sing Sing'. See page 202.*

The **Deutsche Staatsoper** – *classical repertoire, neo-classical design. See page 202*

– except, perhaps, at the Staatsoper, which is as pricey as the Deutsche Oper in the west – but the days of DM5 opera and concert tickets are now nothing but the stuff of nostalgia.

Naturally, most classical music fans want tickets for the Berlin Philharmonic Orchestra at the Philharmonie. The biggest nuisance about the Berlin Phil is that they seem to have lost track of the fact that it's nearly the twenty-first century and don't take reservations over the telephone – not even with a credit card. There's nothing for it but to trek to the box office during opening hours. Arrive early, and be prepared to queue. Even then, tickets can be hard to come by, especially when Abbado is conducting, but *nil desperandum*. It's common to make a sign saying 'Suche eine Karte' ('seeking a ticket') and stand outside the hall. Or try this on people entering: 'Haben Sie vielleicht eine Karte übrig?' ('Have you by any chance got a spare ticket?') With luck, you'll find someone whose companion needed to work late, or you'll spot someone holding a sign reading 'Karte(n) zu verkaufen' ('ticket(s) for sale'). Watch out, there are also sharks about. If you can't get to see the Berlin Phil, tickets are usually to be had for the also excellent Deutsches Sinfonie-Orchester.

The major Berlin music festival is the Berliner Festwochen. Started in 1950, this brings to Berlin the cream of the world's soloists and orchestras and spans the whole month of September. Each of the Festwochen is based on a theme (for example, the 'Berlin/Moscow' or 'France/Germania' festival themes of recent years).

As well as upping prices, cutbacks have also taken their toll on repertoire, which is becoming increasingly less adventurous – the main concern of orchestras and opera houses has become bums on seats rather than artistic adventure. Berlin is still light years behind London for the amount of contemporary music on offer, but the contemporary music festival, the Biennale (every other year in March), as well as regular appearances by Germany's premier group for modern music, the Ensemble Modern, assures that those who want more challenging fare than Bach, Beethoven and Brahms are fairly well looked after. That said, the Biennale is often maddeningly biased towards serial and post-serial composers. Postmodernists scarcely get a look-in.

At the other end of the historical scale, there's the Bach-Tage ('Bach Days') – an annual July feast of Baroque music, usually played on period instruments and taking place at various venues around the city – as well as November's Wochen der alten Musik ('Early Music Weeks') which latterly have included period instrument performances of operas at the Staatsoper. Additionally, 'alternative' opera performances at the small but creditable Neuköllner Oper or by the excellent Berliner Kammeroper are not to be dismissed.

Tickets & information

Tip and *Zitty* (*see chapter* **Media**) can be relied upon for classical listings. Tickets are sold at the concert hall box offices or through ticket agencies,

Konzerthaus – *class joint, classy concerts.*

called Theaterkassen. At box offices, seats are generally sold up to an hour before the performance. You can also reserve by phone, except, as noted above, for the Berlin Phil. The Theaterkassen are convenient but commissions on tickets can run as high as 17 per cent. Some take credit cards, but most accept only Eurocheques or cash. Below we list the major Theatrekassen in central Berlin. For details of the other ticket agencies, consult the *Gelbe Seiten* (Yellow Pages) under *Theaterkassen*.

Hekticket
Rathausstraße 1, Mitte, 10178 (2431 2431). S3, S5, S6, S7, S9/U2, U5, U8 Alexanderplatz. **Open** 4pm-8pm daily. **No credit cards.. Map G3**
Hekticket offers discounts of up to 50 per cent on theatre and concert tickets. For a DM2 commission, staff will sell you tickets for the same evening's performance. Tickets for Sunday matinées are available on Saturday.

Kant-Kasse
Kantstraße 54, Charlottenburg, 10627 (313 4554). S5, S6, S9/U7 Wilmersdorfer Straße. **Open** 10am-6.30pm Mon-Fri; 10am-2pm Sat. **No credit cards. Map B4**

Kartenhaus im Berliner Congress Center
Märkisches Ufer 54, Mitte, 10179 (2758 4190). S3, S5, S6, S7, S9, S10/U8 Jannowitzbrücke. **Open** 10am-6pm Mon-Fri. **No credit cards. Map G4**

Konzertkasse
Oranienstraße 29, Kreuzberg, 10999 (615 8818). U1, U8 Kotbusser Tor. **Open** 9am-7pm daily. **No credit cards. Map G4**

Major Venues

Deutsche Oper Berlin
Bismarckstraße 34-37, Charlottenburg, 10585 (343 8401). U2 Deutsche Oper. **Open** *box office* 11am-7pm Mon-Fri; 10am-2pm Sat. **Tickets** DM17-DM142. **Credit** AmEx, DC, EC, V. **Map B4**
Doesn't have the funding to import the superstars of the international operatic circuit, yet the singing is generally excellent and they still occasionally commission new operas or mount one or two works per season that aren't part of the standard repertoire (such as Carlisle Floyd's *Susannah* or Henze's *Der Prinz von Homburg* in recent seasons). Designed by Fritz Bornemann and built in 1961, the theatre's interior is pleasant enough, but its exterior, a forbidding tranche of granite, has caused Berliners to nickname it 'Sing-Sing'.

Deutsche Staatsoper
Unter den Linden 5-7, Mitte, 10109 (2035 4555). U6 Französische Straße. **Open** *box office* 10am-6pm Mon-Fri; 2pm-6pm, Sat, Sun. **Tickets** DM12-DM200. **Credit** AmEx, DC, EC, V. **Map F3**
The Deutsche Staatsoper has a longer and grander history than the Deutsche Oper. It was founded as Prussia's Royal Court Opera for Frederick the Great in 1742, and designed along the lines of a Greek temple – one of many neo-classical buildings which earnt Berlin the name 'Athens on the Spree'. Although the present building dates from 1955, the façade faithfully copies that of Knobelsdorff's original, twice destroyed in World War II (in 1941 and 1945). The elegant interior gives an immediate sense of the house's past glory, with huge chandeliers and elaborate wall paintings. Daniel Barenboim now divides his time between being musical director of this house and musical director of the Chicago Symphony Orchestra, and is striving to instill new life into its performances and repertoire. If you're lucky, you may discover the likes of Domingo singing Wagner here. Even luckier, and you'll get a ticket. Chamber music is performed in the small, ornate Apollo Saal within the main building.

Komische Oper
Behrenstraße 55-57, Mitte, 10117 (202 600). U6 Französische Straße. **Open** *box office* 11am-7pm Mon-Sat; 1pm-4.30pm Sun. **Tickets** DM15-DM108. **Credit** EC, MC, V. **Map F3**
The Komische Oper is dominated by its artistic director, Harry Kupfer – one of the few 'Ossis' whose career has not just continued but sailed since reunification. He runs a tight ship here, ably assisted by his dynamic, young Russian-American musical director, Yakov Kreizberg. Kupfer, one of the star directors in the German opera scene, is nothing if not bold; his radical but almost always incisive interpretations – especially, appropriately, of comic operas – virtually guarantee a stimulating evening's entertainment. The singing (all operas are sung in German, which seems a pointless indulgence in this age of surtitles) may not always be breathtaking, but prices are accordingly fair. Furthermore, all unsold tickets for an evening's performance can be purchased from the box office for half price after 11am on the day of performance.

Philharmonie
Matthäikirchstraße 1, Tiergarten, 10785 (2548 8132). U1 Kurfürstenstraße. **Open** *box office* 3.30pm-6pm Mon-Fri; 11am-2pm Sat, Sun. **Tickets** DM12-DM154; half-price for students for some concerts 30 mins before the performance begins. No telephone reservations. **No credit cards. Map C4**
Berlin's most famous concert hall, home to the world-renowned Berlin Philharmonic Orchestra, is also its most daring architecturally: a marvellous, fluid piece of organic modernism. It's such a fine, witty, beautiful design, it's hard to see why so many people revile it. The hall, with a golden, reconstructionist vaulting roof, was designed by Hans Scharoun in 1963, and has been nicknamed the 'Karajani Circus'. Its reputation for superb acoustics is accurate, but does depend on where you sit. Behind the orchestra the acoustics are appalling, but in front the sound is heavenly. The structure also incorporates a smaller hall, the Kammermusiksaal, about which the same acoustical notes apply. The Berlin Phil was founded in 1882 and has been led by some of the world's finest conductors. Its greatest fame came under the baton of the late Herbert von Karajan, but current director Claudio Abbado is very much his own man and it is still a magical orchestra. On the other hand, the insufferable, almost exclusively nineteenth-century sadness of their repertoire can be quite frustrating. The Berlin Phil gives about 100 performances in Berlin during its August-June season, with another 20 to 30 concerts worldwide. Tickets for visiting orchestras that play at the Philharmonie are usually easier to come by than those for the Phil itself.

Konzerthaus

Gendarmenmarkt (Platz der Akademie), Mitte, 10117 (2030 92101). U6 Französische Straße. **Open** *box office* noon-8pm Mon-Sat; noon-4pm Sun, Holidays. Tickets DM25-DM75; half-price for students and pensioners for some concerts 30 mins before the performance begins. **Credit** AmEx, EC, MC, V. **Map F**4

Formerly the Schauspielhaus am Gendermenmarkt, the Konzerthaus, an 1821 architectural gem by Friedrich Schinkel, was all but destroyed in the war. Lovingly restored,

it was reopened in 1984. There are two main spaces for concerts: the Großer Konzertsaal for orchestras, the Kleiner Saal for chamber music. Organ recitals in the large hall are a treat, played on a massive organ at the back of the stage. The Berliner Sinfonie-Orchestra, led by their Danish musical director Michael Schønwandt, is based here. This house displays some of the most imaginative programming in Berlin; a healthy mixture of the old, the new, and the rediscovered makes the Konzerthaus a wonderful venue. The Deutsches Sinfonie-Orchester, one of the finest in the land, is also based

Berlin on disc

'Berlin bleibt Berlin' – 'Berlin remains Berlin' goes the title of an old popular song, and for many classical music fans, Berlin remains the Berlin of the inter-war years. Below are listed five CDs of special interest for those who want something a bit more authentic than modern recordings by pseudo-divas warbling Weill songs, plus one of music from a vanished country – East Germany.

You should be able to find all these at **Hans Riedl Musikalienhandel**. *See chapter* **Shopping & Services**.

1. Die Dreigroschenoper/BERLIN 1930

Lotte Lenya, Marlene Dietrich, Lewis Ruth Band and others. (Teldec 9031-72025-2).

Forget your 'original Broadway cast' recording of *Threepenny Opera*. This recording, made in 1930, contains most of the members of the first-ever cast from 1928. The CD is rounded off with vintage 1920s Berlin cabaret songs sung by Berlin-born Marlene Dietrich, Kurt Gerron and others.

2. Ernst Krenek: Jonny Spielt Auf

Kruse, Marc, St Hill and others, Gewandhausorchester Leipzig, Lothar Zagrosek (Decca 436 631-2) (2 CDs).

Jonny Strikes Up was first performed in Leipzig in 1927 and stormed across Europe within months, becoming one of the most frequently performed operas of its time. Often called 'the first Jazz opera', it isn't, but it's one of the first – and one of the best. Not strictly 'Berlin', but a glorious tonal evocation of the times. Part of Decca's praiseworthy series of first recordings of works banned by the Nazis as 'Entartete Musik' ('Decadent Music'); the irony of the Nazi's ban is that the libretto is actually rather racist in its portrayal of the Black protagonist, Jonny. An impeccable recording.

3. Entartete Musik: Eine Dokumentation

(Pool Musikvertrieb CD 65023) (4 CDs)

Not to be confused with Decca's 'Entartete Musik' series mentioned above, this superb, often disturbing, collection of mainly archive and some modern recordings documents Germany from the mid-1920s until the fall of Nazism. From Hitler speeches to Dessau's resistance songs, from Klaus Mann denouncing Richard Strauss for Nazi collaboration to the nauseating 1934 Hitler paean *Gott sei mit unserm Führer* ('God be with our Leader' – played by the Berlin Philharmonic!), this four-CD set is an outstanding work of documentation. Available with either a German or English booklet (specify when ordering). If

you have trouble getting this CD, contact Pool Musikvertrieb directly at Streitstraße 86, 13587 Berlin (355 9370).

4. Paul Hindemith: Neues vom Tage

Werres, Nicolai, Pries and others, Kölner Rundfunkorchester, Jan Latham-König (Wergo 6192-2) (2 CDs).

Premiered in 1929 at Berlin's Kroll Opera (destroyed in the war), *News of the Day* is, incomprehensibly, one of Hindemith's least-known works. A masterpiece of knowing orchestration, it's a hilarious, cynical and urbane opera about a middle-class couple's divorce, abounding in jazzy rhythms, muscular counterpoint and lyrical pastiche. In terms of musical language and social themes, it's perhaps the greatest and most representative operatic *Zeitstück* of the period. Latham-König never lets the pace slacken in his dynamic reading of the score. Essential listening.

5. Hanns Eisler: Historische Aufnahmen

Busch, Kühl, Eisler, etc., Chorus & Orchestra of the Berliner Ensemble. (Berlin Classics 0092302BC).

When it came to singing Eisler songs, nobody, but nobody has ever equalled the dramatic power of the great Ernst Busch. This set of historic recordings, part of Berlin Classics' unreservedly recommended series of vintage Eisler recordings, includes ballads, proletarian marching songs and the stage music to Brecht's adaptation of Gorky's *The Mother*. Displaying the rigorous, fighting flavour of Berlin's pre-war Communist workers' choirs , this music is of such relentless force it's almost hard to believe the Left couldn't stop Hitler in the 1930s simply by singing him down.

6. Musik in der DDR: Vol. 1, Musik für Orchester

(Berlin Classics 0090692) (3 CDs)

Another excellent issue from Berlin Classics' catalogue – orchestral music from the GDR. (Volumes 2 and 3 represent GDR vocal and chamber music, respectively). Recording standards are sometimes less than perfect, but this set represents a broad spectrum of 12 of the former East Germany's major composers such as Kochan, Kurz, Goldmann, Matthus and Dittrich. Worth owning if only for the deliciously kitsch *Festouvertüre 1948* by Ottmar Gerster; a six-and-a-half minute, neo-Brahmsian concert overture which is a kind of 'Greatest Hits of the Dictatorship of the Proletariat' ('The Marseillaise', 'Internationale', 'Brothers, to the sun, to freedom', and so on). Not surprisingly, it was the most frequently performed orchestral work by an East German composer in the GDR. Bet you've never heard it. A fascinating, worthy collection.

here, and their performances, particularly of contemporary music, are top-notch. There are also occasional, informal concerts in the cosy Musik Club in the depths of the building.

Other Venues

Many churches offer regular organ recitals. It's also worth enquiring whether concerts are to be staged in any of the castles or museums in the area, especially in the summer or around holidays. Telephones are often erratically staffed, so check *Zitty* or *Tip* for listings.

Akademie der Künste
Hanseatenweg 10, Tiergarten, 10557 (3900 0764). U9 Hansaplatz. **Open** *enquiries* 10am-6pm Mon-Fri. **Tickets** DM10-DM20. **No credit cards. Map D3**
The Academy of the Arts offers visitors everything from art exhibitions to literary readings, from films to music. It specialises in performances of compositions from the twentieth century. Concerts are either in the large (507 seats) or the small (205 seats) hall. Acoustics in both rooms of the 1960 building are reasonable.

Ballhaus Naunynstraße
Naunynstraße 27, Kreuzberg, 10997 (2588 6644). U8 Moritzplatz. **Open** *box office* open one hour before performances. Reserve tickets by telephone. **Tickets** DM10-DM45. **No credit cards. Map G4**
Don't expect to hear anything ordinary at this Kreuzberg cultural centre: a varied assortment of western and oriental music is on the menu. The long, rectangular hall, which seats 150, plays guest to, among others, the excellent Berliner Kammeroper (Berlin Chamber Opera).

Berliner Dom
Lustgarten, Mitte, 10117 (2026 9136). S3, S5, S6, S9 Hackescher Markt. **Open** *enquiries* 10am-6pm Mon-Fri. **Tickets** DM10-DM20. **No credit cards. Map F3**
Berlin's cathedral, having just been fully restored from its war-damaged state, promptly went up in flames a few years ago. It's now been re-restored and hosts some worthwhile concerts, usually of the organ or choral variety.

Hochschule der Künste
Hardenbergstraße 33, Tiergarten, 10623 (3185 2374). U2 Ernst-Reuter-Platz. **Open** *box office* 3pm-6.30pm Tue-Fri; 11am-2pm Sat. **Tickets** free for student concerts; DM30-DM60 for guest performers. **No credit cards. Map C4**
Berlin's wannabe musical luminaries study in the adjacent building. A grotesquely ugly but thoroughly functional hall plays host both to student soloists and orchestras, as well as lesser-known, under-funded professional groups. There's a great deal of variety here, and the fact that it doesn't attract the best-known artists is certainly no reason to avoid it.

Kulturbrauerei
Knaackstraße 12, Prenzlauerberg, 10405 (441 9269). U2 Eberswalderstraße. **Open** 9am-8pm Mon-Sat. **Tickets** DM10-DM50. **No credit cards. Map G2**
Situated, as the name implies, in a converted brewery, which also houses art galleries and a rather over-priced courtyard bar, this small theatre is rapidly establishing itself among Berlin's black-clad culture vultures who come to see occasional opera or music-theatre pieces.

Meistersaal
Köthener Straße 38, Kreuzberg, 10963 (264 9530). S1, S2 Anhalter Bahnhof. **Open** *enquiries* 11am-9pm Mon-Fri; 1pm-8pm Sat, Sun. **Tickets** DM10-DM50. **No credit cards. Map E4**

Berliner Dom – *restored for recitals.*

The 'Maestro Hall' plays host to solo instrumentalists and chamber groups who can't afford to book the Kammermusiksaal of the Philharmonie. But this indicates lack of cash rather than quality; music-making of the highest rank occurs in this welcoming little salon with superb acoustics.

Neuköllner Oper
Karl-Marx-Straße 131-133, Neoköln 12043 (6889 0777). U7 Karl-Marx-Straße. **Open** *enquiries* 3pm-7pm Tue-Sat. **Tickets** DM30-DM60. **No credit cards. Map H6**
No grand opera here, but a constantly changing programme of chamber operas and music-theatre works much loved by the Neuköllners who come here to see lighter, bubblier (and much less expensive) works than in Berlin's three big opera houses. An informal alternative to the champagne-and-chandeliers atmosphere of the major houses.

Staatsbibliothek-Otto Braun Saal
Potsdamer Straße 33, Tiergarten, 10785 (2661). U2/S1, S2 Potsdamer Platz. **Open** *enquiries* 10am-1pm Mon-Fri. **Tickets** DM20-DM30; DM10-DM15 concs. **No credit cards. Map E4**
Smaller ensembles provide the lion's share of the music in this chamber of the state library.

St Matthäus-Kirche
Matthäi-Kirchplatz, Tiergarten, 10785 (261 3676). U1 Kurfürstenstraße. **Open** noon-6pm Wed-Sun. **Tickets** prices depend on who's performing. **No credit cards. Map E4**
Because it's next to the Philharmonie, this church has been nicknamed the 'Polka Church' by Berliners. Check listings to see who's playing; it might be anything from a free organ recital to a literally heavenly chorus of Russian Orthodox Monks at DM35 per ticket. The acoustics are exquisite.

Music: Rock, Folk & Jazz

Once on the fringes in every sense, Berlin music maintains an experimental edge and thrives in semi-legal dives.

Darkness and isolation have always shaped Berlin's rock scene, rendering its music murky, adventurous and somewhat obscure. West Berlin's physical separation from the rest of western Europe and, in East Berlin, relatively easy access to western radio and records combined with the political necessity of pretending otherwise, has kept Berlin music on the fringes in every sense.

The major players of the post-war West German music industry set up in comfortable western cities; even today only one major label has an office of significance in Berlin. Without a business infrastructure, West Berlin's bands have long depended on independent labels, while East Berlin's scene was beholden to political patronage. This was luxury and curse for both Berlins: rock here had an avant-garde tendency but was rarely taken seriously or even heard by the rest of the country.

Berlin's experimental spirit was reinvigorated by the dozens of clubs and bars that sprouted after 1990. Many of the new semi-legal stages had a provisional air well-suited to outlandish sounds – seemingly derelict buildings still house clubs in brick cellars left largely unrepaired since Allied bombing raids. Thus Berlin bands continue to toil in the unsanitised splendour left by 30 years of shadowy loneliness. From the lo-fi, girlie guitar anthems of the Poptarts to the incendiary, electronic hardcore of Atari Teenage Riot (*see page 210* **The Empire talks back**), from the deep, obtuse grooves sculpted by Rope out of live instruments to the trippy, turntable-friendly Terranova, good shows happen all the time.

SPLENDID ISOLATION

The Allied media in divided Berlin helped spread the music and myth of Anglo-American rock on both sides of the Wall. The earliest example was Berlin Beat. Though the Beatles landed in Hamburg, Beat music made deep inroads in Berlin with groups like The Lords and, in East Berlin, Die Sputniks and the Franke-Echo-Quintett. West Berlin Beat sounded British: upbeat, poppy, usually in English. Purists such as The Ones or The Odd Persons stuck to early models like The Animals

and The Yardbirds. The movement lasted into the 1970s and had time to widen and blossom, like its British counterpart, into psychedelia.

Eastern Beat leaned more towards American surf music, since instrumentals were less controversial than songs. But by 1965 East Berlin's Beat bands were viewed by the authorities as yet another manifestation of Western 'non-culture', and their records were deleted by Amiga, the state record label, in 1967. This was a staggering blow to the Eastern music scene, which would only recover a decade later in a flurry of illegal activity.

Even without official pressure – on the contrary, quite handsomely subsidised by Berlin's Senate – purveyors of pop music in the West grew increasingly uncomfortable with the artificial heritage of Anglo-American rock. While the romance of foreign sounds never dwindled, Berlin musicians sought other foundations for their work. Here Berlin's vanguard parted ways with the fare offered by military radio, and in the early 1970s moved off into experimental avenues led by bands like Ashra Tempel and Tangerine Dream.

The 1980s witnessed a new burst of music from Berlin, though the bulk, with German lyrics, remains unknown in the anglophone world. Industrial pioneers Einstürzende Neubauten stepped from the underground on to an international stage. Frenetic new wave bands, part of the Neue Deutsche Welle trend, emerged with a blaze of enthusiasm and a series of Berlin acts stumbled upon sounds that gained wider attention: Düsseldorf immigrants DAF, new waver Nena, punk ironists Die Ärzte, radical girl group Malaria.

GOING UNDERGROUND

In East Berlin, the last-minute cancellation in October 1977 of an Alexanderplatz open-air concert by City, an official band with a few troublesome songs, proved the impetus for a seething, illegal music scene. Nina Hagen left East Berlin to become one of West Germany's most infamous and successful musical provocateurs, but the underground scene in the East took off at the dawn of the 1980s with punk bands like Planlos.

For the first half of the 1980s, the scene thrived on a tangible sense of danger. Then in 1985 the authorities allowed radio station DT64 to showcase underground 'Schräge Musik' (literally, 'slanting music'), permitting a new generation of punk and experimental bands such as Die Skeptiker, Die Anderen, Feeling B and Cadavre Esquis to perform and record in semi-official peace. A rare 1989 compilation named for the DT64 programme, 'Parocktikum', documented the scene: guttural punk lingers from the truly underground days while bands torturing tape-loops and synths provide startling glimpses of the Eastern avant-garde.

THE POST-TECHNO ERA
In the 1990s the electronic avant-garde came upon techno – a form of music so primeval that it battered its way into the mainstream with a social and commercial strength previously unimaginable in experimental circles. The unfettered post-reunification club culture evolved an infrastructure missing during the Cold War: new studios, graphic artists, promoters, management companies. The way the experimental edge of Berlin music energised the mainstream had far-reaching implications: even U2 managed to reinvent themselves in Berlin with their *Achtung, Baby* album.

While DJs such as Westbam and Paul van Dyk continue to enjoy large-scale success, a new experimentalism has bobbed up in techno's wake. Kitty-yo Records' stable of eclectic bands, for example, most of whom combine modern electronica with traditional elements. From Laub, who mix breakbeats, reverbed guitar strumming, pastoral noise and restrained female vocals, to the heavy machinations of Surrogat, harnessing digital precision to the heft of layered guitars, Kitty-yo offers original sounds reflecting the juxtaposition of demolition and construction at Berlin's heart.

Releases by Maurizio and others on the consistently inspiring Chain Reaction label represent the residual dub-echo of Berlin techno now that the party's over – dampened sounds, vast acoustical spaces and driving, muddy beats that come over like the noises left rattling in your head the morning after the club-night before.

Others ignore the jurassic beats of the 1990s. Le Hammond Inferno, a DJ team, rose from underground clubs to airport lounges, from a pair of plastic turntables to their own record label, on the strength of parties set to the kind of decidedly non-experimental music more frequently heard in lifts and supermarkets. Their sensibility struck a chord, spurring a nationwide easy listening craze and now, through their Bungalow label, a new generation of comfortable German club pop typified by the cocktail-house of the Maxwell Implosion or the eccentric electro noodlings of Dauerfisch.

Of other acts worth catching, Spy produce a rollicking guitar pop that harkens back to Berlin Beat; Mellowbag meld funk and jazz with contemporary French hip hop; Stereo Total update the French Beat of Jacques Dutronc with an array of secondhand machines and instruments; and the Madonna Hip-Hop Massaker hitch loud guitars to programmed beats. A whole slew of bands are churning out sounds perfectly suited to mini-venues like **Galerie berlintokyo**, classic locations such as **Roter Salon** or **Trash**, and an ever-changing array of transient performance spaces.

Venues
Rock

Arena
Eichenstraße 4, Treptow, 12435 (533 7333). Bus 265.
Formerly a maintenance hall for public transport vehicles, now host to big concerts and other events seeking space but not worried about refinement. Prodigy, Chemical Brothers and Smashing Pumpkins have all played here. No seating.

Galerie berlintokyo
Rosenthaler Straße 38, Mitte, 10178 (283 2484). U8 Weinmeister Straße. **Open** from 9pm. **Map F3**
Literally underground, a tiny basement gallery hosting local bands, DJs and artists in makeshift surroundings.

Huxley's Neue Welt
Hasenheide 108-114, Kreuzberg, 10967 (621 1028). U7 Hermannplatz. **Open** box office 10am-6pm Mon-Fri. **Map G5**
Former roller-skating rink with stages both large and small (Huxley's Cantina). Good mid-range venue for mainstream

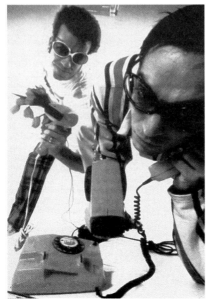

Who ya gonna call? – Le Hammond Inferno.

and not-so-extreme alternative, plus the occasional gangsta rapper and any German band with enough pulling power, with singer-songwriters and indie bands in the smaller room.

Insel
Alt-Treptow 6, Treptow, 12435 (534 8851). S6, S8, S10 Planterwald. **Open** box office noon-6pm.
A three-storey tollhouse on a tiny, wooded island in the Spree converted to a multi-purpose space for concerts by international bands, popular Berlin acts, and a variety of club nights.

Knaack Club
Greifswalder Straße 224, Prenzlauer Berg, 10405 (442 7060). S8, S10 Greifswalder Straße. **Open** from 10pm. **Map H2**
Adventurous booking policy covers the full spectrum of alternative rock. Both dancefloors and performance spaces lurk within this shabby multi-level complex, meaning sometimes as many as three different events on one night.

Loft
In the Metropol, Nollendorfplatz 5, Schöneberg, 10777 (215 5463). U1, U2, U4 Nollendorfplatz. **Open** box office 11am-6pm Mon-Fri; 9.30am-2pm Sat. **Map D5**
Small-to-medium concert venue that's past its glory days, though even now, if they're smallish and you've read about them in the *NME*, they'll still probably turn up here.

Velodrom
Paul Heiser Straße 29, Prenzlauer Berg, 10407 (4430 4714). S8, S10 Landsberger Allee. **Map H2**
Recently completed sports facility hosts mainstream rock shows. Where to see the likes of Genesis or Janet Jackson. *See chapter* **Sport & Fitness.**

Volksbühne/Roter Salon
Rosa-Luxemburg-Platz, Mitte, 10123 (247 6772/Roter Salon 3087 4806). U8 Rosa-Luxemburg-Platz. **Open** noon-6pm. **Map G3**
The Volksbühne (*see chapter* **Theatre**) regularly turns over its stage to bands such as Stereolab, Billy Bragg or German indie stars Tocotronic. In the smaller Roter Salon, which has its own side entrance, stucco moulding and glass chandeliers expect club nights and concerts by more marginal artists.

Folk & World Music

Midway between eastern and western Europe, Berlin offers excellent opportunities to hear all sorts of eastern exotica, from Cossack choruses to Gypsy campfire music. Touring acts rarely use set venues, however, so check local listings for interesting gigs in churches, bars, and theatres.

Several local bands, including Mutabor, 17 Hippies and Inchtabokatables, offer edgy takes on folk music, borrowing strings from eastern Europe or, in the case of Mutabor, influences from long stays in North Africa. Both record for big labels; both put on lively concerts.

For up-to-date info on world music events call in on **Canzone** record shop (*see chapter* **Shopping**), tune to SFB4 MultiKulti radio on 106.8FM, or scan music listings in *Tip* and *Zitty*.

Hackesches Hof Theater
Rosenthaler Straße 40-41, Mitte, 10178 (283 25 87). U8 Weimeister Straße. **Open** box office open 45 minutes before performances. **Map F3**
Intimate seated space offers daily concerts of Klezmer, Yiddish and east European folk music.

Bags of fun at the mighty **Quinn's** *(p207).*

Haus der Kulturen der Welt
John-Foster-Dulles Allee 10, Tiergarten, 10557 (397 870/3970 0566). S3, S5, S6, S7, S9 Bellevue, bus 100. **Open** box office and information 10am-9pm Tue-Sun. **Map E3**
An important venue for the 'high art' end of world music – Indian classical music, for example. The Café Global, which overlooks the river Spree, occasionally features live bands and world music DJs.

Pfefferberg
Schönhauser Allee 176, Mitte, 10119 (449 6534). U2 Senfelderplatz. Bus N52. **Open** hours vary according to events. **Map G2**
Entrance below a colonnaded terrace leads up to a complex that includes a large beer garden and a roomy performance space where reggae and world music predominate.

Irish Pubs

Most of Berlin's many Irish pubs also put on live folk music. Here are three of the better ones.

Irish Harp Pub
Giesebrechtstraße 15, Charlottenburg, 10629 (882 7739). U7 Adenauerplatz. **Open** 11am-2am daily; music from 8pm Fri, Sat. **Admission** free. **Map B4**
Big, rowdy pub in the middle of Charlottenburg. Music at night and fry-up breakfasts in the mornings.

Irish Pub
Europa-Center, Tiergarten, 10787 (262 1634). U2, U9, S3, S5, S6, S7, S9 Zoologischer Garten. **Open** from 11.30am-3pm; live bands from 9pm Mon-Fri; 6pm Sat, Sun. **Admission** free. **Map D4**
Biggest of Berlin's Irish bars, this place is well-frequented by tourists. A bit of a meat-market.

Quinn's
Schönhauser Allee 6-8, Mitte, 10119 (440 6030). U8 Rosenthaler Platz. **Open** 11am-1am Sun-Thur; 11am-2.30am Fri, Sat. **Admission** free. **Map G2**
Huge, lavishly decorated multi-level pub with a basement club space attached. Satellite TV showing Gaelic football and hurling as well as regular live music.

Jazz

Germans take jazz very seriously. Berlin's jazz scene is neither the best nor worst in Germany (the best is almost certainly Cologne's), but it's large and encompasses everything from pub jam ses-

Pedestrians

Possibilities

Time Out | London's Living Guide.

http://www.timeout.co.uk

A-Trane – *jazz for swankers. Page 209.*

sions to major international festivals, and has Germany's only 24-hour jazz radio station.

The Berlin FMP (Free Music Production) label's concerts often feature some of the world's best improvisers, such as FMP founder Peter Brötzmann, an extremely physical baritone sax player. They're sometimes free when the sessions are being recorded. For concerts, check Jazz Radio 101.9, listings magazines, flyers in shops like **Gelbe Musik** (*see* chapter **Shopping**), and see **JazzFest** (*below*).

A-Trane
Pestalozzistraße 105, Charlottenburg, 10623 (313 2550). S3, S5, S6, S9 Savignyplatz. **Open** box office from 9.30pm, music from 10pm, daily. **Map C4**
On the corner of Bleibtreustraße, a swanky attempt at a New York-style jazz bar where events are only occasionally interesting enough to be heard over the yuppy trimmings.

B-Flat
Rosenthaler Straße 13, Mitte, 10119 (280 6349). U8 Rosenthaler Platz. **Open** from 8pm daily. **Map F2**
Cavernous bar fills up on weekend nights for mostly local, mostly mainstream jazz performers and DJ sets.

Badenscher Hof
Badensche Straße 29, Wilmersdorf, 10715 (861 0080). U7 Berliner Straße. **Open** 3pm-1am daily. **Map D6**
Small, friendly club offers semi avant jazz with a mostly African-American cast, occasional blues bands and soul-food brunches, and a nice garden space in summer.

Flöz
Nassauische Straße 37, Wilmersdorf, 10717 (861 1000). U7 Berliner Straße. **Open** box office from 8pm, bands from 9pm daily. **Map C5**
A dark and woody cellar bar in the old Berlin style where the players, usually local groups, blast out a little bebop.

Junction Bar
Gneisenaustraße 18, Kreuzberg, 10961 (694 6602). U6, U7 Mehringdamm. **Open** live music daily, differing start times, usually after 10.30pm. **Map F5**
Jazz in all its varieties – swing, latin, contemporary, jazz poetry – but not all on the same night. Occasionally blues and rock here, too. Obnoxious doorpeople. Count your change. *See also* chapter **Clubs**.

Parkhaus
Puschkinallee 5, Treptow, 12435 (533 7952). S6, S8, S10, S46 Treptower Park. **Open** box office from 7.30pm, music from 10pm, Thur-Sat.
Berlin's oldest jazz venue, with Senate support, puts on a jazz programme Fri and Sat nights in the cellar of an old villa.

Passionskirche
Marheinekeplatz 1-2, Kreuzberg, 10961 (6940 1241). U7 Gneisenaustraße. **Map F5**
Lovely church with great acoustics hosts quieter musical events in all genres.

Podewil
Klosterstraße 68-70, Mitte, 10179 (247 496). U2 Klosterstraße. **Open** box office 2pm-6pm Tue-Fri. **Map G3**
Former HQ of the FDJ (the Communist youth organisation) and 'music-vetting' centre of the GDR. Jazz is one of the more conservative options in their imaginative programmes, ranging across Free Music Meetings, themed concert/arts/theatre seasons, contemporary music and related movies.

Quasimodo
Kantstraße 12A, Charlottenburg, 10623 (312 8086). U2, U9, S3, S5, S6, S7, S9 Zoologischer Garten. **Open** box office from 5pm, concerts from 10pm, daily. **Map C4**
A small and cramped but successful club in the centre of west Berlin and a stopping-off point for many American groups on tour. The programme is mainly jazz but also includes roots and blues. Notoriously the smokiest venue on Europe's jazz circuit, a fact which performers often bemoan.

Schlot
Kastanienallee 29, Prenzlauer Berg, 10435 (448 2160). U2 Eberswalder Straße. **Open** from 8pm. **Map G2**
The east's answer to Quasimodo, but without the international names – a small, cosy venue offering nightly concerts as well as occasional cabaret. Look for the sign, then walk through the arch into the courtyard.

Festivals

Clubs United
Usually on the first weekend of September. One ticket allows entrance to around two dozen clubs and use of shuttle buses between them. Every kind of live and DJ music is on offer, depending on the booking policies of the clubs involved.

Heimatklänge
At the Tempodrom, In den Zelten, Tiergarten, 10557 (394 4045/winter 2175 2761). S3, S5, S6, S9 Lehrter Stadtbahnhof. **Dates** July/August; phone for details. **Admission** free, or nearly so. **Map E3**
Berlin's biggest world music event. The Tempodrom tent-venue in the Tiergarten hosts acts from all four corners of the globe, each of which gets five days of shows. At the time of going to press it seemed the event, and the Tempodrom itself, may move, but probably not until 1999. *See also* chapter **Berlin By Season**.

Jazz Across The Border
Haus der Kulturen der Welt, John-Foster-Dulles Allee 10, Tiergarten, 10557 (397 870). Tickets available from May; phone for details. **Map E3**
Over June and July, around 15 different groups play five weekends of concerts at the **Haus der Kulturen der Welt** (*see page 207*).

Jazzfest Berlin
Haus der Kulturen der Welt, John-Foster-Dulles Allee, Tiergarten, 10557 (397 870). **Dates** Oct. **Admission** varies. **Map E3**
A four-day event aiming to present a cross-section of European jazz along with some American groups and examples of new influences. Usually around 25 bands take the stage, although the days of big names are long gone. Total Music Meeting, a free jazz and improvised music event, runs alongside the more mainstream JazzFest. Its concerts take place mostly at Podewil. *See also* chapter **Berlin By Season**.

Karneval der Kultur

On the last weekend of May – a world music version of the Love Parade. A variety of floats wind their way through Kreuzberg on the Saturday afternoon while an assortment of open-air and traditional venues around town offer everything from drumming to drum 'n' bass over the course of the weekend.

Love Parade

Like a cross between a political demonstration and a techno Mardi Gras, on the second Saturday of every July hundreds of thousands of ravers mass and party through the Tiergarten behind a series of floats blasting house, techno and drum 'n' bass. Over the weekend there are also dozens of raves and parties in venues all over town. In 1997 over a million people turned up. At the time of going to press there was talk of the event moving to Paris. *See also chapters* **Clubs** *and* **Berlin By Season**.

Metrobeat

Berlin's Senate is highly supportive of the city's music scene, particularly when it comes to keeping Berlin musicians in work. In conjunction with the public, music business and the media – all of them invited to vote for Berlin's best bands – the city is establishing Metrobeat as a two-day festival for the known and the new in a number of venues across Berlin. In 1997 this took place in December, a change from previous years when it usually took place in January or February.

The Empire talks back

Of all the apocalyptic noise pranksters to emerge from Berlin, Alec Empire most persistently shoots out its lights. As founder of both the do-or-die! breakbeat brat trio Atari Teenage Riot and the Digital Hardcore Recordings (DHR) record label, Empire has kept up a constant war of attrition against his hometown and, by extension, the rest of Germany. Hardly subtle or subversive, his assaults on German propriety have the immediacy of graffiti spray-painted across rat-a-tat beats. 'I will fuck the system!' shrieks the opening of ATR's 1997 EP *Sick To Death*, which choruses 'Burn Berlin burn! Burn Berlin burn!', while other ATR titles include 'Destroy 2000 Years Of Culture', 'Into The Death' and the inverted anthem 'Deutschland (Has Gotta Die!)'. Though he has also recorded solo under the

alias Destroyer, Empire does have a quieter side, best heard on the triple CD collection, *The Geist Of Alec Empire*. This showcases his talent for minimalist and moodily atmospheric electronics, rippled through with patterned breakbeats.

Shifting back and forth between confrontation and contemplation, Empire is as deliberately difficult to pin down as his music is instantly appealing. Or repellent, depending on your tolerance of ATR's bratbeat politicking. 'Some people,' Empire laughs, 'if they're screamed at all the time, they just close their ears.' Weird, that.

Operating at the insane speed of a video arcade game, ATR's songs were often conceived as rapid response retaliations to tendencies in Berlin's ever-changing club scene. (Alec came of age at the beginning of Germany's Digital Dance era – circa 1990 – and tends to perceive clubland as a microcosm of the world.) ATR's first single stab at notoriety, 'Hunt For Nazis', was their answer to what they perceived as the attempted neo-Nazification of techno, and much of what followed has been aimed at repoliticising the city's post-rave scene. It was released the same year as Empire's own, first widely available 12-inch, the *SuEcide* EP, which proposed that ravers should E themselves into a stupor so as to become a drain on Germany's welfare state. Empire might argue you have to be as garishly loud as a Judge Dredd comic to be heard over the euphoria of the Love Parade.

Despite, or perhaps because of, the heavy localisation of Empire/ATR's songs, they're building large followings in the USA – where their stuff is licensed through The Beastie Boys' Grand Royal label. That's because, argues Empire, audiences can identify their own situation in ATR's cartoon outlines of the system's failings. 'A lot of Americans made this MC5/Public Enemy comparison,' Empire has said, 'that is a brilliant compliment for me.'

Sport & Fitness

The spectating ain't spectacular – but in Berlin participation is the name of the game.

Berlin has a rather ambivalent attitude towards spectator sports. On the one hand the bid to host the Olympics was plagued by constant demonstrations and sabotage, and no Berlin football team seems capable of staying in the Erste Bundesliga for more than one season. On the other, historically moulded loyalties make for passionate rivalries even between third division football clubs, and more recently professionalised sports such as ice hockey and basketball have begun to thrive.

Participating in sports is much more heartily supported. Most every sport has a hierarchical structure headed by a national *Verband*, or federation, to facilitate participation at every level. The regional offices of these bodies can help identify clubs, facilities and events that may be of interest. The city of Berlin also maintains a wide range of inexpensive public facilities, from swimming pools to football pitches.

The Deutsche Pokalendspiele – the German equivalent to the FA Cup Final – takes place in the Olympiastadion every year at the end of May or beginning of June. The same stadium hosts an important annual track and field meet, the ISTAF, in late August. Top female tennis stars rally in Grunewald every May for the German Open – the same month in which an important leg of the German Touring Car Championships takes place along the Avus race course. And on the last Sunday in September, Berlin hosts the world's third-largest marathon run.

Major stadia

Olympiastadion
Olympischer Platz 3, Charlottenburg, 14053 (300 633). U2 Olympia-Stadion. **Map A4**
Built for the 1936 Olympics, the 80,000 capacity structure is one of the best preserved examples of Fascist architecture in Berlin. It's also the biggest arena in town and hosts football matches, track meets and other mass gatherings. Only Mick and Keef, however, seem able to pack it like the old days. Information about the German Cup final can be gleaned at 896 9940. For information about ISTAF, the final leg of the track and field grand slam, admission, call 238 4252/51.

Velodrom
Paul Heiser Straße 29, Prenzlauer Berg, 10407 (4430 4714). S8, S10 Landsberger Allee. **Map H2**
The Velodrom opened in early 1997, one of the only projects linked to Berlin's abortive bid for the 2000 Olympics to have been completed. Since mid-1997 a company called Vélomax has been responsible for managing the facility, and information and tickets are available through their hotline at 4430 4430. In addition to biking competitions such as the

European Championships, the new building hosts wind surfing exhibitions, handball tournaments, and other sporting and cultural events, including rock concerts.

Spectator sports

Athletics
ISTAF Track and Field Meet
Olympiastadion, Charlottenburg, 14053 (238 4251/52). U2 Olympia-Stadion. **Date** late Aug. **Admission** DM20-DM80. **Tickets** Kant-Kasse (313 4554). **Map A4**
Established a year after the 1936 Berlin Olympics, this international one-day tournament is now one of the four venues in the light athletics grand slam. Some 250 athletes from 50 nations compete.

Basketball
Alba Berlin were only founded in 1991, but in 1996-97 won both league championship and German Cup and established themselves as a European

Olympiastadion – *spot the Hertha fans.*

powerhouse. They now play all home matches, the season runs from September to May, in the Max-Schmelling-Halle, a brand-new 10,000-seat arena at one end of Mauerpark, a patch of former no-man's land between Prenzlauer Berg and Wedding. The Alba moniker can be seen scrawled everywhere in the city, but that isn't graffiti: the main sponsor of the team is a rubbish collection and recycling company of the same name.

Alba Berlin e.V. Basketball team

Max-Schmelling-Halle, am Falkplatz, Prenzlauer Berg, 10437 (5343 8000). U2 Eberswalder Straße. **Admission** German league matches DM10-DM35, European matches DM15-DM100. **Map G1**

Football

Despite no lack of enthusiasm for the national obsession, Berlin has problems with football. At the time of writing, Hertha BSC had climbed back into the Erste Bundesliga and were actually managing a decent run while three former first division football clubs languish in the third division. The two eastern teams, 1. FC Union and FC Berlin, competed for decades at the top of the eastern tables; the western one, Tennis Borussia (TB), plans to make it back to the Bundesliga by 2000. But things are never that simple in Berlin. Eastern football fans can agree not to support western clubs but squabble among themselves. FC Union fans maintain a very dim view of FC Berlin because they were once BFC Dynamo and, like all teams called Dynamo in eastern Europe, were affiliated with the secret police. FC Berlin fans like to think their team's numerous GDR championships had nothing to do with blatant favouritism by referees. FC Union have qualified for the second division three times in recent years but been denied promotion on financial grounds. TB have money but lack a fan base. And if Hertha manage to stay in the first division it will be a minor miracle.

1. FC Union

Stadion An der Alten Försterei, An der Wuhlheide 263, Köpenick, 12459 (657 2585). S3 Köpenick. **Tickets** DM8-DM20.
Set up in 1906, the club has been through many phases and is dear to many for largely eluding political pressures over the years.

Fußball Club Berlin

Sportforum Hohenschönhausen, Steffenstraße, Hohenschönhausen, 13053 (975 1178). Tram 23. **Tickets** DM6-DM25.

Hertha BSC

Olympischer Platz 3, Charlottenburg, 14053 (300 9280). U2 Olympia-Stadion. **Tickets** DM12-DM56. **Map A4**
While Hertha remain in the first division expect regular crowds of around 50,000 – which still means it's easy to get a ticket.

Tennis Borussia

Mommsen Stadion, Waldshulallee 34-42, Charlottenburg, 14055 (306 9610). S-bahnhof Grunewald, Bus 119. **Tickets** DM8-DM22

Tennis Borussia are poised to make the second division for the 1998 season, and are pumping funds into their club to take it even further.

Horse Racing

Galloprennbahn-Hoppegarten

Goetheallee 1, Dahlwitz-Hoppegarten, 15366 (033 423 8930). S5 Hoppegarten. **Admission** DM7.
Berlin's race-course is just outside the city limits to the north-east. Races take place between April and October. The betting system in Germany is run pretty much like the English Tote (and is computerised).

Trabrennbetrieb-Karlshorst

Treskowallee 129, Karlshorst, 10318 (500 170). S3 Karlshorst. **Admission** free.
This and Mariendorf (*below*) host trotting events, otherwise known as harness racing. This entails riders pelting around in modern-day chariots. Meetings are held throughout the year on Saturdays at 2.30pm. Races also take place on Tuesday evenings beginning at 6.30pm.

Trabrenn Verein-Mariendorf

Mariendorfer Damm 222, Mariendorf, 12107 (740 1212). U6 Alt-Mariendorf, then bus X76, 176, 179 Trabrennbahn. **Admission** DM3 Sun; free Wed.
Race meetings are on Sundays at 2pm and on Wednesdays at 6.30pm.

Ice hockey

Since German ice hockey clubs set up a completely private national league and broke from the governing *Verband* in 1994, the sport has become big business in Germany. In Berlin two perennial powers, the eastern Eisbären (a Dynamo descendent) and the western Capitals (formerly Prussians), have continued their success under the new system. Derbies between these arch-rivals are wild matches with incredible audience enthusiasm. *See box* **Polar opposites.** The season runs from September to April.

Berlin Capitals Eishockey GmbH

Eissporthalle, Jafféstraße, Charlottenburg, 14055 (885 6000). S3, S9, S75 Westkreuz. **Admission** DM18-DM70. **Map A4**

EHC Eisbären Berlin

Eishockeystadion, Weißenseer Weg 51, Weißensee, 13053 (240 4171). Tram 1, 13. **Tickets** DM22-DM50.

Motor racing

The first race on the Avus course took place in 1921, and the rich history continues with a variety of races. Some Formula series races (though not Formula 1), motorcycles and touring cars all use the course – actually a 2.64 kilometre stretch of the Autobahn heading towards Wannsee. The biggest event of the year are the German Touring Car Championships every May.

Avus

Messedamm 22, Charlottenburg, 14055 (868 6285). U2 Kaiserdamm, S3, S9, S75 Westkreuz. **Admission** DM15-DM70. **Map A4**
Adjacent to the ICC convention center and Funkturm.

Tennis

The German Open, held each May, is the world's fifth-largest international women's tennis championship and draws the top female players.

LTTC Rot-Weiß

Gottfried-von-Cramm-Weg 47-55, Grunewald, 14193 (8957 5510). S3, S7 Grunewald, Bus 119. **Open** 8am-5pm Mon-Thur; 8am-noon Fri.
The German Open uses this club's clay courts. Tickets can be ordered at 8957 5520.

Activities

Verbände (federations) are national umbrella organisations for sports of all kinds. They help with coordination, facilities, financing and other logistical aspects of any sport looking to gain wide participation. The local Berlin branch offices can be invaluable when trying to get involved in a sport here.

Landessportbund Berlin (LSB)

Jesse-Owens-Allee 2, Charlottenburg, 10453 (300 020). U2 Olympia-Stadion. **Open** 9am-3pm Mon-Thur; 9am-2pm Fri.
The central office for Berlin coordinates other sport-specific offices and provides general information. At the same address is the Landesausschuß Frauensport, the office for information about women's sports.

Athletics

The Berliner New Year Fun Run begins every year at the Soviet Memorial on Straße des 17 Juni (*see chapter* **By Area**). Call 302 5370 for information.

'You're *Scheiße* and you know you are!'

Berlin football has given the term 'capital punishment' a whole new meaning. The top team, Hertha BSC, have not won a single trophy since 1931, and although the fan scarves boast a DFB Pokal final appearance in 1993, it was in fact Hertha's reserve team (Hertha Amateure) that made it all the way in Germany's premier knockout competition.

In 1990, the first year of being the unified capital's top side, Hertha gained promotion to the Erste Bundesliga (German first division) but were relegated the following season. The 1997-98 season is Hertha's first back in the top flight.

Watching a football game in the Olympic Stadium, Hertha's home, can be an extraordinary experience. With a capacity of 76,000 it is Germany's largest football arena and when full the atmosphere is exhilarating.

Hertha attract over 50,000 fans for Bundesliga games against top opposition. If Hertha are on top or when they score the massed cries of 'Sieg' send shivers down your spine – this was the stadium where Hitler refused to acknowledge Jesse Owen's record-breaking feats in the 1936 Olympics. You feel shivers of a different kind on a winter's day if Hertha are playing lowly opposition and a 10,000 crowd leaves the stadium feeling empty and eerie.

Berliners love their football, but apart from the occasional flash of top-quality play from Hertha the best chance they have of seeing anything half decent is the German cup final.

The Olympic Stadium has hosted the final since 1985 (on the first Saturday after the season ends – usually at the end of May) as a concession from the German football association (DFB) after the Soviet Union vetoed Berlin as a venue for the 1988 European Championships.

The national team plays in Berlin occasionally. In 1995 Berliners were deprived of the footballing classic of Germany against England after the DFB arranged the game for 20 April. The match was cancelled after much public outcry as it coincided with the 106th anniversary of Hitler's birthday.

The Bundesliga has existed in its current form since 1963 and it is a Berlin team who bear the record of the worst season's performance ever. In 1965-66, after Hertha failed to have their licence renewed, Tasmania 1990 Berlin replaced them at the last minute. They played 34, won two, drew four and let in 108 goals. One nearly as dismal season from Blau-Weiß 90 (1987-88) and two from Tennis Borussia (1974-75, 1975-76) have made the capital the butt of many a footballing joke.

Hertha are currently managed by ex-German national player Dieter Hoeness and in Juergen Roeber they have a top-class trainer. Things are looking up and it seems that after years of mismanagement Hertha have finally arrived in the twentieth century. With a multi-million Deutsche Mark sponsorship from the media giant UFA and the second-highest Bundesliga attendance average they finally have a healthy financial basis for success. Nevertheless some aspects of modernity seem to have passed the club by: all 12,000 season tickets for 1997-98 had the seat and block numbers written by hand.

Berliner Leichtathletik-Verband
Glockenturmstraße 1, Charlottenburg, 14053 (305 7250).
Contact this office for information about tracks, clubs and
events in the city.

Berlin Marathon
Waldschulallee 34, Charlottenburg 14055 (302 5370).
Date Final Sunday in September. **Map A5**
1998 is the Berlin Marathon's 25th anniversary. Upwards of
20,000 people usually participate, making it the world's third-
largest after London and New York. The course winds past
many historic sights. Taking part costs DM70-DM80,
depending on whether or not the registration must be sent
abroad. There's also the Berlin Half-Marathon on the first
Sunday in April. Details can be had from the above address.

Basketball

Though a relatively recent arrival in Germany,
basketball has a strong following. Public courts
remain few and far between, but clubs have access
to gymnasiums and temporary streetball installations pop up during the summer. Contact the
Verband for locations and club information.

Berliner Basketball-Verband
Postfach 33 04 45, 14174 Berlin (893 6480). **Open**
10am-3pm Mon-Thur; 10am-2pm Fri; personal
appointments, 4pm-7pm, must be made in advance.
Sign up for a club or get information about various streetball competitions or the Supercup.

Billiards

Tables can be found in many corner bars and a
slew of pool halls. Most tables are for eight- and
nine-ball, though the halls usually offer a few
caramboulage and snooker tables.

Billardparadies
*Immanuelkirchstraße 14, Prenzlauer Berg, 10405 (442
8270). Tram 1, 5.* **Open** 24 hours daily. **Map G2**
A utilitarian establishment with 32 pool, five snooker and
three caramboulage tables.

Frank's Billard Halle
*Oranienstraße 40-41, Kreuzberg, 10999 (615 6566). U1,
U12, U15, U8 Kottbusser Tor.* **Open** 2pm-4am daily.
Map G4
Roomy and peaceful, despite its location right above Trash
(*see chapters* **Music Rock, Folk & Jazz** *and* **Nightlife**).
Table service, Czech Budweiser, excellent pommes frites, 20
pool tables, two full-size snooker tables, caramboulage too.

Köh
*Sophienstraße 6, Mitte, 10119 (282 8420). U8
Weinmeister Straße, S3, S5, S7, S9, S75 Hackescher
Markt.* **Open** 4pm-3am daily. **Map F3**
Small and cosy, with leather couches and a better bar than
normal halls.

Chess

Berliner Schachverband
Blumenweg 17, Mariendorf, 12105 (705 6606). **Open**
10am-2pm Mon, Tue, Thur, Fri; 2pm-6pm Wed.
Information on joining clubs.

Café Belmont
*Kurfürstenstraße 107, Schöneberg, 10787 (218 6365). U1,
U2, U3 Wittenbergplatz.* **Open** 24 hours daily. **Map D4**

Café Belmont – *pawn to be wild.*

The best place to get into the Berlin chess scene. Most of the
hours this place is open you'll find a cosmopolitan crowd
playing and talking chess.

Cycling

Dedicated bike lanes line most major roads in
Berlin, making cycling an easy way to get around.
Sport cycling is popular, but Berliners also think
of bikes as ideal urban transport. In summer you
can even catch a bicycle taxi. The ADFC
Fahrradstadtplan, available in most bike shops for
DM13, is an excellent guide to Berlin's cycle routes.
For rental shops, *see chapter* **Getting Around**.

Berliner Radsport-Verband
*Priesterweg 3, Schöneberg, 10829 (784 5753). S2, S25
Priesterweg.* **Open** 10am-5pm Mon-Fri.
Information on clubs, races, and events. The International 4
Ettappen Fahrt (a four stage, 600km race) takes place annu-
ally at the end of May.

Fitness Studios

Fit Point
*Wallstraße 9-13, Mitte, 10179 (471 5339).U6
Kochstraße.* **Open** 10am-9.30pm Mon-Fri; 10am-4pm Sat;
10am-3pm Sun. **Map G4**
Facilities include bodybuilding, fitness, aerobics, gymnas-
tics, and saunas for afterwards. Minimum membership peri-
od is six months, with monthly charges ranging from
DM49-DM104.

Gold's Gym
Immanuelkirchstraße 3/4, Prenzlauer Berg, 10405 (442 8294). U2 Senefelder Platz. **Open** 10am-11pm Mon-Fri; 10am-6pm Sat; 10am-4pm Sun. **Admission** minimum per month DM89. **Map G2**
Moderately priced fitness studio offering two weeks free for Gold members

Jopp frauen-fitness-Berlin
five locations in the city, here are the most central:
Tauentzienstraße 13, Charlottenburg, 10789 (210 111). U2, U9, S3, S5, S6, S9 Zoologischer Garten. U1 Kurfürstendamm. Karl-Liebknecht-Straße 13, am Alexanderplatz, 10178 Mitte (243 49 355). U2, U5, U8, S3, S5, S6, S7, S9 Alexanderplatz. **Open** 7am-11pm Mon-Fri; 10am-8pm Sat-Sun. Monthly charges DM75-DM130

Jump!
Togostraße 76, Wedding, 13351 (451 4712). U6 Seestraße. **Open** 10am-10pm Mon-Fri. 11am-6pm Sat; 11am-5pm Sun. **Map D1**
Smallish sport studio run by a friendly, helpful team. Mixed but popular with gays. Universal weights plus a small selection of free weights and regular aerobic step classes on offer. One can buy a ten-day pass for DM150 or a month pass for DM210.

Oasis
Stresemannstraße 74, Kreuzberg, 10963 (262 6661). S2 Anhalter Bahnhof. **Open** 10am-11pm Mon-Fri; 10am-8pm Sat; 10am-4pm Sun. **Admission** DM 79-DM120. **No credit cards**. **Map F4**
Well-equipped, for both men and women, and with a great swimming pool.

Football
Football is Berlin's most popular sport. Pick up games can be found in virtually every park at the weekend.

Berliner Fußball-Verband
Humboldtstraße 8A, Grunewald, 14193 (896 9940/47/48). S6, S9 Westkreuz. **Open** 8am-4.30pm Mon-Thur; 8am-7pm Fri. **Map A5**
Office for information about football clubs, local leagues and competitions.

Ice Sports
Below are the best ice-skating rinks in the city. Plus, many of Berlin's lakes and canals freeze over every year. The Verband has nothing to do with these, so just look for other skaters and hope their judgement is good.

Berliner Eissport-Verband
Fritz-Wildung-Straße 9, Wilmersdorf, 14199 (823 4020). S45 Hohenzollerndam. **Map B6**
Offers information on halls, clubs, and events.

Eislauf an der Glocke
Glockenturmstraße, Charlottenburg, 14055 (305 5020). U2 Theodor-Heuss-Platz, then bus 149 Stößenseebrücke. **Open** from mid November to end of February; 10am-noon Mon-Sat; 3pm-5pm Tue-Fri; 10am-noon, 2pm-4pm, 4.30pm-6.30pm, Sat, Sun. **Admission** DM4 for two hours; DM2,50 concs.

Polar opposites

'All of us are here, all of us are here, apart from Erich Honecker,' announce fans of east Berlin's Eisbären ('Polar Bears') hockey team, alluding to the GDR's last dictator. In matches against their arch-rivals, west Berlin's Capitals, such chants make the rink an arena for lingering resentments and loyalties surrounding reunification.

As cheering Eisbären fans frequently remind their rivals, the team has 15 (East) German championships under its well-padded belt while the Capitals have never won a title. But this glorious history must be qualified. In the late 1960s, East German sporting authorities realised ice hockey would never attain the international stature it had in the USSR or Czechoslovakia. They decided to apply funding elsewhere, spelling the end for all but two hockey clubs – both of which had connections to the police or Stasi. Dynamo Berlin, as the Eisbären were then known, and Weißwasser, the only opponents, refused to let their plight bother them: they played an entire regular season and play-offs every year.

With reunification the Eisbären stepped out from under the Dynamo umbrella and gained entry in the Bundesliga only to be relegated after their first season. They spent only one season in the second division, but several more years at the bottom of the top division.

Their fortunes changed as a result of two developments. In 1994 German ice hockey teams broke from the club system to create a private league and the rabid Eisbär following meant substantial advertising revenues. Then in 1996 a European court struck down limits on foreign players in national football leagues. The Eisbären were the first to see the implications of the Bosman ruling for ice hockey and quickly signed up numerous Canadian players with access to EU passports.

Reinstalled near the head of the table, the Eisbären represent for their fans a heroic David to the Goliath of the western authorities who have swept through east Berlin changing street names and tearing down statues. So with a touch of irony, and a hint of longing, Eisbären supporters trot out their most incendiary songs for crosstown games:

'Two crossed stalks of grain and one big D/That is the Dynamo, our club/We come from the Stasi, we once had the power/And we'll come back with a bang!'

Eisstadion Berlin Wilmersdorf

Fritz-Wildung Straße 9, Wilmersdorf, 14199 (824 1012).
U1 Heidelberger Platz. **Open** October to mid-March; 9am-
6.30pm, 7.30pm-10pm Mon, Wed, Fri; 9am-5.30pm,
7.30pm-10pm Tue, Thur; 9am-9.30pm, Sat; 9am-5pm Sun.
Admission DM3 for two hours; DM1,50 concs. **Map B6**

Kayak & canoe

Much of Berlin is reclaimed land, to which many
canals and embanked waterways can attest. The
regions immediately south (Spreewald), east and
north have additional lakes and rivers. There are
plenty of destinations but be prepared to paddle:
the flat Brandenburg plain means no white water
or strong currents.

Landes-Kanu-Verband Berlin

(439 8070).

Kanu Connection

Köpenicker Straße 9, Kreuzberg, 10997 (612 2686). U1
Schlesisches Tor. **Open** 8am-4.30pm Mon-Wed; 10.30am-
7pm Thur; 7am-2pm Fri. **Map H4**
Canoe and kayak rentals from four different landings. Daily
rentals for DM55, entire weekends for DM120. Guides available. Paddle through Kreuzberg's canals or take off into the
waterways winding through the forests east of Berlin.

Der Bootsladen

Brandensteinweg 8, Spandau, 13595 (362 5685). Bus
149. **Open** noon-4pm Mon-Fri; 9am-4pm Sat.
Good starting point for tours of the western canal system.
The shop rents by the hour, from DM10-DM12 depending
on boat size, but offers better deals for longer rentals.

Sailing

The Wannsee is actually a gigantic bend in the
Havel river, and provides an extensive area for
sailing and connections to Babelsberg and
Potsdam. To the east, Müggelsee is likewise a
swelling of the Spree.

In addition, north of Berlin in Brandenburg and
Mecklenburg are innumerable lakes that offer
more possibilities for boating. Contact the *Verband*
for details.

Berliner Segler-Verband

Bismarckallee 2, Charlottenburg, 14193 (893 8420/fax
8938 4219). **Open** 10am-5pm Mon-Fri.
Information on certification, regulation, and events. If you
want to sail or surf on the lakes, you'll need an Amtlicher
Sportbootführerschein-Binnen – a sailing certificate. To get
one you must pass a theoretical and practical exam administered by this organisation. If you think you have enough
practical experience to pass, register for the six-day theoretical course (to learn the rule and regulations on Berlin's
waterways).

Am Großen Fenster

Am Großen Fenster 1, Nikolassee, 14129 (803 7137).
S1, S7 Nikolassee. **Open** *Apr-Oct* 10am-7.30pm daily.

Sauna

Many of Berlin's public baths have saunas and
women can use the Hamman Turkish Bath at the
Schocko-Fabrik (*see chapter* **Women's Berlin**).

Thermen

Europa-Center, Nurnbergerstraße 7, Charlottenburg,
10787 (261 6031). U1, U2 Wittenbergplatz. **Admission**
DM30 for three hours; DM34 whole day; DM2,200 year
ticket. **Map D4**
Big, central, mixed facility offering Finnish saunas, steam
baths, hot and cool pools, and a garden open until October.
There is a pool where you can swim out on to the roof, even
in deepest winter, a café, and pool-side loungers where you
can doze or read. Also table tennis, billiards and massage.

Squash

An hour on a squash court will cost you about
DM20. You can hire a racket for DM5 from the bigger sports centres.

Squash-City-Club Berlin

For membership details, phone Gene Scites (8037 8959).
The club plays at Tennis and Squash City (*see below*).

Tennis and Squash City

Brandenburgische Straße 53, Wilmersdorf, 10707 (873
9097). U7 Konstanzer Straße. **Open** 7am-midnight
daily. **Map C5**
Apart from seven tennis courts and 11 squash courts, this
centre has four badminton courts (DM25 per hour) and a
small driving range (DM10 for 30 min). There's also a sauna,
solarium and restaurant. Training is given in all games.

Swimming

Almost every Berlin district has at least one indoor
pool. Check the phone book for the nearest one.
Pools will be either *Normale Bäder* (the water temperature will be at or below 26°C/78.8°F) or
Warmbäder (above 27°C/80.6°F).

Berliner Schwimm-Verband

Landsberger Allee 203, Hellersdorff, 13055 (971 0150).
S8, S10 Landsberger Allee. **Open** 8am-4.30pm Mon,
Wed, Fri; 8am-7pm Tue; 8am-3pm Fri.

Schwimmhalle Fischerinsel

Fischerinsel 11, Mitte, 10179 (242 5449). U2 Märkisches
Museum. **Open** 6.30am-9am Mon, Thur; 5am-9.30pm
Tue, Fri. **Admission** DM2,50; DM1,50 concs. **Map G4**

Stadtbad Charlottenburg

Krumme Straße 6a-8, Charlottenburg, 10585 (3430
3241). U2 Deutsche Oper. **Open** 2pm-8pm Mon, Tue, Fri;
2pm-5pm Wed; 2pm-4pm Thur. **Admission** DM3,50;
DM2 concs. **Map B3**

Stadtbad Kreuzberg

Wiener Straße 59, Kreuzberg, 10999 (2588 5813). U1
Görlitzer Bahnhof. **Open** 8am-10pm daily, 2pm-7pm Mon
women only. **Admission** DM3,50; DM2 concs. **Map H5**

The following open-air pools are open from early-
or mid-May to September. There are also plenty of
other places on the western lakes where swimming
is possible. Schlachtensee and Krumme Lanke are
both easily accessible, clean and in attractively
wooded surroundings.

Freibad Halensee

Königsallee 5A, Charlottenburg, 14193 (891 1703). S3,
S6, S9 Westkreuz. **Open** 8am-8pm daily. **Admission**
DM5, DM3 concs. **Map A5**

A gutsy call at **Frank's**. *See page 214.*

Freibad Humboldthain
*Wiesenstraße 1, Wedding, 13357 (464 4986). U8
Voltastraße, S1, S2 Humboldthain.* **Open** call for
information. **Admission** DM5; DM3 concs. **Map F1**
Complete with water slides.

Olympia Schwimmstadion
*Olympischer Platz, Charlottenburg, 14053 (300 633). U1
Olympia-Stadion.* **Open** 7am-7pm daily. **Admission**
DM5; DM3 concs. **Map A4**

Seebad Friedrichshagen
*Müggelseedamm 216, Friedrichshagen, 12587 (645
5756). S3 Friedrichshain.* **Open** 9am-6pm daily.
Admission DM5; DM3 concs.
Bathing beach on the northern shore of the Müggelsee.

Sommerbad Kreuzberg
*Gitschiner Straße 18-31, Kreuzberg, 10969 (2588 5416).
U1 Prinzenstraße.* **Open** 8am-7pm daily. **Admission**
DM5; DM3 concs. **Map F5**

Strandbad Müggelsee
*Fürstenwalder Damm 838, Rahnsdorf, 12589 (645
1826). S3 Rahnsdorf.* **Open** 8am-10pm daily.
Admission DM5; DM3 concs.
North shore bathing beach, complete with nudist colony, on
the bank of east Berlin's biggest lake.

Strandbad Wannsee
*Wannseebadweg, Nikolassee, 14129 (803 5450). S1, S3
Nikolassee.* **Open** 7am-8pm daily. **Admission** DM5;
DM3 concs.
Europe's largest inland beach, equipped with sand, sunbeds,
water slides, snack stalls and lots of Germans – just like
being in the Mediterranean, really.

Table Tennis
If you've got bats and balls, stone tables with metal
nets can be found here and there in most Berlin
public parks.

Berliner Tisch-Tennis Verband
*Bismarckallee 2, Charlottenburg, 14193 (892 9176). S3,
S6, S9 Westkreuz.* **Open** 10am-noon Wed, Fri; 3pm-6pm
Thur. **Map A6**
Information about table tennis clubs and events in Berlin.

Lux Tischtennis Zentrum
*Lobeckstraße 36, Kreuzberg, 10969 (614 9015). U8
Moritzplatz.* **Open** 10am-6pm Mon-Fri; 9.30am-1.30pm
Sat. **Map G4**
Meet all your table tennis needs at this shop. It's also a good
place to get advice about which club to join.

Tennis
Tennis is expensive in Berlin. At the cheapest time
(mornings) it will cost you DM29 to DM42 for one
hour on an indoor court. *See also* **Tennis and
Squash City** listed under **Squash**.

Tennis-Verband Berlin-Brandenburg
*Auerbacher Straße 19, Charlottenburg, 14193 (825
5311). S7 Grunewald.* **Open** 10am-2pm Mon-Fri.
Information about joining leagues and clubs.

tsf
*Richard-Tauber-Damm 36, Marienfelde, 12277 (742
1091). U6 Alt-Mariendorf.* **Open** 7am-11pm daily.
The Marienfelde facility has nine indoor courts, the Spandau
branch has five. Winter prices are highest, ranging from 32-
50DM per hour, depending on day and time. There is no
membership fee.
Branch: Galenstraße 33-45, Spandau, 13597 (333 4083).
U7 Rathaus Spandau. **Open** 7am-11pm daily.

TCW tennis center Weissensee
*Roelckstraße 106, Weisensee, 13088 (927 4594). S2, S8
Greifwalderstraße.* **Open** 7am-midnight. **Map H1**
New hall with eight tennis courts and 12 badminton courts,
all indoors. The surface is meant to approximate clay. Prices
in winter are DM25-DM45 per hour, and include use of the
sauna.

Windsurfing
Windsurfing is popular on Berlin's lakes.

Windchiefs
*Horstweg 33-35, Charlottenburg, 14059 (3260 1777).
U2 Sophie-Charlotte-Platz.* **Open** 10am-6.30pm Mon-
Wed; 10am-8pm Thur-Fri; 10am-4pm Sat. **Map B4**
A shop offering sales, service, and rentals for windsurfing,
in-line skating, and snowboarding. They also have their own
windsurfing school at 803 6634.

Women's sports
See also chapter **Women's Berlin**.

Landesausschuß Frauensport
*Jesse-Owens-Allee 2, Charlottenburg, 14053 (300 020).
U2 Olympia-Stadion.* **Open** 9am-3pm Mon-Thur; 9am-
2pm Fri.
At the same office as the Landessportbund Berlin (*see above*)
this office promotes and provides information about
women's sports.

Theatre

Times are tough for Berlin's formerly flourishing theatres but with vigour and vibrancy the fringe scene is fighting back.

Berliner Ensemble – _house that Brecht built._

No one could dispute the historical importance of Berlin as a world-class theatre centre. The city's two theatrical heydays were the inter-war period with its explosion of stylistic innovations, and the post-war period, when Brecht's Berliner Ensemble went out from the East to conquer the world. The Berliner Ensemble became the theatrical pride of the GDR – although often performances at home were attended by high-ranking party officials or top GDR army brass rather than workers and peasants. Brecht – who conspicuously never joined the Communist Party, ruthlessly plagiarised the works of his mistresses and collaborators, refused to support the GDR workers' uprising of 17 June 1953 and died in East Berlin in 1956 holding Austrian citizenship and millions in his Swiss bank account – had become, ironically, an East German establishment statement.

As the two Germanys became geographically and ideologically entrenched on opposing sides after the war, theatre – ironically – flourished. Determined to showcase their respective systems and concerned more with cultural one-upmanship than turning a profit, governments in both East and West Berlin effectively handed blank cheques to theatres. But when the Wall tumbled, so did the subsidies. Now that there's no political 'need' for culture, times are increasingly hard for Berlin's theatres.

When the world-renowned Schiller-Theater (where, among other legends, Beckett directed the definitive performances of his major works in the 1970s) fell under the governmental axe in the early 1990s, an icy wind blew through Berlin's theatre community. At time of writing it appears that at least two other theatres are about to come a crop-

per. Andrea Breth, Intendant of the Schaubühne, has announced that the house's resident ensemble (the last one at a major west Berlin theatre) is to be disbanded. When this news broke in late 1997, Berlin's liberal daily newspaper, _Der Tagesspiegel_, howled – quite rightly – that this would mean the end of perhaps the last resident ensemble theatre in Berlin where productions regularly merited a journey from Vienna or Hamburg.

Similar news came from the Metropol Theater. Scarcely had it been announced that vocally fading Heldentenor René Kollo would be taking over the leadership, when the word became public that this theatre, too, is being wound up and going the way of the Schiller – a venue to be hired out for touring musical productions.

Compounding matters, the theatre that Brecht made world-famous, the Berliner Ensemble, has, since the death of former Intendant Heiner Müller in early 1996, been proving ungovernable. These days the BE, as it is commonly known, seems to change Intendants as frequently as Italy changes governments. Will Claus Peymann finally be lured from Salzburg to take over the helm? Or might playwright Rolf Hochhut be given the nod?

Despite, or perhaps because of all of this, the fringe theatre scene ('Off-Theater' in German) has been fighting back with renewed vigour. Although natural attrition has led to some fringe theatres closing and fringe groups disbanding, there's still a remarkable, if at times almost desperate, vibrancy in the fringe scene.

Theatre in English can be found at the Friends of Italian Opera and sporadically at other venues such as the Theater Zerbrochene Fenster, STÜKKE, Theater am Halleschen Ufer and the Hebbel-Theater. Some solo performers working in English are also worth seeking out – look for shows by Lindy Annis, Jon Flynn, Bridge Markland and Gayle Tufts.

Tickets & information

Unless otherwise indicated, box offices open one hour before a performance and sell tickets for that performance only. Ticket prices vary from DM15-DM30 for Off-Theater productions to upwards of DM75 for the best seats at a commercial theatre. While student ID should get you a discount at a smaller theatre on the night of a given show, don't expect the same generosity from larger commercial or civic theatres. Audioloops (in German only) for the hard of hearing and full or limited wheelchair access (always ring ahead to book for this) are indicated where available. *See chapter* **Music: Classical & Opera** for other ticket agencies.

Theatershop am Alex
in S-Bahnhof Alexanderplatz, Mitte, 10178 (2758 4190). S3, S5, S6, S7, S9/U2, U8 Alexanderplatz. **Open** 9am-7pm Mon-Fri; 10am-4pm Sat. **Credit** AmEx, DC, MC, V. Booking charge 15 per cent of ticket price. **Map G3**
At the time of writing this agency was temporarily closed due to construction work at Alexanderplatz. Check the *Berlin Gelbe Seiten* (Yellow Pages) in case the information given here proves out of date after going to press.

Civic theatres

Berliner Ensemble
Bertolt-Brecht-Platz 1, Mitte, 10117 (Box Office: 282 3160 or 2840 8155; Info & Ticket reservations: 282 7712 or 2840 8150) S1, S2, S3, S5, S6, S7, S9/U6 Friedrichstraße. **Open** 11am-6pm Mon-Sat; 3pm-6pm; Sun. **Map F3**
The House that Brecht built (and where *Threepenny Opera* was first seen in 1928). Technically speaking, the Berliner Ensemble is only the name of the resident company – the house itself is called Theater am Schiffbauerdamm. If you want to see the classic productions from Brecht's heyday, you've come decades too late. This house simply isn't what it once was, but things are slowly improving. Theatrical deconstructivism were the passwords here under former Intendant Heiner Müller, whose death in 1996 has continued to leave a question mark over future artistic direction. *Wheelchair access and audioloop.*

Love it or leave it – the **Volksbühne**.

Deutsches Theater/Kammerspiele des Deutschen Theaters
Schumannstraße 13a, Mitte, 10045 (2844 1225). S1, S2, S3, S5, S6, S7, S9/U6 Friedrichstraße. **Open** noon-6pm Mon-Sat; 3pm-6pm Sun. **Map E3**
Two lovely adjacent houses on an attractive little courtyard in the quiet backstreets of Mitte provide the venue for hearty bourgeois theatrical fare – mainly German and international classics. One of the most reliable companies in Berlin. *Wheelchair access.*

Hebbel-Theater
Stresemannstraße 29, Kreuzberg, 10963 (2590 0427). S1, S2 Anhalter Bahnhof/U15 Hallesches Tor/U15 Möckernbrücke. **Open** 4pm-7pm daily. **Credit** AmEx, EC, MC, V. **Map F5**
The thinking person's theatre in Berlin. Superb performances by the very best local and international theatre companies and frequently varying programmes make the Hebbel a haven of scintillating, thought-provoking work. Chamber opera, dance and occasional performances in English further enhance this theatre's popularity among the Berlin intelligentsia. One drawback: if you have got long legs, you will probably find that the rows are placed together too closely for comfort. *Limited wheelchair access.*

Maxim Gorki Theater
Am Festungsgraben 2, Mitte, 10117 (2022 1129/2022 1115). S1, S2, S3, S5, S6, S7, S9/U6 Friedrichstraße. **Open** 1pm-6.30pm Mon-Sat; 3pm-6.30pm Sun. **Map F3**
Specialises in modern classics with an emphasis on German, Russian and Scandinavian playwrights, although they've increasingly branched out into contemporary repertoire and have so far survived the ravages of funding cuts. A solid but hardly dazzling house. *Audioloop.*

Schaubühne am Lehniner Platz
Kufürstendamm 153, Charlottenburg, 10709 (890 023). S3, S5, S6, S7, S9 Charlottenburg/U7 Adenauerplatz. **Open** 11am-6.30pm Mon-Sat; 3pm-6.30pm Sun. **Map B5**
Arguably the last of the truly first-class, if somewhat conservative, resident Berlin companies calls the Schaubühne home; but as of going to press plans were afoot to close down the resident ensemble. What the future holds for this three-stage theatre, designed by Erich Mendelsohn, remains a source of concern and uncertainty. *Limited wheelchair access & audioloop.*

Volksbühne
Rosa-Luxemburg-Platz, Mitte, 10178 (247 6472). U2 Rosa-Luxemburg-Platz. **Open** noon-6pm daily. **Map G2**
'The People's Stage' – and if your idea of theatre is neither wildly avant-garde nor extravagantly experimental, you'll probably keep that 'The People' can bloody well keep it. Frank Castorf presides and provocation and re-interpretation rule the day. The sort of ultra-modern theatre one either loves utterly or hates utterly – there must be a surfeit of the former, as it's hugely popular. *Limited wheelchair access.*

Commercial theatres

Theater am Kurfürstendamm
Kurfürstendamm 209, Charlottenburg, 10719 (882 3789). U15 Uhlandstraße. **Open** 10am-8pm Mon-Sat; 2pm-6pm Sun. **Map C4**
Venue catering to the coach-loads of provincial German tourists up in the Big City to see their favourite television stars cavorting in light farce and Boulevard comedy. Same goes for the Kömodie nearby at Ku'damm 206. *Wheelchair access & audioloop.*

Theater des Westens

Kantstraße 12, Tiergarten, 10623 (882 2888). S3, S5, S6, S7, S9/U9 Zoologischer Garten. **Open** *box office* 10am-6pm Mon-Fri; 10am-3.30pm Sat. *Reservations* noon-7pm Tue-Sat; 2pm-5pm Sun, public holidays. **Map C4**
Unchallenging but popular formula of pseudo-American fake-1950s musicals written by Germans, and revivals in German of Broadway chestnuts. The interior design features unspeakably vulgar frescoes on the boxes.
Wheelchair access.

Off-Theater

It's impossible to say exactly how many fringe groups and theatres there are in Berlin, but it's a lot – certainly no less than 100. They're often small, rough-and-ready spaces, but can sometimes provide real theatrical revelations. Quality varies hugely but prices are much lower on the fringe, the audiences less stuffy, and no matter what you see, chances are it will be at worst 'interesting' and at best stunning.

Most theatres will have an answering machine with details of what's on. Box offices usually open only 30-60 minutes before each evening's performance – hence the absence of opening times here. Leave your order, name and phone number on the answering machine and pick up your tickets half an hour before curtain. And forget about paying with a credit card.

Arena

Eichenstraße 4, Treptow, 12435 (533 2030). U1, U15 Schlesisches Tor.
This huge former public transport depot has hosted some of the best theatre in town in recent years, including stellar productions by Paris' Théâtre du Soleil and Theatre de Complicite from London, whose *Caucasian Chalk Circle* taught the Germans a thing or two about how to do Brecht.

Friends of Italian Opera

Fidicinstraße 40, Kreuzberg, 10965 (691 1211). U6 Platz der Luftbrücke. **Map F6**
English-language performances almost every night of the year. There's no opera at this cosy 60-seater – 'Friends of Italian Opera' was how the Mafia camouflaged themselves in the film *Some Like it Hot*. The 'Friends' attracts a loyal and varied crowd of expats and Germans who come to see both resident anglophone Berlin theatre groups such as the consistently excellent Out to Lunch Theatre Company or top-of-the-line international groups.

Theater des Westens *– reviving chestnuts.*

Kulturbrauerei

Knaackstraße 97, Prenzlauer Berg, 10435 (441 9269). U2 Eberswalderstraße. **Map G2**
Performance events and occasional opera can be enjoyed in this space – a converted brewery – now one of Berlin's most fashionable venues. The courtyard is fine for a drink of a summer's evening. *See also chapter* **Music: Classical & Opera**.

STÜKKE

Hasenheide 54 (2nd courtyard), Kreuzberg, 10967 (6940 9869). U7 Südstern. **Map G5**
'Straight plays', experimental theatre and solo performances – frequently in English – have kept this 120-seater afloat as a major fringe site despite funding problems. Nice bar space with limited seating.

Theater am Halleschen Ufer

Hallesches Ufer 32, Kreuzberg, 10963 (251 0941). U7, U15 Möckernbrücke/U15 Hallesches Tor. **Map F5**
A large, modern building with big windows overlooking the Landwehr canal, this is the theatre where Peter Stein made his name. The house hosts a variety of theatre groups and solo performers, some in English.

Theater am Ufer

Tempelhofer Ufer 10 (2nd courtyard), Kreuzberg, 10963 (251 3116). U7, U15 Möckernbrücke/U15 Hallesches Tor. **Map F5**
Not to be confused with the nearby and similarly named theatre listed above. Here you will find the popular Theater Kreatur, the small resident company who perform gestural, highly physical theatre that packs the house every time.

Theater Zerbrochene Fenster

Fidicstraße 3 (entrance on Schwiebusserstraße 16), Kreuzberg, 10965 (694 2400). U6 Platz der Luftbrücke. **Map F6**
Another space where anglophone productions can sometimes be seen, the 'Broken Windows' theatre is in a converted factory building and unexpectedly large for a fringe space.

Theater zum Westlichen Stadthirschen

Kreuzbergstraße 37-38, Kreuzberg, 10965 (785 7033). S1, S2 Yorckstraße. **Map E5**
Mainly local groups provide the theatre, which has proven consistently rewarding. Not quite as monumental as the massive arch at its entrance suggests, but a classy space nonetheless.

Vagantenbühne

Kantstraße 12a, Charlottenburg, 10623 (312 4529). S3, S5, S6, S7, S9/U2, U9 Zoologischer Garten/U9, U15 Kurfürstendamm. **Map C4**
Although they've rather abandoned their experimental roots, this consistently solid house, the 'Vagrant's Stage', is one of the few that still receives government subsidies. Many productions sell out in advance – be sure to book.

Festivals

Berliner Festspiele

Budapester Straße 50, Charlottenburg, 10787 (2548 9100). S3, S5, S6, S7, S9/ U2, U9 Zoologischer Garten. **Map D4**
Oversees most of the major festivals in Berlin and reliable for information about events they are sponsoring, in particular the Berliner Festwochen, each September, when some of the world's greatest theatre companies are invited to town.

Theater Treffen Berlin

A kind of pan-German theatrical trade congress, the 'Berlin Theatre Meeting' occurs each May. Performances and a wide selection of events related to theatre.

Trips Out of Town

Getting Started

Routes, rides and railways out of town.

Berlin is a city in the middle of nowhere. For miles around, fields, lakes and dense woods are scarcely interrupted by small towns and villages.

The hard details about what is to be seen, when and for how much, are available from central tourist offices, usually in or near main railway stations. Most of them keep up-to-date supplies of inexpensive or free tourist maps and leaflets and are indefatigable promoters of themselves and other points of interest within reach.

Berlin Tourismus Marketing

Europa-Center, Budapester Straße, Charlottenburg, 10787 (250 025/fax 2500 2424). S3, S5, S6, S7, S9/U2, U9 Zoologischer Garten. **Open** 8am-10pm Mon-Sat; 9am-9pm Sun. Reduced opening hours on public holidays. **Map D4**

By bus

There are no buses to Leipzig or Weimar.

Bus Station

Messedamm 8, Charlottenburg, 14057 (301 8028). U2 Kaiserdamm/S45 Witzleben. **Open** for information 5.30am-9.30pm Mon-Sat.

To **Babelsberg**: from Platz der Einheit in Potsdam take the 693 bus; journey time ten minutes.
To the **Baltic Coast**: coach from Omnibusbahnhof am Funkturm to Usedom on the eastern German Baltic coast (Saturdays, Mar-Oct only); journey time about four hours.
To **Hamburg**: there are four departures daily from Omnibusbahnhof am Funkturm; journey time about three hours.
To **Prague**: from Omnibusbahnhof am Funkturm on Mondays, Wednesdays, Fridays and Saturdays at 11.55pm; journey time six hours 20 minutes; returns on Tuesdays, Thursdays, Fridays and Sundays at 8pm.

By train

The S-Bahn system is integrated with the DB network (Deutsche Bahn), reaching about 40km beyond the city boundary. Any BVG (Berliner Verkehrsbetrieb Gesellschaft) ticket is valid for unlimited distances within the system.

The welding together of the eastern and western rail systems into the Deutsche Bahn often creates changes in services. Information about timetable alterations is displayed on affected platforms. At popular times of the year longer-distance trains can be fully booked well in advance. You should also book a seat at weekends.

Trains are ruinously expensive in Germany, but trips into eastern Europe are still much cheaper even though services have mostly been modernised.

Deutsche Bahn Information

Zoologischer Garten (Bahnhof Zoo), Hardenbergplatz, Charlottenburg, 10623 (194 19). **Open** 5am-11pm daily.

To **Potsdam**: direct link S-Bahn trains (S7/S3 to Potsdam Stadt) run three times an hour from the centre of Berlin; journey time about 45minutes from Bahnhof Zoo. Cost DM3,90.
To **Babelsberg** from Potsdam take the S3/S5 or R4 from Potsdam Stadt to Griebnitzsee; journey time about 10 minutes. Cost DM2,60 from Potsdam.
To **Sachsenhausen** take the S1 from Friedrichstraße to Oranienburg; journey time about 45 minutes. After that it's a 15-minute walk: east along Straße des Friedens, left into Straße der Einheit, and finally along Straße der Nationen to the camp entrance. Cost DM3,90.
To **Leipzig** (168km) direct from Bahnhof Lichtenberg every two hours from 7.40am to 5.40pm; journey time about two and a half hours; last return 10.22pm. Cost DM51 single; DM102 return.
To **Weimar** (278km) direct from Bahnhof Lichtenberg every two hours from 5.27am to 5.27pm; journey time three hours; last return 7.15pm. Cost DM67 single; DM134 return.
To the **Baltic Coast** (280km) trains to Rügen run from Bahnhof Lichtenberg every hour from 5.47am to 7.47pm; journey time three and a quarter hours; last return 12.06am. Cost DM68 single; DM132.
Trains to **Rostock** (240km) also run from Bahnhof Lichtenberg every two hours from 6.47am to 6.47pm; journey time two and a half hours; last return 7.27pm. Cost DM58 single; DM116 return.
To **Dresden** (198km) trains from Bahnhof Lichtenberg run every two hours from 6.46am to 6.46pm; journey time two hours; last return at 9.15pm. Cost DM53 single DM106 return.
To **Frankfurt Oder** (87km) from Bahnhof Lichtenberg or trains from Warschauer Straße (home to the regional bahn) run every hour at 58 minutes past the hour; journey time one hour; last return 10.50pm. Cost DM17,60 single; DM35,20 return.
To **Hamburg**: there are eight departures a day from Zoologischer Garten; journey time two and a quarter hours; last return 11pm. Cost DM74,20 single; DM148 return.
To **Prague** (377km) trains from Bahnhof Lichtenberg every two hours from 6.46am to 4.46pm and also at 7.45pm; journey time four and a half hours; last return 3.58am. Cost DM81,60 single; DM163,20 return.

By car

If you own, borrow or hire a car, make sure you are well briefed before setting out. Speed limits are ruthlessly enforced; in built-up areas it's usually 30kmph; 50kmph is customary on main arterial roads; the Schnellstrecke – dual carriageway – functions in all but name as a motorway, with a limit of 100- or 120kmph; and on the motorway there is, as yet, no speed limit.

The motorway system has regular service and filling stations which are all listed in free maps issued by the **ADAC** (German automobile association) and available at any of their outlets. Information on car transport can be obtained from the association:

ADAC Berlin-Brandenburg
ADAC Haus, Bundesallee 29-30, 10717 (Information 86 860/breakdown & accident assistance 01802 22 22 22.)

To **Potsdam & Babelsberg**: take the AVUS as far as the Drewitz turn off, then turn right into Großbeeren-straße and follow it until Babelsberg and then Potsdam.
To **Spreewald**: located 100km (62 miles) to the south-east of Berlin, the Spree bisects the area in Unterspreewald and Oberspreewald. For the former, Schepzig or Lübben are the best starting points; for the latter go 15km further on the train to Lübbenau. Journey time approximately 90 minutes.
To **Leipzig**: take the AVUS to the Berliner Ring, then take the A9. A trip to Leipzig by car takes about two and a half hours down the motorway, but be prepared for considerable traffic jams during trade-fair times as you approach the city; a good road map of the Leipzig and its environs will help you make time-saving diversions.
To **Weimar**: as for Leipzig (*above*), but continue on the E4055.Weimar lies 50km (31 miles) to the south-west of Leipzig across the state border in Thüringen (Thuringia). If you travel here by car, you will also be able to explore the stunning Saale valley on the way.
To **Hamburg**: drive north from Jakob-Kaiser-Platz along Kurt-Schumacher-Damm to the A24; journey time two and a half hours.
To the **Baltic Coast**: drive north to the Berliner Ring and then follow the A24 to Rostock (about 2 hours); continue on the B105 to Stralsund and Rügen. The motorway to Rostock affords easy access on the way to the many inland lakes and forests.
By ferry there are regular links between Rügen and the mainland, as well as the Danish island of Bornholm.
To the **Polish border**: take Frankfurter Allee to Münchenberg, heading from there either take the A12 to Frankfurt-Oder or to Seelow. Journey time one hour.
To **Dresden**: take the AVUS to the Berliner Ring and then the A16. Journey time about 90 minutes.

Shared lifts

The well-established national network of lift-sharing was founded in the 1960s and was originally used mainly by students. Each city or town has at least one office, advertised in the phone book or *Yellow Pages* (*Gelbe Seiten*) under *Mitfahrzentrale*. Passengers can call the office, or visit in person, to find out if there are any drivers seeking companions. Usually a small fee is charged by the agent (about DM20). Theoretically, each agent recommends a fixed number of Pfennigs per kilometre, but in practice the deal travellers strike up with each other is more important.

Once, lifts could be arranged a matter of hours in advance, now you should allow two or three days' warning. Very long jaunts (say, Berlin to London) are possible but not as common as short ones; you should prepare at least a week in advance and be flexible.

Pedal power – ever popular in Berlin.

City-Netz
Kurfürstendamm 227, Charlottenburg, 10719 (194 44). U9, U15 Kurfürstendamm. **Open** 8am-9pm daily.
City-Netz has branches in every major German city.

Mitfahrzentrale am Alex
Alexanderplatz U-bahn, Mitte, 10178 (241 5820). S3, S5, S6, S9/U2,U8 Alexanderplatz. **Open** 8am-8pm Mon-Fri; 8am-6pm Sat; 10am-6pm Sun.

Hitching

Hitch-hiking is still widely used in Germany, mostly by the young. Inner-city hitching, especially at night, has almost disappeared and been replaced by a much improved night bus system and two 24-hour tube lines at the weekend. Asking around at lorry parks and filling stations on the main routes out of the city can be a good way to cut your travelling expenses.

If heading to Hamburg take bus 224 direction Henningsdorf and get off at Heiligensee. The bus stop is 150 metres from the car and lorry park known as the Trämperparlplatz.

If heading in the direction of Hannover, Leipzig or Nürnberg take the S1, S3 or S7 to Wannsee; exit towards Potsdamerchaussee, then walk 300m to the slip road leading to the lorry park and petrol station at Raststätte Dreilinden. Standing on the hard shoulder is illegal and you may be moved on by the police. But this is still a busy spot, so arrive early and carry a clear sign indicating your desired destination.

Bicycles

Cycling is a popular way to get about. Especially in fine weather, it is common for Berliners to pack their bikes on to the train and head off into the countryside. On the U-Bahn, there is a limit of two cycles at the end of carriages which have a bicycle sign on them. More may be taken on to S-Bahn carriages, but in each case an extra ticket must be bought for each bike. With a yearly, monthly, Berlin or Kombi-Tageskarte ticket you can take your bicycle for free.

Day Trips

Step out of Berlin's boundaries to Potsdam, Babelsberg and beyond.

The area immediately around Berlin is full of lakes and forest, offering interesting bike rides and plenty of places to swim in summer. Potsdam is to Berlin what Versailles is to Paris, with a collection of palaces and other interesting things to see – almost more, in fact, than is manageable in one day. Neighbouring Babelsberg has the old UFA film studios, Germany's answer to Hollywood. The Spreewald, a forest filigreed with small streams, is good for an afternoon's boat ride. More sombrely, KZ Sachsenhausen offers a reminder of one of history's more chilling passages.

With the exception of the Spreewald, which is only accessible by car, all of the destinations in this chapter can be reached on the S-Bahn. *See chapter* **Getting Started**.

Potsdam

Potsdam is capital of the state of Brandenburg and Berlin's closest and most beautiful neighbour. In 1993 it celebrated its one thousandth anniversary, by which time it had once again become a chic exurb of Berlin, with burgeoning shops, restaurants, and cafés. The main permanent attraction is the grandiose collection of palaces and outbuildings in Park Sanssouci. This is in itself would take a whole day to see. There is plenty to fill another whole day in the baroque town centre as well as nearby Babelsberg.

Large parts of Potsdam town centre were destroyed in a single bombing raid on 14 April 1945, which claimed 4,000 lives. The vagaries of post-war reconstruction produced a ghastly 'restoration' of Schinkel's St Nikolaikirche, whose dome can be seen for miles, as well as acres of featureless 1960s and 1970s flatblocks which crowd out Platz der Einheit (Square of Unity) and the surrounding streets.

Nevertheless, the unusual, mid-eighteenth century, Palladian-style Rathaus (Town Hall) is worth admiring, particularly for its round tower, which until 1875 was used as a prison. It is now an arts centre (Kulturhaus). The Hans-Otto-Theatre, resembling a nuclear plant or a Midwestern Toyota parts warehouse, was intended to be part of the millenium festivities and finished with diminished funds after the fall of the Wall. The park at the Alter Markt here covers the ruins of the first Stadtschloß, and a square of stones marks its oldest tower, from 1200.

Yorck- and Wilhelm-Raab-Straße retain their baroque architecture: the Kabinetthaus, a small palace at Am neuen Markt 1, was the birthplace of Friedrich Wilhelm II (the only Hohenzollern both to have been born and to have died in the royal residence of Potsdam). The baroque heart of the town, originally intended as a quarter to house people servicing the court, is bounded by Schopenhauerstraße, Hebbelstraße, Charlottenstraße and Hegel Allee. The dwellings were built between 1732 and 1742, at the behest of Friedrich Wilhelm I; the best of them can be seen running west along the pedestrianised Brandenburgerstraße. Potsdam's Brandenburg Gate (by Gontard 1733), at the Sanssouci end of Brandenburger Straße, is a delightfully happy contrast to Berlin's sombre structure of the same name.

The Holländisches Viertel (Dutch Quarter), is between Gutenbergstraße, Friedrich-Ebert-Straße, Hebbelstraße and Kurfürstenstraße, and takes its name from the Dutch immigrant workers that Friedrich Wilhelm I, the inveterate builder, invited to the town. He ordered 134 gable-fronted red-brick houses to be built, most of which fell into neglect after the last war, but the survivors, particularly along Mittelstraße at the junction with Benckerstraße, have been scrubbed into shape. With squatters evicted and private money poured into them, they now form a chic shopping and eating district.

The best museum in town is the Filmmuseum, with an excellent documentation of the history of German cinema from 1895 to 1980. Indeed, it's one of the finest of its kind anywhere. Contained in the elegant former Marstall (royal stables), which were given their current appearance by Knobelsdorff during the eighteenth century, it has rooms full of famous props, costumes, set-designs and projection screens showing clips. There's also a good café and a large, comfortable cinema with an art-house programme rivalling anything on offer in Berlin. Ask about talks and special events. Behind it, bounded by Dortusstraße and Yorckstraße, lies another magnificent Baroque neighbourhood awaiting restoration.

The extensive gardens of Sanssouci (French was the language of the Prussian court in the

Sanssouci – *the visitor's main target in Potsdam. See page 227.*

eighteenth century, and this means 'without care') were begun by the francophile Friedrich Wilhelm II in 1740. They were intended to be in stark contrast to the style favoured by his detested father – German history is littered with examples of one generation doing the precise opposite of its predecessor. The first palace to be built, and the one which gives the park its name, forms a semi-circle at the top of a terrace on whose slopes symmetrical zig-zag paths are interspersed with vines and (in summer) orange trees. It houses a collection of paintings.

Voltaire was brought to live in a suite here between 1750 and 1753, supposedly to oversee the library. But he devoted most of his time to his own writing, an act of defiance which eventually brought the relationship with his patron to an acrimonious end. The abundant attractions include Friedrich Wilhelm II's huge Neue Palais, built 1763-69 to celebrate the end of the Seven Years' War. So many statues were needed for the roof that they had to be mass produced in a factory.

The last occupant, Kaiser Wilhelm II, took the Neue Palais' contents with him in 60 railway carriages when he fled into exile in Holland in 1918, where most of the items remained in boxes, unopened until they were returned to fill the restored palace in the 1980s. Also worth visting in Sanssouci are: the gigantic Orangerie, in Italian Renaissance style; the Spielfestung (toy fortress), built for Wilhelm II's sons, complete with toy cannon which can be fired; the Chinesisches Teehaus (Chinese Teahouse), with its collection of Chinese and Meissner porcelain; the Römischer Bäder, an imitation Roman villa by Schinkel and Persius; and Schloß Charlottenhof, with its extraordinary blue-glazed entrance hall and Kupferstichzimmer (copper-plate engraving room) adorned with reproduction Renaissance paintings; and the Drachenhaus (Dragonhouse), a pagoda-style coffee shop which sells truly excellent cakes. If you want to see them all, take a stout pair of walking shoes.

While the park is open all the year round, much of the statuary – as is customary in this part of the world – is protected from the harsh winter by being encased in wooden boxes. For this reason, it's best to visit between April and October, a fact which is well known by vast crowds of tourists. Arrive early on a weekday.

Outside Sanssouci Park is Alexandrowka (between Puschkinallee and Am Schragen), a fake Russian village built in 1826 by Friedrich Wilhelm III to house Russian musicians and their families who came into Prussian hands as prisoners of war during the Napoleonic campaigns. The houses were arranged in the form of a St Andrew's cross and designed to look like log cabins. They still carry the names of the original tenants in inscriptions on their fronts, some in cyrillic. The icon-

Weekend market on Brandenburger Straße.

filled Alexander Newski Kapelle, constructed three years later at the top of the densely wooded Kapellenberg hill, is named – strangely – after the celebrated Russian hero who defeated the medieval Teutonic Knights.

In the Neuer Garten (New Garden), at the end of Johannes-Dieckmann-Allee, the Marmorpalais (Marble Palace), overlooking the beautiful Heiliger See, was where Friedrich Wilhelm II died. Nearby, Schloß Cecilienhof, the last royal addition to Potsdam's palaces, was begun in 1913 and completed four years later: its English-country-house style was unaffected by the war with Britain.

It was here that the Potsdam Conference (17 July to 2 August 1945) took place, and where Stalin, Truman and Attlee signed the 'Potsdamer Abkommen', the treaty which divided post-war Germany. The conference room, including the specially fashioned round table (so that none of 'The Big Three' would take precedence) were left untouched. The room was damaged in an arson attack in 1990, presumed to be the work of neo-Nazis. One wing of the building was converted into a hotel in 1960, and remains an expensive place to stay or dine.

Touristenzentrale am Alten Markt

Friedrich-Ebert-Straße 5, Potsdam, 14467 (0331 275 580, 0331 19433). **Open** *Apr-Oct* 9am-8pm Mon-Fri; 10am-6pm Sat; 10am-4pm Sun, public holidays. *Nov-Mar* 10am-6pm Mon-Fri; 10am-2pm Sat, Sun, public holidays. Some English spoken. Note: A *Potsdam Billett* is available for DM7,50 that allows 24 hours' free travel on public transport, as well as reductions on museum entry fees, concessions on theatre and cabaret tickets, and much else. It is available at both tourist offices, as well as from the VIP (the Potsdam public transport authority) ticket offices in the Platz der Einheit and Luisenplatz. The DM1 map also available here is excellent value, showing all the main attractions and how best to move between them on the public transport system.

Potsdam Information

Brandenburger Straße 18, Potsdam, 14467 (0331 293 038). **Open** 10am-7pm Mon-Fri; 10am-2pm Sat. Mostly useful for purchase of tickets for cultural events.

Altes Rathaus: Kulturhaus Potsdam

Am Alten Markt, Potsdam, 14467(0331 293 175). **Open** 10am-6pm Tue-Sun.

Besucherservice (Information Centre of Park Sanssouci)
Zur historisches Mühle, Potsdam, 14469 (0331 969 4202). **Open** 8.30am-4pm daily.
The visitors service arranges tours around the parks and palaces of Sanssouci. Phone or write in advance.

Filmmuseum
Marstall, Potsdam, 14467 (0331 271 810). **Open** 10am-5pm Tue-Sun. **Admission** DM4; DM2 concs. *Special exhibitions* DM4; DM2 concs. *Cinema admission* DM7, concs DM5; children DM2,50; *Mon* DM5, DM2 children. Cinema tickets must be obtained 15 minutes before programme starts.

Marmorpalais
In the Neuer Garten on the shore of the Heiligen See. **Closed** at present with no scheduled reopening date; contact tourist office for information.

St Nikolaikirche
Am Alten Markt, Potsdam, 14467 (0331 216 82). **Open** *Mar-Oct* 10am-5pm Mon-Sat; *Nov-Feb* 2pm-5pm Mon-Sat. **Admission** free (tours by prior arrangement).

Sanssouci
(0331 969 4202). **Open** *for tours* (every 20 mins) 9am-5pm daily; Park until dusk daily. **Admission** *Palace and exhibition buildings* DM8; DM4 concs; *Park* free. **Note**: Each of the various outbuildings has its own closing days each month, and some are only open 'during the season' of mid-May to mid-Oct. If you have a particular interest, call the number above for full information as to opening.

Schloß Cecilienhof
Am Neuen Garten, Potsdam, 14469 (0331 969 4244). **Open** 9am-5pm daily (closed every 2nd and 4th Mon in month). **Admission** DM4; DM3 children, students, pensioners.

Babelsberg

Across the Lange Brücke, Albert-Einstein-Straße leads past the state parliament building (known as the Kreml, or Kremlin, during the GDR) on to the Telegrafenberg (Telegraph Hill). In 1832 one of the mechanical telegraph stations linking Berlin to Koblenz was built here. When electrification made it obsolete, an astronomical observatory was erected. Its expressionist tower by Erich Mendelsohn, the Einsteinturm, was added in 1920 with the hope of luring Albert Einstein here to test his Theory of Relativity.

From Lutherplatz, a bus down Großbeeren-straße runs along the south side of the Babelsberg Film Studios, whose entrance is just before you reach Drewitz S-Bahn station. The first studio was opened here in 1912 by the Berlin production company Bioscop. But it was not until 1917, when the German General Staff decided that the war effort was suffering because of the inferior quality of their propaganda, that the Universum Film AG (UFA) was founded, with the financial support of the Deutsche Bank.

By the 1920s the studio had become the largest in the world outside Hollywood, making as many as 100 films a year, including the Expressionist

The Cabinet of Dr Caligari, the futurist *Metropolis* and the decadent *The Blue Angel* (the young Marlene Dietrich was so convinced she would not be eligible for the role of Lola, that she came to her audition without a song to sing).

A mixture of success, the Depression and the rise of the Nazis saw most of the studios' talent leave for America, or the concentration camps. *See page 184* **The exile files**.

During World War II, films such as the anti-Semitic *Jew Süß* and the colour, escapist fantasy *The Adventures of Baron Münchhausen* were made. Renamed Deutsche Film AG (DEFA) in the GDR, film-making resumed and included *Der Untertan* (The Subject), possibly the best study of German totalitarianism ever made. It was banned immediately after its premiere in 1952 – a common fate.

The rediscovery, and sometimes reconstruction, of 'lost' DEFA films continues at a time when the studios have ceased feature film production, prior, some suspect, to disappearing forever.

Sadly, the sections of the studio open to the public have been transformed into a cheap and cruddy theme park where the product placement of international soft drink sponsors overshadow the exhibits on display. Avoid, unless you're turned on by inflatable Coca-Cola bottles. A walk by the pretty Griebnitzsee is a far more appealing prospect – even in the rain. *See also page 188* **Babelsberg: the dream factory**.

Studio Babelsberg
August-Babel Straße 26-53, entrance on Großbeerenstraße, Potsdam, 14482 (0331 721 2750 reservations/721 2755 information). S3 Griebnitzsee, then bus 693 direction Bahnhof Rehbrücke or 20 minutes' walk. **Open** 10am-6pm daily (Mar-Oct). Entrance up to 1 1/2 hours before close. **Tickets** DM28; DM25 concs. Special rates for groups.

Touristenzentrale am Alten Markt
Friedrich-Ebert-Straße 5, Potsdam, 14467 (0331 275 580/0331 19433). **Open** *Apr-Oct* 9am-8pm Mon-Fri; 10am-6pm Sat, 10am-4pm Sun, public holidays. *Nov-Mar* 10am-6pm Mon-Fri; 10am-2pm Sat, Sun, public holidays.

Spreewald

This filigree network of tiny rivers, streams and canals, dividing dense patches of deciduous forest interspersed with market garden farmland, is one of the most spectacular, and most touristy, excursions out of Berlin. The area is extremely crowded in season, and particularly at weekends, giving the lie to its otherwise justified claim to be one of the most perfect areas of wilderness in Europe.

Located 100km (62 miles) to the south-east of Berlin, the Spree bisects the area in Unterspreewald and Oberspreewald. For the former, Schepzig or Lübben are the best starting points; for the latter go 15km further on the train to Lübbenau.

The character of both sections is very similar. The Oberspreewald is perhaps better, for its 500 sq km (193 sq miles) of territory contains more than 300 natural and artificial channels, called Fliesse. You can travel around these on hand-propelled punts – rent your own or join a larger group – and also take out kayaks. Motorised boats are forbidden. Here and there in the forest are restaurants and small hotels.

Theodor Fontane described the Spreewald as resembling Venice more than 1,500 years ago. The local population belongs to the Sorbisch Slavonic minority, with their own language much in evidence in street names, newspapers and so on.

Spreewald Information

Ehm-Welk-Straße 15, Lubbenau, 03222 (035 42 36 68). **Open** 10am-6pm Mon-Fri; 10am-2pm Sat.

KZ Sachsenhausen

Many Nazi concentration camps (*Konzentrationslager*) have been preserved and opened to the public as memorials to what happened and how. Sachsenhausen is the one nearest to Berlin.

Immediately upon coming to power, Hitler set about rounding up and interning his opponents. From 1933 to 1935 an old brewery on this site was used to hold them. The present camp received its first prisoners in July 1936 (coinciding with the Berlin Olympic Games). It was designated with cynical euphemism as a *Schutzlager* (Protective Custody Camp). The first *Schutzhäftlinger* were political opponents of the government: communists, social democrats, trade unionists. With time, the number and variety of prisoner widened to include anyone guilty of 'anti-social' behaviour, homosexuals and Jews.

About 6,000 Jews were forcibly brought here after Reichskristallnacht alone. It was here that some of the first experiments in organised mass murder were made: tens of thousands of prisoners of war from the Eastern Front were killed at the neighbouring Station Z, where the cells for *Prominenz* (high-class detainees) housed Pastor Martin Niemöller, a decorated First World War U-Boat captain and one-time supporter of the Nazis.

The SS evacuated the camp in 1945 and began marching 33,000 inmates to the Baltic, where they were to be packed into boats and sunk in the sea. Some 6,000 died during the march before the survivors were rescued by the Allies. A further 3,000 prisoners were found in the camp's hospital when it was captured on 22 April 1945.

But the horror did not end here. After the German capitulation, the Russian secret police, the MVD, re-opened Sachsenhausen as 'Camp 7' for the detention of war criminals; in fact it was filled with anyone suspected of opposing them. Following the fall of the GDR, mass graves were 'discovered', containing the remains of an estimated 10,000 prisoners.

On April 23 1961, the partially restored camp was opened to the public as Nationale Mahn- und Gedenkstätte Sachsenhausen, a national monument and memorial. As far as the GDR was concerned, it was absolved of all complicity in the actions of the Hitler regime, whose rightful successors, they claimed, could be found across the border in West Germany. The inscription over the entrance, Arbeit Macht Frei ('Work Sets You Free'), could be found over the gates of all concentration camps.

The parade ground, where morning roll-call was taken, and from where inmates were required to witness executions on the gallows, stands before two remaining barrack blocks. One is now a museum and the second a memorial hall and cinema, where a film about the history of the camp is shown hourly, on the hour. The scale and the grisliness of the horror remembered here can be very disturbing; but it is worth noting that there are some people today who would like to pretend that none of it ever happened, some of whom burned a couple of the buildings here in 1996. They were being reconstructed at time of writing.

KZ Sachsenhausen

Straße der Nationen 22, Oranienburg, 16515 (033 0180 3715). **Open** 8.30am-6pm Tue-Sun. **Admission** free.

Forced labour at **KZ Sachsenhausen**.

Overnighters

South to the cities of Saxony, north to the Baltic Coast, or clock up some culture in Weimar.

It is possible to get to and from the following destinations within one day, but these would be arduous day trips, especially for inveterate museum-goers. Better, we reckon, to make them an overnight stay, even though affordable hotel accommodation is still relatively scarce in the former GDR.

All these destinations are within the five new federal states, where the economic, political, social and cultural base is of an entirely different character, not only from the west, but also from eastern Berlin, which enjoyed a comparatively favoured position in the former Eastern Bloc. Federal subsidies for rebuilding have been eagerly seized, and construction is rampant, meaning some landmarks, particularly once-neglected churches, may be closed or clad with scaffolding.

Even so, a longer excursion into the east German hinterland not only affords an unrepeatable experience as the continent of Europe continues to move into a new era, but a chance to see some of the country's other regions which played their own parts in Berlin's history.

Leipzig

One of Germany's most important trade centres and former second city of the GDR, Leipzig is both Bach's city and the place where the Wende, or 'change', started. Once one of Germany's biggest industrial strongholds, trade fairs are its bread and butter these days. The recent influx of western businesspeople (and their spouses) has resulted not only in the scrubbing clean of the city, but also in a proliferation of pricey shops and boutiques.

All forms of transport between Berlin and Leipzig are liable to be overcrowded or fully booked during important *Messen* (trade fairs); ask at a tourist information office for details. The advantage of taking a slower train is that it enables you to make stops en route (perhaps Wittenberg, former home of Martin Luther and a pretty, medieval town). Another sight which can not be overlooked by train is the gigantic chemical works at Leuna. The factories were originally built in the early 1900s for the immense conglomerate IG Farben, which produced the poison gas used on the Western Front during World War I and the Zyklon B nerve gas for the Nazi Vernichtungslager (Extermination camp) gas chambers.

Leipzig's Hauptbahnhof ('main station'), one of the largest in the world, has been extensively restored, and features a three-level shopping mall, including an international press shop which has a finer selection of books and magazines than any in Berlin, and plenty of places to catch an inexpensive snack.

The compact town centre is surrounded by the Ring, a wide road built on the site of the old city wall (torn down in the last century). Most things worth seeing are within this ring. Leipzig was heavily bombed during the last war and restoration has been piecemeal, if not chaotic. But examples of grand, turn-of-the-century civic pomp survive dotted among the communist blandness.

The Neues Rathaus (New Town Hall), on Martin-Luther-Ring 2, dates from the end of the last century, and competes well with the University skyscraper for ugliness. At Dimitroffplatz, opposite, the Reichsgerichts-museum with the Museum für Bildende Künste (Museum of Arts, Picture gallery) is worth a visit just to look at the building. Farther along the ring is the Runde Ecke, where the dreaded Stasi had their headquarters. It now houses a museum about their activities. Across the park and back south is the Thomaskirche, where Bach spent the last 27 years of his life as *Kapellmeister* (music director). He is buried in the choir, and fans won't want to miss the Bach Museum, located in the Bosehaus behind the church, or the small monument in the park, which was erected by another Leipziger, Felix Mendelssohn, in Bach's honour.

Continue down Thomaskirchhof as it turns into Grimmaische Straße and you reach the Altes Rathaus, which dates from the Renaissance and has the longest building inscription in the world. It also houses the town history museum. The covered Galerie Mädler Passage across the street has been completely rebuilt, one of the older of the Passages which have sprung up in post-Wende times, attracting expensive shops and boutiques. In its basement is Auerbachs Keller, one of Germany's most famous restaurants. Goethe came here regularly to eat, and especially to drink, and used it as a location for a scene in his epic drama, *Faust*. Two bronze models at the entrance and paintings inside depict scenes from the drama. The restaurant, which is over 300 years old, was extensively refurbished in 1911.

Reichstraße leads past the Alte Börse, sparkling with its gilding, to Sachsenplatz, the city's main outdoor market. But turn just before the market to see the Nikolaikirche, Leipzig's proud symbol of its new freedom. This medieval church, with its Baroque interior featuring columns that imitate palm trees, is the place where regular free-speech meetings started in 1982. These evolved into the Swords to Ploughshares peace movement, which led to the first anti-GDR demonstration on Monday, September 4, 1989 in the Nikolaikirchhof. (Today, there is the excellent Kulturcafé in the church's former school.)

By November 6, 1989, the Monday Demonstrations had swelled into 600,000-strong rallies in Augustusplatz (formerly Karl-Marx-Platz) just down the street by the University. The crowd chanted *Deutschland Einig Vaterland* and *Wir Sind Das Volk* and listened to speakers like Kurt Masur, chief conductor of the Leipziger Gewandhaus Orchester (housed in the brown glass-fronted buildings on the south side), one of the world's finest orchestras.

Augustusplatz was a project of GDR communist party leader Walter Ulbricht, himself a Leipziger, and the staggeringly ugly skyscraper is supposed to represent an open book. Be sure to catch the inscription memorialising the Universitätskirche, a medieval building destroyed to make way for this eyesore. On the north side of the square stands the Opernhaus Leipzig (opera house opened in 1960), which also has an excellent reputation.

Wandering through the city centre, you can see many of the handsome, prosperous homes of Leipzig's industrialists that survived the ravages of recent history. Now most of the stores in the city centre built to cater for this elite have been restored. As a contrast, visit the offices of the Universität Leipzig, Augustusplatz, which have an impressive bronze bas-relief of Marx urging workers of the world to unite.

Tourist Information Leipzig
Richard-Wagner-Platz 1, Leipzig, 04109 (0341 7104 260/265). **Open** 9am-7pm Mon-Fri; 9.30am-2pm Sat, Sun.
The best stop for all enquiries. English is spoken here, and they can provide an excellent information booklet in a dozen languages.

Auerbachs Keller
Mädlerpassage, Grimmaischestraße 2-4, Leipzig 04109 (0341 21610 40). **Open** 11am-3pm, 5pm-12 midnight daily. **Average** DM35. **Credit** AmEx, D, EC, JBC, V
Both the menu and the wine list are of excellent quality at Auerbachs. Their specialities include Leipziger Allerlei, a dish of steamed mixed vegetables and mushrooms with crayfish.

Johann-Sebastian-Bach-Museum and Archive
Thomaskirchhof 16, Leipzig, 04109 (0341 7866). **Open** 10am-5pm daily. **Tickets** DM2; DM1 concs.

Leipziger Gewandhaus Orchester
Augustusplatz 8, Leipzig, 04109 (0341 12700/127080). **Open** 1pm-6pm Mon; 10am-6pm Tue-Fri; 10am-2pm Sat. **Admission** varies.

Museum für Bildende Künste
Dimitroffplatz 1, Leipzig, 04107 (0341 216990). **Open** 9am-5pm Tue, Thur-Sun; 1-9.30pm Wed. **Tickets** DM5; DM2,50 concs.

Museum in der Runden Ecke
Dittrichring 24, 04199 Leipzig (0341 29 44 05). **Open** 2pm-6pm Wed-Sun .

Opernhaus Leipzig
Augustusplatz 12, Leipzig, 04199 (0341 12610). **Open** box office 10am-6pm Mon-Fri; 10am-1pm Sat. **Admission** varies.
Call for information about tours of the building.

Weimar

Lying 50 kilometres south-west of Leipzig and across the state border into Thüringen (Thuringia) Weimar is known as Kulturstadt Deutschlands (Home of German Culture), and the European culture capital for 1999. It is a small, provincial town stuffed to the gunnels with monuments to the country's literature, music and other arts.

Goethe and Schiller both lived and worked here, although the town's charm is such that one can have an enjoyable visit without having read a word by either of them. Weimar was bombed heavily in the last war, but after decades of work, most of it has now been restored. Apart from writing, directing the State Theatre and working on assorted scientific theories, Goethe also held various posts in the government of Weimar. His house is now a museum, and the office where he did much of his writing has been preserved intact – complete with original desk, quills and paper at the ready.

Not very far off is the considerably more modest house (also now a museum) of Schiller, the first German to make a career out of writing plays. Both Schiller and Goethe had their plays performed at the Nationaltheater. The building was the assembly point of the 1919 conference which drew up Germany's first republican constitution, thereafter known as the Weimar Republic. Weimar was also the first German town to elect a Nazi-dominated council – an event which caused the Bauhaus, the famed school of design founded here, to move on to Dessau and Berlin. A small museum devoted to the Bauhaus now stands opposite the Nationaltheater.

Bach lived here and worked at the Stadtkirche St Peter und Paul on Herderplatz. The church is also known under the name Herder Kirche; it was built in 1498 in late Gothic style and renovated in early baroque style. In the mid-nineteenth century, when the Abbé Liszt arrived, music became a

Rügen Island – go out of season and enjoy the solitude.

focal point of town life. Today, regular concerts by the Hochschule für Musik Franz Liszt, the music school of which Liszt was first director, are of the highest quality. The Hochschule is at the Platz der Demokratie 2-3 (03643 652 41). Ticket prices vary.

The castle and former home of the court of Thüringen (Thuringia) is now a Museum, with a collection of Weimar artists from the turn of the century and a superb collection of Lucas Cranach the Elder, who lived here in the year preceding his death. It stands beside a large, handsome park which also holds Goethe's summer home. The town square houses an open-air market selling local specialities like the justly celebrated Thüringer Rostbratwurst sausage, and the Ratskeller has a good selection of inexpensive regional dishes. But for a choice of bars and cafés, explore the pedestrianised section of the town, especially near the Schillerhaus.

Weimar's plans for 1999, its year of being European city of culture, include a bevy of avant-garde art exhibitions and events, and the town is being scrubbed and rebuilt in anticipation. Up-to-date information on events and exhibitons can be found at *www.uni-weimar.de/weimar.*

Tourist Information

Markt 10, Weimar, 99421 (03643 240020). **Open** *Apr-Oct* 9am-7pm Mon-Fri; 9am-4pm Sat, 10am-4pm Sun. *Nov-Mar* 9am-6pm Mon-Fri; 9am-1pm Sun.
Not very helpful, and no English spoken, although some minimal brochures are available for purchase, and the city tours available here (10am and 2pm daily, DM8) can be had in English. Expect this to improve as 1999 comes on.

Castle and Museum: Die Kunstsammlung zu Weimar
Burgplatz 4, 99423 Weimar (03643 618 31). **Open** 10am-6pm Tue-Sun. Until 8pm Thur. **Tickets** DM6; DM3 concs; children under-6 free.

Deutsches Nationaltheater
Theaterplatz, 93401 Weimar (03643 75 50; telephone ticket service 03643 755 334). **Open** box office 2-6pm Mon; 10am-1pm, 4-6pm, Tue-Fri; 10am-noon, 3-6pm, Sat. **Tickets** DM9-DM40; half-price students, unemployed, pensioners.

Goethe House and Museum
Am Frauenplan, 4 (03643 54 50). **Open** 9am-5pm Tue, Fri, Sat, Sun; 9am-7pm Wed, Thur. **Tickets** DM5, DM2.50 students, unemployed, pensioners.

Ratskeller
Markt 10, 99420 Weimar (03643 641 42). **Open** 11.30am-midnight daily. **Average** DM30. **Credit** AmEx, EC, V.

Schiller House and Museum
Schillerstraße, (03643 54 50). **Open** 9am-5pm Fri-Mon; 9am-7pm Wed, Thur. **Tickets** DM5, DM2.50 students, unemployed, pensioners.

The Baltic Coast

The Baltic Coast was the favoured holiday destination of the ordinary GDR citizen; post-reunification it is now the most easily accessible seaside resort for all Berliners. The coast forms the northern boundary of the modern state of Mecklenburg-Vorpommern. Bismarck said of the area: 'When the end of the world comes, I shall go to

Rostock – attractive but melancholy.

Mecklenburg, because there everything happens a hundred years later.'

The large island of Rügen is gradually resuming its rivalry with Sylt in the North Sea – both islands claim to be the principal north German resort. In July and August it can get crowded, and Rügen's handful of restaurants and lack of late-night bars mean visitors are early to bed and early to rise. Go out of season and enjoy the solitude.

Rostock was one of the founder-members of the medieval Hanseatic League, and, until wrecked by bombing in the last war, was an attractive port full of grandiose, gabled merchants' houses and seamen's cottages. The GDR did a good job of putting Rostock back together again and, though it is no longer the vital trading link it once was, it is a quietly attractive, if slightly melancholy town, especially off-season. Much of the past flavour can still be found around the waterfront, where cafés, restaurants and hotels have recently opened. But Rostock's reputation has not yet recovered from the ugly racial incident in 1992, when people and police alike stood and watched as Neo-Nazis stormed and fired a hostel for asylum seekers.

Forty kilometres (25 miles) to the east of Rostock is Peenemünde, site of secret weapons development in the closing years of World War II. Here, a group of engineers and technicians produced the Vergeltungswaffen ('revenge weapons'), V1 and V2, and several rockets were fired from the island. Part of the complex has been preserved as a museum, and examples of the rockets are on display. After the war, both the Americans and Russians were quick to requisition the services of the scientists responsible for the rockets' creation. One of the boffins, Werner von Braun, became the leading expert of NASA's Apollo programme.

Fremdenverkehrsverband 'Insel Usedom'

Insel Usedom Tourist Information Office
Bäderstraße 4, Ueckeritz, 17459 (038375 7693). **Open** 8am-4pm Mon-Fri.

Fremdenverkehrsverband Rügen

August-Bebel-Straße 12, Ostseebad Sellin, 18592 (038303 1470/1). **Open** 8am-4.30pm Mon-Fri .

Regionalverband Mecklenburgische Ostseebäder

Goethestraße 1, Bad Doberan, 18203 (038 203 2120). **Open** 8am-5pm Mon-Thur.

Rostock Information

Schnickmannstraße 13-14, Rostock, 18055 (0381 4925260). **Open** *May-Sept* 10am-6pm Mon-Fri; 10am-2.30pm Sat, Sun; *Oct-Apr* 10am-5pm Mon-Fri, 10am-2.30pm Sat.

The Polish Border

The Polish border region is a must for World War II buffs, since it is the place where the Russians broke through the German lines to start the final assault on Berlin. But it is also a place of peaceful countryside dotted with relatively untouched villages that are quite unlike anything in western Germany. For anything but a day trip to Frankfurt-an-der-Oder, a car and a detailed map are essential, since transport in this part of the country is severely underdeveloped and the places referred to below are way off the usual routes. Floods in 1997 wreaked havoc with many of the small towns here, and reconstruction is still underway at press-time.

Frankfurt-an-der-Oder, is the central metropolis of the border region – a thirteenth century market town that was almost completely destroyed during the War. It has little to recommend it, since the GDR reconstruction was along the usual socialist architectural lines, leaving the centre with some vast open spaces ringed by concrete eyesores, including the 89-metre high Oderturm, built in 1976.

Frankfurt's chief virtue is as a jumping-off point to Poland to the east. A bridge across the river leads to the Polish town of Slubice, where flea-markets depressingly reminiscent of those on the U.S./Mexican border sell cheap cigarettes, meats, cheese, and horrid clothing and knick-knacks.

Seelow, just to the north of Frankfurt, is another thirteenth-century town that suffered horrible wartime devastation. The battle for the Eastern Front is commemorated at the Gedankstätte Seelower Höhen, a hill topped with a statue of a Russian soldier. Until 1990, no mention was made of the 12,000 German soldiers, mostly old men and boys from the Hitler Youth, who perished here, but today, the museum pays homage to both sides, and a slide presentation (available in English) with a light-up map and a rather tendentious narration will explain the struggle to break through and take Berlin. Going back south from Seelow, you'll find an even grimmer reminder in the recent German Military Cemetery in Lietzen, where so far 890 graves have been installed. Few of the inhabitants are over 20.

A drive through the villages near Seelow, in the area known as the Oderbruch, will turn up a

Russian war memorial in every village square. Neu Hardenburg has a Schinkel church, built as part of the reconstruction of the village after a disastrous fire, a project overseen by the teenage genius as one of his first projects. The Schloß was the family home of the Graf von Hardenburg, one of the plotters against Hitler, and it was here that he was captured by the SS and taken to Sachsenhausen. The Oderbruch was a special project of Friedrich the Great after his release from prison in Kostryzn across the Polish border, and he built a huge levee on what is now the German side of the river to control the flooding so that the area could be settled for agriculture. Wilhelmsaue has the area's only windmill, which is sometimes open as a museum. North of Seelow, Neutrebbin was a village personally founded by the king, and today it is a gem which hardly looks touched by the twentieth century, let alone the GDR. The statue of Frederick in the town square is brand-new, a replica of one melted down by the GDR authorities in 1953. The one in the town square at nearby Letschin, however, is original, albeit restored, and the centre of a hilarious story involving the innkeeper at the nearby Zum Alten Fritz and several of his buddies, who hid the statue in a cow stable and managed to drag it out as far as the bus-stop one drunken night in 1986. The steeple in the town's centre is all that remains of one of Schinkel's first churches, the only one the architect did in red brick. Accommodations are available in several Gaststätte in surrounding villages, and there is a small motel in Seelow.

Frankfurt-an-der-Oder Verkehrsverein
Karl-Marx Straße 8a, Frankfurt-an-der-Oder, 510230 (0335 325216). **Open** 10am-noon, 12.30pm-6pm Mon-Fri; 10am-12-30pm Sat; *summer* 10am-1pm Sun.
If their phone manner's anything to go by, don't expect an excess of help here.

Gedenkstätte Seelower Höhen
Küstriner Straße 28a, Seelow, 15306 (03346 597). **Open** 9am-4.30pm Tue-Sun. **Admission** DM2; DM1 concs.

Zum Alten Fritz
Karl-Marx Straße 1, Letschin, 15324 (033475 223). **Open** 10am-6pm Tues, 10am-11pm Wed, Thu, Sun, 10am-12am Fri & Sat. **Average** DM12.
Mammoth portions of typical Oderbruch cuisine in a family-run inn typical of the area. Ask to see the Frederick the Great room, with souvenirs of the notorious battle to rehabilitate the statue.

Dresden

Destroyed twice and rebuilt one-and-a-half times, the capital of Saxony currently looks like one huge building site. But among the tower cranes can be found one of Germany's best art museums and numerous historic buildings.

Modern Dresden is built on the ruins of its past. A fire consumed Altendresden on the right bank of the Elbe in 1685, provoking a wave of rebuilding throughout the city. On the night of 13 February 1945, the biggest of Sir Arthur 'Bomber' Harris's raids caused huge fire storms killing 30,000 to 100,000 people, mostly refugees from the Eastern Front. After the war, Dresden was

The Zwinger – Dresden's stately pleasure garden.

twinned with Coventry, and Benjamin Britten's War Requiem was given its first performance in the Hofkirche by musicians from both towns and soloists from Britain, Germany and the Soviet Union. Reconstruction of the old buildings under the GDR was erratic, but the maze of cranes and scaffolding now in place are evidence that Dresden is making up for the lost time.

Dresden's greatest attraction remains the buildings from the reign of Augustus the Strong (1670-1733). The Hofkirche cathedral (Am Theaterplatz 1), the Zwinger, a pleasure-garden containing a complex of museums, and the Grünes Gewölbe, a collection of Augustus' jewels and knick-knacks in the Albertinium, all give a flavour of the city's baroque exuberance. You get to them by leaving the Hauptbahnhof's Prager Straße exit and walking through the pedestrianised mall that competes with Alexanderplatz for the title of ugliest GDR public space.

Building was continued by Augustus' successor, Augustus III, who then lost badly to Prussia in the Seven Years War (1756-63). Frederick the Great destroyed much of the city in this war, although not the Brühlsche Terrassen in the old part of the city. A victorious Napoleon ordered the demolition of the city's defences in 1809. In 1985 the Semperoper (opera house), named after its architect Gottfried Semper (1838-41), was fully restored to its earlier elegance. Tickets are notoriously hard to come by (you can try to get them from the central theatre box office in Schinkel's Altstädter Wache on the main square). The Gemäldegalerie Alte Meister in the Zwinger has a superb collection of Old Masters, particularly Italian Renaissance and Flemish, including Raphael's Sistine Madonna, that belonged to Augustus (check the AR monogram on the frames) and there are also exhibitions of porcelain from nearby Meißen, and fascinating collections of armour, weapons, clocks and scientific equipment.

The industrialisation of Dresden heralded a new phase of construction that produced the Rathaus (Town Hall, built 1905-10) at Dr Külz-Ring, the Hauptbahnhof (1892-95) at the end of Prager Straße, the Yenidze cigarette factory, designed in the shape of a mosque (1912), in the Könneritzstraße, and the grandiose Landtagsgebäude (completed to plans by Paul Wallot, designer of Berlin's Reichstag, in 1907) at Heinrich-Zille-Straße 11. The finest example of inter-war architecture is Wilhelm Kreis's Deutsches Hygienemuseum (1929) at Lingner-platz 1, built to house the German Institute of Hygiene.

The Frauenkirche at the Neumarkt is, with the Schloß, one of the last of the bombed buildings to be reconstructed. Plans are underway to have the Altstadt reconstructed by the city's 1000th anniversary in 2006. The nearby Müntzgasse, with its pricey Hilton hotel, cafés and restaurants, is wryly referred to by locals as Wessistraße.

The magnificent **Semperoper**.

In the GDR days, this part of the country, behind the Saxon hills, could not receive western television or radio broadcasts and was called Tal der Ahnungslosen ('Valley of the Clueless'). Today's Dresden is catching up, with a vibrant alternative scene in the Neustadt, particularly in the bars and cafés on and around Alaunstraße like Schaune Café, Café 100, Planwirtschaft and Raskalnikov.

The Striezelmarkt (named after the savoury pretzel you will see everyone eating), is held on Altstädtermarkt during December every Year. This Christmas market is one of the most colourful events of the year. Dresden is also home to the best Stollen, a German variety of yuletide cake.

Dresden Tourist Information

Prager Straße 10, Dresden, 01069 (0351 495 5025). **Open** *Nov-Feb* 9am-6pm Mon-Fri; 9am-2pm Sun. *Mar-Oct* 9am-8pm Mon-Sat; 9am-2pm Sun.
Neustädter Markt, Dresden, 01097 (0351 53539). **Open** 9am-6pm Mon-Fri, 9am-4pm Sat., 11am-4pm Sun.

Albertinium (including Grünes Gewölbe)

Georg-Treu-Platz, Dresden, 01067 (0351 4953056). **Open** 10am-6pm Fri-Wed. **Admission** DM7; DM3,50 concs.
For details about museum Tageskarte *see below* **Gemäldegalerie Alte Meister.**

Altstädter Wache

Theaterplatz, Dresden, 01067 (0351 484 2323). **Open** *box office for the Semperoper* noon-5pm Mon-Fri; 10am-1pm Sat. **Tickets** DM5-DM65; DM8 students (occasionally), available half an hour before performance.

Gemäldegalerie Alte Meister

in the Zwinger at the Theaterplatz, Dresden, 01067 (0351 484 0120). **Open** 10am-6pm Tue-Sun. **Admission** DM7; DM3,50 concs. **Note**: If you intend to see several of the local museums, a much better alternative is a Tageskarte, DM10, DM5 concs, which will also get you into the armour and porcelain collection, the Schloß, the Albertinium complex, and other museums.

Mathematisch-Physikalischer Salon

in the Zwinger at the Theaterplatz, Dresden, 01067 (0351 495 1364). **Open** 9.30 am-5pm Wed-Mon. **Admission** DM3, in two instalments for the instrument and clock collections.

Semperoper

Theaterplatz 2, Dresden, 01067 (0351 484 20). **Open** box office see Altstädter Wache.

Hamburg

Art, culture, sleaze and beer in Germany's richest city.

The Freie- und Hansestadt Hamburg (Free and Hanseatic City of Hamburg), home of the flourishing Reeperbahn red-light district, the elegant villas of the Elbchaussee and most of the country's major publishing houses, has an important place in German history. The Hanseatic League was founded here as a protected trade zone stretching along the North Sea and Baltic coasts. The legacy of mercantile independence has continued to give Germany's largest port its unique character: Chancellor Helmut Schmidt turned down the Bundesverdienstkreuz (highest honour of the Federal Republic) because Hamburgers do not accept 'foreign' honours. Hamburg has always been a wealthy city and is today probably the richest in Europe: around one per cent of the population are millionaires. At the same time, there is a long history of Social Democracy and the SPD has a virtual monopoly of power in the Burgschaften (city parliament).

Hamburg is built on the lower reach of the Elbe, where the river is joined by the waters of the Binnen- and Aussenalster lakes (a fine view of both can be seen from the Kennedy Brücke). The city has more canals than Venice, although most are in the harbour area.

Much of Hamburg was destroyed during World War II, but subsequent restoration has created a generally attractive appearance. In winter, the city, located on the flat northern expanse that stretches from the Dutch coast to the Asian steppes, can be both bleak and bitterly cold. But in spring and summer, it is transformed by the abundant greenery lining its lakes and boulevards. Spend the days lazing on the water or in the parks recuperating from heavy club nights in Saint Pauli.

The nineteenth-century Hauptbahnhof (railway station), constructed to resemble a fortress, may be your first view of the town; try the roast mushrooms, a local delicacy, sold from the gallery above the platforms.

Nearby are a number of good, reasonably priced hotels; as well as the Deutsches Schauspielhaus (German Playhouse) which has a programme of everything from classics to musicals, with occasional live, large-screen video relays shown in the square. Within walking distance is the Kunsthalle (Art Gallery) on Glockengießerwall, which has an extensive collection of German medieval, nineteenth-century, Impressionist and Brücke movement artists.

Trip the red-light fantastic on the Reeperbahn.

North-east from the station is the area of St Georg. Along Lange Reihe are many good cafés, restaurants and ice cream parlours. Cut through leafy Danziger Straße on to Steindamm and then to Adenauer Allee for a more commercial atmosphere; in among the concrete and steel are several good nightclubs. Parts of the old town centre are pedestrianised with numerous street cafés and frequent al fresco music and cabaret performances (particularly at the Alter Markt).

On 7 May is 'Überseetag' (Overseas Day), a city holiday commemorating Frederick Barabarossa giving Hamburg the right to trade freely on the lower Elbe in 1189. A variety of events fill the week either side of this day, including the music festival, when all available spaces are occupied with open-air and usually free concerts by rock, folk, jazz and classical performers from around the world. The weather in May is usually particularly good, and the best time to experience the city.

The Reeperbahn on the far western side of the town is unrivalled in Germany for its permissiveness. A long, broad boulevard running practically to the harbour which provided the Reeperbahn with its original pleasure-hungry seagoing clientele, it is packed with over 300 venues. They include raucous drinking bars, where bands in sailor uniforms blast out popular melodies, cheap (and not so cheap) restaurants and kebab bars, and bordellos. The Star Club – where The Beatles played in their infamous Hamburg days – was at Große Freiheit 39, just off the Reeperbahn. Today the same street reverberates with sleazy cabaret sounds oozing out of sex bars and dubious oriental cafes. There's also the infamous side street, Herbertstraße, hidden by a metal barrier and eerily quiet, with men wandering around gaping at the women of varying age and beauty sitting in illuminated bay windows.

At the harbour end of the Reeperbahn lies Hafenstraße, once the scene of pitched territorial battles between squatters, punks, anarchists and riot police. Some oddly interesting, transient bars and clubs can sometimes be found in gone-to-seed stripjoints. There's also Harry's Bazaar: a musty, decidedly bizarre junk shop where sailors come to offload their sharktooth necklaces, stuffed armadillos and other weird souvenirs picked up on their travels. Behind its deceptively small shopfront is a maze of rooms packed with fascinating rubbish. Expect to pay a small admission fee refundable against any purchase.

Rather quieter but no less interesting is the traditional workers' district of St Pauli (with its celebrated football club) just north of the Reeperbahn. In its network of narrow streets and small houses, clustered round the main road Schulterblatt, you can find good, cheap Italian, Greek and Turkish food.

Altona was originally a separate community described in old Plattdeutsch as *all to nah* (all too near). Follow the Elbchaussee, lined with handsome villas and rows of smaller cottages built for merchant marine officers in the last century.

Hamburg – spot all the millionaires.

Explore the Rosengarten en route to the Altonaer Balkon hill, where you can get a good view across the Elbe. Its sandy shore is a favoured bathing spot in good weather.

The gigantic harbour (Hafengelände) occupies ten per cent of the city's area. Completely rebuilt and modernised after the last war it is now second only to Rotterdam as Europe's chief container port. Fascinating dockyard tours (Hafenrundfahrt) are run by HADAG, Hafen-Dampf Schiffarts AG; ticket office is at St Pauli Landungsbrücke 4. Boats leave half-hourly daily from 9am-6pm.

If you can get up early enough, join the throngs at the market at Landungsbrücke around 6am Sundays in time for the fishermen landing their hauls. Other sights include the Binnenalster, a lake in the centre of Hamburg which has a beautiful tall fountain (illuminated at night); and the Rathaus Markt, which has a memorial to wartime destruction and a handsomely rebuilt nineteenth-century Rathaus (Town Hall). Immediately south of here, the Hohe Brücke (High bridge) over the Nikolai Fleet affords a picturesque view of old warehouses and boats on the bend of the canal.

The south-eastern shore of the Aussenalster, An der Alster, is greener and a busy beach in summer, and home to the pricey hotels, Vier Jahreszeiten and Atlantic. To the north is the luxuriant Volkspark garden. Closer to the centre, Planten und Blumen Park and the Botanischer Garten next to it also feature music concerts in summer and a son et lumière fountain display every evening (at 10pm; 9pm out of season).

Hamburg also has one of the oldest breweries in the world, Gröningers, serving its dark and light beers as well as food in the claustrophobic lower ground floor rooms.

Hamburg is a good base from which to venture further afield to Friedrichsruh, where Bismark's family home has been turned into a museum. Off the coast to the north, the long, thin island of Sylt can be reached by train, bus or car, and has a beach stretching the length of its North Sea shoreline. It's a favourite destination for holidaymakers in and out of season.

Tourismus-Zentrale Hamburg
Burchardtstraße 14, 20095 Hamburg (040 30 05 10). **Open** 8.45am-5.15pm Mon-Fri.

Deutsches Schauspielhaus
Kirchenallee 39, 20099 Hamburg (040 24 87 13). **Open** *box office* 10am-6pm Mon-Sat; 10am-1pm Sun, holidays. **Tickets** prices vary. **Credit** AmEX, DC, EC, JBC, MC, V.

Gröningers Brewery
Gröninger Braukeller, Ost-West-Straße 47, 20457 Hamburg (040 33 13 81). **Open** 11am-midnight Mon-Fri; 5pm-midnight Sat. **Average** (meal) DM35.

Kunsthalle
Glockengießerwall, 20095 Hamburg, (040 24 86 26 12). **Open** 10am-6pm Tue-Sun. **Tickets** DM8, DM4 students, pensioners.

Prague

The stunning Czech capital offers a complete contrast to Berlin.

Just four and a half hours from Berlin by train – a beautiful journey on the stretch south of Dresden as the line winds through the mountains along the Elbe – Prague is both one of Europe's most stunning cities and a complete contrast to Berlin.

Unlike most European metropolises, Prague was never bombed. It still retains the look, feel and smell of genuine medieval stonework – the scent of old Europe. There's something ghostly, something dark, something eternal about this ancient city which has survived all the tragic events of the last millennium with barely a scratch. Prague is a city people come to visit for a few months and end up staying for years. But if you've only got a weekend, it's still more than worthwhile to surrender yourself to its mystery and confusion, its wild juxtapositioning of fragments, its jagged clash of old and new.

Sightseeing

Prague, which was ringed by walls right up until the nineteenth century, easily lends itself to sightseeing on foot. And when it all gets too much, there's a wide choice of art nouveau cafés and gothic wine cellars in which to recover.

Prague Castle

Hradčany's main feature is the hrad, or Castle. For over 1,000 years its silhouette has risen above the town, a symbol of the power of the city's rulers, politically and spiritually the centre of the country and still the presidential seat today. Founded in the ninth century by the Přemysl princes, it is not one single building but a complex of different structures. These have been built, destroyed, re-built and expanded until it now resembles a museum of architectural styles from the Romanesque period right up to the early twentieth century. The **Old Royal Palace** was home to six centuries of kings who systematically built new parts over the old, and behind the baroque façade of **St George's Basilica** lies the oldest piece of Romanesque architecture in Bohemia. Other sights worth seeing include the Italian Renaissance-style **Belvedere**: the first royal structure in Prague to be dedicated to pleasure-seeking rather than power-mongering. The extraordinary Golden Lane, where Kafka once lived, is a row of oversized doll's houses clinging to the northern castle walls and painted all the colours of the rainbow. And although the **St**

Strees that time forgot – imagine away the centuries in a Hradčany alley.

Vitus's Cathedral was only completed in 1929, it has always been a holy place, and is undoubtedly the spiritual centre of Bohemia.

The Belvedere
Belvedér
Pražský hrad, Královská zahrada, Prague 1. Metro Malostranská/12, 22 tram.

Old Royal Palace
Starý Královský palác
Pražský hrad, Prague 1 (33 37 31 31). Metro Malostranská/12, 22 tram. **Open** 9am-4.45pm daily. **Admission** 120kč family ticket; 80kč adults; 40kč concs.

St George's Basilica
Bazilika sv. Jiří
Pražský hrad, Jiřské náměstí 33, Prague 1 (33 37 31 16). Metro Malostranská/12, 22 tram. **Open** 9am-4.45pm daily. **Admission** 120kč family ticket; 80kč adults; 40kč concs.

St Vitus's Cathedral
Katedrála sv. Vita
Pražský hrad, Prague 1 (33 37 32 26). Metro Malostranská/12, 22 tram. **Open** 9am-noon, 12.30-4pm, daily. **Admission** 120kč family ticket; 80kč adults; 40kč concs.

Malá Strana

The name means the 'Little Quarter' or 'Lesser Town', and this is a typically Bohemian understatement for an area which contains monumental palaces and ornate, formal gardens, as well as grand baroque churches (such as the ornate **Church of St Nicholas** and the **Church of St Thomas**) and tiny, crumbling cottages. One of the principal sights is a 400-year-old wax effigy of the baby Jesus, Il Bambino di Praga, which draws pilgrims from all over the world.

Today, the character of the quarter is changing rapidly as accountancy firms, bankers and froufrou wine bars set up here. It's still remarkable, though, just how few businesses there are in what is one of the most central Prague districts. Malostranské náměstí now bustles with life all day and deep into the night, but this is mostly the result of the tourist trade and the area's many bars, restaurants and music venues. Apart from stores selling souvenirs and cut glass to the tourists, there is very little shopping in the area.

Il Bambino di Praga
(Pražské Jezulátko)
Kostel Panny Marie vítězné, Karmelitská, Prague 1 (53 07 52). Tram 12, 22. **Open** 8.45am-8pm daily.

Church of St Nicholas
(Chrám sv. Mikuláše)
Malostranské náměstí, Prague 1. Metro Malostranská/12, 22 tram. **Open** 9am-4.45pm daily. **Admission** 20kč adults; 10kč concs.

Church of St Thomas
(Kostel sv. Tomáše)
Tomáška 8, Prague 1 (53 02 18). Metro Malostranská/12, 22 tram. **Open** 10-11am, 1-6pm, daily.

St Vitus's – *Prague's spiritual centre.*

Staré Město

It's almost impossible not to get lost in Staré Město ('Old Town') and much the best way to get a true measure of its charm is to do exactly that. Originally settled in the tenth century it has always been where the nitty-gritty of the town's business got done. While the city's rulers plotted and intrigued high up on the hill, the good merchants of the town got on with the business of making a quick buck, a skill that is re-emerging in post-communist times as the inhabitants learn to wash the tablecloths, smile at the customers and quadruple the bill. Some of the sights well worth seeing are the **Astronomical Clock**, in action since 1490, Every hour on the hour between 8am-8pm crowds gather outside the old Town Hall to watch the wooden statuettes emerge from behind trap doors and enact a tale of medieval morality. The fourteenth-century **Bethlehem Chapel** is also worth a visit, as is the walk across Prague's oldest and most stunning bridge, **Charles Bridge**, which joins Stare Mestto with Mala Strana. The best time to come is at night when he castle is floodlit in various pastel shades and appears to hover above your head. At the stroke of midnight the switch is thrown and the Castle disappears into the night.

Astronomical Clock
Orloj
Staroměstské náměstí, Prague 1. Metro Staroměstská.

Bethlehem Chapel
Betlémská kaple
Betlémské náměstí, Prague 1. Metro Národní třída/6, 9, 18, 22 tram. **Open** 9am-6pm daily. **Admission** 20 kč adults; 10 kč concs.

Charles Bridge
Karlův most
Prague 1. Tram 17, 18.
Staré Město tower **Open** 9am-6pm daily. **Admission** 20kč adults; 10kč children.
Malá Strana tower **Open** 10am-5pm daily. **Admission** 20kč adults; 10kč children.

Staré Město – impossible not to get lost.

Josefov

Pařížská is the main street of Josefov, an elegant, tree-lined avenue of designer shops and airline offices, which leads from Old Town Square down to the Intercontinental Hotel. This is in sharp contrast to the rest of what was once Prague's Jewish quarter. These days it's more of a sad museum to a culture that no longer exists – and an overpriced tourist trap that swarms with visitors. The **Klausen Synagogue** is best seen from the eerie remnants of the **Old Jewish Cemetery**. If you can bear it go to see the 77,297 names painted on the inside of the **Pinkas Synagogue**, listing the men, women and children of Bohemia and Moravia who were dispatched to Nazi concentration camps and never returned home. And the **Rudolfinum** otherwise known as the House of Artists.

Klausen Synagogue
Klauzová synagóga
U starého hřbitova 4, Prague 1 (231 03 02). Metro Staroměstská. **Open** 9.30am-12.30pm Mon-Fri, Sun. **Admission** 80kč adults; 30kč children, students.

Old Jewish Cemetery
Starý židovský hřbitov
U Starého hřbitova, Prague 1. Metro Staroměstská. **Open** 9am-4.30pm Mon-Fri, Sun.

Pinkas Synagogue
Pinkasova synagóga
Široká 3, Prague 1. Metro Staroměstská. **Open** 9.30am-1pm, 1.30-5.30pm, Mon-Fri, Sun. **Admission** 80kč adults; 30kč concs.

Rudolfinum
Dům umělců
Alšovo nábřeží 12, Prague 1 (24 89 33 52). Metro Staroměstská. **Open** 10am-5.30pm daily. **Admission** 30kč adults; 15kč OAPs, 6-15 year-olds.

Nové Město

The 'New Town' is far from new and no longer a township. It was founded in 1348 by Charles IV, who'd had a premonition that the Old Town would be destroyed by fire and flood. The Old Town is still standing, but its far-sighted urban-planning, which led to the creation of wide boulevards and broad squares, has meant the area has adapted well to the rigours of modern life.

Here is where the real business of Prague daily life goes on: offices and department stores, cinemas and theatres, fast-food outlets and financial institutions are all located around here.

Wenceslas Square is the area's main artery. The square is a wide boulevard, half a mile in length, which rises up to the neo-Renaissance edifice of the **National Museum** – the backdrop to a thousand outside broadcasts in 1989. It has always been a popular place for staging revolutions, as it can comfortably accommodate 400,000 people.

National Museum
Národní muzeum
Václavské náměstí 68, Prague 1 (2449 7111). Metro Muzeum. **Open** *Oct-Apr* 9am-5pm, *May-Sept* 10am-6pm daily. Closed every first Tue of the month. **Admission** 40kc adults; 15kc concs. Free first Mon of the month.

Restaurants

Dining in Prague has improved immeasurably since the end of communism, and there are now close to 2,000 places to eat.

Bistrot de Marlene
Plavecká 4, Prague 2 (291 077). Metro Karlovo náměstí. **Open** 11.30am-4.30pm, 7.30pm-11pm daily. **Average** 550 Kč. **Credit** AmEx, MC, V.
Charming small restaurant with attentive service and a short menu of well-prepared traditional French dishes. – an excellent spot for a quiet business confab, a romantic tete-à-tete, or simply a damn good meal.

Parnas
Smetanovo nábje 2, Prague 1 (24 22 76 14). Tram 9, 18, 22. **Lunch served** noon-3pm, **dinner served** 5.30-11.30pm, daily. **Average** 1,000Kč. Set menu 895Kč. **Credit** AmEx, EC, MC, V.
Parnas and its adjoining café changed hands early this century and got the Art Deco treatment. The restaurant has preserved its sumptuous interior, which includes green marble columns, walls of inlaid wood depicting the signs of the zodiac and a mosaic over the bar entitled 'The Absinthe Drinkers'. Service is impeccable and the carefully-prepared international menu is one of the best in Prague.

Avalon
Malostranské Náměsti 12, Malá Strana, Prague 1 (530 263/530 276). Tram 12, 22. **Open** 11am-1am daily.
Average 395 Kč. **Credit** AmEx, EC, MC, V.
In the style of a California eatery offering a well-prepared range of grills, pastas, ribs, salads, sandwiches, seafood and Tex-mex items. Its location on Malostranské náměsti behind the baroque Church of St Nicholas is the main selling-point – the summer tables outside are a wonderful spot for lunch or dinner. Service is erratic but well-meaning.

Segafredo
Na příkope 10, Nové Město, Prague 1 (2421 0716).
Metro Můstek. **Open** 11.30am-1am daily; *café* **open** 8.30am-11.30pm Mon-Wed, 8.30am-1am Thur-Sat.
Average 480 Kč. **Credit** AmEx, DC, MC, V.
Given its coffee company franchise and location on one of the New Town's main tourist drags, this is a surprisingly good Italian place. While the busy café in the front serves coffee, croissants and drinks, dining takes place in a pastel-shaded back room. Probably better for lunch than dinner.

Klub Architektů
Betlemské náměsti 169, Staré Město, Prague 1 (2440 1214). Metro Narodni trida. **Open** 11.30am-midnight daily. **Average** 110 Kč. **Credit** AmEx, DC, EC, MC, V.
Low prices, excellent location and a selection of decent vegetarian dishes keep this place packed to the gills. Meat dishes are hearty and typical, though lighter than is usual for Prague. Outside there's a more limited menu, including a commendable pasta salad.

Noveměstský Pivovar
Vodičkova 20, Prague 1 (421 5999). Trams 3, 9, 14, 24. **Open** daily 11am-1am. **No credit cards.**
While enjoying some of Prague's finest, albeit pricey, microbrewery beer, you can also sample a good menu of upscale traditional Czech food. It's as close to an authentic Czech pub dining experience as your stomach will ever want to go.

Cafes, pubs & bars

The recreational drinker will think he or she has died and gone to heaven. Czech beer is the best in the world and incredibly cheap in Prague.

U Fleků
Křemencova 11, Prague 1 (24 91 51 18). Metro Národní třída. **Open** 9am-11pm daily.
The most famous pub in Prague, U Fleků has brewed fine 13 degree dark beer on the premises for centuries. You are automatically assumed to be here for the beer and well-drilled waiters keep you supplied. The courtyard is shaded by trees; Germans sing and swing glasses to oom-pah music within. Hair-raising atmosphere, but incomparable beer.

U Hynků
Štupartská 6, Prague 1 (232 34 06). Metro Náměstí Republiky. **Open** 11am-2am, pub open 11am-1am daily. **Average** 250kč. **No credit cards.**
Both a wine bar eatery featuring a range from Moravian Znojmo to French Saint Emilion, and a blues pub where frequent live wailing accompanies the quaffing of Lobkowicz beer and Murphy's Extra Stout. Both spaces are relaxingly dingy and attract a noisy young crowd.

Marquis de Sade
Templová 8, Prague 1 (232 3406). Metro Náměstí Republiky. **Open** daily 11am-2am (food until 11pm)
The Old Town's crossover bar, featuring a little bit of everyone who's out, and despite nightly live jazz, enough peace and quiet for them to talk to each other. Good bar for perch-

Heart of the matter – the Old Town Square.

ing, excellent location, mediocre but cheap salads and sandwiches, inexcusably poor Lobcowicz beer.

U Maleho Glena
Karmelitska 23, Prague 1 (no phone). Metro Malostranska; 12, 22 trams. **Open** 7.30am-2am daily.
Two-level pub in Malá Strana. Upstairs is intimate without being suffocating, sporting long wooden benches, margaritas and pita sandwiches. Downstairs you'll find a tiny bar that hosts jazz and reggae shows.

Akropolis
Kubelíkova 27, Prague 3 (no phone) Metro Jiřího z Poděbrad. **Open** Mon-Sat 4pm-2am; 4pm-midnight Sun.
Hip version of a traditional Czech pub, with funky decor, music veering between Eno and AC/DC, a vaguely hip crowd and friendly but occasionally overwhelmed staff.

Nightlife

Though Prague is no major metropolis of the night there is still plenty to do once the traditional pubs start closing between 11pm or midnight.

Radost FX
Bělehradská 120, Prague 2 (25 12 10) Metro IP Pavlova. **Open** 8pm-4am daily. **Average** 80 Kč.
Memories of when this was the hippest place in town have been trampled by guys named Sergio, along with all white except for small fluorescent orange backpacks. That's not to say it isn't worth checking out, especially when a good DJ is playing, but the dancefloor is small and isolated and the prices are high. The long bar can be fun, though, and there's a chill-out area and a bar, gallery and FX café upstairs.

Roxy
Dlouhá 33, Prague 1 (24 81 09 51) Metro Náměstí Republiky. **Open** Tues-Sat from 8pm; **Tea room** daily 5pm-midnight. **Average** 40 Kč.
The space is stunningly cool – a delapidated theatre with a balcony bar and a spacious dancefloor. The cover and drink prices are low but the music is inconsistent and the sound system inadequate. After 1am on Friday is the best time to catch what is probably Prague's best club.

Gay

Riviera Club
Národni třída 20, Nové Město, Prague 1 (2491 2249). Metro Národní třída. **Open** 9pm-6am daily.
Big and raunchy, the Riviera is the epicentre of the gay club scene. The clientele is mixed, though predominantly male. The neutral atmosphere can wear thin after a few visits, but this is a good general introduction to Prague's gay nightlife.

Directory

Directory

Essential Information

Climate

Berlin has a Continental climate, hot in the summer and cold in the winter, especially when the wind blows in from the surrounding lowlands. At the end of October temperatures can fall below zero and in January and February Berlin often ices over. Spring begins in late March or April. The average range of temperatures are: January to February -3°C to 4°C; March to May 8°C to 19°C; June to July 21°C to 24°C; August to September 22°C to 19°C; October to December 13°C to 3°C.

Crime

Though crime is going up, Berlin remains a reasonably safe city by western standards. Even for a woman, it's pretty safe to walk around alone at night in most central areas of the city. Avoid the eastern suburbs if you look gay or non-German. Pickpockets are not unknown around major tourist areas. Use some commonsense and you're unlikely to get into any trouble.

Customs

EC nationals over 17 can import limitless goods for their personal use, if bought tax paid.

For citizens of non-EC countries and for duty-free goods, the following limits apply:
• 200 cigarettes or 50 cigars or 250 grams of tobacco;
• 1 litre of spirits (over 22 per cent alcohol), or 2 litres of

fortified wine (under 22 per cent alcohol), or 2 litres of non-sparkling and sparkling wine;
• 50 grams of perfume;
• 500 grams coffee;
• 100 grams tea;
• Other goods to the value of DM125 for non-commercial use;
• The import of meat, meat products, fruit, plants, flowers and protected animals is restricted or forbidden.

Dentists

See **Health.**

Disabled Travellers

Only some U- and S-Bahn stations have wheelchair facilities; the full map of the transport network (*see pages 288-289*) indicates which ones. The BVG are slowly improving things, adding facilities here and there, but it's still a long way from being a wheelchair-friendly system. You may prefer to take advantage of the Telebus (*below*), a bus service for people with disabilities.

Berlin Tourismus Marketing (*below*) can give details on which of the city's hotels have disabled access, but if you require more specific information, try the Beschäftigungswerk des BBV or the Touristik Union International.

Beschäftigungswerk des BBV

Berlin's Centre for the Disabled
Bizetstraße 51-55, Weissensee, 10388 (927 0360). S8, S10 Greifswalder Straße. **Open** 8am-4pm Mon-Fri.
The Centre provides legal and social advice, together with a transport service and travel information.

Blisse 14 Sozial Therapeutisches Zentrum und Café

Blissestraße 14, Wilmersdorf, 10713 (821 1091/fax 821 5673). U7 Blissestraße. **Open** 10am to 11pm Mon-Fri; 10am-5pm Sat, Sun. **Office** 9am-1pm Mon-Fri. **Map C6**
The café-bar at this social therapy centre, designed specially for disabled people, is popular with a mixed clientele.

Gästehaus der Fürst-Donnersmarck-Stiftung

Wildkanzelweg 28, Frohnau, 13465 (406 060). S1 Frohnau. Call for prices
Berlin's only hostel that's specially adapted for people with disabilities.

Telebus-Zentrale

Esplanade 17, Pankow, 13187 (410 200). U2 Vinetastraße. **Open** (office hours) 7am-5pm Mon-Fri.
The Telebus is available to tourists if they contact this organisation in advance. A pass has to be issued for each user, so give plenty of notice. *See also chapter* **Getting Around**.

Touristik Union International (TUI)

Kurfürstendamm 119, Charlottenburg, 10711 (896 070). S45, S46 Halensee. **Open** 9am-6pm Mon-Fri. Call or write for appointment. **Map B5**
Provides information on accommodation and travel in Germany for disabled people.

Driving in Berlin

Though the city is increasingly congested, particularly in areas undergoing heavy construction, driving in Berlin, with its wide, straight roads, presents few particular problems. Visitors from the UK and US should bear in mind that, in the absence of signals, drivers must yield to traffic from the right, except at crossings marked by a diamond-shaped yellow sign. In the east side of the city, trams always have the

New word order

Learning German was never easy. The language is riddled with so many rules governing grammar and spelling that even native speakers can come unstuck when choosing where to put a comma, how to hyphenate a word, or just how many words can be stuck together to form one of those interminable compound nouns

With such complexities in mind, language experts, politicians and civil servants got together in the mid-1980s to dream up ways of making German easier. Over ten years and much philological hair-splitting later, the result was the *Rechtschreibereform* or 'correct writing reform'.

The reform included a cut in the number of rules governing grammar and spelling from 212 to 112 and in those governing commas from 58 to 9. Compound nouns were to be broken up and the use of the 'ß' would be restricted.

The reformers also proposed new spelling for words to reflect their etymological roots or common pronounciation. The verb *numerieren* ('to number'), for instance, would acquire a

second 'm' to show its provenance from the noun *Nummer*. The reformers also recommended Germanifying foreign words, so that in future people will eat *spagetti* or study *geografie*.

In 1996, the federal states passed the reforms, which are supposed also to be adopted in Austria and the German-speaking parts of Switzerland, Luxembourg, and northern Italy. They set August 1998 as the launch-date for their official introduction. However, the decision of some states (including Berlin) to introduce the reforms early in schools in 1997 unleashed a wave of popular protest. Parents went to court to protest against what they saw as a state diktat to change the common property of language. Writers such as Günter Grass raged against the bureaucratisation of language. Pleas have been made to the constitutional court, the highest body in the land, and the matter has been raised in parliament.

Thus, in a quick bit of backtracking another commission has been set up to consider a reform of the reforms.

right of way. An *Einbahnstraße* is a one-way street.

Parking

Parking is free in Berlin side streets, but spaces are increasingly hard to find. If you park illegally (pedestrian crossing, loading zone, bus lane and so on), you risk getting your car clamped or towed away. Meters are appearing in some areas.

There are long-term car parks at Schönefeld and Tegel airports (*see below*). Otherwise there are numerous Parkgaragen and Parkhäuser (multi-storey and underground car parks) around the city, open 24 hours, that will charge about DM3 an hour.

Schönefeld Airport Car Park

(6091 5582). **Cost** *1 day* DM15; *1 week* DM114; *2 weeks* DM163. **Credit** EC, Visa

Tegel Airport Car Park

(4101 3377). **Cost** *1 day* DM15-DM18; *more than 7 days* DM189-DM390 *per week.* **No credit cards**.

24-Hour Petrol

There are round-the-clock petrol stations on major roads throughout the city. Most also sell rudimentary groceries, chocolate, booze, condoms and cigarettes.

Breakdowns

The following garages offer 24-hour assistance. Like most German businesses, they are credit-card shy. Minimum call-out charge is about DM100.

Eichmanns Autodienst

Rothenbachstraße 55, Weissensee, 13085 (471 9401).

Abschleppdienst West

Mansfelder Straße 58, Wilmersdorf, 10709 (883 6851).

Drugs

By European standards, Berlin is relatively liberal in its attitude to drugs. Despite illegalities, possession of hash or grass has been effectively decriminalised. Anyone caught with an amount under ten grams is liable to have the stuff confiscated, but can expect no further retribution. Joint-smoking is tolerated in many of Berlin's younger bars and cafés. It's usually easy to tell whether you're in one. If in doubt, just ask – they can only say no – but be both considerate and discreet. Anyone caught with small amounts of harder drugs will net a stiff fine, but is unlikely to be incarcerated.

Drogen Notdienst

Emergency Drug Service
Ansbacher Straße 11, Schöneberg, 10787 (19 237). U1, U2 Wittenbergplatz. **Open** (for advice)

8.30am-10pm Mon-Fri; 2-9.30pm Sat, Sun, public holidays. **Map D4** Open 24 hours daily for emergency cases, with overnight stays possible. No appointments are necessary if you are coming for advice.

Education

There are over 160,000 students in Berlin: some 120,000 in the west and 45,000 in the east, spread between three universities and 17 subject-specific colleges (*Fachhochschulen*). Studies last at least four years but most students take longer, since many are forced to work as well as studying.

Since reunification and the selection of Berlin as Germany's new capital, the lot of students has worsened. Rents have risen, libraries and lecture halls are congested, while the official budget is eaten up by reunification programmes. *See opposite* **The student's lot**.

The Universities

Freie Universität Berlin

Kaiserswertherstraße 16-18 (central administration), Dahlem, 14195 (8381). U2 Dahlem-Dorf. What is today Germany's biggest university was founded by a group of students in 1948 after the Humboldt was taken over by East German authorities. It began with a few books, a Dahlem villa provided by the US military government and a constitution which gave students a vote on all decision-making bodies. It was to be free of government interference. But today, the huge anonymous university is far from being a community of professors, tutors and students. The AStA (Allgemeiner Studentenausschuß – General Student Committee) elected by the student parliament, now has no decision-making powers. The financial situation is also getting worse: more students, less books, less professors and tutors, fewer services.

Humboldt Universität zu Berlin (HUB)

Unter den Linden 6, Mitte, 10117 (2016 5850). U6, S1, S2, S25, S5, S7, S75, S9 Friedrichstraße. **Map F3** Berlin's first university, was founded by the humanist Wilhelm von Humboldt in 1810. Hegel taught here in the 1820s, making Berlin the centre of German philosophy. His pupils included Karl Marx. Other departments have boasted Nobel Prize winning chemists van t'Hoff and Otto Hahn; physicists Max Planck, Albert Einstein and Werner Heisenberg; and physicians Rudolph Virchow and Robert Koch. During the Nazi period, books were burned, students and professors expelled and murdered. When the Soviets reopened the university in 1946, there were hopes of a fresh start but these were stifled at birth by the GDR government. After the 1989 revolution, students briefly fought, with partial success, against plans to close whole faculties. Today jobs, not political activism, are the priority.

Technische Universität Berlin (Technical University, TU)

Straße des 17 Juni 135, Tiergarten, 10623 (3140). U2 Ernst-Reuter-Platz. **Map C4** Started life as a mining, building and gardening academy in the eighteenth century. With its focus on engineering, machinery and business, the university was given financial priority by the Nazi government. It was reopened in 1946 with an expanded remit including the social sciences, philosophy, psychology, business studies, computers and analytical chemistry. With roughly 40,000 students, the TU is one of Germany's ten largest universities. It also has the highest number of foreign students (17 per cent). There are special supplementary classes and a Language and Cultural Exchange Programme for foreigners (Sprach- und Kulturbörse, SKB), where you can take intensive language courses, join conversational groups, attend seminars on international issues and apply for language exchange partnerships. The SKB services are open to students at any Berlin university. For further information, contact:

Sprach-und Kulturbörse an der TU Berlin

Franklinstraße 28-29, room 3012, Charlottenburg (3142 2730, fax 3142 1117). U2 Ernst-Reuter-Platz. **Open** 10am-noon Tue; 2pm-4pm Thur. **Map C4**

Information

Studentenwerk Berlin

Hardenbergstraße 34, Charlottenburg (311 2313). U2 Ernst-Reuter-Platz. **Open** 9am-3pm Mon-Fri. **Map C4** The central organisation for student affairs and runs hostels, restaurants and job agencies.

Learning German

Goethe-Institut

Friedrichstraße 209, Mitte 10969 (259 063). U6 Kochstraße. **Open** 9am-6pm Mon, Thur; 9am-5pm Tue; 9am-2pm Wed, Fri. **Map F4** The Goethe Institute is well-organised, solid and reliable. Facilities include a cultural extension programme (theatre, film and museum visits), accommodation for students, and a media centre with computers. Evening and intensive courses last eight weeks and cost DM1,100 and DM3,090 respectively. Exams can be taken at the end of each course.

Tandem

Lychenerstraße 7, Prenzlauer Berg, 14037 (441 3003/fax 441 5305). U2 Eberswalderstraße. **Open** 11am-2pm, 4pm-7pm Mon-Thur; 11am-2pm Fri. **Map G1** For DM30 Tandem will put you in touch with three German speakers who want to learn English, and are prepared to teach you German.

Electricity

Electricity in Germany runs on 220V. To use British appliances (which run on 240V), simply change the plug or use an adaptor (available at most UK electrical-goods shops). American appliances run on 110V and require a converter.

Embassies & consulates

You can obtain a full list from Berlin Tourismus Marketing (tourist information office) for DM10 or look under *Botschaften* in the *Gelbe Seiten* (*Yellow Pages*).

British Embassy

Unter den Linden 32, Mitte, 10117 (201 840). S1, S2 Unter den Linden. **Open** 9am-noon, 2pm-4pm, Mon-Fri. **Map F3**

Irish Consulate

Ernst-Reuter Platz 10, Charlottenburg, 10587 (3480 0822). U2 Ernst-Reuter Platz. **Open** 10am-1pm Mon-Fri. **Map C4**

US Embassy

Neustädtische Kirchstraße 4, Mitte, 10117 (238 5174). S1, S2 Unter den Linden. **Open** 24 hours daily. **Map F3**

The student's lot

Students were responsible for brilliant insights into the physical sciences and philosophy in the nineteenth century, and a revolutionary fervour in the late 1960s that changed the face of German politics in the 1970s. Today, the only thing notable that the Berlin academic community seems to offer is a financial burden totalling millions of marks on the city coffers.

Until only a decade ago, being a student in East Berlin meant you were the hapless spawn of obsequious socialist functionaries, heading for a power job reeking of pesticides and swine faeces in some agricultural *Kombinat*. A bit more sophisticated in West Berlin, but hardly less escapable, it meant absolution from military conscription, generous support from the Federal government, and ten years of driving a taxi or tending a bar waiting for a break in your calendar to complete your final exams.

With something like 131,000 students, Berlin is Germany's largest university city. But it is a population under siege. The local government aims to slash student numbers to around 80,000 in the next few years. There's a virtual freeze on hiring professors and courses are being phased out. For the first time in the history of the Federal Republic, students are having to cough up symbolic amounts in enrollment fees.

With part-time jobs hard to come by, federal student support diminishing, and rents higher than in other German cities, most students lead frugal and fashionless lives. Ambitious ones get involved in small businesses on the side putting in only rare campus appearances. Either way, Berlin students don't travel in packs and are in general an inconspicuous lot.

Pursuing academic careers is hopeless as the city downsizes its university staffs, and suitable, non-academic jobs are simply not being created in the local market. That means graduates must bolt to other cities to escape unemployment. As a result non-locals have little incentive to develop the thick skin necessary for living among gruff Berliners and their often intolerable manners. Where students in Berlin used to live a carefree, fuck-the-system lifestyle, their T-shirts today read 'fucked by the system'.

US Consulate

Clayallee 170, Zehlendorf, 14195 (832 4087). U1 Oscar-Helene-Heim. **Visa enquiries** 8.30-11.30am Mon-Fri; **Consular enquiries** 8.30am-noon Mon-Fri.

Canadian Embassy

Friedrichstraße 95, Mitte, 10117 (261 1161). U6 Oranienburger Tor. **Open** 8.30am-5pm Mon-Fri. **Map F3**

Australian Embassy

Uhlandstraße 181-183, Charlottenburg, 10623 (880 0880). U15 Uhlandstraße. **Open** 8.30-1pm, 2pm-5pm Mon-Thur; 8.30am-4.15pm. **Map C4**

South African Embassy

Douglasstraße 9, Grunewald, 14193 (825 011). S7 Grunewald. **Open** 9am-noon Mon-Fri.

Health

EC countries have reciprocal medical treatment arrangements with Germany. All EC citizens will need form E111. British citizens can get this by filling in the application form in leaflet SA30, available in all Department of Social Security (DSS) offices or over the post office counter. You should get your E111 at least two weeks before you leave. The E111 does not cover all medical costs (for example, dental treatment) so you may wish to take out private insurance before leaving for Germany.

Citizens from non-EC countries should take out private medical insurance before their visit. German medical treatment is expensive: the minimum charge for a visit to the doctor will be DM60.

The British Embassy (*see above* **Embassies & consulates**) publishes a list of English-speaking doctors, dentists and other medical professionals, as well as lawyers and interpreters.

Should you fall ill in Berlin, take a completed form E111 to the AOK (Local Sickness Fund) and staff will exchange it for a *Krankenschein* (medical certificate) which you can present to the doctor treating you, or to the hospital in an emergency.

If you require non-emergency hospital treatment, the doctor will issue you with a *Notwendigkeitsbescheinigung* ('need certificate') which you must take to the AOK. They in turn will give you a *Kostenubernahmeschein* ('cost transferral certificate') which will entitle you to hospital treatment in a public ward.

All hospitals have an emergency ward open 24 hours daily. Otherwise, it is customary in Germany for patients to be admitted to hospital via a practising physician. For a complete list of

Directory

Vocabulary

Most west Berliners will have at least a smattering of English, though not all enjoy using it. In the east, Russian was the first language learned at school; although English is rapidly being acquired, it is useful and polite to have at least a few German words, especially if you intend to venture out of the city.

Pronunciation

z – pronounced ts
w – like English v
v – like English f
s – like English z, but softer
r – like a french r, throaty
a – as in father
e – as in day
i – as in seek
o – as in note
u – as in loot
ä – combination of a and e, sometimes pronounced like ai in paid and sometimes pronounced like e in set
ö – combination of o and e, as in French eu
ü – combination of u and e, like true
ai – like pie
au – like house
ie – like free
ei – like fine
eu – like coil

Useful Phrases

hello – *guten Tag*
goodbye – *aufwiedersehen, tschüss* or *tschau*
yes – *ja; jawohl* (formal)
no – *nee; nein* (formal)
please – *bitte*
thank-you – *danke schön*
excuse me – *entschuldigen Sie mir bitte*
sorry – *pardon*
I'm sorry, I don't speak German – *entschuldigung, ich kann kein Deutsch*
Do you speak English? – *sprechen Sie Englisch?*
sir – *Herr*
madam – *Frau*
waiter – *Kellner*
open – *offen*
closed – *geschlossen*
I would like... – *Ich möchte...*
how much is... ? – *wieviel kostet... ?*
could I have a receipt? – *darf ich bitte eine Quittung haben?*

how do I get to... ? – *wie komme ich nach... ?*
how far is it to... ? – *wie weit ist es nach... ?*
where is... ? – *wo ist... ?*
left – *links*
right – *rechts*
straight ahead – *gerade-hinaus*
far – *weit*
near – *nah*
street – *Straße*
square – *Platz*
gate – *Tor*
good – *gut*
bad – *schlecht*
big – *groß*
small – *klein*

Numbers

0 *null*; 1 *eins*; 2 *zwei*; 3 *drei*; 4 *vier*; 5 *fünf*; 6 *sechs*; 7 *sieben*; 8 *acht*; 9 *neun*; 10 *zehn*; 11 *elf*; 12 *zwölf*; 13 *dreizehn*; 14 *vierzehn*; 15 *fünfzehn*; 16 *sechszehn*; 17 *siebzehn*; 18 *achtzehn*; 19 *neunzehn*; 20 *zwanzig*; 21 *einundzwanzig*, 22 *zweiundzwanzig*; 30 *dreissig*; 31 *einunddreissig*; 32 *zweiunddreissig*; 40 *vierzig*; 50 *fünfzig*; 60 *sechszig*; 70 *siebzig*; 80 *achtzig*; 90 *neunzig*; 100 *hundert*; 101 *hunderteins*; 110 *hundertzehn*; 200 *zweihundert*; 201 *zweihunderteins*; 1,000 *tausend*.

---

hospitals in and around Berlin, consult the *Gelbe Seiten* (*Yellow Pages*) under *Krankenhäuser/Kliniken*.

AOK Auslandsschalter

Foreign Section AOK
Karl-Marx-Allee 3, Mitte, 10957 (253 181). U2, U5, U8, S3, S5, S7, S75, S9 Alexanderplatz. **Open** 8am-2pm Mon, Wed; 8am-6pm Tue, Thur; 8am-noon Fri. **Map G3**

Complementary Medicine

There is a long tradition of alternative medicine (*Heilpraxis*) in Germany and your medical insurance will usually cover treatment costs.

For a full list of practitioners, look up Heilpraktiker in the *Gelbe Seiten* (*Yellow Pages*). There you'll find a complete list of chiropractors, osteopaths, acupuncturists and

homoeopaths. Homoeopathic medicines are harder to get hold of and much more expensive than in the UK, and it's generally harder to find osteopaths and chiropractors.

Contraception & Abortion

Family planning clinics are thin on the ground in Germany, and generally you have to go to a gynaecologist (*Frauenarzt*).

The abortion law was amended in 1995 to take into account the differing systems which existed in east and west. (East Germany had abortion on demand; in the west abortion was only allowed in extenuating circumstances, such as when the health of the foetus or mother was at risk.) In a complicated compromise,

abortion is still technically illegal but is not punishable. Women wishing to terminate a pregnancy can do so only after receiving certification from a counsellor. Counselling is offered by state, lay and church bodies. Counsellors are not there to talk women out of having an abortion, though may seek to persuade women to think again. The following agency can advise you:

Pro Familia

Ansbacher Straße 11, Schöneberg, 10787 (213 9013). U1, U2 Wittenbergplatz. **Open** 10am-1pm Mon, Wed; 4pm-6pm Tue; 1pm-3pm Thur. **Map D5**
Free advice about sex, contraception and abortion. Best to call for appointment. Staff speak English.

Doctors & Dentists

If you don't know of any doctors or are too ill to leave

your bed, phone the Emergency Doctor's Service/Ärztlicher Bereitschaftdienst (310 031), which specialises in dispatching doctors for house calls. Charges vary according to treatment.

In Germany you choose your doctor according to his or her speciality. You don't have to get a referral from a GP. The British Embassy (*see above* **Embassies & Consulates**) will provide you with a list of English-speaking doctors, but many doctors can speak some English. They will all be expensive, so either have your E111 at hand or your private insurance document. The following are English-speaking doctors and dentists:

Dentists

Mr Pankaj Mehta
Schlangenbader Straße 25, Wilmersdorf, 14197 (823 3010). U1 Rüdesheimerplatz. **Surgery hours** 9am-noon, 2pm-6pm Mon, Tue, Thur; 8am-1pm Wed, Fri. **Map B6**

Dr Andreas Bothe
Kurfürstendamm 210, Charlottenburg, 10719 (882 6767). U3 Uhlandstraße. **Surgery hours** 8am-2pm Mon, Fri ; noon-7pm Tue, Thur. **Map C4**

General Practitioners

Frau Dr I Dorow
Rüsternallee 14-16, Charlottenburg, 14050 (302 4690). U2 Neu-Westend. **Surgery hours** 9am-11.30am Mon-Fri; 5pm-7pm, Mon, Thur;Thur; 4pm-6pm, Tue. **Map A3**

Herr Dr U Beck
Bundesratufer 2, Moabit, 10555 (391 2808). U9 Turmstraße. **Surgery hours** 9.30am-noon, 4pm-6pm, Mon, Tue, Thur; 9am-noon Wed, Fri. **Map D5**

Dr Christine Rommelspacher
Gotzkowskystraße 19, Moabit, 10555 (392 2075). U9 Turmstraße. **Surgery hours** 4pm-7pm, Mon-Fri. **Map C3**

Gynaecologists

Dr Lutz Opitz
Tegeler Weg 4, Charlottenburg, 10589 (344 4001). U7

Mierendorffplatz. **Surgery hours** 8am-2pm Mon; 8am-noon Wed, 3-7pm Tue, Thur; 8am-noon Fri. **Map B3**

Pharmacies

Prescription and non-prescription drugs (including aspirin) are sold only at pharmacies (*Apotheken*). You can recognise these by a red 'A' outside the front door. A list of pharmacies offering Sunday and evening services should be displayed at every pharmacy. For information, phone:

Emergency Pharmaceutical Services
(01 141). Open 24 hours daily.

Sexually Transmitted Diseases

For most problems, see a general practitioner.

Berliner Aids-Hilfe (BAH)
Büro 15, Meinekestraße 12, Wilmersdorf 10719 (885 6400; advice line 194 11). U9, U15 Kurfürstendamm. **Open** noon-6pm Mon-Thur; noon-4pm Fri. **Map C4**
The BAH runs a 24-hour advice line; information is given on all aspects of HIV and AIDS. Free consultations, and supplies of condoms and lubricant, are also provided. Staff speak English.

Deutsche Aids-Hilfe (DAH)
Dieffenbachstraße 33, Kreuzberg, 10967 (690 0870. U8 Schönleinstraße. **Open** 11am-5pm Mon; 10am-5pm Tue-Fri. **Map G5**
The Germany-wide version of the BAH (*see above*), which will also provide information on other sexual diseases.

Help-Lines

Alkoholkranken-Beratung (Alcoholic Advice Centre)
Gierkezeile 39, Charlottenburg, 10585 (348 0090). U7 Richard-Wagner Platz. **Open** (for advice) 3pm-6pm Mon; 2pm-4pm Tue, Fri. 10am-noon Thur. Outside of consultation hours, by appointment only. Telephone manned from 9am-noon, 1pm-6pm Mon-Fri. **Map B3**
Provides advice and free information on self-help groups.

KUB
Crisis & Advice Centre
Apostel-Paulus Straße 35, Schöneberg, 10823 (781 85 85). U7 Eisenacher Straße. **Open** 6pm-

midnight Mon-Thur; 10pm-8am Fri-Sun. **Map D5**
Free and confidential advice for people in need of emotional counselling.

Emergency Psychiatric Help

Psychiatrischer Notdienst
Horstweg 2, Charlottenburg, 14059 (322 2020). U2 Sophie-Charlotte-Platz. **Open** 6pm-midnight Mon-Thur; 3pm-midnight Fri-Sun, public holidays. **Map B4**
Staff will be able to put you in touch with your local psychiatric clinic.

Help & Advice Line
(080 0111 0111).
A crisis telephone line for the depressed and suicidal. The staff speak English.

Hitch-Hiking

Western Germany is quite hitcher-friendly but citizens of the east are less used to the practice. Thus, on major routes out of the city heading westwards, you should have little trouble getting a ride, but other directions may prove troublesome.

Mitfahrzentrale match car drivers to prospective travellers for a small fee. This is a safe and cheap method of travel. The following are among the many companies offering this service. *See also chapter* **Gay & Lesbian Berlin**.

Mitfahrzentrale am Alex
Alexanderplatz U-Bahn, in the hall between lines 8 and 2, Mitte, 10178 (241 5820). S3, S5, S6, S9/U2, U8 Alexanderplatz. **Open** 8am-8pm Mon-Fri; 8am-6pm Sat; 10am-6pm Sun, public holidays. **Map G3**

Mitfahrzentrale am Zoo
Zoo Station U-Bahn, platform of line 2 (Vinetastraße), Zoologischer Garten (Bahnhof Zoo), Hardenbergplatz, Charlottenburg, 10623 (194 40). U2, U9, S1, S3, S5, S7, S9, S75 Zoologischer Garten. **Open** 8am-8pm daily.

Internet

For internet access on a short visit, try one of the cybercafés listed below. If staying longer,

Snafu are reputed to be Berlin's best internet service provider. Call them on 2543 1112 or check their website at *www.snafu.de*. Websites with information about Berlin include: *www.berlin.de*; *www.zitty.de* and *www.berlinfo.com*.

Internet Café Alpha
Dunckerstraße 72, Prenzlauer Berg, 10437 (447 9067). Transport U2 Eberswalder Straße. **Open** 3pm-midnight daily.
Using one of their seven computers costs DM6 for 30 minutes. They're proud of their wine selection and also offer beer and assorted snacks such as omlettes and baked camembert.
http://alpha.berlinonline.de

Internet Café Haitaick
Brunnhildestraße 8, Schöneberg, 12159 (8596 1413). U9/S45, S46 Bundesplatz. **Open** 11am-1am daily.
Half an hour on one of their 11 machines costs DM6. Otherwise, expect beer, wine, baguettes, salads, assorted arcade games and a scanner. They also run computer and internet classes.
www.haitaick.de
office@haitaick.de

Website
Joachimstaler Straße 41, Charlottenburg, 10623 (8867 9630). U9, U15 Kurfürstendamm. **Open** 10am-2am daily.
As much a cyber-cocktail bar as a café, they have 40 computers (DM7 for 30 minutes) and virtual reality games plus courses on computers on the internet.
www.cybermind.de
cafe1@cybermind.de

Jaywalking

In Berlin, as elsewhere in Germany, jaywalking is a fineable offence. Even Berliners tend to view the little red man on the traffic light; ignore it and you may well find yourself reproached by solid citizens or spot-fined DM10.

Language Schools

See **Education**.

Legal Help

If you get into legal difficulties, the British Embassy (*see above* **Embassies & Consulates**) can provide a list of English-speaking lawyers in Berlin. If

you can't afford a lawyer, contact your local *Sozialamt* (social services office, listed in the telephone book).

Libraries

There are dozens of *Bibliotheken* (public libraries) and *Büchereien* (the same) in Berlin. To borrow books from them, you will need your stamped *Anmeldungsformular* (certificate of registration, *see below* **Residency**) and your passport. There will also be a small joining fee.

Amerika-Gedenkbibliothek
Blucherplatz 1, Kreuzberg, 10961 (690 840). U1, U6 Hallesches Tor. **Open** 3pm-7pm Mon; 11am-7pm Tue-Sat. **Map F5**
This library has a small collection of English and American literature.

Amerika-Haus Library
Hardenbergstraße 22-24, Charlottenburg, 16023 (3110 7406). U2, U9, S1, S3, S5, S7, S9, S75 Zoologischer Garten. **Open** 1pm-5pm Mon-Fri. **Map C4**

British Council
Hardenbergstraße 20, Charlottenburg, 10623 (3110 9910). U2, U9, S1, S3, S5, S7, S9, S75 Zoologischer Garten. **Open** 2pm-6pm Mon, Wed, Thur, Fri; 2pm-7pm Tue. **Membership** DM50 per year, DM20 for students or teachers. **Map C4**

Staatsbibliothek
Potsdamer Straße 33, Tiergarten, 10772 (2661). U1 Kurfürstenstraße. **Open** 9am-9pm Mon-Fri; 9am-5pm Sat. **Map E4**
Books in English on every subject are available at this branch of the State Library.

Staatsbibliothek
Unter den Linden 8, Mitte, 10102 (201 50). U6 Französische Straße. **Open** 9am-9pm Mon-Fri; 9am-5pm Sat. **Map F3**
This branch has a smaller range of English books than the above, but is still worth a visit. It contains a cheap café that's a good place to get into conversation with Berliners.

Lost or stolen property

If your belongings are stolen, you should go to the police

station nearest to where the incident occurred (listed in the *Gelbe Seiten/Yellow Pages* under *Polizei*) and report the theft and fill in report forms for insurance purposes. If you can't speak German, the police will call in one of their interpreters at no cost.
If you've lost a credit card, phone one of the emergency numbers listed below. All lines are open 24 hours daily.

Mastercard/EC/Visa
(0697 9330).

American Express
(0180 523 2377).

Diners' Club
(069 260 3050).

BVG Fundbüro
Fraunhoferstraße 33-36, Charlottenburg, 10587 (lost property 2562 3040/customer services 194 49). U2 Ernst-Reuter-Platz. **Open** 9am-6pm Mon-Thur; 9am-2pm Fri. **Map C4**
Contact this office with any queries about lost property on Berlin's public transport system.

Zentrales Fundbüro (Central Lost Property Office)
Platz der Luftbrücke 6, Tempelhof, 12101 (6995). U6 Platz der Luftbrücke. **Open** 7.30am-2pm Mon, Tue; noon-6.30pm Wed; 7.30am-noon Fri. **Map F6**

Maps

The city map of choice is the Falk Plan Berlin (DM10) – available in petrol stations, newsagents and bookshops around town. Falk's weird folding system make them difficult to open right out, but this map scores by providing house numbers, bus and tram routes as well as the U- and S-Bahn, places of public interest and most of the larger structures.

Money

The unit of German currency is the Deutschmark, abbreviated to DM. The DM is divided into 100 Pfennigs (pfg). Coins in use are 1 pfennig, 5 pfennigs, 10

Directory

pfennigs, 20 pfennigs, 50 pfennigs, DM1, DM2 and DM5. Notes come in DM5, DM10, DM20, DM50, DM100, DM200, DM500, and DM1,000 denominations.

Berliners prefer to use cash for most transactions, although the larger hotels, shops and most restaurants will accept one or more of the major credit cards (Access/Mastercard, American Express, Diners' Club, Visa) and many will take Eurocheques with guarantee cards, and travellers' cheques with ID. In general, the German banking and retail systems are much less enthusiastic about credit than their UK or US equivalents, though this is slowly changing.

If you want to take out cash on your credit card, banks will give an advance against Visa and Mastercard (Access) cards. But you may not be able to withdraw less than the equivalent of US$100. There are cash machines all over town, linked to the major international systems.

American Express
Bayreuther Straße 37, Schöneberg, 10789 (214 9830). U1, U2 Wittenbergplatz. **Open** 9am-6pm Mon-Fri; 10am-1pm Sat. **Map D5**
Holders of an American Express card can use the company's facilities here, including the cash-advance service.

Banks

Most banks are open from 9am to noon Monday to Friday, from 1pm to 3pm three afternoons a week, and from 2pm to 6pm on the other two afternoons a week (days vary).

German banks are notoriously bureaucratic. If you are staying long enough to warrant opening a German bank account, the Sparkasse (with branches all over the city) is much less trouble than arranging transfers. Otherwise, *Wechselstuben* (bureaux de change) are open outside normal banking hours and generally give better rates than banks.

Reisebank AG
In Zoo Station, Hardenbergplatz, Charlottenburg, 10623 (881 7117). U2, U9, S1, S3, S5, S7, S9, S75 Zoologischer Garten. **Open** 7.30am-10pm daily. **Map C4**
The Wechselstuben of the Deutsche Verkehrsbank offer among the best rates of exchange in the city. There's also a branch at Bahnhof Lichtenberg.

Opening Times
Shops

Shops can stay open until 8.30pm on weekdays, and 4pm on Saturdays. though many close earlier. Most big stores open their doors at 8.30am, newsagents a little earlier, and smaller or independent shops tend to open around 10am or later.

Many Turkish shops are open on Saturday afternoons and on Sundays from 1pm to 5pm. Many bakers open to sell cakes on Sundays from 2pm to 4pm. Most filling stations also sell basic groceries. *See chapters* **Shopping & Services** *and* **After Hours**.

Bars

Bar opening times vary considerably, but most start serving around 6pm and stay open until at least 1am, if not through until the morning. If the bar you happen to be in does close, there's plenty of opportunity to continue partying in cafés and clubs until dawn breaks. *See chapters* **Cafés & Bars** *and* **After Hours**.

Passports

By law you are required to carry some form of ID, which for UK or US citizens will mean a passport. If police catch you without one, they may go with you to wherever you've left it. But if the offence is trivial and you play the dumb foreigner, you'll probably get away with a telling-off.

Pharmacies
See **Health**.

Police

You are unlikely to come in contact with the German police, unless you commit a crime or are the victim of one. Most of the time they seem fairly distant figures, buzzing around town in their green and white vans, though they come out in droves for a riot. There are very few pedestrian patrols or traffic checks (and often they announce on the radio news which areas to watch out for).

Post Offices
Main Post Office
Postamt 120, Charlottenburg, 10612. At Zoo Station, Hardenbergplatz (3110 0234). U2, U9, S1, S3, S5, S7, S9, S75 Zoologischer Garten. **Open** 6am-midnight Mon-Sat; 8am-midnight Sun. **Map C4**
If your mail is urgent, send it from here and it should get to the UK in about three to four days. Letters to the States will take about seven or eight days. Letters for poste restante should also be sent to this post office, addressed: (Recipient's name), Postamt 120, 10612 Postlagernd. They can be collected from the counter marked Postlagernde Sendungen. Take your passport. Fax and Telex facilities are also available here, and at many modern hotels and some copyshops. Most other post offices (Post in German) are open from 8am to 6pm Monday to Friday, and 8am to noon on Saturday. Stamps are sold at all post offices. Letters and cards can be deposited in yellow mail boxes throughout the city. For non-local mail, be sure to use the Andere Richtungen (other destinations) slot as opposed to the Berlin slot. Letters of up to 20 grams (7oz) to anywhere in Germany and the EC need DM1.20 in postage. Postcards require DM1. A 20-gram airmail letter anywhere else costs DM3; postcards cost DM2.

Public Holidays

On public holidays (*Feiertagen*) you will find it very difficult to get things done, but most cafés, bars and restaurants stay open. Public holidays are: New

Year's Day 1 January; Good Friday; May Day 1 May; Ascension Day; Whitsun; Day of German Unity 17 June; Reunification Day 3 October; Day of Prayer and National Repentance third Wednesday in November; Christmas Eve 24 December; Christmas Day 25 December; Boxing Day 26 December.

Public Toilets

Berlin public toilets can be pretty scummy but the authorities have been trying to clean them up. Single-occupancy, coin-operated 'City Toilets' are becoming the norm. The loos in main stations are looked after by an attendant and are relatively clean. Restaurants and cafés have to let you use their toilets by law and legally they can't refuse you a glass of water – though of course they can get stroppy about it.

Religion

For up-to-date information on English-language services, contact the British or American Embassy. **Berlin Tourismus Marketing** (*below*) publishes an extensive list of churches, synagogues and mosques in Berlin.

The American Church in Berlin

Alte Dorfkirche, Zehlendorf, corner of Clayallee and Potsdamer Straße, 14169 (813 20 21). U2 Oskar-Helene-Heim, then bus 110. **Mailing address**: *Onkel-Tom-Straße 93, 14169.* **Services** 11am Sun. Holy Communion 11am 1st and 3rd Sun in month. Sunday school 9.30am Sun. International ecumenical congregation. All services are conducted in English.

International Baptist Church

Rothenburgstraße 13, Steglitz, 12165 (774 46 70). U9 Rathaus Steglitz. **Services** noon Sun. Sunday school 10.45am Sun. Prayer service 7.30pm Wed. Singles bible study Fri 7pm.
All services are conducted in English.

Catholic

St Hedwigs-Kathedrale

Bebelplatz, Mitte, 10117 (203 4810). U6 Hausvogteiplatz. **Services** 8am, 10am, 11.30am, 6pm Sun; 7am, 6pm weekdays; 7pm Sat. **Map F4**
Services in German. In Latin first Sunday of the month.

Islamic

Die Moschee-Islamische Gemeinde

Moshee Islamic Community
Brienner Straße 7-8, Wilmersdorf, (875 703). U2 Fehrbelliner Platz. **Services** 1.30pm Fri. **Map C5**
Services are conducted in English (prayers in Arabic). All religions welcome.

Jewish

Central Information Office

Fasanenstraße 75-80, Charlottenburg, 10623 (8842 0330). U2, U9, S1, S3, S5, S7, S9, S75 Zoologischer Garten. **Open** 8am-3pm Mon-Thur; 8am-1pm Fri. **Map C4**
The Information Office issues a monthly calendar of events listed on an information sheet and advertised every month in the magazines *Zitty* and *Tip*.

Repairs

There are few 24-hour emergency repair services dealing with plumbing, electricity, heating, locks, cars and carpentry. They usually charge a minimum of DM40 for a call-out, plus around DM25 per hour's labour, plus parts.

Water, Gas & Heating

Meisterbetrieb
(703 5050).

Kempinger
(851 5111).

Ex-Rohr
(6719 8909)

Lock-Opening & Repairs

For a local locksmith, look in the *Gelbe Seiten* (*Yellow Pages*) under *Schlösser*. Schlossdienst (834 2292) provides emergency assistance 24 hours daily.

Gas & electricity

In Berlin gas is supplied by Berliner Gaswerke (GASAG) while electricity comes courtesy of the Bewag (Berliner Kraft-und Licht AG).

Berliner Gaswerke (GASAG) Service

Torgauer Straße 12-15, Schöneberg, 10829 (78 720/ Emergency/Störungsdienst 787229). S1 Rathaus Schöneberg. **Open** 24 hours daily. **Map D6**

Berliner Kraft-und Licht (Bewag) AG Service

*Puschkinallee 52, Prenzlauer Berg, 12435
(2670/Emergency/Störungsdienst 2671 2525/heating 267 27106).* **Open** 24 hours daily.

Residence permits

For stays of longer than three months, you'll need a residence permit. EC citizens, EFTA citizens (from Finland, Austria, Sweden, Norway, Switzerland) and citizens of Andorra, Australia, Israel, Japan, Canada, Malta, New Zealand, the United States and Cyprus, can obtain this from the Landeseinwohneramt Berlin (*see below*).

A residence permit is free and can normally be obtained on the day of application. Appointments are not required but queues start at around 6am and you can expect a wait of up to two hours. Once you have queued it only takes a few minutes for the interviewer to process your application and grant you a visa. You will need your passport, two photos and proof of an address in Germany (your *Anmeldungsbestätigung* – a form confirming you have registered at the Anmeldungsamt, or registration office). If you have a work contract, take that along too and you may be granted a longer stay than you would otherwise.

Landeseinwohneramt Berlin

Friedrichstraße 219, Mitte, 10958 (6995). U6 Kochstraße. **Open**

Emergencies

The following emergency services are all open 24 hours daily.
Ambulance/Krankenwagen (*112*).
Fire Service/Feuerwehr (*112*).
Police/Polizei (*110*).
ADAC Auto Assistance/ADAC-Stadtpannendienst (*01802 222 222*).
Emergency Dental Service/Zahnärztlicher Notdienst (*8900 4333*).
Emergency Doctor's Service/Ärztlicher Notdienst (*310 031*).
Emergency Pharmaceutical Services/Apotheken Notdienst (*01 141*)
Emergency Veterinary Care/Tierärztlicher Notdienst (*011 41*).
Poisoning/Giftnotruf (*4505 3555*).

7.30am-2pm Mon, Tue, Thur; 1pm-7pm Wed; 7.30am-noon Fri. **Map F4**

If unsure about your status, contact the German Embassy in your country of origin, or your own embassy or consulate in Berlin. *See above* **Embassies & consulates**.

Smoking

Many Berliners smoke, and though the habit is in decline, there is a lot less stigma attached than in the UK or US. Smoking is banned on public transport, in theatres and cinemas and in many public institutions, but is tolerated just about everywhere else. Berlin bars can get exceedingly smoky and there is little that you, the visitor, can do about this except put up with it, join in, or take your custom elsewhere. It's normal for people to approach you in the street to ask for a cigarette, or for you to do the same. Leave a lighter and cigarettes on a bar or café table, don't be surprised if someone takes this as an invitation to help themselves.

Telephones

Phone Boxes

At post offices you'll find both coin- and card-operated phones, but pavement phone boxes are card-only. You can sometimes find a coin-operated phone in a bar or café. Phonecards can be bought for DM12 or DM50 at post offices and newsstands. The minimum fee for a call from a phone-box within Berlin is 30 pfennigs . If you're here for a while, the DM50 card works out cheaper in the long run by 5 pfennigs per call. Look for phone-boxes marked international and with a ringing-bell symbol — you can be called back on them. The post office at Zoo Station (*see above* **Post Offices**) is your centre for telecommunications. Here you can send telexes, faxes and use the metered pay-phones.

Dialling Codes

If you have any difficulty with codes, ring directory enquiries (*see below* **Operator Services**). Dialling within Berlin, no code is necessary.

International Calls

To phone Berlin from abroad, dial the international code (in the UK it's 010) then 49 30. To phone out of Germany dial 00, then the appropriate country-code: Australia 61; Canada 1; Ireland 353; New Zealand 64; United Kingdom 44; United States 1. For calls to the UK and Ireland, charges start at DM0,96 per minute. Calls to the US and Canada start at DM0,72 per minute and calls to Australia cost DM2,16 per minute at all times. You can call 0130 1118 to check the price at any time.

Phone books

Phone books for public use are found in all post offices. The Telefonbuch (three volumes) lists names of people and businesses alphabetically. The *Gelbe Seiten* (*Yellow Pages*, two volumes) lists businesses under category headings. The initial pages of the first volume give international dialling codes, telephone services and a useful list of services (administrative offices, social and recreational services).

Operator Services

All these services are open 24 hours daily.

Operator assistance/ Telefonauskunft German directory enquiries (*118 33*).

International directory enquiries (*001 18*).

Alarm calls/Weckruf (*011 41*).

Engineers/Störungsannahme, for phone repairs (*011 71*).

Financial markets/ Börsennachrichten (*national 011 68/international 011 608*).

Telegram/ Telegrammaufnahme (*011 31*).

Theatre and concert booking/Theater- und Konzertveranstaltungen (*011 56*).

Time/Zeitansage (*011 91*).

Traffic news/ Straßenzustandberichte (*011 69*).

Travel advice (*national and international 194 19*).

Weather/ Wettervorhersage (*011 64*).

Directory

'It's all sausage to me!'

Ever since Mark Twain's 'That Awful German Language', Deutsch has had something of a bad press. While French is regarded as a lover's tongue, and Italian can sound operatic even when reciting a shopping list, German is either grudgingly complimented for its philosophical exactitude, or else regarded as suitable only for snarling *verboten*. Rampant German polysyllabicisms can indeed be frightening – but then so can English words like 'polysyllabicisms'. Everyday Deutsch is actually rich in bizarre idiom and precise put-downs – many without English equivalents – and Berliners deploy them with zest. Here we present five crucial colloquialisms. Even if you don't get around to using any, they will at least make listening in to bar conversations a more edifying touristic experience.

Feierabend

Literally 'party evening', but when a barkeeper announces this at four in the morning, don't take it as an invitation to dance on the tables. It's actually a more poetic version of the English 'knocking-off time' or the cringeworthy American 'Miller time'. Bond with your local greengrocer by wishing him a *schön Feierabend* ('beautiful party evening') at the end of a long working day, and then nip right out for a *Feierabendsbier* yourself.

Scheißladen

A handy term which, once mastered, can be used time and time again on any visit to Berlin. Literally 'shit shop', but the word *Laden* can also mean a bar, club,

restaurant or any place where you part with your money and expect value in return. When the waiter forgets your order, the barman brings you the wrong drink, or you queue for 20 minutes only to find that some obvious item is out of stock and then get barked at by the shopkeeper, communicate your disdain for their establishment by spitting back *Scheißladen!*

Arsch

German swearing tends to the scatalogical. Literally 'arse', *Arsch* is German's most common amplifier. Weather can be *arschkalt* (very cold), goods might be *arschteuer* (extremely expensive) and someone who talks a lot of crap and gets on your nerves is an *Arschgeige* ('arse violin'). To be the recipient of an *Arschkarte* ('arse ticket') is to get the short end of the stick, if you're *verarscht* (or *gearscht*) you've been tricked or made a fool of, and when everything's going wrong all at once you say there's an *Arschprogramm* going on. Be warned: *Arschloch* ('arsehole') is a way more serious insult than it is in English. Avoid using it unless you want to end up *am Arsch* (fucked up).

Geil

The German equivalent of English 'wicked' or American 'awesome' literally means 'horny' as in 'gagging for it'. Berliners deliver the dipthong with great gusto: '*Guy*-ull!'

Wurst

The centrality of the sausage in German culture is evidenced in a wealth of idiom. For 'I don't care' try *Mir ist Alles Wurst!* – 'It's all sausage to me!'. When things are coming to the crunch, you might say *Es geht um die Wurst!* – 'It goes around the sausage!' And when someone's sulking tell them: *Sei keine beleidigte Leberwurst!* – 'Don't be an insulted liver sausage.'

Time

Germany is on Central European Time – one hour ahead of Britain, except briefly at the end of March and the end of September.

Germany uses a 24-hour system. 8am is 8 Uhr (or 8h), noon is 12 Uhr Mittags, 5pm is 17 Uhr and midnight is 12 Uhr Mitternachts.

Tipping

The standard tip in restaurants is ten per cent, but it is not obligatory. Check for the words *Bedienung Inclusiv* (service included) on your bill. In a taxi round up the bill to the nearest Mark.

Tourist Information

Berlin Tourismus Marketing

*Europa-Center, Budapesterstraße, Tiergarten, 10787 (250 025). U2, U9, S3, S5, S7, S9, S75 Zoologischer Garten.***Open** 8am-10pm Mon-Sat; 9am-9pm Sun. **Map D4**
There's always someone at this number who speaks English.

Universities

See **Education.**

Visas

A valid passport is all that an EC national needs for a stay of up to three months in Germany. Officially, within a week of arriving you are supposed to

register your address at the Anmeldungsamt (local registration office). To find the one in your district phone the Landeseinwohneramt (state registration office) on 6995.Take your passport and expect to queue.

However, your passport probably won't be stamped when you arrive in the country, so unless you need to register to enrol as a student or extend your stay beyond three months, don't worry about registering. *See also* **Residency**.

Working in Berlin

Berlin remains one of the most liberal and open cities in

Germany and offers a wealth of opportunity for people wanting to stay and work. However, the price of accommodation is soaring and the jobs market is beginning to shrink.

The small ads of the magazines *Zitty*, *Tip* and *Zweite Hand* (*see chapter* **Media**) are good places to start the search for work, but jobs are filled quickly so move fast. Teaching English is a popular choice: there is always a demand for native English speakers. Look for adverts around the city.

If you're a studying in Berlin, try the Studentische Arbeitsvermittlung (student job service). You'll need your passport, student card and a *Lohnsteuerkarte* (tax card), available from your local Finanzamt (tax office – listed in the *Gelbe Seiten*). Your tax is reclaimable: get details from

the tax office. Students looking for summer work lasting between two and four months can contact the Zentralstelle für Arbeitsvermittlung.

The British/German Chamber of Commerce publishes a list of English companies who have associates in Germany. There's a copy in the commercial department of the British Embassy (*see above* **Embassies & Consulates**).

The German equivalent of the Job Centre is the Arbeitsamt (employment service). There are very few private agencies. In effect, this makes looking for a job less hassle, as you only have one office to deal with. To find the address of your nearest office in Germany, look in the *Gelbe Seiten* under *Arbeitsämter*.

EC nationals have the right to live and work in Germany

without a work permit. UK nationals working in Germany have the same rights as German nationals with regard to pay, working conditions, access to housing, vocational training, social security and trade union membership. Families and immediate dependants are entitled to join them and have similar rights. For information about registration in Germany and residence permits (*see* **Visas**).

Studentische Arbeitsvermittlung (TUZMA)
Wilhelmstraße 64, Mitte, 10117 (226 546). U2 Mohrenstraße. **Open** 8am-6pm Mon-Fri. **Map F4**

Zentralstelle für Arbeitsvermittlung (ZAV)
Kurfürstendamm 206, Charlottenburg, 10719 (885 9060). U15 Uhlandstraße. **Open** 9am-noon Mon-Fri; 4pm-6pm Thur. **Map C4**

Getting Around

Berlin is served by a comprehensive and interlinked network of buses, trains, trams and ferries. Divided into three zones – though visitors will rarely stray beyond zones 1 and 2, making it effectively a flat-fare system – it's efficient and punctual but hardly cheap. Various ticket deals are detailed below.

The respective transport systems of former East and West Berlin have mostly been sewn back together, though it can still sometimes be complicated travelling between eastern and western destinations. Even within one half of the city, journeys can involve several changes of route or mode of transport.

Taxis are also efficient but also pricey, and subject to the same delays that currently affect traffic all over building-site Berlin. The city is excellent for cycling – flat and criss-crossed by dedicated bike paths.

Arriving in Berlin

From Tegel Airport
Airport Information (4101 2306). **Open** 6am-10pm daily. **Map B1**
Take buses 109 or X9 (the express version) to the Zoologischer Garten (known as Zoo Station or just Zoo) in the centre of the city. This costs DM3.60. From Zoo you can connect by bus, U-Bahn (underground) or S-Bahn (surface rail) to anywhere in the city. You will also find rail and tourist information offices at Zoo (*see below*). Alternatively, you can take bus 109 to Jacob-Kaiser Platz U-Bahn, or bus 128 to Kurt-Schumacher-Platz and transfer to the underground system, for which your bus ticket is valid (*see below* **Tickets & Travel Passes**); whether you use Kurt-Schumacher-Platz or Jacob-Kaiser Platz, depends on your ultimate destination, so pick up a free transport map at the airport (*see below* **Maps**). A taxi to the Zoo area will cost around DM30.

From Berlin Tempelhof Airport
Airport Information (69510). Flight Information (6951 2288). **Open** 6am-10pm daily. **Map F6**
Berlin Tempelhof is just south of the city centre on the U6 line. Connections to the rest of Berlin are easy. The U-Bahn station (Platz der Luftbrücke) is

a short walk from the terminal building, as are bus connections.

From Schönefeld Airport
Airport Information (60910). **Open** 24 hours daily.
The airport of east Berlin is a long way to the south-east of the city. Officials can still be over-scrupulous in the old east German way. A taxi to Zoo station will cost you about DM60. The 171 bus from takes you to the S-Bahn, which provides easy access to the east and west, with S9 going to Alexanderplatz, Friedrichstraße and Zoo (change at Ostkreuz for Bahnhof Lichtenberg), and the S45 taking a southern route to Westend. You can also take the 171 bus on to Rudow U-Bahn station and connect with the rest of the underground via line 7 (it's probably quicker to get to the Zoo this way than on the S-Bahn).

From Train Stations
Deutsche Bahn Information, Zoologischer Garten (Bahnhof Zoo), Hardenbergplatz, Charlottenburg, 10623 (19419). **Open** 5am-11pm daily. **Map C4**
Bahnhof Zoo is the point of arrival from most destinations to the west, including Hamburg, Hanover and Amsterdam. Bahnhof Lichtenberg, out in the wilds of east Berlin on lines U9, S5, S7 and S75, is the main station for destinations to the south and east,

including Vienna, Warsaw, Prague, Budapest, Dresden and Leipzig.

From Bus Stations

Information (301 8028). **Open** 5.30am-9.30pm Mon-Sat.
Buses arrive in west Berlin at the Central Bus Station on the Messedamm 8, Charlottenburg, 14057 opposite the radio tower (Funkturm) and the ICC (International Congress Centrum). From there, continue by U-Bahn line U2, direction Vinetastraße (station Kaiserdamm), to the centre. There is no bus station in the eastern half of the city.

Public Transport

The Berlin transport authority, the **BVG**, operates the bus, **U-Bahn** (underground, some of which runs on the surface), **S-Bahn** (surface rail, some of which runs underground) and tram networks. These, plus a few ferry services on the lakes, are all connected on the same three-zone tariff system. A DM3.60 ticket allows travel for two hours on all forms of transport in two adjacent zones. A three-zone ticket costs DM3.90.

Berlin is also served by the **Regionalbahn** (regional railway) which in former times connected East Berlin with Potsdam via the suburbs and small towns that had been left outside the Wall. It still circumnavigates the entire city. This is run by Deutsche Bahn and ticket prices vary according to the journey.

Renovation work on the S-Bahn system is almost complete, though there are still temporary disruptions. The final piece of the puzzle will be the northern segment of the inner Ringbahn – from Jungfernheide to Schönhauser Allee – scheduled for completion in 2000.

U-Bahn

The first stretch of Berlin's U-Bahn was opened in 1902 and the network now consists of nine lines and 163 stations. The first trains run shortly after 4am; the last between midnight and 1am, except weekends on the U1/15 and U9 lines when trains run all night. The direction of travel is indicated by the name of the last stop on the line.

S-Bahn

Under constant renovation for over a decade, the S-Bahn system is no longer the rattly ride through the city's 'ripped backsides' celebrated in Iggy Pop's *The Passenger*. It's especially useful in eastern Berlin, covers long distances faster than the U-Bahn and is the best means for getting to Berlin's outlying areas.

Buses

Berlin has a dense network of bus lines (155), and a restricted number (45) run in the early hours (*see below* **Travelling at Night**). The day lines run from 4.30am to about 1am the next morning. Enter at the front of the bus and exit in the middle. The driver sells only individual tickets, but all tickets from the orange or yellow machines on the U-Bahn are valid. Most bus stops have clear timetables and route maps.

Tram

There are only 28 tram lines, all originating in the east, though some have now been extended a few kilometres into the western half of the city, mostly in Wedding.

Maps

The Liniennetz, a map of all BVG U-Bahn, S-Bahn, bus and tram routes for Berlin and Potsdam, costs DM2 from ticket offices and includes an enlarged map of the city centre. A simpler, schematic map of the U- and S-Bahn can be picked up free at the same ticket offices or from the grey-uniformed *Zugabfertiger* – Customer Assistance personnel – who can be found loitering in some of the larger U-Bahn and S-Bahn stations. It is also reproduced on pages 288-289 of this Guide.

Tickets & Travel Passes

Apart from the *Zeitkarten* (longer-term tickets, *see below*) and the WelcomeCard (sic), tickets for Berlin's public transport system can be bought from the yellow or orange machines at U- or S-Bahn stations. These take coins and sometimes notes, give change and have a limited explanation of the ticket system in English. Once you've purchased your ticket, validate it in the small red box next to the machine, which stamps it with time and date. If you're caught without a valid ticket you will be fined DM60 on the spot. Ticket inspections are fairly frequent, particularly on weekends and at the beginning of the month, when they hope to collar miscreants who haven't renewed their passes. *See page 256* **Being controlled**.

The BVG says the current ticket system is unlikely to change in the near future, but prices listed here are set to rise sometime in 1998.

Single Ticket (Normaltarif)

Single tickets cost DM3.60 for travel within two zones or DM3.90 for all three zones (DM2.40 or DM2.60 for children between the ages of 6 and 14). Your ticket allows you to use the BVG network for two hours, with as many changes between bus, U-Bahn and S-Bahn and with as many breaks as you like – an excellent system for running around town doing errands.

Short-Distance Fare (Kurzstreckentarif)

The Kurzstreckentarif (ask for a Kurzstrecke) costs DM2.50 (DM2 concessions). It is valid for three U- or S-Bahn stops, or six bus stops. No transfers allowed.

Day Ticket (Tageskarte)

The Tageskarte allows travel anywhere in two zones (DM7.50; DM5 concessions) or all three zones (DM8.50; DM5.50 concessions) until 3am the day after validating.

Group Day Ticket (Gruppentageskarte)

Same as the Day Ticket for a group of up to five people. DM20 in two zones or DM22.50 for all three.

Longer-Term Tickets (Zeitkarten)

If in town for a few days with a family, the WelcomeCard is the way to go. For DM29 it allows 72 hours of travel throughout all three zones with up to three under-14s. If in Berlin longer, it makes sense to buy a **Sieben-Tage-Karte** (seven-day ticket), for DM40 for two zones or DM45 for all three (no concessions available).

A stay of over two weeks makes an

The little traffic light men

Nearly ten years on and the glue binding east and west has yet to dry. Easterners have conceded an entire political and social system, often grudgingly, but cling on stubbornly to a few surviving symbols. Probably no remnant of the GDR, not even the fate of the Palast der Republik, has caused such an uproar as the figures on eastern pedestrian crossing signs – the *Ampelmännchen* (little traffic light men).

It's easy to see why: they're cute and they're endangered. Designed in the 1960s by cartoonist Heinz Behling in cooperation with traffic psychologist Karl Peglau, *der Steher* and *der Geher* (the stayer and the goer) were intended to reach the elderly and the very young. Kids needed something they could identify with, and those with poor eyesight needed something they could see, so the little men are not only appealing and have funny hats, but their design covers more surface area than the glyphs used in the west.

But with unification came compliance with European Community standards, and they said the *Ampelmännchen* had to go. Not only that, argued the city, but the old housings in which they stood weren't environmentally

sound. Protests erupted. In mid-1996, the 'Rescue the Ampelmännchen' campaign committee was formed at Mondos Arts, a company specialising in 'Ostalgic' t-shirts. Enlisting Peglau and Behling, plus some artists who had used discarded *Ampelmännchen* in an installation at the Volksbühne, the committee started a website (*http://www.interactive.de*), began printing the icons on t-shirts and baseball caps and licensed the design to firms making other products.

It wasn't just a commercial move: although new traffic-lights are needed in the east to take advantage of computerised traffic-control systems, manufactured by Siemens, there's no reason why the old icons can't be retrofitted into the new housings, and today, although hundreds of the old lights have been replaced, some of the new ones contain *Ampelmännchen*.

There are still European Community rules to deal with, so victory may be short-lived, but the *Ampelmännchen* are on the move: souvenir shops are jammed with Ampel-paraphernalia, there's a book about the icons' history, and the little fellows have even shown up advertising patent medicine.

Umweltkarte ('environment ticket') economical. Get the basic card free from station ticket offices, and then purchase the validating stamp either there, or from a machine. This costs DM93 for two zones or DM104 for all three. This works for one calendar month across the network, and is transferable to other users. If you decide to settle in Berlin, buy a **Jahreskarte** (year ticket) for DM890 (two zones) or DM990 (all three zones). These are only available at ticket windows in stations and at BVG Customer Service.

Lost Property & Customer Services

BVG Fundbüro

Srauenhof Straße 33-36, 10587 (lost property 2562 3040; customer services 19449). U6 Ullsteinstraße.
Open 9am-6pm Mon-Thur; 9am-6pm Wed; 9am-2pm Fri.
The lost property office of the BVG. The building also houses the BVG's customer service department. Some of the staff speak English.

Travelling at Night

Berlin has a comprehensive **Nachtliniennetz** (night bus network) that covers all parts of town via 60 bus and tram routes running every 30 minutes between 1am-4am. Before and after these times the regular timetable for bus and tram routes applies. In addition, the U12 (Ruhleben to Warschauer Straße) and U9 (Osloer Straße to Rathaus Steglitz) lines run all night on Fridays and Saturdays, with trains every 15 minutes.

Night-line network maps and timetables are available from BVG information kiosks at stations. Ticket prices are the same as during the day. Buses and trams that run at night are distinguished by an 'N' in front of the number.

Note: The N16 to Potsdam runs only once an hour. S-Bahn lines 3 to 10 provide an hourly service. On lines N11 and N41 the bus will actually take right to your front door if it's close to the official route.

The BVG also operates a Taxi-Ruf-System (Taxi calling service) on the U-Bahn for people with disabilities and for female passengers from 8pm every evening until the network closes down for the night. Just ask the uniformed BVG employee in the platform booth to phone, giving your destination and method of payment, since you will have to pay the full taxi fare.

Boat Trips

Besides the BVG there are several private companies operating on Berlin's waterways.

Being controlled

In a hurry, short of change or simply succumbing to an anarchistic urge – sooner or later you'll end up taking advantage of the fact that in Berlin there's absolutely nothing to stop you walking on and off a train without paying. No turnstiles, no ticket collectors, nothing.

But retribution lurks. One minute you'll be sitting there, childishly proud of having bucked the system in this elementary fashion. The next minute you'll be surrounded by officials in blue uniforms, demanding to see your travel documents. Or some fellow passenger will suddenly whip out an ID card and reveal themselves to be secret agent of the BVG, the Berlin public transport authority. No ticket? 'Kommen sie bitte mit.' An interrupted journey and a DM60 spot fine are the almost inevitable result.

'Sie sind kontrolliert worden!', as they say in Germany. 'You have been controlled.'

Germans and expats alike translate the idiom thus. 'I was controlled yesterday,' someone will typically moan. Germans and long-term expats are oblivious to the macabre comedy of the phrase, conjuring as it does visions of electrodes to the head and sinister ticket collectors directing passenger movements with joysticks.

The phrase also broadens out to describe any brush with uniformed authority. Cold War Berlin was the world capital of being controlled. Eastern police, Western police, border guards, customs officials, Allied military police – at every turn there lurked officials empowered, in their various ways, to stop you, search you, detain you, inspect your documents, move you on or stop you smoking.

But the glory days are over and the U-Bahn *Kontrolleure* – 'controllers' – are the last remnant of this grand Berlin tradition. The plain clothes ones are hard to spot. Many wear leather jackets, but then so does half of the population. The 'Blue Meanies', as the uniformed variety are affectionately known, are less common these days, but stand on the platform so you're not sure whether they're coming on the train, or waiting to control anyone who comes off.

Controls are most common at weekends and the beginning of the month, when they trawl for people who haven't yet renewed their travel passes. They're less common after 7pm, though evenings are still no controller-free zone. Playing the innocent foreigner rarely works, unless you catch them just before their knocking-off time and manage to make yourself more trouble than you're worth. 'No, I don't speak German... no money... my passport is at my hotel... ' This strategy can easily backfire, though, and you'll end up sitting for hours in a little office on the station platform, filling in forms and cursing your luck.

Oh, and you can try and leg it, but be warned: solid citizens will leap out, tackle you, and smugly hand you back to the responsible authority.

Directory

Stern und Kreisschiffahrt GmbH

Puschkinallee 16-17, Treptow, 12435 (536 3600). S6, S8, S9 S10 Treptower Park. **Open** 7.30am-4pm daily.
Offers various cruises along the Spree and around lakes in the Berlin area. Departure points and times vary, but timetables are available from the company. A round trip will cost about DM15.

Reederei Heinz Riedel

Planufer 78, Kreuzberg, 10967 (691 3782). U8 Schönleinstraße. **Open** 8am-4pm Mon-Fri. *May-Sept* (also fair weather days in October) daily. **Map F5**
Fascinating excursions are offered which start in the city and pass through industrial suburbs into rural Berlin. Tours also leave in the other direction and explore Neukölln's waterways. A tour through the city's rivers and canals costs about DM19.

Taxis

Berlin taxis are numerous, pricey, reasonably efficient and frustratingly lackadaisical. You can walk for half an hour in the rain without seeing a single cab, and then find two dozen of them parked at a rank. Often they cruise in the outside lane and can't stop even if they see you.

The starting fee is DM4 and thereafter the fare is DM2.10 per kilometre (about DM3.36 per mile) for the first six kilometres. At night this rises to DM2.30 per kilometre (about DM3.68 per mile). For short journeys ask for a Kurzstrecke. For DM5 this will allow you to travel for 2km or 5 minutes, whichever comes first. These are only available when you've hailed a cab and not from taxi ranks. Taxi stands are relatively numerous, especially in central areas, and can usually be found near stations and at major intersections.

You can phone for a cab 24 hours daily on 261 026. In Treptow, Köpenick, Marzahn, Hellersdorf and at Schönefeld

---

airport the number is 33 66. Cabs ordered by phone start at DM6 rather than the normal DM4. Most taxi firms can transport the disabled, but require advance notice.

Most cabs are Mercedes. If you want an estate car (station wagon) ask for a 'combi'. There's also a company called Berlin Taxi which operates vans capable of transporting up to seven people. Call 813 2613.

Car Hire

Car hire in Germany is not generally expensive and all the major companies are represented in Berlin. Look under *Autovermietung* in the *Gelbe Seiten* (*Yellow Pages*) and be sure to shop around.

Bicycle Hire

The western half of Berlin is wonderful for cycling – flat,

well equipped with cycle paths and with lots of parks to scoot through and canals to cruise alongside. East Berlin is no less flat, but has far fewer cycle paths and a lot more cobblestones, tram lines and holes in the road.

Bicycles can be taken on the U-Bahn (though not in the first carriage) and on the S-Bahn (though only in carriages marked with a bicycle symbol) at the cost of a second ticket for the bike. The **ADFC Fahrradstadtplan**, available in bike shops for DM13, is an excellent guide to the city's cycle routes. The companies below are reliable and cheap bicycle-hire firms. Or look under *Fahrradverleih* in the *Gelbe Seiten* (*Yellow Pages*).

Bikes & Jeans

Albrechtstraße 18, Mitte, 10117 (281 6687). S3, S5, S6, S9/U6 Friedrichstraße. **Open** 10am-7pm Mon-Fri; 10am-1pm Sat. **Rates** DM20-DM25 per day. **Map F3**

Pedalpower

Pfarrstraße 116, Lichtenberg, 10317 (555 8098). S5 Nöldnerplatz. **Open** 10am-6.30pm Mon-Fri; 10am-2pm Sat. **Rates** DM10-DM19 weekdays, DM25-DM42 weekends.
They also have a branch servicing the Kreuzberg area, but you still have to call the above address first.

Bardt im Zentrum

Kantstraße 88, Charlottenburg, 10627 (324 7040). U7 Wilmersdorfer Straße/S3, S5, S6, S9 Charlottenburg. **Open** 9am-6pm Mon-Fri; 9am-1pm Sat. **Rates** 15DM per day, DM300 deposit. **Map B4**

Disabled Travellers

Telebus-Zentrale

Esplanade 17, Pankow, 13187 (4102 0123). U2 Vinetastraße. **Open** (office hours) 9am-6pm Mon-Fri.
Telebus, a bus service for disabled people (*see chapter* **Survival**), is available to tourists. You may be able to use this service at short notice if it's not too busy, but it's best to contact the office two weeks before your arrival in Berlin so that you can be issued with a pass that will guarantee you use of Telebus. The service runs from about 7am to 1am.

Business

The economic situation in Berlin has lately been far from rosy. With still-rising unemployment at a post-war high, the monumental cost of reconstruction in the East and the withdrawal of companies who had settled in West Berlin for now vanished Cold War subsidies, it's no wonder that the city's business community is focusing on the future.

The 1999-2000 move of the German capital from Bonn to Berlin – and with it a horde of politicians, government agencies, journalists and bureaucrats – should serve as a major boost to the lacklustre Berlin economy. New jobs will be created, especially in the service industry, and under-utilised real estate (Berlin has approximately 2 million square metres of vacant office space) will be snatched up, raising property values.

Also by the year 2000, the construction on and around Potsdamer Platz is due to solidify into huge office, retail and entertainment facilities. Daimler-Benz' computer services division, Debis, has already moved into their offices there, with Sony's European HQ and a score of other businesses on the way.

Not everything is in a standstill until the magic year 2000, of course. Berlin is, as it has been historically, a centre for both industry and R&D. There are more than 1,500 manufacturing companies registered in Berlin, and the city-state spends more on R&D than any other federal state, employing over 50,000.

One advantage unique to Berlin is its role as the easternmost Western city in Europe (or the westernmost Eastern city, depending upon

how you look at it). It has a long history of serving as the crossroads between east and west, and while this position was hardly enviable during the Cold War, Berlin is now a springboard for businesses looking to expand eastward.

Another advantage the city has is due, ironically, to the complete shambles in the east that was left by four decades of communist rule. The massive renovation necessary to bring the eastern half of town up to western standards means that Berlin is becoming one of Europe's most modern cities. Much of the infrastructure has been constructed (or reconstructed) within the past eight years – for example the around 60,000 kilometres of data-carrying fibre optic cable which has been laid since 1990, outwiring any other European metropolis.

PRACTICALITIES

German efficiency is based not on speed, but on method. Don't expect things to happen fast. Instead, nearly everything – from requesting a telephone to transferring money – will be done methodically, but slowly. But when things get done, they get done properly.

Be prepared for lots of form-filling. If you are signing any contracts you will need to have them notarised by a state-approved notary. By law you are required to be able fully to comprehend the terms of the contract which, if you cannot understand German, means it will need to be professionally translated. One way of avoiding this expense is to give your right of signature to a trusted German-speaking colleague or lawyer.

The same diligence is applied to the working week – arrive on time (early) and leave on time (early). Despite their reputation as a nation of workaholics, Germans now work less hours than anyone else in Europe. Lunch-hours devour afternoons and few are at their desks after 3pm on Fridays.

Finally, foreigners are often surprised at the extent of graft and corruption that accompany even small transactions in Berlin: another reason to be sure you work through a reputable law firm when doing business here.

Stock Exchange

Börsenverwaltung

Stock Exchange Administration
Fasanenstraße 3, Charlottenburg, 10623 (311 0910/fax 3110 9178/79). S3, S5, S6, S9/U2, U9 Zoologischer Garten. **Open** 9am-4pm Mon-Fri. **Map C4**
Groups wanting to be shown round the Börsengebäude (*see below*) should arrange the tours at these offices beforehand.

Börsengebäude

Stock Exchange
Hardenbergstraße 16-18, Charlottenburg, 10623 (315 100). S3, S5, S6, S9/U2, U9 Zoologischer

Garten. **Open** 10.30am-1.30pm Mon-Fri. **Map C4**
Individuals and small groups are permitted to the visitors' gallery during operating hours.

Banks

The following are the head offices for the major banks in Berlin:

Berliner Bank

Hardenbergstraße 32, Charlottenburg, 10623 (310 90/fax 3109 2548). U2, U9 Zoologischer Garten. **Open** 8.30am-1.30pm Mon-Fri; 3pm-6pm Tue, Thur. **Map C4**

Berliner Commerzbank

Potsdamer Straße 125, Schöneberg, 10783 (2653 3762/3953/fax 2653 2746). U1 Kurfürstenstraße. **Open** *9am-7pm Mon-Fri.* **Map E5**
This branch has an 'International Counter', the only such in Berlin, which will deal with your needs in English.

Deutsche Bank

Otto-Suhr-Allee 6-16, Charlottenburg, 10585 (340 70; fax 3407 2788). U2 Ernst-Reuter-Platz. **Open** 9am-3.30pm Mon, Wed; 9am-6pm Tue, Thur; 9am-12.30pm Fri. **Map C4**

Dresdner Bank

Uhlandstraße 9-11 (corner of Kantstraße), Charlottenburg, 10623 (31530/fax 312 4041). U15 Uhlandstraße. **Open** 8.30am-2pm Mon, Wed, Fri; 8.30am-6pm Tue, Thur. **Map C4**

IKB Deutsche Industriebank

Bismarckstraße 105, Charlottenburg, 10625 (310 090/fax 3100 9109). U2 Deutsche Oper, Ernst-Reuter-Platz. **Open** 8am-5pm Mon-Fri. **Map C4**

Embassies & agencies

American Embassy Commercial Department

Neustädtische Kirchstraße 4-5, Mitte, 10117 (238 5174/ fax 238 6296). S1, S2, S3, S5, S6, S9/U6 Friedrichstraße. **Open** 8.30am-5.30pm Mon-Fri. **Map E3**

American Chamber of Commerce

Budapesterstraße 16, Tiergarten, 10787 (261 5586/fax 262 2600). S3, S5, S6, S9/U2, U9 Zoologischer Garten, U2, U3 Wittenbergplatz. **Open** 9am-5pm Mon-Fri. **Map D4**

Berlin Chamber of Commerce

Hardenbergstraße 16-18, Charlottenburg, 10623 (315 100/fax 3151 0278). S3, S5, S6, S9/U2, U9 Zoologischer Garten. **Open** 9am-5pm Mon-Fri. **Map C4**

Berlin Economic Development Corporation

Wirtschaftsförderung Berlin GmbH
Hallerstraße 6, Charlottenburg, 10587 (399 800/fax 3998 0239). U2 Ernst-Reuter-Platz. **Open** 8.30am-5pm Mon-Fri. **Map C3**
Help for foreign investors settling in Berlin.

Brandenburg Economic Development Corporation

Wirtschaftsförderung Brandenburg Stadt Verwaltung,
Neuendorferstraße 90, Brandenburg, 14770 (03381 587 801/fax 03381 530 274). **Open** 9am-noon, 2pm-4pm Tue; 9am-noon Thur.
Ring for appointment to get advice on investment in Brandenburg.

Brandenburg Ministry of Economics

Wirtschaftsministerium Brandenburg
Heinrich-Mann-Allee 107, Potsdam, 14467 (0331 8660). RB Rehbrücke. **Open** 9am-4pm Mon-Fri.
Advice and assistance on investing in Brandenburg.

British Embassy Commercial Department

Unter den Linden 32/34, Mitte, 10117 (201 840/fax 2018 4157). S1, S2 Unter den Linden. **Open** 9am-noon, 2pm-4pm, Mon-Fri. **Map F3**
Basic assistance and advice for British business looking to set up in Berlin.

Senate for Economics and Industry

Senatsverwaltung für Wirtschaft und Betriebe
Martin-Luther Straße 105, Schöneberg, 10820 (787 60/fax 7876 3541). U4 Rathaus Schöneberg. **Open** 9am-3pm Mon-Fri. **Map D6**
Responsible for overall economic planning in the city. Will provide advice and guidelines for investors.

Business services

Accountants & consultants

The major international accountants and consultants are all represented in Berlin.

Bossard Consultants

Bleibtreustraße 38, Charlottenburg, 10623 (886 0694/ fax 883 6958). U15 Uhlandstraße. **Open** 8.30am-5pm Mon-Fri. **Map C4**

Deloitte and Touche

Lützowufer 33, Tiergarten, 10787 (254 6803). U1, U2, U15 Wittenbergplatz. **Open** 10am-6pm Mon-Fri. **Map D4**

EC Harris

Birkbuschstraße 10, Steglitz, 12167 (844 7840/fax 8447 8444). U9, S1 Steglitz. **Open** 10am-6pm Mon-Fri. A construction consultant: this bilingual office handles project management, cost consultancy and quantity surveying.

Price Waterhouse Consulting

An der Mühle 3, Tegel, 13507 (439 020). U6 Alt-Tegel. **Open** 8am-7pm Mon-Fri.

McKinsey and Company

Kurfürstendamm 185, Tiergarten, 10707 (884 520). U7 Adenauerplatz. **Open** 8.30am-5.30pm Mon-Fri. **Map C4**

Conference facilities

Aktiver Büroservice

Leibnitzstraße 58, Charlottenburg, 10629 (323 7588/fax 324 9638). U7 Adenauerplatz. **Open** 8am-5pm Mon-Fri. **Map C4**
Office services and conference organisers.

Messe Berlin

Messedamm 22, Charlottenburg, 14055 (30380/fax 3038 2325) U2 Thodor-Heuss-Platz. **Open** 10am-6pm. **Map A4**
The city's official trade fair and conference organisation, which can advise in setting up small professional seminars and congresses, or big trade fairs.

Regus Business Centre

Kurfürstendamm 11, Tiergarten, 10719 (884 410/fax 8844 1520). S3, S5, S6, S9/U2, U9 Zoologischer Garten. **Open** 8.30am-6pm Mon-Fri. **Map C4**
Offices for short-term rent, multilingual secretarial services and conference facilities in two central locations.
Branch: Lindencorso, Unter den Linden, Mitte, (0130 110 311).

Couriers

A package 1Kg (2.2lbs) or under within Berlin will cost you about DM15-DM30. These companies use both motorbike and cycle couriers.

Heikosprint

(2327 6660). **Open** 7am-7pm daily.

Messenger

(2355 0023). **Open** 24 hours daily.

Moskitos

(616 7900). **Open** 7am-5pm Mon-Fri.

Prices vary considerably, but a package under 1Kg (2.2lbs) delivered within Germany will cost about DM9, to the UK about DM16 and to America about DM30. It might be worth going to the post office and using their express service.

DHL

Kaiserin-Augusta-Allee 16-24, Moabit, 10553 (347 8511/fax 345 7762). U9 Turmstraße. **Open** 8am-6pm Mon-Fri. **No credit cards. Map C3**
Delivers to 180 countries worldwide. Overnight to most European centres and New York.

Federal Express

Friedelstraße 34, Neukölln, 12047 (0130 7573). **Open** 8am-7pm daily. **No credit cards. Map H5**

UPS

(0130 826630).

World Courier

Pariser Straße 35, Wilmersdorf, 10707 (881 7015/fax 882 5824). U1, U9 Spichernstraße. **Open** 24 hours daily. **No credit cards. Map C5**

Estate agents

The estate agents listed below will do business with you in English.

Healey and Baker

Mommsenstraße 68, Charlottenburg, 10629 (882 5724/fax 882 5670). U15 Uhlandstraße. **Open** 9am-5.30pm Mon-Fri. **Map C4**

Saddelhoff Deutschland

Friedrichstraße 60, Mitte, 10117 (201 7050/fax 201 7011). U6 Französischestraße. **Open** 8.30am-6pm Mon-Fri. **Map C4**

Jones Lang Wooton Investment Team Berlin

Charlottenstraße 57, Mitte, 10117 (203 9800/fax 2039 8040). U6, S1, S2, S25, S3, S5, S7, S75. U6 Friedrichstraße. **Open** 10am-5pm Mon-Fri. **Map F3**

Office equipment

L&W Büroeinrichtungen

Groß-Berliner Damm 73C, Treptow, 12487 (639 9630). S-bahn Schöneweide. **Open** 10am-6pm Mon-Fri; 10am-2pm Sat. **Credit** EC, V. Furniture, office software and communications technology.

Pärschke Bürobedarf

Potsdamer Straße 98, Tiergarten, 10785 (264 9130/fax 2649 1326). U1 Kurfürstenstraße. **Open** 9am-6pm Mon-Fri. **Credit** EC V. **Map E4**
A large supply of office essentials, stationery and gimmicks.

Lawyers

The British Embassy (*see above* **Embassies & consulates**) can supply a list of English-speaking lawyers. Here are two that specialise in commercial law and speak English:

Guentsche and Partner

Hr. Johann Peter Sieveking, Hubertusbader Straße 14a, Grünewald, 14193 (825 2085/fax 825 2080). S3 Grünewald. **Open** 9am-6.30pm Mon-Fri.

Peter Evers

Oliver Platz 16, Charlottenburg, 10707 (880 3300/fax 880 3330). U7 Adenauer Platz. **Open** 10am-6pm Mon-Fri. **Map C5**

Relocation Services

The following offer assistance in looking for homes and schools, and will help deal with residence and work permits.

Hardenberg Concept

Burgunder Straße 5, Nikolassee, 14129 (8040 2646). S1, S7 Nikolassee. **Open** 9am-6pm Mon-Fri.

Regus Business Centre

Kurfürstendamm 11, Charlottenburg, 10719 (2092 4000). U9, U15 Kurfürstendamm. **Open** 9am-6pm Mon-Fri. **Map C4**

Staff hire agencies

Here are two temp agencies specialising in technical and sales personnel. A secretary will cost about DM35 an hour.

City Büro

Wexstraße 1 (on Innsbrucker Platz), 10825 (854 1094/fax 854 1097). U4 Innsbrucker Platz. **Open** 8am-4.30pm Mon-Fri. **Map D6**

Personal Partner

Tauentzienstraße 18A, Schöneberg, 10789 (213 1051/fax2 13 2527). U1 Wittenbergplatz. **Open** 8am-4.30pm Mon-Fri. **Map D4**

This agency places multi-lingual secretarial staff.

Translators & interpreters

See also *Übersetzungen* in the *Gelbe Seiten* (*Yellow Pages*) for other translation services. A thousand words will cost about DM500 at professional rates.

Amerikanisch/Englisch Übersetzerteam

Kurfürstendamm 11, Tiergarten, 10711 (881 6746). U9, U15 Kurfürstendamm. **Open** 9am-5pm Mon-Fri. **Map C4**

Specialists in English-language business, technical and legal documents.

K Hilau Übersetzungsdienst

Innsbrucker Straße 58, Schöneberg, *10825 (781 75 84/fax782 2680). U4, U7 Bayerischer Platz.* **Open** 10am-5pm Mon-Fri. **Map D6**

Interpreters for Italian, English, Spanish, French and Arabic. They specialise in the translation of legal, technical and business documents.

Scharpe & Arend Simultaneous Translations

Perelsplatz, Friedenau, 12159 (859 9180/fax 851 8220). U9 Bundesplatz. **Open** 9am-5pm Mon-Fri. **Map D6**

Women

Berlin has an enormous network of organisations for women, from feminist-run garages and carpenters' associations to hotels, didgeridoo classes and even brothels. This well-endowed infrastructure is a testament to the self-confidence of women in a city which, over the last two centuries, has nurtured a distinguished array of female politicans, thinkers and artists.

However, women in 1990s Berlin are still reeling from the shock of reunification. Many cafés, bars and other subsidised projects have closed due to a lack of government funds. Women have also borne the brunt of soaring unemployment, particularly those in the east who were fired in droves after the collapse of the GDR. The same women have had a hard time adapting to the west German version of womanhood, which, for all its freedoms, tends to cast men in the role of breadwinner.

In addition to jobs, easterners lost rights to comprehensive childcare and abortion-on-demand, which was replaced in 1992 by a less liberal law involving compulsory consultations with at least two doctors. They responded to all this by simply not having children. Berlin's birth rate plummeted to one of the lowest in Europe. The result, almost ten years on, is a dearth of children and lots of empty kindergartens.

Despite present economic woes, Berlin's women can look back on a long tradition of success and distinction. In the late eighteenth century intellectuals such as Henrietta Herz and Rahel Varnhagen von Else advanced the cause of emancipation by setting up literary and cultural salons. Another key figure was the communist Clara Zetkin – after the 1871 unification of Germany she presented her groundbreaking 'Theory of Emancipation' before going on to orchestrate the campaign for women's suffrage. The vote for women was eventually won in 1919, the year which saw the murder by the Freikorps of another great revolutionary, Rosa Luxemburg. During the inter-war years women began to make significant inroads into the world of arts and entertainment – before being stripped of their rights by the Nazis. Marlene Dietrich shot to international fame as the femme fatale in Josef von Sternberg's *Der blaue Engel*, and the Anita Berber, immortalised in red by painter Otto Dix, gained notoriety as the city's first nude dancer. After the war it was the *Trümmerfrauen* ('Rubble Women') who rebuilt the city. And in the late 1960s, it was the women of Berlin who instigated a nationwide protest against the country's restrictive abortion legislation.

Such achievements are seared into the consciousness of Berlin women, who tend to be independent, self-assured and aware of their rights. This can be seen in their relationships with men who, after years of feminism, are unlikely to confer unwanted attentions – or even chat you up at all for that matter. The upside is that women can usually move through the city without being hassled – Berlin is safer than most west European capitals. But it also means that women have to use their initiative if looking for conversation or 'interaction' with men other than rose-sellers and tourists.

Help & information

The monthly German-language women's calendar and magazine, *Blattgold* (DM5), will help you negotiate the bewildering number of women's events in Berlin. It's on sale at health food shops and women's cafés. *Selbständige Frauen* ('Independent Women'), a directory of women's businesses in Berlin and Potsdam, is available at women's centres or through Weiberwirtschaft (*see below*).

Directory

Frauenkrisentelefon

(615 4243). **Open** 10am-noon Mon;
10am-noon Thur; 7pm-9pm Tue,
Wed, Fri; 5pm-7pm Sat, Sun.
Women's helpline offers advice and
information on anything and
everything.

Notruf (rape crisis phone line)

(251 2828). **Open** 6pm-9pm Tue,
Thur; noon-2pm Sun; answering
machine at other times.
Advice and help on rape and sexual
harassment, as well as help dealing
with the police and doctors.

Accommodation

artemisia

*Brandenburgische Straße 18,
Wilmersdorf, 10707 (873 8905). U7
Konstanzer Straße.* **Rates** single
DM159; double DM220. **Credit**
AmEx, DC, EC, V. **Map B5**
A shabby elevator brings you to the
fourth floor of this art nouveau
building near the Ku'damm, where
Germany's first and Berlin's only
women-only hotel opened in 1989.
The artemisia is comfortable and
bright. Each room is dedicated to a
famous woman from Berlin's history.
The breakfast buffet on the first floor
is a treat. There are two conference
rooms, and the hotel welcomes groups
and business women. Further extras:
a roof terrace, a small bar and a
Queen's Suite.

Art & museums

Goldrausch Künstlerinnenprojekt

*Dircksenstraße 47, Mitte, 10178
(283 2776). S3, S5, S7, S9
Hackescher Markt.* Answering
Machine. **Map G3**
Organises year-long seminars for
women artists, as well as exhibitions
at venues across the city.

Das Verborgene Museum

The Hidden Museum
*Schlüterstraße 70, Charlottenburg,
10625 (313 3656). S3, S5, S7, S9
Savignyplatz.* **Open** 3pm-7pm Thur,
Fri; noon-4pm Sun. **Map C4**
The amount of art by women that is
rotting unseen in Berlin's museum cellars is alarming. With temporary
exhibitions and lectures, the Hidden
Museum tries to rescue female artists
from historical oblivion.

Baths & massage

Hamam Turkish Bath

*Schoko-Fabrik, Naunynstraße 72,
Kreuzberg, 10997 (615 1464). U1*

Kottbusser Tor. **Open** 3pm-10pm
Mon; noon-10pm Tue-Sun. Closed in
July/August. **Admission** call for
details. **Map G4**
Daylight filters through the glass
cupola of the main hall, where women
sit in small annexes, bathing in the
warm water of the baths. Enjoy
Turkish tea and a reviving massage
afterwards. The bustle of Berlin
seems miles away. *See also below*
Women's Centres.

Bookshops

Adhara Büchertempel

*Pestalozzistraße 35, Charlottenburg,
10627 (312 2462). U7
Wilmersdorfer straße.* **Open** 10am-
7pm Mon-Wed; 10am-7.30pm Thur-
Fri; 10am-6pm Sat. **Map B4**
Stocks a good selection of feminist
and lesbian literature.

Lilith

*Knesebeckstraße 86-87,
Charlottenburg, 10623 (312 3102).
U2 Ernst-Reuter-Platz.* **Open** 10am-
6.30pm Mon-Fri; 10am-6pm Sat.
Map C4
Around 5,000 titles by women.
There's a big selection of British and
American lesbian fiction. Near the
door are noticeboards and piles of
leaflets.

Schwarze Risse

*Gneisenaustraße 2a, Mehringhof,
10961 (692 8779). U7
Mehringdamm.* **Open** 10am-6.30pm
Mon-Fri; 11am-2pm Sat. **Map F5**
In the Mehringhof, a courtyard
housing over 30 leftwing projects
including a kindergarten, school, bar
and bike shop, this is a political
bookshop which sells, among other
things, women's and lesbian literature
from around the world.

Business

Weiberwirtschaft

*Anklamerstraße 38, Mitte, 10115
(440 2230). U8 Bernauer straße.*
Map F2
In October 1992 the Weiberwirtschaft
leased the building complex at this
address, where 5,000 square metres
can be used as a business space for
women. Companies owned and run by
women can meet and liaise here; both
profit- and non-profit-making
organisations.

Cafés

All venues listed below are
women-only. *See also below*
Women's Centres *and
chapter* **Gay & Lesbian**.

Café Ada

*Anklamerstraße 38, Mitte, 10115
(448 4875). U8 Bernauer straße.*
Open 9am-midnight daily. **Map F2**
Women-only café in the
Weiberwirtschaft business centre.

Begine

*Potsdamer Straße 139, Schöneberg,
10783 (215 4325). U2 Bülowstraße.*
Open 6pm-1am daily. **Map E5**
This café and cultural centre is named
after the Beginen, women who shared
a common social and economic
network in the Middle Ages. A
popular meeting place for all kinds of
women. Hot snacks, soups and salads
are available. *See also chapter* **Gay &
Lesbian** .

Schoko-Café

*Marianenstraße 6, Kreuzberg,
10997 (615 1561). U1 Kottbusser
Tor.* **Open** 2pm-1am Mon-Thur;
from 2pm Fri; from 12pm Sat & Sun.
Map G5
Part of the women's centre Schoko-
Fabrik *(see below* **Women's
Centres***)*, this beautiful, factory-style
café is mostly frequented by the
women who participate in the many
courses and activities, or who finish
their afternoon in the Turkish bath.
Cakes, soups and hot snacks are
served. Occasional dancing-parties
are held: call for details. *See also chapter* **Gay & Lesbian**.

Health

Aids Beratungen für Migrantinnen

*Skalitzer straße, Kreuzberg, 10999
(615 3232).* **Open** 10am-8pm Mon;
10am-8pm Tue-Thur; 10am-5pm Fri.
Helpline for female immigrants
offering advice on AIDS in over 20
languages, including English.

Berliner Aids-Hilfe

*Meinekestraße 12, Wilmersdorf (885
6400/24-hour helpline 19 411). U3,
U9 Kurfürstendamm.* **Open** 24
hours daily. **Map C4**
The Berlin equivalent of the Terence
Higgins Trust has a special service
for women. Female counsellors can
help and inform on AIDS-related
problems. There's also a self-help
group for HIV-positive women.

Feministisches Frauengesundheitzentrum (FFGZ)

*Bamberger Straße 51, Schöneberg,
10777 (213 9597). U4, U7
Bayerischer Platz.* **Open** 10am-1pm
Tue, Thur; 5pm-7pm Thur. **Map D5**
Courses and lectures on menstruation,
natural contraception, pregnancy,
cancer, abortion, AIDS, migraines and
sexuality. Self-help and prevention

Directory

are stressed. Information on gynaecologists, health institutions and organisations can also be obtained. The FFGZ's archive holds an international collection of books, magazines and articles on issues concerning women and health.

Music

'Wie es Ihr gefällt'

*Last week of November,
Kulturbrauerei, Knaackstrasse 97,
Prenzlauer Berg (441 9269).*
'As She Likes It' features an eclectic mix of bands, from avant-garde and classical to drum 'n' bass and techno. Set up in 1990 to provide a platform for all-girl bands, it attracts top-notch artists from as far afield as the USA, Japan and the Czech Republic. The standard is extremely high and men make up at least half the audience.

Lärm und Lust

*Feminismusikzentrum,
Schwedenstraße 14, 13357 (491
5304).* **Map E1**
A women's music centre providing rehearsal rooms and courses.

Politics

Die Frauen

*Feministica Partei, c/o Liz Schmidt,
Manteuffelstraße 58, Kreuzberg,
10999 (612 1350).*
Founded in 1995, Die Frauen hold monthly discussion groups on political topics. See *Blattgold* for details.

Sightseeing tours

Compania

*Anklamerstraße 38, Mitte, 10115
(4435 8703). U8 Bernauer straße.*
Open 11am-7pm Mon-Fri. **Map F2**
Berlin's first escort service for women and lesbians organises Friday night city tours which stop off at women's bars and clubs and other places of historical, cultural and architectural interest. The agency also provides individual guides. *See also chapter* **Gay & Lesbian**.

Sport

Seitenwechsel

*Kulmerstraße 20a, Kreuzberg,
10783 (215 9000).* **Open** 5pm-7pm Tue; 4pm-6pm Thur. **Map E5**
This sports club for women and lesbians offers courses in badminton, basketball, aerobics, swimming, self-defence, tennis, volleyball and other disciplines. Events take place at sports centres across the city. Phone for details.

Travel

Frauen unterwegs

*Potsdamer Straße 139, Schöneberg,
10783 (215 1022/fax216 98 52). U2
Bülowstraße.* **Open** 10am-2pm Mon-Fri; 5pm-7pm Mon-Thur. **Map E5**
If you want to take a trip out of Berlin, you can book a women-only cultural tour with this association. Staff will organise tours for small groups, which involve meeting local people and retracing the steps of important women, as well as city trips, sporting and walking vacations, language holidays and workshops.

Women's Centres

EWA Frauenzentrum

*Prenzlauer Allee 6, Prenzlauer Berg,
10405 (442 5542/442 7257). U2
Rosa-Luxemburg-Platz.* **Open** *office* 10am-6pm Mon-Fri; *café, centre and gallery* 4pm-11pm Mon-Fri; 10pm-3am Sat; *library* 4pm-7pm Tue; 3pm-6pm Thur. **Map G2**
The Erster Weiblicher Aufbruch (first feminine awakening) is essentially a meeting place for women from the former GDR. Women at the centre offer legal advice and psychological counselling, but you can also just pop into the café for a great breakfast. Other courses cover computers, sport, foreign languages and art. The collection of the library and archive Hex Libris charts the development of women's groups in the GDR – before and after its demise.

Frieda Frauenzentrum und Frauencafe

*Proskauer Straße 7, Friedrichshain,
10247 (422 4276). U5 Rathaus
Friedrichshain.* **Open** 7am-11pm Tue; 9am-11pm Thur-Fri, various times Sat, 3pm-6pm Sun
The founding women's group (belonging to the New Forum) first met in 1989. Three years later, in August 1992, this new communication centre and café for the women of Friedrichshain opened. The monthly programme includes cultural events like exhibitions and poetry-readings, as well as political debates. There's a disco twice a month and weekly meetings of self-help and conversational groups, plus a variety of courses and advisory services.

Schoko-Fabrik

*Naunynstraße 72, Kreuzberg (615
2999). U1 Görlitzer Bahnhof.* **Open** *office* 10am-2pm Mon-Thur. **Map G4**
In 1981 this old chocolate factory in Kreuzberg was squatted and turned into a centre for Turkish and German women. On the first floor there's a joinery. Women practise self-defence

on the second floor. Cultural events take place on the fifth floor and there's an ecological garden on the roof. And we haven't even mentioned the Turkish Bath Hamam (*see above* Baths & Massage), the café, kindergarten, private flats and the office. There are many groups, projects and collectives living and working in the Schoko: educational support for Turkish girls, fitness classes, language courses, dance, bicycle repair workshops and medical advice. You name it.

Women's Studies

FFBIZ

*Frauenforschungs, -bildungs, und
Informationszentrum.
Danckelmannstraße 47 and 15,
Charlottenburg, 14059 (322 1035).
U1 Sophie-Charlotte-Platz.* **Open** *archive, library and telephone advice* 2pm-6pm Tue; 10am-1pm Thur; 3pm-8pm Fri; *additional telephone service* 10am-noon Mon-Fri. **Map B4**
A women's research, education and information centre. The huge archive files contain leaflets, press cuttings, badges, posters, exam papers and documents, all relating to women's topics, projects and movements. You can also read, though not borrow, books in the library. The centre also offers an extensive programme of historical city walks, lectures, poetry readings, exhibitions and courses.

Zentraleinrichtung zur Förderung von Frauenstudien und Frauenforschung

*Freie Universität, Königin-Luise-
Straße 34, Dahlem, 14195 (838
6254/5/6/838 3044). U2 Dahlem-
Dorf.* **Open** *information and library* 2pm-5pm Tue; 10am-6pm Wed. 10am-noon Fri.
Literally, the department of promotion of women's studies and women's research at the Free University. Twice a year, the department publishes a brochure listing current projects and interdisciplinary seminars relating to women's studies.

Zentrum Interdisziplinäre Frauenforschung (ZIF)

*Humboldt Universität zu Berlin,
Mittelstraße 7-8, Mitte, 10117.
(3088 2301). S3, S5, S6, S9/U6
Friedrichsstraße.* **Open** *information and documentation* 9am-noon Mon-Fri. **Map F3**
This department of the Humboldt University organises seminars and lectures, provides a computer pool and courses for women, and stores information relevant for women's research.

Directory

Further Reading

We've chosen these books for quality and interest as much as for availability. Most are currently in print, but some will only be found in libraries or second-hand shops. The date given is that of the first publication in English.

Fiction

Deighton, Len: *Berlin Game, Mexico Set, London Match* (London 1983, 1984, 1985)
Epic espionage trilogy with labyrinthine plot set against an accurate picture of eighties Berlin.
Deighton, Len: *Funeral In Berlin* (London 1964)
Best of Deighton's sixties novels.
Döblin, Alfred: *Berlin-Alexanderplatz* (London 1975)
Devastating Expressionist portrait of the inter-war underworld in working class quarters of Alexanderplatz.
Eckhart, Gabriele: *Hitchhiking* (Lincoln, Nebraska 1992)
Short stories viewing East Berlin through the eyes of street cleaners and a female construction worker.
Grass, Gunther: *Local Anaesthetic* (New York 1970)
The Berlin angst of a schoolboy who threatens to burn a dog outside a Ku'damm café to protest the Vietnam War is funnily satirised, albeit in Grass's irritating schoolmasterly way.
Harris, Robert: *Fatherland* (London 1992)
Alternative history and detective novel set in a 1964 Berlin as the Nazis might have built it.
Isherwood, Christopher: *Mr Norris Changes Trains, Goodbye To Berlin* (London 1935, 1939)
Isherwood's two Berlin novels, the basis of the movie *Cabaret*, offer finely drawn characters and a sharp picture of the decadent city as it tipped over into Nazism.
Johnson, Uwe: *Two Views* (New York 1966)
Love story across the great East-West divide, strong on the mood of Berlin in the late fifties and early sixties.
Kerr, Philip: *Berlin Noir* (London 1994)
The *March Violets/Pale Criminals/German Requiem* triology now available in one volume. Bernie Gunther is a private detective in a tension-filled Nazi Berlin.
Le Carré, John: *The Spy Who Came In From The Cold* (London 1963)
The primal shot-going-over-the-Wall thriller.
Markstein, George: *Ultimate Issue* (London 1981)

Stark thriller of political expediency leading to an uncomfortably likely conclusion about why the Wall went up.
McEwan, Ian: *The Innocent* (London 1990)
Fascinating tale of naive young Englishman recruited into Cold War machinations with tragi-comic results.
Müller, Heiner: *The Battle* (New York 1989)
Collection of plays and pieces strong on the grimness of the Stalinism and false temptations from the West.
Nabokov, Vladimir: *The Gift* (New York 1963)
Written and set in 1920s Berlin, where impoverished Russian émigré dreams of writing a book very like this one.
Schneider, Peter: *The Wall Jumper* (London 1984)
Somewhere between novel, prose poem and artful reportage, a meditation on the madhouse absurdities of the Wall.

Children

Kästner, Erich: *Emil And The Detectives* (London 1931)
Classic text mostly around Zoo Station and Nollendorfplatz.

Biography & Memoir

Baumann, Bommi: *How It All Began* (Vancouver, 1977)
Frank and often funny account of the Berlin origins of
West German terrorism, by a former member of the June 2nd Movement.
Bielenberg, Christabel: *The Past Is Myself* (London 1968)
Fascinating autobiography of an English woman who married a German lawyer and lived through the War in Berlin.
F, Christiane: *H – Autobiography Of A Child Prostitute And Heroin Addict* (London 1980)
Stark account of life in the housing estates and on the heroin scene of 1970s West Berlin. Later filmed as *Christiane F*.
Friedrich, Ruth Andreas: *The Berlin Underground 1938-45* (New York 1947)
A few courageous souls formed anti-Nazi resistance groups. The journalist-author's diaries capture the day-to-day fear.
Millar, Peter: *Tomorrow Belongs To Me* (London 1992)
Memoir of a Prenzlauer Berg local pub by a former East Berlin Reuter's correspondent.
Rimmer, Dave: *Once Upon A Time In The East* (London 1992)
The collapse of communism from ground level – strange and hilarious tales of games between East and West Berlin and travels through assorted East European revolutions.

Schirer, William L: *Berlin Diaries* (New York 1941)
Foreign correspondent in Berlin from 1931-1941 bears appalled witness to Europe's plunge into Armageddon.

History

Farr, Michael: *Berlin! Berlin!* (London 1992)
Lightweight history, concentrating on cultural life and colourful characters.
Garton Ash, Timothy: *We The People* (London 1990)
Instant history of the 1989 revolutions.
Gelb, Norman: *The Berlin Wall* (New York 1986)
Gripping narrative history of how the Wall went up.
McElvoy, Anne: *The Saddled Cow* (London 1992)
Lively history of East Germany by a former Berlin *Times* correspondent.
Masur, Gerhard: *Imperial Berlin* (London 1971)
Berlin in the days of the Kaiser, from the proclamation of empire in 1871 to the end of World War I.
Read, Anthony and Fisher, David: *Berlin – The Biography Of A City* (London 1994)
Probably the best single-volume history of Berlin.
Schirer, William L: *The Rise And Fall Of The Third Reich* (New York 1960)
Still the most readable history of Nazi Germany.
Tusa, Ann & John: *The Berlin Blockade* (London 1988)
Absorbing account of the 11 months when the Allied sector was fed from the air and Berlin, Germany and Europe proceeded to fall into two.

Architecture

Ladd, Brian: *The Ghosts of Berlin: Confronting German History in the Urban Landscape* (Chicago, 1997)
Erudite and insightful look into the relationship between architecture, urbanism and Berlin's violent political history.
Berlin-Brandenburg – An Architectural Guide (Berlin 1993)
Berlin by building, with quirky text in both English and German.

Miscellaneous

Bertsch, Georg C & Hedler, Ernst: *SED* (Cologne 1990)
Schöne Einheits Design: over 200 illustrations of crazy East German consumer product designs.
Friedrich, Thomas: *Berlin – A Photographic Portrait Of The Weimar Years 1918-1933* (London 1991)
Superb photographs of lost Berlin, its personalities and its daily life, with a foreword by Stephen Spender.

Advertisers' Index

Please refer to the relevant sections for addresses/telephone numbers

Index

buses 254
  arriving by 254
  late-night 166, 255
business services 257-60
  for women 261
BZ 198

c

cabaret 168-9
Café Theater Schalotte 169
Café Aroma 118
Café Belmont 214
Café Sliberstein 134
cafés:
  by district 133-42
  cybercafés 247-8
  women-only 195-6, 261
calendar, cultural events 27-30
camera hire 162
camping sites 113
canoeing 216
cars and driving 242-3
  hire 257
  hitching 223
  out of town 222-3
  parking 243
  petrol, 24-hour 243
  shared lifts 190, 223
  speed limits 222-3
Castorf, Frank 219
cemeteries 17, 57, 66
Central (cinema) 186
Chamäleon Varieté 169
Chambers of Commerce 258
Charlottenburg 64-5
  art galleries 90-3
  bars and cafés 141
  bars for gays 192
Checkpoint (cinema) 186
Checkpoint Charlie 21, 41
Checkpoint Charlie Museum 41, 171
chess 214
Chez Nous 168
children's Berlin 170-3
  attractions 171-2
  babysitting 102, 171
  entertainment 172
  restaurants 173
  shops 148-50, 170-1
Chouakri, Mehdi 94
Christian Democrats (CDU) 26
Christmas Markets 30
Christo 69
Christopher Street Day Parade 28, 189
churches/chapels:
  English-language services 250
  in hotel 102
cinemas *see film*
circus 172
Circus Hostel 98, 111, 113
Classic Open Air 29
climate 242
Clinton, Bill 46
clubs 174-80
  discos 180, 190-1, 193
  gay 193
  gay and lesbian mixed 190-1
  lesbian 196
Cölln 5, 6, 32
Columbushaus 61
Communists 14-15, 22, 45
complementary medicine 246
concentration camps 15-16, 18, 189
  Sachsenhausen 16, 17, 224, 228, 233

Concept Hotel 103
Condomis 145
conference facilities 259
  in hotels 100, 102, 103, 104, 105
Congress of Vienna 9
consulates 244-5
consultants, business 258-9
Contemporary Fine Arts 93
contraception 246
Coppi, Helle 94
costume hire 157-8
Cote, Kevin 199
courier services 259
Cragun, Richard 181
Cranach, Lucas 79-81, 231
credit cards, lost or stolen 248
crime 242
cruising, gay 194
Customs 242
cybercafés 247-8
cycling 214
cycle hire 172, 257
  taking cycles on trains 223

d

DAAD Galerie 89
Dahlem 34, 37, 70, 78
dance 181-2
  classes 182
  listings 181
  performance venues 181-2
  Tango Sommer 29
day trips 224-36
Debis building 41
dentists 247
department stores 150-1
Deutsch-Amerikanischer
  Volksfest 29
Deutsch-Französisches
  Volksfest 28
Deutsch-Russisches Museum
  Berlin-Karlshorst 84
Deutsche Bahn Information 222
Deutsche Guggenheim Berlin 90
Deutsche Oper 12, 181, 202
Deutsche Staatsoper 33, 46, 181, 200, 201, 202
Deutsches Historisches Museum
  7, 32, 84, 187
Deutsches Symphonie-Orchester
  200, 201
Deutsches Theater 45, 219
Diehl, Volker 91
Dietrich, Marlene 184, 189, 227, 260
  grave 66, 71
disabled:
  hotel facilities 102, 103, 242
  travel facilities 242, 257
discos 180
  gay and lesbian mixed 190
  lesbian 196
Dix, Otto 14, 81, 260
doctors 246-7
Domäne Dahlem 171
Dominikuskirche 62
Dorotheenstadt 7, 32
Drake, Friedrich 68
Dreher, Anselm 93
Dresden 233-4
driving *see cars and driving*
drugs 243-4
drycleaners 158-9
Düppler Forst 73-4
Dussmann das Kulturrkaufhaus
  42, 148, 152
Dutschke, Rudi 22

e

Ebert, Friedrich 13
education 244
  women's studies 262
Egyptian Museum
  see Ägyptisches Museum
Einstein, Albert 12, 227
Eiszeit (cinema) 186
electricity 244
embassies 244-5
  Commercial Departments 258
emergencies:
  medical 247
  repair services 250
  24-hour services 251
Empire, Alec 210
Engels, Friedrich 10, 49
Englischer Garten 68
Ephraim-Palais 32, 79
Ernst, Max 81, 89
Ernst Thälmann Park 59
escort agencies for women 262
estate agents 259
Europa-Center 14, 21, 47, 63
Europahaus 41
exports, shipping firms 163

f

Fahrenkamp, Emil 69
farms 171
Fernsehturm 21, 38, 42, 45, 55, 69, 170
festivals:
  dance 181, 182
  film 30, 183-5, 191
  music (classical) 27, 28-9, 201
  music (rock, folk and jazz) 29, 30, 209-10
  theatre 220
fetish venues, gay 193
FEZ Köpenik 173
film 183-8
  Berlin Film Festival 30, 183-5
  cinemas 38, 183, 185-8
  East German 227
  Filmmuseum, Potsdam 224, 227
  Studio Babelsberg 188, 227
  Verzaubert Internationales
    Schwullesbisches
    Filmfestival 191
  video rental 188
Fine Art Rafael Vostell 91
fines, for fare-dodging 256
fitness centres 214-15
  gay 195
  in hotels 98, 100, 102, 103
fleamarkets 67, 147, 159
Flyer 174
Focus 198
food:
  delivery 161-2
  late-night shopping 166
  meals 114
  menu translations 120-1
  shops 132, 159-62
  street 124
  vegetarian 114, 123
football 212, 213, 215
  Deutsche Pokalendspiele 28
Foster, Sir Norman 38, 41, 69
Franck, Eric 93
Frankfurt-an-der-Oder 232
Frankfurter Allgemeine Zeitung
  198
Franz Ferdinand, Archduke 13
Frederick Barbarossa 235
Freie Universität 19, 25, 37, 70, 244

Street Index

Inselstraße - G4
Invalidenstraße - E3/F2
Isingstraße - H5
Isländische Straße - F1

Jablonskistraße - G2/H2
Jacobsohnstraße - H1
Jacobystraße - G3
Jaffestraße - A4
Jäger Straße - F4
Jagowstraße - C3/D3
Jahnstraße - G5
Jakob-Kaiser-Platz - B2
Jannowitzbrücke - G3/4
Jenaer Straße - D5
Joachim-Friedrich-Straße - B4/5
Joachimsthaler Platz - C4
Joachimsthaler Straße - C4/5
Joachimstraße - F3
Johannaplatz - A5
Johannisstraße - F3
Johanniterstraße - F5
John-Foster-Dulles-Allee - E3
Jugend-Platz - A2
Jugendweg - A2
Jülicher Straße - F1
Jungfernheideweg - A1/2
Jüterboger Straße - F6

K.-Niederkirchnerstr - H2
Kaiser-Friedrich-Straße - B3/4
Kaiserdamm - A4/B4
Kaiserin-Augusta-Allee - C3
Kalckreuthstraße - D5
Kameruner Straße - D1
Kamminer Straße - B3
Kantstraße - C4
Kapelleufer - E3
Karl-August-Platz - B4/C4
Karl-Kunger Straße - H5
Karl-Liebknecht-Straße - G3
Karl-Marx-Allee - G3/H3
Karl-Marx-Straße - H6
Karlsruher Straße - B4/5
Kärntener Straße - D6
Kastanienallee - A3/4
Kastanienallee - G2
Katharinenstraße - B4/5
Katzbachstraße - E5/6
Keibelstraße - G3
Keithstraße - D4
Keplerstraße - B3
Kiefholzstraße - H5
Kiehlufer - H6
Kieler Straße - E2
Kienitzer Straße - G6/H6
Kirchgasse - H6
Kirchstraße - D3
Kirschenallee - A3
Kirshstraße - F3
Kissinger Platz - B6
Kissinger Straße - B6
Kleine Präsident Straße - F3
Klausenerplatz - B3
Kleine Hamburger Straße - F3
Kleineweg - F6
Kleiststraße - D4/5
Klingelhöferstraße - D4
Klopstockstraße - D3
Kluckstraße - E4
Knaackstraße - G2
Knausstraße - A6
Knesebeckstraße - C4
Kniprodestraße - H2

Knobelsdorffstraße - A4/B4
Köbisstraße - D4
Kochstraße - F4
Koenigsallee - A5/6
Kohlfurter Straße - G5
Kollwitzplatz - G2
Kollwitzstraße - G2
Kolonnenstraße - E5/6
Kommandantenstraße - F4/G4
Kongostraße - D1
Köningin-Elisabeth-Straße - A3/4
Konstanzer Straße - B5/C5
Kopenhagener Straße - F1/G1
Köpenicker Straße - G4/H4
Kopfstraße - H6
Koppenstraße - H3/4
Korsörer Straße - F1/G1
Körtestraße - G5
Köthener Straße - E4
Kottbusser Damm - G5
Kottbusser Straße - G5
Kottbusserbrücke - G5
Krausenstraße - F4
Kreuzbergstraße - E5/F5
Kronberger Straße - A6
Kronenstraße - F4
Kronprinzenufer - E3
Krügerstraße - G1/H1
Krummestraße - B4
Kruppstraße - D2/E2
Kudowastr - B5
Kufsteiner Straße - D5/6
Kuglerstraße - G1
Kulmer Straße - E5
Kurfürstendamm - B5/C4
Kurfürstenstraße - D4/E5
Kurische Straße - H2
Kurstraße - F3/4
Kurt-Schumacher-Damm - B2
Kyffhäuserstraße - D5

L.-Hermann-Straße - H2
Landhausstraße - C5
Landsberger Allee - H3
Landshuter Straße - D5
Langenscheidt-Straße - E5
Langhansstraße - H1
Lassenstraße - A6
Laubacher Straße - C6
Lausitzer Platz - H4/5
Lausitzer Straße - H5
Leberstraße - E6
Legiendamm - G4
Lehderstraße - H1
Lehniner Platz - B5
Lehrterstraße - E2/3
Leibnizstraße - C4
Leinestraße - G6
Leipziger Straße - F4
Lenaustraße - G5/H5
Lennéstraße - E4
Leonhardyweg - F6
Leopoldplatz - E1
Lesser-Ury-Weg - E3
Lessingstraße - D3
Leuschnerdamm - G4
Leuthener Straße - E6
Levetzowstraße - C3/D3
Lewishamstraße - B4
Leykestraße - H6
Lichtenberger-Straße - G3/H3
Lichtenrader Straße - G6
Lichtensteinallee - D4
Liebenwalder Straße - E1

Liesen Straße - E2
Lietzenburger Straße - D4/5/C5
Lilienthalstraße - G6
Limburger Straße - D1
Lindenallee - A3/4
Lindenstraße - F4
Linienstraße - F3/G2/3
Linkstraße - E4
Littenstraße - G3
Lobeckstraße - G4/5
Loewenhardtdamm - E6
Lohmühlenstraße - H5
Lortzingstraße - F1
Lübecker Straße - D2/3
Lüderitzstraße - D1
Lüdtgeweg - C3
Ludwigkirch-Platz - C5
Luisenstraße - E3
Luitpoldstraße - D5
Lüneburger Straße - D3/E3
Lutherbrücke - D3
Lützowplatz - D4
Lützowstraße - D4/E4
Lützowufer - D4
Luxemburger Straße - D1/E1
Lychener Straße - G1
Lynarstraße - A5/B5
Lynarstraße - E2

Maaßenstraße - D5
Magazinstraße - G3
Mahlower Straße - G6
Mainzer Straße - H6
Mainzerstraße - C6
Malmöerstraße - F1/G1
Manfred-Richthofen-Straße - E6/F6
Manitiusstraße - H5
Mansfelder Straße - B5
Manstein Straße - E5
Manteuffelstraße - G5/H4/5
Marchbrücke - C3
Marchlewskistraße - H4
Marchstraße - C3/4
Mariannenplatz - G4
Mariannenstraße - G5
Marienburger Straße - G2/H2
Marienstraße - F3
Markgrafenstraße - F4
Marshallbrücke - E3
Martin-Lutherstraße - D5/6
Masurenallee - A4
Mauerstraße - F3/4
Max-Steinke-Straße - H1
Maybachufer - G5/H5
Mecklen-Burger Straße - B6/C6
Mehringbrücke - F5
Mehringdamm - F5
Mehringplatz - F5
Meierotto Straße - C5
Meineckestraße - C4
Melchiorstraße - G4
Menzelstraße - A6
Meraner Straße - D5/6
Messedamm - A4
Methfesselstraße - F5
Metzer Straße - G2
Michaelkirchstraße - G4
Michelangelostraße - H1
Mierendorff Platz - B3
Mierendorffstraße - B3
Mindener Straße - B3
Miqueslstraße - A6
Mittelstraße - F3
Mittelweg - H6

Mittenwalder Straße - F5
Möckernbrücke - F5
Möckernstraße - E5/F4/5
Mohrenstraße - F4
Mollstraße - G3/H3
Moltkebrücke - E3
Moltkestraße - E3
Mommsenstraße - B4/C4
Monbijoustraße - F3
Monumentenstraße - E5
Morsestraße - C3
Morusstraße - H6
Motzstraße - D5
Mühlendamm - G3
Mühlenstraße - H4
Mühsamstraße - H3
Mulackstraße - G3
Müllerstraße - D1/E1
Münchener Straße - D5
Muskauer Straße - H4

Nachodstr - C5/D5
Nassauische Straße - C5
Nauheimer Str - B6/C6
Naumannstraße - E6
Naunynstraße - G4
Nazarethkirchstraße - E1
Nehringstraße - B3/4
Nene-Hochstraße - E2
Nestorstraße - B5
Neue Kantstraße - A4/B4
Neue-Roßstraße - G4
Neuenburger Straße - F4/5
Neues Ufer - C3
Neumannstraße - G1
Niebuhrstraße - B4/C4
Niederkirchner-Straße - F4
Niederwallstraße - F4
Nithackstraße - B3
Nollendorfstraße - D5
Nonnendammallee - A2
Nordhauser Straße - B3/C3
Nordufer - D2
Norwegerstraße - F1
Nostitzstraße - F5
Nürnberger Straße - D4
Nußbaumallee - A3

Obentrautstraße - F5
Oderberger Straße - G2
Oderstraße - G6
Ohlauer Straße - H5
Okerstraße - G6
Olbersstraße - B2
Oldenburger Straße - D2
Olivaer Platz - C5
Olof-Palme-Platz - D4
Onckenstraße - H5
Oppelner Straße - H5
Oranienburger Str - F3
Oranienplatz - G4
Oranienstraße - F4/G4/5
Orber Straße - B5
Orthstraße - E1
Osloer Straße - E1/F1
Osnabrücker Straße - B3
Ostender Straße - D1
Ostseestraße - H1
Otawistraße - D1
Otto-Braun-Straße - G3
Otto-Dix-Straße - E3
Otto-Suhr-Allee - B3/C3
Ottoplatz - D3

Palisadenstraße - H3
Pallasstraße - D5/E5
Pankstraße - E1
Pannierstraße - H5
Pappel Allee - G1
Paretzer Straße - C6
Pariser Platz - E3
Pariser Straße - C5
Pascalstraße - C3
Passauer Straße - D4
Pasteurstraße - H2
Paul-Lincke-Ufer/H5
Paul-Lobe-Straße - E3
Paul-Robeson-Straße - G1
Paulsborner Straße - B5
Paulstraße - D3
Perleberger Straße - D2
Pestalozzistraße - B4/C4
Pfalzburger Straße - C5
Pflügerstraße - H5
Pflugstraße - E2
Phillippstraße - E3/F3
Pistoriusstraße - H1
Planufer - G5
Platanenallee - A4
Platz Der Republik - E3
Pohlstraße - E4/5
Pommersche Straße - C5
Popitzweg - A2
Potsdamer Straße - E4/5
Potsdamm Brücke - E4
Prager Platz - C5
Prager Straße - D5
Prenzlauer Allee - G2/3/H1
Prenzlauer Promenade - H1
Prinzenallee - F1
Prinzenstraße - G4/5
Prinzregentenstraße - C5/6
Pücklerstraße - H4
Pufendorfstraße - H3
Putbusser Straße - F1
Putlitzbrucke - D2

Quedlinburger Straße - B3/C3
Quellweg - A2
Quitzowstraße - D2

R.-Luxemburg-Str - G3
R.-Schwarz-Straße - H2
Ramlerstraße - F1
Rankestraße - C4/D4
Rathausstraße - G3
Rathenauplatz - A5
Rathenower Straße - D2/3
Ratiborstraße - H5
Rauchstraße - D4
Raumerstraße - G1/2
Regensburger Straße - C5/D5
Reichenberger Straße - G4/5/H5
Reichenhaller Straße - B6
Reichpietschufer - D4/E4
Reichsstraße - A4
Reichstagufer - E3/F3
Reichweindamm - B2
Reinerstraße - A6/B6
Reinhardtstraße - E3/F3
Reinickendorfer Strasse - E1
Reuterplatz - H5
Reuterstraße - H6
Rheinbabenallee - A6
Richard-Sorge-Straße - H3
Richard-Strauss-Straße - A6
Richard-Wagner-Straße - B3/4
Richardplatz - H6

Richardstraße - H6
Riedemannweg - C1/2
Ritterstraße - F4/G4
Rochstraße - G3
Rodenbergstraße - G1
Roelckestraße - H1
Rohrdamm - A2
Rolandufer - G3
Rollbergstraße - H6
Rönnestraße - B4
Röntgenbrücke - C3
Röntgenstraße - C3
Rosa-Luxemburg-Platz - G3
Rosenheimer Straße - D5
Rosenthalerstraße - F3
Rostocker Straße - C2
Rubensstraße - D6
Rue A. Le Notre - B1/C1
Rungestraße - G4
Ruppiner Straße - F2
Rüsternallee - A3/4
Rütlistraße - H5
Rykestraße - G2

Saarbrücker Straße - G2
Saatwinkler Damm - A1/B1/C1
Sachsendamm - D6/E6
Sächsische Straße - C5
Salzburger Straße - D5/6
Salzufer - C3
Sanderstraße - G5/H5
Sansibarstraße - D1
Savignyplatz - C4
Schaperstraße - C5/D5
Scharnhorststraße - E2
Scheidemannstraße - E3
Schellendorffstraße - A6/B6
Schiffbauerdamm - E3/F3
Schillerstraße - B4/C4
Schillingbrücke - H4
Schillingstraße - G3
Schivelbeiner Straße - G1
Schlangenbader Straße - B6
Schlesische Straße - H5
Schloß Brücke - B3
Schloßstraße - B3/4
Schlüterstraße - C4
Schmidstraße - G4
Schmollerplatz - H5
Schöneberger Straße - E4/F4
Schöneberger Ufer - E4
Schonensche Straße - G1
Schönhauser Allee - G1/2
Schönleinstraße - G5
Schönwalder Straße - E2
Schreiberring - E6/F6
Schuckertdamm - A2
Schulstraße - E1
Schulzendorfer Straße - E2
Schumannstraße - E3/F3
Schustehrus-Straße - B3
Schützenstraße - F4
Schwäbische Straße - D5
Schwedenstraße - E1
Schwedlerstraße - A6
Schwedter Straße - F1/G2
Schwiebusser Straße - F6
Sebastianstraße - G4
Seelingstraße - B3
Seelower Straße - G1
Seesener Straße - B5
Seestraße - D1/E1
Selchowerstraße - G6
Sellerstraße - E2

Senefelderstraße - G1/2
Senegalstraße - D1
Seydelstraße - F4/G4
Seydlitzstraße - E3
Sickingenplatz - C2
Sickingenstraße - C2
Siemensdamm - A2
Siemensstraße - C2/D2
Sigismundstraße - E4
Sigmaringer Straße - C5
Singdrosselstei - A1
Singerstraße - G3/H3
Skalitzer Straße - H5
Solmsstraße - F5
Sömmeringstraße - B3
Sonnenallee - H5/6
Sonnenburger Straße - G1
Soorstraße - A3/4
Sophie-Charlotte-Platz - B4
Sophie-Charlotten-Straße -
A3/B3/4
Sophienstraße - F3
Spandauer Damm - A3/B3
Spandauerstraße - G3
Sparrplatz - E2
Spenerstraße - D3
Spessartstraße - C6
Spichernstraße - C5/D5
Sponholzstraße - D6
Spreeweg - D3
Sprengelstraße - D2
Sredzkistraße - G2
Stahlheimer Straße - G1
Stallschreiberstraße - G4
Stargarder Straße - G1
Stauffenbergstraße - E4
Stavanger-Straße - G1
Steinmetzstraße - E5
Steinplatz - C4
Stephenstraße - D2
Stettiner Straße - F1
Storkower Straße - G2
Stralauer Straße - G3
Stralsunder Straße - F2
Straßburger Straße - G2
Straße Am Schoelerpark - C6
Straße Der Parlser Kommune -
H3/4
Straße Des 17. Juni - C4/D4/E3
Strelitzer Straße - F2
Stresemannstraße - E4/F4
Streustraße - H1
Stromstraße - D2/3
Suarezstraße - B4
Südwestkorso - C6
Sültstraße - H1
Swinemünder Straße - F1/2
Sybelstraße - B4/C4
Sylter Straße - D2

Talstraße - G1/H1
Taubenstraße - F4
Tauentzienstraße - D4
Tegeler Straße - D2/E2
Tegeler Weg - B3
Tempelhof Ufer - E5/F5
Tempelhofer Damm - F6
Tempelhofer Weg - D6/E6
Teplitzer Straße - A6
Teutoburger-Platz - G2
Thielenbrücke - H5
Thomasius Straße - D3
Thorner Straße - H2
Thulestraße - G1

Thüringer Allee - A4
Tieckstraße - F2
Tiergartenstraße - D4/E4
Tiergartenufer - D4
Toepferstraße - A2
Togostraße - D1
Tölzer Straße - B6
Topsstraße - G1/2
Torfstraße - D2
Torgauer Straße - D6/E6
Torstraße - F2/3/G2/3
Trabener Straße - A5
Transvaal-Straße - C1/D1
Trautenaustraße - C5
Triftstraße - D1/E1
Tucholsky Straße - F3
Turiner Straße - D1/E1
Turmstraße - C3/D3

Uferstraße - E1
Uhlandstraße - C4/5
Ulmenallee - A3
Ungarnstraße - D1
Unter Den Linden - F3
Urbanstraße - F5/G5
Usedomer Straße - F2

Varziner Straße - C6
Veteranen Straße - F2
Vinetaplatz - F2
Voltastraße - F2
Vorbergstraße - D5/E5

Wadzeckstr - G3
Waldemarstraße - G4
Waldenserstraße - C2/D3
Waldschulallee - A5
Waldstraße - C2
Wallenbergstraße - C6
Wallotstraße - A5
Wallstraße - G4
Wangenhelmstraße - B5
Warmbrunner Straße - A5/B6
Warschauer Straße - H4
Wartburgstraße - D5
Wartenburgstraße - F5
Wassertorplatz - G5
Waterloobrücke - F5
Wattstraße - F2
Wedekindstraße - H4
Weichselplatz - H5
Weichselstraße - H5/6
Weidendammer Brücke - F3
Weigandufer - H6
Weinbergsweg - F2/G2
Weinhelmer Straße - B6
Weinstraße - G3/H3
Weisestraße - G6
Weldenweg - H3
Welserstraße - D5
Werbellinstraße - H6
Werdauer Weg - D6
Werderstraße - F3/G3
Werftstraße - E3
Werner-Voß-Damm - E6
Wernerwerkdamm - A2
Weserstraße - H5/6
Westfälische Straße - B5
Wexstraße - C6/D6
Weydemeyer Straße - G3/H3
Wichertstraße - G1
Wichmannstraße - D4
Wiclefstraße - C2/D2
Wiebestraße - C2/3

Wielandstraße - C4
Wiener Straße - H5
Wiesenstraße - E1
Wikinger Ufer - C3
Wildenbruchplatz - H6
Wildenbruchstraße - H6
Wilhelmsaue - C6
Wilhelmshavener Straße - D2/3
Wilhelmstraße - F4/5
Willdenowstraße - E1/2
Willibald-Alexis-Straße - F5
Wilmersdorfer Straße - B3/4
Wilmsstraße - F5/G5
Wilsnacker Straße - D2/3
Windscheldstraße - B4
Winkler Straße - A5
Winsstraße - G2
Winterfeldt Straße - D5/E5
Wintersteinstraße - B3
Wisbyer Straße - G1
Wissmannstraße - A5
Wissmannstraße - G6
Wittelsbacher Straße - C5
Witzlebenstraße - B4
Wöhlertstraße - E2
Wolffring - E6/F6
Woliner Straße - F2
Wörther Straße - G2
Wrangelstraße - H4
Wrangelstraße - H5
Wullenweberstraße - C3
Wundtstraße - A4/B4
Württembergische Str - C5

Xantener Str - B5/C5

Yorckstraße - E5/F5

Zähringer Straße - B5/C5
Zehdenickner Straße - G2
Zeppelinplatz - D1
Zeughofstraße - H4
Ziegelstraße - F3
Zillestraße - B4
Zimmerstraße - F4
Zossbrücke - F5
Zossener Straße - F5
Züllichauer Straße - F6/G6
Zwinglistraße - C3/D3

Section sponsored by

B B C WORLD SERVICE

Maps

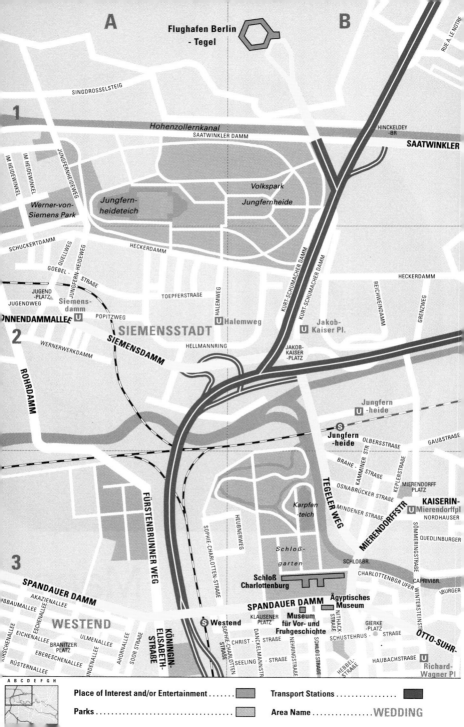

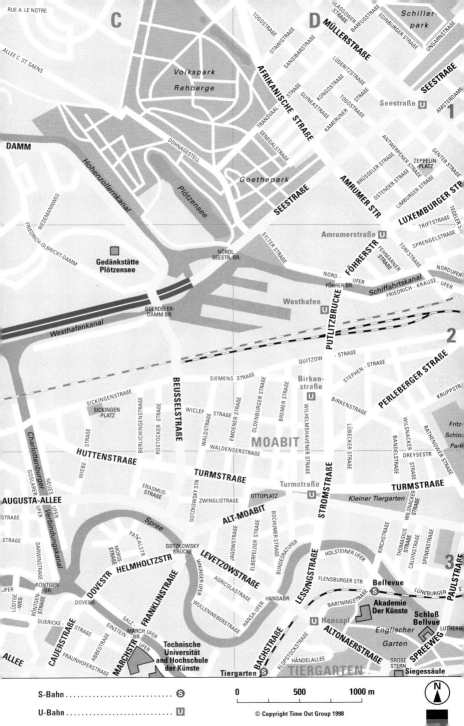

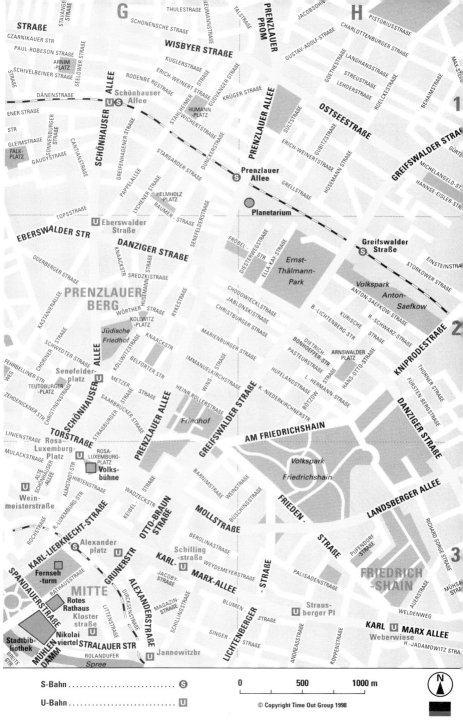

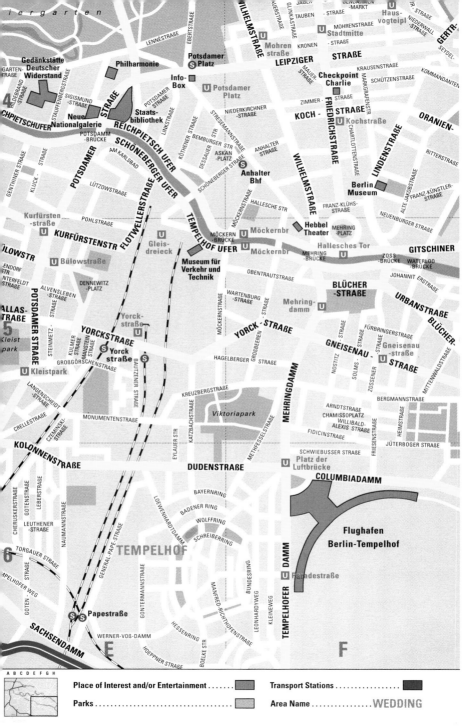

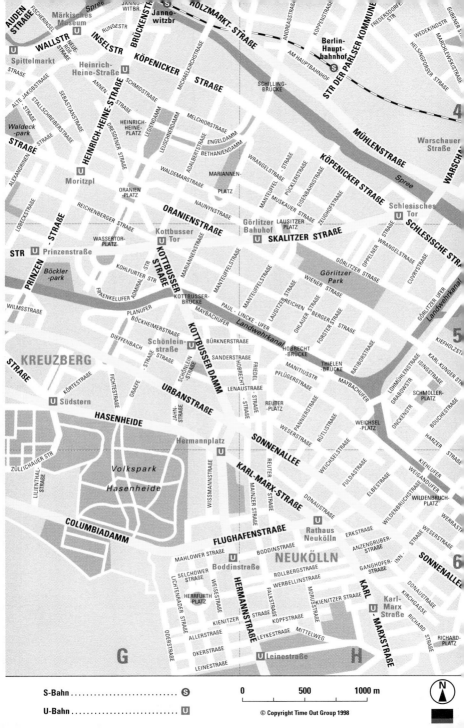

S-Bahn .... ⑤

U-Bahn .... Ⓤ

0   500   1000 m

© Copyright Time Out Group 1998

N

BBC WORLD SERVICE
going abroad ?
Pack the BBC
keep up with
news
current affairs
sport
music
internet: http://www.bbc.co.uk/worldservice
e-mail: worldservice.letters@bbc.co.uk
fax: +44 (0) 171 557 1258 / 1254
phone: +44 (0) 171 240 3456
address: PO Box 76
Bush House
London WC2B 4PH
quote reference: TO.Berlin.1

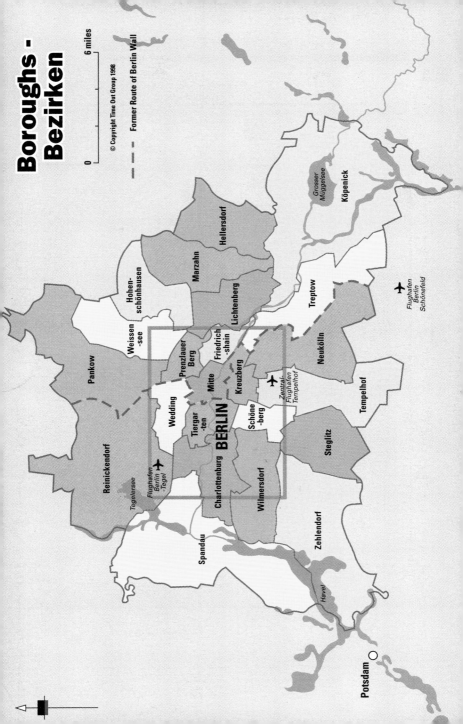

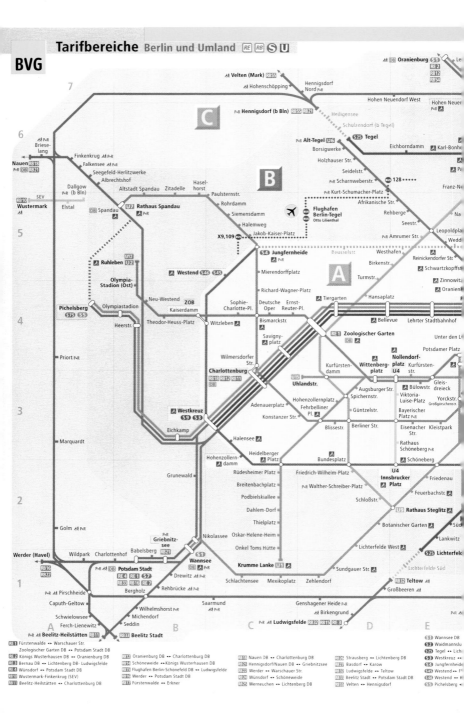